www.wadsworth.com

wadsworth.com is the World Wide Web site for Wadsworth and is your direct source to dozens of online resources.

At *wadsworth.com* you can find out about supplements, demonstration software, and student resources. You can also send email to many of our authors and preview new publications and exciting new technologies.

wadsworth.com
Changing the way the world learns®

International Political Economy

The Struggle for Power and Wealth

Third Edition

Thomas D. Lairson
Rollins College

David Skidmore
Drake University

THOMSON
™
WADSWORTH

Australia • Canada • Mexico • Singapore • Spain
United Kingdom • United States

THOMSON

WADSWORTH

Executive Editor, Political Science: *David Tatom*
Senior Development Editor: *Stacey Sims*
Assistant Editor: *Heather Hogan*
Editorial Assistant: *Dianna Long*
Technology Project Manager: *Melinda Newfarmer*
Marketing Manager: *Janise Fry*
Marketing Assistant: *Mary Ho*
Advertising Project Manager: *Brian Chaffee*
Project Managers, Editorial Production:
  Erica Silverstein, Katy German

Print/Media Buyer: *Jessica Reed*
Permissions Editor: *Robert Kauser*
Production Service: *UG / GGS Information
  Services, Inc.*
Illustrator: *UG / GGS Information Services, Inc.*
Cover Designer: *Sue Hart*
Cover Image: *Lois & Bob Schlowsky/Stone*
Text and Cover Printer: *Webcom*
Compositor: *UG / GGS Information Services, Inc.*

For more information about our
products, contact us at:
**Thomson Learning Academic
Resource Center
1-800-423-0563**
For permission to use material from
this text, contact us by:
Phone: 1-800-730-2214
Fax: 1-800-730-2215
Web: http://www.thomsonrights.com

Library of Congress Control Number: 2002109288

ISBN-13: 978-0-15-507497-2
ISBN-10: 0-15-507497-0

Wadsworth/Thomson Learning
10 Davis Drive
Belmont, CA 94002-3098
USA

Asia
Thomson Learning
5 Shenton Way #01-01
UIC Building
Singapore 068808

Australia
Nelson Thomson Learning
102 Dodds Street
South Melbourne, Victoria 3205
Australia

Canada
Nelson Thomson Learning
1120 Birchmount Road
Toronto, Ontario M1K 5G4
Canada

Europe/Middle East/Africa
Thomson Learning
High Holborn House
50/51 Bedford Row
London WC1R 4LR
United Kingdom

Latin America
Thomson Learning
Seneca, 53
Colonia Polanco
11560 Mexico D.F.
Mexico

Spain
Paraninfo Thomson Learning
Calle/Magallanes, 25
28015 Madrid, Spain

Contents

❖

Preface

This edition of our book carries over many of the objectives and themes central to the first two editions while also addressing a number of new topics and issues. Once again, our goal has been to produce a clear and readable textbook without sacrificing sophistication or rigor. We recognize the difficulties that students face in mastering a subject that lies at the intersection of two complex fields—political science and economics. We therefore take great care to explain basic economic concepts and to offer a balanced blend of theory, history, and policy. We believe that the resulting volume is accessible enough to be used as a supplement in an introductory course on international relations, but challenging enough to be assigned as a main textbook for upper level courses.

As before, we depict the international political economy as a realm of both struggle and cooperation. We show how these contrary imperatives coexist and how the mix between the two varies over time, across countries, and within issues. In pursuing this theme, we weave together theory, concepts, and arguments throughout and tie these ideas closely to the topics under discussion.

The third edition includes a number of pedagogical aids, including illustrations and tables, anecdotes, an annotated bibliography at the end of each chapter, a glossary of essential terms, a list of acronyms, and a list of relevant Web links.

The third edition has been updated throughout to reflect current events and new data. The new edition also includes expanded coverage of a number of important topics, including:

- Expanded discussion of global economic interdependence between 1890 and 1914

- Analysis of the impact of the Euro on the European Union and on the world economy

- New evidence on the political consequences of the globalization of finance

- New evidence on the direction and consequences of foreign direct investment

- Discussion of the impact of multinational corporations on developing states

- The impact of global production networks created by multinational corporations

- Examination of the impact of information technology and the Internet on the political and economic strength of states

- Evaluation of the impact of freer global markets on income inequality, on economic growth, on welfare and tax policies, and on the ability of nations to control their economies

- Extended discussion of the continuing economic crisis in Japan

- Examination of Silicon Valley as a primary example of competitiveness in the information age

- The launching of a new round of global trade negotiations

- The role of social capital in development

- Recent efforts to reform official development assistance

- The emergence of a transnational anti-globalization movement led by nongovernmental organizations

- The consequences and lessons of the Asian financial crisis and its spread to Russia and Latin America

- New proposals for reforming the international financial system

- The HIV/AIDS crisis in Africa and other parts of the developing world

- The debate over the production and trade of genetically modified food products

- A discussion of the "tragedy of the commons" and the relationship of this concept to international negotiations over ozone depletion and climate change.

We thank the editors at Wadsworth, including David Tatom, Acquisitions Editor, who has actively supported this project from its genesis; Stacey Sims, Developmental Editor, who provided valuable assistance at different stages in the preparation of the manuscript; and Erica Silverstein, Project Manager, who guided the book through production. We also appreciate the advice offered by reviewers of the second edition, including Mark Amen, University of South Florida; John A. C. Conybeare, University of Iowa; Paul D'Anieri, University of Kansas; Patricia Davis, University of Notre Dame; Roe Goddard, Thunderbird University; Harold K. Jacobson, University of Michigan; and Mark Rupert, Syracuse University. Finally, we each thank our spouses, Sally Lairson and Charlene Skidmore, for their patience and support.

1

❖

Introduction:
The Political Economy
of International Affairs

Understanding international affairs is exceedingly difficult and perhaps impossible without a clear sense of how politics and economics are related. This assertion, very controversial even fifteen years ago, may still provoke dissent and perhaps confusion from students today. After all, political science is taught in one department and economics in another. One looks at power and the other at money and products. The study of international political economy is premised on the view that such distinctions are artificial and, ultimately, unproductive. Rather, international political economists promote the view that great gains in understanding may be had by focusing on the intersections between political and economic relationships in world affairs.

One way to see the benefits of thinking in terms of international political economy is to consider some of the events in international affairs and observe how closely politics and economics are entangled. Examine the following account of a recent international financial crisis. Why is the crisis happening to Mexico, and why is this a problem for the United States?

> During the winter of 1994–1995, the collapse of the Mexican peso threatened the stability of the international financial system. The United States and several important international economic organizations responded by providing Mexico with large loans. They did this not out of beneficence, but rather because an unchecked crisis in Mexico could have brought on a global financial crisis with great potential harm to many countries. What caused the crisis? Primarily, it was serious economic

problems in Mexico that became clear in late 1994. Beginning in the mid-1980s, the Mexican government chose economic opening and liberalization and moved toward freer trade with the United States and Canada in the North American Free Trade Agreement (NAFTA). The Mexican economy expanded, trade grew, and foreign investors moved into Mexico. But Mexico experienced a large deficit in its international accounts, inflation was high, savings were low, and the exchange rate of the peso (managed by the government) was too high. This all became clear when the government attempted to reduce the peso's value. The result was that domestic and then international investors began to flee Mexico, driving the peso's value much lower. With Mexico standing at the precipice of a default on its international debt, President Bill Clinton moved to support Mexico. Along with the International Monetary Fund and the Bank for International Settlements, the United States organized a $50 billion line of credit for Mexico with $20 billion from the United States. The falling peso had by now spread to other emerging market countries in Latin America and Asia. Had Mexico been unable to meet the payments due on its debt, a collapse of the peso and Mexican securities would have followed, along with a major economic decline in other countries, including the United States. For its part, Mexico moved to reduce government spending, lower money supply growth, and increase the privatization of its state enterprises.

This was not the first time something like this had happened. During a serious recession in 1982, the U.S. government took steps to prevent a loan default by Mexico to U.S. and other foreign banks. The U.S. government provided additional loans to Mexico, supported loans by the International Monetary Fund, and lowered interest rates, thereby reducing the annual payments of Mexico and other debtor states. These actions also served to protect the interests of those U.S. banks who had lent Mexico and other Third World states nearly $100 billion. U.S. Secretary of the Treasury Donald Regan—a former Wall Street tycoon—defended this policy before Congress. He pointed out that a loan default would invariably lead to a contraction in U.S. bank lending at home and would probably force interest rates higher.

> ... We are not talking here just about the big money-center banks and the multinational corporations. Well over 1,500 U.S. banks, or more than 10 percent of the total number of U.S. banks, have loaned money to Latin America alone.... Those loans, among other things, financed exports, exports that resulted in jobs, housing and investment being maintained or created throughout the United States.[1]

For Mr. Regan, an immensely practical man with a strong commitment to private enterprise and American interests, it was essential that the U.S. government spend considerable sums on protecting and preserving the international financial system.[2]

Notice first how much the Mexican government influences the way the Mexican economy operates. The value of the country's currency in international markets, the way in which trade is carried out between Mexico and the rest of the world, and borrowing from international banks all are directly affected by the government's decisions. This doesn't mean the Mexican government is in control of these matters, just that they have a big impact. Things can go very badly. Pay attention also to the fact that the U.S. government's attitude is about the same in the 1980s, when a conservative Republican administration is in office, as in the 1990s, when a more liberal Democratic administration is in control. Both care a great deal about what happens to Mexico and are very concerned. Why? As Regan said, many U.S. banks have a direct interest in Mexico's fate. What does the United States do? It acts to help Mexico and to support international financial and economic stability. That is, the U.S. uses its considerable financial and political resources to support Mexico, but also forces the Mexican government to make changes in its policies. Try to imagine understanding these events without using both politics and economics. Ask yourself whether our thinking would be very different if we looked only at one part.

Students of international political economy have begun to develop a systematic approach to understanding how politics and economics are related. This involves developing categories to identify different types of relationships that can help us economize and organize our thinking. By way of introduction, we will focus on two broad categories: the political economy of relationships within a nation and those among nations. As we work through some of the basic ideas of international political economy and some of the stories about these categories, notice the variety of connections between politics and economics. We will see how international political negotiations can lead to significant changes in the ways people live and work; how almost everyone is caught up in an immense world economy of production, technology, and competition that can affect the very foundations of their societies; how systems of economic interdependence can have unexpected consequences for prices and profits as a result of political changes thousands of miles away; and how deeply involved governments are in helping private businesses succeed in the world economy.

DOMESTIC POLITICAL ECONOMY

The nature and scope of a country's participation in the world economy are greatly affected by political decisions made within its borders. The politics of this decision making is often influenced by the fact that different groups are affected in different ways by involvement in the world economy: some groups win, while others are disadvantaged, which sets up a political struggle over what to do. Taxes, interest rates, decisions about tariffs, and economic negotiations with other nations are but a few of the choices involved in this process.

The outcome is typically a result of both the power relationships and resources of the groups involved, and the degree to which governmental leaders can act independently of those interests.

A more general version of this process is the long-standing question of how governments and private business interests are to be related in making economic decisions. Within Western capitalist states, the experience of depression and war from the 1930s to the 1950s worked to politicize economic choices and to focus them on the national government. Political leaders became much more deeply involved in regulating the economy, and national prosperity became their responsibility. Presidents and prime ministers now regularly win and lose elections based on whether the economy is expanding or contracting. Further, the intensification of international economic competition has prompted many governments to play a much more important role in supporting particular industries.

Here are three different examples of this deep concern by governments for how their nations' economies function. Notice both the similarities and the differences.

Those who believe that private enterprise freed of governmental interference is the only source of dynamism in the world economy will find the close cooperation between business and government in the development of high technology industries somewhat perplexing. Perhaps the most important governmental role has come from an obscure unit of the Defense Department known as the Advanced Research Projects Agency (ARPA). Its bureaucratic location is a consequence of Americans' willingness to tolerate close government-business ties in defense production and illustrates the strong connection between technology and national security. ARPA has played a key role in the development of several industries, especially computers and software. The Internet, now used by millions daily, was originally created in the 1960s as ARPAnet. Though some try, it is hard to escape the conclusion that ARPA was an essential player in developing and accelerating the development of the core features of the most technologically advanced industries in the United States. Today, ARPA has a budget of over $1 billion to support the development of dual-use technologies. These are technologies with both defense and commercial applications. But ARPA also provokes strong criticism from those who fear any governmental role in defining industrial development and from others who support the principle underlying the agency but who object to the role of the military. Perhaps the key question raised by ARPA is whether success in the world economy today demands a major role for government in subsidizing and even selecting where research and development funds for expensive and risky high technology should be spent.[3]

In 1986, the Communist leaders of Vietnam faced a severe crisis. Having won the thirty-year war to gain independence and reunite the country in

1975, they found the economic and political program that followed was in tatters. Close association with the Soviet Union produced aid and some tourists. But the effort to collectivize the agricultural breadbasket in the south had failed, generating serious food shortages. The shelves of state-run stores were starkly bare, and economic growth had failed to keep pace with population increases. A huge Vietnamese army was bogged down in Cambodia, and the nation faced diplomatic isolation. Radical change seemed afoot in the Soviet Union, while Vietnam's neighbors in China, Malaysia, Thailand, and Indonesia were moving toward even more rapid economic growth. Many members of the Communist Party's ruling politburo saw their nation falling very far behind these other state's economic capabilities. Vietnamese leaders, their entire lives devoted to achieving national independence and scarred by many years of terrible war, were nonetheless moved by desperate circumstances to engage in a somewhat open debate about the failings of their system. In the end, they chose to join the world capitalist economy. Over the next ten years, markets were freed of much state control; many thousands of small enterprises selling plentiful goods emerged; rice production soared to make Vietnam a big exporter; foreign direct investment poured in; Vietnam withdrew from Cambodia and received diplomatic recognition from the United States; and economic growth jumped to more than 8 percent annually.[4]

The politics of business and government relations is also a crucial element of the world aircraft industry. Recent gains in global market share by the European consortium Airbus have hurt U.S. companies that have historically dominated this market. And the fact that Airbus is partially state owned has led to complaints of unfair subsidies and threats of a trade war. Between 1988 and 1990 Airbus increased its world market share for commercial jet aircraft from 15 percent to 34 percent, cutting Boeing's from 59 percent to 34 percent and McDonnell Douglas's from 22 percent to 15 percent. Government subsidies for development costs may have permitted Airbus, which is owned by private companies from Germany and Great Britain and state-owned companies in France and Spain, to undercut the prices of the American firms. The Airbus case has helped prompt calls for similar actions by the U.S. government in order to preserve America's market share. Meanwhile, Boeing and McDonnell Douglas are independently scrambling to devise a plan to counter this new competitive environment. One option was for a merger between the two companies, which took place in 1997. The U.S. government sanctioned such a merger of two giant firms because global competition made McDonnell Douglas nonviable on its own.[5]

The increasing role of the state in economic affairs is a defining element in our study of international political economy. Even in the United States, with its long-standing and now mostly mythological notions of a sharp separation of government and business, political leaders are deeply involved in business decisions. Regulating banks and bailing out failing banks, subsidizing basic research, giving tax breaks to investors, spending on defense, maintaining incomes for the poor, imposing regulations on polluters, and attempting to manage the economy through fiscal and monetary policy are but a few of the many areas of government direction of the economy. At the same time, many other nations—especially those first moving toward industrialization in the twentieth century—have gone beyond the Western model toward an intimate business-government partnership in promoting economic growth. These governments mobilize national resources and energies, build up certain industrial sectors, and manage and even restrict access to their markets in the name of a national economic strategy. The result is the establishment of a competitive environment in which the capabilities of entire nations are being harnessed to succeed in the world economy.

Political economy pays a great deal of attention to how governments affect economic systems and vice versa. But government actions and economic outcomes are the result not only of what happens inside a nation but also of what happens outside. We can see this easily in the case of the United States and ARPA: the military competition with the Soviets pushed the U.S. government to accelerate the development of technology that might provide the United States with military advantages. The Vietnamese government was more worried about its ability to keep up with its neighbors than with the mandates of communist ideology. And European governments and the U.S. government were equally and deeply involved in working to insure the preservation of a strong aircraft industry capable of selling its products in international markets. All these examples illustrate the importance of examining the international dimensions of political economy.

INTERNATIONAL POLITICAL ECONOMY

The frequent and extensive economic interactions among nations define our second category. Perhaps the most general and least obvious point here is the relationship of the world economy to the power politics among nations. The organization of international markets is made possible by the political agreements that nations reach. It is international power that defines legal relationships, creates and destroys economic opportunities, and raises and lowers profits. These processes come about in many ways. The French conquest of Indochina in the nineteenth century opened that area to French entrepreneurs, many of whom made vast fortunes. The creation of the International Monetary Fund in the 1940s, made possible by the preponderance of U.S. power, eventually helped create legal rules that today permit the movement of money around the world. And raising or lowering tariffs, which affect whether and how much of a good is imported, is closely linked to simultaneous negotiations among more than one hundred nations.

Similarly broad in its relevance to world affairs is the fact that the international military and political power of a nation rests largely on the dynamism of its economy. The ability to support a large military system depends on a nation's wealth, and its success in war depends on how this wealth and productive capability compares to other nations. Both a nation's technological prowess and its ability to turn its new developments into profitable products and implements of war are central to the nation gaining its objectives in the international arena. The extraordinary advantages enjoyed by the United States in the 1990–1991 war against Iraq, the 2001–2002 war against Afghanistan, and the temporary American monopoly of atomic weapons are but three of many examples of this fact. Over the past 150 years, international competition has been defined by an ever tightening relationship among military, economic, technological, and political processes.

When we probe these links between power and economics, matters become more complex. Things are usually not quite as simple as "the strong always win, and the weak lose," though this sometimes happens. One of the most important ways of thinking about the origins of a world economy examines the role of the most powerful state in establishing an open international economy, where goods and money move about with few hindrances. But this process gets complicated very quickly. An especially powerful nation—what political scientists call a hegemon—wants other, weaker nations to participate in the system voluntarily. This may require bribing them or winning the support of their political and economic leadership. At the same time, the hegemon must be careful not to let its economic advantages wipe out the economies of those nations whose cooperation it needs. Much less clear is whether this process of spending money to support the system actually weakens the hegemon in the long run. Also uncertain are the consequences of hegemonic decline. Does it mean the international economic system will also decline?

Power relationships are also crucial when we shift attention to the interactions of nations of sharply different capabilities. Much of the developing world is at a considerable disadvantage in the world economy. Many of these nations were subjected to Western imperialism in the nineteenth and twentieth centuries and have poorly developed mechanisms for international competition. Their corporations are small and undercapitalized, their educational and technological systems are underfunded, and their political systems are fragmented and conflictual. It is unclear whether this state of affairs is primarily the result of the capitalist world economy and the power disadvantages of these countries or the result of weaknesses in their societies. Equally uncertain is whether the few Third World states that have been able to accomplish strong economic growth are exceptions or are models that others need to emulate. What is clear is that different nations, groups, and individuals bring very unequal resources to their interactions with the world economy. There are many ways to see this inequality, but here is the story of a small village in Mexico.

Zinacantan is a small village in the southernmost Mexican state of Chiapas, just north of Guatemala. Chiapas has been an area of considerable political and even military strife in recent years. But that is not the focus of our interest. Rather, Zinacantan is one of many places where people face enormous difficulties when they encounter global economic forces. This is an area of picturesque mountains, but that means at best most families have land on a hillside. Zinacantan is a village of subsistence farmers, able to produce just enough for their families and animals to eat and then have a bit more to sell for a cash income. Population growth is high, resulting in increasing pressure on the land. Most homes have electricity but no running water. The people of Zinacantan have limited resources and are often at the mercy of global forces.

The North American Free Trade Agreement (NAFTA) is designed to reduce tariffs between Mexico, the United States, and Canada so as to increase trade. Efficiency of production and low prices for consumers are its goals. This does not work to the advantage of the farmers of Zinacantan, who cannot grow corn as efficiently, on mountainsides with no machinery, as in the Midwest of the United States. Cheap corn from the United States has reduced the cash incomes of farmers here. Some farmers tried to grow flowers as a cash crop. When Mexico suffered a financial crisis in the mid-1990s (partly the result of opening up its economy in response to NAFTA), many of the government's support systems for small farmers had to be eliminated. A fungus in the flowers grown in Zinacantan wiped out the crop because farmers could no longer borrow money to purchase the fungicide that would have saved it. The farmers of Zinacantan are placed in very difficult circumstances, and efforts to solve the problems sometimes make matters worse. Logging of the nearby forests produces erosion that destroys the village's farmland. And selling off land to the loggers only reduces the resources of Zinacantan's people.

One of the most important features of the study of international political economy is the inequality among different actors in the world economy. Sometimes this inequality produces tragic results.

Also of interest is how nations more equal to each other in power interact. The growth of the world economy in trade and money connects nations in webs of interdependence, forcing them to work together in order to manage the consequences. Interdependence sets up a tension between the domestic politics of making decisions and the international politics of reaching agreements. When we remember that national decisions are related to domestic interests, we can see that making compromises and sacrifices to smooth out international problems may be difficult. Equally important, nations may try to manipulate the fact that they are less dependent than others on the world economy to gain advantages in negotiations; winning their support for an agreement may require that more-dependent nations make special concessions. The economic conflicts between the United States and Japan—two very close allies—is instructive.

> With some frequency after 1975, the United States and Japan have experienced significant political conflict over their trade relations. First over textiles, then automobiles, next semiconductors, then with automobiles again, these two countries have struggled to manage the level of their trade. Conflict over trade is neither new nor unusual; nations have often turned to political negotiations to try to resolve economic disagreements. The U.S.-Japan conflict is noteworthy because these are the two largest economic powers in the world and because they are bound together in a very close security alliance. Each episode of conflict involved significant public rancor, occasioning repeated threats, deadlines, and recrimination. At one point, a U.S. member of Congress resorted to demolishing Japanese goods with a sledgehammer. Many others in Congress wanted to retaliate against Japan by blocking the sale of Japanese goods in the United States. In 1995, it was revealed that the U.S. Central Intelligence Agency provided the U.S. trade negotiator with a daily briefing about secret communications among members of the Japanese negotiating delegation. Behind the disputes is a complex mix of somewhat conflicting economic interests. The United States and Japan are caught up in a web of economic relations that benefit both nations: their economies are linked by large and increasing amounts of trade, investment, technology, and security interdependence. At the same time, the results of this interdependence have often favored Japan more than the United States. The consequences of the trade conflicts have been significant. Leaders in both countries have engaged in a debate over the merits of free trade and protectionism and over the nature of the U.S. and Japanese economies. Negotiations have led to politically arranged trade outcomes and to discussion about the need to alter the basic structure of each nation's economic system. "Voluntary" restrictions on Japanese auto sales in the United States, a quota for sales of U.S. semiconductors and autos in Japan, reduction of the U.S. budget deficit, and changes in Japanese public spending were among the deals. One important byproduct of the trade conflicts was worry over whether these disputes would lead to bigger problems. The continuing weakness in the Japanese economy after 1995 has led the U.S. to soften and redirect its criticisms of Japan.[6]

Thus cooperation among nations, even when there are important gains from such arrangements, may not be easy. This is also true because nations that are partners in cooperation are also engaged in competition. The politics of cooperation and of competition in the world economy are never far apart. For example, many of the nations in Europe have recently accelerated their cooperation in creating a free market for goods, services, and people. A main motivation is these nations' need to improve their ability to compete against the Japanese and the United States. But even the benefits of closer cooperation in Europe are not always sufficient to bind these nations' interests together. Sometimes one nation's circumstances can lead to significant conflicts with other nations, often because of the close interdependence between economies.

The end of the Cold War brought considerable changes in Europe. Perhaps the most important was the reunification of West and East Germany. The size of the West German economy and the role of the government bank, the Bundesbank, in managing the monetary affairs of Europe had made this country the dominant economic power in Europe. Other countries in Europe were required to follow the Bundesbank's leadership to make their system of fixed exchange rates work effectively. Stability of exchange rates required European countries to coordinate their monetary policies and interest rates, and they did this by following the Bundesbank. This became much more difficult after the reunification of the two Germanys. The dislocation and even trauma associated with integrating East and West and especially converting the East from a communist to a capitalist economy were sources of the problem. For East Germans, prices rose dramatically, and many enterprises closed in bankruptcy. Perhaps as many as 40 percent of those previously employed lost their jobs. Large sums were spent by the German government to stabilize and rebuild the East. The resources came from government borrowing and amounted in 1991 to almost 5 percent of total output. To stem the feared inflation, the Bundesbank used its economic powers to raise interest rates to more than double the level before reunification. This confronted other countries in Europe with a choice between raising interest rates and abandoning the fixed exchange rate system. Because many of these countries were in a serious recession, they resisted interest rate hikes. Eventually some, like the British, dropped the fixed exchange rate system. The pound fell by nearly 25 percent in less than a week, producing shock waves throughout Europe and the world. Some foreign exchange rate speculators made hundreds of millions of dollars by correctly predicting the outcome of the crisis.[7]

Sometimes these efforts to promote competitiveness can have unexpected and even unwanted consequences. In the 1950s and 1960s, the United States promoted the efforts of its multinational corporations to set up operations in Europe and elsewhere. But over time, the logic of the global marketplace has turned many of these corporations into truly transnational firms that produce and sell based on costs and markets around the world. In many ways, their identity as American firms may have declined, and their profit-based decisions may not further U.S. interests in competition with other countries. How does nation-based politics, intent on promoting national economic interests and supplemented by limited arenas of international cooperation, cope with the development of transnational firms that carry out a large proportion of world trade and innovation?

Equally interesting is the emergence of a range of nongovernmental and transnational organizations that operate around the globe. Their membership and funding comes from people of many nations, and their activities range from promoting health, literacy, and democratic institutions to mounting political efforts to press for trade policies and environmental improvement. The Internet now makes possible a variety of activities that elude government control but eventually affect government choices. Before 1980, only governments could afford the costs of setting up secure systems of real-time global communications. In the 1980s and 1990s most corporations came to afford such systems. Today, almost any group can achieve the communications systems that previously only the wealthy and powerful could have.

The shifting tides of world affairs have helped reveal the enormous importance of international political economy for understanding global politics. The processes of struggle, competition, and cooperation—always the main elements of international relations—have become increasingly focused on national capacities for generating wealth and technological innovation and for supporting institutions capable of adjusting rapidly to a changing environment. New and powerful interests in preserving and extending a global economy have been created. Nations and their leaders are involved as never before in each other's "domestic affairs." More and more, issues must be decided in international forums because behaviors and consequences spill across borders. And the global economy itself has advanced to the point that markets and exchange can sometimes constrain nations and corporations.

APPROACHES TO INTERNATIONAL POLITICAL ECONOMY

What is the best way to learn about international political economy? Before answering that question, you should realize that economic and political interests are deeply engaged by how people think about this subject. That is, individuals and groups who control different kinds of resources and/or have different kinds of opportunities also have quite distinct preferences about how the world should be arranged. Further, different forms of analysis contain different implications for organizing political-economic relations and thus for determining who wins and who loses. The consequence is that several strongly held ideologies have grown up around international political economy. Historically, three broad perspectives (sometimes theories) compete for our loyalties: Liberalism, Mercantilism, and Radicalism. Each makes an important contribution, but each also has important limitations; each has its best day in answering certain questions and in pointing us in the right direction.

Liberalism can trace its lineage more than two hundred years to economic philosophers Adam Smith and David Ricardo. Today liberals are found among economists; much of the business community in the West; writers for the *Wall Street Journal, The Economist,* and the *Far Eastern Economic Review;* and officials at the International Monetary Fund and the World Bank. Liberalism, also known as neoclassical thinking, extols the virtues of free markets and trade. Its

ideas are complex and often provide a convincing case for the power and efficacy of markets. Perhaps liberals' most important contribution is the idea that
all participants in a system of free markets and trade are beneficiaries. But the
arguments of liberals sometimes extend beyond respecting to worshipping
markets; their views often have the effect of rationalizing the interests of powerful groups; and liberals almost never understand the role of politics and
power in creating and conditioning markets. Liberals generally have a somewhat negative and even hostile view of government. They see government
spending as harming economic efficiency and reducing liberty. And they
often see the state as composed of self-seeking individuals who use power
only to promote their own narrow ends. More recently a new version of liberalism, neoliberalism, has built on older versions of political economy. Neo-
liberals make broad claims about the impact of markets, international
interdependence, and the possibilities for cooperation among nations.[8]

Mercantilists can lay claim to the longest intellectual tradition because this
perspective emphasizes the importance of nations and power in thinking
about economic issues. The mercantilist perspective is an aspect of nationalism, and mercantilists often call on governments to manipulate markets so as
to capture special benefits for their nation. The criterion used for judging
policies and actions is the need to preserve and enhance the power and prosperity of the nation. Mercantilists contrast most sharply with liberals in asserting that the gains of one nation usually come at the expense of others. The
international economy is closely linked to the competitive system of states.
Consequently, mercantilism sees a close relationship between economic
strength, technological prowess, economic competitiveness, military strength,
and national influence. Mercantilists can be found among the military and
economic planners of most nations. Frequently, groups disadvantaged by international trade will cast self-serving arguments in terms of protecting national economic and military strength. Military and economic planners in
countries like the United States, Japan, South Korea, and China pay close attention to the relative capabilities of other nations. The contribution of mercantilists is to recognize that international economic relations operate within a
world of competitive and conflictual nations. Economic capabilities do make a
major contribution to military and political influence. Power and politics are
always a part of economics. But, like liberalism, mercantilism is frequently tied
closely to the interests of certain groups or at most to a nation-centered view.
This leads to proposals that privilege these groups over others or that undermine cooperation among nations.[9]

A third perspective, "Radicalism," by contrast holds that the system of national and international capitalism biases economic outcomes to the benefit of
certain social classes within the most powerful capitalist nations. Drawing their
ideas from a Marxist perspective on political economy, radicals focus our attention on the area of greatest weakness for liberalism and mercantilism: the
way that economic power and political power create interests and shape outcomes. The merit of radical arguments is that they tend to see power relationships that others miss (or want obscured). The central purpose of radical

analysis is to uncover the role of power in seemingly "voluntary" market relations. An important benefit of the radical perspective is that it presses us to see beyond national economies or even a world economy created by transactions among states. Instead, they want us to see a global capitalist economy framed by the logic of capitalist exchange. One variant of radical theory is the idea of dependent development, which argues that market relations between rich and poor states are based on and reinforce inequality. Radical research is especially useful in identifying the impact of inequality on political economy and in critiquing the self-satisfaction in liberal analysis. Though radicals help us see how power can affect the distribution of economic benefits, they may not adequately appreciate how nations that are organized effectively for economic competition can turn the weak into the strong in a market system.[10]

Beyond the three broad categories are dozens of permutations and combinations of these and other forms of thinking, most with great confidence in one point of view. There sometimes seem to be nearly as many theories as facts. This buzzing confusion of theories and facts is a sign of the complexity of the study of international political economy, its political and economic significance, and of its newness. For scholars, complexity and even confusion make this an exciting field; for the uninitiated student, these are surely frightening and even intimidating. The authors of this book find merit and weakness in each of the three approaches and seek to write about international political economy by using each effectively. Thus, we find that markets work (sometimes), states matter (but maybe less than before), and the operation of markets is always embedded in power relationships and affects those relationships. One-sided books may bring out the nuances of a single perspective but usually fail to enlighten students.

We are also of the view that simply learning the intricacies of theories won't "stick" with you without a rich sense of context and, likewise, that mere presentation of the facts devoid of analysis is equally doomed. Understanding theories is much easier when they can be related to concrete events and situations. And the real significance of events can be comprehended only through theories. The key to learning about international political economy is to strike the right balance between theory and information. We hope we have found such a balance. Throughout the book, the many approaches to the study of international political economy are emphasized as the topic requires. No one approach is privileged, because no one has a monopoly on truth.

We will follow the lead of contemporary research in international political economy and focus on a set of overlapping and specific theoretical questions. The questions we address include:

- How do governments and domestic interests affect foreign economic policy?
- How do we understand the different ways that political leaders and institutions are entangled in managing and conditioning market outcomes?
- What are the roles of political power and international institutions in shaping the terms of trade flows and capital transfers?

- How does the globalization of finance and production alter the options and behaviors of nations and multinational corporations?
- How does a nation's economic growth and technological prowess affect its international influence?
- What are the sources of the development gap between the North and South?
- What alternatives exist to enable the poor and weak to survive and even succeed in the world economy?
- How do domestic and international factors affect the choice of development strategies?
- What are the sources of and barriers to international cooperation?
- How has the character of international economic competition been changed by new technologies?
- Why do different development strategies succeed or fail?
- How do we understand the relative bargaining power of North and South over the terms of foreign investment and borrowing?

These analytical themes are always wrapped in a context of background, events, stories, and anecdotes.

The purpose of this approach is to give students information they can use both to appreciate and to evaluate theoretical arguments. Much attention is devoted to the history of the world economy before 1945. This period is rich in events that offer perspective on the main points of analysis: the political origins of free trade; industrialization by poor states; the shifting tides of competitive advantage; the effects of war on economic relationships; and examples of cooperation, conflict, and competition. These and many other topics are considered in the post-1945 era in terms of the rise and decline of U.S. power, the explosion of interdependence and globalization, and tenuous efforts at development in the Third World.

The plan of this book advances the student toward a deepening understanding of the issues involved in international political economy. Chapters 2 and 3 are designed to serve as a further orientation to the subject. Chapter 2 does this by offering a basic literacy in economics, developing those concepts that are indispensable to understanding international political economy; Chapter 3 gives some historical depth to the concept of a world economy, offering a sense of how we got to the present and some perspective on the outcome of past efforts at cooperation and struggles for international economic and political power. Chapter 4 moves on to consider the special role of the United States in creating the political and economic basis for the new shape of the world economy and international interdependence after 1945. Chapter 5 examines the complex matter of the globalization of finance and production after 1973. Chapters 6 and 7 address two central concepts in international political economy as applied to relations among advanced industrial states. Chapter 6 considers international cooperation in managing the global economy and in forming economic blocs. Chapter 7 focuses on the problems of conflict and competition. We look at Japan and the implications for international competition, along with the rise of a new protectionism as a response to an uncertain world economy.

Chapter 8 begins a section new to this edition focusing on developing nations. It gives you a clear understanding of the different ways of thinking about the problems of development and the relationship of North and South. Poorer nations have followed several strategies of economic development. Chapter 9 evaluates these strategies in terms of case studies of success and failure. Chapter 10 evaluates the role of foreign aid in promoting or inhibiting development. Chapter 11's topic is the bargaining power and distribution of benefits between multinational corporations and developing nations. The political issues involved in the Third World debt crisis and the problems associated with suggested solutions are the focus of Chapter 12. The critical questions associated with food, population, and sustainable development are the subject of Chapter 13. And Chapter 14 offers some general conclusions concerning possible future directions for the world economy, in particular the balance between struggle and cooperation and the competitive positions of several nations.

International political economy is certainly not an easy subject. It takes two areas of intellectual inquiry and mixes them together in new and complicated ways, but we expect that the following presentation will help you sort through these difficulties and emerge with a much clearer understanding of an immensely important area. With patience and some dedication on your part, this will be the case.

NOTES

1. As quoted in John C. Pool and Steve Stamos, *The ABCs of International Finance,* Lexington, Mass.: Lexington Books, 1987, 80.

2. The debt crisis of 1982 is detailed in Chapter 12? The 1994–1995 crisis is discussed in International Monetary Fund, *World Economic Outlook,* Washington: IMF, May 1995, 90–97.

3. James Kitfield, "The New Partnership," *National Journal,* August 6, 1994, 1840–1844. See also Michael Hauben and Rhonda Hauben, *Netizens,* Los Alamitos: IEEE Computer Society Press, 1997, 96–126.

4. Adam Fforde and Stefan De Vylder, *From Plan to Market: The Economic Transition in Vietnam,* Boulder, Colo.: Westview Press, 1996.

5. Eric Vayle, "Collision Course in Commercial Aircraft," Cambridge: Harvard Business School Case, 1993.

6. Kenneth Flamm, *Mismanaged Trade?* Washington, D.C.: Brookings Institution, 1996; Leonard Schoppa, *Bargaining with Japan,* New York: Columbia University Press, 1997; C. Fred Bergsten et al., *No More Bashing,* Washington, D.C.: Institute for International Economics, 2001.

7. Alexander Dyck, "Germany in the 1990s: Managing Reunification," Cambridge: Harvard Business School Case, 1994.

8. David Baldwin (ed.), *Neorealism and Neoliberalism: The Contemporary Debate,* New York: Columbia University Press, 1993; and Peter Evans, *Embedded Autonomy,*

Princeton, N.J.: Princeton University Press, 1995, 21–42. You can find examples of liberal thinking on the editorial pages of *The Economist* and the *Wall Street Journal*.

9. Theodore Moran, *American Economic Policy and National Security,* New York: CFR Press, 1993; James Fallows, *Looking at the Sun,* New York: Pantheon, 1994; Wayne Sandholtz et al., *The Highest Stakes,* New York: Oxford University Press, 1992.

10. Stephen Gill and James Mittelman (eds.), *Innovation and Transformation in International Studies,* Cambridge, England: Cambridge University Press, 2001; Randolph Persaud and Robert Cox, *Counter-Hegemony and Foreign Policy: The Dialectics of Marginalized and Global Forces in Jamaica,* Albany: State University of New York Press, 2001.

2

❖

The Economics
of International
Political Economy

tudying the intersection of politics and economics at the international
level cannot proceed very far without a firm grasp of basic economic relationships. Reading this or any book on international political economy
requires that you understand a somewhat diverse set of economic concepts.
This chapter is designed to introduce these ideas in a straightforward and non-
technical manner. At each stage of the book we will mix economic and political matters, with the balance sometimes shifting in one direction or another.
This is just such an occasion, and its purpose is to provide a basic literacy in
economics.

The most important task is to see how international and domestic
economies are related, especially the ways in which the international environment constrains and directs national decisions. Governments strive to maintain
control over their economies and at the same time to reap the benefits of international trade. Increasing global interdependence makes this effort much
more difficult and uncertain. Understanding how these two spheres of economic activity affect each other requires a common conceptual language that
summarizes the most elemental features of each.

Acquiring a command of the language will involve a mastery of five basic
tasks. First, we need a clear sense of why trade takes place among nations in the
first place. The prevailing understanding of this is the theory of free trade, and
the basic elements of this theory and some alternative approaches will be considered. Second, we need to learn how to measure the movement of goods, services, and money across national boundaries—the balance of payments—and

how to interpret this somewhat complex and daunting array of statistics. Third, we must understand the tools of economic management by the central government that define the basic features of domestic political economy. The most important of these tools is fiscal and monetary policy, by which the government, through its spending, taxing, and banking policies, has a major impact on the economy. Fourth, the fact that international transactions require the exchange of one national currency for another creates a special set of problems that must be explored. Fluctuation in exchange rates not only influences the level of imports and exports but also creates an opportunity and need for political intervention. Finally, we need to bring these concepts together by examining the dynamics of monetary and fiscal policy, interest rates, exchange rates, financial markets, and the balance of payments.

These are complex matters, but they must be understood for the rest of the material in this book to make sense. Consider reading this chapter at least twice and playing with the ideas and relationships so that you can quickly see causal linkages. After these are clearly in mind, the rest is much easier.

FREE TRADE

Free trade is a variant on the notion of free markets and is probably the most important contribution that liberals make to the study of international political economy. It may also be the most controversial idea promoted by economists, as many people around the world react negatively to the idea of free trade. The central assertion is that, if trade is unrestricted, production will take place where it is most efficiently done, and as a result, all nations will benefit. Standing behind this is a preference for allocating resources to the most efficient way of producing goods; that is, a division of labor should operate among nations so that each concentrates on the set of goods to which it is best suited as compared with other nations and with all the kinds of goods it could produce. Economists focus their assessment of the benefits and costs of free trade on this idea of efficiency and the benefits to consumers in lowest prices for goods. They focus less on the politically relevant costs of the economic adjustments that people must make to satisfy the demands of free trade.

Why shouldn't a nation just produce and consume for itself? Why trade at all? One undesirable consequence of such a strategy is that it cuts the country off from goods that might be especially desirable and that cannot be produced at home. Thus one somewhat eccentric but popular view of trade sees it as an involuntary act: buying those goods that you cannot produce for yourself and selling goods abroad in order to make these purchases. Another, more mercantilist view sees trade as a sort of weapon used to enrich the country. By selling more than it buys, the nation will be better off. Somehow the nation needs to restrict imports and make sure that others do not respond by blocking its goods. The notions of trade as compulsion and comparative enrichment have frequently dominated thinking. By contrast, liberals argue that trade should be seen as mutually beneficial—where all nations are better off trading than in restricting trade.

How does the argument for free trade work? It rests on the fact that countries differ in their ability to produce goods. Often any given nation will possess an absolute advantage in the cost of producing a particular good. That is, one country can produce a good at a lower cost than can another. This concept can be illustrated very easily with some simplifying assumptions: two countries, Great Britain and the United States, and two products, wheat and iron. Workers in each country are better at producing one good than the other; this can be seen from the per-worker production of each.

	Wheat (bushels/worker)	Iron (tons/worker)
Britain	100	250
United States	200	150

Clearly, Britain has an absolute advantage in iron, whereas the United States enjoys an absolute advantage in wheat.

Suppose that each country has 200 workers. If both devote half their workforce to each good and avoid trade, they obtain the following output:

	Wheat (bushels)	Iron (tons)
Britain	10,000	25,000
United States	20,000	15,000
Total Output	30,000	40,000

Inspecting the figures reveals the benefits of specialization and trade. The United States can produce 200 bushels of wheat per worker, and Britain can produce 250 tons of iron per worker. If each shifts all its workers into the production of the good at which it is best, the total output of both will increase. Britain will produce 50,000 tons of iron by itself, and the United States will produce 40,000 bushels of wheat. Then trade can take place at the rate of four bushels of wheat for every five tons of iron, and both countries will benefit.

The amount of trade depends on how much of each good is needed. But notice that Britain can trade five tons of iron for four bushels of wheat. If Britain itself produces wheat, it will need to give up ten tons of iron for every four bushels of wheat.[1] For simplicity's sake, assume that Britain and the United States are happy trading 16,000 bushels of wheat for 20,000 tons of iron. The following is the amount of wheat and iron that each can consume as a result of this specialization and trade:

	Wheat (bushels)	Iron (tons)
Britain	16,000	30,000
United States	24,000	20,000
Total Output	40,000	50,000

Both the United States and Great Britain end up with more wheat and iron in this scenario than if they try to produce both commodities by themselves.

The benefits of trade in instances of absolute advantage are intuitively plausible and can be measured by the increase in total output and in the additional consumption in both countries. But economists argue convincingly that trade can benefit both nations even if one is inferior in the production of both goods. As long as the inferior nation has a comparative advantage in one good over the other, trade can be beneficial. This can be illustrated by assuming that the Britain-U.S. production ratios are now as follows:

	Wheat (bushels)	Iron (tons)
Britain	300	1,200
United States	100	200

This depicts a situation in which a British worker has an absolute advantage in the production of both wheat and iron. But because the United States is not equally inferior in both goods, the basis for trade is available. Notice that the trade-off in transferring resources from the production of iron to wheat is 4:1 for Britain, whereas it is only 2:1 for the United States. It is this comparative advantage that can be used to make trade profitable.

The easiest way to show this relationship is to examine the difference between the cost of producing the goods at home and the cost of buying them from the other country. If it costs less to buy the good abroad, specialization and trade make the best path. If we assume that cost is measured in terms of the ratios of production capabilities, comparative advantage is somewhat obvious. Thus for Britain the cost of producing the good in which it has a comparative disadvantage—wheat—is four units of iron. But the U.S. cost is only two units of iron, and Britain should be able to buy the wheat at that price. For the United States, the domestic cost of each unit of iron is one-half unit of wheat, but Britain should be willing to trade iron at its cost, which is one unit of iron per one-quarter unit of wheat. The United States is clearly better off paying the British price for iron, and Britain is better off paying the U.S. price for wheat. Thus comparative advantage makes trade beneficial for both countries. Although the benefits of trade are less pronounced under a situation of comparative advantage, this is the most difficult and unlikely case. Most nations will possess an absolute advantage in the production of some goods. But demonstrating the benefits of trade under comparative advantage makes a very strong case for free trade.

David Ricardo first explained the merits of free trade nearly two centuries ago, just at the start of Great Britain's industrial transformation. He made some assumptions to simplify the scope of his argument that were appropriate then but are less so today. Ricardo assumed a world of simple national firms and a fixed distribution of the factors of production, where large firms have no cost advantages over small ones and trade is mostly exchanging manufactured goods for agricultural goods. Does this still work in a world of complex and rapidly changing technology, large transnational firms, governmental involvement with firms and markets, and international trade much more centered on the exchange of manufactured goods? One necessary change is that, instead of seeing comparative advantage as coming from fixed natural endowments, we need to entertain the possibility that advantages now come more from the ability to create capabilities through new technology, skills, and innovation. And this may derive from malleable features of the national and international environment in which firms operate. These differences may indicate that free trade and free markets are only part of the story.

Those more sensitive to the political consequences of trade—radicals and mercantilists—have raised other arguments against an unrestrained enthusiasm for free trade. Specialization may not produce the type and degree of economic development desired. If a country concentrates on food and raw materials whose price relative to manufactured goods is declining over time, it will inevitably fall behind industrial states in national income. Further, the state concentrating on low-value added and low-technology production will miss out on the great gains in income and social development to be had from advanced technological production. The population of such a state will be condemned to a permanently inferior position in the international hierarchy.

In addition, certain goods are often thought to be essential to national security—for example, those used to produce armaments. An infrastructure of technological capability may be critical to maintaining military parity with other states. Specialization can expose nations to dependence on external supplies of such goods and thereby compromise security and other international goals. For example, many U.S. defense analysts have worried that purchasing high-technology goods from Japan compromises defense capabilities by exposing the United States to the possibility of a cutoff during a crisis. Lastly, movement toward free trade and specialization requires shifting resources away from some goods and toward others. This entails political consequences because those affected are likely to resist the personal costs and disruption associated with change. Adopting free trade or protection is an intensely political process involving conflicts over who will receive the benefits and who will bear the costs. When we consider the added dimensions of changed circumstances, development, security, and redistribution, the choice of free trade becomes somewhat less clear; it should not be surprising to learn that free trade has been the exception and not the rule over the past 175 years.

Why this is so can be understood through a consideration of the political economy of free trade. We have seen that free trade leads a nation to shift resources from the production of goods for which it has a comparative disadvantage to the production of goods for which it has a comparative advantage. Exactly what does *shift* mean? Businesses unable to compete because their products are at a comparative disadvantage in global markets will go broke and workers will lose their jobs. Only if businesses move to production of goods where the nation has a comparative advantage can these resources be profitably employed. How are we to understand this process politically? After all, this "shift" is likely to be difficult; some workers and businesses will not be able to make the transition. By the same token, those already producing goods with a comparative advantage will benefit from free trade.

If we think of national politics in terms of different groups based on their economic positions, several important conclusions about how trade affects politics are possible. A nation will have a comparative advantage in goods whose main factor of production (land, labor, or capital) is plentiful relative to that factor's availability throughout the world. By contrast, that nation will be at a comparative disadvantage in producing a good using a factor that is scarce relative to the rest of the world. From this we can see that increased or freer trade will produce significant benefits to those groups whose economic position is based on an abundant factor and that it will harm those whose economic position is based upon scarce factors. The key point is that free trade does not help all producer groups (although it will help consumers).

Free trade will benefit those in a nation who control relatively abundant resources that give them a comparative advantage in global markets; it will damage those who produce goods using a relatively scarce factor. This sets up a political conflict between such groups as they struggle over whether the nation will have free trade or trade barriers. For example, suppose that labor in a nation is scarce relative to labor's much greater abundance in the rest of the world. Closing off this nation to trade will permit labor there to receive higher wages than if free trade were adopted. An open economy would force workers to compete against the much more plentiful workers in the rest of the world, and their wages would fall. If capital (banking and finance) is abundant there relative to other nations, owners of capital will prefer openness because it can increase their returns through trade. The choice the country makes will probably depend on the political strength of labor versus capital.[2]

THE BALANCE OF PAYMENTS

One of the most basic and essential concepts for understanding the international economy is the balance of payments, which focuses on a particular nation and its transactions with the rest of the world. This accounting technique records the movement of goods, services, and capital across national boundaries over some period of time (month, quarter, year). The notion of "balance" here is somewhat misleading, for although this statistic always balances (because of the requirements of double-entry bookkeeping), we are really interested in the imbalances that inevitably appear in its various components.

Given that the parts are more important than the whole, what are the main items in the balance of payments? First, note that we want to measure all transactions of resources and claims on resources that the citizens of one nation have with the rest of the world.[3] For the purposes of this book, we will focus on eight major categories:

1. **Merchandise Exports and Imports**
   This refers to tangible goods produced at home and sold abroad (exports) and tangible goods produced abroad and sold in the home country (imports). This is the most familiar item in the balance of payments and includes all goods from clothing to computers to auto parts.

2. **Exports and Imports of Services**
   This refers to more intangible items, such as the transportation costs for goods and people, consulting, insurance, information, satellite transmissions, and banking.

3. **Investment Income and Payments**
   When someone invests resources in another country, he or she expects a return in the form of interest or dividends. This item measures foreigners' payments of investment income to citizens of the home country and the home country's payments to foreigners.

4. **Government Exports/Imports and Foreign Aid**
   The government may be engaged in selling or buying goods internationally, such as weapons. Additionally, the government may give or receive foreign aid.

5. **Balance on Current Account**
   The Balance on Current Account is a summary measure of items 1–4, that is, Merchandise, Services, Investment Income, and Government. Along with the Merchandise Account taken alone, the Current Account balance is the most frequently used measure of a nation's international transactions.

6. **Capital Account**
   This measures the actual investment of resources abroad or in the home country by foreigners. Typically a distinction is made between short-term investments, which have a maturity of less than one year, and long-term

investments, which have a maturity beyond one year. For example, when a Japanese bank purchases a U.S. government security, such as a treasury note, which matures in 180 days, this is recorded in the short-term Capital Account. (When the government pays interest to the Japanese bank, this is recorded in the Investment Account, which is described in number three above.)

7. **Official Reserves**

   A country's central bank holds reserves of foreign exchange and gold that it uses when it conducts transactions with the central banks of other nations and when it intervenes in foreign exchange markets to buy or sell currency. The effect of these actions is to balance the net differences of other items in this list.

8. **Statistical Discrepancy**

   The measurement of the balance of payments is an inexact process, owing to its complexity and to the fact that some transactions are concealed (for example, trade in illegal drugs). This item is a statistical device used to express the imprecision of measurement and to bring the overall credits and debits into balance.

A handy way to think of the balance of payments is to consider whether a transaction results in a payment to the country (credit) or a payment to a foreigner (debit). Or as a famous student of politics once said, "Follow the money." Table 2.1 offers a hypothetical example.

The balancing in the balance of payments is due not only to the accounting technique but also to the fact that everyone must get paid in one form or another. For example, imbalances in the merchandise, services, and investment accounts tend to be offset by the capital account. A current account surplus permits investment abroad, or to put it another way, it allows the accumulation of foreign assets. The nation gets paid for its current account surplus with the assets of foreign countries. In Table 2.1, the $39.9 billion surplus on current account is partly offset by the outflow of funds recorded in the capital account. A trade deficit, in contrast, encourages foreigners to invest in your country. This would mean that a deficit in the current account would be offset by an inflow of funds in the capital account.

To see how this process works and also gain some practice in understanding the balance of payments, look at Table 2.2. This is a comparison of our hypothetical country A's balance of payments over a four-year period. Note that the figures for Table 2.1 are in year 3. What can we learn about the dynamics of the balance of payments from Table 2.2? Perhaps the simplest matter is comparison of each item across the four years. The hypothetical country experiences a growth in exports, but imports grow even more rapidly. These different growth rates produce a shift from a current account deficit to a surplus and then back to a deficit. You can see this as the current account swings from a deficit of $21.4 billion to two years of surplus and then back to a deficit of $30.9 billion. The capital account tends to mirror these changes, with a net inflow of funds followed by two years of outflow and then a return

Table 2.1 Country A's Balance of Payments

	Credit	Debit	Balance
		(in billions of dollars)	
1. Merchandise			
Exports	164.3		
Imports		129.6	
2. Services			
Exports	21.1		
Imports		19.3	
Trade balance	185.4	148.9	+36.5
3. Investment income and payments			
Income	14.6		
Payments		21.4	
4. Government			
Exports	13.5		
Imports		2.6	
Aid (net)		.7	
5. Balance on current account	213.5	173.6	+39.9
6. Capital account			
Exports (long and short term)		58.4	
Imports (long and short term)	31.7		
Balance on capital account			−26.7
7. Official reserves		7.0	−7.0
8. Statistical discrepancy		6.2	−6.2

Table 2.2 Country A's Balance of Payments over Four Years

	YEAR			
	1	2	3	4
Goods/services				
Exports	102.2	156.7	185.4	191.4
Imports	119.9	140.1	148.9	227.5
Investments				
Income	3.2	3.7	14.6	20.2
Payments	8.4	11.9	21.4	23.1
Government	1.5	11.8	10.2	8.1
Current account balance	−21.4	20.2	39.9	−30.9
Capital account				
Exports	12.2	32.6	58.4	27.7
Imports	26.8	29.1	31.7	50.3
Capital account balance	14.6	−3.5	−26.7	22.6
Reserve account	3.2	−11.0	−7.0	4.1
Statistical discrepancy	3.6	−5.7	−6.2	4.2

Table 2.3 Country A's Creditor/Debtor Status

Assets abroad	
Official (government held)	$ 41.4
Private (direct investment and securities)	219.6
Foreign holdings of country assets	
Official (government held)	49.0
Private (direct investment and securities)	238.0
Net position (debtor)	$ −26.0

to an inflow. In this hypothetical case, country A is able to invest more abroad and reap the benefits in income in the two intermediate years as a result of surpluses. The swing back to a deficit, however, sharply curtails this investment and, instead, pulls in foreign investment. This process can be traced in the sharp drop in capital exports and the rise in capital imports in year four.[4]

This may seem to be good given that other countries are willing to make investments in our hypothetical country. Nevertheless, this situation has important and potentially costly consequences for the future. The increase in capital imports means country A must pay income to foreign investors in the future, while future payments from abroad will diminish due to the decline in capital investments overseas. If the combination of a trade deficit and an increase in capital imports persists for a long period, it will set up some unpleasant choices for the future. One option is to reverse the current account deficit in order to pay income on investments to foreign investors, perhaps by curtailing imports. Alternatively, continuing the current account deficit will force the country to borrow more from abroad to pay income on past investments. But the ability to use foreign debt to pay for a deficit depends on the willingness of foreigners to invest; they are not compelled to do so.[5] Thus, the need for everyone to get paid means that the nation must make adjustments for a current account deficit. The adjustments may come in market responses and/or in political action.

A related measurement is the nation's international standing as a creditor or debtor. This denominates the accumulated investment abroad by your citizens and by foreigners in your country, including governments and private actors. The position of our hypothetical state in year four might look something like Table 2.3.

The table reveals that country A is a debtor in the sense that foreigners own more of its assets than its citizens own of foreign assets. This is the result of the fact that deficits in the current account have, on a net basis over several years, been financed by investment from abroad. If the investment comes in the form of foreign direct investment, so much the better.[6] If the investment comes in the form of a debt it is less of a benefit and contains potential problems. Worthy of note is the fact that a debtor state will likely pay out more in interest and dividends to foreigners than it receives (notice in Table 2.2 the payments in year four of $23.1 billion and $20.2 billion in receipts), which is a further negative item in the balance of payments. This will continue until the current account can be brought into surplus for several years.[7] Had the situation been the opposite, and had the nation had more assets abroad than were held by foreigners, then it would be described as a creditor state. It then would likely receive a net income from abroad, a positive addition to its balance of payments.

To repeat, the balance of payments is most important for what it reveals about imbalances, especially persistent ones in the current account. But how do deficits and surpluses affect a nation's prosperity and financial position? What options does a government have for correcting or ameliorating these problems? To answer these questions, we must clearly see the relationships between national and international economies, and this requires a discussion of some of the basics of macroeconomic management: interest rates, money supply, and monetary and fiscal policy.

MONETARY AND FISCAL POLICY

For much of the twentieth century, governments have expanded their role in influencing the overall level of national prosperity. The two most basic and well-established areas are fiscal and monetary policy. Fiscal policy refers to decisions about spending, taxes, and borrowing by the central government, whereas monetary policy involves efforts by the central bank to manage the money supply and interest rates. Of the two, monetary policy has the longest tradition, is the most institutionalized, and generally is the most effective. Fiscal policy, by contrast, tends to be much more politicized because interest groups are easily able to identify its costs and benefits and act to influence decisions. The result is that efforts to use fiscal policy as a tool of macroeconomic management have a checkered legacy.

The decision to establish a central bank in the United States came early in 1913. The combination of financial panics and the management capabilities of other nations' central banks pushed even conservative leaders to create the Federal Reserve. One of the recurring features of capitalism and free markets is a boom-and-bust cycle, often characterized in financial arenas by a panic followed by a rapid drop in prices of financial assets.[8] The United States was much later in creating a central bank than were other large and prosperous countries. Great Britain did so in the 1840s, Germany in the 1870s, and upstart Japan in the 1880s.[9] One important distinction among central banks is the degree to which they act independently or are subject to political control. On that score, the German central bank—the Bundesbank—is certainly the most independent, with the Bank of England and the Banque de France generally following the direction of the government. The Federal Reserve falls

somewhere between the two extremes, able to act on its own but often responding to political pressure to expand the money supply or lower interest
rates.[10] The new European Central Bank (ECB) has yet to establish a clear
pattern. It is founded on the model of the German Bundesbank (which it replaces), and this would lead us to expect independence. But operating a central bank for a group of twelve nations is a very difficult task, and several years
will be needed to see if the ECB lives up to it model.

Monetary Policy

Today, the Federal Reserve, or Fed, as it is commonly called, has two major
tools for managing the economy: open market operations and the discount
rate. The purpose of both is to affect the availability of credit—that is, the
willingness of banks to make loans and of individuals and corporations to
borrow.

Most of what we treat as money is intangible, found in checking accounts
and not in bills and coins. Usually we pay for goods and services by ordering a
bank to transfer a computer entry from ourselves to someone else (writing a
check). Moreover, increases and decreases in the money supply for a nation
typically come much more from banks making loans than from the government printing money. The Fed manages the money supply by affecting this
process. When banks lend money to their customers, whether to buy a boat,
computer, or office building, this expands economic activity. The production
of goods and services to meet this demand boosts employment, and these additional workers spend their incomes and perhaps borrow money for purchases. The process also works in reverse: when banks decrease the rate of
lending, purchases of goods and services shrink, unemployment increases, and
further decreases in spending result.

How do actions of the Federal Reserve affect this process? First, we need
to know that the Fed is connected to member banks in several ways: it determines the proportion of bank assets that must be held as reserves; it has the
right to inspect, without notice, bank records and force changes in lending
policies; and it lends money to member banks. The most commonly used
technique for managing the money supply is open market operations. Here
the Fed is either pumping funds into or draining funds from the banking system by buying or selling U.S. government securities. When several billion
dollars of securities are purchased, by the Fed, the selling institutions (usually
banks and insurance companies) will receive a check from the Fed that will
expand the money available for lending. In adding funds to the banking system, and thereby increasing the potential lending power of banks, the Fed is
pursuing an expansionary monetary policy. By contrast, a policy designed to
contract or tighten the money supply would involve selling government securities. In this case, the Fed receives payment and effectively drains resources
from the banking system.[11]

The discount rate is also a powerful instrument for managing the money
supply. This is the interest rate charged by the Fed to member banks when

they borrow money from it. The discount rate also functions as an anchor interest rate; changes in it tend to spark changes in other interest rates. If the discount rate is 7.5 percent, the prime rate (the rate that banks charge their most creditworthy customers) might be 9.5 percent, first mortgage loans at 10.5 percent, and credit cards at 18 percent. When the discount rate increases, other interest rates also rise, though not always in lockstep. The reverse is also true: a fall in the discount rate will probably produce a drop in other interest rates.[12] Once again, the object is to expand or contract the money supply and thereby the economy as a whole. Raising the discount rate increases the price of money, discourages borrowing, and should slow down economic expansion. Lowering the rate encourages borrowing and should accelerate economic activity.

The Federal Reserve's role in the United States is to provide stability to financial markets during times of crisis and to promote economic growth consistent with low inflation. The Fed was created in the early twentieth century largely to moderate the financial panics that had become increasingly severe. A panic is a time when frightened investors attempt to sell securities all at once or when depositors lose confidence in the banking system and try to remove their money. The Fed also serves as a lender of last resort to provide liquidity (meaning a money supply sufficient for the transactions people want to make) to the economy when fear paralyzes the actions of other lenders. An equally important role of the Fed is to control inflation while encouraging economic growth. Inflation is especially harmful to persons who lend money or who have their assets in fixed-income instruments (such as government bonds). The fixed rates of future income are effectively reduced by inflation, because rising prices mean that interest received in the future has less purchasing power. In acting to control inflation, the Fed is protecting the interests of lenders and others who are hurt by rising prices.[13]

Fed decision makers pay close attention to the capital and credit markets, as well as the indicators of economic expansion and contraction. If the evidence suggests that expansion is moving too fast and inflationary pressures are increasing, the Fed is likely to take action. The quiet and short-term method of attacking inflation would be open market sales of government securities, thereby reducing the money supply and pushing up interest rates. A more public declaration of policy would be an increase in the discount rate. Depending on the severity of the problem, some combination of these actions may continue for many months or even years. During much of the 1970s and 1980s, when inflationary pressures were strong, the Fed pursued a "tight money" policy, pushing interest rates to unprecedented levels. In early 1994 the Fed acted in anticipation of rising inflation to push up interest rates and slow the U.S. economy. Following several years of economic expansion and rapidly rising stock prices, the Fed in 1999 began to raise the Fed funds rate and push up interest rates, all in the hope of slowing down the economy and stock market. Then in 2001, after a stock market collapse and warning signs of a recession, the Fed began a series of drops in the Fed funds rate to cushion these economic declines.

Fiscal Policy

The other major instrument of economic management is fiscal policy—the use of taxing and spending by the national government to affect the economy. The basic ideas of fiscal policy can be traced to the thinking of John Maynard Keynes, an influential British economist. Keynes and others argued that fiscal policy need not, and should not, be tied to the rigid orthodoxy of a balanced budget but instead could be used to manage the economy and smooth out the business cycle of expansion and recession (or depression).[14]

The notion of "pump priming" by the government to stimulate economic expansion involves deficit spending. Here, government spending exceeds tax revenue, with the difference made up by having the Treasury Department sell government bonds. Before about 1960 the theory supporting deficit spending was that selling bonds and spending the funds on government projects stimulated the economy by returning unused savings into the spending and income stream. With the Kennedy-Johnson tax cut of 1964, the rationale changed. Rather than rely on increased government spending, economists promoted cutting taxes and maintaining spending to produce a stimulative deficit. Here, recipients of lower taxes were expected to spend their increased income to accomplish the same result.[15]

The great weakness of fiscal policy as a means of macroeconomic management is that decisions about spending and taxes are rarely based on judgments about the "correct" size of deficit or surplus to fine-tune the economy. Not only do many groups—from the military to Social Security recipients—use political pressure to increase government spending, but politicians often use tax cuts to win votes, whether or not this is best for the economy. In 1966 and 1967 President Johnson chose not to increase taxes to pay for the Vietnam War because he felt that this would undermine an already weakened base of support for his policies. These extraneous factors may be rational as short-term political calculations, but they are harmful for economic management purposes. Often, the tendency to increase spending and to decrease taxes has overstimulated the economy, resulting in inflation. This was clearly the consequence of Johnson's decisions in the 1960s. In the 1980s, presidential budget proposals became blatantly political documents in a struggle with Congress. Budgets served more as a way to score points with constituents than to manage the economy.[16] In the mid-1990s, following years of gargantuan fiscal deficits, Congress and the president began to compete for votes by proposing several versions of a balanced budget and even a constitutional amendment to require such a balanced budget. In Chapter 5 we will see how the globalization of finance puts pressure on governments to control deficits.

EXCHANGE RATES AND TRADE DEFICITS

The one remaining set of concepts essential to understanding international political economy concerns the relationship between exchange rates and international trade. For trade to occur, money must change hands. But in international trade, one country's currency must be exchanged for another country's currency, and the rate of this exchange has significant consequences for the terms of trade and for the network of relationships linking domestic and international politics. This section explains how foreign exchange trading works and how exchange rates can affect trade, explores the reasons for government intervention in foreign exchange markets, and examines the impact of interest rates on exchange rates.

The exchange rate for a currency is simply how much of another country's money can be purchased with a specified amount of your own country's money. In 2002 one U.S. dollar would purchase 133.9 Japanese yen, 0.71 British pound, and 1.15 Euros.[17] Or reciprocally, one Japanese yen would buy 0.0075 U.S. dollar (just less than one cent); one British pound would purchase 1.41 U.S. dollars; and one Euro could be exchanged for 0.87 U.S. dollar (87 cents). These values are the result of daily trading in foreign exchange markets. That is, one currency is used to purchase another currency, and this trading comes at different rates of exchange, or different prices for currencies. Most of this trading is by private individuals, banks, financial institutions, corporations, and occasionally governments. Part of the reason for foreign exchange trading is that these individuals and corporations are engaged in international trade or finance and need to buy or sell currencies. But a very large part of trading is to speculate on changes in the price of currencies.

The exchange rate, or price, of a currency is determined by the demand for and supply of one currency in relation to another. Buying and selling currencies is partly the result of transactions recorded in the balance of payments between the two countries.[18] For example, trade between two countries generates a demand and a supply of both currencies as exporters seek to change their buyers' foreign currencies for their own. Exchange rates can be measured in terms of a single foreign currency or as an average of several currencies. The volume of foreign exchange trading is truly enormous, generally averaging in 1998 $1.6 trillion per day around the world. By comparison, all equities trading in the United States for one day is about $100 billion. Global foreign exchange trading is sixteen times bigger than stock trading in the United States.

The exchange rate is something in which governments are vitally interested. Governments use several ways to influence exchange rates. One way is to establish fixed rates, which typically involve substantial governmental intervention in foreign exchange markets to keep the price of a currency from moving up or down. A fixed exchange rate system operated in much of the world during the forty years before World War I and from 1958 to 1973. The opposite is a floating rate system, in which a currency's value is determined entirely by market forces without government intervention. The current set of arrangements is a complex mixture. About fifty countries have some form of modified float, whereby the government intervenes periodically to affect markets. Fewer than twenty states have adopted arrangements that provide for somewhat fixed rates in relation to a group of other currencies. The vast majority of states, mostly small and poor, have fixed their currency's value to one or more stronger currencies. An important distinction to remember is between hard and soft currencies. Hard currencies are those few currencies that

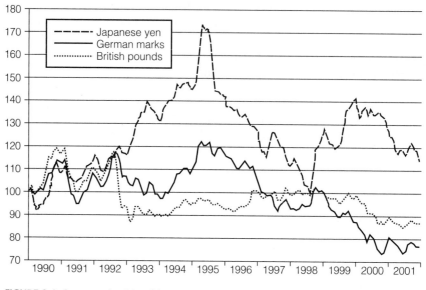

FIGURE 2.1 Comparative Monthly Average
Exchange Rates: Relative to U.S. Dollar

SOURCE: Pacific Exchange Rate Service.

are especially stable and secure, that may be accepted in payment for international transactions, and that international financiers can readily exchange for other currencies. Soft currencies lack these characteristics and are used only within the nation of issue.

Figure 2.1 demonstrates the erratic changes in the exchange rates of four major currencies—the U.S. dollar, German mark, British pound, and Japanese yen—between 1990 and 2001.[19] We can clearly see significant volatility in the value of the four currencies. The widest variation comes in the dollar-yen exchange rate, but there are also considerable changes in the value of the pound and the mark. Each of these currencies is considered hard, yet we still see significant changes.

There are almost no examples of exchange rates determined entirely by market forces. As we have seen, the central bank (government-owned) of a country sometimes intervenes in foreign exchange markets, buying or selling in hopes of influencing the price of its currency. But why would a central bank want to influence the value of its money? What effect does a particular exchange rate have on a nation's economic prosperity? Economists and government officials have long recognized that the value of a nation's currency affects the prices of its goods involved in foreign trade and the prices of foreign goods sold in its home market. By changing the value of their nation's currency, these officials typically want to change the prices of imports and exports and thereby affect the nation's overall balance of trade.

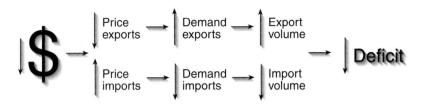

FIGURE 2.2 Exchange Rates, Trade, and Balance of Trade

How Exchange Rates Affect Trade

How is this supposed to work? First, remember that when people engage in foreign trade, they must price their goods in the currency of the selling market, whereas they want to end up with their own currency. This means that the money received from selling goods must be exchanged for the home currency. Thus, changes in the exchange rate directly influence the prices that can or must be charged.

To see this in action, consider the following situation. A U.S. exporter is selling computer disc drives in Great Britain. The exchange rate is £1 equals $2 (or $1 equals one half of a pound). The disc drives sell for $500 apiece in the United States, and the exporter is prepared to absorb the costs of transportation in order to establish a position in Britain. Thus, he or she prices the disc drives at £250 because this can be exchanged for the $500 he or she actually wants. Now suppose the exchange rate changes to £1 equals $3. The pound has appreciated in value (it now brings $3 instead of only $2), while the dollar has depreciated (because you need $3 instead of only $2 to get £1). What effect does this have on our exporter? Remember that he or she wants to end up with $500. To do this, the exporter now needs to charge only £166.67 in order to convert to $500 (166.67 times 3). A depreciating dollar permits (but does not require) U.S. exporters to lower their prices abroad.

The opposite result occurs when the dollar appreciates in value. Suppose that the original exchange rate of £1 equals $2 becomes £1 equals $1. The pound has depreciated while the dollar has appreciated. Our exporter now has a big problem. In order to end up with $500, he or she must increase the price to £500. Thus an appreciating dollar virtually forces exporters to raise prices or else see their profits fall. As an important aside, we should note that these effects also work, but in the opposite direction, for British exports to the United States.

This example gives us the basis for understanding how the government hopes to influence the nation's trade balance. We have a convenient historical example, namely the effort by the Reagan administration, beginning in 1985, to first "talk down" and later push down the value of the dollar. This came in the face of an unprecedented deficit in the balance of trade. Why try to force down the value of the dollar? The purposes can be summarized in Figure 2.2 as a causal chain. Verbally, this shows the expectation that a drop in the exchange rate of the dollar should lead to a drop in the prices of U.S. exports

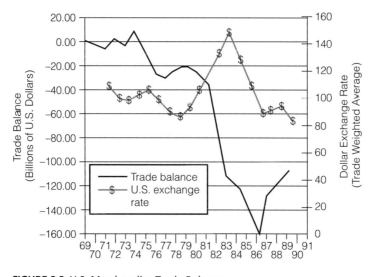

FIGURE 2.3 U.S. Merchandise Trade Balance
Compared to Dollar Exchange Rate

SOURCE: The data are taken from Department of Commerce,
National Trade Data Bank, October 1991.

while the prices of imports rise. A decline in export prices should also lead to an increased demand for these goods, while rising import prices should lead U.S. citizens to purchase fewer imported goods. As a result, the amount of exports should rise while imports decline, and the trade deficit should improve.

But there are important limits on the ability of an exchange rate depreciation to eliminate a deeply entrenched deficit such as that of the United States. Look at Figure 2.3, which shows a trade-weighted average of the value of the dollar and the U.S. merchandise trade balance.[20] It should be clear that the U.S. trade deficit has been only marginally affected by previous declines in the dollar. Although the dollar generally fell from 1971 to 1980, the trade balance worsened. Since 1985 the dollar has fallen by as much as 50 percent, whereas the trade deficit continued rising until 1987. The figures for 1988–1990 recovered to only about 1984 levels.

There are several fairly simple reasons why the desired reduction in the trade deficit has been limited. Perhaps the most important unrealized expectation is that, instead of falling, imports have continued to rise in spite of a falling dollar. Look at Figure 2.4, which shows an increasing trend line for imports after 1983. Two factors contribute to this problem. First, U.S. consumers believe that many foreign-made products are superior to those made in the United States, so even when the prices of imports rise, demand may not fall very much.[21] A second reason is that businesspersons who are selling goods in the United States may choose not to raise prices but instead to absorb some of the effects of a declining dollar. They might take this step to remain competitive, retaining their market share in hopes of a rising dollar. Or

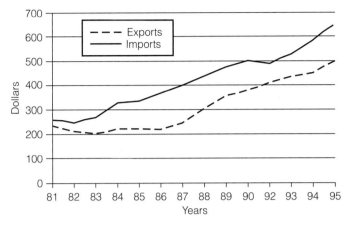

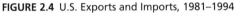

FIGURE 2.4 U.S. Exports and Imports, 1981–1994

SOURCE: The data are taken from International Monetary Fund, *International Financial Statistics Yearbook*, 1995.

they might decide to hold their money in dollars, investing in U.S. assets rather than reverting to a foreign currency. (Indeed, the growth of multinational firms with permanent operations abroad and less need to convert to a "home" currency increases the chances of this happening.) On the export side, those who sell abroad have options that would not necessarily help the trade deficit. Remember that a declining dollar permits but does not require the exporter to lower prices. But if exporters are already competitive in price, they may choose to keep prices about the same and reap the extra profits when the pounds (or whatever the currency of transaction) are exchanged for dollars. Once again, the presence of large multinational firms, which are in a position to benefit from continuing exchange rate transactions, may nullify much of the anticipated impact of a declining dollar.[22]

EXCHANGE RATES, TRADE, AND MACROECONOMIC POLICY

We can now begin to see how the complexities of national and international economies work. Frequently, actions in one economic arena complicate the situation elsewhere. International economic interdependence creates important difficulties for economic management. This section discusses some of the ways this can happen.

First, we need to extend our earlier discussion of exchange rates to see how a purely economic or market-based analysis of this process might work. In a system in which exchange rates are a result only of the forces of supply and demand for foreign exchange as generated by exports and imports, market processes can act to adjust trade balances automatically. For example, a trade deficit in country X adds to the supply of its currency in the hands of foreigners. (If you don't see why this is true, review the sections on exchange rates and the balance of payments.) When foreigners exchange country X's currency for their own, assuming other factors remain unchanged, the price of X's currency should fall. This decline activates the process, discussed earlier, of falling export prices and rising demand for exports, accompanied by rising import prices resulting in lower demand. This fall in prices should continue until the trade deficit has disappeared. A trade surplus brings the same arrangements into play, except in the opposite direction. But caution should be used in accepting this rather neat system. We have already considered how the connections among exchange rates, prices, and demand are subject to important qualifications. Another major problem with market-based solutions to trade imbalances is that foreign exchange trading has become disconnected from international trade. As we shall see in Chapter 5, the foreign exchange market is influenced by trade in only a small way. Speculators in foreign exchange make up the lion's share of actual trading. Equally significant are other complications that emerge when we consider the political and other economic dimensions of the relationship between domestic and international economic systems.

Allowing exchange rates to cure a trade deficit or attempting to manipulate these rates toward the same end can have unpleasant consequences. A fall in the dollar, if it works right, should force up import prices, thereby increasing inflationary pressures and even permitting domestic producers to raise their prices. Equally significant, export prices may fall abroad, leading to increased demand that spurs the domestic economy. But the combination of rising import prices and accelerating economic growth also creates the specter of inflation. This brings on the Federal Reserve (or the central bank of most countries), which, as we know, has a major commitment to fight inflation.

As we have seen, one of the main weapons in the Fed's arsenal for combating inflation is interest rates. Specifically, the Fed may, in anticipation of the inflationary effects of a falling dollar, use the discount rate and open market operations to force interest rates to rise, in anticipation of the inflationary effects of a falling dollar, so as to reduce business investment and consumer spending. This, the Fed hopes, will reduce overall economic activity and hold down inflationary pressures. In other words, the Fed may try to induce a recession, or at least an economic slowdown, to counteract the inflationary consequences of a falling dollar. In addition to helping control inflation, a recession can result in a declining demand for imported goods as the economy contracts.[23]

But this effort to counter the effects of the falling dollar can have negative consequences for the stock market, which is very sensitive to changes in interest rates. The individuals and institutions that own stocks pay closer attention to the somewhat more certain returns from securities that pay a fixed return rather than to the more speculative form of dividends or price appreciation. When interest rates rise, especially if the expectation is for continuing increases, many investors may sell stocks and buy securities that offer the new (increased) interest rates. Rising interest rates frequently lead to a declining stock market. The sequence can work like this: The trade deficit for the month is announced, and it shows a larger than expected gap between imports and exports. People who own stock, anticipating Fed actions to cope with the expected inflation from a falling dollar, will sell stocks, sometimes creating frightening declines. This is part of what happened in October 1987, when the Dow Jones Industrial Average fell more than one thousand points, or more than one third of its total value, over the space of a few days.

Thus, the effort to improve the trade deficit through a declining dollar can lead to inflation, higher interest rates, and even a recession. But matters do not stop here. Interest rates themselves also affect exchange rates. Remember that the value of a currency is a result of the demand and supply in foreign exchange markets. Interest rates affect the capital account portion of the balance of payments by influencing the level of investment in a country. To see this, suppose you are a foreign banker with the choice of investing in the government bonds of five countries. The interest rates on these bonds are as follows:

U.S.	Japan	France	Britain	Germany
8.7%	3.6%	6.1%	9.2%	4.8%

If the Fed raises the discount rate and drives U.S. bond yields up to 10 percent, this will attract investors. To purchase U.S. bonds, the foreign banker must first buy dollars with his or her currency. If large numbers of investors do this, the increased demand for dollars will drive up the exchange rate.[24]

So what do we have? A declining dollar designed to improve the trade deficit ignites inflation. This prompts the Fed to raise interest rates, attracting foreign investors. And this pushes up the value of the dollar, which we know could make the trade deficit expand. Economic interdependence makes policy choices much more complicated because the international and domestic consequences of actions may negate each other. The result of this set of counteracting complexities is that nations are often forced to choose whether they will focus on inflation or trade; an effort to solve both simultaneously is difficult.

The complexities of operating economic policies in an open economy are even greater than we have already seen. If one country chooses to pursue an expansionary economic policy, it must consider the international consequences of its actions. An expanding economy, especially if accompanied by inflation, pulls in imports. If this occurs when other nations' economies are not expanding, the consequence is likely to be a weakening of the current account balance. Because other countries are experiencing an economic slowdown, they are not likely to be very good markets for exports. A declining current account surplus or widening deficit acts as a drag on the overall gross national product (GNP) and may even negate the expansionary stimulus. This was the situation confronting the French government in the early 1980s as it sought to stimulate its economy at a time when other Western capitalist economies were in or entering a recession. The result was a serious worsening in the current account balance. As exports faltered and imports poured in, the value of the franc fell and inflation rose.

Clearly, international economic interdependence means that domestic economic policies frequently must be coordinated with other states in order to be effective. Furthermore, it is too simple to say that market systems, left alone, can solve the problems created by a payments imbalance or that intervention by governments can always smooth out market imperfections. There are several markets at work, sometimes operating at cross-purposes, and always functioning both with some autonomy and with powerful linkages to each other. Exchange rates, interest rates, and the markets for exports and imports certainly share this interesting combination of contradictory effects, independent operation, and interdependence.

Beyond the economics, there is the politics of the problem of managing domestic and international economic relations. Two situations are worth emphasizing here. Manipulating exchange rates, either by active intervention or passive acceptance of market forces, is a politically cheap way of trying to solve a trade deficit. Because most persons do not understand the mechanisms involved, the costs of such a policy can be disguised or hidden. A limited political impact is produced by assertions that a trade deficit results in transferring claims against a nation's resources to the rest of the world or that the deficit means that a nation is consuming more than it is producing. Certainly exchange rates are politically preferable to a strategy of economic restructuring or deflation and recession. But equally clear is the possibility that exchange rates may fail to solve the problem.

Also worthy of emphasis is the complex problem of achieving international political cooperation to manage interdependent economic systems. Obviously such cooperation is influenced by the status of political relationships in other matters. As we shall see in later chapters, success in cooperation is entangled in a web of conflicting and common interests and in the ability of leaders to maneuver and build a set of acceptable compromises among internal and external constituencies. This game of complex interdependence is at the heart of the problems of cooperation and conflict. But before we can talk intelligently about the present, we need to understand the historical origins of a world economy.

CONCLUSIONS

This chapter was designed to give you many of the concepts of economic analysis that are essential for understanding international political economy. At this point you should be comfortable with the following:

1. The concepts of free trade, absolute advantage, and comparative advantage are the keys to understanding why trade occurs and how the benefits of free trade are spread to all who participate. But remember that the

benefits are not equal and that nations seeking security do not always gain what they need.

2. The components of the balance of payments, including some of the summary measures, such as the current account and related terms like *creditor* and *debtor nation,* should be familiar concepts. Additionally, you need to understand the relationship of the current account and capital account.

3. The differences between fiscal and monetary policy and the basic mechanisms of their operation must be almost second nature. Pay special attention to the use of monetary policy and interest rates to manage the domestic economy.

4. The lines of influence between exchange rates and the prices of and demand for exports and imports are an especially important set of relationships. You need to be able to work through this process quickly and to apply it to various policy options. Equally significant, however, is the plethora of factors that undermine and distort this process.

5. Finally, the most difficult but also most important matter is the interacting effects of the balance of payments, monetary and fiscal policy, and exchange rates. This is a major topic, in more complex form, in subsequent chapters.

There are other important economic concepts left for consideration in subsequent chapters, including the gold standard, fixed exchange rate systems, key currency, and protectionism. But with the ideas of this chapter in mind, you are now prepared to begin thinking seriously about international political economy.

NOTES

1. Remember that British workers can produce 2.5 times as much iron as wheat in bushels. So to get four bushels of wheat from their own workers, they will need to give up 4 times 2.5, or 10 tons of iron.

2. Ronald Rogowski, *Commerce and Coalitions: How Trade Affects Political Alignments,* Princeton, N.J.: Princeton University Press, 1989.

3. There are many complicated issues concerning who counts as a citizen. An example is a company with units operating abroad: the branches or facilities abroad are treated as foreigners.

4. The relationship between the current account and capital account is not a necessary one. A surplus in the current account means that the country in question is accumulating foreign exchange. This permits but does not require it citizens to use those resources to make investments abroad. By contrast, a current account deficit results in foreigners accumulating the country's currency (or claims on its currency), and this allows them to purchase its assets. What happens if these investments don't take place? The balancing factor then becomes the official reserve account, which entails the transfer of

reserve currencies or other liquid international assets among central banks. So a current account deficit not offset by investments from abroad will produce the transfer of official reserve assets to foreign countries.

5. When this investment fails to happen, several things may occur. The country's exchange rate may fall, interest rates may rise to attract investment, and/or the reserve account may be drawn upon to pay the bills for imports.

6. Foreign direct investment (FDI) involves foreigners purchasing business assets in a nation with the purpose of managing those assets as a business. When Intel buys land and builds a plant to package semiconductors in Malaysia, this is foreign direct investment. By contrast, when a U.S. citizen buys stock in a Malaysian company hoping its price will go up, this is a portfolio investment. The key point for balance of payments purposes relates to how fast funds can be withdrawn. FDI involves a long-term commitment to the nation. Removing the funds requires selling an entire business, a slow process. Portfolio investment is much easier to withdraw, and its potentially negative impact on the balance of payments is much greater.

7. In Country A's case, the size of the debtor position is small and not terribly worrisome. However, the trends toward a current account deficit in this country's balance of payments create the possibility of continuing additions to its international debt. Should this debt become large, as measured by the ratio of interest payments to exports, the potential for trouble will grow. The composition of the debt also matters, especially the maturity of the debt. When large portions must be repaid within twelve months (short term), the possibility for trouble is much higher. Thus, when debt reaches high levels and when it is mostly short term (as with some nations in Asia in the late 1990s), the

debtor status takes on important consequences.

8. Charles Kindleberger, *Manias, Panics, and Crashes,* New York: Basic Books, 1989.

9. Charles Goodhart, *The Evolution of Central Banks,* Cambridge: MIT Press, 1988. For establishment of the Federal Reserve, see Richard Timberlake, *The Origins of Central Banking in the United States,* Cambridge: Harvard University Press, 1978.

10. John Wooley, *Monetary Politics: The Federal Reserve and the Politics of Monetary Policy,* Cambridge, England: Cambridge University Press, 1984; Ellen Kennedy, *The Bundesbank,* London: Pinter, 1991.

11. These actions also affect interest rates. Changes in the supply of money cause changes in the price of money, that is, in interest rates. Two key interest rates that often reflect open market operations are the Federal Funds rate and the Treasury bill rate. A rise in these rates may indicate that the Fed is following a tight money policy by selling government securities (the price of T-bills falls, and the effective interest rate rises). When rates fall, the Fed may be pursuing an expansionary policy through open market purchases (the price of T-bills rise, and the effective interest rate falls). Similar policies are associated with the Fed funds rate, which is the interest rate charged by banks when they borrow money from each other for very short periods of time. The Fed manipulates its open market operations to achieve a target Fed funds rate, thereby affecting interest rates throughout the economy.

12. Note that interest rates mostly rise and fall independent of Fed action, based on market-driven changes in the supply and demand for funds.

13. For a discussion of the contending interests over inflation, see William Grieder, *Secrets of the Temple,* New York: Simon and Schuster, 1987.

14. There was great resistance to Keynes's ideas among conservatives, especially

from the 1930s to the 1960s. An interesting discussion of the political struggles over Keynesianism is Robert Collins, *The Business Response to Keynes,* New York: Columbia University Press, 1981.

15. Some economists, known as "supply siders" justified the Reagan tax cuts in 1981 by predicting that the increased work and risk taking would produce an additional economic stimulus.

16. Another complicating factor is that fiscal policy and monetary policy are made in different political settings. The president and Congress are the chief actors in fiscal policy, whereas the Fed makes decisions about monetary policy. There is no guarantee of policy consistency, and actions at cross-purposes are not uncommon

17. Most newspapers carry reports of daily transactions in foreign exchange markets, usually in the business pages. The are many Internet sites for near real-time information. Two are <http://pacific.commerce.ubc.ca/xr/> and <http://finance.yahoo.com/m3?u>.

18. In addition, speculators hoping to profit from fluctuations in currency prices also affect demand and supply. The transactions of speculators may or may not be recorded in the balance of payments.

19. Note the value of the U.S. dollar is revealed by examining the value of each of the other three in relation to the dollar.

20. A trade-weighted average means an average value of the currencies of the nation's main trading partners. The average is weighted by the amount of trade conducted; more trade with a particular partner leads to a higher weighting.

21. The relationship between the change in price and the resulting change in demand is the *elasticity of demand.* When demand changes are large, elasticity is high. But this process is more complicated. Changes in elasticity, especially in international trade, may vary over time and this is often referred to as a "J curve." The J curve reflects this time-based relationship of exchange rates and prices of exports and imports, and demand may be curvilinear. At first, prices of imports and exports may change immediately, while demand may take some time to change (low initial elasticity, followed by higher elasticity later). The J curve indicates that the immediate result of a fall in a currency may be a *worsening* of the trade balance. If export prices fall and import prices rise, with little initial change in demand, then exports (measured by volume times price) will actually fall and imports will actually rise. This deterioration in the trade balance should be followed by improvement (thus the J curve) as elasticities in demand for exports and imports take over and swell export volumes by more than the fall in prices, and the reverse occurs for imports.

22. A detailed discussion of the adjustment process is in Paul Krugman, *Has the Adjustment Process Worked?* Washington, D.C.: Institute for International Economics, 1991.

23. This set of actions is similar to the adjustment often forced on a nation by the International Monetary Fund (IMF). Typically a country will have persistent balance of payments deficits and will have trouble paying its foreign debts. The "belt tightening" usually involves cuts to government spending, increases in taxes, and increasing interest rates.

24. An additional consideration for investors is the stability of the exchange rate, because this affects the actual yield. A falling exchange rate reduces the net return because you will need more foreign currency to purchase that home currency. Conversely, a rising exchange rate adds to the overall return; thus the combination of high interest rates and a rising exchange rate reinforce each other. Remember, the key is relative interest rates—relative to the rest of the world.

ANNOTATED BIBLIOGRAPHY

Richard Caves et al. *World Trade and Payments: An Introduction.* New York: HarperCollins, 1993. Provides an excellent introduction to the entire field of international economics.

Paul Erdman. *Tug of War.* New York: St. Martin's/Griffin, 1997. A lucid discussion of international financial crises.

Robert Heilbroner and Lester Thurow. *Economics Explained.* New York: Touchstone, 1982. A very clear and basic introduction to economics.

Paul Krugman. *The Age of Diminished Expectations.* Cambridge: MIT Press, 1991. Offers a series of clearly written essays relating to many of the central topics of economics and economic policy.

Michael Melvin. *International Money and International Finance.* New York: HarperCollins, 1992. Provides a very clear and understandable introduction to the complications of exchange rates.

John C. Pool and Steve Stamos, *The ABC's of International Finance.* Lexington, Mass.: Lexington Books, 1987. A theoretically limited but very clear introduction to the basics of international economics.

Paul Samuelson. *Economics.* New York: McGraw-Hill, 1990. The standard textbook in the field of economics.

3

❖

The Origins of a World Economy

In some respects a world economy is very much like other economic systems: goods are produced and services provided, wealth is accumulated and destroyed, investments are made on the basis of maximizing returns, and prices fluctuate according to supply and demand. And yet, because these things are taking place across national borders, we know that something different is happening. We are accustomed to thinking of economies as coextensive with the nation. Historically, nations have guarded their borders jealously; after all, this is one of the things that defines them as nations. Governments have always tried to place some controls on trade, immigration, and monetary transactions with the outside world. Consequently, the stupendous growth of a world economy over the past 150 to 175 years calls for understanding on its own terms.

The purpose of this chapter is to provide the student with the tools and information needed to begin thinking about the world economy as a special phenomenon. The approach is historical so the student can appreciate the long-term background to contemporary events and gain some perspective on the many different outcomes of international economic cooperation and conflict. Especially important is learning how the transformation of the world economy is inextricably enmeshed with international political and military developments. The discussion will follow two related lines. The first deals with developments within nations, such as technology and production, special advantages in raw materials, labor skills, and entrepreneurial strategies and behaviors. The second line considers economic relations among nations, including the flow of goods, capital, information, and technology, and competitive advantages and their effects on political and military relations. The focus includes the beginnings of international trade in manufactured goods in the early nineteenth century, the formation of a world economy of expanding trade and interdependence from 1840 to 1875, and the breakdown and collapse of this system in World War I and the Great Depression.

INDUSTRIALIZATION
AND INTERNATIONAL TRADE

We begin our story with the late eighteenth and early nineteenth centuries. This is when the industrial system spread from England across Europe and, in conjunction with the explosion of British trade in manufactures, began to create a world economy somewhat like our own. Of course, international economic relations of substantial proportions did exist before this time. For example, during the sixteenth and seventeenth centuries a complex economic system grew up in Asia. It was organized by the British, Dutch, Spanish, and Portuguese around cloth, spices, and silver.[1] But what distinguishes our starting point from previous periods is the sense of potential economic gains for all from world trade, the growing importance of manufactured goods in foreign trade, and the enormous increase in the degree of interdependence among nations.[2] These factors combined to create new forms of production and thereby expanded dramatically the benefits from trade. Prior to the mid-eighteenth century, a mercantilist view of trade defined the way virtually all states thought about economic policy. This meant that protectionism—efforts to prevent goods from entering the country and laws controlling the way trade is conducted—ruled the day. The growth of world trade changed nations' willingness to participate in this new system of freer trade, even as expanding profits encouraged overseas investments at unprecedented levels. This process extended from 1780 to 1850 and resulted in the creation of a world economy with features resembling that of our time.[3] As we shall see, the interdependence established in this new world created a variety of political problems that contributed to the breakdown of this system during World War I.

British Industrialization

An enduring and exceedingly important characteristic of the world economy is its unevenness. Nations compete with each other on quite unequal terms based on distinct advantages in technology, economic organization, and resources. Such was the case with the industrial development of Britain in the late eighteenth century and with the changes in the world economy that followed. The British enjoyed the benefits of being the leaders in new manufacturing processes because of a particular configuration of factors favoring this development.

In 1750, Britain was already a highly commercialized society with the largest market in Europe. Rising agricultural productivity over much of the eighteenth century supported a rapidly increasing population. A monetary economy (in contrast to one based on barter) was widely accepted, and the country had a long and successful tradition of international trade.[4] In terms of labor, Britain had few restrictions on movement from agriculture to manufacturing and also possessed a significant number of persons competent in the somewhat low-level technical skills needed for the period's manufacturing processes. Additionally, sufficient capital was available for the scale of investment needed in manufacturing processes.[5] The focus of these activities was initially in the production of wool cloth and, by the late eighteenth century, in manufacturing cotton cloth. Buoyed by the opportunities in domestic and foreign markets, British entrepreneurs quickly adopted new techniques of production. The result was a dramatic decline in costs and prices and a consequent explosion in sales.[6]

British political and military power also mattered. Already a major power, Britain became the world's foremost state during the period of the industrial revolution. This meant Britain could defend itself and could capture and preserve the benefits of its new capabilities. Had the industrial innovations in Britain taken place elsewhere—in India, for example—the Indian ability to retain these advantages would have been compromised, as the country was already dominated by foreign powers and interests. India could not have prevented control over these new industrial processes from slipping into others' hands.[7]

It was the sale of cotton goods abroad that fueled a general rise in British exports from 1784 to 1814. "Exports became, for the first time, a powerful 'engine of growth' of national income."[8] Sales abroad accounted for 18 percent of national income in 1801, and the cotton industry alone represented 7 percent of all national products in the same year.[9] Of equal significance was the fact that markets and sources of supply increasingly came from areas that were outside the Empire and, consequently, not under British political control. Trade relationships with other sovereign states were eventually to take on quite a different color than those with colonial areas. Unfortunately, these tendencies were interrupted somewhat by the international conflicts of 1792–1814 (the wars between revolutionary and Napoleonic France and much of Europe). The combination of the British blockade of continental ports and extreme protection by the French from British products retarded economic development in Europe and permitted Britain to move into French overseas markets.

But we should not overestimate the impact of industrial production or international trade on Britain during this period. Industrialization, although rapid, did not transform Britain or the world economy all at once. For this to happen, British political and economic leaders had to develop an understanding of trading relationships based on something other than a mercantilist effort at national aggrandizement. That is, we need to understand how developments in British political economy, the adoption of industrial systems and the growth of markets in Europe, and the unilateral British decision for freer trade produced a world economy with familiar features.

After 1815 many continental European nations, fearing competition and the political consequences of a flood of foreign goods, raised protectionist barriers to British goods. Mercantilism and protectionism remained the ideological core of foreign trade policy.

> The cardinal fact for most French producers after 1815 was the existence of an overwhelmingly dominant and powerful industrial producer not only as their nearest neighbor but as a mighty force in all foreign markets and sometimes in their own heavily-protected domestic market.[10]

For several reasons, these same nations were unable to match British productivity quickly, often taking nearly fifty years to catch up in any meaningful sense. The barriers to advancing among Europe and states were varied. In some cases it was technological backwardness (often rectified by industrial spies); in other cases, the growing scale of competitive enterprise had outpaced the capital capacities of family firms. Many European countries were disadvantaged by higher costs, by attitudes that undermined effective entrepreneurship, and most of all by the patchwork nature of their countries and markets. The complex set of political and cultural divisions often carved markets up into areas too small to support the most efficiently sized production unit.[11] In some instances patterns of industrialization can be linked to abundant coal reserves (Belgium), whereas others took advantage of human capital, awaited political efforts at national unity, depended on the agricultural sector, or simply failed in their efforts to make the transition.[12] In spite of the myriad paths and fitful efforts at industrialization, many European states had made a significant beginning by mid-century, and this process accelerated considerably thereafter.[13]

THE TURN TO FREER TRADE

Repeal of the Corn Laws

Meanwhile, several developments in the British and world economies contributed to a British-led effort to create a more open international economy. In Britain agriculture remained an important but declining sector. Indeed, between 1815 and 1845 Britain lost the capacity to feed itself as population growth outstripped agricultural output. At the same time, exports failed to expand at a rate sufficient to provide employment to a growing population. Stagnation in exports was due mainly to falling prices and to successful efforts in mainland Europe and the United States to protect their infant industries. The combination of greater dependence on imported food and slow economic growth fueled radical political challenges to the government and helped prompt a somewhat novel political and economic response.[14]

Traditionally, Britain had followed a policy, reflecting the political power of its landed interests, of protecting agriculture with tariffs and other restrictions—the Corn Laws. But these restraints on trade increasingly came to be seen by manufacturing and financial interests and by political leaders as a barrier to solving the problems of food and exports. Manufacturers were especially adamant that the Corn Laws kept agricultural prices artificially high and prevented other nations from selling Britain food and then purchasing British manufactured goods. Some hoped that a unilateral reduction in British tariffs would induce a freeing of trade elsewhere and that this would lead to an international division of labor resting on British manufacturing with agricultural and raw material production. (Not inconsequentially, this arrangement would nip in the bud the growing industrial competition from Europe and the United States.) These views gathered strength as manufacturing rose in relation to agriculture, but the shift was accelerated by the potato famine in Ireland. The 1840s produced repeal of the Corn Laws and of the Navigation Acts restricting transport to British ships. In addition, many of the duties on manufactured imports were eliminated. In the years after 1846, British manufactured exports rose dramatically.[15]

The repeal of the Corn Laws is important for two reasons. First, it helps us see the role of domestic political alignments in producing foreign economic policy. "Economic theories prevail ... only when they have mobilized political authority, that is, only if those who believe the theories get the resources that enable them to take authoritative action."[16] For decades before 1846, economists had promoted the benefits of free trade. But only when the coalition of political forces favoring free trade was able to convince government leaders and defeat protectionist agriculture could this become national policy.[17] Second, this unilateral move to free trade was of crucial importance in shaping the world economy. In 1860, Britain and France signed the Cobden-Chevalier Treaty, substantially reducing tariffs on trade between the two nations. This was followed by tariff reductions in eight other European countries and ushered in the first major period of relatively free trade.[18] Equally important, a system of multilateral trade and capital flows, centering largely on Britain, emerged to form a world economy of substantial proportions. One increasingly important nation—the United States—moved in the opposite direction and adopted more restrictive tariff policies after 1865.

The Expansion of the World Economy

The movement toward freer and increased trade was influenced by and in turn helped to advance several related developments between 1850 and 1875. The political unification of Germany, pushed by the need for unified markets and the desire for greater international influence, changed the economic landscape in central Europe. Much of the process of economic change was centered on building railroads—an activity that required substantial amounts of capital and had the consequence of expanding dramatically the scope and scale of markets. Initially, much of the capital for railroads in Belgium and France came from Britain. Later, France became a capital exporter, even as Germany was able to meet its own needs.

In the midst of these developments, industrial progress in Europe produced a widened scope of economic relationships. Expansion of textile production in France and Germany, along with continuing growth in Britain, resulted in sharp increases in wool and cotton imports from the United States, Australia, and New Zealand. Improvements in continental and oceanic transportation, beginning especially in the 1860s and 1870s, led to dramatic increases in European imports of grain and meat. A multilateral division of labor, based on geography and the level of industrialization, developed within Europe. British goods, especially railroad equipment, machinery, coal, and textiles, were sold in economically advanced sections of Europe, while German industry, for example, was successful in central and eastern European markets. Ironically, British trade in machinery and railroads helped the newly industrializing areas of Germany and France to utilize their own advantages (for example, German wages were lower than those in Britain) to close the gap with Britain and to adopt the role of leading other European states into the world economy.[19]

Equally telling, in addition to these general reservations about free trade, are the calculations made by countries who chose to participate in freer trade in the mid-nineteenth century. France used the 1860 treaty to deflect Britain from interfering in its conflict with Austria over Italy. The German free trade area—the Zollverein—recognized that its substantial sales of grain in Great Britain would be protected by lowering tariffs on British goods. In the United States, the new possibilities for trade with Britain created by lower tariffs helped solidify a political coalition supporting lower U.S. tariffs. These examples strongly reinforce the importance of understanding matters like free trade in terms of political economy—a perspective that acknowledges a close relationship between economic and political influences.[20]

THE PERILS OF INTERDEPENDENCE:

1873-1914

Transformation of the World Economy

The period from 1873 to 1914 produced changes in the world economy equal in importance to those of the preceding hundred years. The pace of change accelerated, with an extraordinary shift in the distribution of relative international economic power resulting from the decline of Great Britain and the rise of the United States and Germany. Accompanying this acceleration were the first stirrings of industrialization in what we today call the Third World. This was true in India, China, and especially Japan. The continuing expansion of international trade and finance led to a growing interdependence among national economies, as measured by price movements, common financial crises and economic fluctuations, increasing proportions of foreign trade and investment, and a more coherently organized international monetary system centered on gold.

At the same time, the free trade system created after 1846 was eventually dismantled and reversed by widespread protectionist sentiments. Higher tariffs were a reflection of intensified competition for markets and of the political and economic dislocations caused by dramatic increases in trade. Finally, the very character of industrial life began to change in fundamental ways. New industrial systems, such as chemicals, oil, electricity, and steel, emerged in the late nineteenth century not only as leading but even as dominant sectors. In these and other industries a new type of enterprise developed—one of much greater size and designed to take advantage of significant economies of scale in production and national and international marketing and distribution networks.

The changes in the distribution of international economic and industrial power can be seen in Tables 3.1 to 3.5. The precipitous decline of Great Britain and France and the equally rapid rise of the United States, and to a lesser extent Germany, are the most striking features of Table 3.1. That Britain, in the space of two generations, could fall relatively so far in spite of a growing economy over most of this period is testimony to the tenuous position of all nations in the modern world economy.[21] The United States and Germany, along with Russia, also experienced a rapid expansion in population, with growth from 1890 to 1913 of 55 percent, 36 percent, and 50 percent, respectively. By contrast, British population growth for the same period was only 22 percent, while in France it amounted to less than 4 percent.[22] In selected areas the shift toward a U.S. and German advantage was even more dramatic. Clearly, by 1913 British dominance of world industrial capabilities had been swept away.

How are we to understand this remarkable transformation? There are really two matters to explain: first, the extraordinary economic growth by these nations taken as a whole; second, the dramatic differences among the nations. The broad base of growth is best understood as a result of freer trade (though this diminishes with time), extraordinary technological changes, and the declining costs of production, transportation, and communication. Steamships had become by 1870 the dominant form for the international transport of goods. About the same time, railroads began to connect more and more of the cities of Europe and the cities and rural areas of the United States. In the 1850s, the telegraph began to connect cities within the United States and within parts of European nations. By the late 1860s effective transoceanic cables began to connect significant parts of the world and permit rapid and relatively inexpensive communication. By the 1870s, refrigerated ships began delivering meat across oceans. And at the end of the nineteenth century, electricity and chemicals emerged as new sources of power and products. The confluence of these technological developments produced a dramatic decline in the cost of moving goods from previously remote areas to almost anywhere

Table 3.1 Distribution of World Industrial Production, 1870–1913 (in percentages)

Years	United States	Great Britain	Germany	France	Russia	Japan	India	Rest of World
1870	23	32	13	10	4	—	—	17
1881–1885	29	27	14	9	3	—	—	19
1896–1900	30	20	17	7	5	1	1	19
1906–1910	35	15	16	6	5	1	1	20
1913	36	14	16	6	6	1	1	20

SOURCE: Walt Rostow, *The World Economy,* Austin: University of Texas Press, 1978, 52–53.

Table 3.2 Iron and Steel Production, 1890–1913 (millions of tons)

	1890	1900	1910	1913
United States	9.3	10.3	26.5	31.8
Great Britain	8.0	5.0	6.5	7.7
Germany	4.1	6.3	13.6	17.6

SOURCE: Adapted from Kennedy, *The Rise and Fall of the Great Powers,* New York: Random House, 1987, 200.

Table 3.3 Energy Consumption, 1890–1913 (in millions of metric tons of coal equivalent)

	1890	1900	1910	1913
United States	147	248	483	541
Great Britain	145	171	185	195
Germany	71	112	158	187

SOURCE: Adapted from Kennedy, *The Rise and Fall of the Great Powers,* New York: Random House, 1987, 201.

on the planet. It became possible to raise livestock and grow wheat in the land-rich United States and sell it effectively anywhere in the world. Additionally, the cost of producing goods fell when larger markets allowed fixed costs to be spread over many more units.[23]

Perhaps the best explanation for the differential rates of growth across nations lies in the simple but powerful fact that certain special advantages in the United States and Germany were well suited to the industrial developments of the age. In Germany, an extensive and diversified system of scientific education produced large numbers of trained scientists and technical personnel who were able to take advantage of a cascade of theoretical innovations. This was especially true in the newly emerging chemical industry

**Table 3.4 Gross Domestic Product: United States, Great Britain, and Germany
(1970 U.S. prices)**

Country	1870	1913
United States		
Gross domestic product (billions)	$3.050	$17.628
Gross domestic product (per capita)	$764	$1,813
Great Britain		
Gross domestic product (billions)	$3.036	$6.808
Gross domestic product (per capita)	$972	$1,491
Germany		
Gross domestic product (billions)	$2.099	$7.184
Gross domestic product (per capita)	$535	$1073

SOURCE: Albert Chandler, *Scale and Scope: The Dynamics of Industrial Capitalism,* Cambridge: Harvard University Press, 1990, 52.

and in the production of complex machine tools. Further, Germany used its raw materials and industrial capabilities to press rapidly ahead in steel and coal production and in railroad construction (including in central and eastern Europe).[24] Similarly, the United States used its substantial raw material resources and very large and affluent domestic market as the base for creating the largest economy in the world.

The unification of markets produced by the introduction of the railroad and the telegraph had its greatest impact in the United States. It was here that the system of modern managerial capitalism was born and developed furthest in the pre-World War I era. Over a wide array of products, U.S. firms launched into mass production, distribution, and marketing for the giant domestic market, thereby taking advantage of substantial returns to scale.[25] The organization and direction of these firms rapidly shifted from owner-managers to professional, hierarchically arranged, salaried managers. It was this structural innovation that permitted the coordination and direction of these vast enterprises.[26]

The evolution of the world economy in the forty years before World War I generated substantial levels of financial and trade interdependence. In many ways, similar levels of interdependence have been reached again only in the 1990s. As Table 3.5 shows, international financial transactions before World War I were large and growing. Purchase of international stocks and bonds was common throughout Europe, where few regulations or restrictions existed to limit these transactions. The gold standard (discussed later) operated to stabilize currency values and establish an environment facilitating financial flows. As we have seen, trade grew dramatically after 1850 in spite of growing protectionism. The difficulty was that interdependence generated the need for greater international cooperation. Unfortunately, arrangements to manage the system of financial and trade flows were mostly ad hoc and private.[27]

Table 3.5 Overseas Investments of the Major Economic Powers, 1870–1914 (in millions of dollars)

	1870	1900	1914	% of World in 1914
Great Britain	4,900	12,000	20,000	44.0
France	2,500	5,800	9,050	19.9
Germany	—	4,800	5,800	12.8
United States	100	500	3,500	7.8
Others	500	1,100	7,100	15.5

SOURCE: Sidney Pollard, "Capital Exports, 1870–1914: Harmful or Beneficial?" *Economic History Review*, 38.4, November 1985, 492.

British Hegemony?

What about Great Britain during this period? One important point to recognize is that Britain remained the dominant force in international trade and finance. Even in 1913, Britain accounted for 31 percent of world trade in manufactured goods, with Germany at 27.5 percent, and the United States at 13 percent.[28] In 1914, the British share of international investments was clearly in a commanding position and perhaps still growing. But this strong international investment position cannot disguise the serious relative decline in the British economy—a decline from which Britain never really recovered.

One important source of difficulty was Britain's incomplete adaptation to the emerging world of capital-intensive, large-scale, scientifically based, and professionally managed firms. British businesses and investors were content with retaining a much more personal system of management, often resting with the founder's family. This meant smaller enterprises with relatively limited managerial hierarchies. The reasons for these developments are complex but lie mainly in the fact that British advantages contributing to their leading role in the first industrial revolution did not transfer into advantages for the second industrial revolution. The British domestic market, once the largest in Europe, not only was small in comparison with the United States and Germany, but also grew much more slowly. Large domestic markets were crucial in supporting U.S. and German industries in their move into new industrial areas and provided the justification for creating large and sophisticated enterprises. The domestic British market simply did not support the widespread adoption of this kind of business organization. Moreover, the areas of early British advantage—textiles, iron, and ships—did not lend themselves to economies of scale, nor were they greatly affected by the new systems of communication and transportation. Thus, British export markets remained in the older industries even as the United States and Germany, resting on the base of a large domestic market, pushed their exports in the new industries such as "refined oil, processed foodstuffs, mass-produced light machinery, and electrical equipment." In the emerging age of large-scale production, marketing, and distribution, British industry lacked the advantages that would push its entrepreneurs to take the lead in developing these areas.[29]

Almost certainly, the most important British roles in the world economy during this period were to extend international capital markets, contribute to a loosely organized international monetary system based on gold, and maintain open markets in a time of increasing protectionism. Britain's dominance resulted from the importance of the city of London in short-term financing of international trade, from the role of sterling as virtually equivalent to an international currency, and from the vast sums of capital that flowed abroad into long-term foreign investments. These bases of power enabled the London banking system to affect interest rates around the world, to provide international liquidity during times of crisis, and to finance, over many years, the balance of payments deficits of a variety of countries without harsh adjustments.[30]

Central to this process was an international monetary system based on the gold standard and the pound sterling. This developed in the 1870s, when several countries in addition to Britain adopted a gold backing for their currencies and permitted the free movement of gold exports and imports. A unit of a country's currency could be exchanged for a fixed amount of gold. The effect was to fix the exchange rates of these currencies based on the ratio of gold backing. That is, the exchange rate between any two currencies was simply the ratio of the amount of gold backing those currencies. The result was a rudimentary but evolving international monetary system, built around British management and protection of Britain's own position along with an almost constant outflow of British capital to cushion the adjustment problems created by its perpetual current account surplus.[31]

The combination of economic growth (especially in the United States and Germany), increasing world trade, and expanding capital flows generated both greater interdependence among nations and a reaction designed to reduce the costs of this connectedness. The links among nations and the importance of these links can be seen in the increasing tendency for simultaneous expansion and contraction in national economies, including both production and finance. By the late 1850s the price of wheat in any given country was heavily influenced by world market conditions. In 1857, both an oversupply of wheat in the world and falling prices produced a financial panic in the United States that had serious effects in Great Britain and Germany. Throughout the 1860s, the U.S. Civil War greatly affected financial conditions in Britain and land prices in India. By 1873 the French indemnity payment to Germany (following their 1870 war) produced such imbalances in the international financial system as to precipitate an international depression.[32]

This depression coincided with a growing supply of wheat, especially from the United States, made possible by improvements in land and sea transportation and in production technology. Price declines in many commodities were substantial, accelerating a trend common to much of the nineteenth century. This continued until an upturn began in the 1890s. The result was to rearrange the economic and political interests of several groups, especially with regard to tariff questions. Many agricultural and industrial producers were confronted with being forced out of business, suffering major losses, or substantially changing their methods of production. Their demands for protection were not ignored, and several governments, led by Germany and France, began raising tariffs. By 1890 much of the system of freer trade had been reversed.[33]

The major exception to these trends was Britain, which resisted domestic pressure for protection and refused to retaliate against other nations. Yet any consideration of Britain's behavior during the late nineteenth century raises questions about the role and importance of the world's leading economic power in creating and sustaining a stable and orderly world economy. How important was British leadership for the nineteenth-century world economy? Did British leaders see themselves as responsible for maintaining a system of free trade and international economic prosperity? Or rather, did they simply look to extend their position and engage in leadership only when it could be linked to narrow national interests?

This question has usually been framed in terms of whether Britain acted as a hegemonic state, that is, whether the British were willing to apply over-whelming economic, military, and political strength to the formation and preservation of an international economic order. The evidence for this is mixed. Clearly, British market power in the 1840–1860 period helped move several nations toward freer trade, while British financial power was key to the functioning of a world trading and monetary system for much of the century. Further, British policies, capital, and businessmen served to transmit technology and bring many peripheral areas into the world economy. Perhaps most important was the willingness of private financiers to supply credit during periods of financial distress.[34] But on the whole, Britain acted as a passive hegemon, reflecting the laissez-faire political economy of the day. It led largely by example and not by organizing multilateral efforts to manage the system. The instruments and practices of domestic economic management were limited, thereby restricting similar efforts at the international level. The failure to punish those nations who increased tariffs after 1873 suggests a much more aloof Britain rather than one which saw itself as responsible for keeping an open system in place.

If we think beyond economic relationships, British military power was certainly important for forcibly opening China and Japan to the world, controlling India, and preserving free movement on the world's oceans. But Britain was equally important in the process of expanding imperialism and thereby closing off areas from the world economy (except as trade went through Britain itself). Britain certainly made no effort to oppose the principle of international aggrandizement in the non-Western world (again, except as it encroached on British interests). We can safely say that the link between British security, international security, and the world economy was a tenuous one. The effect of this was to remove a key incentive for a stronger British involvement in managing world affairs. Thus when nations began raising trade barriers in the 1870s,

Britain stuck to its policy of splendid isolation from the continent, accepted this outcome, and shifted much of its trade to the Empire.[35]

The first great test of Britain's and other nations' ability to manage the vicissitudes of economic interdependence and international competition resulted in failure. Economic and political nationalism reinforced military competition, and nations increasingly found themselves unable to find a secure basis for pursuing prosperity within an open international system. The growing tide of protectionism and destructive competition did not eliminate the web of interdependence in the world economy. At the same time, the level and nature of political and economic cooperation were stunted and, consequently, failed to provide mechanisms for collective gain. The spiral of struggle, alliances, armaments, and planning for war overwhelmed the logic of comparative advantage and mutual benefits from trade.

JAPAN AND LATE ECONOMIC DEVELOPMENT

One of the most important and enduring questions of international political economy concerns the relationship between more developed and less developed states. Do advanced states, through trade and capital investments, serve to transmit the technology, money, and ideas for industrialization? Or do these more powerful states use their leverage to exploit weaker states and perpetuate underdevelopment? We will reserve a more thorough treatment of these questions for Chapter 8. For now, one very important part of the answer lies in determining whether any less developed and non-Western states have been able to break through from backwardness to industrialization. Japan during the last third of the nineteenth century surely presents the most remarkable example of such a case.

It was Western determination to gain access to Japan that set this process into motion. Isolated for more than two hundred years and beset by a feudal system and a weak government, the Japanese were overwhelmed by Western military technology. In 1853–1854, and continuing over the next fifteen years, Japan was subjected to demands by the United States and Great Britain (among others) for special privileges and rights that compromised its sovereignty. The effort to cope with these demands without inviting war destroyed the legitimacy of the Japanese government. At the same time, the Western presence activated a virulent antiforeign reaction among the *samurai* (a military caste that had declined over the preceding two centuries of peace). Additionally, access to and the ability to utilize Western military technology effectively became the decisive factor in determining the outcome of the domestic political struggle that ensued. The result was a new Japanese government with the political strength and unflinching determination to make Japan into a modern nation capable of maintaining its independence.

Nonindustrialized states entering the world economy at such a late date are often said to face a special set of disadvantages in comparison with early industrializers. Late arrivers encounter established competitors who have more-complex systems of technology and education and a set of institutions experienced in adjusting to the demands of international competition. Those who hope to succeed must adopt some way of compensating for their weaknesses. Often this has meant relying on the government to finance, or even establish, enterprises, especially when the capital requirements for large industries such as coal or steel are needed.[36] Equally important, the state has usually provided the means for creating the broad social infrastructure needed for a modern society.

The pattern of Japanese development conforms in several respects to these expectations, but in others it deviates in significant ways. In 1868, the year of the Meiji Restoration, Japan had already developed a substantial market economy based largely on rural enterprises.[37] Over the next thirty years, much of Japan's economic growth derived from agricultural improvements and from rural industrial enterprises. These small-scale industries were primarily silkworm-raising, silk-reeling, and cotton textile operations, and most of the production was for export.[38] Unlike the tendency toward large-scale, capital-intensive, heavy industries found in other late industrializers, the first wave of Japanese industrialization was concentrated in areas of comparative advantage.

This may have been the result of a convergence of two factors: Japan's forced exposure to the world economy and changes in the competitive position of several more-advanced states. One of the consequences of the unequal treaties of the 1850s and 1860s was that Japan forfeited control over its tariff policy. In addition, a decline in Britain's ability to dominate the cotton industry opened the door for Japan. The technology of production was readily available and inexpensive (compared to that for heavy industry) and much easier to adopt. Sensitivity to the world market, the presence of a disciplined, reliable labor force, and entrepreneurial experience in the countryside gave Japan enough of an advantage to enter the world market successfully.

The greatest similarity between Japan and other late industrializers is the role of the state. The new Meiji government acted rapidly to reshape the country based on the needs of centralized power and economic development. It abolished the regional authorities (the domains), enacted a centralized tax system, eliminated the special status of the *samurai,* started conscription, and created a national educational system, all within seven years.[39] This extraordinary capacity for moving Japan so far so fast constitutes the distinctive quality of the Japanese state.[40] But, like most European states in the 1820–1870 period, the Japanese government mobilized capital, invested in infrastructure, started demonstration enterprises, offered subsidies, promoted market unification, and regulated industries needing help in establishing common production standards.[41] Yet the greatest part of the industrialization process came from private action, even when supported by the state. This is true not only of Japan but also of France and Germany in the mid-nineteenth century.

What may have been most unusual about Japan was the extraordinary cooperation of private and public actors.

THE WORLD ECONOMY ON THE EVE
OF WORLD WAR I

The century prior to World War I led to the transformation of the world economy, making it unlike the time that preceded it. Economic growth in the nineteenth and early twentieth centuries dwarfs that of any century before; the process of production and the nature of the goods produced was categorically different than before; and the level of interdependence across the world economy was higher than ever before. A finer brush permits us to see a complex system of global economic relations.

During this 100-year period, large differences in the level of economic development among nations emerged as a limited number of Western nations plus Japan industrialized. We have seen the impact of differential growth rates on these industrializing nations. But this process also affected other nations in dramatic ways.[42] The nineteenth century was one of imperialism, in which economically and militarily advanced nations increased their control over less advanced nations. This took two main forms. One was direct, in which the imperial power maintained political control over the colonial territory. For example, in the 1860–1890 period, the French used military force to conquer and establish direct rule over the Vietnamese and other peoples in Indochina. The other form was more indirect, in which influence was based on the dependence of the ruled peoples. An example is in much of Latin America, where British influence was preponderant. An important effect of direct and indirect imperialism was external control over tariff levels, almost always forcing the colonized nation to maintain open markets. Thus the industrial products of the advanced nations could freely enter the markets of less advanced nations whose economic policies were largely controlled from the outside. Remember that for 25 years, Japan was affected by indirect imperialism and was required to maintain open markets. For much of the world similarly affected, the result was deindustrialization. That is, existing industrial capabilities were destroyed by the much more competitive industries in the now advanced industrial world. This was especially evident in India, an area of direct British rule. A vibrant Indian textile industry was unable to compete with cloth and yarn produced through the much more advanced industrial techniques in Britain. Because its markets were held open by British control, during the 1850–1900 period, perhaps 75 percent of domestic consumption of textiles in India was of imported goods.[43] Many nations similarly affected were left to selling primary products and raw materials to industrial nations.

Among advanced nations, interdependence advanced dramatically through increased trade, finance, and migration. This came in spite of rising protectionism through increased tariffs. One nation—the United States—

rose to industrial supremacy behind the walls of high tariffs. But the United States was not alone, as most other advanced states (the major exception was Britain) also increased tariffs after about 1870. Nonetheless, trade levels grew much faster than output, and by 1913 merchandise exports stood at an average of almost 13 percent of gross domestic product (GDP) for the most industrially developed nations. The bulk of this trade was among advanced states, often in the same industry and frequently based on direct investments in these markets.[44] But the driving force of interdependence was finance. In 1913 international capital flows were 5 percent of advanced states' GDP, leading to the substantial integration of these nations' financial markets. The main vehicle of investment was bonds, and the primary investors were British. These investments were directed at raw materials, railroads, utilities, and public works, and very often the lending was to governments.

Missing from the world economy just before World War I were effective international institutions capable of managing this emerging interdependence. In one important sense, the gold standard was designed to regulate trade and financial flows. This system was supposed to regulate problems in international accounts through fluctuating price levels and unemployment whenever problems arose. This sometimes worked but at a price many found unacceptable. But effective adjustment was uncertain, especially to the problems of overinvestment and speculation that come with free capital markets. Financial crashes in the 1890s and early twentieth century spread quickly around the industrial world and prompted calls for stronger controls. Perhaps most inadequate were the ideas associated with increasing interdependence. National leaders in most countries continued to see trade in largely mercantilist terms, that is, as a weapon in international competition. Taking territory and establishing exclusive trading relations was a common objective of foreign policy. The ideas of mutual gain from trade found in liberal notions of free trade were in retreat in the years before 1913. Consequently, the substantial ties of interdependence did little to stop the impending disaster of 1914.

WORLD WAR I AND ITS AFTERMATH

The world war that began in August 1914 was the culmination of the failure of nations to find security and prosperity within a context of tightening interdependence. Even more important was the extraordinary restructuring of the world economy caused by the war: it redistributed international economic power, disrupted the world economy, and destroyed trade and financial relations. The period from 1919 to 1939 is largely the story of limited and somewhat unsuccessful efforts to reorganize a functioning and prosperous world economic system. It also marks an era when much of the interdependence established from 1873 to 1914 was destroyed.

There were three major impediments to international economic stability after World War I. First, most governments lacked the political strength and experience to design and carry out a managerial role in their domestic economies and were even less able to design a managerial role for the international economy. This meant that important problems were left unsolved. As a result, the world economy lacked effective mechanisms for transferring capital from surplus to deficit countries, especially during times of economic distress. Second, the failure of the world's largest economic power, the United States, to accept a leadership role opened a major void. British weakness prevented a resumption of its nineteenth-century role, and the U.S. political system was too immature to support an assumption of this responsibility. Third, the ferocity of the downturn in the world economy after 1929 almost guaranteed a retreat into autarchy and protection as nations struggled to defend their domestic economies. But in spite of these barriers, there were significant elements of reconstruction and cooperation. Private efforts frequently attempted to fill the vacuum created by government reticence. In the 1930s the United States became less timid about organizing international cooperation. As it happened, though, these actions almost never proved sufficient.

The Economic Consequences of World War I

The pattern of participation and fighting in the war helps explain many of its economic consequences. Britain and France, allied with Russia, fought Germany and Austria-Hungary for nearly three years before the United States joined the war. The United States declared its neutrality but emerged quickly as the chief supplier of war-related material to Britain and France. Before the United States entered the war in April 1917, the Allies paid for these goods by liquidating their overseas investments and by using credit provided by private U.S. banks. After the U.S. entry, credit for purchases was supplied by the U.S. government. By the war's end, Britain and France had accumulated more than $10 billion in debts, and the United States had become the largest creditor nation in the world.[45] Equally significant, European reliance on external suppliers and the disruption of export markets provided a major boost to production in several peripheral states but especially in the United States and Japan.[46] Japan experienced dramatic improvements in its industrial and technological development from expanded markets in Europe and Asia. For other states the breakdown of trade patterns provided incentives to develop domestic industries that could substitute for European imports. Thus, the European focus of the war helped shift industrial production to outlying nations and created an immense international debt burden.

Added to these hardships were problems created by worn-down and destroyed production facilities in Europe and by the financial disruption from measures used to finance the war. Four years of maximum production and difficulties in replacing old equipment reduced European competitiveness in the world economy. The war also forced abandonment of the gold standard at home and abroad—meaning that currency could no longer be exchanged for gold—along with a rapid expansion of the money supply to support deficit spending by the government. The result was unparalleled inflation, further deterioration in Europe's competitive position, and continuation of a large trade deficit into the postwar period.[47] On top of the imbalances experienced by the war's victors were the problems Germany faced. The political importance of vengeance and the economic need to recoup losses combined to prompt Britain and France to demand reparations (payments for war losses) from Germany.[48] But reparations had to come from a German current account surplus or from capital supplied from abroad. Neither was likely. The combination of trade imbalances and debt payments created a very unstable situation for the world economy.

A Failure of Political Vision

Effective solutions to these difficulties were hampered by the failure of political thinking to keep up with the real changes produced by the war. Statesmen and publics in many countries were eager to return to the world of 1914 and acted as though they expected few problems in so doing. This was reflected in the almost blind faith in the need to reestablish the gold standard, create monetary stability, and fix exchange rates. Wartime governmental controls were lifted quickly, and at the same time, little thought was given at the peace conference to the importance of continuing intervention by governments in stabilizing the world economy.[49] Perhaps most shortsighted was the U.S. insistence on repayment of all war debts. This overlooked the payments deficit position of the Europeans and the negative impact that repayment would place on recovery. The U.S. commitment to war debt repayments made France especially determined to force Germany to make large reparation payments. But lest we see war-debt forgiveness as an easy matter, to do anything other than exacting payment would have required the United States to raise taxes to absorb the debts into the U.S. budget. Although such a plan was highly rational in terms of world reconstruction and stability, the U.S. government did not have the political strength required for such an act. Conservatives and nationalists rejected any U.S. responsibility for these problems and demanded the debts be repaid.[50]

In spite of domestic pressures to ignore any international responsibilities and to insist on war-debt repayment, the leadership of the U.S. government and financial community could not ignore the difficulties created by such a policy. They understood only too well the potential for great trouble resulting from imbalances in the world economy. The current account deficits of European states obviously hampered the payment of reparations and war debts. But in 1922, the already protective U.S. tariff rose (even if only by a small amount), thereby undermining the ability of Europeans to sell in the United States, achieve a current account surplus, and make debt payments. Exchange rates, due to financial dislocations caused by the war, could not be fixed. These fluctuations undercut the ability of businesspersons to make calculations for investments. From the standpoint of American leaders, European stability was judged to be an important but not vital interest. The domestic economy took priority over U.S. efforts to promote European recovery.[51]

A more active U.S. policy had to await French military action in 1923 to collect German reparations and the virtual financial and economic collapse of Germany over the next year. A coalition of U.S. government officials and private financial interests took steps to deal with the situation. The Dawes Plan, negotiated in conjunction with Britain and France, called for reductions in annual reparations payments and provided for private American loans to Germany. Over the next five years, a large volume of foreign loans, mostly from the United States, provided Germany with the capital to make its reparations payments and achieve an uneven economic recovery.[52] But this was a fragile and precarious arrangement, dependent as it was on an unending supply of foreign capital, which itself was contingent on private bankers' calculations of profit. Any interruption in foreign loans would prompt a return to the chaos of 1923–1924.

A second and equally problematic effort at producing stability came from Britain's decision to restore the gold standard and fix the value of the pound at the prewar rate. Wartime inflation had exacerbated the problem of British competitiveness, which was evident well before 1914. Rather than use a postwar recession to drive prices down and recoup some of its competitive position, Britain chose to let the pound float. Its price initially fell but by 1925 had returned to near prewar exchange rates, at which point the pound was placed on the gold standard. The success of such a system depended on two crucial factors. London had to be able to meet the demand for gold, which was complicated by the emergence of New York and Paris as alternative international financial centers. The greater strength of the dollar and the franc put pressure on the weaker pound and produced a constant drain of gold from London. Equally important was the need to provide for capital flows from surplus to deficit countries (which was part of the Dawes Plan). But Britain's ability to fulfill this function was greatly damaged by the financial restructuring of the war, and the U.S. ability to take its place was hampered by the domestic priorities of the government and private bankers. When U.S. lending and imports both contracted from 1928 to 1930, the strains on the world economy were simply too great, and the system collapsed.[53]

Collapse of the World Economy

Although the imbalances created by the First World War and the patchwork efforts to resolve these problems were not the precipitating cause of the Great Depression, they did serve to transform a downturn in the business cycle into a hurricane of deflation and unemployment. The Federal Reserve in the United States, worried about the boom and speculation in the American economy, moved to restrict credit in 1928. The result was the aforementioned decline in U.S. foreign lending, a drop in U.S. production, and a bursting of the stock market bubble in October 1929. U.S. foreign lending was cut in half from 1928 to 1929 and halved again by 1930. This led to a decline in investment and production in Europe, which, combined with the slowdown in the United States, meant a sharp fall in commodity prices and contributed to the break in stock prices.[54]

The rush of world economic decline between 1930 and 1931 exposed the weaknesses in the system of trade, finance, and economic management. In the United States during 1930, manufacturing production declined by 20 percent and exports by 35 percent. In the same year, unemployment rose in Britain from 10 percent to 16 percent and in Germany from 13 percent to 22 percent.[55] Initial government reaction was largely to accept these events based on the expectation that investment would revive when prices fell far enough. What finally prompted government action was the impending collapse in May and June 1931 of the debt system built up around reparations, war debts, and U.S. loans. Fearing a "complete collapse of Germany's credit structure within a day or two" and the impact of that collapse on the American banking system, President Herbert Hoover granted a moratorium on reparations payments.[56]

When this proved insufficient to halt the German banking crisis, Hoover pulled back, preferring to shift any additional relief burden to private U.S. bankers. But this was impossible, and in mid-July the German government closed German banks and placed severe restrictions on foreign-exchange transactions. The effect was to freeze all foreign assets in Germany. The crisis then shifted to London, and the threat to international financial stability moved Hoover to reverse the ten-year-old U.S. policy of refusing official participation (direct and open) in European affairs. He agreed to send Secretary of State Henry Stimson to a conference in London to address the crisis. Notwithstanding this break with the past, the U.S. government remained hamstrung by a deep reluctance to expand its budget deficit and by political forces insisting on domestic solutions to the depression. Consequently, the London Conference failed to solve the problem.[57]

The crisis continued throughout August and September as Britain was forced to exchange gold for pounds. When additional credits from private and central bankers were exhausted, the British abandoned the gold standard in a dramatic decision on September 21, 1931. The next day, the United States suffered massive gold withdrawals and, by the end of October, the first of an unceasing wave of bank failures. The spiral of declining world trade and domestic production; falling prices, investments, and profits; and rising loan defaults and bank failures continued throughout 1931 and 1932. By early 1933 the banking system in the United States was perilously close to complete collapse. Only a decision to close the entire system and rebuild it from the ground up averted this outcome.[58]

Autarchy and Cooperation

The disintegration of international monetary and trading systems ushered in a period in which many countries tried to cope with the depression apart from the world economy.[59] Earlier, in 1930, Congress passed and President Hoover signed the Smoot-Hawley Tariff, which increased U.S. protection substantially. This triggered a round of tariff increases around the world.[60] In 1931 Japan invaded Manchuria in China, hoping to secure markets and resources.[61] After Britain left the gold standard in 1931, the pound fell in value by more than 30 percent, producing a substantial boost to the competitiveness of

British exports. Britain also tried, with limited success, to organize a trading bloc of nations tied closely to the use of sterling. Coupled with cheap money and a housing boom, these measures helped Britain to begin crawling out of its economic hole in 1932.[62] France also organized a trading bloc of states remaining on the gold standard, but with little effect on recovery.[63] Germany, under the Nazis, used a vicious form of national economic planning, deficit spending, conscription, and arms production to spark recovery.[64] And in 1933 President Franklin Roosevelt left the gold standard to foster depreciation of the dollar, rejected international cooperation, and concentrated on using government reorganization of the domestic economy to encourage recovery.[65]

Notwithstanding the retreat into autarchy and the recovery that this sometimes produced, most nations could not ignore their relation to the broader world economy. In June 1934, only one year after launching a strongly nationalistic recovery program, the United States adopted the Reciprocal Trade Agreements Act (RTAA). This authorized the president to negotiate substantial tariff reductions on a reciprocal and bilateral basis with other nations. Although many agreements did result and tariffs fell on many items, the importance of the RTAA is mostly symbolic in indicating a shift by the United States away from a nationalist-protectionist tariff policy.[66] Also important for its symbolic value was the Tripartite Monetary Agreement of 1936, among the United States, Great Britain, and France. This agreement was designed to stabilize currencies and to end the process of competitive devaluation. The scope of the agreement was somewhat limited, and stabilization continued to be an elusive goal.[67] A more thoroughgoing and effective organization of the world economy awaited the restructuring of domestic and international politics produced by World War II.

CONCLUSIONS

This chapter has focused on the development of a world economy over the century from the repeal of the Corn Laws to the Great Depression. Several key themes emerge that will help us understand later events, in particular the processes of competition, economic transformation, and the growing importance of international cooperation for managing the world economy. This new system of economic relations originates with the growing industrial power of Britain and its special needs for imports and ability to sell abroad. By 1870 tariffs had fallen substantially, and a system of freer trade encompassing much of the globe had formed around Britain. The accumulated profits from British manufacturing began flowing into foreign investments, which helped to finance sales abroad as well as to transmit the technology of a modern economy. The availability of technology and improvements in infrastructure meant that many countries could begin competing with Britain on equal terms. But changes in technology, transportation, and communication—especially the ability to deliver goods and manage large and dispersed organizations—altered the nature of business firms and markets. These changes worked to Britain's disadvantage and benefited the United States and Germany. By 1914 Britain had lost its position as the world's leading economy.

Understanding the world economy in these terms helps to underline its extraordinary dynamism. This dynamism can be seen in the tremendous growth in productive capacity, self-sustaining economic growth, and the rapid changes in technology. Competition among states meant that these economic changes produced substantial shifts in the balance of world power. The capacity for war and international influence was rearranged along with the world economy. Further, circumstances that provided advantages at one point in time did not last. Leading states, by selling, buying, and investing in other states, transferred their advantages. Moreover, the deep structural dynamism of the world economy transformed the very bases of advantage. What works to benefit a nation at one time is eroded, and new arrangements of competition emerge that privilege other nations at a later time.

The management of the world economy, a necessarily political process, became both more problematic and more important over this century. British interests and power worked to provide leadership and organization in the early stages, and Britain's financial predominance supported an international monetary system until 1914. But the move away from free trade and toward economic nationalism in the last quarter of the nineteenth century marked the limits of British power. The intensification of competition and conflict accompanying these trends suggests a general failure to cope with the new relationships of interdependence. World War I itself generated massive changes in economic power, but these did not lead to corresponding procedures for effective international cooperation. This made the world economy especially vulnerable and contributed greatly to the catastrophic depression of the 1930s. Only the combination of war and depression would produce new forms of domestic and international political power committed to new arrangements of international management.

NOTES

1. Mark Borthwick, *Pacific Century,* Boulder, Colo.: Westview, 1992, 77–89. Peter Hugill, *World Trade since 1431,* Baltimore: Johns Hopkins University Press, 1993. The best analysis of the world economy over the long run is Fernand Braudel, *Civilization and Capitalism: 15th–18th Centuries,* New York: Harper and Row, 1984.

2. Free-trade thinking contrasts sharply with that of mercantilism, the dominant position prior to the middle of the eighteenth century. Operating from a zero-sum concept of the world economy, mercantilism asserts that the gains from trade *must* come at the expense of other nations. In this view, nations try to protect their own markets while seeking to take export markets from others. See Jacob Viner, "Power versus Plenty as Objectives of Trade in the Seventeenth and Eighteenth Centuries," *World Politics,* 1.1, October 1946.

3. Between 1500 and 1750 local exchange and barter were predominant, with international trade

largely confined to luxury goods. These included foodstuffs, silk, hides, copper, metals, spices, and timber. The slow and very uneven growth of world trade at this time contributed to this zero-sum attitude (Kristof Glamann, "European Trade, 1500–1750," in Carlo Cipolla (ed.), *The Fontana Economic History of Europe: The Sixteenth and Seventeenth Centuries,* Glasgow: Fontana Press, 1974, 427–526; P. J. Cain, *Economic Foundations of British Overseas Expansion, 1815–1914,* London: Macmillan, 1980).

4. Eric Hobsbawm, *Industry and Empire,* New York: Penguin, 1969, 53; E. L. Jones, "Agriculture, 1700–1800," in Rodrick Floud and Donald McCloskey (eds.), *The Economic History of Britain since 1700,* Cambridge, England: Cambridge University Press, 1981, 66–86; P. K. O'Brien, "Agriculture and the Industrial Revolution," *Economic History Review,* 30.1, 1997, 166–181; David Landes, *The Unbound Prometheus,* Cambridge, England: Cambridge University Press, 1969, 46–54. Landes reports that Britain had the highest per-capita income in Europe, which means it also had the highest wages and a significant market for consumer goods.

5. Hobsbawm, *Industry and Empire,* 39; Landes, *The Unbound Prometheus,* 61–66.

6. D. N. McCloskey, "The Industrial Revolution, 1780–1860: A Survey," in Floud and McCloskey (eds.), *Economic History,* 110–111.

7. Cain, *Economic Foundations,* 112.

8. P. J. Cain and A. G. Hopkins, "The Political Economy of British Expansion Overseas, 1750–1914," *Economic History Review,* 33.4, November 1980, 472.

9. McCloskey, "Industrial Revolution," 112.

10. Alan Milward and S. B. Saul, *The Economic Development of Continental Europe, 1780–1870,* London: Allen and Unwin, 1979, 307–309.

11. Landes, *Unbound Prometheus,* 125–150.

12. Rondo Cameron, "A New View of European Industrialization," *Economic History Review,* 38.1, February 1985, 9–16. France, for example, was restrained by relatively high cost coal. Behind a wall of protection, however, it was able to develop a textile industry but could export only specialized and high-priced textiles (Milward and Saul, *Economic Development,* 312–331.

13. A helpful discussion of the various means for transmitting industrialization from Britain to Europe is Sidney Pollard, *Peaceful Conquest: The Industrialization of Europe, 1760–1970,* Oxford: Oxford University Press, 1982, 142–190.

14. Ralph Davis, *The Industrial Revolution and British Overseas Trade,* Leicester, England: Leicester University Press, 1979, 15.

15. This paragraph is based on Cain and Hopkins, "Political Economy," 474–481; and on Cain, *Economic Foundations,* 17–21. Accompanying the move toward freer trade was an end to efforts designed to prevent other nations from obtaining British technology and manpower skills. In the 1820s, laws barring the export of machinery and the immigration of skilled artisans were relaxed and, by 1843, repealed. See Pollard, *Peaceful Conquest,* 144. The Navigation Acts are discussed in R. P. Thomas and D. N. McCloskey, "Overseas Trade and Empire, 1700–1860," in Floud and McCloskey, *Economic History,* 94.

16. Peter Gourevitch, *Politics in Hard Times: Comparative Responses to Economic Crises,* Ithaca: Cornell University Press, 1986, 54.

17. An alternative interpretation of the end of the Corn Laws, emphasizing free-trade ideas, is Charles Kindleberger, "The Rise of Free Trade in Western Europe, 1820–1875," in his *Economic Response: Comparative Studies in Trade, Finance, and Growth,* Cambridge: Harvard University Press, 1975, 53.

For other approaches to the emergence of free trade, see Paul Rohrlich, "Economic Culture and Foreign Policy: The Cognitive Analysis of Economic Policy Making," *Internatinal Organization,* 41.1, Winter 1987, 61–92; Cheryl Schonhardt-Bailey, "Specific Factors, Capital Markets, Portfolio Diversification, and Free Trade: Domestic Determinants of the Repeal of the Corn Laws," *World Politics,* 43.4, July 1991, 545–569; Scott James and David Lake, "The Second Face of Hegemony: Britain's Repeal of the Corn Laws and the American Walker Tariff of 1946," *International Organization,* 43.1, Winter 1989, 1–29.

18. Kindleberger, "Rise of Free Trade," 54–56. For a view of French behavior, emphasizing domestic political and economic interests, see Michael Smith, *Tariff Reform in France 1860–1900: The Politics of Economic Interest,* Ithaca: Cornell University Press, 1980.

19. Pollard, *Peaceful Conquest,* 172–183; E. J. Hobsbawm, *The Age of Capital, 1848–1875,* New York: New American Library, 1975, 27–71; William Woodruff, "The Emergence of an International Economy, 1700–1914," in Carlo Cipolla (ed.), *The Fontana Economic History of Europe,* London: Fontana Press, 1973, 658–672; and Milward and Saul, *Economic Development,* 309–414.

20. James Foreman-Peck, *A History of the World Economy,* Totowa, N.J.: Barnes and Noble, 1983, 57–58.

21. The effects of compound growth can be seen in the statistics of economic expansion spread out over forty years. The average annual growth rate from 1870 to 1913 was 1.6 percent for Britain, 5 percent for the United States, and 4.7 percent for Germany. Seemingly small differences, spread out over many years, led to the dramatic *relative* decline for Britain (Aaron Friedberg, *The Weary Titan: Britain and the Experience of Relative Decline,* Princeton, N.J.: Princeton University Press, 1988, 25).

22. Paul Kennedy, *The Rise and Fall of the Great Powers,* New York: Random House, 1987, 199. Britain retained second position in per-capita industrialization (Kennedy, *Rise and Fall,* 200).

23. Peter Hughill, *Global Communications since 1844,* Baltimore: Johns Hopkins University Press, 1999, 25–51; Kevin O'Rourke and Jeffrey Williamson, *Globalization and History,* Cambridge: MIT Press, 2000, 33–36.

24. Alan Milward and S. B. Saul, *The Development of the Economies of Continental Europe, 1850–1914,* Cambridge: Harvard University Press, 1977, 19–38.

25. The concept of economies of scale refers to a decline in the per-unit cost of production as a result of increases in the volume of production. Typically, this is greatest for those firms with large fixed costs. Larger production volume permits such firms to spread these fixed costs over more units, thereby reducing the per-unit cost.

26. Chandler, *Scale and Scope,* 52–89.

27. Giulio Gallarotti, *The Anatomy of an International Monetary Regime: The Classical Gold Standard, 1880–1914,* Oxford: Oxford University Press, 1995.

28. Friedberg, *Weary Titan,* 24.

29. Chandler, *Scale and Scope,* 235–294, quote on 250. Also see Derek Aldcroft, *The Development of British Industry and Foreign Competition, 1875–1914,* Toronto: University of Toronto Press, 1968, 11–36; Foreman-Peck, *World Economy,* 94–110.

30. Robert Skidelsky, "Retreat From Leadership: The Evolution of British Economic Policy, 1870–1939," in Benjamin Rowland et al. (eds.), *Balance of Power or Hegemony: The Interwar Monetary System,* New York: New York University Press, 1976, 152–163; Foreman-Peck, *World Economy,* 67–84.

31. Barry Eichengreen, "Editor's Introduction," in Eichengreen (ed.), *The Gold Standard in Theory and History,* New York: Metheun, 1985, 5–19; Barry Eichengreen, "Conducting the International Orchestra: Bank of England Leadership under the Classical Gold Standard," *Journal of International Money and Finance,* 6, March 1987.

32. Foreman-Peck, *World Economy,* 84–88, 161–163.

33. Gourevitch, *Hard Times,* 71–123. What was the consequence of increasing protectionism? Politically, it solidified conservative regimes. Economically, protectionism redistributed the costs and benefits of production and trade. Tariffs almost always raise the prices paid by consumers for goods linked to international trade, increase government revenues, and provide protected domestic producers with greater profits. The decline in competition usually reduces the pressures on domestic producers for innovation.

34. Charles Kindleberger, "International Public Goods without International Government," *American Economic Review,* 76.1, March 1986, 1–13; Kindleberger, *Manias, Panics and Crashes,* New York: Basic Books, 1989, 201–231. British power was also very important in promoting "a politically stable environment for trade and investment" (Charles Lipson, *Standing Guard,* Berkeley and Los Angeles: University of California Press, 1985, 42). Skidelsky, "Retreat from Leadership," provides the strongest statement of Britain as hegemon.

35. In some ways, this acquiescence to increasing tariffs is similar to acceptance of German unification.

36. Alexander Gerchenkron, *Economic Backwardness in Historical Perspective,* Cambridge: Harvard University Press, 1962.

37. Thomas C. Smith, *Native Sources of Japanese Industrialization, 1750–1920,*
Berkeley and Los Angeles: University of California Press, 1988, 71–235.

38. Sidney Crawcour, "Industrialization and Technical Change," in Marius Jansen (ed.), *Cambridge History of Modern Japan,* Cambridge, England: Cambridge University Press, 1989, 388–414; W. G. Beasley, *The Rise of Modern Japan,* New York: St. Martin's Press, 1990, 102–114; Osamu Saito, "Commercial Agriculture, By-Employment, and Wage Work," in Maurius Jansen and Gilbert Rozman (eds.), *Japan in Transition: From Tokugawa to Meiji,* Princeton, N.J.: Princeton University Press, 1986, 400–420.

39. Richard Rubinger, "Education: From One Room to One System," in Jansen and Rozman (eds.), *Japan in Transition,* 191–230; W. G. Beasley, *The Meiji Restoration,* Stanford, Calif.: Stanford University Press, 1973.

40. I am grateful to Albert Craig for clarifying this point for me.

41. Barry Supple, "The State and the Industrial Revolution, 1700–1914," in Cipolla (ed.), *Fontana Economic History,* 301–357; William Lockwood, "The State and Economic Enterprise in Modern Japan, 1868–1938," in Simon Kuznets et al., (eds.), *Economic Growth in Brazil, India, and Japan,* Durham, N.C.: Duke University Press, 1955, 540–563; David Landes, "Japan and Europe: Contrasts in Industrialization," in William Lockwood (ed.), *The State and Economic Enterprise in Japan,* Princeton, N.J.: Princeton University Press, 1965, 93–182.

42. The discussion that follows is based on Paul Bairoch and Richard Kozul-Wright, "Globalization Myths: Some Historical Reflections on Integration, Industrialization and Growth in the World Economy," Geneva, Switzerland: UNCTAD Discussion Paper no. 113, March 1996; and Paul Bairoch, *Economics and World History,* Chicago: University of Chicago Press, 1993.

43. Bairoch, *Economics and World History,* 88–90.

44. Once again, the major exception in 1913 was Britain. Trade with colonial areas and with poor nations was much more important to the British and typically consisted of exchanging manufacturing goods for primary products and raw materials.

45. Kathleen Burk, *Britain, America and the Sinews of War, 1914–1918,* Boston: Allen and Unwin, 1985; Ross Gregory, *The Origins of American Involvement in the First World War,* New York: Norton, 1971, 63. The interallied financing system was more complex than simply sending funds from the United States to Britain and France. Several states operated as both borrower and lender, creating a tangled web of debts. See Derek Aldcroft, *From Versailles to Wall Street, 1919–1929,* Berkeley and Los Angeles: University of California Press, 1977, 93.

46. Aldcroft, *From Versailles,* 37–41.

47. Aldcroft, *From Versailles,* 30–33, 63.

48. The amount of reparations was never fixed in a permanent sense. But in 1921 the Reparations Commission determined the amount to be equal to $33 billion (Aldcroft, *From Versailles,* 81).

49. Aldcroft, *From Versailles,* 3–6.

50. Joan Hoff Wilson, *American Business and Foreign Policy, 1920–1933,* Boston: Beacon Press, 1971, 70–133.

51. Melvyn Leffler, *The Elusive Quest: American Pursuit of European Stability and French Security, 1919–1933,* Chapel Hill: University of North Carolina Press, 1979, 40–81. Many U.S. officials believed that economic expansion abroad was beneficial but did not think that U.S. prosperity depended on it. At the same time, major figures in the New York financial community were committed to making New York the world's financial center, displacing London (Leffler, *Elusive Quest,* 147, 173; Carl Parrini, *Heir to Empire: United States Economic Diplomacy, 1916–1923,* Pittsburgh: University of Pittsburgh Press, 1969, 101–137).

52. Aldcroft, *From Versailles,* 84–86; William McNeil, *American Money and the Weimar Republic,* New York: Columbia University Press, 1986. A view giving more weight to the stability of this era is Charles Maier, *Recasting Bourgeois Europe,* Princeton, N.J.: Princeton University Press, 1974.

53. Skidelsky, "Retreat from Leadership," 168–173; Aldcroft, *From Versailles,* 168–186. Because the U.S. Government could not appear to be intervening in European affairs, the task of managing the unavoidable U.S. involvement fell to the relatively invisible Federal Reserve Bank of New York and its governor, Benjamin Strong. Strong developed a close working relationship with Montague Norman, governor of the Bank of England. The men understood that the international financial system could not function on its own and acted to supply the leadership needed to keep an unbalanced system in place, at least until the late 1920s (Stephen V. O. Clarke, *Central Bank Cooperation, 1924–1931,* New York: Federal Reserve Bank of New York, 1967).

54. Aldcroft, *From Versailles,* 231–284.

55. Leffler, *Elusive Quest,* 231–232; Charles Kindleberger, *The World in Depression, 1929–1939,* Berkeley and Los Angeles: University of California Press, 1973, 128–145.

56. Leffler, *Elusive Quest,* 238–246. The crisis in Germany started in neighboring Austria, where a major bank, Credit-Anstalt, failed Kindleberger, *World in Depression,* 146–153.

57. Leffler, *Elusive Quest,* 248–256.

58. Susan Kennedy, *The Banking Crisis of 1933,* Lexington: University Press of Kentucky, 1973, 152–223; Kindleberger, *World in Depression,* 167–177; Leffler, *Elusive Quest,* 256–272.

59. Kindleberger, *World in Depression,* reports that world trade shrank from

an average of $2.9 billion per month in 1929 to $1.1 billion per month in 1933.

60. Leffler, *Elusive Quest,* 195–202.

61. Michael Barnhart, *Japan Prepares for Total War,* Ithaca: Cornell University Press, 1987, 22–58.

62. Kindleberger, *World in Depression,* 162–181; Skidelsky, "Retreat from Leadership," 178–188.

63. Kindleberger, *World in Depression,* 247–264.

64. Gourevitch, *Hard Times,* 140–147.

65. Albert Romasco, *The Politics of Recovery: Roosevelt's New Deal,* New York: Oxford University Press, 1983.

66. Robert Pastor, *Congress and the Politics of U.S. Foreign Economic Policy,* Berkeley and Los Angeles: University of California Press, 1980, 84–93; Stephan Haggard, "The Institutional Foundations of Hegemony: Explaining the Reciprocal Trade Agreements Act," *International Organization,* 42.1, Winter 1988, 91–119.

67. Skidelsky, "Retreat from Leadership," 186–188.

ANNOTATED BIBLIOGRAPHY

Paul Bairoch. *Economics and World History: Myths and Paradoxes.* Chicago: University of Chicago Press, 1993. A short but immensely useful historical analysis of many of the major issues of international political economy.

W. G. Beasley. *The Rise of Modern Japan.* New York: St. Martin's Press, 1990. A detailed history of Japan from the 1850s to the present.

P. J. Cain, *Economic Foundations of British Overseas Expansion 1815–1914.* London: Macmillan, 1980. Provides a political economy approach to understanding nineteenth-century British foreign economic relations.

P. J. Cain and A. G. Hopkins. *British Imperialism, Innovation and Expansion: 1688–1914.* London: Longman, 1993. A remarkable overview, emphasizing the impact of financial interests.

Albert D. Chandler, Jr. *Scale and Scope: The Dynamics of Industrial Capitalism.* Cambridge: Harvard University Press, 1990. A masterful study of the competitive capacities of the largest firms in the United States, Germany, and Great Britain between 1890 and 1914.

James Foreman-Peck. *A History of the World Economy: International Economic Relations since 1850.* Totowa, N.J.: Barnes & Noble Books, 1983. Perhaps the best general overview of the world economy for the nineteenth and twentieth centuries.

Aaron Friedberg. *The Weary Titan: Britain and the Experience of Relative Decline.* Princeton, N.J.: Princeton University Press, 1988. A very important study of the domestic politics, economics, and foreign policy related to British economic decline in the late nineteenth and early twentieth centuries.

E. J. Hobsbawm. *The Age of Capital, 1848–1875.* New York: Mentor, 1975; *Industry and Empire.* New York: Penguin, 1969. Two indispensable studies of the origins and development of nineteenth-century capitalism.

Paul Kennedy. *The Rise and Fall of the Great Powers.* New York: Random House, 1987. An important comparative study of the relationship between economic and military power.

Charles Kindleberger. *The World in Depression.* Berkeley and Los Angeles: University of California Press, 1973. The best single source for understanding the world economy during the Depression years of the 1930s.

David Landes. *The Unbound Prometheus.* Cambridge, England: Cambridge University Press, 1969. The classic study of technological and economic change over the past two centuries.

Charles Maier. *Recasting Bourgeois Europe.* Princeton, N.J.: Princeton University Press, 1974. The most important examination of the interaction of European interest groups, domestic politics, and the world economy in the 1920s.

Alan Milward and S. B. Saul. *The Economic Development of Continental Europe, 1780–1870.* London: Allen and Unwin, 1979. An important study of industrial change in Europe.

Joel Mokyr (ed.). *The British Industrial Revolution: An Economic Perspective.* Boulder, Colo.: Westview, 1999. A thorough review of recent research.

Kevin O'Rourke and Jeffrey Williamson. *Globalization and History: The Evolution of a Nineteenth-Century Atlantic Economy.* Cambridge: MIT Press, 2000. A data-rich analysis of international market convergence in the nineteenth century.

Sidney Pollard. *Peaceful Conquest: The Industrialization of Europe, 1760–1970.* Oxford: Oxford University Press, 1982. An important study of industrial change in Europe.

Walt Rostow. *The World Economy.* Austin: University of Texas Press, 1978. A very rich source of data on the history of the world economy.

Peter Sterns. *The Industrial Revolution in World History.* Boulder, Colo.: Westview, 1993. An effective discussion of industrial changes across the world from 1760 to the present.

4

❖

The Political Economy
of American Hegemony,
1938–1973

The years following World War II produced dramatic, even epoch-making, changes in the world economy. Unprecedented prosperity, the development of new international economic institutions, an explosion in world trade, and an extraordinary expansion in international cooperation were the key elements in this new international economic order. This chapter will describe these developments and the political structures that supported them and also examine in detail the reasons for these events. How and why did these changes in the world economy occur? A considerable portion of the answer to this question rests with the actions of the United States. We have seen that prior to 1940 the United States was unwilling to commit any substantial resources to stabilizing either the world economy or the international political system. The consequence was a catastrophic depression and, ultimately, war. But during and after the World War II, the United States moved assertively to reconstruct the world economy. Understanding the political sources of this change and the consequences of this activity occupies the greatest part of this chapter.

This 35-year period offers a rich set of events for understanding international political economy. Several of the most important empirical issues and theoretical questions are linked to this era. The first part of this chapter provides a detailed discussion of the essential features of the postwar international economic order, in particular the patterns of economic growth and the basic institutions created to manage the system. These include the International Monetary Fund (IMF), the World Bank, and the General Agreement on Tariffs and Trade (GATT). The second part of the chapter examines the very important question of how political power affects economic outcomes. What were the nature and significance of U.S. leadership in producing the postwar international economic order? What were the motives for U.S. actions? Could the United States design the system alone? Who benefited from this system? The third part of the chapter considers several crucial developments that emerge from the era of U.S. hegemony: the growth of multinational corporations, the political economy of U.S. foreign policy, and European economic integration. Finally, the last part of the chapter examines the two events that marked a change in the world economy: the collapse of fixed exchange rates and the end of cheap oil, both of which took place between 1971 and 1973.

STRUCTURES AND TRENDS
IN THE POSTWAR WORLD ECONOMY

Growth of the World Economy

International trade and investment grew more quickly between 1938 and 1973 than in any other previous period after 1815 (see Table 4.1). Comparison of the rates of change in gross national product (GNP) for the pre- and postwar eras shows a substantial acceleration of growth after 1950. Most industrial countries experienced a near doubling of the rates of growth between 1950 and 1960 as compared with the 1913–1950 period.[1] International trade was a key ingredient in this growth, with world trade in manufacturing expanding faster than world manufacturing output by a ratio of 1.4:1 between 1950 and 1970.[2] The importance of the United States to this process is evident from Table 4.2.

The recovery of Western Europe and Japan was also a driving force in this economic growth. The surge in exports of industrial nations is a measure of this process. The expansion in world trade was in many ways generated by declining tariff levels, convertible currencies, and more openness. The near elimination of tariffs shown in Table 4.3 is also found in tariff levels for advanced capitalist states.

Also contributing to this process of economic growth was the availability of oil at stable prices (Table 4.4). Inexpensive imported oil became the primary energy source supporting the dramatic increases in economic output. The shift from reliance on coal to imported oil occurred principally in Europe and Japan. Between 1950 and 1970 Western Europe increased its dependence on oil for total energy needs from 14.3 percent to 55.6 percent, while Japan's oil dependence increased from 5 percent to 68.8 percent. From 1962 to 1972, combined Western European and Japanese imports of oil rose from 6.17 to 18.84 million barrels per day.[3]

Table 4.1 World Exports, 1938–1974 (current value in billions of U.S. dollars)

Year	Value
1938	21.1
1948	53.9
1958	96.0
1960	107.8
1965	156.5
1970	265.7
1972	355.3
1974	729.2

SOURCE: Robert A. Pastor, *Congress and the Politics of U.S. Foreign Economic Policy,* Berkeley and Los Angeles: University of California Press, 1980, 99.

Table 4.2 U.S. Trade and World Trade, 1949–1973 (exports at current value in billions of U.S. dollars)

Year	U.S.	Industrial Nations	World Exports	U.S. as % of Industrial Nations	U.S. as % of World
1949	12.1	33.8	55.2	35.8	21.9
1960	20.6	78.8	114.6	26.1	17.5
1970	43.2	208.3	283.7	20.7	15.2
1973	71.3	376.8	524.2	18.9	13.6

SOURCE: International Monetary Fund, *International Financial Statistics Yearbook,* 1979, 62–67.

Table 4.3 Average Global Tariffs

Year	Average Tariff
1940	40%
1950	25%
1960	17%
1970	13%
1980	7%
1990	5%

SOURCE: Peter Dicken, *Global Shift,* New York: Guilford, 1992, 153. For additional comparative data on tariffs, see United Nations, *World Economic Survey,* New York, 1991, 52.

Table 4.4 World Energy Consumption by Source, 1950–1972 (percentage shares)

Source	1950	1960	1965	1970	1972
Coal	55.7	44.2	39.0	31.2	28.7
Oil	28.9	35.8	39.4	44.5	46.0
Natural gas	8.9	13.5	15.5	17.8	18.4
Electricity	6.5	6.4	6.2	6.5	6.9

SOURCE: Joel Darmstadter and Hans H. Landsberg, "The Crisis," in Raymond Vernon (ed.), *The Oil Crisis,* New York: Norton, 1976, 19.

International Institutions

The growth of the world economy took place within a context created by several new international institutions, conceived of and established near the end of World War II at an international conference in Bretton Woods, New Hampshire. These include the International Monetary Fund (IMF), the International Bank for Reconstruction and Development (commonly known as the World Bank), and the General Agreement on Tariffs and Trade (GATT). The IMF was designed to manage exchange rates and payments imbalances among nations, the World Bank to supplement private capital for international investment, and GATT to serve as a negotiating forum for the reduction of tariffs and other barriers to trade. The purposes of these institutions—indeed, their very existence—derives from the power and purposes of the United States.

One of the most distinctive and important features of the post-1945 world economy was this set of formal and informal institutions for managing the economic relations among nations. During the 1920s a significant array of mostly informal institutions had been created to deal with the new complexity of economic ties among nations.[4] Those designed and established between 1942 and 1948 were framed by certain principles of international economic relations. These principles included a preference for convertible currencies, a lowering of trade barriers, a system of fixed exchange rates, and generally the promotion of a multilateral system of trade and payments.

The desire for fixed exchange rates was the result of a deeply felt need for stability in international transactions—a sentiment reinforced by the negative experience of floating exchange rates in the 1930s and memories of the "golden age" of fixed rates under the nineteenth-century gold standard. The United States possessed the vast majority of the world's gold in 1945, and this was used as the basis for establishing fixed rates.[5] The dollar was fixed in value to gold at $35 per ounce, while other governments fixed their currencies to the dollar and pledged to intervene in foreign exchange markets to keep values within a narrow band around the fixed rate. All this came within the basic rules of operation of the International Monetary Fund, which itself was established through payments of gold and national currencies from member states. The United States provided the lion's share of the IMF's resources, 31 percent, and consequently received the largest share of voting power.

The primary purpose of the IMF was to provide short-term loans to countries experiencing a current account deficit in their balance of payments. The loans would typically be used to support the fixed value of a country's currency and were usually contingent on adoption of a national policy designed to reverse the deficit. This often meant some combination of cutting government spending and restricting the money supply. This "belt tightening" would produce an economic downturn, higher unemployment, and lower inflation, which were expected to lead to higher exports and lower imports.[6] The IMF became the enforcer of the views of a conservative U.S. financial community, in which trade deficits were seen as an indicator of a country's domestic profligacy and adjustments were expected to come in the domestic economy so as to make it more competitive internationally.[7]

If a nation's current account deficit were serious enough—that is, if it were structural and not just temporary—the IMF would permit an alteration of the exchange rate (called a "devaluation" when the rate falls against other currencies). The British devaluation of the pound from $2.80 to $2.40 in 1967 is an example of this process. Burdened by an uncompetitive manufacturing sector, Britain consistently experienced a larger current account deficit whenever the economy expanded. Because of the importance of the pound to the world economy, the United States and the IMF were ready to provide financial aid to help support the currency. Eventually, the British government concluded that only a devaluation would produce a current account surplus and stay the need for additional borrowing. The British made this decision in conjunction with the IMF.

The International Bank for Reconstruction and Development, or World Bank, was also established at Bretton Woods. Eventually, the bank was allocated $10 billion in capital and given the ability to borrow funds in capital markets. Over its first decade, the World Bank played only a marginal role in the postwar reconstruction process. But in the late 1950s and early 1960s an increasing interest in the Third World prompted lending at the rate of well over $1 billion annually in new loans.[8] In Chapter 9 we will consider in more detail the role of the World Bank in providing aid to developing states.

The mechanisms for managing international trade in the early post war era had a somewhat more checkered history. Originally, the United States hoped to create an international organization for this purpose but found the goals of other states to be incompatible with its own. Concurrent negotiations in 1947 and 1948 produced first a General Agreement on Tariffs and Trade and an International Trade Organization. But the U.S. government was dissatisfied with the ITO because it placed restrictions on the United States while creating exceptions for other nations, and the president refused to submit the treaty to the Senate for ratification.[9] GATT was acceptable and served for the next forty-six years as the chief international organization for trade.[10] It provided a forum for negotiating reductions in tariffs and some other barriers to trade. In a series of meetings beginning in 1947 and continuing with various "rounds" through 1994, GATT produced a substantial drop in world tariff levels.[11] In the period from 1890 to 1935, U.S. tariff levels fluctuated between 30 percent and 45 percent of dutiable imports. By 1955 these had been cut to 15 percent and by 1970 to 12 percent.[12] This helps illustrate a key fact about GATT and U.S. postwar trade objectives: American leaders strongly favored lowering tariffs and other barriers to trade, that is, they were interested in freer trade; they were really not interested, in spite of much rhetoric to the contrary, in free trade. But GATT did embody a commitment by its members to establish a schedule of tariff rates and a set of trade principles designed to produce uniformity and predictability in international commercial relations. Although tariff barriers on manufactured goods fell substantially, trade in agriculture and services remained largely outside GATT (as did the communist bloc and many Third World nations). Beginning with the Tokyo Round in 1973–1979, negotiations moved on to tackle nontariff barriers to trade, and the Uruguay Round (1986–1993) took up these matters along with the areas of agriculture and services.

The growth and dynamism of the world economy, along with the new set of international institutions, produced an epochal change in international economic relations. How this change came about, in particular the United States' role, is the subject of the next section.

U.S. HEGEMONY
AND THE WORLD ECONOMY

A common characteristic of all the social sciences, especially those as new as international political economy, is disputation over the most basic of theoretical and empirical relationships. Perhaps the most important question for this emerging field—and the topic producing the greatest discussion—is the relationship of politics and power to the creation and management of the world economy. Many scholars have traced the emergence of a liberal international economic order to the presence of a single dominant power in the international system. The "hegemonic stability" theory holds that such a nation has the opportunity to construct an open and stable international economic system. Because this hegemonic state possesses a preponderance of military and economic power, it is in a position to convince other nations to enter into a system of relatively free trade and regular procedures for monetary relations. That is, the hegemon has the capacity and the motivation "to make and enforce the rules for the world political economy."[13]

Application of these ideas to understanding the period after World War II has produced a set of important insights but also several points of intellectual conflict. What follows is a consideration of these issues in terms of asking and answering five basic questions. First, what was the nature of U.S. leadership? For which issues or problems was U.S. power the key element? Second, what were the United States' aims? Was it primarily interested in acting for the benefit of all states in providing international peace and prosperity, or was it more concerned with designing a system to benefit itself even to the extent of turning a profit from its position? Third, what factors motivated the United States to assume the responsibilities of world leadership? What mixture of domestic interests and external political, military, and economic concerns provided the incentives for these actions? Fourth, how important was U.S. leadership to international cooperation and political and economic stability? What were the extent and limits to U.S. power in engineering and/or coercing these outcomes? Fifth, what were the consequences of U.S. hegemony, particularly the distribution of benefits? These are broad and complex questions, and the answers are sometimes not yet clear. But they point out the basic elements of international political economy for the postwar world.

Economic Consequences of World War II

Some historical background about the World War II and its political and economic impact is helpful in providing a context for answering these questions. First and foremost was the importance of productivity in fighting and winning the war. World War II was essentially a contest of physical capabilities, with victory going to the side best able to amass the implements and manpower of war. Events from 1939 to 1945 both revealed and accentuated the productive advantages of the U.S. economy. Not only did the United States possess the greatest concentration of productive resources, but also its productivity—output per unit of input, usually labor—was far higher than that of any other nation. By 1944 the United States was producing 40 percent of the world's armaments, and its productivity was twice that of Germany and five times that of Japan.[14] The result was that the U.S. gross national product increased, in real terms, from $88.6 billion in 1939 to $135 billion in 1944.[15]

The war had equally profound effects on patterns of international trade and finance. The United States supplied vast quantities of Allied war material and financed this through the Lend Lease program. In spite of this largess, Britain liquidated its foreign reserves and large portions of its overseas investments to pay for imports from the United States. By the war's end, the pattern of British trade deficits financed by U.S. capital was firmly established. In addition, the rupture created by military operations made reestablishing prewar trade practices difficult. This was most evident in central and Eastern Europe, where Soviet control served to remove this area from its traditional role in European trade. Added to this was the physical destruction of the war, which represented approximately 13 percent of the prewar capital stock in Germany and 8 percent in France.[16] The result was a high demand for imports, significant barriers to exports, and a substantial payments imbalance between Europe and the United States.

The war and depression from 1929–1945 also had psychological and political consequences that influenced economic choices. The fear of recurrent depression helped reinforce affirmative government action in guaranteeing domestic prosperity. The depression left a legacy of significant barriers to trade and a memory of the dangers of economic warfare. More ominous were the German and Japanese experiences of military and economic organization designed to secure access to the resources needed for autarchy.[17] Finally, the military outcome not only disrupted traditional European trade but also brought a politically and economically alienated great power—the Soviet Union—into the heart of Europe.

The United States and World Order

What are the main issues in which U.S. power played the key role in defining the postwar international order? We will emphasize four: trade and finance, international security, vital resources, and international and domestic politics.[18] First, the United States was consistently the central actor in establishing and managing a framework of rules for international trade and finance and also in making the system work by providing financial support. We have seen how the Bretton Woods institutions and GATT were created largely through political initiatives from the United States. At the same time, these institutions confronted striking imbalances in the world economy measurable in terms of the sizable current account deficits between Europe and the United States.[19] Continuing the policy established under Lend Lease, in 1946 the United States provided additional funds to Britain and France to make up the payments gap. When this proved insufficient, political leaders in the United States moved to supply even more funds so that the recovery of Europe could continue. The Marshall Plan provided the financing needed to cover this imbalance. This can be seen in Table 4.5.

During the first four years after the war, the U.S. government and private sources supplied $28 billion to finance the payments imbalance with the rest of the world. This pattern continued with Marshall Plan aid in 1950–1951 and largely with military aid thereafter. The chief consequence of these actions was to ensure European recovery and to enshrine the dollar as the key international currency. That is, the dollar became the primary medium of international payment and the currency serving as the store of value for all others participating in the system.[20]

Beyond these immediate economic issues lay a set of political and security matters that cried out for U.S. attention. Further, the U.S. ability to persuade the leadership of many nations to participate in the new liberal world order depended on their confidence in the United States and its willingness to ensure their security. The recent war had demonstrated the vulnerability of many parts of the world to a determined and aggressive state. Many of the European leaders who were considering joining the U.S.-defined system were deeply worried about the political effects of Soviet military power in the heart of Europe. Thus when events such as the Soviet-inspired coup in Czechoslovakia or the Soviet blockade of Berlin intensified these fears, the United States felt compelled to act. The result by 1949 was the North Atlantic Treaty Organization (NATO), which represented a standing U.S. commitment to defend

**Table 4.5 World Payments Imbalances, 1946–1949
(billions of U.S. dollars)**

	1946	1947	1948	1949
U.S. current account balance	+7.8	+11.5	+6.8	+6.3
Financed by:				
U.S. government	−4.9	−5.8	−5.1	−5.9
Private loans and gifts	−1.1	−1.5	−1.6	−1.1
IMF and World Bank	0.0	−0.8	−0.4	−0.1
Liquidating foreign assets	−1.9	−4.5	−0.8	0.0
Errors and omissions	+0.1	+1.1	+1.1	+0.9
Total	−7.8	−11.5	−6.8	−6.3

SOURCE: W. M Scammell, *The International Economy since 1945*, 2nd ed., New York: St. Martin's Press, 1983, 21.

Western Europe. U.S. international leadership depended on the ability to use its superior power to reassure allies and contain the Soviet Union. Especially critical was preventing Soviet actions from undermining confidence in and encouraging challenges to the United States. Many in the U.S. government concluded that the success of the postwar system rested on the image of U.S. power in Europe and on preventing the use or threat of force from affecting the shape of international politics.

A related set of political and security issues was defined by the relationships among states in the emerging Western system. The United States played a crucial role in encouraging cooperation, including convincing some—like the French—that their security would be ensured even as the German economy was being revived. A U.S.-imposed requirement for receiving Marshall Plan aid was European cooperation in coming together to define the scope of their economic problems and in coordinating administration of the funds. Much of the impetus for European unity came from the United States' constant encouragement. The occupation of Germany (a collective enterprise with the British and the French)[21] and the occupation of Japan (entirely by the United States) produced substantial efforts to change the domestic politics of these nations.

A final and equally important element of U.S. hegemony was ensuring access to vital resources through the normal course of market relationships. Nations should not feel the need to use military force to gain a special position or access to these resources. Perhaps the most important of these resources was oil. The principal agents of control of this resource were the large American, British, and Dutch multinational oil corporations, but U.S. political and military power in the Middle East was an equally important ingredient.[22] This was especially evident in the U.S. effort to force the Soviets out of Iran in 1946, the U.S. intervention in Iran in 1953, and the United States' close relationship with Saudi Arabia. The consequence was to ensure plentiful supplies at relatively cheap and stable prices.

U.S. Purposes?

Although we can identify the main issues of international order in which U.S. hegemony played an essential role, scholars have disagreed about the basic aims of U.S. policy. Some have seen U.S. actions in trade, money, politics, security, and resources as an effort to provide many nations with the generalized benefits of peace and prosperity, sacrificing U.S. short-term interests for the good of the world community. In this case, the United States was involved in providing what are called collective or public goods. Considered very precisely, collective goods refer to identifiable benefits that are available to all who participate in the system (even if they pay no part of the cost) and consumption of the good by one participant does not diminish consumption by others. In one version of hegemonic stability theory, collective goods, such as security and prosperity, will emerge only if the most powerful nation accepts the costs of providing them and defers its own benefit to the future. This country, in effect, must be willing to think in terms of benefits to a wide set of nations.[23]

A second perspective proposes that the collective benefits of international order will be supplied only if the dominant state can extract a disproportionate amount of the benefits. This view sees the United States as able to use its leverage to gain special privileges or to compel member states to make contributions to the costs of world order, so as to make providing international order a profitable venture.[24] A third perspective rejects the collective goods concept of international order and suggests instead that hegemonic power produced a substantial array of private benefits to the United States.[25]

As is often the case, the actual situation contains a complex mixture of all three perspectives. In terms of bearing the costs of international order, the United States was clearly the only state capable of providing capital and guaranteeing the security of nations. The proportion of GNP the United States spent on defense was much higher than that of other states in the "free world," and U.S. troops did a disproportionate share of the fighting and dying in wars for international stability. At the same time, free trade can provide great benefits to the most productive and low-cost nations because their exports are likely to expand relative to others. Further, the nation with the world's key currency receives special benefits by avoiding the need to adjust its domestic economy to payments deficits. Because the dollar functioned as a key currency and because other nations accepted it as payment for goods, the United States was able to force these nations to bear some of the costs of its international operations.[26] At the same time, peace and prosperity in the postwar period were general, at least for developed nations.[27]

But the real key to understanding U.S. motives in promoting international stability lies with the perceptions of U.S. leaders about the military and political costs that would come from dissolution of world order. The experience of depression and war convinced many key government officials that U.S. prosperity and security depended on prosperity abroad and on eliminating or blocking the acts of hostile and aggressive states. Should the United States not act to ensure these outcomes, international economic conflict would doom any chance for full employment and free enterprise in the United States, while control of the resources of Europe and Asia by a hostile power would certainly force a garrison state in the United States and cause another world war.[28] In an important sense, the benefits of a liberal world order derived from the unacceptable costs that could be forgone with its presence.

Power and Outcomes

Should we conclude from this discussion that U.S. power was so dominant that the United States could get whatever it wanted? The answer is certainly "no," but for reasons that may not be obvious. Two critical examples help illustrate the point. Throughout the war, in negotiations leading to Lend Lease, in the discussions of the Bretton Woods institutions, and in the agreements for the British loan in 1945–1946, the United States pressed the British very hard to dismantle the Imperial Preference System. This was the trade and monetary bloc created by Britain among past and present colonial areas to cope with the depression and the war. The U.S. position was consistent with a multilateral and open world order and would have eliminated the various mechanisms used to protect British trade.[29] The British grudgingly gave verbal assurances and, as a first step in 1947, moved to make the pound fully convertible. The result was to expose the weaknesses in the British economic position as the British were forced to use most of the $3.75 billion loan to support the pound. After a six-week trial, the idea of convertibility was shelved.

The U.S. objective of European political unity, a key element of Marshall Plan aid, suffered a similar fate. The idea was to create a stronger and more prosperous Europe through political and economic integration, and the expectation was for rapid movement toward this goal. One important consequence would be to establish an offsetting system of power in Europe and thereby reduce U.S. responsibilities. The other consequence would be to move more rapidly toward a multilateral trading system based on convertible currencies. This plan ran headlong into British resistance. The British genuinely feared the economic and political effects of integration into Europe. British leaders worried about ties to Commonwealth nations, about the loss of political and economic independence, about the economic consequences of competition with the United States and the rapid swings in the U.S. business cycle, and about their status as a world power. Other countries also feared the consequences of a single integrated market in Europe.[30]

Despite its overwhelming power advantages and the apparent leverage created by the importance of Marshall Plan aid to Europe, the United States could not always obtain its objectives.[31] Three factors contributed to this result. First was the audacity of the proposal: bringing Europe—an area of intense political conflict for centuries—toward political and economic integration within a few years was probably unrealistic. Moving Britain and Europe toward a liberal system had to wait until their economies could compete with the United States'. Second and more interesting was the effect of European and British weakness. The importance of bringing these nations into a Western political and economic bloc meant that overt intimidation and coercion were likely to prove counterproductive. At the very least, adopting the U.S. vision of an unbridled multilateral world would have proved devastating to the economies of Europe. Pushing too hard would have produced either collapse of U.S.-oriented political elites or cooperation without actual consent. Finally, the very nature of U.S. hegemony placed sharp limits on the ability to achieve U.S. demands. From the U.S. standpoint, world stability required a collective and collaborative effort to contain the Soviet Union and to create a more liberal international system. Achieving a genuinely cooperative arrangement among Western nations forced the United States to make many compromises. U.S. hegemony was based mostly on leadership and not on coercion.[32]

The Consequences of U.S. Hegemony

Understanding the overall effects of U.S. hegemony is a very difficult problem, and much of the rest of this book can be seen as an extended answer to this question. One major consequence of this hegemony was an extraordinary level of peace and prosperity, certainly with disproportionate benefits accruing to developed states, but also with some previously poor states gaining in economic strength. The rapid recovery of West Germany, most of Europe, and Japan owed much to U.S. aid, investment, and a favorable political and security climate. The Third World as a whole did not fare as well, losing in share of world trade and total output. Much of this came as a result of a relative decline in the importance of primary products and food and an increase in the importance of manufactured goods. After the mid-1960s, some poor states were able to break into the world market for manufactures. (See Chapters 8 and 12 for more discussion of this process.) For the United States, many special benefits flowed from hegemony—the foreign policy benefits from having the key currency and the advantages to its corporations of operating on a world scale are two examples—but it too experienced a relative decline in world product and trade. After 1971, U.S. policy took on a much more unilateral cast in trying to manipulate the world economy to its advantage. The Vietnam War experience, from 1961 to 1973, also made the United States much more resentful of the military costs of hegemony and led to pressures on allies to share more of the burdens.

Unquestionably, U.S. economic, military, and political power shaped the post-1945 world economy. Examining in more detail the costs and benefits of that system for industrial states is the subject of the next section.

THE HEYDAY OF U.S. HEGEMONY:
1958–1970

Although the United States commanded great power resources after World War II, it was not until 1958–1959 that its vision of a multilateral and liberal world economy began to be realized. The 10 years from 1948 to 1958 produced several new and significant features in the world economy, the most important being the development of new institutions for economic cooperation, dramatic economic growth in Europe, rising U.S. military spending, increased U.S. foreign aid in the Third World, and the emergence of U.S.-based multinational corporations. These factors helped to generate the stability and prosperity that gave nations the confidence to participate in this liberal system. But each factor also contributed to an outflow of dollars from the United States, and this ultimately brought down the Bretton Woods system. In this section we will briefly consider these developments and then turn to the problems they created.

The European Economic Community

Perhaps the most important event during these 10 years came in March 1957 with the signing of the Treaty of Rome. This treaty, signed by France, the Federal Republic of Germany (West Germany), Belgium, Luxembourg, Italy, and the Netherlands, called for the creation of the European Economic Community (EEC) beginning on January 1, 1958.[33] Several steps had preceded this decision. Marshall Plan aid had been made contingent on European cooperation, and the United States pressed hard for much greater levels of economic and political unity.[34] But in Europe, leadership for integration was supplied by the French, who were motivated initially by the need to bring German industrial power under international supervision and later by a recognition of the importance of creating a European system capable of dealing with the United States and the Soviet Union on equal terms. Under the U.S. concept of world leadership, this notion of independent power centers was actually encouraged, and the tariff discrimination and political independence that almost inevitably followed were tolerated. Further, the United States wanted German power accommodated to Germany's other European partners and available to deal with the Soviets. Initial steps came, first in 1948, as Belgium, Luxembourg, and the Netherlands established a customs union,[35] and then in 1950, when the European Coal and Steel Community was created to manage and control German industrial power.[36] In 1955 negotiations began for a broader customs union, which reached fruition in the 1957 Rome treaty.

The basic purpose of the agreement was to establish a schedule for reducing tariffs and quantitative restrictions on trade. On the whole, the timetable was met or exceeded, with tariffs slashed dramatically and quotas eliminated entirely.[37] Shortly after the inauguration of the EEC (late 1958 and early 1959) fourteen European nations, including Great Britain, moved to accept full convertibility of their currencies.[38] The same economic growth in the 1950s that made the EEC possible also gave these and other nations the financial strength to close their payments gap and to accumulate the reserves needed to support a currency at a fixed price against the dollar. This also coincided with an expansion of resources and a more liberal lending policy at the IMF, both of which facilitated convertibility.[39]

Military Keynesianism and Foreign Aid

The 1950s also witnessed important developments in U.S. political economy, in particular the increasing role of military spending, the rise of foreign aid, and a persistent balance of payments deficit. The combination of Soviet development of an atomic bomb in 1949 and the outbreak of the Korean War in 1950 produced a militarization of the Cold War and a consequent rise in U.S. military spending. Actual spending increased more than threefold by 1952 and stood at more than 10 percent of GNP by 1953. The legacy of 1930s Keynesianism, the postwar commitment to high levels of employment, and the need for high military spending merged to form a relatively coherent national policy. In the 1930s, Keynes proposed to use increases in government spending during periods of economic recession to stimulate the economy. From a political standpoint, the easiest way to raise spending was to pay for the military requirements of the Cold War. By the early 1960s, the new Kennedy administration had added the notion of reducing taxes while increasing spending so as to provide an extra boost to the economy.

A key element in U.S. postwar aims was dismantling the nineteenth-century colonial system established by the European powers. The late 1940s and 1950s produced a wave of new nations as this process came to fruition. However, the Soviet Union moved to take advantage of this development and increased its political and economic activities in what emerged as the Third World. The U.S. response was to utilize its military capabilities to engage in selective intervention and to increase its aid—economic and military—to reinforce its political and military position in the Third World. Castro's victory in Cuba and his swing toward the Soviet Union in 1959–1960 gave strong incentives to accelerate this trend. The Third World and its economic and military orientation in the Cold War became important enough to warrant much more attention and resources.

Dollar Glut

The revival and integration of Western Europe and the growing demands of the Cold War came against the backdrop of troubling trends in the U.S. international economic situation. The 1950s, which began with a dollar shortage, ended with the United States wanting to reverse a persistent balance of payments deficit. In the early part of the decade, a payments deficit was created through military and economic aid; this was desirable because it helped close the dollar gap with the still economically weak Europeans. By the late 1950s Europe had recovered, and the deficit presented new problems. Although the United States enjoyed a substantial surplus in its goods and services and investment income accounts, this was more than offset by foreign aid, military expenditures abroad, and private overseas investment.[40] The sudden shrinkage in the surplus accounts in 1958–1959 produced a much wider payments deficit and instability in the dollar.

Remember that under the Bretton Woods system the dollar was fixed in terms of gold at $35 an ounce. This meant that the U.S. government was required to redeem dollars held by foreigners at that price—a commitment that served as the core of the fixed exchange rate system. The likelihood of exercising this option was based on the ratio of dollars held by foreigners to the gold held by the United States. If the amount of dollars abroad surpassed the amount of U.S. gold, all claimants could not be paid unless the United States changed the price of gold. Raising the price of gold in terms of dollars—in effect devaluing the dollar—automatically increased the dollar quantity of gold. Speculators in foreign exchange and others who feared this possibility would anticipate such an action and convert their dollars for gold—producing a "run" on the dollar and contributing to the very outcome they wanted to profit from or avoid. Because confidence in the dollar was a key element of the Bretton Woods system and because this confidence meant persuading those holding dollars to continue doing so, the U.S. balance of payments became a prime indicator of the system's stability. A larger payments deficit meant more dollars abroad and more potential claimants on U.S. gold.

Political Economy and Hegemony

It was this problem that dominated international monetary management in the 1960s and ultimately led to the demise of the Bretton Woods system. In a sense, the requirements of hegemony—as expressed in U.S. foreign and economic policies from the late 1940s—undermined a major pillar of that system. Kennedy and Johnson are the clearest examples of presidents who not only had policies guided by the political, military, and economic demands of hegemony but also point out the costs and contradictions of such policies. President Kennedy was determined to marshal U.S. power in order to contain the Soviet Union and communism on a global scale. Expansion of military power and foreign aid was the chief means to this end. Kennedy was also concerned about the United States' economic performance at home and abroad. He expected rapid domestic economic growth—the result of a fiscal policy based on military Keynesianism—to ameliorate the costs of the military buildup. Coupled with accelerating the liberalization of world trade, the improved productivity from growth was also expected to solve the balance of payments problem.

Links between domestic and international economies were more tightly drawn in the 1960s than in previous years. Expectations about economic growth were driven by the requirements of competition with the Soviet Union. Moreover, the U.S. position in the world economy, as measured by the balance of payments, became a serious concern of Kennedy and his successor. One important advisor warned that "[we] will not be able to sustain in the 1960s a world position without solving the balance of payments problem."[41] But the harder the United States tried to meet its global responsibilities, the more it damaged the balance of payments and undermined its ability to act as hegemon. This behavior also began to prompt a backlash from allies, who came to resent the privileges and consequences of the dollar as key currency. Their chief complaint was that the unrelenting U.S. payments deficit—a product of U.S. foreign operations—presented a major policy dilemma.

They were forced either to hold dollars and expand their money supply and inflation rates or to exchange the dollars for gold and undermine the value of the dollars remaining in foreign hands. The French were especially critical, arguing that they and others were being required to pay part of the costs of a mistaken U.S. policy in Southeast Asia.

Over the decade, the U.S. response was to reject the option of devaluation and instead to devise a variety of mechanisms to cope with what was hoped to be a short-run balance of payments problem. These mechanisms included persuading Europeans to use their gold and currencies to support the dollar, taking voluntary and mandatory measures to restrict the movement of U.S. private capital abroad, and defending the value of the pound as the dollar's first line of defense. The most lasting result of the efforts to salvage the dollar-gold connection was the establishment of a new form of international money. The Special Drawing Rights (SDRs) established in the International Monetary Fund was a checking account that central banks could use to supplement their international reserves. Nations in deficit could use this overdraft privilege to settle international accounts with other central banks. The hope was that the dollar's liquidity role could be eased by SDRs. But the small size of SDR allocations and reluctance to rely on "fiat" money limited the usefulness of SDRs.[42]

On a more fundamental level, the United States pushed for additional liberalization of world trade. Congress passed the Trade Expansion Act in 1962, giving the president broadened powers to negotiate lower tariffs. In large part, this act was a response to the challenges presented by the new European Economic Community. The EEC created a common external tariff on goods from outside the six member countries while reducing tariffs within the group. This threatened to hurt U.S. trade and to further weaken the balance of payments. The resulting Kennedy Round of GATT lasted from 1963 to 1967 and produced significant tariff reductions over a broad range of goods.[43] But, as we shall see, the U.S. trade balance, and with it the balance of payments, did not improve.

The Emergence of Multinational Corporations

The efforts to cope with the EEC and payments difficulties also affected another very important development in the U.S. economy and the world economy: the rise of the multinational corporation and new international capital markets. The combination of the EEC and convertibility helped spur U.S. corporations to invest in Europe after 1958. The fear of tariff walls around the EEC provided the incentive, and the ability to convert profits back into dollars offered large U.S. corporations the opportunity, to establish production facilities in Europe.[44] Multinational corporations (MNCs)—with production and/or marketing facilities in at least two countries—have given rise to a new language for the analysis of international relations. Scholars now speak of the internationalization of production, the integration of national economies, global calculations of market relations, and the power of transnational actors in relation to nations themselves. The term *globalization* now stands for all these

**Table 4.6 U.S. Foreign Direct Investment: 1950–1970
(book value in billions of U.S. dollars)**

	Total	Manufacturing	Petroleum & Mining	Trade & Public Utilities
1950	11.79	3.83	4.52	2.18
1960	31.82	11.05	13.76	4.95
1970	78.18	32.26	27.88	9.42

SOURCE: Adapted from Mira Wilkins, *The Maturing of Multinational Enterprise: American Business Abroad from 1914 to 1970*, Cambridge: Harvard University Press, 1974, 330.

**Table 4.7 U.S. Foreign Direct Investment in Manufacturing,
1955–1970
(book value in billions of U.S. dollars)**

	EEC	U.K.	Europe Other	Canada	Latin America	Other	Total
1955	0.6	0.9	0.1	2.8	1.4	0.5	6.3
1960	1.4	2.2	0.3	4.8	1.5	0.9	11.1
1965	3.7	3.3	0.6	6.9	2.9	1.9	19.3
1970	7.2	5.0	1.5	10.1	4.6	3.9	32.3

SOURCE: Adapted from Wilkins, *Multinational Enterprise*, 331.

trends. These are matters that we will take up in subsequent chapters. For now, our concern is with understanding the political consequences of MNCs and the economic motivations behind their expansion abroad.

A key feature of multinational corporations is direct investment abroad designed to establish and control a production and/or distribution unit.[45] The levels of foreign direct investment (FDI) and its geographic and business direction can be seen in Tables 4.6 and 4.7. Clearly, expansion abroad is substantial in all categories but especially in manufacturing. Table 4.7 shows the geographic distribution of foreign direct investment in manufacturing. Several areas of the world, but especially Canada, the EEC, and Asia, received U.S. direct investment.

The process of foreign direct investment was overwhelmingly an American phenomenon. By the early 1970s, the book value of U.S. international investments was $86 billion, which represented 52 percent of all foreign direct investment for all market economies. Even more impressive is the $172 billion worth of goods and services that U.S. companies produced abroad. This is compared with $43.5 billion worth of goods produced within the United States for export. That is, production abroad by U.S. firms was almost four times as great as all U.S. exports.[46]

The growth of multinational corporations in the period from 1958 to 1970 was the consequence of a complex mixture of political and economic factors. In political terms, the interests of the United States and European nations were accommodated, and this created the climate within which U.S. MNCs in Europe could flourish. Specifically, this meant acceptance by the United States of the EEC and its discriminatory and competitive effects on American trade and, in return, the Europeans' (especially the Germans') agreement to finance the U.S. balance of payments deficit by holding dollars. This would permit operations such as stationing U.S. troops in Europe to continue and helped to make possible other major U.S. actions, such as in Vietnam. As part of this process, the United States persuaded the Europeans to give U.S. MNCs access to the EEC and to treat them as if they were European companies.[47]

Considered only in economic terms, multinational corporations had a somewhat cloudy set of benefits for the United States. In 1971 U.S. MNCs engaged in $4.8 billion in foreign direct investment (remember that this is a negative item in the balance of payments), while generating $9 billion in investment income (a positive item).[48] More difficult to measure is the loss of jobs in the United States to overseas production, the transfer of technology abroad, and the exports back to the United States (our imports) of goods produced elsewhere by U.S. MNCs. But in terms of the immediate political needs of generating a positive return in the balance of payments, multinational corporations represented a support system for U.S. international responsibilities.[49]

From the standpoint of the multinationals themselves, the political climate created by U.S. hegemony and the economic climate of stability and opportunity intersected with a set of more specifically economic motivations. Several somewhat complementary explanations have been offered for the expansion of multinationals, each of which begins with the fact that typically these are firms that are operating in an oligopolistic environment and are seeking to maintain or extend their competitive advantages.[50] Because market share is an important asset for oligopolistic firms, these companies may expand operations abroad simply to make certain that they are positioned to participate in any new or expanding market. Or a giant firm that enjoys some special competitive advantage may look to production in foreign markets to exploit this advantage. Finally, the firm may be at a particular point in the evolution of its products such that foreign production becomes an economic necessity. Initially, the combination of a large home market and technological advantages makes production for export a profitable strategy. But as the technology of the product and its production processes become more commonplace and available, the company may be forced to move abroad to take advantage of lower costs and/or to compete with a foreign producer. This "product cycle" theory may be especially relevant to understanding U.S. firms in the 1950s and 1960s that faced competition from rising European firms moving into markets that U.S. firms had pioneered in the preceding ten to fifteen years.[51]

Lagging somewhat behind multinational corporations were U.S. banks, which began in the mid-1960s to expand substantially their foreign operations. Once again, several factors were at work. The dollar as key currency, acceptable for most international transactions, and the U.S. payments imbalance must be judged as critical ingredients. The transition from a dollar shortage to a dollar surplus in 1957–1958 resulted in the accumulation of dollars in foreign banks. London bankers, an ingenious lot, decided to lend these dollars rather than return them to the United States. Thus was born the Eurodollar or Eurocurrency (because some other currencies were also involved) market—essentially an unregulated international money supply. When the U.S. government acted in 1963 to stem the dollar outflow for loans through the interest equalization tax, many U.S. banks established operations abroad to continue their foreign lending and thereby took advantage of the Eurodollar process. The rise of the Eurodollar market, the expansion of U.S. international banking, and the growth of U.S. multinational firms were linked together throughout the 1960s.

Beyond this relationship, the Eurocurrency system became a phenomenon in its own right. Because no single state could regulate it effectively and because of the unceasing U.S. payments deficits, a Euromarket system developed consisting of the dollar and other currencies, a system of bank credit, and a Eurobond market (bonds denominated in dollars but floated outside the United States). A massive volume of funds emerged that, without much restriction, could move across borders in search of the highest yields available on a global basis (discounting for risk). By 1970 this market approached $70 billion and would triple in size in the next three years.[52]

The 1958–1970 period produced an extraordinarily complex set of developments for the world economy. It was simultaneously a time of American dominance and American decline. Bearing the burdens of military competition and Vietnam, the United States was acutely aware of the continued importance of preserving global security and stability. The United States also encouraged the establishment of the EEC and the economic revitalization of Japan, both to marshal its assets against the Soviets and to facilitate the multilateral economic order sought since the 1940s. U.S. resources flowed abroad to preserve a liberal world order even as allies improved their competitive position in the world economy. But neither planned nor entirely desired was the acceleration of U.S. private investment abroad. As we shall see, this combination of events led to the breakdown of the Bretton Woods system, so important to the United States, and contributed to dramatic changes in the control of oil.

MONEY AND OIL, 1971–1973

Between 1970 and 1973, two of the pillars of U.S. hegemony—fixed exchange rates and control of oil—came under pressure and eventually disintegrated, only to be replaced by new relationships. Several of the Bretton Woods system's basic weaknesses were exposed by the continuing U.S.

payments deficit and growing international financial interdependence, and between 1971 and 1973 the system largely collapsed. The ability of the United
States to guarantee ample oil supplies at low prices ran aground on imbalances
of supply and demand and growing nationalism in those Third World nations
where the oil was located. Notwithstanding the collapse of these arrangements, U.S. power remained sufficient to organize new mechanisms for
money and oil. But these new regimes required even greater coordination,
cooperation, and compromise and cast doubt on the future of the world
economy.

The End of Bretton Woods

The economic growth of Western Europe and Japan, a weakening position in
the U.S. balance of trade, and the growth of international capital markets
spelled doom for the Bretton Woods system of fixed exchange rates based on
a fixed dollar-gold exchange rate. As early as 1960, the liabilities created by
foreign-held dollars exceeded the U.S. supply of gold. In that same year, the
price of gold in private markets rose to $40 an ounce. During the next decade
and more, the situation deteriorated.[53]

This deterioration can be seen in several ways but especially in the growing importance of several countries in world trade and in the U.S. balance of
payments. Table 4.8 shows a steady decline in the world proportion of home-
based exports by the United States. (Remember the jump in U.S. MNC production abroad.) The same was true for Great Britain. At the same time, West
Germany, France, and especially Japan made steady relative gains. U.S. exports
rose throughout the period, but not as fast as those of the world or of the
United States' industrial competitors. By 1972 West Germany had nearly
equaled the United States in dollar volume of exports.

A close examination of the U.S. balance of payments for this period reveals
some important refinements for our understanding of the U.S. problem. Several points stand out in the data shown in Table 4.9. Perhaps most important is
the slow growth of exports relative to imports, especially after 1967, and the
development of a trade deficit in 1971. Although investment income (remember MNC direct investments) grew steadily and the capital account and military spending abroad were mostly under control, the U.S. deficit persisted and
grew much worse because of the deteriorating trade balance.[54] Another perspective on this process is revealed from data on exports and imports of manufactured goods (see Table 4.10). Two points are notable from this evidence.
First, imports of both low- and high-technology manufactures were growing
more rapidly than were exports of these goods. Second, by 1971 the deficit in
low-tech goods equaled the surplus in high-tech goods.

The difficulties in the U.S. trade and payments balances can be traced in
substantial part to the interaction of domestic and foreign policy in the mid-
1960s. The decision to escalate U.S. involvement in the Vietnam War in 1965
came in the context of substantial increases in domestic spending for new
poverty and welfare programs and was followed by the decision not to raise

Table 4.8 Proportion of World Exports
(billions of U.S. dollars with percentage of world totals)

	1960	%	1965	%	1970	%	1971	%	1972	%
U.S.	20.6	18.0	27.5	16.5	43.2	15.2	44.1	13.9	49.8	13.2
Great Britain	10.6	9.3	13.8	8.2	19.6	6.9	22.6	7.1	24.7	6.6
W. Germany	11.4	9.9	17.9	10.7	34.2	12.1	39.1	12.3	46.7	12.4
France	6.9	6.0	10.2	6.1	18.1	6.4	20.8	6.6	26.5	7.0
Japan	4.1	3.6	8.5	5.1	19.3	6.8	24.1	7.6	29.1	7.7
World exports	114.6		167.1		283.7		317.4		376.8	

SOURCE: The figures are calculated from International Monetary Fund, *International Financial Statistics Yearbook,* 1979, 62–63.

Table 4.9 U.S. Balance of Payments, 1960–1972
(billions of dollars)

Year	Exports	Imports	Net	Military	Invest Inc.	Current Account Balance	Capital Account Balance	Error	Net Liquidity Balance
1960	19.7	−14.8	4.9	−2.8	2.8	1.8	−3.0	−1.1	−3.7
1965	26.5	−21.5	5.0	−2.1	5.3	4.3	−6.1	−0.5	−2.5
1967	30.7	−26.9	3.8	−3.1	5.8	2.1	−5.5	−0.9	−4.7
1968	33.6	−33.0	0.6	−3.1	6.2	−0.4	−3.4	−0.4	−1.6
1969	36.4	−35.8	0.6	−3.3	6.0	−1.1	−2.0	−2.4	−6.1
1970	42.0	−39.8	2.2	−3.4	6.4	0.4	−3.4	−1.2	−3.9
1971	42.8	−45.5	−2.7	−2.9	8.9	−2.8	−6.8	−10.8	−22.0
1972	48.8	−55.7	−6.9	−3.6	9.8	−8.4	−1.5	−3.1	−13.9

Note: Some items in the balance of payments have been omitted. The result is that only net exports/imports adds across.

The use of different sources for trade and balance of payments produces a slight variation in the exports totals.

SOURCE: Table reconstructed from data in John Odell, *U.S. International Monetary Policy,* Princeton, N.J.: Princeton University Press, 1982, 203–205.

Table 4.10 U.S. Trade in Manufactured Goods, 1960–1971

	1960	1965	1970	1971
Low-technology goods				
Exports	3.573	4.409	6.778	6.262
Imports	4.494	7.350	12.928	14.550
Balance	−0.921	−2.941	−6.150	−8.288
High-technology goods				
Exports	9.010	13.030	22.565	24.187
Imports	2.369	3.895	12.978	15.898
Balance	6.641	9.135	9.587	8.289

SOURCE: Data from Robert Gilpin, *U.S. Power and the Multinational Corporation,* New York: Basic Books, 1975, 193.

taxes. In many ways this combination of choices was consistent with the Keynesian notions of fiscal policy except that it came at a time of near full employment and a booming economy. During the period from 1965 to 1973, the inflation rate rose (as measured by the Consumer Price Index), and the budget deficit widened.

In simple terms, the budget deficit contributed greatly to the rise in inflation, both through overstimulation of the economy and by increases in the money supply encouraged by the Federal Reserve to help finance the deficit. (See Table 4.11.) The rising price of U.S. goods encouraged imports and discouraged exports. In 1968–1969, policy changed with a tax increase and tighter money. The result of this "belt tightening" was a budget surplus, an improvement in the balance of trade, and a stronger dollar. But the economy also went into recession even as inflation remained high. Later, in 1970, economic policy shifted back to stimulation.[55]

The overall trade deficit in 1971 represented the culmination of several years of deterioration and, combined with the deficit in military and capital accounts, produced a major international monetary crisis. With pressure mounting against the dollar, on August 15, 1971, President Nixon announced a new policy. The United States suspended indefinitely the commitment to redeem gold for dollars, imposed domestic wage and price controls, demanded depreciation of the dollar, and placed a 10 percent tariff surcharge on U.S. imports. These actions amounted to a unilateral rejection of the basic rules of the international monetary system largely established by the United States and presented a demand to the United States' military and economic allies to adjust their economic systems. This was an audacious act and can be seen as the beginning of a much more unilateral position by the United States as global hegemon.

What followed was more than eighteen months of coercion and pressure, resistance, seemingly solid agreements, and continued market instability. At issue was the future of the dollar-gold link, fixed exchange rates, the rate of exchange, and which countries would be forced to make the adjustments and trade concessions. The United States wanted substantial revaluations of major currencies, elimination of "unfair" restrictions on trade, and greater sharing of the costs of keeping U.S. forces abroad. The French and the Japanese resisted these demands most strongly, with the French refusing to alter the franc-gold price and the Japanese arguing that the United States should change its domestic economic system. Only after National Security Adviser Henry Kissinger became concerned about the damage this resistance was doing to the alliance system did the United States accept the need for concessions. In December 1971, at the Smithsonian Institution in Washington, D.C., a compromise agreement was reached. The United States devalued the dollar in terms of gold (but made no commitment to redeem dollars for gold) and dropped the import surcharge. The other major capitalist states revalued their currencies against the dollar by an average of 8 percent (Japan's was 16.9 percent against the dollar) and adjusted their currencies against each

Table 4.11 Budget Deficits and Inflation

	1965	1966	1967	1968	1969	1970	1971	1972	1973
CPI (%)	1.7	2.9	2.9	4.2	5.4	5.9	4.3	3.3	6.2
Budget deficit ($)	−1.6	−3.8	−8.7	−25.2	+3.2	−2.8	−23.0	−23.4	14.8

SOURCE: Data on Consumer Price Index taken from David Calleo, *The Imperious Economy,* Cambridge: Harvard University Press, 1982, 201. Data on budget deficit taken from Calleo, *Beyond American Hegemony,* New York: Basic Books, 1987, 243.

other. Trade issues were postponed. The result was a temporary return to fixed rates.[56]

This system held together through 1972 in spite of continuing U.S. trade deficits. But in February 1973, renewed selling of the dollar produced another currency crisis and a U.S. decision to devalue the dollar 10 percent (without consultation) accompanied by the threat to devalue another 10 percent unless the Japanese and the Western Europeans agreed to float their currencies against the dollar. Acceptance of this arrangement led not to stability but rather to further selling of the dollar and the complete collapse of fixed exchange rates in March 1973.[57]

Two main reasons can be identified for the decline and fall of the Bretton Woods system. First, the system was inherently unstable because the mechanisms for adjustment of exchange rates were so inflexible. This was particularly true for the United States, where the value of the dollar also became the measure of the stability of the world economy, especially in the minds of U.S. leaders. The economic relations that developed after 1948 were structured by these fixed values even as the shift from U.S. surplus to deficit increasingly demanded adjustment of exchanges rates. The world of 1971 was significantly different from the world of 1945–1950, but the Bretton Woods system made few accommodations to that reality.

Second and perhaps most reflective of those changes was the massive growth of the market power of international capital and its impact on fixed rates. This is reflected in the emergence between 1958 and 1973 of transnational actors—multinational corporations and international banks—and in the vast Eurocurrency market. As late as 1966, the Eurocurrency market and U.S. international reserves were of approximately equal size. But by 1973 the Eurocurrency market was almost nine times bigger than U.S. reserves.[58] Such an immense collection of resources was capable of overwhelming even concerted government action. Between 1971 and 1973 these new transnational actors collectively lost confidence in the system of fixed exchange rates and the ability of governments to establish any viable system. Eventually, in March 1973, the governments of the capitalist world were forced to accept the immense market power of these actors and to adopt a new system of floating exchange rates.[59]

Loss of Control over Oil

Concurrent with these dramatic changes in the international monetary order was an equally significant structural transformation of the international oil market. Several basic forces converged in the early 1970s to lead to an overturning of the Western control of oil. These forces included changes in the political and military relationship of the United States and Great Britain in the Middle East, shifts in supply and demand for oil, increasing political control over oil exercised by Third World countries, and the 1973 Yom Kippur War. U.S. domination of the international oil market, operating through large multinational oil companies, came to an end as the price for oil skyrocketed and an embargo created shortages in the United States.

Between 1968 and 1971, Great Britain withdrew from its military commitments in the Middle East, leaving a political and military vacuum that it had filled for more than a century. During this time the United States was mired in the Vietnam War, which greatly hampered its ability to use military force anywhere else in the world. These developments damaged the West's ability to defend its interests in cheap and plentiful oil.[60]

The early 1970s also saw the culmination of the trends of the preceding fifteen years, during which the world became increasingly dependent on oil from the Middle East. From 1957 to 1972, the proportion of world oil produced in the United States declined from 43.1 percent to 21.1 percent, whereas the Middle East raised its proportion from 19.4 percent to 41 percent. Over the same period, U.S. oil imports rose from 11 percent of consumption to 35.5 percent.[61] Rapid increases in world production were linked to even more rapid increases in demand for oil. However, by the early 1970s, world supplies of oil failed to match increases in demand, primarily due to flat U.S. production growth. This combination created the potential for substantial price increases.[62]

Accompanying these trends was a growing boldness by the countries where the oil was located to challenge control over production and pricing decisions by the great oil multinationals. Beginning in Libya in 1970 and soon spreading to other states, governments used various forms of intimidation to increase their take, their level of participation in ownership of the oil, and even in the price charged. The tightening supply situation helped accelerate this process as countries began leapfrogging each other in terms of price and control. The devaluations of the dollar in 1971 and 1973 also prompted price increases because oil was denominated in dollars. When the United States was forced to lift import quotas for oil in April 1973, the signal was given for a new round of negotiations.[63]

It was in this context of growing dependence on Middle East oil that Anwar el-Sadat, president of Egypt, launched an attack on Israel that began the Yom Kippur War. U.S. support of Israel led several members of the Organization of Petroleum Exporting Countries (OPEC) to push prices up dramatically (from $3.01 to $5.12 per barrel) and to impose an embargo. This consisted of reductions in overall production and a ban on shipments to the

United States (and the Netherlands). By January 1974, prices had risen to $11.65 a barrel, and the United States was confronted with a shift in power relations that, in Henry Kissinger's words, "altered irrevocably the world as it had grown up in the postwar period."[64]

CONCLUSIONS

In 1941, Henry Luce, publisher of *Life* magazine, wrote effusively of "the American Century." In many ways he was right; the United States was the key player in determining the outcome of World War II and the shape of the post-war world. American money and military might provided the base for pro-jecting a vision of a liberal world order of peace and prosperity. Confrontation with the Soviet Union pushed the United States beyond its original plans and led to a major effort to organize the political and economic resources of the industrial world for containment. Out of this process came a new set of inter-national institutions, new forms of cooperation, and an unprecedented expan-sion of international trade, capital transfer, and world economic growth. Seen against the record of the preceding century, the years after 1945 were truly epochal.

The economic relationships of the American Century did not last as long as the political and military relationships. The United States largely retained its ability to foster military security but in the process lost many of its economic advantages. The effort to rebuild Europe and Japan as economic powers capa-ble of resisting Soviet pressure worked very well. In the meantime, military spending, foreign aid, and direct investment—the sine qua non of U.S. hege-mony—kept the balance of payments in deficit and undermined the dollar-gold link that stabilized the international monetary system. When America's political and economic allies took advantage of the liberal system of interna-tional trade and greatly expanded their exports in the 1960s, the United States found itself unable to maintain a favorable trade balance. Further, when the growth of the world economy and demand for oil expanded in the 1960s and early 1970s, the United States was unable to prevent Western loss of control over oil production and pricing.

Nevertheless, the United States retained great strength; it was by far the largest economy in the world, the predominant source of capital, the biggest export market, and the continuing guarantor of Western security. But in im-portant ways, the game of international political economy had changed. In the first decade or so after the war, the Europeans and Japanese gained their leverage in negotiating with the United States from weakness; and the United States accepted the necessity for sharply limiting any use of coercion to bring about actions it favored. Instead, providing aid and accepting and even pro-moting discriminatory arrangements such as the EEC were common fare. By the 1970s, increasing European and Japanese economic strength tilted the bar-gaining relationship. Now adjustments had to come from them, and the

United States sometimes found it necessary to coerce these concessions. A much more complex system emerged in which the major capitalist states found that their economic interdependence created a new balance of opposing and conflicting interests. Even parts of the Third World, long simply an arena of military and economic struggle with the Soviets, gained the capacity for independent action. The trick to international order changed from one of U.S. dominance to one of bargaining over the terms for creating and recreating a framework within which economic competition on a global scale could take place.

American hegemony was essential to creating a political context for restoring international stability and reconstructing a world economy. One very significant consequence was increasing levels of interdependence, especially among industrial states. Paradoxically, the events of the early 1970s led not to fragmentation in the world economy but rather to an explosion of international financial flows, rapidly growing trade, and an increasingly complex interdependence. This globalization process over the next quarter-century is our next subject.

NOTES

1. W. M. Scammell, *The International Economy since 1945,* 2nd ed., New York: St. Martin's Press, 1983, 53.

2. Scammell, *Intenational Economy,* 127. Scammell notes that between 1876 and 1913, this same growth ratio was less than 1:1. For additional data on growth rates, see Walt Rostow, *The World Economy,* Austin: University of Texas Press, 1978, 67; and David Landes, *The Unbound Prometheus,* Cambridge, England: Cambridge University Press, 1969, 512.

3. Joel Darmstadter and Hans Landsberger, "The Crisis," in Raymond Vernon (ed.), *The Oil Crisis,* New York: Norton, 1976, 19.

4. Michael Hogan, *Informal Entente,* Columbia: University of Missouri Press, 1977. The formal institution of this era was the Bank for International Settlements, which served as a predecessor to the International Monetary Fund. See Frank Costigliola, "The Other Side of Isolationism: The Establishment of the First World Bank, 1929–1930," *Journal of American History,* 59,

December 1972, 602–620.

5. Benjamin Cohen reports the level at 75 percent, whereas David Calleo sets it at 60 percent (Cohen, *Organizing the World's Money,* New York: Basic Books, 1977, 95; Calleo, *Beyond American Hegemony,* New York: Basic Books, 1987, 227).

6. Remember, a recession typically leads to declining prices or at least a decline in the rate of increase of domestically produced goods. This should make these goods more competitive abroad.

7. This somewhat harsh policy is usually applied more to poorer nations than to economically advanced nations. But in any country the tension over domestic adjustment to international requirements presents a classic case of a conflict of interests between debtors and creditors. This is easily seen in the negotiations of the Bretton Woods agreements, especially between the creditor United States and debtor Britain (Alfred Eckes, *A Search for Solvency: Bretton Woods and the International*

Monetary System, 1941–1971, Austin: University of Texas Press, 1975; and Fred Block, *The Origins of International Economic Disorder,* Berkeley and Los Angeles: University of California Press, 1974).

8. For details on the origins and development of the World Bank, see Edward S. Mason and Robert Asher, *The World Bank since Bretton Woods,* Washington, D.C.: Brookings Institution, 1973.

9. Robert Pastor, *Congress and the Politics of Foreign Economic Policy,* Berkeley and Los Angeles: University of California Press, 1980, 96–98.

10. Following negotiations that were completed in 1994, the GATT system was incorporated into the new international organization, the World Trade Organization (WTO).

11. The GATT Rounds include 1947, Geneva; 1949, Annecy; 1950–1951, Torquay; 1955–1956, Geneva; 1959–1962, Geneva (Dillon round); 1963–1967, Geneva (Kennedy Round); 1973–1979, Tokyo; 1986–1993, Uruguay.

12. Pastor, *Congress,* 78.

13. Robert Keohane, *After Hegemony,* Princeton, N.J.: Princeton University Press, 1984, 37. Other works elaborating hegemonic stability theory are Stephen Krasner, "State Power and the Structure of International Trade," *World Politics,* 27, April 1975, 313–347; Charles Kindleberger, *The World in Depression,* Berkeley and Los Angeles: University of California Press, 1973; Robert Gilpin, *U.S. Power and the Multinational Corporation,* New York: Basic Books, 1975; Gilpin, *War and Change in World Politics,* Cambridge, England: Cambridge University Press, 1981.

14. Alan Milward, *War, Economy and Society, 1939–1945,* Berkeley and Los Angeles: University of California Press, 1977, 63–68. Much of this advantage came from government investment that promoted the ability to reap large economies of scale. U.S. productivity advantages were so great

that the nation was able to expand war production without reducing nonmilitary production below 1939 levels.

15. Milward, *War,* 63.

16. Milward, *War,* 333. The gross value of U.S. Lend Lease aid to the British was about $30 billion.

17. For a discussion of resource needs in Japanese war decisions, see Jonathan Marshall, *To Have and Have Not: Southeast Asian Raw Materials and the Origins of the Pacific War,* Berkeley and Los Angeles: University of California Press, 1995; and Michael Barnhart, *Japan Prepares for Total War,* Ithaca: Cornell University Press, 1987.

18. This list builds on and extends Robert Keohane, *After Hegemony,* 139; and Susan Strange, "The Persistent Myth of Lost Hegemony," *International Organization,* 41.4, Autumn 1987, 565.

19. Remember that the main reason for the imbalance was the war itself. U.S. productivity growth, European destruction, disruption of traditional trade patterns, and the political significance of economic recovery all contributed to the outcomes in the 1945–1948 period.

20. Michael Hogan, *The Marshall Plan,* Cambridge, England: Cambridge University Press, 1987.

21. The Soviet Union occupied the eastern third of Germany. The failure of joint occupation in May 1947 moved the United States to press forward on the Marshall Plan and unification of the three western occupation zones of Germany.

22. Lawrence Frank, "The First Oil Regime," *World Politics,* 37.4, July 1985, 586; Keohane, *After Hegemony,* 150–181; John Blair, *The Control of Oil,* New York: Pantheon, 1976.

23. Kindleberger, *World in Depression.*

24. Gilpin, *U.S. Power.*

25. Bruce Rusett, in "The Mysterious Case of Vanishing Hegemony, or, Is Mark Twain Really Dead?"

International Organization, 39.2, Spring 1985, 207–231, promotes this view. For more on this issue, see John Conybeare, "Public Goods, Prisoners' Dilemma, and International Political Economy," *International Studies Quarterly,* 28, March 1984, 5–22.

26. U.S. allies, like Germany and France, accepted dollars in payment for U.S. current account deficits, which increased their money supply and affected inflation rates. This feature of a key currency is discussed more later in this chapter.

27. The postwar system of a liberal world does not precisely qualify as a collective good because some nations could be excluded from the institutions and from U.S. aid.

28. Waldo Heinrichs, *Threshold of War: Franklin D. Roosevelt and American Entry into World War II,* New York: Oxford University Press, 1988; John Gaddis, *Strategies of Containment,* New York: Oxford University Press, 1982; Gaddis, *The Long Peace,* New York: Oxford University Press, 1987.

29. Similar actions were taken against the French bloc as part of a U.S. effort to break down the structure of colonialism built up in the nineteenth century.

30. Stafford Cripps, the British chancellor of the exchequer, asserted in November 1949 that "trade liberalization had gone far enough" and that the American proposal for European integration "amounted to a fifty-year programme." The quote and discussion of the U.S.-British dispute on European union are in Michael Hogan, *The Marshall Plan,* Cambridge, England: Cambridge University Press, 1987, 291. Cripps seems to have had the timetable about right, as real economic union in Europe took until the 1990s.

31. A very useful discussion of these questions, along with a detailed historical analysis, is found in G. John Ikenberry, "Rethinking the Origins of American Hegemony," *Political Science Quarterly,* 104.3, 1989, 375–400.

32. The last point, relating to the nature of hegemony, is not the same as the second point, relating to weakness. U.S. leadership was based primarily on persuasion even, and perhaps especially, had Europe and Japan been strong. The United States needed a commitment of political, economic, and military resources from its allies that derived from a belief in the justice of their cause. Given the cooperative nature of the U.S. hegemonic system, neither weak nor strong states could be coerced into being effective members.

33. Continuing its reluctance to join in European economic integration, Britain was not a founding member of the EEC. Instead, the British in 1960 helped organize the European Free Trade Area (EFTA), along with Norway, Switzerland, Austria, Sweden, Denmark, and Portugal. The main difference from the EEC was that EFTA did not have a common external tariff.

34. In response, the Organization for European Economic Cooperation (OEEC) was set up in 1948 to coordinate Marshall Plan aid and reconstruction efforts.

35. A customs union operates to lower tariffs and other trade barriers among a particular set of nations and also works to establish a common trade policy with outside states.

36. The year 1950 also produced the European Payments Union, designed to manage payments imbalances within Europe.

37. Scammell, *International Economy,* 137–138.

38. Convertibility in the 1958–1971 era occurred when a currency could be freely traded for gold or for a foreign currency. The economic dislocations from the war led most countries to place substantial restrictions on convertibility until 1958. After 1971, gold no longer operated as part of convertibility.

39. Eckes, *Searach for Solvency,* 231–233; Scammell, *International Economy,* 109–116.

40. The late 1950s are discussed in Robert Pollard and Samuel F. Wells, Jr., "1945–1960: The Era of American Economic Hegemony," in William H. Becker and Samuel F. Wells, Jr. (eds.), *Economics and World Power,* New York: Columbia University Press, 1984, 379–381.

41. The quote, by Walt Rostow, special assistant to the president for national security, is from William Borden, "Defending Hegemony: American Foreign Economic Policy," in Thomas G. Paterson (ed.), *Kennedy's Quest for Victory: American Foreign Policy, 1961–1963,* New York: Oxford University Press, 1989, 63.

42. Michael Moffitt, *The World's Money,* New York: Simon and Schuster, 1983, 33; Eckes, *Search for Solvency,* 256–257.

43. Pastor, *Congress,* 104–120; Borden, "Defending Hegemony," 69–80.

44. Gilpin, *The Political Economy of International Relations,* Princeton, N.J.: Princeton University Press, 1987, 233. An additional factor in the growth of MNCs was the decline in transportation and communication costs with the inauguration of regular jet travel and the telex.

45. This process of foreign direct investment (FDI) can be distinguished from portfolio investment, in which the investor seeks merely to receive some return on the investment in the equity or debt of a firm. British investment in the nineteenth century emphasized portfolio investment (Gilpin, *U.S. Power,* 9–11).

46. Gilpin, *U.S. Power,* 15. The propensity of U.S. firms to invest and produce abroad (rather than export from a U.S. base) is indicated by the fact that only two other country's firms—Britain and Switzerland—produced more abroad than at home for export. And neither country did so to the same degree as the United States.

47. Gilpin, *U.S. Power,* 107–108, 124–125, 154–155. Gilpin points out the importance of the dollar as the key currency, especially as the U.S. balance of payments deficit persisted

and the U.S. dollar became overvalued. This situation allowed U.S. firms to use an overvalued dollar to purchase assets abroad and establish branches (mostly in Europe).

48. United Nations, "Multinational Corporations in World Development," in George Modelski (ed.), *Transnational Corporations and World Order,* San Francisco: W. H. Freeman, 1979, 25.

49. Gilpin, *U.S. Power,* 156–157.

50. The term *oligopoly* is used to describe a market system in which the number of firms in an industry is very small, with each firm controlling a significant portion of the market. This control allows each firm to influence the price for its products (keeping them higher than in a more competitive system). This power permits the firm to maintain some level of control over its competitive environment.

51. John Dunning, "The Eclectic Paradigm of International Production: A Restatement and Some Possible Extensions," *Journal of International Business Studies,* 19.1, 1988, 1–31; Lorraine Eden, "Bringing the Firm Back In: Multinationals in International Political Economy," *Millennium,* 20.2, 1991, 197–224; Peter Cowhey and Jonathan Aronson, *Managing the World Economy,* New York: CFR Press, 1993, 43–55; Raymond Vernon, "The Product Cycle Hypothesis in a New International Environment," *Oxford Bulletin of Economics and Statistics,* 41.4, November 1979, 255–267.

52. Jeffrey Frieden, *Banking on the World: The Politics of American International Finance,* New York: Harper and Row, 1987, 79–85; Benjamin Cohen, *In Whose Interest? International Banking and American Foreign Policy,* New Haven, Conn.: Yale University Press, 1986, 19–33; Moffitt, *World's Money,* 43–55.

53. John O'Dell, *U.S. International Monetary Policy,* Princeton, N.J.: Princeton University Press, 1982, 85–87.

54. The large "Error" item in Table 4.9 reflects the substantial volume of speculation against the dollar.

55. Discussion of the links between domestic and foreign economic policy can be found in David Calleo, *The Imperious Economy*, Cambridge: Harvard University Press, 1982, 25–61; and Odell, *U.S. International Monetary Policy*, 110–111.

56. The most detailed discussion of these events is Odell, *U.S. International Monetary Policy*, 188–291.

57. Odell, *U.S. International Monetary Policy*, 292–326.

58. Calleo, *Imperious Economy*, 208. Additional measures can be found in Robert Keohane and Joseph Nye, *Power and Interdependence* (2nd edition), Glenview, Ill.: Scott Foresman, 1989, 812–882; and Eckes, *Searach for Solvency*, 240–241.

59. Odell, *U.S. International Monetary Policy*, 229–305. The arrangement adopted was a "dirty float," in which governments periodically intervene to keep exchange rate fluctuations within some acceptable bounds.

60. Daniel Yergin, *The Prize: The Quest for Oil, Money, and Power*, New York: Simon and Schuster, 1991, 563–652.

61. Darmstadter and Landsberger, "The Crisis," 31–33.

62. Rostow, *World Economy*, 257, reports that the growth of U.S. oil consumption outstripped domestic production throughout the postwar era. U.S. domestic production peaked in 1970 and fell each year from 1971 to 1975.

63. Edith Penrose, "The Development of Crisis," in Vernon (ed.), *Oil Crisis*, 39–57; and Yergin, *Prize*, 577–587.

64. Quoted in Yergin, *Prize*, 588.

ANNOTATED BIBLIOGRAPHY

William H. Becker and Samuel F. Wells (eds.). *Economics and World Power*. New York: Columbia University Press, 1984. Contains several insightful pieces on the history of U.S. foreign economic policy.

Fred Block. *The Origins of International Economic Disorder*. Berkeley and Los Angeles: University of California Press, 1977. Offers a penetrating analysis of U.S. international monetary policy for the postwar era.

Benjamin Cohen. *Organizing the World's Money*. New York: Basic Books, 1977. Very helpful on the economics of international finance.

Jeffrey Frieden. *Banking on the World: The Politics of American International Finance*. New York: Harper & Row, 1987. A very useful study of the internationalization of U.S. financial institutions and the international financial system.

Robert Gilpin. *U.S. Power and the Multinational Corporation*. New York: Basic Books, 1975. Perhaps the best theoretically informed analysis of U.S. multinational corporations.

Robert Keohane and Joseph Nye. *Power and Interdependence*. Glenview, Ill.: Scott Foresman, 1989. The most important study of the politics of bargaining within a framework of economic interdependence.

Charles Maier. "The Politics of Productivity: Foundations of American International Economic Policy after World War II," *International Organization*, Autumn 1977, 607–633. A very perceptive argument concerning the expression of domestic political economy in foreign policy.

John Odell. *U.S. International Monetary Policy*. Princeton, N.J.: Princeton University Press, 1982. The best study of the breakdown and collapse of the Bretton Woods system.

Robert Pollard. *Economic Security and the Origins of the Cold War, 1945–1950*.

New York: Columbia University Press, 1985. The best single source for understanding the relationship of U.S. political economy and national security from 1945 to 1950.

John G. Ruggie (ed.). *Multinationalism Matters.* New York: Columbia University Press, 1993. A collection of articles that help in understanding the multilateral dimension of U.S. hegemony.

W. M. Scammell. *The International Economy since 1945.* New York: St. Martin's Press, 1983. An excellent overview.

Daniel Yergin. *The Prize: The Quest for Oil, Money and Power.* New York: Simon and Schuster, 1991. A comprehensive survey of the role of oil in twentieth-century international politics.

Studies of U.S. hegemony include:

Simon Bromley. *American Hegemony and World Oil.* University Park: Pennsylvania State University Press, 1991.

David Calleo. *The Imperious Economy.* Cambridge: Harvard University Press, 1982. Defends the thesis that U.S. spending on foreign commitments undermined the domestic economy.

David Calleo. *Beyond American Hegemony.* New York: Basic Books, 1987. Relates the end of U.S. hegemony to Europe and NATO.

Stephen Gill. *American Hegemony and the Trilateral Commission.* Cambridge, England: Cambridge University Press, 1990. A brilliant investigation of elite interests in hegemony.

Robert Gilpin. *War and Change in World Politics.* Cambridge, England: Cambridge University Press, 1981. A theoretical investigation of the relationship of international systems, hegemony, and economic decline.

G. John Ikenberry. *After Victory.* Princeton, N.J.: Princeton University Press, 2000. Provides a historical analysis of the nature of hegemonic systems.

Robert Keohane. *After Hegemony.* Princeton, N.J.: Princeton University Press, 1984. A very important study of international cooperation in the period after U.S. hegemony.

Stephen Krasner. "State Power and the Structure of International Trade," *World Politics,* April 1975, 314–347. A key statement of the hegemonic stability thesis.

Joseph Nye. *Bound to Lead.* New York: Basic Books, 1990. Counters the thesis that U.S. hegemony has waned.

5

❖

Globalization
and the World Economy

The combination of the collapse of the Bretton Woods system of fixed exchange rates and the end to Western control of oil prices and production not only served to end the postwar international economic system. These events also unleashed powerful forces of change that have progressively transformed the world economy. During much of the last quarter of the twentieth century, cascading waves of change generated widespread commentary about rising unemployment levels, uncontrolled inflation, skyrocketing interest rates, debt crises, increasing economic integration, massive trade and fiscal deficits, rapid technological change, intensified economic competition, and enormous growth in the international economy. The concept of globalization is perhaps the most effective way to begin to understand the nature and consequences of many of these changes.

This chapter uses research on globalization to gain an understanding of the contemporary world economy. We will define globalization and discuss several ways of thinking about its causes and consequences. Rising levels of involvement in the world economy; increasing interdependence; the establishment of global markets, prices, and production; and the diffusion of technology and ideas all serve to define globalization. We daily witness an explosion of international transactions in money, including foreign direct investment by transnational corporations, declines in the cost of transportation and communication, and astonishing technological developments. The results of globalization include new constraints on states' ability to manage their economies, shifts in domestic political conflict, increasing hostility from sectors and groups harmed by growing economic integration, new forms of production relationships among transnational firms, dramatic potential and actual changes from the global expansion of the Internet, and alterations of the terms and stakes associated with international cooperation and competition. Further, the complexity of globalization raises a number of problems for the way we think about international affairs, especially the basic architecture of the world economy and the relationship between firms and states.

The globalization of the world economy is a continuation and extension of trends present since the 1950s, but at levels that require new concepts and understanding.[1] One of the easiest ways to see globalization is to imagine a situation in which it has not occurred: in which all production and consumption of goods and services takes place within nations, that is, where there is no trade or capital movement between nations. By contrast, globalization refers to a situation in which the economic activity that takes place between nations grows in relation to economic activity that takes place within nations. The enlargement of international economic relations leads to a deepening and tightening of the interdependence among actors in the world economy. In recent years, such a process of globalization has occurred: international economic exchange has grown as a proportion of total economic activity, linkages among actors have been intensified and restructured, and new forms of economic relationships have emerged to define a distinctive stage in the development of the world economy. As we shall see, globalization is a process of ongoing change rather than an end state in which borders are meaningless. We do not have a fully globalized world economy, but instead we have experienced new levels and forms of interdependence.

What has happened to provoke observers of the world economy to develop new terminology for thinking about recent changes? We can identify five major developments that define globalization: (1) extremely rapid growth in international financial transactions; (2) rapid growth in trade, especially among transnational firms; (3) very rapid growth in foreign direct investment (FDI), especially by multinational corporations; (4) a decline in market segmentation, the emergence of global markets, and the convergence of many prices on a global scale; and (5) dramatic declines in the cost of global communication and transportation and the global diffusion of technology and ideas. We will regroup these developments into changes involving finance, production, and technology.[2]

THE GLOBALIZATION OF FINANCE

The most important single indicator of globalization is the explosive growth of international financial transactions. The beginnings of this trend can be traced, in large part, to events in the early 1970s. A series of economic shocks, political reactions, and market forces intersected to produce an exponential rise in international lending and borrowing, foreign exchange transactions, and global investment. As we have just seen in Chapter 4, in the 1960s the combination of widespread currency convertibility, the pumping of dollars into foreign hands via U.S. current account deficits, the expansion of U.S. multinational corporations abroad with the ability to transfer funds across national boundaries, and the emergence and growth of the Eurodollar market generated a large volume of internationalized resources. What is more, many of these resources were very liquid; that is, they could quickly be converted to cash. The actual and potential conversion of dollars into gold, combined with speculative purchases of undervalued currencies, such as yen and deutsche marks, helped precipitate the financial crises that ended the Bretton Woods system.

The collapse of fixed exchange rates in 1973 opened the door to much greater volatility in exchange rates and the growth of foreign exchange markets. But the most important immediate spur to internationalization came from the quadrupling of oil prices in 1973–1974 and the tripling of prices in 1979–1980. The massive transfer of funds from global consumers to oil producers had complex consequences for international finance. Many oil states preferred keeping balances of dollars and other convertible currencies in large Western banks. These banks needed to find investment outlets for their new-found deposits and turned to developing countries who were often eager to borrow. Over the rest of the 1970s, loans to such nations were readily available, and Third World debt grew rapidly. Between 1973 and 1979, the debt of Third World nations rose sixfold, from $100 billion to $600 billion.[3]

The growth of international deposits and debt—of a system of markets for international borrowers, investors, and speculators—exploded in size and complexity in the 1980s. Two events played a key role: the financial and trade imbalances of the United States after 1981 and a series of decisions by governments to end controls on the movement of capital across their borders.

The unprecedented increase in oil prices in 1973–1974 and 1979–1980 forced several important adjustments to the world economy. Paying for higher oil prices had a major impact on the economies of the developed and developing worlds. Because oil was essential for the functioning of all these economic systems, demand can be described as highly inelastic. That is, the short-term and near-term demands for oil remained about the same in spite of the price increases. The consequence was a combination of reduced purchases of other goods and a substantial rise in inflation as monetary authorities increased the quantity of money in circulation to offset oil price increases. Between 1974 and 1976 and between 1980 and 1982, many countries in the developed world experienced a serious case of stagflation—declining economic activity and rising prices. Historically, these events rarely occurred together, because recessions were thought to be a cure for inflation and vice versa. For the first time since the end of World War II, significant and persistent economic dislocation descended on the world economy.

In addition to rising prices and a stagnant economy, the United States also faced a declining dollar. But politically there was very strong support for addressing the problems of inflation and the dollar, even if that led to a weaker economy. The Federal Reserve, under board chair Paul Volcker, adopted a very tight monetary policy that pushed interest rates to unprecedented levels and brought on a deep recession in 1981–1982. These actions also contributed to a serious world recession.

Largely in response to the economic difficulties of the 1970s and early 1980s, several strategies for economic revitalization emerged in the United States and elsewhere. Deregulation and large tax cuts were thought by many conservatives to be the mechanism for a return to strong economic growth and higher rates of savings and investment. Parallel to these ideas were worries about Soviet military power and risk taking, which reached a peak following the Soviet invasion of Afghanistan in late 1979. The solution was seen in much higher U.S. defense spending. The election of Ronald Reagan in 1980 brought together, once again, the political economy of the early 1960s: tax cuts and sharply higher defense spending. The result was a series of the largest peacetime budget deficits in U.S. history.

Imbalances in the U.S. economy spilled over into the world economy. Indeed, it was this link to the rest of the world that permitted some success for Reaganomics. The large budget deficits, combined with a looser monetary policy, produced a significant stimulus to demand and economic growth in the United States after 1982, including a significant rise in consumer and business spending. But as proportions of gross domestic product (GDP), both savings and investment fell while consumption rose. The greatest beneficiaries of the Reagan years were those at the highest income levels. Also accompanying the budget deficits were interest rates that were high relative to those in other countries. This served to attract funds into U.S. investments (these investments provided the funds that otherwise would have to be diverted from U.S. consumption to buy the government debt that closed the government spending gap), which produced large increases in the exchange rate of the dollar. The rising dollar tended to raise the prices of U.S. exports and to lower the prices of imports. This led to massive increases in the trade deficit, especially with the Japanese. The effort at revitalization worked in the sense that world economic growth occurred. But this came at a price: large trade deficits, even larger budget deficits, massive increases in the national debt and U.S. foreign debt, and very large swings in exchange rates.

The imbalances in the world economy are shown in Figure 5.1, which details the current account balances of the three major trading states between 1978 and 1994. The current account balances of the United States, Germany, and Japan hovered around zero until 1981, when the expansion of the U.S. deficit was mirrored in the large German and Japanese surpluses. Remember from the earlier discussion of the balance of payments that a deficit (or surplus) in the current account is offset by a surplus (or deficit) in the capital account. The large and persistent U.S. current account deficit of the 1980s was sustained by a flow of capital into the United States from abroad, and this contributed much to the globalization of capital. This process has continued and even expanded throughout the 1980s and 1990s and has resulted in a cumulative debt by Americans to the rest of the world of $5 trillion.[4]

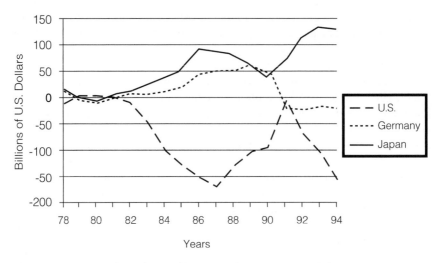

FIGURE 5.1 Comparative Balance of Payment: Current Account Balance

SOURCE: International Monetary Fund, *International Financial Statistics Yearbook,* 1995, 144.

Also important to this process was a series of decisions, from the mid-1970s to the early 1990s, by many nations to eliminate long-standing restrictions on the ability of capital to cross their borders. Following the onset of the world depression in 1929, many governments had turned to capital controls to insulate themselves from the impact of short-term capital flows on economic policy. The Bretton Woods system provided for extensive controls, and until the 1980s most states had used them to restrict (but not prevent) international flows of capital. The end of Bretton Woods led most wealthy states to end capital controls. These decisions both reflected and contributed to the progression of globalization.

The initial step away from capital controls was taken by the United States. Between 1971 and 1973, when the Bretton Woods order was in severe crisis, Europe and Japan preferred efforts by all states to cooperate in establishing new and much more restrictive controls on capital movement. In an effort to save the system, they wanted to reduce the speculation against currencies that was undermining fixed exchange rates. These efforts were blocked by the United States, thereby ensuring the end of Bretton Woods. And in 1974 the United States moved unilaterally to end its own capital controls.[5]

The U.S. decision did not lead immediately to similar actions by other states. Before others would follow the U.S. lead, several states needed to learn the growing ability of capital markets to influence their choices. In 1976, Great Britain was engaged in deficit spending (financed in part by foreign borrowing) to recover from the deep recession that had begun two years earlier. When creditors withdrew from providing additional lending, some British leaders looked to the option of extreme capital restrictions. This would prevent capital from exiting Britain, reduce pressure on the pound, and permit domestic borrowing to resume. The Labour government eventually rejected this option and instead accepted an internationally arranged deal that required Britain to cut government spending in return for additional loans.

Similarly, in 1978–1979 the United States was pursuing a stimulative policy, the effect of which was to require international support for the dollar. When this support faltered, the dollar began to plummet. Like Britain, the United States rejected capital controls and moved toward restricting government spending and higher interest rates rather than return to capital controls.

And the French, suffering from economic recession in the wake of oil price increases, in 1981 elected a government committed to unilateral economic expansion. Financial markets quickly began selling francs, and the French government confronted the same choices that the British and Americans had. Over a two-year period, the Mitterrand government was forced to adopt an ever more restrictive economic policy to preserve France's international financial position. In each of these cases, the British, French, and Americans had the option of imposing capital controls as a way of avoiding unpleasant economic choices. This was rejected because to do so would require a withdrawal from the world economy at enormous political and economic costs.[6]

The U.S. capital liberalization of 1974 and the weakening of capital controls as an option in the three cases just discussed came against a backdrop of rapidly growing international financial markets (see below for more detail). During the 1980s and 1990s, most nations in the advanced world removed all controls on capital movement—actions that acknowledged the power of these markets and contributed to their growth. In large part, these decisions were motivated by competition among states to attract international financial business or simply to avoid being left behind. In 1981, looking to shift some of the burgeoning Euromarket business to its shores, the United States legalized international banking facilities. In 1984, desperately needing international funds to finance its massive budget deficits, the United States reached a yen–dollar agreement with Japan that liberalized Japanese finance and made possible large Japanese investments in the United States. Propelled by competition from the United States, the British government of Margaret Thatcher abolished all capital controls and in 1986 opened the London Stock Exchange to foreign securities dealers. The competitive dynamic between the United States and Great Britain resulted from the fact that international capital was attracted to those areas with the greatest freedom of action and the most liquid markets.

The American and British adoption of capital liberalization was followed by most other industrial countries. Japan, since 1950 the most vigorous practitioner of capital restrictions, was moved toward relaxation by a combination of U.S. pressure, lobbying by foreign multinationals and segments of Japanese business, and the huge profit opportunities available to Japan in international finance. After 1981 the enormous current account surpluses with the United States and the rest of the world provided Japan with hundreds of billions of dollars for international investment. These realities helped shift the Japanese government to expand the limited liberalization adopted before 1981, primarily by permitting yen-based activity in Euromarkets, progressively lifting de facto capital controls, and allowing international banking facilities (offshore operations) in Japan.[7]

Led by Germany, Denmark, and the Netherlands, states in the European Economic Community also took steps to liberalize policies on capital movement in the early 1980s. Later in the decade, they were joined by France and Italy. In many ways these were defensive acts, made necessary by the U.S. and British liberalizations. In order to keep capital from migrating to New York and London, these states needed to lift existing restrictions. In the late 1980s, jumping onto the bandwagon, New Zealand, Australia, Norway, and Finland engaged in the deregulation and liberalization of finance. During the late 1980s and early 1990s, many states in East Asia loosened capital controls in the wake of huge investment opportunities coming from Japan.[8]

In one sense, removing restrictions on capital movement simply restored the openness of the late nineteenth and early twentieth centuries. Liberals would see this as the natural and most efficient state of affairs. But this view is too easy because these changes were really a continuation of the demise of Bretton Woods. Fixed exchange rates and capital controls went together, and the end of fixed rates made controls less viable. Why did these changes happen? The Bretton Woods order resulted, in part, from an effort by states to manage markets to their own ends—mainly expanding domestic economic growth. Events after 1971 suggest a sharp decline in the ability of states to control markets. This is not to say that states were not essential for creating a political context for market activity. Rather, what happened was a shift in the power relationship of states and markets.

Indicators of Financial Globalization

The basic point for understanding the globalization of finance is to see the extent to which international financial flows have grown in proportion to other international activity and in proportion to national resources. One way to comprehend the trends discussed below is to understand that by the late 1990s more than $30 trillion (about the same size as global GDP) was managed by institutional investors in developed economies.[9] The declining barriers to the global movement of these funds means that truly titanic sums are available for international financial activity, whether that be foreign exchange trading, international lending, or investing in equities. Between 1980 and 1996, global trading in bonds and equities rose at a compound rate of 25 percent and in foreign exchange at a rate of 23 percent; international bank lending rose at a rate of 9 percent; and foreign direct investment at 8 percent. During the same time, global trade grew at an annual rate of 6 percent, while world GDP grew at just over 2 percent.[10]

During the 1980s, global trading in foreign exchange came to dwarf global trade in goods and services and, until very recently, has grown much more rapidly than trade. This can be seen in Figure 5.2, which displays the

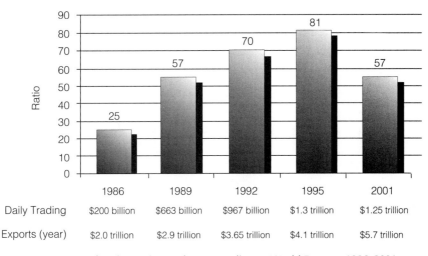

FIGURE 5.2 Ratio of Daily Foreign Exchange Trading to World Exports, 1986–2001

level of daily foreign exchange trading in relation to the level of global trade. In 1986 foreign exchange trading was 25 times the level of world trade; by 2001, it had expanded to 57 times the level of trade, down significantly from 1995. Historically, most buying and selling of foreign exchange was the result of international trade, as buyers and sellers of foreign goods and services needed another currency to settle their transactions. But clearly, trading in foreign exchange markets is now largely disconnected from trade. The players in these markets are large banks and corporations attempting to make money and/or defend profits.

Other indicators of financial globalization include the growth of foreign exchange trading relative to the reserves of foreign exchange held by states, the dispersal of these reserves away from the United States, growth in international lending and equities trading, and the increasing integration of global financial markets. Figure 5.3 provides data about the relationship between foreign exchange trading and the foreign exchange reserves of states. It is these reserves that nations use to intervene in markets to try to influence exchange rates. Thus, nations whose markets are increasingly integrated into global financial markets can intervene effectively in those markets when they hold large reserves of foreign exchange. We can see from Figure 5.3 that even as late as 1983 the foreign exchange reserves of the largest industrial countries were more than double the level of daily foreign exchange trading. By 1995 trading was double the level of reserves. This probably overstates the ability of states to influence foreign exchange markets, because reserves are now much less concentrated and much more globalized. Table 5.1 presents data about changes in the distribution of foreign exchange reserves among nations.

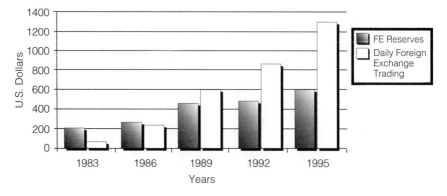

FIGURE 5.3 Foreign Exchange Trading/Reserves (billions of U.S. dollars)

SOURCE: *The Economist,* October 7, 1985.

The data make clear the dramatic shift in foreign exchange holdings over the 36 years from 1964 to 2000. Resources have shifted away from the United States toward Japan and away from industrial countries generally and toward developing states. The impact of this globalization is to make it much more difficult for nations to affect foreign exchange markets through buying and selling currency.

The volume of international borrowing and trading in equities has also increased substantially. As Table 5.2 shows, the annual level of international lending more than doubled from 1990 to 1994. By 1994 outstanding international bonds and international bank loans totaled $6 trillion. Regarding international equity markets, in 1991 there was approximately $1.1 trillion in transactions involving just the United States, Britain, and Japan.[11]

Perhaps the strongest indicators of financial globalization and also for understanding the limits of globalization come from analysis of the degree of integration of financial markets. There are several ways to think about market integration. One way is accessibility: can trading take place in various markets at roughly the same cost for transactions? The immense volume of international financial markets indicates a high level of accessibility and rapidly declining barriers to trading. A second and more precise indicator of market integration is whether the same security asset trades at the same price in different markets. One measure shows that after capital controls were eliminated, the wide differences in French franc-denominated interest rates declined to practically zero.[12] This is not to say that international financial markets are completely integrated. Domestic savings is still much more important for investment, and investors still prefer domestic investment over foreign. But stock markets and interest rates now increasingly move together, driven by the vast sums that do cross borders.[13]

The explosion in international financial transactions has not created a fully integrated global market for securities, but integration is sufficient to create

**Table 5.1 Globalization of Foreign Exchange Reserves, 1964–1995
(billions of U.S. dollars)**

Country	1964	1973	1986	1995	2000
Industrial:					
United States	16.7	11.9	39.8	33.0	24.0
Germany	7.9	27.5	45.6	52.3	38.1
France	5.7	7.1	28.6	15.6	24.7
Japan	2.0	10.2	35.4	116.0	266.5
Switzerland	3.3	7.1	20.7	23.3	23.7
United Kingdom	2.3	5.4	15.7	26.4	30.1
Developing:					
Taiwan	0.3	0.9	38.1	84.0	122.0
China	—	—	9.8	49.5	127.0
Singapore	0.4	1.9	10.6	46.0	61.1
Hong Kong	—	—	—	37.2	82.5
Brazil	0.2	5.3	4.8	33.4	24.9
Thailand	0.7	1.1	2.4	23.9	24.5
Industrial total	58.2	111.6	279.6	441.0	595.6
Developing total	10.9	41.1	172.7	491.0	878.4
World total	69.1	152.7	452.3	932.0	1474.0

SOURCE: International Monetary Fund, *International Financial Statistics Yearbook,* 2001; *The Economist,* November 18, 1995, 82.

**Table 5.2 International Capital Markets Annual Borrowing
(billions of U.S. dollars)**

1990	1991	1992	1993	1994
$435	$536	$610	$819	$955

SOURCE: Organization for Economic Cooperation and Development, *International Financial Markets,* 1995.

significant connections among markets across many countries. This integration is clearest in the way price changes in one market affect those in others and is most manifest in financial crises, such as the global financial crisis of 1997–1998.[14] In the years leading up to 1997, international investors and lenders were eager to purchase equities and extend loans in the emerging economies of Asian nations. Current account imbalances and the sometimes corrupt relationships of business and government were not a barrier to high levels of involvement. Market psychology changed in 1997, when expectations of changes in fixed foreign exchange rates led to speculative attacks on the Thai baht. When the Thai government let the baht float in July 1997, its value plummeted, and this led to speculative attacks on other currencies throughout Asia. Declines in currencies helped push down stock prices across the region, and in the end most currencies lost half or more of their value and stock markets fell even further. The downdraft in Asian asset values spread to Russia in 1998, leading the Russian government to default on its foreign loans. Later that year the crisis of confidence affected the United States with a large decline in stock prices and prompted the U.S. Federal Reserve to lower interest rates to restore calm to markets. Because large institutional investors—such as banks, investment firms, and mutual funds—are now able to scan the globe for investment opportunities and carry out instant and essentially cost-less transactions in markets anywhere in the world, markets everywhere are linked together far more tightly than in the past. Indeed, the global character of the financial crisis of 1997–1998 is a powerful indicator of the interdependence of markets around the world.

Explaining the Globalization of Finance

Trying to understand the reasons for the globalization of finance is entangled with sorting out the consequences of these changes. Put another way, scholars have not been able to agree about cause and effect. As with most important phenomena in the study of political economy, identifying causation is a complex matter. Disagreement often results from accepting different broad theories about how political and economic life is constructed. And such theories sometimes turn on whether causal priority is given to states or to markets. When governments acted to liberalize capital markets or to shift from fixed to floating exchange rates, were they being carried along by overwhelming market forces, or were they acting to manage market forces to their advantage?

How you answer this question may depend on whether you believe that politics or markets have primal force in moving events.[15] Or you might adopt the view, as we do, that politics and markets are always codetermined but that over time the primacy of one over the other can change. Another way to see this process is to notice that actors whose main arena is markets—banks and corporations—sometimes gain strength relative to actors whose main arena is politics—presidents, prime ministers, and heads of central banks. A useful way to think about globalization is to ask why the evident power shift from state actors to market players has taken place. One important answer emphasizes the way changes in technology have been seized upon by market players to their great benefit.

We have seen how political and economic events such as the breakdown of Bretton Woods, the oil crisis, and the debt crisis contributed to globalization. But in significant ways, these events were made possible by the extraordinary changes in technology after 1970. The combination of developments in computers, telecommunications, and satellites has altered the cost and the scale of communications systems. Trading in foreign exchange and global equities is almost entirely a matter of information flows—about prices, events, and actions. When the cost of creating, storing, and transmitting information falls, this serves as a spur to globalizing trading. Between 1965 and the present, these costs have fallen consistently and dramatically—at a rate of about 35 percent every year.[16] By the 1990s costs fell enough for even small economic units to maintain or participate in an instantaneous and continuous communication system on a global scale. Moreover, the creation of a global system with millions of members—the Internet—has made information and its interpretation an extremely important commodity. Events like those we have considered helped create the opportunities for profit and the need for sophisticated global communications, and advances in microcircuitry have made possible a larger and larger scale for communication systems at continuously lower costs. Responding to market opportunities made possible by technology, firms have developed a much greater variety of international financial instruments that have the effect of expanding markets further. And as markets grew larger and gained more participants, they became more regularized, understanding increased, and more banks and corporations became participants.[17]

The rapid growth in international financial markets confronted states with difficult choices related to monetary policies and capital controls. Over the 1970s and 1980s, an increasingly large volume of money controlled by many global actors could be moved across borders in search of profit and often in response to government policies. And these actors—usually banks, large institutional investors, and multinational corporations—developed strong interests in this freedom of international financial maneuvering. The size of markets and changes in technology made certain government policies—especially capital controls—more and more difficult. And markets would reward other policies, especially liberalization, by increasing resources and business in the most liberal locations. Governments essentially confronted the choice between absolute controls—which were very difficult to enforce and required virtual withdrawal from the world economy—and no controls at all. Over time, most countries chose to attract or retain their share of these resources by eliminating controls and liberalizing the opportunities for investment. At stake was the competitive position and future prosperity of the nation and its firms.[18]

So why has financial globalization expanded so much? First, technological advances have reduced the transaction costs and information gathering/monitoring costs to practically nothing, making financial globalization feasible. Various capitalist firms have found many profitable opportunities in the new global markets, and with the low costs of entry many other firms followed. The effect of these processes was to expand the size of markets many times. Second, governments made decisions that often facilitated the expansion of markets, usually by reducing or eliminating capital controls that acted as barriers to the movement of money. The reasons for these decisions are varied. For some, like the United States and Britain, an ideological commitment to free markets by economic and political elites coincided with the interests of American and British financial capitalists who foresaw great profits from expanding global investments. Others, like France, found themselves caught up in a competitive relationship with early liberalizers and felt compelled to open their markets. Still others, like Malaysia, saw opportunities for much greater investment by multinational firms and decided to drop restrictions on capital movement. And there were many states, like South Korea, that received considerable pressure from the United States to liberalize their markets for money and goods. The decisions for opening by governments created new opportunities for global investors and markets grew even larger. Only the Asian financial crisis, which became a global financial crisis, put a major wrinkle in the growth of global investing.

The Consequences of Financial Globalization

In the most elemental sense, the globalization of finance means that money moves quickly in large volume and with few restrictions across national boundaries. The decisions of money managers and speculators are very sensitive to expectations about financial, production, and political conditions, and their task is to act before events occur. They want to profit from change or at least to avoid losses.[19] What does this mean? As globalization proceeds, financial capital, responding to conditions judged adverse to profits, is increasingly able to leave a country and shift to currencies and societies where profit opportunities are relatively better. This ability to leave—capital holders essentially "vote" with their "feet"—enhances greatly the structural power of capital. That is, "international capital mobility systematically constrains state behavior by rewarding some actions and punishing others."[20] This impact is clearly evident in the global financial crisis of 1997–1998. The large and rapid inflows of funds, especially for loans and the purchase of equities, reversed rapidly and plunged even more quickly.

Increased power to capital has significant political and economic consequences. Capital mobility and flexible exchange rates tend to negate the monetary policy adopted by a single nation. That is, a nation acting to establish its monetary policy alone may have its purposes thwarted by globalized capital. Consider the following situation. Nation A wants to dampen inflation in its country by raising interest rates and slowing the growth of its money supply. But the effect of raising interest rates alone is to attract international capital, which results in increasing the money supply. The reverse situation is also common. Nation B wants to stimulate its economy by lowering interest rates and expanding government spending and deficits. Holders of liquid assets in B's currency are likely to flee because interest rates are falling relative to the rest of the world. Further, increasing budget deficits in B point to higher inflation. The decline in the money supply and in international investment could easily offset any expansion from monetary and fiscal policy.

The key point is that global capital flows penalize states whose economic policies are not in sync with the rest of the world. The only way to engage in an effective monetary policy is to cooperate, overtly or tacitly, with other states so as to raise and lower interest rates together.[21] In this way, relative changes in interest rates are minimal, and international capital flows should be small. But in practice, this often means that monetary and fiscal policies are sharply constricted, because coordination among several states may be difficult to organize. Politically, this challenges the viability of basic arrangements worked out after World War II.

A fundamental element of the Bretton Woods system of fixed exchange rates was to shield each nation from having international trade and exchange rates influence its domestic economic policy. Remember that liberalization of the world economy under Bretton Woods was limited by the belief that governments could and should promote economic growth through independent actions. Memories of the 1930s Great Depression were strong, as was the need to diffuse radicalism among workers through sustained economic growth. Expanding the economic pie through managed economic growth was seen by many as the best strategy. A compromise between capitalists and workers could be arranged through government efforts to pump up the economy whenever growth waned. The Bretton Woods system of fixed exchange rates and limits on capital movement insulated domestic economies from international pressure to reverse growth policies.

This arrangement—known as Keynesianism or "embedded liberalism"—has been distinctly eroded by the globalization of capital markets.[22] Moreover, various groups in many countries have seen their economic and political positions helped and hurt by the same changes. Globalization generates quite distinct sets of losers and winners. Generally, holders of mobile capital have seen their rewards and bargaining power enhanced relative to groups whose resources are less mobile. Put another way, those commanding resources that are information and knowledge based have seen their incomes rise in relative terms. Those who hold resources unrelated to knowledge and information have seen their incomes fall relative to others. This usually means workers and manufacturers with large fixed investments in low-skilled, labor-intensive industries that cannot easily be liquidated and moved. Once again, it is the option to shift resources to places with higher returns that enhances the structural power of capital. The rise of global capital opportunities means that mobile capital will invest in areas where, for example, the cost of labor relative to productivity is lowest. This puts downward pressure on wages and diminishes bargaining leverage by workers in high-cost countries. Some of the consequences of globalization are the lack of growth in real incomes in the United States for twenty years (in spite of growth in productivity) and very high unemployment rates in Europe. That globalization has quite negative consequences for some groups should not be surprising; after all, capitalism and free markets have always had this effect. These outcomes should help us understand why responses to globalization have become increasingly negative and violent.

Many countries' political leadership has been forced to shift efforts away from growth via monetary and fiscal policy. Instead, most leaders have concentrated on actions that enhance their nation's competitiveness. That is, governments focus on making their territory as attractive to global capital and business as possible. This can include giving tax and other incentives, creating a favorable regulatory environment, and giving subsidies that shift costs of production to the entire society. The competitiveness strategy chosen may differ, depending on whether the government in power is left or right. Left governments may be more likely to facilitate efforts by workers to adjust quickly to changes in the world markets. This usually means increasing the productivity of labor and granting subsidies to investment rather than forcing down wages. Right wing governments are more likely to reduce welfare programs so as to reduce wage levels and lower tax levels in order to increase returns to business.[23]

In brief, the consequences of the globalization of capital are substantial. The basic structure of political arrangements in postwar domestic politics has been undermined, and the autonomy of states has been reduced. Prior to about 1980, governments throughout the industrialized world regularly focused substantial attention on domestic economic management through fiscal and monetary policy. Today, maneuverability on fiscal policy has been restricted, and monetary policy is closely tied to the interests of global capital. Governments devote much more attention to coordinating monetary and fiscal policies. And a chief concern is to adopt policies that are consistent with the investment priorities of global capital. The previous concerns over raising wages and expanding employment have given way to fears of the effects of too much growth and employment on inflation. Governments cannot take steps that might lead holders of liquid capital to shift their funds to other sites. Holders of global capital have a distinct preference for slow economic growth in the production of goods and services—an environment conducive to low inflation and preserving the value of liquid capital. Reports of "excessive" economic growth or falling unemployment rates spark rising interest rates and quick government efforts to reassure global capital thorough restrictive monetary policy. Labor unions have declined in political influence, and welfare states have been stymied or eroded, whereas active market players have seen their interests, positions, and incomes enhanced.

THE GLOBALIZATION OF PRODUCTION

Advances in the globalization of production and direct investment have not been as dramatic and fast paced as those in finance. Nevertheless, changes in the past 25 years have been very significant and are the result mainly of the growth and development of multinational corporations (MNCs) as major actors in world affairs. Indeed, the actions of multinational financial, production, and distribution enterprises are primarily responsible for globalization. In this section, we will examine both the reasons for the increasingly international activities of these organizations and the consequences of this activity. Especially important are the sheer size of MNCs, the expansion of foreign direct investment, changing patterns of the organization of international production and trade, the diffusion of technology, and new forms of relationships among firms.

Trade Globalization

The globalization of trade since the 1970s has restored and even surpassed the levels of trade interdependence found earlier in the twentieth century. World exports as a proportion of world production rose consistently after 1840, peaked in 1913, recovered after 1950, but surpassed 1913 levels only in the

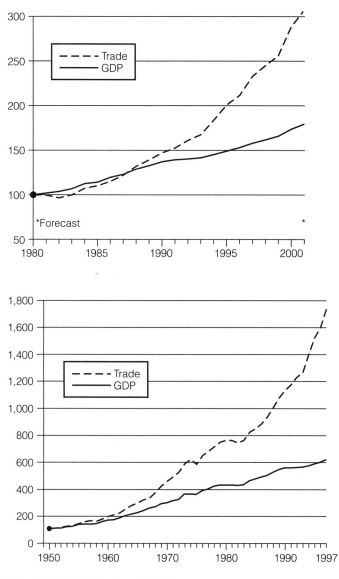

FIGURE 5.4 World Trade and GDP

SOURCE: World Trade Organization.

mid-1970s. That is, since 1970 more and more production has been destined for international trade.[24] Compare the two parts of Figure 5.4. When we begin in 1950, the rate of growth of trade is obviously greater than that of overall world product (GDP). But as a focus on the period after 1980 makes clear, in the late 1980s the growth in trade accelerated even more. During the decade from 1985 to 1994, trade grew about twice as fast as global output. Periods of global economic expansion are especially prone to rapid increases in trade. For example, in 1994 world output grew by 5 percent, whereas world trade increased by over 9 percent. Trade has increased not only as a proportion of global production but also as a proportion of national production. The United States and Canada have experienced more change than most advanced countries, roughly doubling the proportion of exports and imports of goods and services as a proportion of GDP between 1980 and 2000.

The United States has become more dependent on the export of goods and services but even more so on the import of goods produced abroad. Similar trends exist for most other advanced nations (Japan's import dependence has increased but by less), as we can see from Table 5.3.

What is the geography of global trade? Unquestionably, most global trade occurs among the nations of Europe and between Europe and the rest of the world. More than 20 percent of world trade occurs among European states and another 30 percent between these European states and North America, Asia, and the rest of the world.[25] Which countries have the greatest impact on trade? Table 5.4 shows a "top 15" list of exporters and importers for 1998. From this data, we can see that the absolute size of trade is in the hundreds of billions of dollars for each of these countries. Further, it is not just the most advanced nations that are the biggest traders. China, Hong Kong (now a special administrative region of China), South Korea, and Mexico are also major players in world trade.

The expansion of international trade is the result of private firms, mostly multinational firms. The term *multinational corporation* refers to a corporation that controls resources and conducts operations (including sales and production) in several nations. For example, Toyota—the Japanese car company, which in 1975 operated mostly in Japan—has substantially globalized its operations. In 1995 Toyota had 9 parts plants in seven countries other than Japan, 29 assembly plants in twenty-five countries, and 4 research and development facilities in two countries. During the 2000 fiscal year, Toyota's international production was more then 25 percent of total production, and its international sales represented almost 60 percent of its total sales.[26] The United Nations estimated in the early 1990s that parent company MNCs totaled 35,000 worldwide, with 147,000 foreign affiliates. More than 85 percent of the parent companies are from developed countries.[27] Thus, it is multinational corporations that dominate international production and trade, controlling "over one quarter of the world's economic activity outside their home countries; over half the world trade in manufactured goods and even more of the growing trade in services; 80 percent of the world's land cultivated for export crops; and the lion's share of the world's technological innovations."[28] Such firms control vast and vital resources: access to investment capital, the ability to produce goods and services and market them around the world, management expertise, participation in global research and development (R&D) systems, and the capacity to organize and use technology for production and communication on a global scale. At the same time, such firms lack the ability to control territory, make laws, or fight wars—things nations do well.[29]

**Table 5.3 Trade in Goods and Services as a Percent of GDP
(real terms)**

	1981–1991	1995	1999	2000
United States	7.9	11.6	13.9	14.8
Euro Area	11.9	14.3	17.6	19.0
Japan	7.1	8.4	9.1	9.9
Canada	23.7	35.9	43.7	46.3
Switzerland	28.8	33.1	39.2	41.4

SOURCE: Bank for International Settlements, Annual Reports, 2001, 31.

**Table 5.4 Global Top 15 in Trade: Exports and Imports of Goods
and Services (billions of current dollars; figures are for 1998)**

Country	Exports Goods	Exports Services	Total G&S Exports	Imports Goods	Imports Services	Total G&S Imports
United States	781	291	1,072	1,216	217	1,433
Germany	549	84	633	492	134	626
Japan	459	69	528	342	117	459
France	296	82	378	294	63	357
U.K.	283	102	385	327	85	412
Italy	239	56	295	228	56	284
Canada	281	38	319	245	42	287
Netherlands	206	54	260	187	53	240
China (PRC)	202	41	243	211	25	236
Belgium	162	43	205	157	39	296
South Korea	145	27	172	117	27	144
Mexico	166	14	180	174	17	191
Singapore	139	27	166	127	21	148

SOURCE: WTO; IMF, *International Financial Statistics Yearbook*, 2001.

Many of these companies rival large nations in the resources they control. This can be seen in Table 5.5. Notice that nations dominate the first 21 spots on the list. But of the remaining 54 spots, 34 are corporations. What are we to make of this list? Liberals sometimes argue that it is wrong to compare nations and firms in terms of power: nations have power over citizens through taxation and laws backed by force, whereas firms operate through voluntary exchange with workers and customers and therefore have little power.[30] One of the most important reasons for the development of the study of *political economy* is to challenge the simplistic conception of power used by liberals. A few minutes' conversation with the political leaders of almost any nation would quickly reveal the importance and influence—and therefore the

Table 5.5 The 75 Largest Countries and Industrial Corporations
This list represents the 75 largest economic entities in the world as of 2000. Nations are measured by GDP, firms by sales.

Rank	Nation or Firm	GDP/Sales (billions $U.S.)
1.	United States	8,351
2.	Japan	4,079
3.	Germany	2,079
4.	France	1,427
5.	United Kingdom	1,338
6.	China (incl. Hong Kong)	1,142
7.	Italy	1,136
8.	Brazil	743
9.	Canada	591
10.	Spain	551
11.	India	442
12.	Mexico	429
13.	Korea (South)	397
14.	The Netherlands	384
15.	Australia	381
16.	Russia	332
17.	Argentina	278
18.	Switzerland	273
19.	Belgium	250
20.	Sweden	222
21.	Austria	210
22.	Exxon-Mobil	210
23.	Wal-Mart	193
24.	Turkey	186
25.	General Motors	184
26.	Ford	180
27.	Denmark	170
28.	Poland	153
29.	Daimler-Chrysler	150
30.	Royal Dutch Shell	149
31.	British Petroleum	148
32.	Norway	146
33.	South Africa	133
34.	General Electric	129
35.	Mitsubishi	127
36.	Greece	124
37.	Finland	122
38.	Toyota	121
39.	Thailand	121
40.	Indonesia	119

Table 5.5 (continued) The 75 Largest Countries and Industrial Corporations

Rank	Nation or Firm	GDP/Sales (billions $U.S.)
41.	Citigroup	112
42.	Iran	111
43.	Itochu	110
44.	Portugal	106
45.	Total Fina Elf	106
46.	NTT	103
47.	Enron	101
48.	Singapore	95
49.	Colombia	94
50.	AXA	93
51.	Sumitomo	91
52.	IBM	88
53.	Egypt	87
54.	Venezuela	87
55.	Marubeni	85
56.	Volkswagen	79
57.	The Philippines	78
58.	Malaysia	77
59.	Hitachi	76
60.	Siemens	75
61.	Ireland	71
62.	ING Group	71
63.	Alianza	71
64.	Matsushita	69
65.	EON	68
66.	Nippon Life Insurance	68
67.	Deutsche Bank	67
68.	Sony	66
69.	AT&T	66
70.	Pakistan	64
71.	Verizon	65
72.	U.S. Postal Service	65
73.	Philip Morris	63
74.	CGNU	61
75.	Peru	60

SOURCE: *Fortune* Global 500, 2000; World Bank, *World Development Report,* 2000–2001.

power—of multinational firms. Such firms control most of the world's investment capital, access to markets, global production chains, technology, research
and development, management expertise, and ability to operate across national boundaries. These resources make for power—the ability to influence
economic and political outcomes—and nations must negotiate with such
firms. This is not to say that firms have taken power away from states, as we
will see in the discussion below.

Foreign Direct Investment

An important measure of the global activity of multinational corporations is
foreign direct investment (FDI).[31] We have seen how international trade has
grown as a proportion of world production. But FDI has grown even more
rapidly than trade: in the 1960s, FDI grew twice as fast as GDP; in the 1980s,
FDI grew four times as fast as GDP; since 1984, FDI has grown about five
times as fast as merchandise trade.[32] Table 5.6 shows the sharp rise in FDI
flows from Europe and Japan after 1985 and from other Asian states in the
1990s; major recipients of FDI include the United States, Europe, China and
Asia, and Latin America.

Foreign direct investment at these levels has created the need for a new
measure of international production—one that captures not just goods and
services crossing borders but also goods and services produced abroad by foreign affiliates. This measure includes not only an automobile produced in
Great Britain for sale in Germany but also a U.S. company's production of a
car in Britain for sale in Britain. Analysts have concluded that trillions of dollars of international production are not counted by traditional balance of payments accounting because no good or service crosses a border. Instead, FDI
crossed a border. When a U.S. firm establishes a production facility in Britain,
FDI takes place, and international production follows. But unless the goods
produced in Britain are exported, this global production is not counted. Estimates from 1989 of international production are almost twice as large as international trade alone. Because the United States has a long history of FDI, the
ratio of global production to international trade is even greater for its firms. In
1989 the global production of U.S. firms (operating outside the United States)
was $1.266 trillion. For the same year, U.S. firms exported only $307 billion—a ratio of more than 4:1. In 1998, the affiliates of U.S. firms abroad
sold $2.4 trillion, as compared to the total of all exports of goods and services
from the United States that year of $933 billion (a ratio of just less than 3:1).[33]

What are the broad global patterns of FDI; what nations supply it and
what nations are its recipients? Figure 5.5 gives us a sense of the overall volumes of FDI. As expected, FDI explodes in the mid-1980s. Another indicator
of the role of FDI in globalization is the increasing proportion that is geographically dispersed. FDI historically has mirrored the trade triad of North
America, Europe, and Japan.[34] This triad, of course, includes the major developed states. But FDI is increasingly directed toward developing states.

Table 5.6 provides more detail about where the largest FDI flows take
place for the richest nations. The enormous role of the United States as both

**Table 5.6 FDI Inflows and Outflows, 1990–1998
(ranked by total flows, in billions U.S. dollars)**

Country	Inflows	Outflows
United States	625,776	657,672
United Kingdom	237,507	365,120
France	177,620	257,437
Germany	60,246	320,012
China*	282,653	18,900
Netherlands	114,515	175,802
Japan	13,509	219,953
Belgium-Luxembourg	104,493	79,540
Canada	74,918	93,118
Sweden	66,767	79,820
Switzerland	25,870	100,690

*Data are for 1992–1999.

SOURCE: Stephen Thomsen, "Investment Patterns in a Longer-Term Perspective," OECD Working Papers on International Investment no. 2000/2, April 2000, 7. Data for China from OECD, "Main Determinants and Impacts of Foreign Direct Investment on China's Economy" *Working Papers on International Investment*, 2000/4, December 2000, 5.

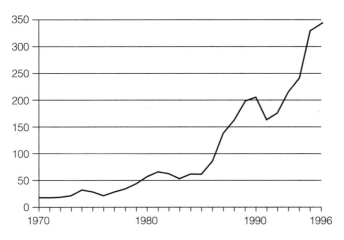

FIGURE 5.5 Growth of Foreign Direct Investment (annual flows, billions of U.S. dollars)

recipient and source of FDI is striking. Other states show greater imbalances, such as Germany, Japan, and Switzerland. In these states, FDI outflows are considerably greater than inflows.

Developing states are also major recipients of FDI. At their most recent peak in 1997, FDI inflows to such states reached $160 billion. Over the 1990s, between 25 and 38 percent of global FDI flows were directed at developing nations.[35] Recently, the largest single recipient has been China. In the early 1980s, FDI began to flow into China at significant levels, reflecting the changes in the government's attitude toward capitalist investors. In the early 1990s FDI inflows rose dramatically, reaching levels above $40 billion annually. China has become the second largest recipient in the world (behind the United States) and by far the largest among developing nations.[36] The most important source of investment into China has been Hong Kong, with considerably smaller amounts from Japan, Taiwan, and the United States. Other developing countries that have been major recipients of FDI include Brazil, Mexico, Singapore, Argentina, and Malaysia.

The patterns of FDI flows are further evidence of accelerating globalization. The consequence of large and persistent FDI flows has been an increasing globalization of assets and production, not just trade. Approximately one-third of the assets of the largest U.S. MNCs are foreign; for Great Britain, the figure is almost one-half; and for Switzerland, Sweden, and Canada, almost all assets are foreign.[37] The fifty largest MNCs have approximately 40 percent of their assets located abroad.[38] Data on several of the largest MNCs and the size of international sales, assets, and employment are give in Table 5.7, which indicates these firms have a very large global presence as a proportion of their overall activities.

Foreign direct investment, like other private global financial flows, moves to places where multinational firms expect a profitable return. But for nations, FDI is a crucial (in many cases, *the* crucial) factor determining whether that nation achieves satisfactory levels of economic growth—that is, whether it becomes richer or remains poor. The ability to attract FDI has come to represent a global "seal of approval" for a nation and its prospects. Along with the capital (usually quite scarce in a developing country), FDI brings technology and management skills (often even more scarce). The investment and the goods produced also frequently open up access to global markets for manufactured goods. Thus, FDI is the door to participation in the global economy, and those nations able to attract FDI tend to fare far better than those that do not.[39]

Sources of the Globalization of Production

The enormous growth of FDI and international assets raises several important questions. Why has this globalization occurred? How do these levels of FDI affect the behavior of firms, their organization, and the way they interact? What are the consequences for nations?

We have seen in Chapter 4 that explanations for the expansion abroad of U.S. corporations in the 1955–1975 era have focused on the hegemonic position of the United States and on the cyclical process of product development. The decline of U.S. hegemony and the global complexity of FDI make these arguments more appropriate for the pre-1975 era.[40] The best explanation for the acceleration in FDI growth can be found in the organizational advantages of MNCs over domestic-based firms. The surge of FDI is a result of the widespread conclusion by the executives of multinational enterprises that profits

Table 5.7 Top 15 Global Firms by Assets

Company	Industry	Foreign Assets (as % of total)	Foreign Sales (as % of total)	Foreign Employment (as % of total)
Royal Dutch Shell	Energy	67.8	73.3	77.9
Ford	Automotive	29.0	30.6	29.8
General Electric	Electronics	30.4	24.4	32.4
Exxon	Energy	73.1	79.6	53.7
General Motors	Automotive	24.9	29.2	33.9
Volkswagen	Automotive	84.8	60.8	44.4
IBM	Computers	51.9	62.7	50.1
Toyota	Automotive	30.5	45.1	23.0
Nestlé	Food	86.9	98.2	97.0
Bayer	Chemicals	89.8	63.3	54.6
ABB	Electrical equipment	84.7	87.2	93.9
Nissan	Automotive	42.7	44.2	43.5
Elf Aquitaine	Energy	54.5	65.4	47.5
Mobil	Energy	61.8	65.9	52.2
Daimler-Benz	Automotive	39.2	63.2	22.2

SOURCE: UNCTAD.

could be expanded or protected through a global expansion of their productive assets. Recent innovations in FDI involve moving beyond the process of simply producing in the home market and selling abroad; FDI means acquiring productive assets in another country and selling there and/or elsewhere. For firms to take on the expense and problems associated with a system of global operations, MNCs must be able to gain some competitive advantage from moving abroad. They must have, or believe they have, the ability to compete more effectively through globalization.

What are the advantages enjoyed by MNCs that enable them to generate large amounts of FDI?[41] Typically, observers attribute MNC investments abroad to an effort to locate the lowest unit labor costs and/or avoid environmental or other forms or regulation. There are certainly many instances where these motives are present. But the most important benefits from international investment lie elsewhere; these involve the ability to operate a global enterprise and derive benefits from that operation. Of great importance is the ability to gain access to new markets. The globalization of technology raises the stakes and the costs associated with innovation and increases the risks involved with new-product competition. The ability to sell in global markets permits MNCs to spread the risks and costs of innovation over a much larger number of sales units. This allows MNCs to accept risks and undertake innovation that otherwise would not happen and thereby to gain competitive advantages. In a similar sense, location-specific assets can also include specialized suppliers, pools of labor with specialized skills, or research facilities. Access to these resources is often a crucial factor in a firm's ability to engage in innovation. Innovation can yield improvements in the product and in the process of production, in marketing techniques, and in management skills. Global operations also give MNCs a much greater scope of access to resources and capital. They can borrow funds and mobilize resources over a much wider set of opportunities.

In a context of globalizing technology, innovation, and information, MNCs increasingly gain advantages by operating an effective global scanning capacity: gathering, integrating, and cross-fertilizing knowledge drawn from around the world. This process presents a major organizational challenge. Solving these difficulties requires a special ability to use the MNC's organization to control and reduce costs and to create advantages in the many sites where it operates. An example might be the ability to coordinate the supply of materials, production, and distribution over several geographically distant locations through an information-processing system created by sophisticated global telecommunications. A successful MNC may use its global locations to obtain the latest technology, integrate that technology into product or production innovation, and organize production and distribution on a global scale to take maximum advantage of the new knowledge.[42] The advantages of an MNC increasingly come from the ability of its units to act effectively as "knowledge brokers" within and outside the organization.[43]

One of the best tests of the thesis that firms simply seek low wages comes in Penang, in Malaysia. There, Western semiconductor and other high-tech firms built plants beginning in the early 1970s, mostly for the purpose of finding low wages. Over time, as more firms entered this area and as more domestic firms developed to provide specialized manufacturing services to the global giants, Penang developed new attractions. A local science university emerged to provide highly trained workers, and firms began to find synergies from the close location of other high-tech firms (in Penang and close by). Local suppliers emerged with capabilities specially attuned to the needs of the MNCs operating there. Even as wages rose dramatically, more global firms located in Penang. Today, there are many lower cost areas for production, but for many global firms Penang provides a source of innovation and access to markets in Asia. Much the same story can be told for the disk drive industry in Southeast Asia.[44] Such firms compete intensely on cost, but equally on the ability to bring new products to market and produce them in volume and with high quality. The globalization of the U.S.-based hard disk drive industry—and the associated system of FDI—provided it with an array of competitive advantages beyond lower labor costs.

Consequences of the Globalization of Production

Several developments of great significance are associated with the globalization of production. We will examine three: changes in the technology of production, the emergence of complex systems of global production, and the establishment of an increasing number and variety of intercorporate alliances.

Globalization increases the channels for the diffusion of technology and expands the abilities of more nations to use technology effectively. One example comes from the development and diffusion of new production techniques in Japan. The intensification of globalization since 1973 has magnified the impact of a new technology of production that found its highest development in Japan. There, largely as a result of intense competition and resource scarcity, many Japanese companies developed production forms that deviated dramatically from the mass production of standardized units typically known as "Fordism."[45] In its place, the Japanese organized a complex system of information-based, flexible manufacturing that emphasized lean production and very high quality standards. Using computer-directed production, Japanese companies began to produce small batches of significantly different products for different customers using the same production line. These production lines were designed to be reorganized quickly and cheaply to accommodate production of goods to customer specifications. Cost control was improved through "just in time" inventory control, in which the part reached the plant just as it was needed for production. Perhaps most stunning, Japanese producers were able to achieve much higher quality control than under Fordism.[46]

One important consequence of globalization has been the rapid transmission of this new technological system to the United States, Europe, newly industrialized countries (NICs), and even to developing states. The system of information-based, flexible manufacturing defines the standard for efficiency, quality, and the ability to meet customer needs. The combination of increased international competition, global information and technology flows, and intercorporate alliances has led to rapid emulation of the Japanese system. Increased globalization produces a more rapid and geographically wider spread of innovation. Not only does information move faster and to more recipients, but globalization also expands the institutional and infrastructural bases that permit firms in many countries to adopt and use these innovations.

Another example is the rapid globalization of the Internet as a technology of communication. Because of past global diffusion of computers and the technical knowledge these machines involve, the Internet achieved global scope about five to seven years after its introduction in the United States. The Internet emerged as a medium for business in the mid-1990s in the United States. By 2000–2001, not only had the technology of the Internet diffused to much of the planet, but many of the emerging e-business strategies as well.

A second institutional consequence of the globalization of production is the development of new and more complex forms for the organization of production. Typically, when we think of international production, the following image comes to mind: a firm organizes all of the steps of production in its home country, manufactures the good, and then sells it abroad. However, this image is increasingly outdated due to the more common organization of production that spans several nations, the growing use of outsourcing,[47] and the connections among firms from strategic alliances. The term *production network* is much better suited to understanding how production actually takes place. In a production network (often organized across a geographic region, but sometimes globally) a firm organizes production of the components of final product in several countries, assembles them in another, and sells the actual product around the world. For example, Ford manufactures the parts for its Fiesta car in Ireland, England, Belgium, Germany, and France and then assembles the car in Spain. Other examples come from the hard disc drive and microprocessor industries. Each locates the research and design process in the United States and then locates production around the world. More frequently, MNCs have begun to raise capital and locate sales offices around the world, place specialized R&D operations outside home countries, and produce goods for very differentiated markets.

The rapid decline in the costs of communication and information processing, the growth of flexible manufacturing, and the emergence of global networks of production, outsourcing, finance, innovation, and communication have altered the nature of many MNCs. They have become global knowledge brokers: knowledge-based producers, acquirers, processors, and appliers of knowledge. In this environment, the global division of labor among nations is much more fluid than in the traditional way of thinking about trading raw materials for manufactured goods. What is increasingly emerging is a specialization that cuts across nations with a division defined by technological sophistication: some areas are knowledge generators, others may be capable of producing the high-technology components of the product, while others are responsible for the low-technology elements of a product.[48] The location of the various elements of the production chain has become sufficiently globalized that placement decisions are based on cost-productivity calculations and much less on geography.[49]

In spite of the considerable strengths of MNCs, these organizations face increasingly daunting problems in coping with globalization. With the pace of technological change and global competition accelerating, the costs of innovation have increased dramatically, and the life cycle of products has declined significantly. This is especially true in the semiconductor industry, where every 18 months microprocessor speeds double and the manufacturing process becomes equally demanding and costly. The Intel plant completed during 1995 in New Mexico cost $1.8 billion, and the next-generation facilities cost over $3 billion.

Changes in semiconductors have dramatic consequences for computers and information processing. Processing power has made quantum leaps, and the cost per computation has fallen as rapidly. Every 18 months the processing speed of computers doubles. In 1987 a $2,000 personal computer could process roughly 4 million commands per second, operated with 512 kilobytes of random access memory (RAM), and could store thirty million bits of information. In 1995 the same-price computer could process 100 million commands per second, operated with 16 million bytes of RAM, and could store 1.2 billion bits of information. In 2002 the $2000 computer will process 2 billion commands per second, possess 512 million bytes of memory, and store 60 billion bits of information.[50] Such is the power of exponential growth. Firms producing semiconductors and computers must deal with rising costs to remain competitive and with shorter periods of time in which to recover these costs. The dynamism in global markets created by global competition simply adds to the risks and uncertainties that firms must manage. The response is to turn to strategic alliances, in which firms pool resources to share costs and spread risks.

A strategic alliance is an arrangement between two or more independent firms. It involves an ongoing and continuous relationship, which could include production, marketing, and/or research and development, that involves the sharing and transfer of information, products, and even production.[51] A key element in the bargain is that each firm needs access to the capabilities generated by or available to the other. The most interesting strategic alliances have increasingly come from MNCs in different countries. Firms that are otherwise competitors and that have strong connections to different countries develop a formal and continuing relationship. They may jointly produce a product, share the costs of development, organize a joint research facility, or simply exchange vital information.

One example of an international strategic alliance is an arrangement begun in the 1980s between General Motors and Toyota in which Toyota was responsible for producing in California an automobile sold by GM. Toyota wanted experience in producing cars in the United States, while GM needed to learn the technology associated with flexible, lean manufacturing. Similar alliances have occurred between Mazda and Ford and between GM and Isuzu. Rapid technological change in semiconductors and computers has led to a dense network of global strategic alliances. A complex system of strategic alliances in microelectronics during the late 1980s included Intel (United States), NEC (Japan), Siemens (Germany), Advanced Micro Devices (United States), Philips (the Netherlands), Toshiba (Japan), Thomson (France), Motorola (United States), and Matsushita (Japan). An even wider web of arrangements linked more than 30 additional firms from an equally wide array of countries.[52]

The rising number and significance of strategic alliances are a response to globalizing processes in technology and markets; these alliances also serve to deepen globalization in new and important ways. Firms find that they are unable to cope with rapid changes in markets and the rising costs of innovation. Thus strategic alliances are a response to some of globalization's consequences. But strategic alliances also affect globalization. These relationships among firms from different countries alter the way we need to think about the nationality of firms in international competition. In some ways, strategic alliances, in conjunction with growing trade and FDI, undermine the connection between nation and firm. Some analysts believe that the emerging global networks of finance, trade, information, and innovation operate in contradiction to the territorial world of states. This can be seen most easily in the difficulties of traditional national trade policy. Efforts to promote or control the trade activities of "national" firms tend to ignore the geographic fluidity and flexibility generated by international strategic alliances, in conjunction with FDI and global production. The competitive advantages of firms seem to rest more with transnational relationships than simply with advantages given by one nation.[53] In addition, strategic alliances increase the pace of innovation and add to the world economy's dynamism. Innovations now spread globally more quickly by increasing the "mobility of capital, information, technology, and personnel."[54]

Evaluating Globalization

Evaluating globalization's consequences has become a central issue in defining political fault lines in many societies. This is testimony to the power of globalization, but also makes any dispassionate discussion very difficult. We will work along two dimensions, one that tries to sort out the discernable effects of globalization and another that attempts to determine whether these effects are positive, negative, or neutral.

How we understand globalization and its consequences is closely related to broader estimates of the future of the world economy and international relations. Consequently, liberals, mercantilists, and radicals see these matters very differently. For liberals globalization is overwhelmingly positive, largely because it increases the efficiency of resource use on a global scale. This aids growth and development, expands trade, and generates significant gains for all. Liberals generally applaud any shifting of power from states to markets. Mercantilists, by contrast, express great skepticism about globalization, arguing that it was more important in the late nineteenth century. Moreover, they believe that states and national economies remain very important and that the present-day impact of a global economy is greatly exaggerated. From this perspective, multinational corporations are still creatures of their home nations, and regional economic systems organized by nations matter more than global systems. Radicals see globalization as significant, powerful, and overwhelmingly negative. The process of freeing markets is bad mainly because it permits MNCs to destroy jobs and harm the environment. Free markets make it easy for MNCs to invest anywhere, and this results in jobs shifting from rich nations to poor ones. This cuts jobs and wages in parts of richer nations and replaces them with jobs paying exploitative wages in poorer nations. Further, this same process permits MNCs to escape environmental regulations and thereby engage in environmentally harmful actions in poor nations that are prohibited in their home countries. To attract investment by MNCs, nations begin a "race to the bottom" to have the lowest wages and most lax environmental regulations. Radicals also criticize international institutions such as the World Bank, International Monetary Fund, and World Trade Organization as undemocratic instruments for the promotion of globalization. They charge that these organizations work to destabilize the economies of many nations, perpetuate poverty, and widen the gap between rich and poor.

Which of these very different conclusions do we find valid?[55] Each perspective offers useful insights into globalization. Liberals and radicals are both right in assessing the impact of widening free markets, because they look at different sides of the same coin. Markets do increase efficiency and thereby produce more growth. This is because markets direct resources toward higher-payoff investments and direct resources away from lower-payoff options. But such abstractions represent real people, with the latter especially significant because these owners and workers have their economic position damaged by the expanding free markets of globalization. Globalization hurts the economic interests of those people whose economic livelihood involves resources with relatively high costs and low productivity. And the wider arc of free markets from globalization brings more and more groups into global competition over costs and productivity. Growth comes because resources are shifted away from those with lower returns to those with higher returns, but this means real economic pain for some. Liberals, in their praise for the growth generated by globalization, usually ignore the dislocation and significant difficulty this also causes. Radicals generally have no viable alternative means to generate economic growth, and to follow the path of market controls will result in other kinds of negative consequences. At the same time, existing mechanisms of response to globalization's ills are inadequate, resulting in a growing political challenge.

Globalization does increase economic growth, but it does not raise all boats equally.[56] There are two ways by which incomes grow farther apart: the harm done to some groups' incomes by efficiency gains and the continuing weakness of the many across the world who are unable to participate in any income gains from globalization. Couple this with the extensive gains for those who possess mobile and highly productive resources, and increasing inequality is not surprising. The size of the problem is difficult to gauge. We need to remember that globalization has produced significant gains for many in poor nations: in urban China, parts of Vietnam, Singapore, Malaysia, Korea, Taiwan, and many other areas of Asia, huge absolute and relative jumps in income have happened since 1965. Most of this can be attributed to the ability of these societies to seize the opportunities presented by globalization. At the same time, rural China, most of Africa, and large parts of Central and South Asia have made little progress in the same period. Broader measures of income distribution suggest a widening gap between the richest 10 percent and the poorest 10 percent in recent years, with a significant part of the reason related to different abilities to reap gains from globalization.[57] In more developed societies, the negative effects of globalization on incomes are concentrated in groups whose labor and skills have significant substitutes in poorer nations. (Remember, this process usually leads to increasing the incomes of workers in these poorer nations.) The process of shifting production to a developing nation generates both efficiency gains *and* lower incomes for those whose jobs are displaced. Even workers possessing similar skills who face no job losses can see their incomes fall in real terms and find their bargaining power in negotiations decline.

Globalization also seems to encourage government policies that have the effect of shifting the tax burden, usually from holders of mobile resources to holders of more fixed-in-place resources. Countries' efforts to attract investment typically involve providing some kind of tax break in return for the investment. To make up for the loss of revenue, those firms and individuals who cannot leave have their taxes increased. Often this means middle and lower classes make up the shortfall—groups that control few mobile resources. These changes can be seen in tax rates: between 1986 and 1995, the standard corporate tax rate fell in OECD (Organization for Economic Cooperation and Development) countries from 43 percent to 33 percent; between 1978 and 1995, the marginal tax rate for a one-income couple raising two children and earning only two-thirds of average wages almost doubled. And between the 1960s and 1990s, taxes on labor grew by more than 8 percent, while taxes on capital grew by less than 1 percent.[58]

Can we say whether on balance globalization is a net positive or negative? One way is to consider the alternatives—a large increase in protectionism and reduction in capital mobility. The consequences of such a program almost certainly would be a sharp decline in economic growth, increasing economic conflict, and an end to any chance for bringing the world's desperately poor out of poverty. Another possibility is found in asking whether globalization can be reformed so as to reduce the bad while keeping the good. One of the main features accompanying globalization is the rise of liberal ideology, extolling the virtues of free markets and dismissing the need for any policy that thwarts the freedom of capitalists to make as much money as possible. "Greed is good" is rarely tempered by a recognition of the negative consequences of free markets. The main barrier to a reformed globalization—one that provides support systems for those damaged by efficiency gains and provides much greater infrastructure support to bring the world's poorest into the game—comes from the narrow-mindedness of the very groups that benefit the most from globalization. Ignoring the need for reform can generate an intense political backlash with tragic consequences for all. Left unreformed, globalization is most vulnerable in economic downturns, when its opponents can seize the political initiative. The ability to make globalization a positive force depends on the political sophistication of the global elites who gain the most but who also stand to lose the most.[59]

Globalization's impact on states is an equally contentious issue. In many ways this relationship is the essence of the study of political economy. The main question is whether and to what extent governments have had their powers and prerogatives compromised through the forces created by the globalization of finance and production and, if so, whether the changes have been for good or ill.

One of the strongest advocates of the view that globalization has reduced the capacities of states to control their own economic life is Susan Strange:

> The impersonal forces of world markets, integrated over the postwar period more by private enterprise in finance, industry and trade than by the cooperative decisions of governments, are now more powerful than the states to whom ultimate political authority over society and economy is supposed to belong. Where states were once the masters of markets, now it is the markets which ... are the masters over the governments of states.[60]

Strange rejects the notion that markets produce an efficient allocation of resources, finding instead a "casino" logic of rampant speculation and often irrational investing. But it is the huge size of these markets that give them such power. Only through sustained cooperation can states hope to influence global financial markets. This capacity for cooperation is usually wanting, leaving many nations at the mercy of wild changes in the value of their currencies during financial crises. Further, MNCs control resources of such enormous value that states must negotiate with them as if they were sovereign entities. As the bearers of money, technology, managerial expertise, production and distribution capabilities, and access to global markets, these transnational firms have become indispensable to accomplishing state goals of economic growth. Thus, firms have assumed the power to negotiate with states and with each other, and this power has grown relative to the power of states.[61]

A second perspective pointing to the decline of state power emphasizes restrictions on the ability to engage in deficit spending and inflationary policies to manage economic growth. When we examine events carefully, however, this argument needs qualification. Government spending by nations in the advanced world has risen with little letup, even as globalization has intensified. Financial market penalties have not eliminated deficit spending; states have actually expanded the gap between revenue and spending in recent years. Between 1974 and 1994, the public debt of OECD states has increased from 15 percent to 40 percent of GDP.[62] This may be the result of the fact that markets need a growing supply of high-quality investments and thus are willing to finance this debt. And the globalization of financial markets means that states can regularly borrow abroad. At best, the rate of increase has been slowed by globalization, and the ability of governments to implement new programs may have been reduced. However, the commitment to broad categories of welfare spending has continued, and it is the growth of these programs that only recently may have been slowed. Perhaps the clearest example of coerced cuts in spending and deficits is in the European Union in the years following the Maastricht Agreement, setting criteria for participation in the Euro.[63] Another example is the effort by the United States to reduce and eliminate the large budget deficits of the 1980s and early 1990s. Nonetheless, the restraints on governments are narrowly focused and less intense than some have argued. States will pay penalties for rapid increases in spending and deficits if financial market players see this as promoting inflation. And the failure to coordinate monetary and fiscal policies can also lead to market penalties.

An opposing view of the impact of globalization on the state points to states' continuing strength. As we have just seen, governments remain at the center of economic life in most advanced capitalist economies, where they account for 40 to 50 percent of all economic activity. Others argue that states continue to play a central role in the creation of effectively working market economies: such markets could not exist without the support systems provided by states. Ethan Kapstein argues that states were themselves key actors in the globalization of finance through policies of deregulation and other efforts to encourage the adoption of open financial markets in developing nations.

And banks and other financial actors still depend on governments to gain market access and make sure competition occurs on a "level playing field."[64] But the globalization of finance has also created a new set of problems that states have needed to deal with. The interdependence among nations created by the globalization of finance means that a financial crisis in one nation can have almost immediate and profound consequences for other nations. Although banks are heavily regulated and central banks remain lenders of last resort to protect domestic banking systems, these arrangements have proved insufficient in dealing with globalized finance. Nations have responded to this problem, according to Kapstein, through increased international cooperation designed to enhance control over international finance from their home countries. This involves establishing a common set of regulatory criteria through a series of agreed-upon principles and then national governments establishing and enforcing these rules.

Steven Vogel adds to the view that markets have not overwhelmed states through a microanalysis of the liberalization and deregulation policies of advanced industrial countries. He makes clear that the widespread series of liberalization policies from the 1970s to the 1990s required a new system of regulations—that is, reregulation. The result has been "freer markets and *more* rules."[65] In contrast to those who see deregulation as the triumph of markets and private interests over governments, Vogel shows that governments retain the power to impose new sets of regulations and that much deregulation was a result of state initiative, not of private interests. Clearly powerful forces were at work on governments: technological change and associated market developments were making existing regulatory systems obsolete; the United States initiated liberalization policies, and its material and ideological power led to imitation by other states; and difficulties from slowing growth and increasing fiscal deficits prompted the use of deregulation and privatization. Even so, governments in the United States, Britain, Japan, France, and Germany were able to shape these forces and respond based on their institutional capacities and goals. In areas as much affected by globalization as telecommunications and financial services, nations found the need to impose new regulations to replace the old ones.

Similar propositions come from Peter Evans, who emphasizes the essential political supports necessary for the operation of a market economy. Hence, rather than globalization leading to a diminished state role, it actually places a greater burden on governments.[66] Only when analysts view globalization through the prism of liberal ideology do they conclude that states can, are, and should be dispensed with in the global economy. International financial actors and those who produce and market intellectual property on a global scale need states to establish rules for regulation and enforcement and to gain the cooperation of other states in abiding by these rules. Thus, "modern [global] markets depend on economic decisions being nested in a predictable institutional framework." Such a framework can only be had through state actions; markets cannot provide these collective goods.

Additional evidence for the continued importance of the state in an era of globalization is drawn mainly from East Asian examples. This research suggests that participation in the global economy works best for societies where the state bureaucracy is effective in creating a set of national institutions that attract international capital and generate economic activity by its citizens. Much of this research focuses on the "developmental state," with the capacity to direct resources and shape the domestic economy to encourage private investment in industries producing for global markets. Several East Asian states, including Singapore, Korea, Japan, and Taiwan provide examples of successful governmental efforts to turn the globalization process to their advantage.[67]

Shifting ground again, other scholars argue that globalization—especially if understood in terms of the revolution in information technology—has so altered the rules of economic and political relationships that we need to rethink the political economy of states and firms. The most interesting and provocative arguments come from those trying to understand how an economy increasingly based on information technology and directed toward knowledge-intensive production changes the ways governments behave and the power they have. The changing relationships of production in an information-based economy are thought to alter power arrangements and the position of states. In many ways this is an extension of—but also a radicalization of—the early arguments regarding the devolution of state power.

What happens when many goods produced are incorporated into digital form and transmitted instantly all over the globe? Further, what does it mean when the consumption of such a good by one person not only does not reduce its utility to another, its consumption by one person actually increases its utility to another? What does international trade mean when the goods are produced, distributed, and consumed in cyberspace—a region where national boundaries have little meaning?

Any answers to these questions must necessarily be somewhat speculative, for the information technology revolution is still in its infancy. One vein of thought asserts that a "dematerialized" economy undermines the concepts of distance, place, and geography—the terms we usually associate with nations, territoriality, and sovereignty. The ability to operate anywhere, without the interference of states, may well reconfigure the very concept of a state, creating a variety of new political forms each of which shares some of the allegiance of individuals. Because we cannot locate the nationality of economic relations, the distinction between internal and external politics is blurred. The emerging contradiction between concepts of geographic space and cyberspace may be accelerated by the adoption of electronic cash. In the form of smart cards and digital money, this e-cash will facilitate global electronic commerce, but it may also undermine a key form of sovereignty: the ability of the state to issue money and control the supply available.[68]

A significant consequence of the information revolution is its impact on large centralized bureaucracies: it makes these entities counterproductive in that they cannot keep up with the pace of change; but more important, by delivering information at practically zero cost to anyone connected, the information revolution dissolves the reason for hierarchies.

> In their place, a complex system of networks and alliances is emerging in which information technology facilitates the integration and coordination of geographically dispersed operations. An international system of production is being replaced by a complex web of interlaced global electronic networks.[69]

Perhaps the most direct, immediate, and indisputable consequence of instant and virtually costless communication is the expansion in the opportunities for transnational associations to emerge and use this technology to pressure the governments of many states to act in a particular way. At elite levels, and expanding as the Internet expands, may be the establishment of new transnational communities of ideas, identities, and interests. Nongovernmental organizations (NGOs) such as Amnesty International already carry more financial and political weight than the human rights units of the United Nations. The capacity for global organization expands in dramatic fashion with the expansion of the Internet, and so likely will the impact of NGOs.[70] John Ruggie takes these themes one step farther. He argues that the scale of operation by multinational corporations is such that it alters the intellectual foundation of the state system. Drawing an analogy to changes during medieval times, Ruggie suggests that

> the new wealth they produced, the new instruments of economic transactions they generated, the new ethos of commerce they spread, the new regulatory arrangements they required, and the expansion of cognitive horizons they effected all helped undermine ... [the ideas upon which the existing system of government rested].[71]

Keohane and Nye offer a more skeptical reading of information technology's impact on states. For much of the twentieth century, analysts have predicted that technology and interdependence would transform world politics. But existing relationships of power and culture often persist in spite of shifts in economic life. Although information moves across borders with ease, it still exists within a political space already occupied by nations, their leaders, and systems of identity. And states retain the capacity to influence what comes through and how it is used. Information technology is also an increasingly important source of power in world affairs, and states still are able to capture some of its benefits and do this in an uneven manner—some have much more than others. The ability to generate, disseminate, and act on intelligence provides considerable power resources to those with advantages in these areas. And clearly, some nations with advanced positions in the information revolution possess these advantages, with considerable military implications.[72]

The expanded globalization of the last quarter of the twentieth century has had profound effects, but most of these are too recent and too unfinished for any certainty in our evaluation. Like capitalism, of which globalization is but a feature, expanding markets have both positive effects for economic growth and disruptive effects that can destroy people's lives. If poverty reduction is a high priority, there are no viable alternatives to developing the institutions needed to moving headlong into production for global markets. This process can have devastating environmental consequences, as China now shows. The process of economic growth in poor nations via global investment can also undermine the opportunities for low-skilled labor in rich countries. And some firms operating in poor nations use exploitative wages and avoidance of environmental regulations to increase profits. But on balance, globalization has a positive impact—expanding economic growth, transmitting democratic ideas, and widening the arc of environmental awareness. If globalization is threatened, it is because of resistance to efforts to ameliorate its negative effects. For states, globalization forces shifts in policy and negotiating partners and renders them much less able to expand social programs through widened deficits. However, there is little clear evidence that states have had their position eroded in any fundamental way.

CONCLUSIONS

Many of the most important features and trends in the world economy can be traced to the process of globalization. We have concentrated on the arrangements in finance and production. The combination of flexible exchange rates, new and less expensive technologies in communication and computing, and a series of historical events has produced a genuine sea of change in global finance. A veritable explosion of foreign exchange trading and huge leaps in international lending and international equities trading have generated a major advance in the globalization of finance. Additionally, the expansion of the operations of multinational corporations through foreign direct investment has altered the world economy in the direction of greater globalization. The vast web of investment generates international production and a complex system of international corporate alliances. These arrangements both reflect and accelerate the processes of technological change, innovation, and global competition.

At the same time, most will acknowledge that globalization has not proceeded to the point where national economies are simply a subset of international transactions and relationships. National economies still account for the preponderance of economic activity: trade, investment, capital formation, and economic decision making. Globalization is taking place at an increasing pace, but the world economy does not overwhelm most national economies. Whether globalization will proceed to such a point is uncertain. Nations remain very important actors in the world economy. The economic strength of the MNC's home base is a very important (some would say the most important) factor in determining the MNC's competitiveness in the world economy.[73] Not only do nations retain the capacity for regulation, but also their efforts to control MNC behavior are essential features of a stable world economy. The liberalization of the past 20 years could be reversed by states; MNCs are not stateless; and borders retain great significance.

But these qualifications must not divert us from understanding the profound consequences for nations, for the relations among nations, and for other actors in world affairs of the current level of globalization. The nature and significance of the nationality of MNCs are anything but clear. MNCs are not stateless, but they are not "stated" or national in the same way as before 1970. The ability to operate a large business enterprise across many countries and to control investment, technology, and innovation makes MNCs very important actors in world affairs. Some scholars argue that the expansion of multinational corporations and globalization has proceeded to the point that the "game" of international politics has been altered. Because states must now compete for the opportunity to create wealth within their borders, they must bargain with MNCs.[74] These firms are the main agents of wealth creation because they control the necessary resources—in particular the ability to move and organize capital on a global scale. There is now tremendous pressure on states to make their territory more attractive to MNCs for production and investment. Leaders of governments understand that for funds and production to move to or remain in their territory, the incentives and advantages must be clear to the holders of these resources. The government of most countries has been focused on their nation's competitive strength.[75] Not only are states driven to organize their societies for global economic competition, they also have increased incentives for cooperation. It is now much more difficult for states to initiate economic expansion via monetary and fiscal policy. Unless most states act together, international financial markets will impose penalties through interest rates and exchange rates. Additionally, when nations cooperate, they still are able to affect prices in foreign exchange markets. Success usually requires acting in a manner consistent with underlying market forces; and long-term or strong trends cannot be controlled by governments. But if market timing is right, as with the 1995 effort by Japan and the United States to push up the dollar against the yen, governments can still influence prices.

Thus, globalization simultaneously pushes states toward greater cooperation and greater competition. The incentives for cooperation can be seen in efforts to create and manage the political context needed for markets to function effectively. International cooperation has become more important in the process of managing exchange rates, coordinating economic policies, homogenizing regulations, negotiating rules for trade and investment, and coping with the difficulties in integrating postcommunist states into the world economy. Globalization can proceed only as states cooperate to maintain an effective framework for these transactions.

At the same time that cooperation increases in response to globalization, there are strong pressures for greater competition. The rising number of players in the world economy—both states and firms—intensifies the struggle for markets and growth. The very nature of this competition is in dispute. Economists argue that only firms compete, whereas the trade and investment crossing national boundaries can only benefit all states. Others point out that rates of economic growth differ substantially in response to international exchange and that many people care about these differences. Globalization may increase a state's need to enhance the ability of firms operating within its territory to compete in the world economy. Certainly the leadership and populace of most states see themselves in competition with each other for the means to wealth and power.

The following two chapters address the issues of cooperation and competition. In Chapter 6 we will explore the nature of international cooperation in relation to globalization. We will consider the problems and prospects for cooperation, understand the conflicting incentives for cooperation, and apply these ideas to several cases of successful and attempted cooperation. Chapter 7 explores the nature and impact of competition and conflict among advanced states. We will examine the indicators of national competitive advantage and disadvantage, the challenge posed by Japan, the competitive strategies available, and the costs and benefits of these strategies.

NOTES

1. Indeed, a longer perspective shows that we have now returned to levels of interdependence found at the beginning of the twentieth century. For a detailed comparison of earlier and present-day interdependence, see David Henderson, "International Economic Integration: Progress, Prospects and Implications," *International Affairs*, 68.4, 1992, 633–653. Also see Paul Bairoch and Richard Kozul-Wright, "Globalization Myths: Some Historical Reflections on Integration, Industrialization and Growth in the World Economy," Geneva, Switzerland: UNCTAD Discussion Paper no. 113, 1996. Chapter 3 of this book provides an extended discussion on the earlier period.

2. The literature on globalization is vast, and we must necessarily limit our discussion to matters immediately relevant to international political economy.

3. John C. Pool and Steve Stamos, *The ABCs of International Finance*, Lexington, Mass.: Lexington Books, 1987, 86. See Chapter 12 below for more detail on the debt crisis.

4. Robert Gilpin, *The Challenge of Global Capitalism*, Princeton, N.J.: Princeton University Press, 2000, 6. Gilpin argues this imbalance represents a significant threat to international economic stability. See the discussion below of international capital flows.

5. Eric Helleiner, *States and the Reemergence of Global Finance*, Ithaca, N.Y.: Cornell University Press, 1994, 102–112.

6. Helleiner, *Global Finance*, 123–145.

7. Helleiner, *Global Finance*, 152–156; Frances M. Rosenbluth, *Financial Politics in Contemporary Japan*, Ithaca, N.Y.: Cornell University Press, 1989, 50–89; John Goodman and Louis Pauley, "The Obsolescence of Capital Controls? Economic Management in an Age of Global Markets," *World Politics*, 46.1, October 1993, 64–70.

8. Helleiner, *Global Finance*, 156–166.

9. International Monetary Fund (IMF), *International Capital Markets*, 2001, 5.

10. "One World," *The Economist*, 1997.

11. The data on outstanding international lending are found in IMF, *World Economic Outlook*, May 1995, 80; the information about equity trading is in

Andrew Sobel, *Domestic Choices, International Markets,* Ann Arbor: University of Michigan Press, 1994, 52.

12. "The World Economy," *The Economist,* October 7, 1995, 6; IMF, *World Economic Outlook,* 80–81; Sobel, *Domestic Choices,* 92.

13. There is evidence of a declining relationship between national savings rates and national investment. See Bank for International Settlements (BIS), Annual Report, 2001, 32–33, which reports a significant decline in the correlation during the 1990s.

14. We discuss these events in more depth in Chapter 12.

15. For an example of the position that markets have primacy, see Richard McKenzie and Dwight Lee, *Quicksilver Capital,* New York: Free Press, 1991. For the view that political actors retain significant influence, see Philip Cerny, "The Limits of Deregulation: Transnational Interpenetration and Policy Change," *European Journal of Political Research,* 19, 1991, 173–196.

16. This refers to the well-known Moore's Law, named for Gordon Moore, a cofounder of the world's most important manufacturer of microprocessors, Intel. In 1965, Moore predicted that the capacity of semiconductors used for computer memory would double every 12 to 24 months at the same cost. Later, the same prediction was extended to logic chips, such as microprocessors. This increasing capacity cuts the effective cost by one-half over the same time period. And this decline in price, when continued over many years, turns costly computing power into cheap and affordable computing power.

17. A very detailed discussion of the role of information technology in investment decisions is "Frontiers of Finance," *The Economist,* October 9, 1993. Also relevant is "Virtual Finance," *The Economist,* May 20, 2000.

18. There is a considerable discussion about whether placing capital controls on the short-term movement of money has substantial benefits, especially for small and vulnerable nations. In the midst of the Asian financial crisis in 1998, Malaysia imposed capital controls that resulted in a stabilization of finances in that nation. Chile has controlled short-term capital flows to its advantage. And the People's Republic of China has an inconvertible currency and capital controls, even as it receives many billions of dollars in FDI each year. For a general discussion of global capital, see "Global Finance," *The Economist,* January 28, 1999. For discussion of Malaysia, see Mark Landler, "The Ostrich That Roared," *New York Times,* September 4, 1999, B1.

19. A very small number of currencies constitutes the great bulk of foreign exchange trading. Most short-term trades involve five currencies: the U.S. dollar, Japanese yen, German deutsche mark, British pound, and Swiss franc. (This, of course, will change with the Euro in 2002.) More than 70 percent of the pairs (remember, foreign exchange trading involves one currency for another) involve these five currencies. Further, 80 percent of all foreign exchange trading has the U.S. dollar as one of the pairs. See David Eitenman, *Multinational Business Finance,* Reading, Mass.: Addison-Wesley, 1995, 87, 90.

20. David Andrews, "Capital Mobility and State Autonomy: Toward a Structured Theory of International Monetary Relations," *International Studies Quarterly,* 38, 1994, 197. Also see, Vincent Cable, "The Diminished Nation State: A study in the Loss of Economic Power," *Daedalus,* Spring 1995, 21–53. Also see the discussion at the end of this chapter.

21. This assumes that states want to influence monetary policy and are not willing to let the exchange rate of the currency rise and fall to any level. If a

government is willing to forfeit any influence on exchange rates, then an independent monetary policy is possible.

22. For the concept of "embedded liberalism," see John Gerard Ruggie, "International Regimes, Transactions, and Change: Embedded Liberalism in the Postwar Economic Order," *International Organization,* 36.2, 1982, 379–415.

23. Geoffrey Garrett and Peter Lange, "Political Responses to Interdependence: What's Left for the Left?" *International Organization,* 45.4, 1991, 539–564; Geoffrey Garrett, "Capital Mobility, Trade, and the Domestic Politics of Economic Policy," *International Organization,* 49.4, Autumn 1995, 657–687.

24. For reasons discussed below, using measures of international trade understates the level of international production. This measure leaves out production by multinational firms that takes place abroad for sale in the country of production. That is, trade measures don't count a significant part of the production that results from foreign direct investment (FDI).

25. In Chapter 6 we will consider whether this and other data demonstrate globalization or regionalization.

26. Toyota Annual Report, 2001.

27. United Nations, *World Investment Report, 1992: Transnational Corporations as Engines of Growth,* New York: United Nations, 1992, 2.

28. John Stopford and Susan Strange, *Rival States, Rival Firms: Competition for World Market Shares,* Cambridge, England: Cambridge University Press, 1991, 15.

29. See below for further discussion of the impact of globalization and of firms on nations. For a useful commentary on MNCs, see Paul Doremus et al., *The Myth of the Global Corporation,* Princeton, N.J.: Princeton University Press, 1998.

30. This wholly negative concept of power is frequently found among liberals, who see states as a necessary evil, exercising power by restricting (their) economic freedom. A version of this argument is found in "Globalisation and Its Critics," *The Economist,* September 29, 2001, 14–15.

31. Foreign direct investment, remember, occurs when a corporation purchases assets in another country and when the purpose is to manage those resources as an enterprise. So when a Japanese auto company invests in the United States to open a production plant, that counts as FDI. When that same firm buys stock in Microsoft, obviously with no prospect of managing Microsoft, that counts as portfolio investment.

32. DeAnne Julius, *Global Companies and Public Policy,* London, Pinter, 1990, 6; World Trade Organization (WTO), Annual Report, 1998.

33. United Nations, *World Investment Report,* 1992, 52–56; Julius, *Global Companies and Public Policy,* London: Pinter, 1990; *The Economist,* February 5, 1994, 71; Joseph Quinlan and Marc Chandler, "The U.S. Trade Deficit: A Dangerous Obsession," *Foreign Affairs,* 80.3, May June 2001, 88.

34. United Nations, *World Investment Report,* 1992, 21.

35. Stephen Thomsen, "Investment Patterns in a Longer-Term Perspective," Organization for Economic Cooperation and Development [OECD] Working Papers on International Investment no. 2000/2, April 2000, 14.

36. OECD, "Main Determinants and Impacts of Foreign Direct Investment on China's Economy," Working Papers on International Investment no. 2000/4, December 2000, 5.

37. "Big Is Back," *The Economist,* June 24, 1995, 15. The overall scale of FDI in relation to GDP is a reminder that we are studying a process of globalization and not an end result. If we add

together one year's inflows and outflows of FDI for a nation, this represents only a small fraction of GDP. The figures for 1994 are Belgium, 7%; Sweden, 6.5%; Great Britain, 4%; United States, 2%; Germany, 1%; Japan, 1%.

38. Calculated from "Multinationals," *The Economist,* March 27, 1993.

39. FDI that flows to developing nations goes overwhelmingly to those higher on the income scale. If we divide developing states into two groups, middle income and lower income, and compare the relative shares of FDI, we see this pattern: those in the middle income group received more than 93% of FDI, whereas lower-income developing states received only 7% of FDI. Even so, FDI into chronically poor areas such as Africa grew from under $2 billion in 1992 to over $6 billion in 1999 World Bank, *Global Development Finance,* Washington, D.C., 2001, 39–40.

40. Raymond Vernon, "The Product Cycle Hypothesis in a New International Environment," *Oxford Bulletin of Economics and Statistics,* 41.4, November 1979, 255–267.

41. We should note that firms in different industries often have quite different circumstances. The following list is a set of generalizations valid for many but not all firms.

42. The concept of technology used here refers not only to the physical technology in machines but also to the "soft" technology involved in the tacit understanding of how machines and people can best be organized.

43. John Dunning, "The Eclectic Paradigm of International Production: A Restatement and Some Possible Extensions," *Journal of International Business Studies,* 19.1, 1988, 1–31; Lorraine Eden, "Bringing the Firm Back In: Multinationals in International Political Economy," *Millennium,* 20.2, 1991, 197–224; Peter Cowhey and Jonathan Aronson, *Managing the World Economy,* New York: CFR Press, 1993, 43–55.

44. David McKendrick, Richard Donor, and Stephan Haggard, *From Silicon Valley to Singapore,* Stanford, Calif.: Stanford University Press, 2000. For additional discussion, see: Richard Donor and Eric Hershberg, "Flexible Production and Political Decentralization in the Developing World: Elective Affinities in the Pursuit of Competitiveness?" *Studies in Comparative International Development,* 34.1, Spring 1999, 45–82. Also see, Alasdair Bowie, "The Dynamics of Business-Government Relations in Industrialising Malaysia," in Andrew MacIntyre (ed.), *Business and Government in Industrialising Asia,* Ithaca, N.Y.: Cornell University Press, 1994, 186–187.

45. David Friedman, *The Misunderstood Miracle,* Ithaca, N.Y.: Cornell University Press, 1988; and Laura Tyson and John Zysman, "Developmental Strategy and Production Innovation in Japan," in Chalmers Johnson et al. (eds.), *Politics and Productivity,* New York: Harper and Row, 1989, 59–140.

46. "Manufacturing Technology," *The Economist,* March 5, 1994,; Michael Piore and Charles Sabel, *The Second Industrial Divide,* New York: Basic Books, 1984; and Mitchell Bernard, "Post-Fordism, Transnational Production, and the Changing Global Political Economy," in Richard Stubbs and Geoffrey Underhill (eds.), *Political Economy and the Changing Global Order,* New York: St. Martin's Press, 1994, 216–229.

47. *Outsourcing* refers to the use of an outside or separate firm to handle part of all of the production process. A good example is Cisco, the global leader in manufacturing the equipment that manages information flow on the Internet. But Cisco doesn't actually make most of the products it sells. Rather, it outsources the production to other firms that specialize in manufacturing. And these other firms—Jabil Circuit, for example—may produce the various

components in a variety of countries and assemble them in yet another. Cisco designs and markets the products. Outsourcing is especially common in the electronics and technology industries. Computers are made in the same way. Interestingly, so are shoes, especially athletic shoes. Nike operates in much the same way as Cisco, outsourcing production of its shoes.

48. OECD, *Globalization of Industrial Activities, Four Case Studies: Auto Parts, Chemicals, Construction, and Semiconductors,* Paris: OECD, 1992; Dieter Ernst and David O'Connor, *Competing in the Electronics Industry: The Experience of Newly Industrialising Economies,* Paris, OECD, 1992; Michael Hobday, *Innovation in East Asia,* Aldershot, England: Edward Elgar, 1995.

49. Martin Carnoy et al., *The New Global Economy in the Information Age,* University Park: Penn State University Press, 1993, 31.

50. One way to grasp the profound changes and innovations in computers would be to consider a hypothetical comparison in automobiles. To duplicate the changes in computers over the 14 years from 1987 to 2001, auto manufacturers would need to be able to move from producing and selling a Model T for $2000 to producing and selling a Lexus 430 for $2000 in the same time.

51. Cowhey and Aronson, *Managing,* 7.

52. For strategic alliances in information technology firms, see John Hagedoorn and Jos Sahakenraad, "Leading Companies and Networks of Strategic Alliances in Information Technologies," *Research Policy,* 21, 1992, 178; and Cowhey and Aronson, *Managing,* 148–149. For automobiles, See Cowhey and Aronson, *Managing,* 91–124; and "The Car Industry," *The Economist,* October 17, 1992. Also see, "Multinationals," *The Economist,* March 27, 1993, 16.

53. Mitchell Bernard and John Ravenhill, "Beyond Product Cycles and Flying Geese: Regionalization, Hierarchy, and the Industrialization of East Asia," *World Politics,* 47, January 1995, 171–172.

54. Cowhey and Aronson, *Managing,* 34.

55. Two very useful discussions of these matters are: Dani Rodrik, "Sense and Nonsense in the Globalization Debate," *Foreign Policy,* Summer 1997, 19–37; Dani Rodrik, "Has Globalization Gone Too Far?" *California Management Review,* 39.3, Spring 1997, 29–53.

56. Very useful discussions of inequality and globalization are Robert Wade, "Winners and Losers," *The Economist,* April 26, 2001; United Nations, *Human Development Report,* 1999, New York: Oxford University Press, 1999; Jeffrey Sachs, "A New Map of the World," *The Economist,* July 1, 2000.

57. See Wade, "Winners and Losers."

58. "World Economy Survey," *The Economist,* September 20, 1997, 33; IMF, *World Economic Outlook,* 1998, 132.

59. Discussions of globalization often are dominated by neoclassical or liberal thinking about political economy, which tends to privilege free markets, efficiency, and benefits to consumers over the difficulties of adjustment by producers. Perhaps most important, liberalism tends to disguise the political interests that stand behind its propositions: it speaks for those who are very good market players and those who have the resources that permit them to be winners, at least as a group. It defines narrowly the interests of those who are much less well positioned. It assumes that the sometimes savage changes demanded of some groups are both necessary and beneficial in the long run, if we measure in terms of production efficiency. That is, it defines the interests of losing groups in terms of social benefits spread over the entire society that emerge over time. This political and ideological process is not always clear, but it is always there.

Neoclassical thinking takes demonstrably accurate assessments of the societywide benefits of free trade but downplays countervailing logics of those who must endure the costs of creating these benefits. Rather than ignore these costs, a less ideological liberal position would acknowledge the essential importance of easing the costs of the globalization of free markets and acknowledge the legitimacy of complaints about having to bear these costs. Instead of shifting costs only onto those who are hurt by globalization, liberalism should acknowledge the responsibility of winners to help losers. Otherwise, the field is left to reactionary protectionists to articulate the fears and anguish of losers.

60. Susan Strange, *The Retreat of the State: The Diffusion of Power in the World Economy,* Cambridge, England: Cambridge University Press, 1996, 4.

61. Susan Strange's work can also be found in: *Casino Capitalism,* Oxford, England: Blackwell, 1986; John Stopford and Susan Strange, *Rival States, Rival Firms: Competition for World Market Shares,* Cambridge, England: Cambridge University Press, 1991; *Mad Money: When Markets Outgrow Governments,* Ann Arbor: University of Michigan Press, 1998.

62. "The World Economy," *The Economist,* October 7, 1995, 16; International Monetary Fund, *International Capital Markets,* Washington, D.C., September 1994, 35.

63. See Chapter 6. See also Layna Mosley, "Room to Move: International Financial Markets and National Welfare States," *International Organization,* 54.4, Autumn 2000, 737–773; and "The World Economy: The Future of the State," *The Economist,* September 20, 1997.

64. Ethan Kapstein, *Governing the Global Economy: International Finance and the State,* Cambridge: Harvard University Press, 1994, 6.

65. Steven Vogel, *Freer Markets, More Rules: Regulatory Reform in Advanced Industrial Countries,* Ithaca, N.Y.: Cornell University Press, 1996, 3.

66. Peter Evans, "The Eclipse of the State? Reflections on Stateness in an Era of Globalization," *World Politics,* 50.1, 1997, 62–87. For additional perspective, see Peter Evans, *Embedded Autonomy: States and Industrial Transformation,* Princeton, N.J.: Princeton University Press, 1995.

67. The best work on this topic includes Robert Wade, *Governing the Market,* Princeton, N.J.: Princeton University Press, 1990; Alice Amsden, *Asia's Next Giant: South Korea and Late Industrialization,* Oxford, England: Oxford University Press, 1989; Chalmers Johnson, *MITI and the Japanese Miracle,* Stanford, Calif.: Stanford University Press, 1982; John Mathews, "High-Technology Industrialization in East Asia," *Journal of Industry Studies,* 3.2, 1996, 1–77; Linda Weiss, *The Myth of the Powerless State,* Ithaca, N.Y.: Cornell University Press, 1998.

68. Stephen Kobrin, "Electronic Cash and the End of National Markets," *Foreign Policy,* 107, Summer 1997, 65–77. A similar argument is made in Eric Helleiner, "Electronic Money: A Challenge to the Sovereign State?" *Journal of International Affairs,* 51.1, Spring 1998, 387–409.

69. Stephen J. Kobrin, "Back to the Future: Neomedievalism and the Postmodern Digital World Economy," *Journal of International Affairs,* Spring 1998, 361–386. Also see, David J. Rothkopf, "Cyberpolitik: The Changing Nature of Power in the Information Age," *Journal of International Affairs,* Spring 1998, 325–359.

70. Jessica Mathews, "Power Shift," *Foreign Affairs,* January–February 1997, 50–66.

71. John Gerard Ruggie, "Territoriality and Beyond: Problematizing Modernity in International

Relations," *International Organization,* 47, Winter 1993, 155.

72. Robert Keohane and Joseph Nye, "States and the Information Revolution," *Foreign Affairs,* September–October 1998, 81–94.

73. Michael Porter, *The Competitive Advantage of Nations,* New York, Free Press, 1998; Yao-su Hu, "Global or

Stateless Corporations Are National Firms with International Operations," *California Management Review,* 34, Winter 1992, 107–126.

74. Stopford and Strange, *Rival States.*

75. Stephan Haggard, *Developing Nations and the Politics of Global Integration,* Washington, D.C.: Brookings Institution, 1995.

ANNOTATED BIBLIOGRAPHY

Peter Cowhey and Jonathan Aronson. *Managing the World's Economy.* New York: CFR Press, 1993. The best discussion of global strategic alliances among multinational corporations.

Peter Dicken. *Global Shift.* New York: Guilford, 1998. The most comprehensive analysis of the globalization of production, with a special emphasis on multinational corporations.

Barry Eichengreen. *Globalizing Capital.* Princeton, N.J.: Princeton University Press, 1996. An excellent history of international monetary relations.

Paul Erdman. *Tug of War.* New York: St Martin's/Griffin, 1997. A very readable analysis of financial crises.

Ronie Garcia-Johnson. *Exporting Environmentalism: U.S. Multinational Chemical Corporations in Brazil and Mexico.* Cambridge: MIT Press, 2000. Argues that U.S. MNCs advance environmental policies and ideas in developing nations.

Edward M. Graham and C. Fred Bergsten. *Fighting the Wrong Enemy: Antiglobal Activists and Multinational Enterprises.* Washington, D.C.: Institute for International Economics, 2000. A thorough and balanced analysis of globalization.

Gary Gereffi and Migueal Korzeniewicz (eds.). *Commodity Chains and Global Capitalism.* Westport, Conn.: Praeger, 1994. Provides an important conceptualization and analysis of the globalization of production.

Randall Germain. *The International Organization of Credit.* Cambridge, England: Cambridge University Press, 1997. Offers a world-economy perspective on the international monetary system.

Stephan Haggard. *Developing Nations and the Politics of Global Integration.* Washington, D.C.: Brookings Institution, 1995. A very useful short discussion of the impact of globalization on developing states.

Eric Helleiner. *States and the Reemergence of Global Finance.* Ithaca, N.Y.: Cornell University Press, 1994. The best discussion of capital liberalization.

Richard Herring and Robert Litan. *Financial Regulation in the Global Economy.* Washington, D.C.: Brookings Institution, 1995. A detailed examination of the problems of harmonization of financial regulations.

R. J. Barry Jones. *Globalisation and Interdependence in the International Political Economy.* London: Pinter, 1995. Offers insights into theoretical and empirical aspects of globalization.

Sylvia Maxfield. *Gatekeepers of Growth.* Princeton, N.J.: Princeton University Press, 1997. An analysis of the shifting power of central banks in developing countries.

David McKendrick, Richard Donor, and Stephan Haggard. *From Silicon Valley to Singapore: Location and Competition in the Hard Disk Drive Industry.* Stanford, Calif.: Stanford University Press, 2000. Examines the forces for the globalization of production.

Gregory Millman. *The Vandal's Crown.* New York: Free Press, 1995. A description of foreign exchange traders.

Henk Overbeek (ed.). *Restructuring Hegemony in the Global Political Economy: The Rise of Transnational Neo-Liberalism in the 1980s.* London: Routledge, 1993. Offers a very insightful radical perspective on liberal ideology.

Steven Solomon. *The Confidence Game: How Unelected Central Bankers Are Governing the Changed Global Economy.* New York: Simon and Schuster, 1995. A useful description of international financial crises.

John Stopford and Susan Strange. *Rival States and Rival Firms.* Cambridge, England: Cambridge University Press, 1991. The best discussion of the impact of globalization on the relationship of states and firms.

Susan Strange. *Mad Money.* Ann Arbor: University of Michigan Press, 1998. A critical examination of international finance and the impact on states.

William K. Tabb. *The Amoral Elephant: Globalization and the Struggle for Social Justice in the Twenty-First Century.* New York: Monthly Review Press, 2001. A reasoned and scholarly critique of globalization.

Andrew Walter. *World Power and World Money.* New York: St. Martin's Press, 1991. Provides a very good short discussion of political power and international finance.

6

❖

Cooperation among Advanced Industrial States

Four major structural trends define much of the background for the contemporary world economy: (1) the decline, or at least change, in American hegemony, (2) the globalization of finance and production, (3) the development of a web of institutions of international cooperation, and (4) the intensification of competition among states and firms. We have seen how the economic weight of the United States has declined from the lofty levels immediately after World War II. And consequently, the behavior of the United States has changed from broad support of the stability of the world economy to leadership based on a narrower definition of national self-interest. Perhaps surprisingly, the decline of U.S. hegemony has been accompanied by increasing levels of global interdependence. Restrictions on the flow of money and goods have fallen dramatically. Rapid expansion of financial flows, the organization of production on a global scale, the rapid transmission of information and technology around the world, and new forms of relationships among firms and states are indications of these trends.

Often responding to the effects of U.S. decline and the globalization of finance and production, many institutions of global and regional cooperation have expanded the scale and scope of their activities. One of the sharpest differences between the nature of interdependence in the late nineteenth century and that in the early twenty-first century is the presence today of many significant international institutions reflecting and contributing to cooperation. The scale and intensity of trade and financial flows have produced new efforts at cooperation and coordination, along with an accentuation of international competition. Nations and corporations frequently have found their interests bound together by the need to manage the burgeoning system of interdependence and thereby continue to reap the mutual benefits of free trade and capital movement. This process has given rise to new attempts at cooperation. Some of the most important are recurring efforts to manage newly floating exchange rates and to coordinate macroeconomic policies. Heads of state, finance ministers and their staffs, and central bankers have become deeply involved in these matters. Also interesting for the mixture of cooperative and competitive features is the growth of trading blocs in Europe, North America, and perhaps in Asia.

Even as we consider the role of cooperation, we must also keep in mind an appreciation of the impact of conflicting interests, because a capitalist world economy generates powerful competitive incentives for nations and firms alike. Those that are able to define the rules for exchange or bring the best or least expensive product to the marketplace win a disproportionate set of the gains. Similarly, those that consistently fail to meet these demands fall further and further behind, whether in market share, technological innovation, ability to attract investment, standard of living, or military competition. Thus the need for international cooperation is often tempered by a countervailing need for institutions and national strategies capable of adapting to and flourishing in an intensely competitive environment. In recent years the rising levels of world trade, the swiftness of change, the significant swings in the level of economic success in Japan and the United States, and the emergence of several newly developing economies have combined to raise significant concerns about competitiveness across much of the world.

This chapter is the first of two that will focus on the complex mixture of cooperation and competition among advanced capitalist states. We begin with a detailed discussion of the concept of cooperation. This is an elusive term, and it requires some extended discussion in order for us to understand its several dimensions. Under what conditions can we expect cooperation to occur? What are the main obstacles to resolving problems through cooperation? Is cooperation likely to increase? In answering these questions, our goal is to provide an understanding of the contexts in which cooperation is possible. We follow a discussion of the factors supporting and obstructing cooperation with a consideration of four very important cases: macroeconomic coordination through economic summits, management of exchange rates, the Uruguay Round and creation of the World Trade Organization, and the creation of economic blocs, especially the European Union (EU), the North American Free Trade Agreement (NAFTA), and a potential Asian bloc. These cases will offer some basis for conclusions about the effectiveness of and prospects for cooperation among the largest and most prosperous states.

THEORIES OF COOPERATION

Examination of the incidence and potential for cooperation engages some of the most basic questions about international politics. Why should we expect any meaningful cooperation to take place in an international system based on sovereign states whose security depends on their own efforts? One answer to this question sees anarchy among nations as the central obstacle to cooperation, driving states to compete for relative gains and thereby making any cooperation difficult and tenuous. Another perspective holds that, in spite of these barriers, cooperation is both possible and even likely. Operating to displace the effects of anarchy is the mutual ability of states to affect each other's fate, the constant interaction and expectation of entanglement into the foreseeable future, and the gains from cooperation. When cooperation produces international institutions, it stabilizes and even enhances future cooperation.

This section examines this debate and considers the circumstances under which cooperation can occur. In particular, we will set out those factors that support cooperation and those barriers that stand in its way. We will discuss the basics of this debate and follow it with three case studies of recent efforts at cooperation in the areas of macroeconomic policy, the management of exchange rates, and the formation of economic blocs.

Why Nations Cooperate

Although the discussion to this point may seem to set cooperation and conflict apart as two distinct kinds of situations, the real world almost always consists of varying mixtures of the two. Harmony is both rare and uninteresting in analytical terms. Instances in which the actions of one nation have no unwanted consequences for others are simply too unlikely to warrant our attention. Perhaps especially in world politics, cooperation is almost never a situation in which two nations simply recognize and act in a harmonious relationship. Rather, cooperation involves bargaining between two or more nations that modify their behavior and/or preferences in order to receive some reciprocal act from each other. The aim is to arrive at a situation in which these nations coordinate their behavior so as to achieve some important purpose that they cannot achieve by themselves.[1]

There are several important implications for this way of thinking about cooperation. First, cooperation does not require that the nations' purposes be identical but rather that some degree of parallel or overlapping interests exists such that the actions of each make some contribution to the purposes of the other. Second, the most interesting forms of cooperation are those that persist over time. These are the cases most likely to have the greatest impact. Third, cooperation may reach the point where tacit or explicit rules and regularity occur; scholars use the term *regime* to describe this situation. Finally, cooperation differs in terms of its scope—that is, broad or narrow issues—and in the terms of the importance of the issue. Cooperation over issues of whaling can be distinguished from those of nuclear weapons or the control of a nation's money supply.

Why should we expect cooperation to occur? What factors help bring it about? Perhaps the most obvious, but slippery, factor is the interests of the nations involved. Some degree of overlap of purpose is needed, but how much and of what kinds? No clear answers exist at this point. But from the perspective of international interdependence, the interests most likely to be engaged are those affected by the benefits of coordination and/or the costs of not cooperating. National leaders must expect to receive significant payoffs or the avoidance of major penalties from working together. However, this process becomes much more cloudy when we remember that nations are rarely unitary actors. Rather, governments are a collection of bureaucratic interests, each of which sees the issues relating to cooperation in a quite different way. Further, governments in the advanced capitalist world generally rest on coalitions of domestic interests that may be affected in very different ways by the proposed arrangements with other nations.

Also relevant to the potential for cooperation are the existing relationships among the nations involved. Certainly affecting a nation's calculations is the prior existence of regimes or institutions facilitating cooperation. Previous experience of cooperation, especially if successful and routinized in institutions, can pave the way for more in the future. Why might institutions, such as the European Union, matter? Institutions, especially in a context of anarchy and uncertainty, frequently supply information that can positively influence national decisions to continue and/or expand cooperation with other states. Institutions can help attenuate concerns that a nation may reap extra gains from cooperation and use those in military and political competition. Institutions also reduce worries about cheating and can bring closure to choices among alternative procedures and arrangements. Through provision of "unbiased" information, institutions clarify the distribution of gains from cooperation and legitimize this distribution. These activities can increase the chance of reciprocity in bargaining and can improve the climate for cooperation.[2] And successful institutions generate gains for participants that cannot be had without cooperation. Among similarly situated states this can produce costs from not cooperating that may demonstrate the value of participation.

Does this mean that states are less important for understanding the reasons for international cooperation? One answer would assert the continuing primacy of states over international institutions but also acknowledge that institutions do affect choices and contribute considerably to cooperation. Institutions matter because they provide a framework of rules whose operation facilitates global order and stability. This order is not a neutral one; rather it is the order desired by the most powerful states. But the rules embedded in institutions constrain the behavior of powerful and less powerful states and channel that behavior in certain prescribed and acceptable directions. This is what is meant by stability—and a certain kind of order. In the postwar era, institutions have generally fostered a liberal set of rules and order—based on the preferences of the United States. In important ways, postwar institutions have been a projection of American power and interests. Creating the institutions and the rules provides a particular coloring to the international order that comes to exist. These institutions and rules facilitate the indirect exercise of U.S. power by shaping choices and sustaining decisions even when the United States is not directly involved. The United States has a significant stake in the success of most global institutions. And yet these institutions are not just creatures of U.S. will. The rules sometimes constrain U.S. choices too, and the cooperation involved requires compromises that are different from U.S. choices that would be made in the absence of such institutions. And the inherent necessity for reciprocity—needed to keep institutions functioning—means that deviation from U.S. preferences is common. Thus, cooperation and its nurturing and preservation as an international norm become a vital U.S. interest, requiring policies and actions other than those flowing from a narrow calculation of national interests.

Of equal or even greater importance for understanding cooperation is the power relationship among nations. The existence of a single powerful state with significant economic resources and a strong commitment to international cooperation can play a key role in whether nations are able to work together. This hegemon's power advantages can be used to win, or even coerce, support from other states that otherwise might be reluctant to participate in cooperative ventures. There are two important corollaries to this argument. First, cooperation among states of relatively equal power is somewhat difficult because no state is in a position to bear the costs of promoting and encouraging cooperation. Second, when the power of the hegemon begins to wane, cooperation may also decline unless the institutions created have continuing value to the nations involved.[3]

What then are the main barriers to cooperation? Perhaps the greatest is the fact that nations operate as sovereign entities that must provide for their own security within an environment of anarchy. The absence of any central political authority capable of making and enforcing peace among nations makes international politics quite different from politics within (most) nations. The result is that national leaders must be wary about the ultimate consequences of agreements with other nations. They must pay attention not only to whether an arrangement produces a gain or a loss for themselves but also to whether it leads to greater gain for other nations.[4] The conditions of anarchy in the system mean that nations must be concerned about whether the gains of another nation might be used to augment that nation's power and to direct it toward some coercive or military purpose. One of the clearest patterns of the past 150 years is the tightening of connections among economic, technological, military, and political dimensions of national power. In a world where anarchy and self-help are the defining features, the fear of relative gain by other states may block cooperation that otherwise would prove beneficial.[5] We need to qualify this pessimism, however, by noting that there are likely to be different mixes of relative and absolute gains calculations depending on the situation. Bargaining with a longstanding rival will probably mean emphasis on the relative gains from the negotiation; but in settings of broad multilateral negotiations over trade liberalization, the emphasis will probably shift to the absolute gains from the bargain.

A second barrier to cooperation results from the fact that a nation's interests are rarely unified and that any agreement may well help some groups within that nation while harming others. Understanding cooperation means that we need to inquire into the politics of interest representation in national decisions and how domestic needs can be linked to international agreements.[6] For example, choosing to lower tariffs and join a free trading system will benefit those producers who are competitive within this new marketplace, probably damage those producers who are not competitive, and improve the choices for consumers. Whether the nation will drop its tariff protection depends in considerable part on the relative political strength of these three groups. If noncompetitive groups have control of the government or veto power over any policy change, they will prevent cooperation, even though it is in the interests of the nation as a whole.

A further barrier to cooperation lies in the structure of the incentives available to a nation. Using the example of participating in a free trade system again, each nation that joins can expect to receive some important benefit. But an even greater benefit, at least in political terms, may come from selling in the open markets of other nations while maintaining protected markets at home. Thus nations may fail to reach agreement because they want to have their cake and eat it too or because they fear that others will try to accomplish this for themselves. These fears and opportunities for profit inhibit cooperation, even when there are significant benefits available to all. But even here we can turn this point around and see how cooperation can still take place. If all nations refuse to cooperate and protectionism becomes the norm, then the costs of this failure may press nations to agree to cooperate. If those that defect can be punished, then the expectation of a continuing need for cooperation to maintain free trade may be sufficient to make this happen.[7]

The question of the extent and degree of cooperation among nations frequently depends on whether leaders focus more on the absolute gains they receive or on the relative gains; on the presence and success of existing institutions; on whether the domestic politics of nations contributes to or detract from cooperation; and on whether the costs of not cooperating are sufficiently painful for nations to overcome the inclination toward defection. To help illustrate these arrangements, we will now consider three cases of efforts at cooperation: one concerning macroeconomic policy coordination, a second involving attempts to manage flexible exchange rates, and a third looking at the formation of economic blocs. The first focuses on the economic summits beginning in 1975, the second focuses on the agreements to bring down the value of the dollar in 1985, and the last examines cooperation to promote economic integration in Europe, North America, and East Asia.

CASE I: MACROECONOMIC POLICY COOPERATION

As we discussed in Chapter 2, macroeconomic policy involves government efforts to manage the overall level of economic activity through fiscal and monetary policy. Traditionally, this means decisions regarding taxes and spending (usually made jointly by chief executives and legislatures) and decisions on expansion and/or contraction of the money supply and interest rates (usually made by central banks). Cooperation among nations on these decisions would include efforts to adjust and coordinate fiscal and monetary policy so as to produce some desired economic outcome that would otherwise prove elusive. In examining the economic summit process, we are interested in understanding the factors that promoted and inhibited cooperation and the outcomes of these efforts.

The fact that economic summits began in 1975 is not an accident.[8] Over the preceding four years, several events combined to produce incentives for cooperation among heads of state. The collapse of the Bretton Woods system of fixed exchange rates, the expansion of the EEC to ten members, the oil crisis of 1973–1974, and the world economic recession in 1974–1975 all created circumstances in which cooperation could improve many nations' positions. Elections in advanced industrial economies had increasingly come to depend on the fates of those economies. When the prosperity of virtually all was swept by external events, this gave national leaders a very good reason to become directly involved in managing the trade-offs associated with the resulting discussions and agreements with other nations. Finally, U.S. leadership, traditionally the linchpin in coordinating the world economy, seemed to fail in the early 1970s as the United States tried to solve its problems through efforts that frequently forced adjustment on other nations.

Perhaps the two most important factors promoting cooperation were the manifest ties of interdependence and the shared experience of working together under the Bretton Woods system. The leadership of the Western world had developed a strong recognition and understanding of their common fate since at least 1945. The events of 1971–1975, even as they often produced conflicting policies, nonetheless reinforced that understanding. Later events helped to bring home the consequences of not cooperating. In 1977 the United States pursued an expansionist macroeconomic policy but paid an important price when that policy resulted in a much larger current account deficit. This deficit came about when other nations failed to stimulate their economies, resulting in a poor showing for U.S. exports even as foreign goods were moving to the United States to take advantage of growth there. A similar fate befell France in 1981, when it too expanded alone. Eventually this helped force a socialist government to devalue the franc twice and to adopt a deflationary fiscal policy. Clearly, nations needed each other's export markets in order to pursue policies of balanced growth.

The economic summits, which began at Rambouillet, France, in 1975, can be divided into four groups. The first four summits, 1975–1978, were driven by the need to recover from the 1974–1975 recession. As such, they focused on the level and timing of economic stimulus and the management of demand, with secondary interests in protectionism and exchange rates. By 1978, after several years of discussion about coordinated fiscal stimulus, a genuine agreement was reached. It called for additional budget stimulus by Germany and Japan in return for a pledge by the United States to reduce its dependence on external oil. Although less than successful in the end, the 1978 Bonn agreement was perhaps the best example of nations adjusting their policies in ways that would not have happened in the absence of cooperation.[9]

The 1979 oil crisis and subsequent inflation and recession, from 1980 to 1982, not only scuttled the Bonn agreement but also shifted the economic summits' tone and substance. The hammer blows produced by these events prompted many nations to search for ways to protect themselves, by either securing oil supplies or finding domestic economic solutions.[10] Between 1979 and 1983 several nations shifted their efforts toward attacking inflation through applying monetary brakes and raising interest rates and toward making structural changes that transferred economic responsibility to their private sectors. The most nationalist-oriented in its policies was the United States, which combined a very restrictive monetary policy with a strong fiscal stimulus. The results were a massive federal budget deficit, rising interest rates, and a rising dollar. Following the dollar's rise was a rapidly increasing deficit in the U.S. current account. The summits of this period, reflecting the situation created by U.S. policies, involved limited efforts at coordination coupled with criticism of the looming imbalances in the world economy.[11]

By 1985 the enormous size of the U.S. current account deficit forced the United States to acknowledge these imbalances, and the summits shifted back toward international cooperation. The primary focus was management of a realignment of exchange rates, with the dollar falling and other currencies rising. The major agreements (to be discussed later) were made outside the summits, but these agreements were the core of the discussions within them, along with increasing recognition of the need for a new round of trade negotiations under GATT. The Uruguay Round began in 1987 as a result of the endorsement of the 1986 Tokyo Summit.

After 1991, the coordination of macroeconomic policies declined in importance. Several factors worked to produce this result. Foremost is the common commitment among U.S. political elites to ending the large U.S. budget deficits. As a result, manipulation of taxes and spending to promote economic growth in the United States fell into disuse. In its place came first a balanced budget and then rising surpluses. Much of this was made possible by the substantial and uninterrupted growth in the U.S. economy after 1992. By contrast, during this same time the Japanese economy has been mired in stagnation, and the Japanese government has attempted to use massive deficit spending to restore growth. The divergence in macroeconomic policies in the two largest economies could hardly be wider.

Taken together, the summits have only a spotty record of accomplishment. Probably the greatest barrier to success lies in each nation's domestic politics. Although all are tied together by interdependence, this has rarely created a politics that will produce decisions based on this interdependence. The formation of political power is based on interests that remain inward looking. At most, about one-third of a typical nation's GNP is based on exports (the United States is closer to one-tenth), and the combination of trade with internationalized capital has not yet formed a dominant political bloc in any nation. Political institutions represent national interests and their own bureaucratic interests, both of which reinforce the concept of sovereignty. Leaders of these groups will be very reluctant to surrender power to international institutions or systems of international cooperation. Further, the policy predispositions of nations reflect their domestic politics. Germany has consistently resisted inflationary policies, while the United States has frequently supported them. These differences have often prevented agreement on macroeconomic coordination.

At best, economic summits may work much like nuclear arms control negotiations in the 1970s: leaders exchange information about policy, build a sense of common purpose, and occasionally produce agreements with limited but desirable results. The key factor in such agreements over the 1975–1998 cycle was the convergence of domestic political developments and the United States' ability to assume the task of leading other nations to cooperate. When these agreements take place, as in 1978 and 1985, cooperation of some significance is the result. Otherwise, results are much more limited.[12]

CASE II: MANAGING EXCHANGE RATES

Does this somewhat gloomy conclusion hold up when we examine efforts to deal with the wild swings in currencies in the 1980s? Cooperation over exchange rates is much more substantial and continuous in some respects. At the same time, many of the same barriers to macroeconomic coordination can be found here. Perhaps the best conclusion is that the tension between cooperation and conflict may be more intense over exchange rates than over macroeconomic policy. Exchange rates engage internationally minded domestic interests more clearly than does macroeconomic policy, but the level and intensity of cooperation required are also much greater and more identifiable.

Exchange rates, whether under fixed or flexible systems, affect the interests of politically organized groups in a direct and intense way. The prices that exporters charge are greatly influenced by a falling or rising currency, especially for those who operate using the nation as a home base to manufacture goods for sale abroad. A rising currency confronts an exporter with the choice of absorbing the change and reducing profits or raising prices and risking lower sales. (Review the discussion in Chapter 2 if this does not make sense.) Meanwhile, importers must face the same choice when the currency falls in price. Banking interests engaged in overseas investments prefer a rising currency because this reduces the price of assets abroad and increases their buying power. The impact of exchange rates on domestic interests is reflected in the choices of a government concerned about its international accounts and about the votes of those interests.

Cooperation among nations over exchange rates engages a common interest in stability because this is the arrangement that strikes a balance between the different domestic interests involved. In a system of fixed exchange rates, this cooperation takes the form of establishing an initial price relationship of currencies and governmental intervention in foreign exchange markets to maintain the currency's value. Whenever a currency becomes out of line with the nation's balance of payments, cooperation is required to adjust the fixed rate of exchange.[13] The same circumstances in a flexible system may call for governmental intervention to move the exchange rate more into line with a current account balance. Flexible systems may also result in such rapid swings in a currency's rate that governmental intervention is needed.

Any significant effort to manage exchange rates under the flexible system operating since 1973 cannot hope to succeed unless the major economic powers cooperate. No nation acting alone can possibly control its currency. Without the combined resources and the overt and coordinated efforts of other nations, a single nation is essentially at the mercy of the market. Along with these powerful incentives for cooperation is the fact that exchange rates contain an inherent and substantial dimension of conflicting interests. A fall in one nation's currency and subsequent improvement in its current account are always matched by a general or more focused rise in the currencies of other nations, which then must suffer a worsened current account. At the same time, a failure to act in response invokes the immediate costs associated with price swings generated by the market. Indeed, one nation might coerce others into cooperation by acting to exacerbate market moves. These other nations will act to prevent an even worse outcome from inaction.

This interesting mixture of cooperative and conflictual dimensions associated with exchange rates is complicated further by several structural realities. Exchange rate markets are driven by many factors of supply and demand for currency in addition to those created by exports and imports. Differences in interest rates among nations can generate capital movements that move exchange rates up or down.[14] Thus, decisions about monetary or fiscal policy that affect interest rates can also influence the exchange rate. Markets are also affected by speculators trying to anticipate fluctuations in exchange rates. A currency's price sometimes changes as a result of perceptions of the nation's economic strength: stronger economies are expected to have stable or higher exchange rates and thereby attract those who want a stable store of value. What is clear is that exchange rates very often do not move in such a way as to adjust a nation's current account imbalances.

When intervention does take place, governments recognize that markets are simply too big for even coordinated action to control them over extended periods of time. The hope from intervention is to move markets in the direction of fundamental forces and to stabilize movements that might prove damaging if left alone. In pursuing these goals, central banks can rely on the market's tendency toward a herd instinct whereby traders play "follow the leader." This makes it possible for small amounts of actual intervention, when coupled with clear signals of cooperation and resolve by major nations, to produce major moves in exchange rates. The risk, of course, is that the herd instinct will go too far and lead to precipitate changes or even panic selling.

A final and perhaps most crucial feature of government involvement in foreign exchange markets is the role of market confidence in government policies and leaders. Fiscal, monetary, and exchange rate policies must be made with an eye toward how they will be received in world markets for equities, bonds, and foreign exchange. A clear negative reaction to a nation's policies can veto those decisions before they have an opportunity to succeed or fail. Because money markets are the main suppliers of credit to governments, the latter cannot ignore how these entities respond collectively to their actions.[15]

Managing Exchange Rates: 1985–1987

The context for international cooperation on exchange rates in 1985 was more than a decade of floating rates following the collapse of the Bretton Woods system of fixed rates, and severe imbalances in the world economy created by the U.S. budget and trade deficits. This meant that leaders needed to create a system for coordinating their behavior in the midst of serious economic difficulties.

Before 1981, U.S. international accounts were in equilibrium, while U.S. fiscal accounts were at historically high deficit levels. The tax cuts of 1981, coupled with increases in government defense and welfare spending, produced massive increases in the budget deficit. Between 1983 and 1986 deficits hovered around $200 billion, nearly three times the level in 1980. A tight monetary policy pushed interest rates to record levels, and this served to attract foreign funds, driving up the exchange rate of the dollar. The dollar rose from about 200 yen in 1981 to 270 yen in 1983 and moved between 230 and 250 for the next two years. The dollar rose much more against other currencies. It moved up about 60 percent against a weighted average of currencies and rose steadily from 1981 to 1985 from 2 German marks to 3.3.[16] The consequence was to put great pressure on U.S. exporters to raise their prices, while importers enjoyed the luxury of keeping prices low. U.S. merchandise exports, which had been growing at the same pace as imports from 1976 to 1981, stagnated and even declined from 1981 to 1986. Merchandise imports rose from $260 billion in 1981 to more than $340 billion in 1986.[17]

The United States had two basic alternatives for dealing with this problem: the policies of the 1980s could have been reversed and efforts made to make the United States more competitive internationally, or price levels could have been readjusted through a lower dollar without altering basic policy. Adopting the first alternative would have meant a rejection of the basic premises of the Reagan administration. Attacking the budget deficit through higher taxes would have permitted lower interest rates and thereby a lower dollar, but it also would have meant undermining both the administration's political position with upper-income groups and its image with others. Further, this policy almost surely would have produced a serious recession.[18] A corollary policy would involve lowering costs and increasing savings, investment, and spending on research and development to improve U.S. competitiveness.

Rather than take on the political dynamite of this option, the Reagan administration actually pursued two contradictory policies between 1981 and 1989.[19] For the first half of this period, the administration chose to ignore the international consequences of its policies (this is sometimes referred to as "benign neglect") and concentrated instead on the domestic economic boom that resulted. Officials simply accepted the large deficits, the rising dollar, and the subsequent growth of U.S. debt that was needed to finance the boom. But after the 1984 election, a policy of reducing the dollar while preserving existing fiscal policy emerged. Exporters were provided with price incentives to attempt to regain lost overseas markets, and importers were forced to raise prices. Domestically, the costs of adjustment were borne by consumers but were disguised by the intricacies of the connections between the dollar and imported goods.

Beginning in 1985, the new U.S. Secretary of the Treasury, James Baker, and his assistant, Richard Darman, moved to organize an international effort to lower the value of the dollar.[20] In a meeting at the Plaza Hotel in New York, the finance ministers and central bank heads of the G-5 (United States, Germany, Japan, France, and Great Britain) orchestrated a collective effort to increase the exchange value of the main nondollar currencies. This was to be accomplished by coordinated market intervention and other signals of determination to see this achieved.[21] Each country pledged a substantial sum of foreign exchange for this operation. Although initially scheduled for six weeks and a 10 to 12 percent drop, the dollar's fall actually extended until December 1987. Much of this period involved something other than smooth cooperation, as there was considerable disagreement over the wisdom of the dollar's continuing fall.

Between the Plaza Accord in September 1985 and the Louvre Agreement in January 1987, the dollar fell from 240 to 140 yen and from 2.8 to 1.8 deutsche marks.[22] The German government was ready to stop after a 7 percent mark appreciation. The Japanese became concerned at 180 yen. At the Louvre, in Paris, in February 1987, the United States reversed its position and supported a stabilization of its currency. This proved ineffective until after the stock market crash in October of that year.

How can we understand this effort to manage exchange rates and the taut mixture of cooperation and conflict involved? In terms of interests, the Reagan administration by 1985 was being subjected to a barrage of complaints from U.S. exporters about the high dollar, and sentiment in Congress, which also received these concerns, was increasingly protectionist. Some in the administration who were most committed to letting markets set exchange rates were replaced by more pragmatic officials. From the U.S. perspective, the ideal arrangement would have been to engineer a coordinated effort to push dollar values down while preserving the levels of foreign investment needed to sustain the budget deficit.

For the Germans, concerns centered on the importance of removing the imbalances in the world economy produced by the U.S. deficits without generating a dollar collapse. Further, a rising deutsche mark would help hold down inflation in Germany—always a key element of policy choice in that country. But German leaders also thought the imbalances were largely a U.S.-Japanese problem and preferred that most of the exchange rate adjustment come between the dollar and the yen. Perhaps most important from the

German perspective was preservation of the European Monetary System (EMS). This was an arrangement among 10 European states in the EEC to fix exchange rates for their currencies with each other and to coordinate fiscal and monetary policies. The Bundesbank, the German central bank, played the key role in this system, setting the standard for conservative policies and using its resources to maintain currency parities. German leaders feared that a precipitous decline of the dollar would put intense pressure on the EMS for realignment and might even force its breakup.[23]

By contrast, the Japanese were more receptive to dollar depreciation. They worried about the consequences of rising protectionist sentiments in Congress much more than did the Germans. Japanese financial sectors hoped to benefit from a higher yen, while some political figures saw exchange rate adjustment as preferable to structural changes in terms of openness to the world. Even so, the yen's massive appreciation eventually led to the disintegration of the domestic political coalition favoring this policy. Small- and medium-sized exporters were battered, and even large firms found themselves pressed to deal with the trade-off between raising prices and accepting lower profits. But the United States seemed determined to allow or to cause the dollar to fall and used noncooperation to prevent stabilization.

We should remember that the strategy of a lower dollar had the effect of rescuing the Reagan Administration from acknowledging the costs of its economic policies. Japan and Germany were being forced to bear most of the politically difficult costs of adjustment. These countries (especially Japan) had simply taken advantage of a situation created by the United States. But as the dollar continued to fall, the United States refused to participate in a stabilization effort. Instead, it attempted to hold out the possibility of sanctioning additional decline unless these countries agreed to stimulate their economies and/or make structural changes. The United States pressed this position because of the very slow improvement in the U.S. current account deficit. Only when fears of an end to foreign investment in the United States became intense did the United States reverse its position.

Conclusions

What conclusions can we reach about the process of cooperation in the two case studies? The study of international political economy has not developed a clear understanding of the sources of cooperation, nor can we predict its future direction. This brief review points out both the weakness of cooperation in macroeconomic coordination and the coercive elements of cooperation in managing exchange rates. The most interesting and important theoretical question raised by the exchange rate case concerns the behavior of the United States as hegemon. For much of the postwar period, the United States accepted the burdens of world leadership. Providing grants and loans, maintaining open markets for foreign goods, and supplying military security are but a few of many examples. The United States behaved as a liberal, somewhat benevolent, hegemon. The exchange rate case of the 1980s continues a trend

beginning in 1971 to emphasize a much more narrow and nationalistic definition of U.S. interests. The United States has been willing to use its continuing
power to force adjustments onto other, often allied, states. The implications of
this pattern for multilateral cooperation may turn out to be very negative and
to support the view that cooperation can diminish in the wake of a declining
hegemon.

At the same time, the globalization of finance has profound effects for
macroeconomic and exchange rate decisions. When we look more closely,
cooperation and coordination may be greater than the case studies initially
suggest. Much of this cooperation may derive from pressure generated by the
structural power of capital: mobile capital frequently punishes states whose
policies conflict with market expectations. There are three different contexts
in which cooperation may occur on macroeconomic and exchange rate policies: among national leaders, among central bankers, and during times of crisis. Efforts by national leaders to set and coordinate policies at annual summits
have had limited success. Because the politics of matters such as spending and
taxes is overwhelmingly domestic, agreement on timing and outcomes will
usually be difficult. Punishment of outliers by global markets may be the most
effective pressure on domestic policy makers. But this can take a long time.

A second context is the coordination of national monetary policy by central bankers and midlevel officials. Here it is possible on a daily, weekly, and
monthly basis to make interest rate, monetary, and exchange rate decisions
that follow markets and operate to coordinate results. Although mostly ratify-
ing market shifts and coordinating responses to markets, these fine-tuning operations occasionally succeed in making marginal adjustments to global
markets. The forums for this cooperation are periodic meetings of G-7 finance ministers, central bankers, and deputy finance ministers (sometimes
known as "sherpas") and regular meetings of national and supranational officials at the Bank for International Settlements, International Monetary Fund,
and Organization for Economic Cooperation and Development (OECD).

A third context, which somewhat recombines the first two, involves crisis
situations that threaten or potentially threaten the stability of the world economy. On several occasions—the 1982 debt crisis, the 1987 stock market crash,
the 1994–1995 Mexican peso crisis, and the 1985–1987 dollar exchange rate
misalignment—national leaders and financial officials have been able to act together to resolve serious problems. Often this is a result of the ongoing contact among lower-level officials. These efforts sometimes yield actions to
establish arrangements that anticipate crises. For example, in 1995 the United
States' central bank, the Federal Reserve, worked out a procedure to purchase
large amounts of U.S. government securities from Japanese banks in the event
that these banks are experiencing liquidity problems. And on a multilateral
level, members of the G-7 have proposed creating an emergency reserve of
money that could be used to support a country facing severe but temporary
financial difficulties in paying its debts.

From the early 1970s and the breakup of the Bretton Woods system, the incentives for cooperation on economic policies have increased, but its incidence

is less consistent. Although a calamity has not happened and stability has eventually occurred, no real institutions for macroeconomic or exchange rate cooperation have developed. The interests that produce stability seem ad hoc and uncertain. Perhaps most disturbing is the role of the United States, which has taken an increasingly nationalistic and even bullying posture in its international economic negotiations. The United States retains the power to force adjustments on other states while avoiding making difficult adjustments itself. This behavior may have undermined the ability of the major economic powers to work together effectively and may account in part for the movement toward economic blocs.

At the same time, institutional manifestations of and efforts at cooperation are much more substantial than at any previous time. A massive array of cooperative activities sustains the world economy every day. We now turn to a brief look at an example of multilateral cooperation with a much better track record, the World Trade Organization and its predecessor the General Agreement on Tariffs and Trade.

CASE III: THE URUGUAY ROUND AND THE WORLD TRADE ORGANIZATION

There is no better example of the entangling of cooperation and competition than the General Agreement on Tariffs and Trade (GATT) and the World Trade Organization (WTO). Tariff reductions, new trade rules, and new trade institutions derive from and amplify cooperation; at the same time, these actions not only provide the context for competition among nations and firms but also actually accelerate competition. The easing of trade restrictions accelerates the capacity for competition, at least among firms if not among states themselves. Further, the competitive process associated with nations and firms depends on the common rules and open system created by GATT and the WTO.

The WTO came into existence as a result of the successful completion of the Uruguay Round of GATT negotiations. Although eventual success was delayed by the difficult issues being addressed, the Uruguay Round was concluded with a comprehensive agreement among 117 nations reached in December 1993 and signed in Marrakech, Morocco, in April 1994. The new WTO, with a status equal to that of the IMF and World Bank, has more than 132 members, 29 with observer status.[24] The WTO is perhaps the best example of international cooperation based on a complex and detailed system of agreed-upon rules. It embodies a system of agreements relating to tariffs (GATT), trade in services (General Agreement on Trade in Services—GATS), and intellectual property (trade-related intellectual property rights—TRIPs). Collectively, these rules constitute much of the global multilateral trade regime. As such, this set of rules defines the laws and regulations nations may enact relating to international trade. Moreover, nations use these same rules as the basis for regulating their trade interactions and for settling disputes with each other. For example, the United States and the European Union have engaged in a series of trade conflicts relating to beef, bananas, tax policies, and airplane production. Each of these conflicts has been taken to the WTO for resolution.

In important ways the future of the free trade order erected after World War II came to be focused on the success of the last negotiating session of GATT, the Uruguay Round. Throughout the postwar era, the United States has served as the chief instigator and supporter of GATT, and the substantial decline in tariff levels can be attributed to its leadership. But from the outset in 1982 the Uruguay Round was beset by problems. Its purpose was to move GATT regulations into new areas and to deal with long-standing trade barriers and problems. These include tariffs and issues of trade in financial services, tourism and construction, trade involving copyrights and patents, and regulations restricting foreign direct investment.

The greatest stumbling block to an agreement came over agricultural trade—an area of U.S. strength and European and Japanese weakness. The United States has pressed Europe (with its [CAP]) (see Chapter 7) for 30 years to lower subsidies and tariff barriers on food products; it has pushed Japan to replace its total ban on rice imports and with tariffs. Because of the political power of farmers in these countries and the likelihood that freer trade would put many out of business, governments in Europe and Japan have resisted liberalization. The price of these actions is a high cost of agricultural products for consumers there and lost markets for U.S. producers. The United States was ready to open its markets (and thereby damage its producers) in textiles, sugar, and dairy products. But on several occasions the talks collapsed when the United States and Europe could not agree on the level of tariff reductions in agriculture.[25]

The Uruguay Round also took up the Multi-Fibre Arrangement and its restrictions on textiles and apparel. Proposed changes included replacing the MFA and its many bilateral agreements with a global quota. Dismantling this protectionist system for developed states' textile and clothing industries will be a boon for many Third World states. In return, developed states looked to gain better protection in the Third World for intellectual property, especially patents and brand names. Another arena for expanding GATT is trade in services like shipping, banking, tourism, and investment. Proposals at the Uruguay Round involved removing various restrictions, such as requirements for local content in production facilities owned by foreigners and shipping that must take place only in containers owned by the host nation.[26]

From the beginning, the Uruguay Round faced the problem of confronting the most difficult and entrenched trade barriers. Furthermore, the threat of a U.S. pullout if U.S. terms were not met has also hung over negotiations. The deadline of December 1990 failed to produce an agreement, and the talks moved into overtime. The main obstacle was the difficulty over CAP. The United States and other agricultural exporters wanted a dismantling of the CAP subsidies, whereas the Europeans resisted making anything but minor changes. The talks continued throughout 1991 with oscillating moods of optimism and pessimism about their ultimate success. In December, after another breakdown, the director general of GATT moved to break the impasse by confronting the parties with a "take it or leave it" set of compromises. But even this was met with much hostility in both Europe and the United States. In April 1992, further efforts to reach agreement failed, leading to a delay of serious negotiations until after the 1992 U.S. elections. Settlement of a trade dispute between the EU and the United States over oil seeds in late 1992 helped pave the way to compromise proposals and a final agreement.[27]

The difficulties in achieving a global trade agreement can be seen better if we think of this process as a complex and multilayered bargaining game. This is a game with a set of domestic winners and losers in each nation. Further, the game is being played without a hegemon that can make concessions, dispense rewards, and punish defectors across the system. The trick to a successful outcome is to gain international terms through agreement among many nations (by adjustment and compromise) that will provide domestic winners with strong enough incentives to convince them to back the agreement and overcome the resistance of losers. This becomes a series of simultaneous bargaining games—at the international and domestic levels—in which national political leaders try to manage toward a favorable conclusion. They are subject to pressure at home from a shifting balance of winners and losers based on the terms of the international agreement. And these leaders are also subject to pressure from abroad owing to the need to make concessions and adjustments in order to reach an agreement. Among the most powerful and advanced states, the national executive and other political leaders have a varying commitment to the postwar institutions of free trade and international cooperation. We should not be surprised when such negotiations frequently seem to reach an impasse, especially when a hegemon is absent. But also constraining choices is the importance of preserving the global economic order itself and fear of the consequences of a decline in cooperation.[28]

The Uruguay Round agreement signed in 1994 made important advances in many areas. Average tariff levels are to be cut by one-third, from just over 5 percent to 3.5 percent. The problems of nontariff barriers and trade conflicts have been addressed by clarifying the standards for dumping, quotas, voluntary export restraints (VERs), and subsidies. In agriculture, tariff levels will be slashed, subsidies cut, and the use of quotas restricted. And the Japanese and Korean rice markets will be partially opened to imports. The MFA's quota system will be phased out over 10 years, leaving tariffs in this area similar to those for other goods. Standards were also established for intellectual property. A General Agreement on Trade in Services was reached. It contains a statement of broad principles, but the lack of clarity and the exemption of areas such as shipping limit its impact.[29]

The most important part of the new agreement is the establishment of the World Trade Organization. GATT was never more than a limited institution to coordinate the negotiation of agreements; it never had the ability to adjudicate disputes or to enforce the rules. The WTO is a much more formal and robust international organization, similar to the World Bank and International Monetary Fund. High-level national representatives will meet at the WTO twice each year. Most significant is the new role in settling trade disputes among nations. Fact-finding bodies will issue reports to the WTO council that will serve as the basis for decisions. These outcomes may be taken to an appellate body, whose decisions are binding. Failure to comply with WTO rulings will result in fines and/or punitive actions by the aggrieved nation(s). The creation of the WTO shifts the process of managing trade relations from bilateral conflicts to a strong international organization, using rules established by multilateral agreement. One analyst has called the WTO "an International Court of Justice for world trade, with the institutional strength and legal mandate to ensure fair trade and global economic integration."[30]

The principles of the WTO represent a significant body of shared understandings about the process of multilateralism and about how international trade should be conducted.[31] This "code of conduct" established in the system of treaties is embodied in the legislation and regulations established by the nations that are members of the WTO. There are four main principles: nondiscrimination, reciprocity, market access, and fair competition. Perhaps the key principle is market access, which means that other nations have the right to sell goods and services in other nations' markets. Achieving this goal requires transparency for the rules of access. Nations must create an openly available system of rules and procedures providing for market access. The rules should establish a system of fair competition, or a level playing field for foreign firms operating within a nation. This principle is sustained, in part, by the idea of nondiscrimination, which requires that foreign goods be treated no less favorably than domestic goods. Additionally, nondiscrimination incorporates the concept of most favored nation, which requires that any trade concession granted to one nation be extended to that of all WTO members. Finally, WTO sustains the process of reciprocity in the negotiation of agreements. All of the treaties were worked out on the basis of a balanced set of concessions made by the various nations; none was required to make a concession that was not balanced by a concession made by other nations.

Completion of the Uruguay Round demonstrates the continued viability of multilateral support for free trade and provides considerable impetus for further advances in globalization. The WTO's political task is the creation of as seamless a global market as is possible in a world of sovereign states. Under the WTO regime, local political actors cannot adopt rules that have the effect of blocking trade. This marks a significant step away from protectionism and reduces the momentum toward regional trade as a basis for trade restriction. But this comes at a price. In the nineteenth century, the U.S. government assumed responsibility for establishing rules for the regulation of commerce across state lines. States and localities could no longer adopt rules designed to privilege local firms. Only later did the national government adopt rules that actually protected the interests of consumers and workers and even later such interests as environmental preservation. The creation of such rules on a global scale faces even more formidable obstacles, chiefly the sovereignty of states and the vast differences in standards and cultural values across the world. Cooperation among states to achieve global rules on the quality of goods, the treatment of workers, and the standards of environmental quality will be very difficult. However, the continuing importance of the WTO for establishing global rules seems assured. In November 2000, agreement was reached at a ministerial meeting in Doha, Qatar, to begin a new round of trade negotiations. And in December 2000, both China and Taiwan entered the WTO. The negotiations over China were especially protracted, partly because the transformation of China as a result of WTO membership will be substantial.[32]

At present, the WTO is framed to address the problem of protectionism, and it is supported in this effort by the tremendous web of global trade and financial interdependence and the domestic political interests and transnational coalitions tied to this connectedness. Nonetheless, there is considerable hostility to the WTO and to the globalization project it promotes. The meeting of the WTO in Seattle in 2000 witnessed a series of violent demonstrations and confrontations. The balance of power still remains with the political bloc favoring free trade and, except in the case of a prolonged global downturn, protectionism will not win the day.

Undoubtedly, the most important and far-reaching effort at international cooperation is the European Union. Less developed but also significant are other economic blocs, including the bloc between the United States, Canada, and Mexico and a potential bloc in Asia. We turn now to a consideration of these more narrowly focused systems of international cooperation.

CASE IV: ECONOMIC BLOCS

Globalization or Regionalization?

Does the evidence of globalization presented in Chapter 5 really represent greater international activity that is confined to nations in close geographical proximity? Are we seeing not the integration of a global economy but instead an acceleration of ties within several separating regions of the world? Should we be talking about the regionalization of the world economy instead of globalization? Is the future of the world economy one of fragmentation into exclusionary blocs? Does increasing cooperation among the nations of a region lead to decreasing cooperation with nations outside that region?

These are some of the questions raised by the growth of regional economic blocs like the European Union and the North American Free Trade Agreement. We need to understand better whether increasing regional integration leads to an expansion of intraregional trade that comes at the expense of trade with the rest of the world. This may have much to do with how open the regional arrangement is to the world and with how much it participates in multilateral trade agreements; in other words, with how much its rules and practices discriminate against outside goods and investment.

We believe that globalization and regionalization, at present, are not conflicting processes. Financial flows and trade destinations may have a regional bias, but the terms on which regionalization occurs are global. Competitive standards are global; tariff levels and trading rules are mostly established globally; capital is raised in global markets; technology and innovation meet global standards; and communication and innovation systems are globally based. At the same time, economic blocs have an inherently discriminatory bias: they involve the reduction of trade barriers only for members. The greatest threat to world trade could come if protectionist forces gain control of governments involved in economic blocs and use the machinery of the blocs to raise barriers.

The European Union

The European Union (EU) is by far the most significant and extensive effort at international economic cooperation.[33] It is the focal point of the most radical effort to shift political and economic responsibility to a transnational level; the EU seeks to expand its geographical scope even as it increases the scope of issues under its jurisdiction; and the EU is the most far-reaching effort to achieve monetary cooperation. The European Union is something of a real-life experiment in studying international cooperation, and its fate will help scholars judge the future of world politics.

Established in 1958, the European Economic Community (EEC), as today's EU was then called, has successfully promoted the reduction of tariffs and quotas among its members. The motives of its founding members contained an interesting mixture of political and economic thinking. France, in particular, wanted to incorporate Germany into a European system and tame any lingering aggressive German tendencies. Also important was the desire to expand the size of the market in which firms could sell their products. Reducing tariffs across the six original member states was designed to reap the benefits of freer trade and to improve the position of European firms in world markets. When *economies of scale* exist—that is, when the cost per unit of production falls as output rises—the costs of a firm would fall and global competitiveness would improve if the firm could sell in a larger market. The 1970s and 1980s produced expansion of the EEC from six to twelve members (see Table 6.1). But after the early 1970s there was little additional progress toward economic integration. This changed in December 1985, when the twelve EEC members signed the Single European Act (SEA).[34] This agreement moved integration beyond tariffs and sought to remove the myriad nontariff barriers created by having 12 countries enacting different laws.

The goal of the 1985 agreement was the free movement of trade, people, and money, and a specific timetable (December 31, 1992) was established for states to adopt more than 300 rules and procedures that would establish common standards throughout a newly named European Community (EC). The consequence has been more uniform standards, free banking across all EC nations, and lower costs of doing business. A single market of 340 million persons makes it much easier for companies to lower costs by expanding

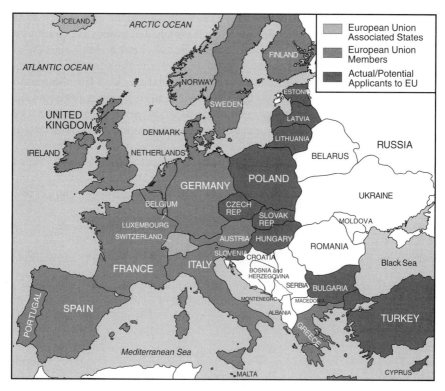

FIGURE 6.1 Expansion of the European Union

SOURCE: Organization for Economic Cooperation and Development.

production to sell to many more consumers. Progress toward a single market has been substantial but remains incomplete. In most (but not all) of Europe, passport controls have ended, and more than 93 percent of the 300 specific measures have been adopted. Beyond specific rules, the SEA also made important advances in decision-making procedures within the EC Council of Ministers (discussed later in more detail). Previously, the Council of Ministers operated with a national veto rule; with the SEA, many decision arenas are now decided by majority vote of the nations. This innovation greatly increased the policy flexibility of the EC.

In late 1991 the EC took steps to expand its membership and to shift its cooperation to a much more intense and significant level. In October the EC reached agreement with the seven members of the European Free Trade Area (EFTA) to bring them into the new trading system after 1992. EFTA nations would initially participate only as associated states and later apply for full membership. In January 1995 Austria, Finland, and Sweden were admitted as members. Several other nations, identified in Figure 6.1, are now lining up to become members.[35]

In December 1991, at Maastricht, the Netherlands, the European Community reached agreement on a broad set of goals that would bring about a much greater degree of integration. The Treaty on European Union (TEU) increased the range of issues subject to majority vote in the Council of Ministers, added to the European Parliament's responsibility, called for a common foreign and security policy, and defined a timetable and criteria for establishment of economic and monetary union (EMU). The result of this last process is a common currency. Implementation of the TEU in 1993 led to renaming the EC as the European Union (EU).

Organization of the European Union

The European Union's governing structure, especially after passage of the Single European Act (SEA), is a complex system of overlapping responsibility, decision making, and representation. The EU has four main units: one executive, two legislative, and one judicial. These include:

European Commission The Commission holds the executive power, vested in a president of the Commission (currently former Italian prime minister Romano Prodi). The Commission, composed of the president and 19 other commissioners appointed by the 15 heads of government (two commissioners each from the four largest nations) of the EU nations and supported by a staff of 15,000, is located in Brussels, Belgium. The commissioners, though appointed by member governments, are pledged to act in the EU's interest. The Commission has the responsibility for initiating legislation and legal action against member nations.

In 1999, the Commission experienced a political crisis of significant proportions when its entire membership was forced to resign as a result of an ethics scandal. The appointment of Romano Prodi was expected to lead to considerable changes in the Commission's organization and reform of its alleged cronyism and fraud.

Council of Ministers The Council is composed of representatives of member states and is the primary decision-making body in the EU. The Single European Act of 1987 broadened the scope of majority-rule decisions in the Council to include all actions required for creation of a single market. This enhances the Council's ability to act, as compared with a single state veto system. Voting is weighted by national population, which creates a complex system of coalition building.[36]

European Parliament The Parliament is composed of members elected by the populations of individual states for five-year terms. It is the only part of the EU that directly represents EU citizens. Traditionally restricted in its power over the budget, the Parliament could well gain wider authority over the budget, the right to initiate legislation, and the ability to approve the Commission. Members of the Parliament are grouped by political affiliation, not by nationality.

Table 6.1 Expansion of the European Union

Original Members

Country	Population	Per-Capita Income (PPP)	Percent Exports to EU States
Belgium	10.1	18,600	74.9
France	58.0	19,440	62.7
Germany	81.6	20,700	54.4
Italy	58.1	18,070	57.8
Luxembourg	0.4	21,500	n.a.
Netherlands	15.4	18,000	76.1
1973 Additions			
Denmark	5.2	16,400	54.4
Ireland	3.6	12,420	74.3
United Kingdom	58.2	16,400	56.0
1981–1986 Additions			
Greece	10.5	8,360	64.1
Portugal	9.4	9,890	75.1
Spain	39.2	13,310	71.2
1995 Additions			
Austria	7.8	18,700	66.1
Finland	5.0	15,500	53.2
Sweden	8.7	18,000	55.8
Associatied States			
Iceland	0.3	17,400	66.8
Norway	4.3	18,600	66.5
Switzerland	6.9	22,000	58.9
Actual/Potential Applicants			
Cyprus	0.7	15,470	40.8
Czech Republic	10.3	7,770	49.5
Hungary	10.3	6,260	49.5
Malta	0.4	8,280	74.4
Poland	38.5	5,010	55.6
Slovak Republic	5.4	6,450	49.5
Slovenia	2.0	8,100	n.a.
Turkey	57.7	5,550	51.7
Aspirants			
Albania	3.1	900	n.a
Bulgaria	8.6	4,470	40.8
Estonia	1.6	3,200	n.a.
Latvia	2.7	5,400	n.a.
Lithuania	3.7	5,000	n.a.
Romania	23.2	2,370	32.5

Population in millions   *PPP = purchasing power parity*

Per-capita income in U.S. dollars   *n.a. = not available*

SOURCES: OECD, World Bank, *The Economist,* IMF.

European Court of Justice The Court is composed of justices nominated by member states. Its responsibility is to render final decisions on disputes among EU institutions, member states, or on suits against EU institutions.[37] The process of political decision making in the EU is very complex but mainly involves the initiation of legislation by the Commission, its modification by the Parliament, and a final decision by the Court of Justice.

The European Union's expansion raises many important issues. Perhaps the most significant include problems brought about by incorporating several small and sometimes quite different countries. Voting in the European Commission is directly affected by expansion such as that in 1995. Already the distribution of votes gives much greater weight to smaller countries, but the locus of real decision making is with the four largest states. Whatever arrangement is made, expansion creates new dynamics of coalition building. Expanding membership also raises questions about political and economic compatibility. Some postcommunist states, such as the Slovak Republic, retain vestiges of authoritarianism. Many potential members have per-capita incomes far below the EU average. And those states with a combination of extensive agriculture and low-cost labor present special competitive problems for existing EU states.

Economic and Monetary Union (EMU)

The incentives for cooperation can be understood even better by considering in detail the process leading toward EMU. Here again, we draw on the earlier discussion of cooperation, especially the role of interests as defined by the benefits and costs of cooperation, the costs of not cooperating, and the impact of existing institutions on the calculations of member states.

In important ways, an economic and monetary union can be traced to the breakup of the Bretton Woods system of fixed exchange rates in the early 1970s. The chief result of that breakup was a realignment of currencies, with the dollar falling against all others. Many European nations (in and out of the EEC) attempted to set up a system of fixed exchange rates with each other so as to offer some protection against the falling dollar. This ultimately proved impossible because of the growth of private financial transactions, especially for purposes of speculation. Another round of dollar depreciation in the late 1970s helped rekindle the idea of a European system for managing exchange rates.[38] In 1978 most of the EEC (Britain was the main exception) joined in creating the European Monetary System (EMS). Its main feature was a system of linked exchange rates. Against a backdrop of fears of lost sovereignty and higher inflation, an exchange rate mechanism (ERM) was created. The ERM defined a small range of fluctuation for each currency in the system. The benchmark was a weighted average of currencies called the European Currency Unit (ECU). Each currency had a fixed rate against the ECU plus or minus 2.25 percent, and as a nation's currency approached this limit, its central bank was obligated to intervene to preserve the parity.[39]

The European Monetary System contributed to the movement toward monetary union through a conditioning of the major states' interests. In other words, the EMS demonstrated both the possibility of monetary cooperation and its benefits. Fluctuations in exchange rates narrowed considerably in the 1980s because of the EMS and the efforts to foster a greater coordination of monetary and fiscal policies. Over time, the ECU gained in credibility as an important denominator of EC transactions. By the late 1980s several defectors from the EMS were moved by its successes to join.[40] They found that the costs of not cooperating were substantial and that the benefits of participating in the system were significant enough to warrant joining. Specifically, the stability provided by fixed rates facilitated investment and planning by multinational firms, and this supported economic growth.

The key to the success of the EMS was the role played by Germany and its central bank, the Bundesbank. With Europe's strongest economy and the most intense commitment to monetary stability and low inflation, Germany offered the deutsche mark as a de facto key currency for the EMS. This role meant that participant nations used the deutsche mark for intervention in currency markets and, consequently, used German inflation rates and monetary policy as benchmarks for their decisions on these matters. The operation of this system resulted in a convergence of macroeconomic policies and inflation rates over the decade of the 1980s and opened the door for closer monetary cooperation.[41]

The decision to move toward an open market for goods in the European Community in the mid-1980s created a powerful momentum for a closer monetary union. Free trade also required the free movement of money. Permitting money to move freely, allowing banks to establish branches across the EC, and promoting the development of an integrated market for financial services contained a set of robust incentives for political cooperation designed to extend the EMS.

Also important as a conditioning factor was the further globalization of finance during the 1980s. Prompted by the massive U.S. trade and budget deficits, this process accelerated with the computer and telecommunications advances that made global financial markets possible.[42] European firms that were engaged in global trade demanded new financial services, and financiers saw new profit opportunities. The Single European Act of 1985 created a timetable for free capital movement and an integrated market for financial services throughout the EC. This tapped into the interests of these firms and provided an enormous boost for monetary union.

The Maastricht Agreement

The most important step toward Economic and Monetary Union (EMU) was taken at the meeting in Maastricht, the Netherlands, in December 1991. The goal established there was nothing less than creation of a single currency to replace the national currencies of the EC members. Perhaps more than any other action in the integration of Europe, a single currency would require the surrender of national sovereignty. Consequently, this is the most difficult move in the integration process.

Why take such drastic action? As with other events, the decisions for EMU and a common currency are a result of political and economic factors. The EU states share powerful interests in the success of the integration venture. At the same time, there is a complex mixture of complementary and conflicting interests that sometimes moves countries toward opposing views on the shape of future cooperation. And reaching agreement involves a process of negotiation whereby countries modify their preferences in order to gain an agreement. Germany—certainly the key player in the European Monetary System and the strongest advocate of financial stability—pressed for a rapid transition to a system modeled on the Bundesbank. This means a bank largely independent of control by politicians and capable of acting effectively to manage inflation. Ironically, many other EU states also prefer an independent bank because that would reduce German influence as compared to the EMS. In this arrangement, decisions about interest rates would no longer be set by the Bundesbank. The Maastricht Agreement meant that the Germans will give up the deutsche mark itself in return for a powerful European central bank. Other EU states likewise surrender an important element of their sovereignty, gain some additional role in policy making, and must lower their inflation rates and budget deficits.

Beyond this, interests begin to diverge and re-form in interesting ways. Many in France have long seen closer cooperation in Europe as an essential element in establishing a new political and economic entity capable of dealing effectively with the United States and Japan. French influence within a strengthened EU would be important, whereas dealing alone with the United States and Japan puts France in a position of weakness. Others in France take a more traditional view and see a renewed EU as the best means of containing German power.[43] Many British, especially among the Conservatives, fear the implications for national sovereignty of moves toward common monetary, economic, foreign, and social policies. Then British prime minister John Major urged delay in the timetable and less power for a central bank. Several EU countries with a tradition of an easy monetary policy, large budget deficits, and high inflation have expressed concern over the deflationary implications of a central bank. Some, including Spain, Greece, Portugal, and Ireland, pressed for more economic aid from the wealthier EU countries as the price for entering the new system. Despite the difficulties, these nations have accepted the responsibility to work toward these goals.

The economics of European integration also created powerful incentives for EMU and a single currency. Throughout the 1970s and 1980s, goods and especially capital moved more freely throughout Europe. And the SEA provided for an end to all capital restrictions and for free banking across the EC. As we have seen earlier, capital mobility forces states to choose between exchange rate stability and an independent monetary policy. The globalization of finance undermines the ability of all states to pursue an independent monetary

Table 6.2 Timetable for the Euro

July 1990	Capital controls are abolished.
December 1991	Maastricht Treaty is signed.
January 1994	European Monetary Institute is created.
December 1995	Single currency name is chosen—the Euro.
May 1998	Participants in the Euro are chosen. Exchange rates among participants are fixed. European Central Bank is established.
December 1998	Conversion rates for the Euro are fixed.
January 1999	Euro takes effect.
January 2001	Greece joins the Euro.
January 2002	Euro notes and coins are introduced.
July 2002	National notes and coins are withdrawn.

policy, so states concentrate on the costs of floating exchange rates. These are substantial, especially as trade and capital flows increase. One important cost is the resources that businesses devote to protecting themselves from exchange rate risks. Just the cost of foreign exchange transactions in Europe is estimated at $30 billion. Additionally, a common currency facilitates planning over the near and long term and will likely increase investment. The periodic realignment of exchange rates in the EMS made this only a partial solution. Thus a single currency came to be regarded by business and political leaders as the most efficient solution that would support closer integration.

How does the process of achieving a single currency work, and how has it fared since 1991? On a somewhat mundane, but practical level the actual effect of the Euro differs over time. (See Table 6.2.) In 1998, the 11 nations locked their exchange rates and then linked them to the calculated value of the Euro on January 1, 1999. Coins and bills of these nations will remain in circulation until 2002, but their value in foreign exchange until then is based solely on the Euro. Beginning in 1999, all stock and bond trading was denominated in Euros, as was all transactions between banks. And checks, credit cards, and even traveler's checks now come in Euros. One interesting problem that has arrived in 2002 is converting all machines that currently accept bills and coins. This may have the effect of increasing the use of various forms of electronic cash, such as "smart cards," for these purchases.

The machinery to make this transition happen is a bit more complex. The Treaty on European Union and subsequent agreements called for the formation of supranational institutions, a timetable of events (see Table 6.2), and a set of economic criteria that nations must meet to join the single currency. The institutional focus of the EMU is an EU-wide central bank, initially established in 1994 as the European Monetary Institute and succeeded by the European Central Bank (ECB) in 1998. The bank is run by its president—initially Wim Duisenberg, a former governor of the Dutch central bank—along with five other persons on an executive board. They are joined on a governing council by the governors of the central banks of the 12 Euro countries. Like its model, the Bundesbank, the European Central Bank will have as its main focus the task of maintaining price stability. This focus, the Germans' preference, will probably be challenged by those who prefer a looser monetary policy emphasizing economic growth. The ECB's considerable political independence probably means that the traditional concern of central bankers and financial elites—low inflation—will win out. But the lack of a track record makes any prediction very uncertain.[44]

For a nation to join the Euro, it had to meet the macroeconomic criteria established by the Maastricht Agreement. The nation's inflation rate, interest rates, public debt, currency stability, and budget deficit had to conform to certain standards. This is because a common currency can work only if monetary and fiscal policies are closely related. Inflation needed to be within 1.5 percent of the average of the three lowest in the EU, and long-term interest rates no more than 2 percent higher than the three best. The exchange rate must have remained within the narrow EMS band for the preceding two years without realignment. The budget deficit cannot be more than 3 percent of GDP, and public debt cannot be more than 60 percent of GDP. Those that initially did not qualify may join later after they meet the requirements.

There was considerable doubt throughout the 1990's about how many nations would be able to meet these criteria. Several countries were forced to cut spending substantially and also raise taxes in order to meet the budget deficit standard. As late as 1994, Italy's budget deficit was 10 percent of GDP and Spain's was 6 percent of GDP. Spain and Italy both were able to reduce their inflation rates from 6 percent in the mid-1990s to 2 percent by 1998, and Sweden slashed its inflation from 10 percent at the time of Maastricht to about 1 percent in 1998. The intensity of commitment to the Euro and the expectations of its benefits can be measured in part by the political difficulty of the efforts to meet the entrance criteria. In many cases, budget cuts provoked considerable political protest.[45] The leaders of Italy, Spain, France, and other countries believed they simply could not afford to be left out of the Euro. The criteria also convinced the Germans that they can safely exchange their stable deutsche mark for the untested Euro.[46]

Three of the EU fifteen initially chose not to participate in the Euro: Sweden, Britain, and Denmark. And one, Greece, initially did not meet the macroeconomic criteria.[47] The three who opted out share a common concern about the implications of the Euro for the level of cooperation and integration and the loss of national control over their own economic fate. For example, in Britain much of the opposition to participating in the Euro comes from conservative nationalists with an intense commitment to preserving British sovereignty. From the beginning of the negotiations for a single currency, conservative British governments have expresses reservations and even outright hostility. Within Britain, as within the other two naysayers, there is considerable disagreement over accession to the Euro. The Labour government under Prime Minister Tony Blair has begun to inch its way toward joining, but the sentiment in Britain is by no means clearly for participation. Perhaps the strongest reason for participation is the potential for being left behind, politically and economically. This was the centerpiece of the argument favoring the adoption of the Euro during the referendum in Denmark. But Danish voters were not persuaded and in September 2000 rejected the idea of adopting the Euro.

There are significant reasons for being inside the system. Management of the Euro will require a new level of cooperation among the Euro 12, and those outside the system cannot participate in formulating the precedent-setting initial policies. Moreover, the investment decisions of multinational corporations almost surely will be drawn toward the stability and opportunity created by the Euro zone. The elimination of exchange rate risk and the greater integration of these economies will provide powerful reasons for the expansion of investment. Outsiders risk being placed at the margin of global investment. Further, operating outside the Euro has considerable costs for British manufacturers. More than one-half of British trade is with the Euro area. This means a British firm's sales are in Euros (declining in value), whereas its costs are in pounds (rising against the Euro), creating a serious profit squeeze. Nonetheless, there are countervailing feelings among a considerable portion of the European electorate that the Euro forces too much homogenization by undermining a nation's ability to have a distinct set of political and economic policies.

There is a continuing question as to whether it is possible to design a common monetary policy that will apply to the great diversity of states and regions in the EU. In Spain unemployment is very high, and presumably this would call for low interest rates and a stimulative monetary policy. However, in Germany a policy of higher interest rates might be more appropriate. How to reconcile these differences is the task of the European Central Bank. Parallel concerns follow from a policy on exchange rates. A Euro exchange rate that might be fine with high-tech Germany may be devastating for low-tech Portugal. Of course, these decisions will be made against a backdrop of national interests, power relations, bargaining, and anticipations of reactions by international capital. One scholar has posed the economic choices as residing in a political space created by a loose and tight monetary policy for one dimension and a stronger or weaker Euro for the other.[48] The issue of exchange rate policy sets financiers (who can use a stronger currency in global markets more effectively) against exporters and manufacturers competing against imports (these groups find a lower exchange rate helps them compete in global markets). And monetary policy engages similar concerns: a tight policy raises interest rates and pushes up the currency, whereas a loose policy lowers interest rates, allows the currency to fall, and stimulates economic and job growth. This places exporters in league with labor unions on both issues and financiers allied with those who benefit from imports—often multinational firms—on the same side. Given the conflicting interests produced by the long-standing German preferences for high interest rates and low inflation and the continuing high levels of European unemployment, the ECB's choices will not be easy.

Some of the Euro's benefits and consequences have already been mentioned. The costs of doing business will decline, and firms' ability to make long term plans will increase. But the really important impact of the Euro will be the efficiency gains it spurs. One indicator of the remaining national character of most of the EU economies is the substantial gaps in the prices for the same goods across the different economies. These differences are often disguised through pricing in national currencies and the calculations involving exchange rates. For example, in early 1999 the same Japanese-made camera sold for the equivalent of $350 in France and $240 in Germany. Pricing in Euros will make comparison easier and encourage arbitrage buying in low-price areas and selling in high-price areas. The increased competition will mean that overall prices are likely to fall and more closely approximate world prices. And falling prices will shift resources from high-cost to lower-cost areas, resulting in efficiency gains. The greater ease in selling across the entire region will lead many firms to restructure, again boosting efficiency. The Euro-wide banking system and capital markets that emerge should lower average interest rates and improve firm decision making. These efficiency gains depend on the flexibility of resources like capital and labor moving across borders and out of inefficient industries and into more efficient areas (remember the discussion of comparative advantage in Chapter 2).[49]

The Euro's global implications come in the rising competitiveness of EU-based firms and in the Euro's potential role as a global currency. Since World War II, the U.S. dollar has operated as the primary global, or reserve, currency. This is because the dollar has been accepted in payment almost everywhere and people around the world are willing to hold dollars without converting them to their own currency. Goods in international trade frequently are priced in dollars, international lending frequently is done in dollars, and the United States has reaped the benefit of paying for its trade deficits with dollars. There has been some recent erosion in the dollar's role as reserve currency, but not much. Between 1980 and 1997, global reserve currency holdings in dollars declined from almost 69 percent of the total to about 57 percent. This reflected mostly growth in the world economy of Asian states; there was little change, for example, in the role of the deutsche mark. Also in 1997, 52 percent of all international debt issues were in dollars, and 28 percent in EU currencies; in the same year, 45 percent of all international lending was in dollars, with 17 percent in EU currencies.[50] The existence of a single EU currency, used in an area that now rivals the U.S. in population, trade, and GDP, may produce inroads into the dollar's dominance. If this happens, the United States may need to pay higher interest rates to sell its bonds around the world. So far, most U.S. leaders have expressed little concern, preferring instead to concentrate on the global benefits of a more competitive Europe.

These hopes for the Euro have been placed on hold because of its weakness in global foreign exchange markets. When inaugurated, the Euro was trading at US$1.17; only 21 months later it had fallen to near US$0.85. Why this decline? Much of it comes from the relative dynamism of the U.S. economy and global investors' desire to place their funds there. This means they will need to buy U.S. dollars and some of them will be selling Euros. Other global investors did not see Europe as an equally attractive place for investment. Foreign exchange traders and speculators, seeing the same preferences of global investors, sold Euros to take advantage of the expected decline. As often occurs in markets, the momentum of the process carried the Euro lower and lower until a coordinated intervention by U.S., European, and Japanese central banks stabilized its exchange rate. What are the consequences of the falling Euro? The prices of Euro-area exports fall, the prices of goods imported into the Euro area rise, and the earnings of many multinational firms operating in Europe fall in terms of their home currencies. But most significantly, the Euro's ability to challenge the U.S. dollar as a store of value has been undermined by its drop. The decline in the Euro abated in late 2001, but the Euro's potential as a global currency remains unrealized.

Now that the Euro has been implemented successfully, the next great issue for the EU is enlargement—the expansion of its membership into eastern and southern Europe. As with other great decisions in the EU, this also is a complex tangle of political and economic motivations. Perhaps the most important is the effort to end the remaining vestiges of the Cold War and its division of Europe, a division that mirrors the lines of pre-Cold War days in economic terms. Bringing the nations of eastern and southern Europe into the EU would extend the institutional system that brought peace and prosperity to Europe. The EU system of diminished nationalism, expanding democracy, and open markets would come to areas marked in the past by war, authoritarianism, and poverty and would lead, it is hoped, to the same historic shift as in western Europe. These goals are especially strong in Germany, a nation that historically coveted control of eastern and southern Europe but today wants to ensure "stability and democracy through European integration."[51] And a clear majority of the populations of many of the potential entrants also wants to be part of the EU, even with the difficulties and changes this would produce.

The substantial gap in income and wealth between east and west is both the attraction and the barrier.[52] The obvious benefit is the promise of higher incomes for those holding resources conveying a comparative advantage— knowledge workers eager to work for relatively lower wages are the best example. By contrast, those who work in old state-owned enterprises or who operate one of the many inefficient farms will find themselves in economic difficulty. Politically, the new EU members will be required to demonstrate acceptance of democratic principles and must adopt the body of EU law—the *acquis communautaire*. The widespread enthusiasm for the EU could become much more divisive as some of the consequences of integration become clear. Among the large states of the EU, only the Italians and the Spanish are positive toward enlargement. This is because the difficulties associated with enlargement are less daunting there. Can the EU maintain its focus and political cohesion with a membership nearly twice as large and much more diverse? Can the EU afford to extend existing social policies and agricultural support systems to the new and much poorer states to the east and the south? How will the integration of these large, mostly poor populations into the duty-free markets of the EU affect the location of industries and employment? Of course, this last matter is a point of significant conflict between labor and management in Europe. Workers fear the competition of "cheap labor" even as the owners and managers of firms see this as an avenue of greater competitiveness and profits.

Conclusions

Developments in the EC and EU after 1985 are certainly the most far-reaching efforts in international cooperation. Given the history of conflict in Europe in the twentieth century, the possibility of a politically and economically united Europe is an extraordinary accomplishment. The driving forces behind these recent moves are powerful structural changes in the world economy, including the decline in U.S. economic leadership, the explosion of globalization, and the new competitive climate in the 1980s and 1990s. The SEA decisions should be seen as a response by elements of the European political and economic elite to changes in the world economy of the 1980s. Most important were the decline of the United States as the primary source of cutting-edge technologies and the most innovative production techniques and the U.S. abdication of responsibility for the international monetary system. Much of the political and economic elite of Europe concluded that they could no longer rely on a U.S.-based system for economic organization. Relying on the Japanese for technological developments—much as the Europeans had done on the United States for 30 years—was not seen as a viable option. The Europeans did not have common security or cultural interests with Japan, a country that many saw as an economic predator. Contributing to these conclusions was the failure of the individual national economic strategies of the 1975–1985 period. The decision was to establish a system that could be much more self-sufficient. A single large market would justify bigger research-and-development expenditures and would promote cost savings from economies of scale. A single monetary system could also help protect from the vagaries of U.S. exchange rate policies, and the newly competitive European firms could defend Europe from the Japanese.[53]

The Maastricht decisions to move toward a European Union are closely related to the end of the Cold War in Europe in 1989–1990. For approximately 40 years the integration process in Europe was bolstered by a common European and American need to deter and counter Soviet power in Europe. Though separate institutions, the EEC and the North Atlantic Treaty Organization (NATO) had similar origins and derived from similar purposes. The fear of the Soviets helped overcome deep and historical conflicts in Europe. With the Soviet threat receding, many Western European countries felt that further progress toward integration was needed to avoid losing the existing gains from closer integration. This goal was further sustained by feelings in France and Germany that a united Germany needed to be retied to Europe and in a more fundamental manner through a common currency. It is telling that the response of European states to structural changes in the international security and economic environment is to increase cooperation.

Today, the state of cooperation in Europe is both more advanced and more insecure than in the recent past. Much of this is due to the economic and political weakness of the Euro. The new currency has not been the resounding economic success many had expected, and this has degraded its support among economic elites. And rejection of the Euro by Danish voters in September 2000 probably means the British and the Swedes will wait even more before deciding to join. The political economy of the Euro presses nations in Europe even harder to structure their economies for international competition, which usually means tax cuts and deregulation favorable to capitalist investment. Often this position collides with welfare state preferences common in much of Europe. The preference for globally competitive firms and closer political cooperation does not have the same political resonance among much of the European public as with its elites. Most likely, European cooperation will be forced into a holding pattern, with its fate in the hands of global investors and European voters. This outcome is made even more likely by the difficulties of enlargement. The burdens on the populations of the EU will be considerable even as the benefits seem remote. Achieving global economic competitiveness and establishing a bigger sphere of peace are noble but demanding goals, and the they will sorely test Europeans' capacity for cooperation.

A North American Trade Bloc?

Building on prior trade arrangements, the United States, Canada, and Mexico negotiated a North American Free Trade Agreement (NAFTA) with the purpose of eliminating virtually all barriers to trade among the three nations.[54] The first step was a free trade agreement between Canada and the United States, which took effect in January 1989. By 1999 essentially all tariffs on goods and services had been eliminated between these nations. NAFTA was signed by Mexico, Canada, and the United States in December 1992 and was ratified by the U.S. Congress in November 1993 after additional side agreements were reached. The terms of the massive document call for reduction of trade barriers spread over a 15-year period, with different schedules for different products. But most of the reductions come quickly, and the consequences for trade growth could be seen almost immediately. The United States' concerns that Mexico would be used as a production platform by third parties to the agreement were restricted, and Canadian worries about the onslaught of U.S. cultural products and Mexico's desire to retain control of its energy production led to these areas being treated as exceptions to the agreement. The principal institution established by NAFTA is the North American Trade Commission, which is designed to settle trade disputes.[55]

The motivations for the United States in pursuing these agreements stem primarily from difficulties in multilateral trade negotiations in GATT and from the competitive pressures generated by the movement toward a single market in the EC. Urged on by its own trade problems—the need to expand

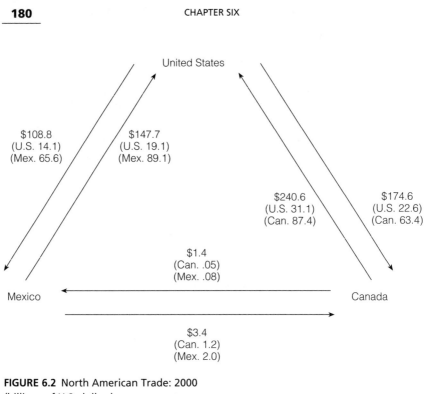

United States

$108.8
(U.S. 14.1)
(Mex. 65.6)

$147.7
(U.S. 19.1)
(Mex. 89.1)

$240.6
(U.S. 31.1)
(Can. 87.4)

$174.6
(U.S. 22.6)
(Can. 63.4)

$1.4
(Can. .05)
(Mex. .08)

Mexico   Canada

$3.4
(Can. 1.2)
(Mex. 2.0)

FIGURE 6.2 North American Trade: 2000
(billions of U.S. dollars)
(figures in parentheses = percent of total exports)

SOURCE: International Monetary Fund. *Direction of Trade Statistics Quarterly, 2001.*

markets for exports and to close a yawning trade deficit—the United States in the early 1980s pushed for a new round in GATT to reduce barriers to trade even more. For much of the decade this was a slow and frustrating process. Negotiating free trade agreements (FTAs) proved to be a quicker way of establishing trade relationships more to the liking of U.S. political leaders. These leaders also hoped that bilateral agreements involving preferential access to the large U.S. market would spur negotiations in GATT. One additional purpose of extending free trade to Mexico was to reinforce the liberalization of that country's economy undertaken after 1985.

For Canadians, preserving access to the U.S. market and developing a clear set of mechanisms for settling trade disputes constituted the main considerations. Canada and the United States represent the world's largest bilateral trading relationship, and Canada is very dependent on the United States for markets and investment. Much of this trade was in automobiles and auto parts, spurred by the 1965 agreement that established free trade in cars. American firms employ 1 million Canadians, while Canadian firms employ 740,000 American workers. Canadian leaders wanted to stabilize and improve access to the United States. Some also saw Mexico as a potential market and production site.[56]

Mexico's decisions relating to an FTA with the United States are conditioned by the size of its trade with the United States and similar fears of U.S.

protectionism. Further, the acceptance of free trade represents a radical departure in Mexico's foreign economic policy. In 1985 Mexico adopted a strongly liberal policy in trade, thereby casting aside a long tradition of protectionism. Reacting to an enormous foreign debt, a collapse in oil prices, and years of low increases in productivity, the Mexican government moved toward opening its markets to foreign competition and toward stimulating exports of manufactured goods. By 1987 tariff rates had been cut in half, quantitative restrictions drastically reduced, and price controls virtually eliminated.[57] This strategy accentuated the importance of access to the U.S. market. Perhaps the clearest result of the liberal trend was the expansion of the *maquiladoras,* or export-processing zones in Mexico. Here imports of parts and exports of assembled goods take place without tariffs. These zones expanded dramatically after 1985, to the point that nearly 500,000 Mexican workers were directly employed in *maquiladora* factories before NAFTA took effect.

Each country has significant political opposition to freer trade. In Canada the 1988 agreement became the major issue in national elections, with opponents warning that jobs would be lost to the United States. There was significant resistance in the United States to the deal with Mexico, due mostly to the substantial differences between the two economies. Labor unions objected strongly, as did many environmentalists; producers in low-tech, low-skills industries; and some agricultural interests, such as citrus growers. These groups are bound together by fears of a loss of sales and jobs to imports from Mexico or from the transfer of production to what they see as a low-wage, environmentally lax Mexico. In Mexico, opposition centered on nationalistic fears of U.S. corporations overwhelming Mexican-based businesses. Many worried about the loss of economic sovereignty.

Recall that in the discussion of free trade in Chapter 2 we argued that free trade is on balance beneficial but that it can produce major adjustments and restructuring that are very difficult for some groups. Free trade usually undermines the economic position of owners and workers in sectors that are not competitive in global terms. Businesses in these areas will go bankrupt, and workers will lose jobs as resources are shifted to areas of the economy enjoying a comparative advantage. The psychological and cultural costs of this process can be very great. The benefits of free trade come in the form of higher-quality and lower-priced imports that replace domestic production. Those groups in a country that are able to compete effectively in global or regional markets will be strong supporters of free trade, as they were in the case of NAFTA. The strongest supporters of NAFTA in the United States and Canada were multinational firms and investment capital, which were eager to consolidate and take further advantage of a regional production-and-investment system.[58]

The short-term consequences of NAFTA have been much as expected. Perhaps the clearest beneficiary is Canada, where exports to the United States have risen sharply and have helped increase support for free trade.[59] Trade between the United States and Mexico has grown but was adversely affected by the peso crisis of the mid 1990s. The 50 percent drop in the peso's value against the dollar has hurt U.S. exports and benefited Mexican exports. Nevertheless, there is evidence that the restructuring based on efficiency gains is proceeding. Taking advantage of the power of global communications, firms have begun to locate different parts of the production process where the combination of cost and productivity is the greatest. This often means low-technology production and assembly in Mexico and high-technology manufacturing and research and development in the United States. The regionalization of automobile production, already developed before NAFTA, fits this pattern. A large proportion of the trade crossing borders is intrafirm or affiliated-firm trade in automobiles and parts. This pattern has spread to other industries as falling tariffs combine with global finance and communications to permit regionalization of production for smaller and smaller firms.[60] The employment consequences of the regionalization of production are unclear, especially for the United States. Because Mexican tariffs were much higher than for the United States, several years may be needed to determine the net results.

Perhaps the most significant overall effect of NAFTA is the boost given to liberal tendencies throughout Latin America. In Mexico the severe peso crisis led not to nationalism and protectionism but rather to accelerating privatization of state enterprises. In 1994 Chile reached an agreement with NAFTA states to negotiate full membership in the FTA. Other Latin American states have already moved substantially toward free trade. As part of establishing and invigorating small regional free trade agreements, Latin American states between 1984 and 1994 cut tariffs for goods from the rest of the world from an average of 56 percent to 12 percent. A series of sometimes crosscutting free trade agreements now structures much of the trade relationships within Latin America: Group of Three (Mexico, Venezuela, and Colombia), Caricom (Trinidad and Tobago, Jamaica, Suriname, and several microstates), Andean Pact (Venezuela, Colombia, Peru, Ecuador, and Bolivia), Mercosur (Brazil, Argentina, Uruguay, and Paraguay), and the Central American Common Market (Guatemala, Costa Rica, El Salvador, Honduras, and Nicaragua). Basic agreements have been reached to establish a Free Trade Area of the Americas by 2005. Many states see the advantages that Mexico has through privileged access to the U.S. market, including the attraction this provides to global capital. NAFTA's existence and success appear to demonstrate the costs of not cooperating in establishing free trade and thereby to generate additional cooperation among states.

An East Asian Trade Bloc?

East Asia is the most complex and dynamic of the three regions and is the least organized in political terms. The dominant power in Asia—the United States—has not pushed for regional economic cooperation, preferring instead to work out bilateral relationships. The natural leader of the integration process is Japan because of the size and level of development of its economy. But Japan carries significant political burdens from World War II. Before the war, Japan organized what it called the Greater East Asian Co-Prosperity Sphere at the point of a gun, and many Asians have negative memories of Japanese imperialism. This limits the ability to organize any formal political framework for economic integration. Unlike Europe and North America, Asia has no regionwide institutions and has only very limited panregional agreements or subregional institutions. The Association of South East Asian Nations (ASEAN) has historically operated as a political forum for seven nations and in 1992 took steps to organize a free trade area.[61] The Asia-Pacific Economic Cooperation Conference (APEC) has existed as a broad forum for discussion and limited coordination of data collection. But APEC shows no signs of advancing toward a regional political and economic institution to regulate trade.[62]

Even a brief consideration of East Asia's complexity quickly reveals some of the problems for broad cooperative arrangements similar to those in Europe and North America. East Asia lacks the similarity of economic development of Europe or even NAFTA. There is one large developed state (Japan), three small states with high incomes (Australia, Singapore, and New Zealand), several small states of middle to lower incomes (Korea, Taiwan, Malaysia, Thailand, and the Philippines), one large and low income state (Indonesia), one very large but poor state (China), and several small and very poor countries (Burma, Cambodia, Laos, Vietnam). East Asia is the fastest-growing region in the world, with many countries achieving sustained GDP growth above 6 percent. The dynamic properties of globalization may be affecting this region in significant ways, producing new forms of economic integration.[63] The creation of complex production networks, based around information technology and different aspects of the production value chain and located in countries at very distinct levels of development, may require unprecedented mechanisms for integration.

East Asia contains many actual and potential poles of economic power, and this diversity may undermine the capacity for cooperation. In addition to Japan, the newly industrialized economies (NIEs) of Korea and Singapore have become important actors in their own right. A Chinese economic area (CEA) consisting of China, Taiwan, and Hong Kong unites advanced industrial capabilities and substantial capital resources with a huge labor pool. And ASEAN states have developed to the point that they have begun to formulate independent economic ambitions. Laced through each of these subregional situations is Japanese foreign direct investment, but also present are U.S. investors and sometimes a very large presence by Korea, Hong Kong, and Taiwan. Japanese FDI directed toward manufacturing production is mainly a result of the rising yen that followed the Plaza Agreement in 1985 and expanded rapidly until 1990. Since 1990 Japanese FDI has leveled off and even begun to decline. The economic links across East Asia established by Japan are important and have resulted in emulation of the Japanese system at the governmental and firm level. But there is little evidence of bloclike activity here.[64] The diversity of levels of development and the number of actors in East Asia make the political organization of economic integration quite difficult.

Economic Blocs and the Future of the World Economy

Regional economic blocs are significant focal points for cooperation among economically advanced states. In the European Union, real and important transfers of sovereignty have taken place, and more are in sight. The persistence of the EU following the end of the Cold War, and especially its moves toward greater integration and expansion of membership, provide strong support for the view that cooperation is possible and that institutions enhance cooperation.[65] Although NAFTA has few institutional parallels and cooperation is far less important, it too is moving toward expansion of membership. Once begun, economic blocs generate a logic of expansion. Those outside the bloc want to gain the benefits of cooperation and to avoid the costs of not cooperating. This process is evident in Europe and in the Western Hemisphere.

The main concern generated by economic blocs is the potential for fragmentation in the world economy. The guiding trade principle since 1945 has been *multilateralism*—meaning the establishment of a widening arc of states, all of which participate in the world economy on basically the same terms. Thus nations negotiate together the terms for access to each other's economies and extend these terms to virtually all nations. Economic blocs represent discrimination and exclusion and suggest the possibility of economic struggle extending to political and even military hostility. Economic blocs establish the institutional framework for much greater discrimination and separation, should the political basis within nations shift in this direction.

At present, the chances of this shift are remote; such an outcome would require a revolutionary political change within states over free trade and protection. This political transformation not only would need to include constructing a plausible strategy for bloc self-sufficiency but also would need to overcome the very large interests that each bloc has in access to other areas of the world. A rough measure of this interdependence across blocs is Table 6.3.

The evidence indicates a growing tilt toward intraregional trade in each area, with the most pronounced internal shift coming in East Asia. But there are other significant trends: an increasing interdependence between North America and East Asia and growing connectedness between the EU and East Asia. Further, notice the absolute levels of trade: 40 percent of EU trade is with non-EU members, 16 percent of EU trade is with North America and East Asia, 55 percent of East Asian trade is outside the region, and more than 60 percent of North American trade is with other parts of the world. The largest and most powerful states are the most interdependent with the world outside their region. For example, Germany, Italy, France, and Britain have more than the EU average of 40 percent of non-EU trade; the United States conducts only 28.6 percent of its trade with other NAFTA states; and more than one third of Japanese exports are to the United States and Germany alone. Any move toward significantly exclusionary blocs would need to overcome the substantial interdependence among regional blocs indicated by this data.

Perhaps the most convincing evidence that regional blocs are unlikely to lead to global fragmentation is the successful conclusion of the Uruguay

**Table 6.3 Intrabloc and Interbloc Trade
(in percent of total exports and imports)**

		With: EU	North America	East Asia
EU	1975	51.2	8.7	3.7
	1992	59.8	8.0	8.0
NAFTA	1975	18.8	34.8	15.7
	1992	17.0	38.9	27.4
East Asia	1975	11.5	22.6	30.6
	1992	14.3	22.9	45.0

SOURCE: Adapted from Masami Yoshida et al., "Regional Economic Integration in East Asia: Special Features and Policy Implications," in Vincent Cable and David Henderson (eds.), *Trade Blocs?* London: Royal Institute of Internation Affairs, 62–63.

Round of GATT in December 1993 and the creation of the WTO. Long delayed by conflict, the Uruguay Round attempted to deal with several important exceptions to and areas of exclusion from previous GATT agreements, in addition to reducing tariffs. As we discussed earlier, since the 1940s GATT has been a very important multilateral forum because of its membership of more than 100 nations and the significance of its ability to gain global agreement on substantial tariff reductions. The new GATT agreement extends its jurisdiction to agriculture, services, intellectual property, investment, and textiles. But most important is the establishment of the World Trade Organization (WTO) as the successor to GATT, with new authority for managing and enforcing the rules of international trade. The WTO and the new Uruguay Round agreement significantly undermine the ability of regional blocs to engage in additional discrimination and strengthen the forces of multilateralism. The most important consequence of regional blocs is to increase market access, and for now, regionalization and globalization are complementary, not contradictory, processes.

CONCLUSIONS

Cooperation among advanced industrial states has become both more essential and more difficult over the past two decades. The ability of these states to bargain over concessions and thereby to produce a mutually beneficial coordination of behaviors is much more important now because of the growth of globalization. Failure to coordinate macroeconomic policies can have sudden and rude consequences; ignoring exchange rate effects can result in enormous and persistent international imbalances. Nonetheless, the political relationships needed for cooperation to succeed are problematic.

Much of this can be traced to the decline of U.S. hegemony. The United States can no longer create the world economy's cooperative structures and gain acceptance for them. For perhaps the last 30 years, U.S. officials have been much more conscious of the costs of leadership, especially a growing current account deficit and the burdens of defense spending. The considerable power remaining to the United States has sometimes been used to push other states to accept some of these costs. But U.S. weaknesses, measured by the relative decline in its weight in the world economy and by large budget and trade deficits, undermine the capacity for creating order. U.S. power is big enough to be an essential element of any multilateral system and big enough that other states will sometimes have to cooperate (exchange rate cooperation in the 1980s is a good example). And yet the U.S. ability to fashion a multilateral system of cooperation has largely vanished. The era of U.S. hegemony has been replaced by a system of U.S. dominance in which genuine bargaining and meshing of interests are prerequisites for cooperation. Frequently, cooperation has required disproportionate concessions by the Japanese and Europeans.

The European Union is certainly the best example of an effective system of cooperation responding to the ties of interdependence. This is a result of efforts to cope with the rush toward connectedness in the 1980s, the need to protect member nations from some of the unfavorable consequences of U.S. decline, and the rise of Japan and the end of the Cold War. Along with the North Atlantic Treaty Organization, the EU provides a powerful institutional context promoting cooperation in Europe. Circumstances favor incorporating additional members into the EU and establishing closer economic and political union by the end of the century.

The record of cooperation in the EU has not always extended to multilateral arrangements among the EU, United States, and Japan. Interdependence here has advanced enough to matter significantly in national political life, but not enough to generate frequent and effective cooperation. Powerful incentives for cooperation exist, but very strong barriers frequently prevent this from taking place. When we remember that interdependence also has uncomfortable consequences—competition, involvement of other nations in what once were domestic political choices, and constant adjustment to external demands—we are reminded that conflict is often a partner in efforts at cooperation.

NOTES

1. This definition relies on Robert Keohane, *After Hegemony*, Princeton, N.J.: Princeton University Press, 1984; Joseph Grieco, *Cooperation among Nations*, Ithaca, N.Y.: Cornell University Press, 1990; and Robert Putnam and Nicholas Bayne, *Hanging Together*, Cambridge: Harvard University Press, 1987.

2. Robert Keohane and Lisa Martin, "The Promise of Institutionalist Theory," *International Security*, 20.1, Summer 1995, 39–51. A critical review of the efficacy of international institutions in promoting cooperation is John Mearsheimer, "The False Promise of International Institutions," *International Security*, 19.3, Winter 1994–95, 5–49.

3. Robert Keohane, "International Institutions: Can Interdependence Work?" *Foreign Policy,* 110, Spring 1998, 82–96.

4. Scholars have used the terms *absolute gains* and *relative gains* to describe the differences in the ways the leaders of a nation might evaluate the benefits from a bargain with other states. *Absolute gains* refers to a situation in which leaders focus only on the size of the gains their nation receives and ignore the gains made by other states. If the benefit justifies the bargain, they favor it. By contrast, *relative gains* describes a situation in which leaders focus intently on how much other states receive relative to theirs. If others get more, they oppose the deal without regard to how much they stand to gain.

5. A useful discussion of this issue is Michael Mastanduno, "Do Relative Gains Matter?" *International Security,* 16.1, Summer 1991, 73–113.

6. For a series of case studies considering this question, see Peter Evans et al. (eds.), *Double-Edged Diplomacy,* Berkeley and Los Angeles: University of California Press, 1993.

7. For a discussion of the various sides of this question, see Keohane, *After Hegemony;* and Grieco, *Cooperation.* The central question in this matter is that of collective action. See Mancur Olson, *The Logic of Collective Action,* Cambridge: Harvard University Press, 1965.

8. This discussion draws heavily on Putnam and Bayne, *Hanging Together: Cooperation and Conflict in the Seven Power Summits.* Cambridge: Harvard University Press, 1987. Richard Cooper et al., *Can Nations Agree?* Washington, D.C.: Brookings Institution, 1989; and Martin Feldstein, *International Economic Cooperation,* Chicago: University of Chicago Press, 1988.

9. Robert Putnam and C. Randall Henning, "The Bonn Summit of 1978: A Study in Coordination," and Gerald Holtham, "German Macroeconomic Policy and the 1978 Bonn Economic Summit," both in Cooper et al., *Can Nations Agree?* 12–177.

10. Somewhat contrary to this trend was the Tokyo summit, which served to produce agreement on targets for controlling oil imports. However, these targets were inflated and were achieved mostly as a result of the recession. See Putnam and Bayne, *Hanging Together,* 110–118.

11. Criticism was somewhat muted after 1982, when the United States relaxed its monetary policy and experienced an economic boom produced by the stimulus of the budget deficit. This, in conjunction with the rising dollar, pulled in record levels of imports and helped to stimulate the economies of Europe and Japan.

12. Putnam and Bayne, *Hanging Together: Cooperation and Conflict in the Seven Power Summits.* Cambridge: Harvard University Press, 1987. One of the best studies of cooperation relating to macroeconomic coordination.

13. This was the role of the IMF under the Bretton Woods system.

14. In general, higher or rising interest rates (especially relative to interest rates in other countries) lead to a rise in the currency's value; lower or falling (relative) interest rates produce a falling currency.

15. An excellent discussion of this process is found in Jeffrey Frieden, *Banking on the World,* New York: Harper and Row, 1987.

16. I. M. Destler and C. Randall Henning, *Dollar Politics,* Washington, D.C.: Institute for International Economics, 1989, 17–25.

17. John Pool and Steve Stamos, *The ABCs of International Finance,* Lexington, Mass.: D.C. Heath, 1987, 77.

18. Instead, the United States experienced a recession for middle- and lower-wage groups, whose real incomes rose little from 1973 to 1995. Although jobs were being created at record levels, these jobs were primarily at low wages. Households maintained

buying power by increasing the number working, usually teenagers and mothers (Kevin Phillips, *The Politics of Rich and Poor,* New York: Random House, 1989).

19. There is no evidence that anyone in the Reagan administration contemplated this strategy, although Richard Darman indicated sympathy for some of its elements.

20. Yoichi Funabashi, *Managing the Dollar,* Washington, D.C.: Institute for International Economics, 1989.

21. *Market intervention* means actions by a government to become a buyer or seller in foreign exchange markets. In this case, each government would sell dollars and buy one of the four main currencies: pound, deutsche mark, yen, or French franc.

22. By December 1987, the dollar fell to 120 yen and to 1.6 deutsche marks.

23. The Germans often made a distinction between themselves and the Japanese: Germany was closely tied to Europe, with one-half its trade there, whereas only 10 percent was with the United States, and 3 percent with Japan (Funabashi, *Managing the Dollar,* 120–121.

24. In 2002, two of the three most important countries that were not members entered the World Trade Organization (WTO): China and Taiwan. Russia, the third, remains outside.

25. Steven Greenhouse, "Industrial Nations Agree to Push for Trade Accord," *New York Times,* June 5, 1991; Peter Passell, " Adding Up the World Trade Talks: Fail Now, Pay Later," *New York Times,* December 16, 1990; Bruce Stokes, "*Apres GATT, le Deluse?" National Journal,* January 12, 1991.

26. H. B. Junz and Clemens Boonekamp, "What is at Stake in the Uruguay Round?" *Finance and Development,* June 1991, 10–15; Sylvia Ostry, "The Uruguay Round: An Unfinished Symphony," *Finance and Development,* June 1991, 16–17.

27. The best overall discussion of the Uruguay Round is the four volume set: Terence P. Stewart (ed.) *The GATT Uruguay Round: A Negotiating History,* Dordrecht, The Netherlands: Kluwer, 1993–1999.

28. Robert Putnam, "Diplomacy and Domestic Politics: The Logic of Two-Level Games," *International Organization,* 42.3, Summer 1988, 427–460.

29. Valerie Brown and Louis Wells, *The Uruguay Round of the GATT: Choices in U.S. Policy,* Cambridge: Harvard Business School Case, 1994.

30. Salil Pitroda, "From GATT to the WTO: The Institutionalization of World Trade," *Harvard International Review,* 17.2, Spring 1995, 47.

31. An excellent and detailed examination of the WTO is Bernard Hoekman and Michel Kostecki, *The Political Economy of the World Trading System: From GATT to WTO,* Oxford, England: Oxford University Press, 1995.

32. Peter Nolan, *China and the Global Business Revolution,* New York: Palgrave, 2000.

33. The European Union has gone through several episodes of increasing integration, and its name has changed with each major episode: from *European Economic Community (EEC; also Common Market)* in 1958–1986, to *European Community (EC)* in 1986–1993, to *European Union (EU)* since 1993.

34. Details on these events are in Andrew Moravcsik, *The Choice for Europe,* Ithaca, N.Y.: Cornell University Press, 1998.

35. In addition to Austria, Finland, and Sweden, the former members of EFTA are Norway, Switzerland, Iceland, and Liechtenstein. In November 1994, Norway voted not to join the EU. Along with Norway, the other former EFTA states have an arrangement with the EU as associated states. In early 2002, there was a long list of applicant states:

Estonia, Latvia, Lithuania, Poland, Czech Republic, Slovakia, Slovenia, Romania, Hungary, Bulgaria, Turkey, Malta, and Cyprus. See Figure 6.1.

36. There are still areas where the veto system (or unanimity) prevails, primarily in taxes and social policy. The weighting in 2000 was as follows:
    10 votes (each)—U.K., Italy, Germany, France
    8 votes—Spain
    5 votes (each)—Netherlands, Belgium, Greece, Portugal
    4 votes (each)—Austria, Sweden
    3 votes (each)—Finland, Denmark, Ireland
    2 votes—Luxembourg

    This gives Germans one vote for each 8,000,000 persons. Luxembourg has one vote for each 200,000 persons.

37. Ann-Marie Burley and Walter Mattli, "Europe before the Court: A Political Theory of Legal Integration," *International Organization,* 47.1, Winter 1993, 41–76; Geoffrey Garrett and Barry Weingast, "Ideas, Interests, and Institutions: Constructing the European Community's Internal Market," in Judith Goldstein and Robert Keohane (eds.), *Ideas and Foreign Policy,* Ithaca, N.Y.: Cornell University Press, 1993, 173–206.

38. This was the period of 1977–1979, when the United States in several economic summits tried to persuade West Germany to adopt an expansionary economic policy.

39. Several states with weaker currencies were permitted a wider range. The weighting for establishing the ECU was based mainly on five currencies, with the German deutsche mark accounting for 30 percent alone. See Jonathan Pinder, *European Community,* Oxford, England: Oxford University Press, 1991, 119–130. The best detail is in Moravcsik, *Choice for Europe.*

40. This was the U.K., Greece and Portugal.

41. Ellen Kennedy, *The Bundesbank,* London: Pinter, 1991, 79–103.

42. "Ebb Tide," *The Economist,* April 21, 1991.

43. Michael Baun and Stanley Hoffman (eds.), *An Imperfect Union,* Boulder, Colo.: Westview, 1996.

44. Another uncertainty results from placing responsibility for exchange rate policy (obviously, for the Euro) in the hands of the finance ministers of the Euro 11. This probably means that monetary policy will take precedence over exchange rate policy for the near term. See the discussion of this trade-off below.

45. Nonetheless, public support for the Euro rose over the decade, reaching 65 percent approval in 1998 across the Euro 11.

46. The need for coordinated fiscal policies continues after the coming of the Euro. The Euro 11 adopted a "stability pact" in which they agree to keep their budget deficits at or below 2 percent of GDP.

47. Sweden and Denmark also missed on some of the criteria. Greece has since met the criteria and will join the Euro.

48. Jeffrey Frieden, "The Euro: Who Wins? Who Loses?" *Foreign Policy,* Fall 1998, 25–40.

49. For an excellent discussion of the consequences of the Euro, see "Work in Progress," *The Economist,* December 1, 2001.

50. International Monetary Fund, *International Financial Statistics,* 2000, 123.

51. An excellent overview of the enlargement question is "Europe's Magnetic Attraction," *The Economist* May 19, 2001, quote at page 5.

52. Extending the EU from 15 to 26 members would increase the population by 34 percent, while reducing the per-capita GDP by 16 percent "Magnetic Attraction," *The Economist,* 4.

53. Jeffrey Anderson, "The State of the (European) Union," *World Politics,* 47, April 1995, 411–465.

54. A free trade agreement (FTA) can be distinguished from the cooperation in the European Union in terms of the scale and scope of the system. An FTA generally does not have a common external tariff and, aside from arrangements for settling trade disputes among the parties, does not have significant institutions that advance economic or political cooperation. For example, NAFTA is unlikely to produce anything resembling linked currencies or the Euro.

55. A useful overview of NAFTA is Robert Pastor, "The North American Free Trade Agreement: Hemispheric and Geopolitical Implications," *The International Executive*, 36.1, January–February 1994, 3–31.

56. Stephen Thomsen, "Regional Integration and Multinational Production," in Vincent Cable and David Henderson (eds.), *Trade Blocs?* London: Royal Institute of International Affairs, 1994, 112. A Canadian perspective on NAFTA is Ricardo Grinspun and Maxwell Cameron (eds.), *The Political Economy of North American Free Trade,* New York: St. Martin's Press, 1993.

57. Ignacio Trigueros, "A Free Trade Agreement between Mexico and the United States," in Jeffrey Schott (ed.), *Free Trade Areas and U.S. Trade Policy,* Washington, D.C.: Institute for International Economics, 1989, 255–267.

58. Marc Busch and Helen Milner, "The Future of the International Trading System: International Firms, Regionalism, and Domestic Politics," in Richard Stubbs and Geoffrey Underhill (eds.), *Political Economy and the Changing Global Order,* New York: St. Martin's Press, 1994, 259–276.

59. *The Economist,* January 14, 1995, 26–27.

60. Lorraine Eden and Maureen Molot, "Continentalizing the North American Auto Industry," in Greenspun and Cameron (eds.), *Political Economy,* 297–313.

61. The membership of ASEAN includes Brunei, Indonesia, Malaysia, the Philippines, Singapore, Thailand, Vietnam, and recent addition Myanmar.

62. The members of APEC are Brunei, Canada, China, Indonesia, Japan, Korea, Malaysia, New Zealand, the Philippines, Singapore, Taiwan, Thailand, and the United States.

63. Mitchell Bernard and John Ravenhill, "Beyond Product Cycles and Flying Geese: Regionalization, Hierarchy, and the Industrialization of East Asia," *World Politics,* 47.2, January 1995, 171–209.

64. For a contrary view about the potential for an economic bloc in Asia see Jeffrey Frankel and Miles Kahler, *Regionalism and Rivalry: Japan and the Untied States in the Pacific Area,* Chicago: University of Chicago Press, 1993.

65. For a different view relating to Europe, see Joseph Grieco, "The Maastricht Treaty, Economic and Monetary Union, an the Neo-Realist Research Program" *Review of International Studies,* 21, 1995, 21–40.

ANNOTATED BIBLIOGRAPHY

Vincent Cable and David Henderson (eds.). *Trade Blocs? The Future of Regional Integration.* London: Royal Institute, 1994. A collection of very insightful articles discussing different aspects of regional trade blocs.

Nicholas Colchester and David Buchan. *Europower.* New York: Times Books, 1990. A detailed and excellent, but dated, description of the European Community.

Richard N. Cooper et al. *Can Nations Agree? Issues in International Economic Cooperation.* Washington, D.C.: Brookings Institution, 1989. A series of excellent case studies in international macroeconomic coordination.

I. M. Destler and Randall Henning. *Dollar Politics: Exchange Rate Policy-Making in the United States*. Washington, D.C.: Institute for International Economics, 1989. A very useful case study of the domestic politics of efforts in the 1980s to manage the value of the dollar.

Wendy Dobson. *Economic Policy Coordination: Requiem or Prologue?* Washington, D.C.: Institute for International Economics, 1991. A broad assessment of international economic cooperation.

Jeffrey Frankel and Miles Kahler (eds.). *Regionalism and Rivalry*. Chicago: University of Chicago Press, 1993. A detailed examination of the existence of an economic bloc in East Asia.

Yoichi Funabashi. *Managing the Dollar: From the Plaza to the Louvre*. Washington, D.C.: Institute for International Economics, 1989. A detailed description of the process of cooperation in the international financial system's operation in the 1980s.

Joseph M. Grieco. *Cooperation among Nations*. Ithaca, N.Y.: Cornell University Press, 1990. A theoretically informed study of cooperation in international trade.

Lisa Martin. *Coercive Cooperation: Explaining Multilateral Economic Sanctions*. Princeton, N.J.: Princeton University Press, 1992. Considers the impact of institutions on economic cooperation.

Kathleen McNamara. *The Currency of Ideas: Monetary Politics in the European Union*. Ithaca, N.Y.: Cornell University Press, 1997. Examines the roles of elite opinion in the formation of the Maastricht Agreement.

Andrew Moravcsik. *The Choice for Europe: Social Purpose and State Power from Messina to Maastricht*. Ithaca, N.Y.: Cornell University Press, 1998. Examines in great and valuable detail the major agreements in the evolution of European integration.

John Pinder. *European Community*. Oxford, England: Oxford University Press, 1991. The best study of the European Community.

Robert Putnam and Nicholas Bayne. *Hanging Together: Cooperation and Conflict in the Seven Power Summits*. Cambridge: Harvard University Press, 1987. One of the best studies of cooperation relating to macroeconomic coordination.

John G. Ruggie (ed.). *Multilateralism Matters*. New York: Columbia University Press, 1993. A collection of sophisticated studies of different aspects of postwar multilateralism.

Jeffrey Schott (ed.). *Free Trade Areas and U.S. Trade Policy*. Washington, D.C.: Institute for International Economics, 1989. A series of detailed studies of free trade areas.

Arthur A. Stein. *Why Nations Cooperate*. Ithaca, N.Y.: Cornell University Press, 1990. A game-theoretic analysis of international cooperation.

Stephen Thomsen and Stephen Woolcock. *Direct Investment and European Integration*. New York: CFR Press, 1993. A detailed look at the impact of foreign direct investment on cooperation in Europe.

Michael Webb. *Global Capital and Policy Coordination: International Macroeconomic Adjustment since 1945*. Ithaca, N.Y.: Cornell University Press, 1995. Sees growing international cooperation on macroeconomic policy, even after the decline of U.S. hegemony.

7

❖

Competition
and Conflict
among Advanced
Industrial States

One of the preceding chapter's main themes is worth repeating: discussions of conflict and competition cannot be far removed from an analysis of cooperation. The world economy simply could not function without the manifold layers of international cooperation.[1] The notion of a global marketplace existing outside a framework of cooperative political relations among nations is as mythological as the bloodless world of perfect competition. Thus we need to remember that competition among firms or nations is possible only in a context in which the rules for trade, investment, and profit making have been created and are maintained through international cooperation.

That having been said, competition and conflict are inherent elements of capitalism. Productive power and the military power linked to it generate an enormous prize to be won by sovereign states. Domestic political power frequently rests on economic growth and dynamism. International rivalry over at least the past two centuries has been caught up in the efforts of capitalist firms to secure markets and resources. The two great wars of the twentieth century began as conflicts among capitalist states. Late in the twentieth century and into the twenty-first, fears abound about the ability to compete in the world economy. Many of the same factors that undermine cooperation also serve to enhance competition and conflict.

The ebb and flow in the balance between cooperation and conflict has led some to express concern about a shift toward the latter. This chapter offers some perspective on this possibility. We begin with a discussion of the concept

192

of competitiveness, considering its appropriateness for understanding the economic relationships among nations. This involves showing two things: first, how economic advances in one nation can harm the economic, political, and military positions of other nations; second, that governments must be able to act effectively to improve national competitiveness for *competitiveness* to become a meaningful political term. There are many strategies used to enhance the competitiveness of nations. We will review these and explain how they might succeed or fail.

The three great arenas of global economic competition are Japan, the United States, and Europe. Japan deserves a detailed look as a nation that recently established a new competitive standard for others to match. Moreover, the Japanese experience has often operated as a model for many Asian states to emulate. This section will examine the postwar rise of Japan and the special business-government relationship often cited as the source of its extraordinary growth. But Japan's competitive decline has now lasted for more than a decade, and its recent weaknesses help us understand the shifting criteria for success in international competition. Japan's difficulties have been mirrored by a surge in the U.S. economy. In the 1980s the United States found itself under considerable competitive pressure. This changed dramatically in the 1990s with the longest economic expansion in U.S. history. How did these turn-arounds happen? Many believe it is linked to the emergence of an information economy in the United States that has begun to spread to the rest of the world. We will review the issues associated with competitiveness in the "New Economy." Europe remains in somewhat of a middle position between the United States and Japan, with important competitive advances and significant remaining problems. Our review identifies the successes and the most troubled areas and the somewhat distinctive strategies designed to improve Europe's competitive position. The advent of the Euro may help spur greater competitive capabilities in Europe.

The traditional reaction to increased competition is protectionism, whereby a government attempts to help its nation's firms by shielding them from the outside world. We will examine the nature of contemporary protectionism. In the wake of a general decline in tariffs, nontariff barriers (NTBs) and efforts at managed trade have assumed a much greater role. This "new" protectionism, along with a consideration of the political economy of decisions to adopt such a policy, receives our attention.

THEORIES OF COMPETITIVENESS

From the beginning of the industrial era, the ability of specific industries and firms in certain nations to achieve advantages over those industries and firms in other nations has defined competitiveness and has distinguished nations from one another. Further, these same economic capabilities have been closely related to the capacity for producing military and political power. Whether in terms of generating wealth that facilitated a large military establishment or the technological infrastructure to support building railroads, dreadnoughts, or ICBMs, economic competitiveness has been linked with national power. Today the military, political, economic, and technological dimensions of international competition are bound together very tightly. World influence demands accomplishment in all four areas, while each increasingly depends on the other three.

For our purposes, competitiveness can be defined as the ability of a nation to achieve economic growth and a rising standard of living, even when exposed to international trade and capital flows.[2] Understanding competitiveness calls for an analysis of nations' broad characteristics along with a consideration of specific industries and firms, because it is that actual competition takes place. Our interest lies in identifying those attributes of a nation that help or hurt an industry or industry segment in global competition. But additionally, examining competitiveness turns the economic performance of a business system, along with the general relationship of the political system to business activity, into intensely political questions.

The competitiveness debate raises questions about the type of international trading system that is most desirable. The notions of free trade and comparative advantage—now nearly two centuries old—define the most desirable system as one in which each nation should specialize in a world of open trade based on each nation's existing factor endowments. In this system, no nation is better off defecting and engaging in autarchy or mercantilism. Those who pursue these paths will eventually produce and consume fewer goods at higher prices (less for more). One of the key issues of competitiveness is whether important gains can be had for one nation by taking steps to boost its proportion of high-profit and knowledge-intensive industries. Although this corresponds to historical experience, such an option does not fit well with the theory of comparative advantage.

The very notion of thinking about nations as engaged in economic competition is one that divides economists from most political economists. The former, operating from a liberal perspective on trade, argue that economic relationships among nations are positive sum. That is, the economic development of one nation helps the economic position of other nations. Growth in nation A provides a market for the goods of nation B, and more important, as Nation A improves its comparative advantage, it is able to supply better goods at lower prices to Nation B.[3] Scholars who approach this matter from the perspective of political economy often acknowledge the correctness of the liberal view but add that conflict is an equally important, and sometimes more important, aspect of international economic relations. Conflict arises because economic growth occurs at different rates, thereby affecting the relative strength of nations involved in international political and military competition. Additionally, the success rate of a nation's firms, and thus the prosperity of its citizens, depends partly on the government's actions. Thus the citizens of a nation have an employment and income interest in the success of some firms—those operating in the nation—over that of other firms. The combination of the political and military implications of different rates of growth, the input of the success or failure of national firms, and the interest of citizens in economic growth in "their" nation.

To sustain their contention that nations do not engage in economic competition, liberals must rely on a version of reality that distorts as much as it reveals. In the economist's idealized world of free trade and investment, market resources are employed at their most efficient. The geography of production is irrelevant, because that production always takes place in the most efficient location. When and where resources are inefficiently used, they must be redeployed to more efficient uses and locations. In the case of labor or capital, it must move to places of greater efficiency. In such a world, nations are simply irrelevant boundaries. Each place (nation) produces goods in which it has a comparative advantage; trade allows all places (nations) to benefit from global efficiencies. Thus, places (nations) do not compete but instead gain from the collective efficiencies of all places (nations). The real competitors are firms, which struggle with each other for profits and market share; one firm's gains usually come at the expense of other firms'.

In the idealized world of global perfect competition, nations cannot change the fate of their geographic area and have no purpose except collectively to provide the political rules for enforcing contracts. But in real life, nations exist and struggle with each other for power and position. Most important, a nation is a political organization whose main purpose is to advance the interests of (at least some) of its population. National leaders cannot be indifferent to the fate of their part of the world economy. Firms are but the front line of competition, the most visible part of a complex system of (mostly) nation-based institutions that support interfirm competition. Simple comparison of the firms in the United States and those in Vietnam shows clearly the dramatic differences in the capacity for competition and the contribution of national institutions to these differences.

It is also true that in their trade relations, the United States and Vietnam share complementary interests. But the same can be said for firms competing against each other. IBM and Toshiba can cooperate to the benefit of both and simultaneously compete for customers. Although firms and nations both compete with and benefit from each other, this is not to say the process is the same. Rising Japanese incomes do not reduce incomes in the rest of the world, but we cannot let this positive sum relationship obscure arenas and dimensions of economic conflict between nations.

A further theoretical grounding for competitiveness as a political issue depends on showing how the actions of governments can make industries grow faster or even make industries develop that otherwise would not evolve. One version of this analysis, known as strategic trade theory, argues that government intervention can work if one of two situations holds. First, government action targets a high-profit industry with large economies of scale,[4] and this action helps to dissuade foreign firms from entering the market or compels them to leave. The nation's objective is to enable its firms to capture a share of the global market large enough to reap the greatest economies of scale worldwide. This serves to drive out other competitors because they can never gain a large enough market share to bring down costs through economies of scale. The nation that establishes such a position in an industry first will come to dominate global production. A second element of strategic trade theory focuses on actions that help establish industries with important economic spin-offs or externalities. Here the purpose is to make sure that your nation contains its share of industries whose operations generate benefits for other industries. The best examples are those knowledge-intensive industries that generate demand for other advanced businesses. The relationship between the computer industry and the computer software industry is an obvious case. The nation containing the greatest proportion of high-externalities industries will likely produce the highest rates of economic growth.[5]

The concept of comparative advantage (discussed in Chapter 2) provides another approach to thinking about political efforts to improve international competitiveness. Research today rejects the standard view that factor endowments controlling comparative advantage are fixed, especially in certain high-technology fields. Rather, the factors that most influence production may be created in part through government action. Again, the proportion of knowledge-intensive industries—those characterized by high research-and-development costs, high risk and payoff, and rapid change—in a society can be a consequence of government decisions. A combination of policies designed to develop the infrastructure for knowledge generation and application may be a necessary ingredient for establishing these industries. Thus education policies, efforts to enhance knowledge and technical skills in the population, and actions to assume some of the risks and costs of product development can have a major impact on where knowledge-intensive firms locate. Further, this process may be subject to a period of increasing returns: the more knowledge-intensive firms a nation has, the more it will get. Nations thereby compete in creating a comparative advantage that affects which ones will capture the largest proportion of these companies. The presence of high-tech industries makes a major contribution to a nation's wage rates, economic growth rates, and standard of living.[6]

STRATEGIES OF COMPETITIVENESS

If we assume that nations are in conflict over power and position, that economic development is closely related to this process, that the success of firms and governments is of vital concern to citizens and leaders, and that government actions can sometimes affect rates of growth, then what strategies have governments followed to improve the competitive position of the nation and its firms? Perhaps surprising, nations engage in a wide variety of actions designed to expand the economic well-being of firms and citizens. Additionally, firms adopt many strategies to promote competitiveness. There are three broad categories of national competition strategies: liberalization, state investment and regulation, and protectionism. For firms, the main categories include actions affecting costs, improving quality, and expanding markets.

There are three main types of state competitiveness strategies:

1. *Liberalization:* the main goal is to expand the scope of markets and thereby to reap the benefits of increased firm competition and of larger markets, or to attract firms to an environment with fewer restrictions. States use deregulation, tax reduction, lower deficits, free trade agreements, and antitrust enforcement to create, expand, and promote markets.

2. *State investment:* the main purpose is to bolster supporting institutions and to increase opportunities for firms. Examples include spending on infrastructure such as telecommunications, education, and other public goods; targeted aid to industries in the form of tax breaks, state purchases of production, and direct and indirect subsidies; the creation and funding of research and development (R&D) in a variety of institutions; business-government partnerships; and exchange rate manipulation. Recently, scholars have begun to recognize that state policies need to emphasize the creation and application of intellectual capital and emphasize less the accumulation of physical capital.

3. *Protectionism:* the purpose is to manipulate the government's ability to control trade access so as to increase national production and sales. This might be accomplished by tariffs, nontariff barriers, state subsidies, managed trade, coerced trade, and linking protection of the domestic market to increased exports.

The competitiveness options available to firms are equally diverse:

1. *Decrease costs:* when a firm faces competition, it needs to reduce costs and thereby reduce the prices of its products. This can be done by downsizing; by slashing workers, including managers; by engaging in foreign direct investment to relocate production so as to maximize the labor cost-productivity relationship; by adopting new production strategies, such as lean production; by improving management communication capabilities; and by making strategic alliances to gain knowledge and/or secure preferential capital and organize suppliers.

2. *Increase quality:* an equally effective but sometimes more difficult strategy is to improve the quality of the product. This might be done by adopting flexible production techniques to increase the ability to offer customers greater variety; by intensifying quality control to reduce defects; by investing in new technology; and by making strategic alliances to gain knowledge.

3. *Expand markets:* firms often compete to gain market share and to expand into new markets. These objectives can be met by foreign direct investment to produce and sell in new markets; by new product development; by the purchase of an existing firm and its markets; and by strategic alliances to gain market access, cartelize markets, or stabilize sales.

4. *Innovation:* the ability to develop new ways of operating can be found in each of the examples above. Beyond this is the capacity to develop new products and processes.

As we examine the competition practices of nations and firms, the strategies will become clearer. However, the success or failure of these activities may be more difficult to determine.

THE RISE AND DECLINE(?) OF JAPAN

At the end of World War II Japan was devastated, with 40 percent of its industrial system in ruins, and occupied militarily by the United States. In the next three years, U.S. officials used their special powers to make important economic and political changes. Japan's immense economic conglomerates, *zaibatsu,* were broken up, many persons associated with the war were purged from positions of responsibility, the military establishment was dismantled, and the economic system was liberalized. The harshest policies began to change in 1947. As the Cold War between the United States and the Soviet Union intensified, pressure on Japan was relaxed and replaced by a policy emphasizing economic recovery. Concern over the Soviet ability to exploit instability around the world prompted a shift of U.S. policy in Europe and Asia. The revival of the Japanese economy and its integration into the rest of East Asia became the primary means for establishing an economic and political bulwark against Soviet expansion there. Perhaps the most important by-products of this were the 1951 U.S. commitment to Japanese security and Japan's complete dependence on the United States for military protection. From the U.S. perspective, this arrangement bound Japan to a U.S.-based definition of international order. For Japan, this U.S. economic and security umbrella opened the door to economic recovery and security.[7]

The political system that emerged in Japan from the U.S. occupation represented a complex mixture of new democratic institutions and traditional oligarchic practices. In 1947 the United States imposed a constitution establishing a representative democracy elected by universal adult suffrage and requiring, through Article 9, that Japan renounce the right to use military force for national ends. By the mid-1950s, a dominant political coalition had been formed composed of the bureaucracy, big business and finance, and a conservative political organization, the Liberal Democratic Party. Business interests provided the money, and the bureaucracy supplied much of the political leadership. Genuinely liberal or radical political interests were systematically excluded from political power.[8] This coalition was able to establish a very strong state based on its institutional resources and a national consensus on the need for economic growth.

The Strategy of Growth

In the 1950s and 1960s Japan faced a situation not unlike that of the nineteenth and early twentieth centuries: catch-up. Almost from the beginning of the postwar era, Japan's political and economic leaders were determined to move into the ranks of the major industrial nations. They were unwilling to

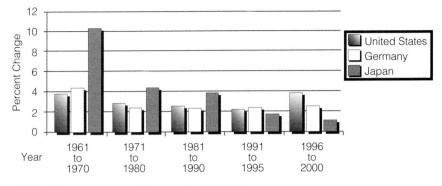

FIGURE 7.1 Comparative GDP Growth: 1961–1995
U.S., Germany, and Japan

rely on the obvious comparative advantage of low wages and instead aimed to make Japan a nation of capital-intensive and high-technology production. This came in spite of capital deficiencies and poor resources and the great advantages of Western nations. The government acted to move the economy in these directions by mobilizing capital, establishing economic priorities, organizing large and economically powerful cartels, protecting certain industries, managing the foreign trade process, and providing guidance for investment. This industrial policy was designed to direct economic development and compensate for Japanese backwardness and economic weakness.[9]

The Japanese were extremely successful in promoting economic growth, as demonstrated in Figure 7.1. Until recently, Japan's GDP growth rate (remember that this excludes exports) has consistently exceeded those of the United States and Germany by wide margins. Over time, the gap narrowed, and there was an overall decline in the rate of increase. Especially during the 1980s, Japan's advantage came from greater consistency of growth. The German and U.S. patterns were subject to more fluctuation, with much sharper swings in the business cycle than in Japan. Since 1991 Japan has generated much slower growth due partly to the bursting of the "bubble economy." This developed in the late 1980s, when bank lending exploded, leading to excessive increases in stock and real estate prices (more on this later).

The initial strategy of development in the 1950s was to reestablish the textile industry, long the mainstay of the Japanese economy. But this quickly expanded to include building infrastructure and the strategic targeting of industries expected to expand rapidly as incomes around the world grew. The Japanese government was unwilling to accept the "natural" position indicated by Japan's comparative advantage: concentrating on low-wage and low-technology industries. Instead, a series of capital-intensive and relatively high-technology industries was given special support by the government. These industries included: steel, electric power, shipbuilding, chemical fertilizers, petrochemicals, synthetic textiles, plastics, autos, and electronics.

Because capital, especially equity capital, was scarce, the Japanese government acted to mobilize resources for these industries. The Bank of Japan guaranteed loans made by private banks to designated industries, and government-controlled bank resources were used as supplements. Over time, private loans were made available to certain industries when the government made clear its priorities. The nurturing of special industries was accompanied by strict protection of the Japanese market for finished goods. The need for foreign technology was satisfied through licensing production by Japanese firms. Thus rather than import goods based on advanced but foreign technology, the Japanese used the attractiveness of their market to obtain licensing and patent agreements that allowed Japanese firms to gain the knowledge and production experience. That is, several American firms (IBM, for example) were willing to transfer licenses and patents to Japanese firms in order to gain access to the Japanese market. Japan was certainly helped by a large and protected domestic market; but it also benefited from relatively open access to large foreign markets. This permitted Japanese industries to reap the cost advantages of high-volume production. Between 1955 and 1970 Japan was able to move beyond production of low-wage, technologically limited goods into much more advanced areas.[10]

By the 1960s the emphasis on exports resulted in a current account surplus and the beginnings of significant outward foreign direct investment. Initially this investment was concentrated in raw materials and in low-tech manufacturing facilities located in developing countries, and it had the effect of providing inputs that would result in Japanese exports to third countries. The great boom in Japanese foreign direct investment came after 1980 and especially after 1985, in conjunction with large Japanese international surpluses, corresponding U.S. deficits, and the Plaza Agreement and rising yen. Accumulating foreign resources permitted Japan to invest abroad. Annual outflows of FDI peaked in 1989 at almost $68 billion and by 1994 had fallen to $41 billion. This was increasingly focused on advanced countries and on industries where Japan was exporting. Protecting export markets, only a modest motive in the 1960s, became a much more important factor in the 1980s. Recently Japanese FDI has been increasingly directed toward other Asian states in order to take advantage of lower manufacturing costs.[11]

The role of international trade in Japanese economic growth is sometimes misunderstood. The rise in U.S. imports from Japan and U.S. concern over this would suggest that Japan lives and dies from this relationship. Although quite important, foreign trade has a more limited impact on the Japanese economy. Table 7.1 provides a comparison of the role of international trade in the economies of four major industrial nations. Clearly Japan's dependence on foreign trade is much less than that of the United Kingdom or Germany and is somewhat less than that of the United States.

But this obscures some important elements in Japanese international trade policy. Japan, more than most other countries in the U.S.-organized world economy, has rejected the notion of mutual gains from free trade. Although Japan joined GATT in 1955, it was slow in removing restrictions on imports

Table 7.1 Ratio of Exports and Imports to GDP (in %)

Country	1994	2000
Japan		
Exports	11.1	11.3
Imports	8.7	9.8
Total	19.8	21.1
United States		
Exports	10.0	11.4
Imports	11.3	15.5
Total	21.3	26.9
United Kingdom		
Exports	21.4	26.1
Imports	21.9	28.0
Total	43.3	54.1
Germany		
Exports	26.1	29.3
Imports	25.5	28.4
Total	51.6	57.7

Exports and imports include both goods and services.

SOURCE: IMF, *International Financial Statistics Yearbook, 2000,* Washington, D.C., 2001; and author's calculations.

because of fears of its own backwardness and dependence on external resources. The Kennedy Round of tariff negotiations in the mid–1960s represented an important shift in viewpoint, with Japan accepting the need for lower tariffs. This was due to the increasing competitiveness of Japanese exports and the expectation that lower world tariffs would spur these exports. By the early 1980s Japanese tariff rates were generally as low as the EEC's and somewhat lower than United States'.[12] At the same time, many countries continue to charge, correctly, that substantial nontariff barriers to imports still exist. These barriers include restrictions based on fear of disease, special regulations, and cultural resistance to foreign products. Further, as a result of legal restrictions and the structure of Japanese business, foreign direct investment in Japan has been very small. Although many of the legal barriers were lifted after 1982–1984, inward FDI remains very low by comparison to other developed states.[13]

The combined effects of export strength and restrictions on imports and inward FDI have skewed Japan's international trade. Most advanced industrial states exchange manufactured goods, often the same kinds of manufactured goods, in their trade with each other. Japan, by contrast, looks much more like a nineteenth-century state. It exports manufactured goods and imports raw materials. Roughly 70 percent of all world trade is in manufactured goods. And Japan, like most, has three-fourths of its exports in manufactured goods. It is in imports that Japan looks unusual. At best, about 50 percent of Japan's imports are manufactured goods, whereas nearly one-half of Japan's imports are raw materials, foodstuffs, and various mineral fuels.[14] Part of this distinctiveness can be explained by Japan's extreme resource dependency on the rest of the world. But much also is due to governmental and business policies.

The first great test of the Japanese economy came in the 1970s, with the collapse of Bretton Woods and the oil shocks that followed. The combination of a rising yen and a massive jump in oil imports put pressure on Japan's international accounts and on its domestic inflation rates. Oil imports rose from 20 percent of total imports in 1970 to more than 50 percent by 1981. Wholesale prices rose by 35 percent in 1974, a year which also saw a large current account deficit.[15] Although the oil shocks slowed Japanese growth, the bursting of the "bubble economy" in 1989–1990 has brought on the longest and most painful period of low growth since Japanese industrialization in the nineteenth century. Between 1992 and 1999, real GDP growth averaged only 1.0 percent.[16] Over several years growth rates have fallen to near zero, and economic stagnation has persisted in spite of the political costs and considerable pressure from abroad for a revival of Japanese economic growth. Moreover, economic expansion in the United States—Japan's largest export market—accelerated throughout the 1990s without leading to increases in Japanese economic growth. How can we understand both Japanese economic successes and failures? What factors could lead to such different outcomes?

Explanations for Japanese Growth and Weakness

Although growth rates for the Japanese economy have declined over time, only recently have they fallen below those for other industrialized countries. Setting aside (for the moment) the most recent period, postwar Japan clearly achieved a miraculous feat of economic recovery and growth. Efforts to explain this record have emphasized a wide variety of factors. Not surprisingly, economists have traced Japan's successes to market relationships. Here the generally accepted ability of the market to sort out the most efficient producers suggests that Japanese entrepreneurs were adept at responding to market incentives. But this approach fails to explain why the Japanese possessed this special market sensitivity.[17] Other economists have pointed to unusual features of the Japanese economy and culture, such as the harmony of labor and management and the high savings rate, or to the benefits of free riding on the open world economy and the security system provided by the United States.[18]

Perhaps the strongest argument, at least for many students of international and political affairs, is made by tracing the Japanese market perspicacity to the role of the government and its relationship with the economy. From the beginning of the modern era in 1868, the state has played a special role in rearranging Japanese society and politics so that Japan could compete effectively with the West. The focus of that effort in the post–World War II era has been the Ministry of International Trade and Industry (MITI).[19] MITI and other important bureaucracies, such as the Ministry of Finance (MOF), helped provide "domestic producers with the support and guidance they needed to achieve competitive advantages in global markets."[20] This "developmental state" sought to create or at least to shape the incentives—market and otherwise—that directed the actions of Japanese firms.[21] Sometimes this took the form of subsidies to young or ailing industries, which is also somewhat common in the West. More important were efforts at organizing industries to achieve lower costs, defining national priorities in technological development, and developing national plans to share the risks associated with corporate decisions.

The texture of the relationship of MITI to the Japanese economy is not constant over time. Rather, it is affected in important ways by the external environment and by the Japanese business system's level of development. Shifts in the world economy and the increasing strength of Japanese business have forced MITI bureaucrats to change their style and strategies for national economic management. Moreover, close analysis reveals that structural characteristics of the Japanese enterprise not only make it an effective partner for government but also offer numerous points of access for MITI influence.

MITI's role reflects a long-standing judgment in the Japanese government about the proper role of the market in directing the economy. Although respecting the power of market forces, MITI officials have rejected the view that a policy of laissez-faire would necessarily produce the best possible use of Japanese economic resources. Left alone to follow the market's signals, investors could easily direct resources toward areas such as real estate that would do little for the nation's international competitive position. Acutely conscious of Japan's backward status and fearful of the effects of weakness on the country's security and independence, MITI designed a strategy for making Japan an industrial power. It sought to identify specific industries in which Japan might make major gains, anticipate changes in the world economy, and organize the Japanese economy to make it competitive in areas that market forces, left alone, would likely avoid.[22]

As we have seen, in the 1950s MITI used control over foreign exchange, technology imports, financial support, and tax breaks to target certain industries for development. In steel, shipbuilding, machine tools, plastics, petrochemicals, and automobiles—traditionally the province of countries with large natural resources or a big domestic market—MITI moved to establish a Japanese presence. The basic objectives were to drive down costs, improve productivity, protect the domestic market from foreign competition, and expand market share abroad. The long production runs permitted by a large market share would take advantage of economies of scale that would further reduce costs.

Two aspects of the Japanese industrial structure assisted in this process. First, MITI was able to reconstitute the large business conglomerates *(zaibatsu)* of the prewar period into similar systems (now known as *keiretsu*) whereby banks, industrial firms, and trading companies functioned much like a cartel. The *keiretsu* distinguish the Japanese business system from that of most other advanced capitalist states. *Keiretsu* can be organized around a large bank, or they can involve bringing together most of the aspects of the manufacturing of a particular product. There is usually a mixture of intra-*keiretsu* relation-ships, from lending and borrowing capital to interlocked ownership and stable trading arrangements. Ownership of stock is more of a long-term partnership than in the West, often involving participation in the firm's management, trade relationships, and loans. *Keiretsu*-like relationships often exist between large firms and suppliers, with very close forms of technology transfer, man-agement, and trade. The result is a system of giant enterprises alongside a large number of small firms. What has distinguished Japan in the past is the com-plex web of intrafirm cooperation.[23]

Second, the reliance on debt rather than equity as the chief source of capi-tal helped focus firms on MITI-style goals. Firms tended to look to the longer term and to growth of market share rather than to short-term profits. Sup-porting this was the Japanese central bank, which acted to guarantee the debt of preferred industries. The combination of *keiretsu* organization and depen-dence on guaranteed debt cushioned the downside risks for certain businesses and thereby directed them toward national goals.[24]

Changes in these arrangements began in the early 1960s with external pressure for liberalization of trade and, later in the decade, for loosening con-trols on Japanese capital markets. Both efforts were prompted by the spectacu-lar success the Japanese economy enjoyed and the seemingly free ride the strict policy of protection created. These events had several important conse-quences. The pressures for liberalization eventually produced results, with trade and capital barriers gradually falling between 1960 and 1982. Largely in response to these changes, MITI was forced to adopt a new strategy for inter-nal economic management. It surrendered direct control over allocating scarce resources and began to rely more on persuasion and the adaptive skills of the *keiretsu* themselves.[25]

One of the most significant recent developments came as a result of the two great changes in the world economy in the early 1970s—the collapse of the Bretton Woods system of fixed exchange rates and the price revolution in oil. Also important were growing domestic political concerns over pollution and the increasing independence of Japan's very successful and powerful busi-ness empires. The result was a lengthy debate within MITI that brought a new bureaucratic faction into power, one more cosmopolitan and interna-tional in outlook. This led to a major policy shift toward energy conservation, reduction of pollution and overcrowding, and a drive to develop knowledge-intensive, high-technology industries.[26]

Japan's move into the realm of high tech has been immensely successful and has produced a dramatic shift in the competitive environment around the world. The once comfortable lead enjoyed by the United States has evaporated in many areas, and other nations have been both encouraged and threatened by Japan's achievements. The primary impetus behind these developments has been a combination of government and private industry efforts. MITI con-tributed research subsidies, and Japanese firms devoted a much larger propor-tion of company resources to research and development and capital investment than did similar U.S. firms. During the 1970s Japan worked to develop and adapt its production capabilities to certain areas, especially semiconductors, computers, and consumer electronics. In the 1980s Japan caught up in computers, surged ahead in semiconductors, consumer electronics, and robotics and redirected research and development toward supercomputers, optoelectronics, and next-generation fighter planes.[27] At the beginning of the 1990s Japan had established itself as a powerful international force in high technology. A 1990 report by the U.S. Defense Department acknowledged a Japanese lead in five high-technology industries crucial to U.S. national security: semiconductors, superconductivity, robotics, supercomputers, and photonics.[28]

MITI's role in this process has continued to evolve as its control over the Japanese economy has waned. This is due in large part to the size and economic strength of Japan's private business enterprises. The largest corporations now have the resources to support high levels of research and development and to absorb investment risks. Further, the most intense competition for many of these corporations is other Japanese firms, thereby undermining their interest in MITI-sponsored cooperation. Funds for research and development continue to flow from MITI, and it still provides an important sanction for investment decisions and supports businesses involved in strategically vital technologies. However, MITI's ability to command has decreased with the maturing of the Japanese economy.[29]

Some scholars find the emphasis on the role of Japan's government excessive in trying to explain rapid economic growth. In particular, they argue that this view pays too little attention to Japan's firms and gives too much credit to the directive power of the state.[30] According to this alternative view, the combination of the developmental state and the complex system of Japanese firms created a special kind of environment that generated especially innovative firms. The Japanese government's developmental policies (mostly targeted subsidies and protection of the home market) produced an unexpected response from some Japanese businesses. Rather than become satisfied and inefficient producers, firms engaged in a fierce investment-driven competition for market share in anticipation of rapid growth in demand. Business leaders understood the large economies of scale (unit costs fall as output rises) to be won from increasing output. Preserving or increasing market share would permit a firm to reap the economies of scale and cost competitiveness. Market share required a capital investment race to increase production capabilities. The major uncertainty in the system was the impact of foreign (and later, domestic) technology. Unable to control or predict the pace and direction of technology change, Japanese firms focused much of their competition on continuous innovation in the way goods were produced. These firms developed new forms of production that were much more efficient and led to goods of much higher quality, making them very competitive in global markets.

Japanese firms (first in the machine tool and auto industries) generated a new form of production: one that combines very high quality control, organizational innovations (such as teams of producers), "just in time" inventory control, and flexibility of production. The cumulative effect was to introduce a dynamic flexibility into the Japanese economy as the production externalities of lead industries were fed into associated industries. The consequences were dramatic. In the late 1980s Japanese automotive firms were able to produce a vehicle in 33 percent less time than U.S. producers and 55 percent less time than European producers. But Japanese autos were made with much higher quality control: 27 percent fewer defects than U.S. autos and 38 percent fewer defects than European cars. This was accomplished with smaller plants and less than 10 percent of the average inventory size of U.S. firms.[31]

One need not choose between a state-centered and a firm-centered explanation of Japan's success. The Japanese economy's effectiveness comes from the ability to organize resources in such a way that firms were able to gain comparative advantages in world markets and generate new arrangements of learning and innovation. Innovation was encouraged by institutional arrangements (government and industry) that absorbed risk and provided incentives for adaptive behavior. The key to understanding Japan lies in focusing not on the state or on corporations but rather on the way that many institutions—markets, firms, government, and industry organizations—relate to each other to create a particular and very successful national innovation system. In Japan, markets are powerful and mold economic decisions; the state shows dexterity in targeting industries for special support; and some firms have an unusual mixture of intense competition and cooperation that makes them juggernauts in the world economy.[32]

The same Japanese institutions that brought so much success have not been able to cope as effectively with recent changes in the global economy. Most important, Japanese institutions have worked at cross-purposes with new circumstances and have thus far failed to make the needed adjustments. The problems originate with the collapse of the bubble economy, but the recent economic difficulties have exposed long-standing weaknesses in the institutions of Japanese political economy.

The proximate cause of economic stagnation in Japan can be traced to the rise of the yen following the Plaza Accord in 1985 and the subsequent bursting of the asset bubble in 1989–1990. The rising yen had several important consequences. Predictably, it meant that producers of goods exported from Japan would be forced to raise prices in order to be profitable in yen terms. In order to compensate, Japan's exporters—its best and brightest firms—began to shift production overseas to avoid some of the costs of the higher yen and to seek out lower cost labor. Waves of outward foreign direct investment permitted the creation of a huge manufacturing production system outside Japan, mostly across Southeast Asia and in the United States. Some have argued that this investment splurge outside Japan by its most competitive firms has led to a hollowing-out of these firms' capacity to manufacture from Japan.[33]

Most certainly, the rising yen made possible the cheap purchase of assets outside Japan and contributed to a massive expansion of the money supply. The Plaza Accord had been designed to adjust the large trade imbalance between the United States and Japan. Its more significant effect was a hyperliquidity in Japan, with large and rapid increases in bank lending, a surge in purchases of foreign assets, and a huge jump in real estate and stock prices in

Japan. The yen doubled in value against the dollar (and effectively against many other currencies tied to the dollar) between 1985 and 1988, giving Japanese buyers of foreign assets a huge advantage. Concurrently, the Japanese monetary authorities lowered interest rates, thereby pumping up the money supply. The process of spiraling asset prices continued as along as banks were willing to make loans to buy these assets at ever rising prices. Between 1985 and 1989 bank lending rose as much as 25 percent per year, feeding annual growth of as much as 11 percent in the money supply, and this fueled a tripling of stock prices and a near-doubling of land prices.[34]

The asset bubble exposes one key weakness in Japan's institutions: its banks are not adequately regulated in terms of evaluating the quality of the loans made to customers.[35] As long as a customer holds an important relationship with a bank or has real estate as collateral, loans are made. The ability to repay the loan from cash flow is not considered. So as long as prices of real estate rose loans were available to buy more real estate and thereby keep prices of real estate and stocks and other assets rising. The result was a self-reinforcing spiral of debt, a global buying binge, and an asset bubble in Japan.

Bubbles cannot expand forever; they eventually burst, usually with very unpleasant consequences. The Japanese financial authorities hoped to let the air out slowly in 1989–1990, when they began increasing interest rates. The bubble was too fragile for such a delicate operation and the collapse of stock and real estate prices after 1990 was traumatic. In the year after May 1989, the discount rate went from 2.5 percent to 6 percent. And in April 1990, the Finance Ministry ordered lenders to place limits on the volume of loans for real estate. The consequences for the Japanese stock market are the easiest to gauge: a drop of about 65 percent of its value from peak to bottom during the next two years. Real estate values fell by one-third to one-half.

How did the drop of roughly 50 percent in stock and real estate prices produce such damaging consequences for the Japanese economy? The main effect was in the banking sector. Many banks were left with a huge volume of bad loans following the bubble's burst. Loans were made based on asset values as collateral; when those values dropped, the borrower was unable to make the payments and the bank faced losses. The large overhang of unproductive loans made banks unable or unwilling to make additional loans, thereby keeping the economy in restraint. Corporations saddled with large debt balances used to purchase assets now worth much less or sitting idle made large cuts in investment, including for research and development.[36] In the United States or the United Kingdom, banks with large numbers of bad loans and unable to function would have been declared bankrupt and closed, and the assets sold. Such a practice violates deeply held cultural norms in Japan, where society is a complex system of relationships, duties, and responsibilities. This led to many delays and difficulties in the government, which was facing the bankruptcy of many Japanese banks and financial institutions, and it has postponed recovery. Moreover, by the mid-1990s, the overall weakness of the Japanese banking system led to the international judgment of Japanese banks as poor credit risks. Many banks around the world cut back on their exposure to Japanese banks, further reducing the lending process. Fears were expressed about the possibility that Japan's banking crisis could damage the global financial system.

The government's response to the unexpectedly severe decline was to take steps to halt the stock market debacle, and these efforts succeeded in stemming the tide of declines after 1992. Beginning soon after, stimulative fiscal policies were adopted in order to restore economic growth. In a classic case of Keynesian strategy, Japan's government has tried to boost the economy through deficit spending. The idea is to provide spending power for consumers, whose purchases will lead to economic expansion. Though significant, these efforts have not had the desired effect. There are three main reasons. First, Japan's banks remain mired in difficulty, as do its debt-ridden companies. Thus, the banks cannot lend and firms cannot borrow. Second, consumer confidence has been deeply shaken by the persistent economic stagnation and fears about the solvency of the nation's pension system. Thus, additional income is placed in savings rather than spent. And third, much of the government spending has gone for pork barrel projects that contribute little to enhancing productivity.[37]

Japan's government receives plenty of advice from the United States about how to fix its problems, much of it designed to persuade the Japanese to adopt Western standards for its financial system. The Japanese economic development strategy has been centered on using the government to control (or heavily influence) capital investment. This has meant that interest rates have been low and the corresponding return to capital has been low. U.S. officials, relying on the U.S. model in which capital investment is privately controlled (and rates of profits for capitalists much higher), call for the deregulation of capital. Additional pressure calls for a liberalization of Japan's relationship with the world economy. This suggestion usually receives a polite response from Japanese authorities coupled with actions that fail to produce this desired liberalization. It is here that the distinctiveness of Japanese institutions is most evident and where we may find the most telling weakness in the Japanese economy. The economic stagnation in Japan has made clearer the existence of a dual economy: one sector is composed of the familiar firms, globally competitive and powerful; the other sector is noncompetitive and protected and acts to hold Japanese growth back.

Between 1950 and 1990, the institutions of Japanese political economy were very effective in generating economic growth when facing the task of catch-up. The Japanese were able to mobilize and invest capital in areas with significant potential for growth. They were successful in technological learning, absorbing and applying knowledge from abroad. And they were able to advance to innovation so as to take a world leadership role in manufacturing of autos and semiconductors. But the economic crisis of the 1990s suggests that these institutions are less effective in coping with the requirements of a world-class economy in the twenty-first century. Specifically, Japan is saddled with a large underdeveloped economy with significant economic ties to the globally competitive sector. And the competitive sectors have not been able to make the leap from high technology producers to a high technology economy.

The noncompetitive economic sector in Japan is large and pervasive, stretching from food processing to retail sales, construction, telecommunications, and service. These industries are substantially protected from international competition and so are very inefficient by international standards. The economic gap between the competitive and noncompetitive sectors in Japan is wide, seemingly much wider than in many other advanced societies. For example, in food processing, Japan's productivity is barely more than one-third that in the United States; in textiles and in wholesale and retail trade Japanese productivity is less than one-half that of the United States. Overall manufacturing productivity is only about 78 percent of the United States'. From the perspective of economic efficiency, these sectors have very negative consequences: high prices for consumers and for other businesses and the inability to create growth from within the industries themselves. For example, food costs in Japan are almost three times that in the United States, and construction costs are about double. As a result of high prices and low productivity, the trailing sectors act as a drag on the Japanese economy. And because these industries are protected from external competition (and often from internal competition), they have little incentive for change. External protection has come mainly from the difficulty for foreign firms to engage in direct investment in Japan. One of the most striking features of the Japanese economy, as compared to other developed economies, is the very small level of inward FDI. In Japan, this has averaged less than 1 percent of GDP; by contrast, other developed nations average 7 percent to 10 percent of GDP, a difference amounting to hundreds of billions of dollars. The barriers to internal competition are also significant. Industries such as construction are linked into a political kickback system and rigged bidding system that work against efficiency and change.[38]

The non-competitive sectors of the Japanese economy remain protected, despite the negative effects for the economy, because of the political economy of their position in Japan. The Japanese drive toward economic success lacked the commitment to free markets found in the West; consequently, efficiency criteria as measured by world prices do not have the same political impact as in the United States. The rush to develop Japan brought with it the political need to retain the support of Japanese firms that could not meet globally competitive criteria. Economic regulations and policies frequently have been used to maintain such producers because they represent a key source of support for the government, including the policies of preparing some Japanese firms for the rigors of global competition. Moreover, many of these same noncompetitive firms have close ties (often through *keiretsu* relationships) with the most competitive of Japanese firms. The result is a political economy that generates some globally competitive firms while pursuing deeply conservative and protective policies at home. The noncompetitive sectors in Japan employ far more workers than the competitive sectors and thereby represent an additional political support for the status quo. Japanese development has always rested on a mercantilist sensibility toward the world and the desire to protect traditional values at home.[39] The result in the 45 years after World War II was a stable political economy of two Japans; in the last decade, the creation of a more thoroughly competitive Japan has been stymied by this same political economy.

A step of potentially great significance was taken in 1998: a "Big Bang" in Japanese finance came as the financial system sank to its lowest depths. The failure of several banks and financial firms helped promote reforms to increase public information about banks' financial condition, relax state controls and regulations, and permit the emergence of new competitors. An unprecedented level of FDI has begun flowing into the Japanese financial sector, with expectations that this will promote more competition. Access to (and the need for) foreign capital may even loosen the *keiretsu* relationships that prop up weak firms. The high-tech sector outside the traditional *keiretsu* has come to life, with a nascent "Silicon Valley" emerging in a part of Tokyo. NTT DoCoMo is the world leader in the development of wireless telecommunication, including the wireless Internet and wireless e-commerce. Nonetheless, Japan continues to lag behind the United States in the degree to which computers and information technology penetrate the economy and households.

Future Prospects

Japan's future is both uncertain and very important. With the world's second largest economy and the largest in Asia, stagnation in Japan harms everyone. Continuing economic weakness has not yet led to political dislocation in Japan, but this cannot be postponed forever. Cataloging the strengths and weaknesses of the Japanese economy produces a long list on both ends.[40]

What steps could the Japanese take to reverse this decline? Not surprisingly, the answers cover the waterfront. One school of thought proposes fixing the macroeconomic imbalances caused by the deficit spending of recent years. By reigning in this spending and reducing debt, capital markets can begin to function more effectively and growth can resume. Others have much more radical proposals, arguing that only serious structural reforms can bring the economy back to life. Some of these include ending the state role in capital allocation and creating a functioning private system; writing off the bad loans and accepting the many bank failures that will result; broadly deregulating the economy to increase competition; restructuring *keiretsu* to end relationships and increase competition as the basis for Japanese capitalism; exposing the noncompetitive sectors of the Japanese economy to much greater external and internal competition and accepting the resulting changes in business bankruptcy and employment. The Japanese prime minister in 2002, Junichiro Koizumi, proposed a program of substantial reform and has significant popular support. However, as in all societies, there are considerable forces resisting change, and progress to 2002 was slow.

Much of the difficulty lies in the state's long-standing effort to manage the capital allocation process central to a capitalist society. During the catch-up phase, Japan was very successful in organizing and directing capital, but today much greater flexibility is needed in making future capital decisions on allocation and especially reallocation. Only when a much larger portion of the economy operates according to the demands of the world economy can sustained growth resume. And this can happen only if the mercantilist culture that pervades Japan's society is diminished. Some observers believe the "Big Bang" of 1998 will produce a much more efficient allocation of resources, with competitive firms gaining at the expense of noncompetitive ones. But years of deficit spending in a mostly futile effort to boost the economy have left the nation saddled with an enormous debt burden. And resistance to change is strong, especially given the cultural traditions and the pain that change will bring. A very large portion of the Japanese population is directly or indirectly employed in firms facing dramatic changes. For reform to be effective many firms will need to go out of business, and many people will need to learn new skills. Coupled with a political system wedded to preserving existing interests, the opposition to reform in Japan is formidable.

Japan is the most spectacular example of postwar economic growth fueled by the extraordinary development of the ties of international economic interdependence. But most other advanced capitalist states have also experienced dramatic economic growth and are likewise caught up in the expanding web of international interchange. Such an environment contributes to deepening relations of cooperation, competition, and even conflict among nations. We turn now to a consideration of the capabilities of the United States in global economic competition.

THE UNITED STATES AND COMPETITIVENESS

Not surprisingly, discussion of the question of competitiveness in the United States increased dramatically in the 1980s and early 1990s, a time of economic difficulty. Concern has declined since 1995, when the U.S. economy entered the longest expansion in its history. Although the hand-wringing has decreased, we still need to understand the sources of the shifting tides in growth and development. The difficulties in Japan have been mirrored by a strong resurgence in the United States. How did this happen and can the success be transferred? In 1990, scholars and policy makers sought to figure out what Japan had done and try to emulate it; in the early twenty-first century, attention around the world was riveted on replicating Silicon Valley.

How can we organize our thinking about shifting trends in competitiveness? Perhaps the most common perspective is promoted by liberals (usually economists), who focus on a nation's ability to manage its macroeconomic fundamentals so as to produce a smoothly functioning market economy. A second approach examines the government's ability to take a leadership role in directing the economy (considered above in relation to Japan). And a third approach looks at the broad configuration of institutions and the ability to create a national system of innovation, especially in the nation's firms. We will consider all three: there is considerable data relating to the macro-economic position of the United States; the decline and resurgence of the U.S. semiconductor industry offers considerable insights into government-business relations; and the competitive strengths of Silicon Valley highlight the importance of a complex system of institutions for competitiveness.

Macroeconomic Measures of Competitiveness

The standard way for understanding the competitiveness of a nation's econ-omy considers changes in the overall ability of an economic system to gener-ate sustained growth in output and income. Often this means comparative measures of output, trade, savings, investment, productivity, and income growth. Sometimes these measures give conflicting indicators. Such is the case for the United States. Consider Figure 7.2, which compares industrial pro-duction for six of the most advanced states from 1990. It clearly shows much faster growth in the United States and stagnation in Japan, along with more modest growth by several European states. By this measure, the United States was doing very well. Similarly, examine Table 7.2, which offers details regard-ing proportions of world trade. Here the evidence suggests stagnation to de-cline in Europe and Japan, with a small rising trend for the United States and considerable increases for developing nations.

Contrast this rather rosy view of the United States with another standard measure of a nation's competitiveness in world markets: its current account balance. We have described the dramatic collapse in the U.S. position during the first half of the 1980s and the effort to reverse this collapse through a pol-icy of dollar depreciation. Did it work? Table 7.3 provides detailed informa-tion about the trade balance, the balance on services, and income. The picture is not very favorable. Although the trade balance did improve for a time after 1987, it has since returned to levels of the mid-1980s. The initial improve-ment in the deficit as a percent of GDP has since been reversed. The size and persistence of the trade deficit suggests to some an important weakness in the United States' competitive position. The most favorable data are from the ser-vices accounts, where the United States runs a continuing and growing sur-plus. However, the surplus in services, combined with the declining net return on foreign assets, is too small to compensate for the trade deficit.

The globalization of production (discussed in Chapter 5) complicates the use of the trade balance as a measure of national competitiveness. Multina-tional corporations based in the United States (or elsewhere) now locate pro-duction and other facilities around the world using calculations of wage rates, productivity, and market access. Indeed, the ability of MNCs to compete in global markets depends substantially on their ability to organize production globally. The fact that IBM is based in the United States has only a limited bearing on which of its facilities will be located in the United States. IBM has more than one-half of its assets, sales, and workers located outside the United States. This means we need to distinguish between those processes that make multinational firms competitive and those that make the United States attrac-tive as a site for production, research, or distribution facilities. Indeed, at the

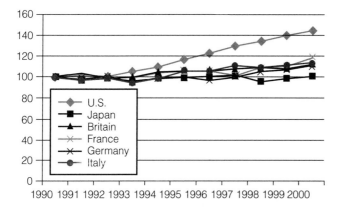

FIGURE 7.2 Industrial Production, 1990–2000 (1990 = 100)

SOURCE: WTO.

**Table 7.2 Shares of World Trade
(in %)**

	1990	1991	1992	1993	1994	1995	1996	1997	1998
Euro area	20	19	18	17.5	17.5	18	17.5	17.7	17.5
United States	12.5	12.9	12.8	13.3	13.5	13.2	12.8	13.5	14.0
Developing countries	15.5	15.2	15.1	15.8	16.4	16.5	16.6	17.5	18.3
Japan	7.5	7.7	8.0	8.3	8.5	8.2	7.6	7.3	7.3

SOURCE: IMF, *World Economic Outlook,* October 1998, 123.

same time that U.S. trade deficits have expanded, U.S.-based MNCs have remained very competitive on a global basis, as indicated by an expanding share of world trade. Thus U.S. multinational corporations show competitive strength at the same time that one measure of the competitiveness of the United States as a geographical area shows weaknesses. Which measure of U.S. competitiveness is the most accurate in an age of globalization? The U.S. trade balance may be a better measure of changes in the world economy, in which production of larger proportions of labor intensive goods occurs outside the United States. And it may tell us more about foreigners' willingness to invest in the United States. For a trade deficit is the flip side of a capital account surplus. As long as foreigners are ready to invest in the United States, a trade deficit will take place.[41]

Perhaps the most important broad measure of a nation's competitiveness involves its productivity, savings, and capital investment. These represent the ability to generate higher output with the same resources, and the related abilities to withhold resources from present consumption and devote them to investments that permit production of more and better goods in the future. It is

**Table 7.3 U.S. Current Account, 1987–2000
(billions of dollars)**

Year	1987	1990	1991	1992	1993	1994	1997	2000
Exports:								
Goods	250.2	389.3	416.9	440.4	456.9	502.7	680	774
Imports:								
Goods	409.8	498.3	491.0	536.5	589.4	669.1	899	1224
Trade balance	−159.6	−109.0	−74.1	−96.1	−132.5	−166.4	−197	−450
Exports:								
Services	97.7	147.1	163.1	176.4	184.6	195.1	255	291
Imports:								
Services	89.4	115.9	116.5	119.7	126.6	133.9	166	217
Services balance	8.3	91.2	46.6	56.7	58.0	61.2	89	74
Balance:								
Goods and services	−151.8	−77.8	−27.3	37.4	−18.5	−105.1	−108	−376
Investment income (net)	7.2	19.7	−13.8	3.5	3.8	16.4	9	−15
Balance on trade, services, and investment income	−144.1	−58.1	−13.7	−35.9	−71.7	−121.6	−99	−391

SOURCE: IMF, *International Financial Statistics Yearbook, 2000*, Washington, D.C., 2001;

Table 7.4 Comparative Savings and Investment as a Percent of GDP (average for 1970–1992)

	U.S.	Britain	Germany	France	Japan	Canada
Gross investment	18.5	18.4	21.6	23.1	32.0	21.7
Gross savings	17.8	17.0	23.6	23.4	34.0	20.0

SOURCE: *The Economist,* June 24, 1995, 73.

Table 7.5 Technology Spending, 1997 (billions of U.S dollars)

		Percent of World
U.S.	640	35.6
Japan	310	17.6
Germany	110	6.6
Britain	95	5.7
France	85	5.1
Italy	48	2.8
Canada	42	2.6
Brazil	36	1.9
Austria	35	1.9
China	28	1.6

SOURCE: World Information Technology and Services Alliance, cited in *New York Times,* May 11, 1999.

this capacity for improving and innovating that makes an economy competitive and makes possible rising incomes and living standards.

The evidence on U.S. savings and investment is generally mixed, whereas that on productivity is more positive. Table 7.4 indicates the similarity of the British and U.S. economies, with the lowest levels of savings and investment of six advanced economies. Germany, France, and Canada save and invest 3 to 4 percent more of their GDP than do the United States and Britain. The real exception is Japan, with much higher levels of savings and investment than any other advanced state. However, the quality of Japanese investment—in relation to the productivity benefits—can be questioned. This is because a significant portion of Japanese investment is politically directed toward the least productive sectors of the economy. When all industrial countries are combined, the gross savings rate for 1994 was 20 percent, making the United States and Britain look even less effective in providing for future growth.[42]

But these broad measures of investment may be misleading, as the quality of the investment may be more important than absolute levels. Japan spends large sums on public infrastructure—not surprising given its need to catch up. But the U.S. invests much more in technology, as Table 7.5 indicates. In spite

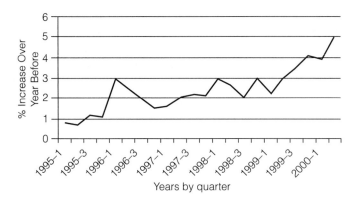

FIGURE 7.3 U.S. Productivity Growth, 1995–2000

SOURCE: IMF.

Table 7.6 Comparative Productivity in Manufacturing (index based on U.S. productivity = 100)

Industry	United States	Germany	Japan
Computers	100.0	90.0	95.0
Automobiles	100.0	62.0	113.0
Consumer electronics	100.0	58.0	110.0
Auto parts	100.0	75.0	122.0
Steel	100.0	100.0	145.0
Metalworking	100.0	100.0	117.0
Food	100.0	74.0	34.0
Average	100.0	77.0	82.0

SOURCE: *The Economist,* October 23, 1993, 88.

of the poor showing in savings and investment, U.S. productivity measures have given rise to encouragement. Productivity measures the quantity of output per worker, and its growth is usually tied closely to growth in income. During the 1970s U.S. manufacturing productivity grew at only 1.4 percent, whereas that of other industrial nations grew at nearly 4 percent. The 1980s led to a turnaround in U.S. productivity growth. Between 1979 and 1989 the United States matched these same nations at 3.6 percent growth. Much of this gain came from downsizing U.S. plants, laying off workers, and increasing the productivity of those who remained.[43] The rising productivity of U.S. workers, especially in the 1990s, reverses a long period of stagnation and is surely the best measure of the current revival in U.S. economic capabilities. Rising productivity is essential to economic growth and has the added benefit of supporting growth in income without inflation. Beginning in 1995, U.S. productivity has shown substantial increases, as Figure 7.3 shows. Aside from changes in productivity, the absolute level of output per worker considered on a comparative basis provides a useful measure of a nation's competitiveness. Table 7.6 offers such data organized by industry. These data show the United States enjoying a broad lead over Germany and Japan in average productivity and especially over Germany in most manufacturing industries. The massive U.S. lead in areas such as food is offset by Japanese advantages in manufacturing productivity.

Competition in Chips

The semiconductor is perhaps the most important product anyone makes. Entry into semiconductor production is a key test of a nation's ability to be a player in the global high-technology game and can pay large dividends for downstream and related industries. The production process is a marvel of high technology, requiring immense capital investment in the most precise of machines and the ability to make improvements and innovations that effectively double the capacity of semiconductors every two years.[44] Further, semiconductors sit at the base of several industry value chains, ranging from electronics, computers, and the Internet to automobiles and appliances. The semiconductor industry was born in the United States and was essential to its dominant position in high technology. The Japanese ability to grab a leading market share in semiconductors by the mid-1980s cast a deep pessimism over the United States' future ability to compete. But almost as fast, U.S. firms have reversed this position and have emerged as global leaders once again. How did this happen and what are its implications?

This story relates to our earlier discussion of government-business ties in Japan, with some interesting twists. The semiconductor industry began in the United States, reflecting the immense technological advantages the victor enjoyed after World War II. Beginning in the 1950s the U.S. government (mainly the Defense Department and later NASA) provided substantial funding for research that led to the integrated circuit, and for another two decades was the major customer for semiconductors. This provided stable demand even when consumer demand was limited and when production and research costs were so high that government purchases amounted to an industry subsidy. In the 1970s commercial demand surged, and many new corporations were started to supply semiconductors and take advantage of technological breakthroughs. By 1975 U.S.-based firms produced over 60 percent of all the semiconductors in the world.[45]

In Japan, the Ministry of International Trade and Industry supported a crash effort to catch up and then surpass the United States in product development. Even though U.S. firms possessed overwhelming advantages, MITI realized the importance of semiconductors to high-technology production and innovation. MITI's support, plus closing the Japanese market for a time to foreign-made semiconductors, gave Japanese producers the opportunity to develop production experience and an assured market. The production wizardry of Japanese firms soon enabled them to surpass U.S. producers in quality. These same Japanese firms took large losses by selling below cost in order to capture a large segment of the U.S. market (a strategy frequently used by firms in an industry with large economies of scale). The combination of quality and price led to rapid sales growth, to falling costs of production (economies of scale), and to additional price cuts. The results were catastrophic for U.S. firms. Between 1981 and 1989 the share of the global semiconductor market held by U.S.-based firms declined from 51 percent to 35 percent. Japanese-based firms mirrored this change, rising in world market share from 35 percent to 50 percent. As we see from Figure 7.4, the U.S. turnaround began that same year, and since 1989 American firms have recovered as Japanese firms have slipped.

Stabilization of global competition was the result of a complex set of factors: large investment efforts by U.S.-based firms, effective shifts in firm strategy, efforts to manage trade through government agreements, a major R&D partnership between the U.S. government and several semiconductor firms that permitted improvements in manufacturing technology, and dynamic changes in global markets. The threat to U.S. economic and national security could be measured by the government's intervention in markets. In 1986, the U.S. and Japan signed the Semiconductor Trade Agreement. This sought greater access for U.S. firms to the Japanese market and acted to block alleged dumping by Japanese firms in the United States. The agreement's real effect was to cut back production and raise prices through cartel-like arrangements. The agreement had the effect of raising prices and profits for over two years and may have saved several U.S. firms.[46]

A second government initiative was an effort to improve U.S. firms' manufacturing capabilities. Created in 1987, this government-business partnership, Sematech, is a consortium of firms organized and partially funded by the U.S. government. Motivated by the tremendous losses suffered by U.S. companies and by the possibility of dependence on Japan for semiconductors, government and industry officials focused their efforts on improving manufacturing capabilities. With $100 million supplied by the Defense Advanced Research Projects Agency (DARPA) and matched by $100 million from the industry partners, Sematech became a catalyst for improving the precision and quality of semiconductor manufacturing technology. By most measures, this goal was accomplished. By early 1993 Sematech had achieved a level of production tolerance unmatched in the world. But U.S. firms, most notably Intel, have also engaged in a binge of their own investment and R&D that has contributed much to their revival.[47] At the beginning of the 1980s, U.S. semiconductor firms' defect rates were two to ten times higher than for Japanese firms. In the early 1990s, this gap was essentially closed. Thus, a major competitive advantage enjoyed by Japanese firms was eliminated.

These improvements were reinforced by a more successful strategy by U.S. firms: shifting to a much more specialized focus on designing the most complex and high-margin computer chips and leaving the production of commodity chips to the Japanese and Koreans. The most spectacular of these was the decision by Intel in 1985 to abandon the memory market and focus on logic chips, notably microprocessors.[48] The explosive growth of personal

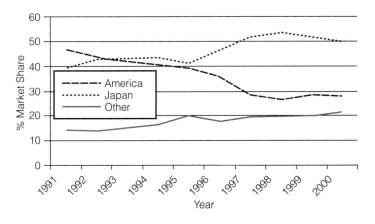

FIGURE 7.4 Global Semiconductor Market Share

SOURCE: Semiconductor Industry Association.

computers has made Intel the largest semiconductor firm in the world, on the strength of its dominance of the microprocessor market. Because microprocessors are now essential to many products other than computers, these market trends continue to favor U.S. firms.

As in previous cases, reaching firm judgments about competitiveness is complicated by globalization. The revival after 1989 has been in U.S.-based firms, not so much in the United States as a production platform. Although many firms are establishing new plants in the United States, only about 50 percent of semiconductor production by U.S. firms occurs in the United States. The 10 years after 1989 witnessed an acceleration of global production by U.S.-based firms. Further, Sematech's goal was to provide support to U.S. firms, but it found that the globalization of production and technology development makes that quite difficult. Many of the U.S. firms involved in Sematech are engaged in strategic alliances for sharing technology with Japanese, Korean, and European firms. And some of the small U.S. firms associated with Sematech have been purchased by Japanese firms. Creating and capturing competitive advantages within national boundaries is a very difficult task in a world of globalization.

The semiconductor case illustrates many of the important features of competitiveness among advanced industrial states. It is a vital technology that affects many aspects of the emerging information-based economic system. Having successful firms in the semiconductor industry provides many positive consequences for other high-technology industries; failing to have such firms can mean dependence on foreign sources, which creates the risk of falling behind in more than semiconductors. The military applications of semiconductors and other high technology add to the competitive element of this industry. And the development and production of semiconductors are extraordinarily dynamic processes, requiring very strong firms, plentiful capital, and occasional government support to create and re-create competitive advantages. The semiconductors case points out that the quality and strength of a nation's innovation systems greatly affect the success of firms based in that nation.[49] At the same time, globalization undermines the national focus of high-technology innovation and the ability of nations to capture the benefits of their investments.

Silicon Valley

Competitive strengths increasingly reside in the ability of firms to operate effectively in two related arenas: (1) the information-based and knowledge-intensive elements of almost all products have been used to lower costs, increase speed to market, and apply information to production, all in the name of innovation; and (2) the ability to manage operations across the globe has been used to reap the localized strengths of a multitude of geographic areas. One of the seeming paradoxes of globalization has been to heighten the importance of regions, where specialized knowledge and capabilities reside. There are several important "clusters" located around the world: Hollywood for movies, Italy for leather goods, and Taiwan for semiconductor foundries. But no region defines competitive strength in this new environment better than Silicon Valley, just south of San Francisco.

Silicon Valley is home to the world's greatest concentration of information-based, knowledge-intensive firms and the human talent that runs them. Ranging from semiconductors, software, computer hardware, and biotechnology to Internet-based firms, this area attracts venture capital, immensely productive workers, and rapid innovation. High technology concentrations exist elsewhere in the United States—in Seattle for software, Austin for computer production, Orlando for computer simulation, northern Virginia for Internet firms, and Cambridge for genomics. Nonetheless, across the world, the primary model for high-technology development is Silicon Valley. In the late 1980s, scholars were debunking Silicon Valley's capabilities while praising the model established by Japanese *keiretsu*. In the early twenty-first century, that has changed to a focus on the American model established in Santa Clara County.[50]

The key point to draw from the Silicon Valley case is the importance of the immediate environment for firms in creating continuing competitive advantages. It is not just the internal capabilities of the individual firm but also the network of institutions in which the firm is embedded that count. This environment includes the various firms in complementary industries—such as suppliers and end users—along with the service firms providing legal advice and capital. In addition, research institutes, universities, and government agencies have significant roles. The combination of firm capabilities and related institutions affects the productivity of firms, their rates of innovation, and the ability to spawn new firms. The Silicon Valley cluster provides firms with access to a pool of highly trained and talented employees, a wide variety of specialized suppliers and customers, and many partners for strategic alliances. The result is to increase productivity, accelerate innovation, and create many new firms that expand technology and increase competition.

What institutions have been essential to the creation of Silicon Valley? Foremost are the firms, from the early semiconductor firms, to the birth of much of the personal computer industry and its related suppliers of microprocessors, disk drives, and memory, to the vast number of software firms providing applications to the PC, and most recently, the array of Internet-related firms. But behind the scenes for many of these firms are four vital creative institutions: Stanford University, the Defense Department, Xerox PARC, and venture capitalists. Stanford University has long played a central role in the creation and dissemination of the intellectual capital at the core of Silicon Valley's success. From the 1930s and 1940s, when inventions by Stanford students and faculty led to the formation of Hewlett Packard, Litton Industries, and Varian Associates, to the 1980s, when the same pattern led to the creation of SUN Microsystems out of the Stanford University (computing) Network, Stanford has been a catalyst of innovation and entrepreneurship. The U.S. Department of Defense was essential to the development of Silicon Valley, through its role in the aerospace industry, which was a major early employer, through its role as the primary customer for the output of integrated circuit firms, and by its support of microprocessor technology at Stanford that led to SUN Microsystems. Xerox PARC (Palo Alto Research Center) was established by the Xerox Corporation as its specialized R&D unit. Its role, like that of many other research institutes, was the invention and development of new technology. Xerox PARC is famous for the first modern PC, with a mouse, GUI-based software, a monitor, and networked through an Ethernet, all by 1978.[51] And venture capitalists, along with specialized law firms, provided the funding, deal making, advice, and managerial expertise to sustain the myriad of start-up firms that have emerged in Silicon Valley.

Efforts to duplicate the set of Silicon Valley institutions across the world have met with limited success, leading to a mystery over how to explain this region's success. To understand Silicon Valley better requires some speculation and focuses mainly on the region's shared culture. Firms in Silicon Valley have been able to develop a remarkable set of complementarities; that is, they are able to build on each other's strengths. This is partly due to the tradition of shared knowledge. The "open source" tradition, in which the basic software standards are available to all, not proprietary with one firm, is a basic value in Silicon Valley. Knowledge sharing is reinforced through the rapid circulation of knowledge workers from one firm to another, based on their high mobility. Perhaps the most striking feature of Silicon Valley is the culture of technological entrepreneurship, which grows out of the network of firm relationships and knowledge networks in the Valley. This involves an acceptance of high levels of risk in attempting to develop radically new products and services. The rapid pace of technological change, itself a product of the system of innovation in the area, is sustained by the universities, research institutes, and venture capital firms that seek out and finance new ideas. The "start up" culture not only accepts risk; it also has a high tolerance of failure, which is seen as a normal consequence of entrepreneurial activity in such uncharted waters. Silicon Valley is distinctive because of its ability to create new firms and new technologies, not once or twice, but continuously.

Does the Silicon Valley culture extend to other U.S. firms not in this area? During much of the 1980s and 1990s, criticisms of U.S. firms were mostly based on economic weakness in the U.S. economy. The concerns included a tendency toward short-range thinking driven by the enormous influence of institutional investors in stock ownership and their concern for the next earnings report; an unwillingness to invest in workers; an excessively hierarchical organizational culture; and a poor ability to see opportunities abroad and operate in a non-U.S. setting. Some of these criticisms are less relevant now. U.S. enterprises have made major adjustments to improve their competitive position. Exports, initially prodded by large declines in the dollar, have grown substantially, and an international emphasis has increased throughout the U.S. business system. The rapid rise of international strategic alliances, the new emphasis on production and commercialization R&D, and the increasing use of new manufacturing systems show the ability to borrow from abroad and to cooperate. Less clear is whether time horizons have expanded: a company' stock price is still battered when earnings fail to match or exceed analysts' expectations. And the most common (and controversial) competitiveness strategy—downsizing by making large cuts in the workforce—suggests that companies still do not understand the value of investing in employees. But in the years after 1990, most U.S. firms made massive investments in technology and with that came some of the Silicon Valley culture. Especially with the emergence of e-business, the value of linking a firm into a network of suppliers and customers—the "extended enterprise"—has gained acceptance. In such an environment, knowledge sharing and innovation are the touchstones of success. Compared to firms in Japan and Europe, U.S. firms have led the way in developing new business practices based on information technology. This may account for some important part of the competitive resurgence of U.S. firms.

EUROPEAN APPROACHES
TO COMPETITIVENESS

The Europeans have not been unmindful of the new competitive environment. As we noted in Chapter 6, both the decision to move toward a single market and the plans for enlargement into much of Eastern Europe have been designed to increase the competitiveness of European firms. The removal of nontariff barriers to trade is being advanced through the development of 282 measures drafted by the European Commission, passed by the European Parliament, and sent on to national governments for enactment into law. Perhaps the most significant is the widespread adoption of the Euro as the single currency for most EU states. The effect is to create a single set of rules across the

EU for commercial transactions and reduce the wide price disparities across the EU. There are two main consequences of these actions for competitiveness: reducing costs made unnecessary by the elimination of various trade barriers and encouraging the creation of EU-wide firms capable of operations in all of these markets. This will lead to additional cost savings from economies of scale and firms large enough to afford the investments needed to compete in world markets. Beyond these results, the elimination of internal trade barriers still leaves external barriers in place. The consequence is to force many non-European firms to locate facilities within the EU in order to sell in this market. Although this strategy displaces imports and maintains employment, it may also present European firms with significant competition in their home market.

The free market approach, embedded in the new single market in Europe, contrasts sharply with more traditional industrial and competitiveness policies within EU countries. All of these countries have made extensive use of subsidies and other state aid in agriculture and manufacturing and have substantial experience in state-owned firms, and many have supported development of cartels for industries in distress.[52] The movement toward the Single European Act (SEA) and deregulation has prompted the European Commission to press for an end to subsidies, cartels, and other forms of market distortions. However, the clash between these competing perspectives has not been sorted out. In the electronics and computer industries—areas of major importance to advanced industrial economies—EU states have acted to support private firms. And pressure on governments from these same firms—especially in computers and semiconductors—to do more has increased. Nonetheless, the states in the EU are sufficiently different to make a common competitiveness policy unlikely for the moment. Some, like France and Italy, are much more interventionist than others, like Germany and Britain. Equally relevant is the fact that industries are not always in the same position in every country; some are competitive and some are not. This makes it difficult for the EU to opt for anything other than freeing up the market to improve competitiveness.

Despite these qualifications, the states and firms of the European Union possess many competitive disadvantages in the world economy. These derive mainly from the relative cost of production in Europe, which generally is quite high. Several of the largest and most developed European states are areas of high wages, high taxes, high welfare expenditures, and low productivity. Table 7.7 provides comparative data on several indicators relating to this problem. One factor contributing to high wage costs in Germany is the large expenditure for social welfare benefits and for vacations. Together, these make up $12, or 46 percent, of the $26-per-hour wage rates in German manufacturing. By comparison, the figure for the United States is $5, or 25 percent, of the $20 rate, and for Japan the figure is $7.50, or 36 percent, of the $22 rate. Alone, wage rates do not necessarily indicate the actual costs of production; we must also include worker productivity to generate a unit labor cost— that is, the cost of labor in producing one unit. Since 1980 unit labor costs in the United States have fallen by 20 percent, while in Germany they have risen

Table 7.7 Comparative Competitiveness Indicators

	Germany	France	Belgium	Italy	U.S.	Japan
Manufacturing wages ($/hour 1999)	26.00	16.23	22.82	16.60	20.00	22.20
Total tax revenues (% of GDP, 1994)	39	44	46	45	30	29
Budget deficits (surplus) (% of GDP, 2000)	2.7	1.3	.3	1.5	(2.4)	5.8
Unemployment (% of total labor force, 2001)	9.6	9.7	10.9	10.5	5.1	4.8

SOURCE: IMF.

by 30 percent. The costs of welfare and unemployment also show up in budget deficits, which are much higher in Europe than in the United States or Japan.[53] Budget deficits in Europe, like those in the United States, declined through the 1990s, resulting in lower interest rates. But labor markets in Europe remain highly regulated, making the normal adjustment of people to jobs more difficult.

Specific European industries also show important weaknesses. European automobile firms have been slow to adopt flexible, lean manufacturing and consequently have trouble competing in global markets. European producers take more than twice as long to make a car as the Japanese, but the cars Europeans produce are plagued by two-thirds more defects. When Porsche shifted to a Japanese-based system of flexible, lean manufacturing, production time dropped by 40 percent, defects by 50 percent, and inventory levels by 81 percent. However, the barriers to accepting such a system have been formidable. Flexible manufacturing requires changes in work rules, downtime, and worker-manager relations that conflict with traditional European practices.[54]

High-technology industries are also a major problem for European competitiveness.[55] This is especially true for semiconductors, computers, and consumer electronics. Somewhat brighter conclusions can be reached about telecommunications. In semiconductors, European producers were the main losers in the struggle between U.S. and Japanese firms in the 1980s and 1990s. World market shares for European firms have fallen to 10 percent and show little signs of recovery. Even inside Europe, domestic producers maintain only a 40 percent market share. European firms control even less of their market for computers, only 34 percent, and seem to be falling behind in the capacity to innovate and gain competitive advantage. Consumer electronics is somewhat better, with European firms stronger than U.S.-based firms but still weaker than the Japanese. Only in telecommunications do European firms dominate their home markets and compete effectively in global markets. But some part of this strength derives from protected markets and preferential policies by home governments. Liberalization of telecommunications markets on a global scale in the 1990s provides a good test of European firms' long-term capabilities.

Individual governments and the European Union have made efforts to reverse the competitive weaknesses of European high-technology firms. Business and government elites across Europe have understood quite well the strategic nature of many of these industries. They have recognized that strength in high technology shapes the trajectory of economic development and growth for entire economies; weakness closes off possibilities that can limit growth in many areas. In the past, these concerns led to national policies designed to promote a national firm capable of competing in world markets. These efforts failed because the scale of such enterprises and markets was too small. EU leaders realized that only when the European market was a genuine reality could scale problems be overcome. This helped propel the decision for a single market in 1992. Additionally, the EU has moved to support interfirm cooperation through large-scale R&D projects. Four of these projects deserve mention. The European Strategic Programme for Research and Development in Information Technology (ESPRIT) was created by the EEC in 1984 to provide funds for collaborative R&D. Nearly $10 billion was allocated to this program by 1994, half from government sources. R&D in Advanced Communications-Technologies in Europe (RACE) is a somewhat smaller program established in 1985 to promote collaboration in such areas as high-definition television. The European Research Coordination Agency (EUREKA), established in 1985, sponsored such projects as Joint European Semiconductor Silicon (JESSI) to catch up in semiconductor manufacturing. And Basic Research for Industrial Technology in Europe (BRITE) was directed at special materials related to superconductivity.[56] The results of these efforts remain unclear but are testimony to the intense concern in Europe over lagging behind in high technology. Much recent evidence from other nations (such as Japan), however, suggests that large government-directed consortia are ineffective in advancing competitiveness. The key to improvement is the ability to use knowledge rapidly to develop products and new markets. Only firms can do this.

Early in the twenty-first century, European firms have begun to display some bright signs. The late 1990s found many of these firms engaged in the same process of cost cutting and shedding of extraneous divisions as U.S. firms. Much of this leads to a greater focus on the firm's most important competitive competencies, while outsourcing (buying from other firms) those activities that can be done better by others. Mergers and acquisitions—by which the ownership of firms is reshuffled—has increased dramatically as firms seek more effective partners. This intense specialization makes firms more efficient and more competitive. These changes have resulted partly from the EU's unification of markets and partly from national deregulation and privatization, which leads to lower prices for such things as telecommunication services. Europe now is developing a single capital market, which facilitates the buying and selling of companies.[57] And the advent of the Euro makes operating across borders much easier, which portends an even more dynamic process of restructuring for European firms.[58]

The terms of international competition have changed, making obsolete the advantages that once propelled Europe, and then the United States, to world economic preeminence. For a time in the twentieth century, Japan seemed to have taken control of setting a global competitiveness standard. But the resurgence of the United States, and possibly Europe, has changed matters. Competitiveness now seems to reside in the firm that can use information and knowledge the most effectively to cut costs, develop new products, and deliver these products in the fastest and most flexible manner. This capability often involves not only firms but also the complex system of institutions that surround and support firms. A much wider hearing needs to be given to the call for policies designed to create comparative advantage through investments in infrastructure supporting knowledge-intensive industries, higher levels of national savings, and actions to cushion or even assume risks for certain key industries. This approach involves thinking in terms of national systems of innovation.[59] But beyond these proposals is the traditional strategy for responding to the new climate of international competition: protectionism.

PROTECTIONISM

Ironically, the acceleration of the world economy toward freer trade and even greater interdependence has also led to a revival of pressures for protectionism. This should not come as too much of a surprise because more interdependence means that the most competitive and innovative foreign producers have more opportunities to sell their goods. Those who cannot meet this competition invariably begin to call for government help. But in an international climate where GATT/WTO has led to very low tariffs, protectionism has become somewhat more sophisticated.[60]

Protectionism without Tariffs

These "new" protectionist measures are typically designed to help a particular industry. In the broadest sense, these measures are designed to "manage" trade outcomes without regard to the results of (seemingly) free markets. Examples of managed trade include efforts to use the threat of legally mandated restrictions to compel importers to restrict the sale of their goods "voluntarily," and negotiated arrangements that establish quotas to limit imports. A second form involves efforts to arrange a quota for exports of a particular product and in this sense might be understood as trade promoting rather than trade restricting.

Sometimes known as voluntary export restraints (VERs) and orderly marketing agreements (OMAs), these arrangements have been used to establish quotas for the sale of goods in the United States.[61] In 1981 the Japanese government acted "voluntarily" to restrict the number of automobiles sold in the United States so as to reduce pressure in the U.S. Congress for much more restrictive protectionism.[62] The Reagan administration did not want to violate its free trade ideology but could not ignore the rapid growth of Japanese auto sales in the U.S. market. Subtle pressure on Japan led it to choose the least painful option and announce that no more than 1.68 million cars per year would be shipped to the United States. The arrangement remained in place for more than 10 years, with several interesting consequences. Japanese penetration of the U.S. auto market was slowed but not stopped, with the Japanese share of the U.S. auto market rising from less than 19 percent in 1980 to 23.1 percent in 1994. Automakers in Japan have modified the mix of cars sold in the United States toward more expensive models, and prices for autos have risen much more rapidly than for other goods.[63]

From the perspective of U.S. autoworkers and executives, the VER was insufficient. Much more needed to be done to restrain the competitive pressure generated by Japan. From the position of U.S. consumers, qualitative improvements (and some jobs) were purchased at a very high cost.[64] In effect, U.S. consumers, through higher prices, subsidized both the U.S. and the Japanese auto industries. From the position of political leaders, the VER can be a relatively quiet way to provide relief to a threatened industry without challenging the concept of free trade either at home or abroad. Of course, this works only so long as the exporting country cooperates.[65]

Perhaps the best example of managed trade is in the semiconductor industry, discussed earlier. In 1985, after several years of losing market share to Japanese firms, the Semiconductor Industry Association (a cooperative alliance of U.S. semiconductor firms) filed a petition under Section 301 of the Trade Act of 1974.[66] This petition and subsequent legal actions charged that Japanese firms were "dumping" semiconductors (selling in the United States at prices below the cost of production) and that the Japanese semiconductor market was closed to U.S. firms. The main purpose of this action was to force the Japanese government to begin negotiations on a division of market share between U.S. and Japanese firms. The result was an agreement reached in 1986 in which Japanese firms promised to stop dumping semiconductors in the United States and to increase the Japanese market share for U.S. firms to 20 percent within five years. After punitive tariffs were imposed in 1987 to force compliance, the U.S. share of the Japanese market began to increase. An extension of the agreement was needed in 1991 to give Japan time to meet the 20 percent quota, which it did in 1993.[67]

The longest-standing VER is the Multi-Fibre Arrangement (MFA), which can be traced back to the early 1960s. The textile and apparel industry—where the industrial revolution began 200 years ago—is a good example of a labor-intensive, low-capital-investment, low-technology industry in which comparative advantage comes largely from relative wage levels. High-wage nations have typically been unable to compete with low-wage nations in the absence of some form of protectionism. The MFA is a multilateral agreement designed to place quantitative limits on imports of textiles and apparel into high-wage countries. Associated with it is a series of bilateral agreements designed to serve the same purpose. Well over half of all world trade in this industry is subject to one of these agreements.[68] The 1994 GATT agreement in the Uruguay Round of negotiations phases out the MFA to the great benefit of low-wage, high-productivity countries.

Important variations on protectionism in the West can be found in Japan, which has increasingly become the target of those who are harmed by its exports. Many have argued that Japan continues to operate as a free rider—benefiting from free trade while blocking the import of many goods. Documenting this charge is difficult because overt barriers to trade in Japan—tariffs and quotas—are generally lower than in most other advanced capitalist countries.[69] Rather, Japan retains a number of cultural and structural arrangements that effectively stand in the way of many imports. The result is a skewing of Japanese imports toward raw materials and semiprocessed manufactures and away from high-value-added and high-tech goods, as compared with other advanced capitalist states.

In general, barriers in Japan fit into one of several categories. They include:

1. Product standards (more important before 1980 than today), which indirectly or directly discriminate against foreign products

2. A distribution system, composed of many small retailers linked through exclusive arrangements with manufacturers and protected by price fixing, that blocks market access by foreign firms[70]

3. Government favoritism toward Japanese firms in its purchases

4. A predominant form of business organization—*keiretsu*—that effectively creates a closed system of intrafirm purchases and suppliers which blocks entry by foreign firms

5. Cultural and business structural barriers to foreign direct investment, especially the foreign purchase of Japanese firms

6. A strong cultural preference for Japanese goods and a bias against foreign goods that makes Japan a difficult market, requiring a substantial investment of time and resources

7. Substantial overt protection of Japanese agriculture that is tied to political support for the predominant party, the Liberal Democratic Party[71]

The large Japanese trade surplus, the special Japanese government-business system, and the large Japanese consumer market help draw attention to these trade barriers. During the 1980s and 1990s, many in the U.S. Congress have called for trade retaliation unless Japan opens its markets and reduces the trade surplus by a specified amount. And these sentiments have been responsible for various VERs and managed trade agreements. This may make good politics, but it fails to deal with the fact that many of these same practices exist in the United States and most other nations.

The Common Agricultural Policy (CAP) in the European Union also represents one of the most formidable systems of protection. As with many other things in the history of the EEC, EC, and EU, the Common Agricultural Policy was originally part of a compromise between France and Germany. French farmers were permitted to sell in Germany, while German farmers were protected from world prices. CAP established a free internal market for food within the EEC, a system of price supports through purchases of foodstuffs when prices fall below world levels, and a tariff and internal tax to pay for the program. Further, surplus food was often exported at subsidized prices. Because European farmers have consistently been inefficient relative to the rest of the industrialized world and because plans for modernization of agricultural production have been blocked by farmers' resistance to change, the gap between world prices and community support prices has widened over time. This has meant that the budget for support payments also has had to grow and by 2000 accounted for 50 percent of the entire EU budget. The political basis for this system was the close relationship between farmers' organizations and the agricultural ministry in each state, which maintained effective control over CAP. Additionally, CAP is woven into the many political compromises and agreements that sustain the EU. This makes it a difficult arrangement to change. Even so, the distortion of world trade caused by CAP is substantial because the EU should be a major importer but instead is a major exporter of food. Prices inside the EU are much higher and world prices lower because of the oversupply of food.[72]

Why Do Nations Choose Protection?

Why should we expect countries to adopt protectionism? The politics of the decision to place barriers on imports in any particular industry or as a general national policy is linked to a maze of interests, power relationships, and institutions. Political economists at this point can provide only a list of the main forces at work and cannot specify the circumstances under which protectionism will succeed or fail.[73]

1. Because the benefits of protection are concentrated in a small number of owners and workers in the affected industry while the costs of protection are spread across many consumers, political organization for protection is easier than for free trade.[74]

2. A nation's position in the world economy affects its foreign economic policy. That is, its relative proportion of world trade and the competitiveness of its products generate incentives and opportunities that largely define whether it pursues free trade or protection or some combination. Very large and competitive states—hegemons—will prefer a multilateral free trade system. Middle-ranking states will mix desire for free trade in the system with desire for some level of domestic protection, but they also realize that too much free riding on their part can lead to a collapse of the system. Small and/or uncompetitive states are likely to prefer protectionism at home and to hope for free trade in the system.[75]

3. The fate of the world economy—depression or prosperity—intersects with the structure of a nation's domestic interests—the relative power of protectionist versus free-trade groups—to affect national decisions on foreign economic policy. It is much more difficult to sustain free trade in a depressed world economy.[76]

4. As a variation of number 3, the growth of global interdependence and a nation's extensive participation in the world economy lead to more and more firms with interests in promoting free trade. As these firms depend on global markets, they actively oppose efforts to increase protection for other industries because of fear of retaliation.

5. Choices about free trade and protection are constrained by ideas, political institutions, and political relationships framed during particular historical periods. After ideas come to permeate elite thinking and institutions are established, the institutions create rules for the evaluation of policy.[77]

6. Likewise, when a particular set of ideas and institutions achieves predominance at the international level, it also structures choices in bilateral and multilateral negotiations. The extension of free trade ideas and institutions since 1945 has conditioned the nature and extent of protectionist policies.[78]

7. Finally, protectionist or free trade proposals or policies may be used as part of a bargaining strategy designed to alter the preferences of other states. The efforts by U.S. presidents to negotiate trade outcomes with Japan violate the principles of free trade. But these agreements are partly designed to alter the Japanese trading system and to appease protectionist forces in the United States.

The new protectionism just described is often an effort to strike a political balance between a general commitment to freer trade and the genuine economic damage that such a policy can have on inefficient domestic producers and their workers.[79] The leadership of advanced industrial nations understands that withdrawal from the world economy would have disastrous economic and political consequences. The incentives to keep an open system functioning are simply too great to permit its demise.[80] At the same time, this viewpoint is politically viable only as long as the system produces a rising standard of living, and this requires that nations continually adjust to its inherent dynamism. Prolonged recession would surely unravel the political supports that make such a system possible. The recent growth of protectionism, the difficulties in negotiating the Uruguay Round of GATT, and the rise of economic blocs do not clearly portend the end of an open system. But in a stagnant or shrinking world economy, these developments certainly could serve as a basis for fragmentation and even disintegration.

CONCLUSIONS

Especially in the context of an open world economy, competition among nations and among firms takes place. The global system of relatively free trade generated in large part by GATT/WTO makes substantial and mutual gains from trade possible. Nonetheless, nations and firms compete for additional gains from trade: nations compete by supporting their own firms, national and multinational; nations compete to attract firms and business from around the world; and firms compete with each other on a global basis for market share and profits. Finally, nations see economic competition as intimately linked to political and military competition in the international system.

Economic competition and conflict rarely get out of bounds because nations and firms understand the mutuality of gains from the present world economy and the potential damage from its demise. This helps sustain the immense effort that nations must also make to cooperate in creating a political context for competition. And when different national practices or unpleasant outcomes produce conflict, nations typically moderate their demands to resolve the differences. The international institutions for resolving trade conflict have been weak and the rules sometimes unclear. But trade conflict, such as between the United States and Japan, is unlikely to lead to real political hostility.

What is the future direction for competition? The era in which Japan's successes are the object of condemnation seems over, partly because those successes have dimmed and partly because of U.S. resurgence. Although protectionism has been increasing in the wake of Japan's success and the new climate of global competition, more energy has been directed toward other strategies. These usually involve aid directed toward increasing the productive capabilities of specific high-value industries, improving the national infrastructure of competition (such as in education and training), creating larger markets through free trade agreements, and attracting firms by making markets freer of regulation or through regulations that help firms operate effectively. The new standard of competitiveness is Silicon Valley and the high-tech opportunities and challenges this presents. Although the stampede toward the Internet and e-business has faded, this arena is likely to define the next set of global competitive standards.

Perhaps the greatest uncertainty in understanding competition is the impact of globalization. This makes identifying the nationality of firms more difficult, disperses the benefits of national investments throughout the world through technology transfer and strategic alliances, and places the locus of competitive power in the hands of geographically mobile multinational corporations. In the near and long term, globalization may have its greatest effect by incorporating the Third World into the competitive process on much more equal terms. The globalization of production, investment, finance, and communications transfers to the Third World much of the infrastructure of competition formerly located exclusively in rich nations. The emergence of Newly Industrialized Countries (NICs) and many other candidate NICs expands dramatically the scope of competition. It is to this arena of rapid change and development that we now turn our attention.

NOTES

1. For a useful examination of many different arenas of international cooperation, see the various articles in Peter Haas (ed.), "Knowledge, Power and International Policy Coordination," *International Organization,* special issue, 46.1, Winter 1992.

2. The ability to produce rising standards of living while maintaining a policy of autarchy or without selling in world markets is an interesting but empirically rare case. We are interested in those nations involved in the world economy.

3. This view is most forcefully presented in Paul Krugman, "Competitiveness:

A Dangerous Obsession," *Foreign Affairs,* March–April 1994, 28–48. Critical responses are in "The Fight over Competitiveness," *Foreign Affairs,* July–August 1994, 186–202. A more scholarly analysis is David Rapkin and Jonathan Strand, "Is International Competitiveness a Meaningful Concept?" in C. Roe Goddard, et al. (eds.), *International Political Economy: Readings on State-Market Relations in the Changing Global Order,* Boulder, Colo.: Lynne Rienner, 1995.

4. Remember, *economies of scale* refers to a situation in which the cost of each unit of production falls as output rises. Typically, a firm experiencing significant economies of scale has substantial fixed costs and somewhat modest marginal costs. Economies of scale result as the fixed costs are spread over higher and higher levels of output, resulting in falling per-unit costs.

5. Paul Krugman, *Rethinking International Trade,* Cambridge: MIT Press, 1990. Paul Krugman and Alasdair Smith, (eds.), *Empirical Studies of Strategic Trade Policy,* Chicago: University of Chicago Press, 1994. For a critique of strategic trade theory, see J. David Richardson, "The Political Economy of Strategic Trade Policy," *International Organization,* 44.1, Winter 1990, 107–135.

6. For some perspective on this process, see B. A. Lundvall, *National Systems of Innovation,* London: Pinter, 1992; and Richard Nelson (ed.), *National Innovation Systems,* New York: Oxford University Press, 1993. Also see Michael Porter, *The Competitive Advantage of Nations,* New York: Free Press, 1990. A very useful review is in John Clark and Ken Guy, "Innovation and Competitiveness: A Review," *Technology Analysis and Strategic Management,* 10.3, 1998, 363–395.

7. Three insightful sources on the postwar era and U.S. occupation are Michael Schaller, *The American Occupation of Japan,* New York: Oxford University Press, 1985; Bruce Cumings, "Power and Plenty in Northeast Asia: The Evolution of U.S. Policy," *World Policy Journal,* 5.1, Winter 1987–88, 79–106; John W. Dower, *Embracing Defeat,* New York: Norton, 2000.

8. Useful sources on the development of the postwar Japanese political system include Chalmers Johnson, *MITI and the Japanese Miracle,* Stanford, Calif.: Stanford University Press, 1982; and T. J. Pempel, *Regime Shift: Dynamics of the Japanese Political Economy,* Ithaca, N.Y.: Cornell University Press, 1998. Between 1956 and 1986, 7 of the 10 Japanese prime ministers had also served as minister of international trade and industry (W. G. Beasley, *The Rise of Modern Japan,* New York: St. Martin's Press, 1990, 246).

9. Daniel Okimoto, *Between MITI and the Market,* Stanford, Calif.: Stanford University Press, 1989, 23.

10. Access to foreign markets was made possible by U.S. pressure on its Western allies to admit Japan to full status in GATT despite several countries' resistance (Ryutaro Komiya and Motoshige Itoh, "Japan's International Trade Status and Trade Policy, 1955–1984," in Takashi Inoguchi and Daniel Okimoto [eds.], *The Political Economy of Japan,* Volume 2, Stanford, Calif.: Stanford University Press, 1988, 174–179).

11. Note the similarity of motivation between Japanese MNCs and U.S. MNCs. See Young Kwan-Yoon, "The Political Economy of Transition: Japanese Foreign Direct Investment in the 1980s," *World Politics,* 43, October 1990, 1–27; Makihiro Matsuoka and Brian Rose, *The DIR Guide to Japanese Economic Statistics,* Oxford, England: Oxford University Press, 1994, 144–149.

12. For data comparing these nations and the ratio of tariff revenue to imports, see Komiya and Itoh, "Japan's International Trade Status," 193.

13. Between 1980 and 1997, inward FDI to Japan was always less than 1 percent of GDP and hardly increased

at all, whereas in the United States, Italy, Germany, and France during the same period, inward FDI increased from about 3 percent of GDP to about 8 percent. Some increases in Japan did occur between 1995 and 1999, but the overall level remains very small ("Business in Japan," *The Economist,* November 27, 1999).

14. Matsuoka and Rose, *DIR Guide,* 132; David Yofee, *Beyond Free Trade: Firms, Governments and Global Competition,* Boston: Harvard Business School Press, 1993, ix.

15. The deficit recurred in 1980, following the second wave of oil shocks (Komiya and Itoh, "Japan's International Trade Status," 198–200; Stephen Weatherford and Haruhiro Fukui, "Domestic Adjustment to International Shocks in Japan and the United States," *International Organization,* 43.4, Autumn 1989, 600–617).

16. Bank of Japan, Economic Statistics. A very useful account of the bubble economy is George Lodge, "Japan Confronts an Interdependent World," Harvard Business School Case, March 1994.

17. David Friedman, *The Misunderstood Miracle,* Ithaca, N.Y.: Cornell University Press, 1988, 4–6.

18. Johnson, *MITI,* 11–17.

19. The name of this bureaucracy has now been changed to "Ministry of Economy, Trade and Industry" (METI).

20. Friedman, *Misunderstood Miracle,* 3.

21. In his discussion of MITI, Chalmers Johnson coined the phrase "developmental state" to describe the situation in Japan. The term has since been used to describe many governments in Asia and elsewhere (Meredith Woo-Cumings, *The Developmental State,* Ithaca, N.Y.: Cornell University Press, 1999).

22. Okimoto, *MITI and the Market,* 11–36; Johnson, *MITI,* 81.

23. Michael Gerlach, *Alliance Capitalism,* Berkeley and Los Angeles: University of California Press, 1992.

24. Johnson, *MITI,* 199–212. Of special significance in this process was access to the U.S. market, which offered an enormous opportunity to utilize economies of scale, cut costs and raise productivity.

25. Johnson, *MITI,* 249–272.

26. Johnson, *MITI . . . ,* 275–301.

27. Okimoto, *MITI and the Market,* 55–85.

28. Martin Tolchin, "Pentagon Says It Lags in Some Technologies," *New York Times,* March 22, 1990.

29. David Sanger, "Mighty MITI Loses Its Grip," *New York Times,* July 9, 1989. Also see Marie Anchordoguy, "Mastering the Market: Japanese Government Targeting of the Computer Industry," *International Organization,* 42.3, Summer 1988, 509–543.

30. The following discussion draws on Okimoto, *MITI and the Market;* Friedman, *Misunderstood Miracle;* and Laura D'Andrea Tyson, "Developmental Strategy and Production Innovation in Japan," in Chalmers Johnson et al. (eds.), *Politics and Productivity,* New York: Harper and Row, 1989, 59–140.

31. Stephen S. Cohen, "Geo-economics: Lessons from America's Mistakes," in Martin Carnoy (ed.), *The New Global Economy in the Information Age,* University Park: Penn State University Press, 1993, 107.

32. This view is adapted from several sources: Richard Samuels, *The Business of the Japanese State,* Ithaca, N.Y.: Cornell University Press, 1987; Jeffrey Hart, *Rival Capitalists,* Ithaca, N.Y.: Cornell University Press, 1992; Richard Nelson (ed.), *National Innovation Systems,* Oxford, England: Oxford University Press, 1993.

33. Walter Hatch and Kozo Yamamura, *Asia in Japan's Embrace,* Cambridge, England: Cambridge University Press, 1996, 187–188.

34. "The Japanese Economy: From Miracle to Mid-Life Crisis," *The Economist,* March 6, 1993; George

Lodge, *Japan Confronts an Interdependent World,* Harvard Business School Case, March 1994.

35. This same problem is common throughout Asia and helps account for the Asian financial crisis of 1997–1998. See Chapter 12. For more detail on the Japanese banking system and the bubble crisis, see Peter Hartcher, *The Ministry,* Boston: Harvard Business School Press, 1998, 60–122. By contrast, in the United States banks are closely scrutinized by bank inspectors from the U.S. government, who examine the quality of loans on a regular basis.

36. Hartcher, *The Ministry,* 100.

37. Ultimately, the size of deficit spending has been so great as to threaten the Japanese economy. Government debt now is 130 percent of GDP. Most other developed states have ratios far below that level. During the 1990s Italy, Britain, Canada, Germany, France, and the United States all dramatically reduced deficits or shifted from deficits to budget surpluses. By contrast, Japan moved from a budget surplus of 3 percent of GDP in 1990 to a deficit of 8 percent of GDP in 1999.

38. Details on the economically weak sectors of the Japanese economy are found in Richard Katz, *Japan: The System That Soured,* Armonk, N.Y.: M. E. Sharpe, 1998. Also see "Business in Japan," *The Economist,* November 27, 1999. Data on relative prices are from Michael Porter et al., *Can Japan Compete?* Cambridge: Perseus, 2000, 6.

39. For discussion of this interpretation of Japanese political economy, see Steven K. Vogel, "Can Japan Disengage? Winners and Losers in Japan's Political Economy, and the Ties that Bind Them," *Social Science Journal Japan,* 2.1, April 1999, 3–21; T. J. Pempel, "Structural Gaiatsu: International Financial Movements and Domestic Political Change," *Comparative Political Studies,* 32.8, 1999, 907–932; Lonnie Carlile and

Mark Tilton, *Is Japan Really Changing Its Ways?* Washington, D.C.: Brookings Institution, 1998; Kent Calder, *Crisis and Compensation,* Princeton, N.J.: Princeton University Press, 1988.

40. Contrasting viewpoints about Japan's future are found in M. Diana Helweg, "Japan: A Rising Sun?" *Foreign Affairs,* 79.4, July–August 2000, 26–52; and Aurelia George Mulgan, "Japan: A Setting Sun?" *Foreign Affairs,* 79.4, July–August 2000, 40–52.

41. Joseph Quinlan and Marc Chandler, "The U.S. Trade Deficit: A Dangerous Obsession," *Foreign Affairs,* 80.3, May–June 2000, 87–97. This article reports that total U.S. exports to the United Kingdom, Germany, and Japan in 1998 were $124 billion; that same year, U.S. firms produced and sold $464 billion in goods in those three countries.

42. *The Economist,* May 6, 1995, 78. The main source of the savings deficiency in the United States is households. In 1973, the household savings rate was 9 percent; by 1994, it was 4 percent (*The Economist,* January 21, 1995, 19).

43. Lawrence Klein, "Components of Competitiveness," *Science,* 241, July 15, 1988, 308–313.

44. This refers to Moore's Law, named for Gordon Moore, a founder of Intel. In the 1960s, Moore predicted that the number of transistors that could be etched on a semiconductor device would double every one to two years, effectively doubling computing power.

45. The early years of the global semiconductor industry are discussed in Laura D'Andrea Tyson and David Yofee, "Semiconductors: From Manipulated to Managed Trade," in Yofee (ed.), *Beyond Free Trade,* 29–48; and Timothy O'Shea, *The U.S.-Japan Semiconductor Problem,* Washington, D.C.: Pew Case Studies, 1994.

46. The most complete discussion of the trade agreement is Kenneth Flamm, *Mismanaged Trade?* Washington, D.C.: Brookings Institution, 1996.

47. David Gibson and Everett Rogers, *R&D Collaboration on Trial,* Cambridge: Harvard Business School Press, 1994, 467–533. Sematech, now known as International Sematech, has morphed into an international consortium and is privately funded (see its Web site at <http:www.sematech.org/public/index.htm>).

48. There are, broadly speaking, two major types of semiconductor chips, memory and logic. The former were the focus for much technological innovation until the 1990s, when it assumed more of a commodity position. About the same time, logic chips assumed a more important role because of their greater complexity and diversity (Richard Langlois and W. Edward Steinmueller, "The Evolution of Competitive Advantage in the Worldwide Semiconductor Industry, 1947–1996," in David Mowery and Richard Nelson [eds.], *Sources of Industrial Leadership,* Cambridge, England: Cambridge University Press, 1999, 19–78). Japanese firms' decision to remain in memory chips was further undermined by the emergence of Korean firms such as Samsung, which continually took market share after 1985.

49. If you doubt this, imagine the barriers to establishing a successful semiconductor industry in Vietnam.

50. Evidence of this interest can be found in the number of books and articles on the topic. A sample includes Annalee Saxenian, *Regional Advantage,* 2nd ed., Cambridge: Harvard University Press, 1996; Chong-Moon Lee et al. (eds.), *The Silicon Valley Edge,* Stanford, Calif.: Stanford University Press, 2000; Martin Kenney (ed.), *Understanding Silicon Valley,* Stanford, Calif.: Stanford University Press, 2000; Michael Porter, "Clusters and the New Economics of Competition," *Harvard Business Review,* November–December 1998, 77–90.

51. Details on Xerox PARC are in Michael Hiltzik, *Dealers of Lightening: Xerox PARC and the Dawn of the Computer Age,* New York: HarperCollins, 1999.

52. Several articles detailing industrial policy in France, Germany, and the United Kingdom are in Richard E. Foglesong and Joel Wolfe (eds.), *The Politics of Economic Adjustment,* New York: Greenwood Press, 1989.

53. *The Economist,* January 15, 1995, 66.

54. Nathaniel Nash, "Putting Porsche in the Pink," *New York Times,* January 20, 1996, 17.

55. This discussion of European high technology relies on John Zysman and Michael Borrus, *Failure to Fortune? European Electronics in the Changing World Economy,* Berkeley: BRIE Working Paper, 1994; Wayne Sandholtz, *High-Tech Europe,* Berkeley and Los Angeles: University of California Press, 1992; and Kirsty Hughes (ed.), *European Competitiveness,* Cambridge, England: Cambridge University Press, 1993.

56. The best discussion of these programs is found in Sandholtz, *High-Tech Europe.*

57. One consequence of having a firm bought out is that its management is often replaced. Thus, increasing merger and acquisition activity is a spur to management to do a better job so that the firm's value is high. The firms that are the most likely candidates for takeover are those that could be managed better and therefore have the most potential for firm value increase.

58. An optimistic survey of the competitiveness of European firms is "European Business," *The Economist,* April 29, 2000.

59. Richard Nelson (ed.), *National Innovation Systems: A Comparative Analysis,* Oxford, England: Oxford University Press, 1993.

60. A still useful, but dated, overview of protectionism is David Greenway, *Trade Policy and the New Protectionism,* New York: St. Martin's Press, 1983.

61. Others include countervailing duties (CVD) and antidumping arrangements, which result from what are thought to be unfair trading practices. When foreign firms sell below "fair value" or receive a state subsidy, these methods are used to raise prices so as to establish a "level playing field." A useful overview of protectionist trends in the United States is I. M. Destler, *American Trade Politics*, 3rd ed., Washington, D.C.: Institute for International Economics, 1995. Case studies are found in Gary Hufbauer et al., *Trade Protectionism in the United States*, Washington, D.C.: Institute for International Economics, 1986.

62. A similar agreement exists between the EU and Japan.

63. The machine tools industry is another area where VERs have been used with mixed results. The uncompetitive producers support this policy; whereas more competitive firms oppose VERs (Steve Lohr, "A Split over Machine Tools Imports," *New York Times*, October 7, 1991).

64. One estimate is that each job saved cost consumers $110,000 to $145,000 (Charles Collyns and Steve Dunaway, "The Cost of Trade Restraints: The Case of Japanese Automobile Exports to the United States," in King [ed.], *International Economics*, 13–21).

65. The best reviews of the auto VERs are Simon Reich, *The Reagan Administration, the Auto Producers, and the 1981 Agreement with Japan*, Washington, D.C.: Pew Case Studies, 1992; and Simon Reich, *Restraining Trade to Invoke Investment: MITI and the Japanese Auto Producers*, Washington, D.C.: Pew Case Studies, 1992.

66. Section 301 and its successor, Super 301, from the Trade Act of 1988, give the president the authority to impose punitive tariffs on countries engaging in "unfair" trade practices.

67. See Flamm, *Mismanaged Trade?* for a detailed discussion of the semiconductor trade agreement.

Discussion of trade conflict is in David Rowe, *Trade Wars: The Political Economy of International Economic Conflict*, Cambridge: Institute for Strategic Analysis, 1994.

68. William R. Cline, "The Evolution of Protection in Textiles and Apparel," in King (ed.), *International Economics*, 34–40.

69. But it is the case that in the recent past Japan has had much higher tariff barriers.

70. Perhaps the most famous arrangement supporting the system of small, specialized retailers is the "Large Store Law," which was used to block large discount stores from opening. Such stores would likely stock more foreign goods at lower prices and eliminate many small retailers. See Leonard Schoppa, *Bargaining with Japan*, New York: Columbia University Press, 1997, 146–180. The demise of the Large Store Law has opened the door to U.S. retailers such as Walmart.

71. For the link between the LDP and farmers, see Gerald L. Curtis, *The Japanese Way of Politics*, New York: Columbia University Press, 1988, 49–61. Also see, Dorothy Christelow, "Japan's Intangible Barriers to Trade in Manufacturers," in King (ed.), *International Economics*, 41–56.

72. See "The Future of Europe," *The Economist*, October 21, 1999.

73. Richard Friman, "Rocks, Hard Places, and the New Protectionism: Textile Trade Policy Choices in the United States and Japan," *International Organization*, 42.4, Autumn 1988, 689–723; Benjamin Cohen, "The Political Economy of International Trade," *International Organization*, 44.2, Spring 1990, 261–281.

74. Real P. Lavergne, *The Political Economy of US. Tariffs*, New York: Academic Press, 1983.

75. David Lake, *Power, Protection, and Free Trade*, Ithaca, N.Y.: Cornell University Press, 1988, 1–65.

76. Peter Gourevitch, *Politics in Hard Times*, Ithaca, N.Y.: Cornell

University Press, 1986; Ronald Rogowski, *Commerce and Coalitions,* Princeton, N.J.: Princeton University Press, 1990.

77. Helen Milner, *Resisting Protectionism,* Princeton, N.J.: Princeton University Press, 1988.

78. Judith Goldstein, "The Political Economy of Trade: Institutions of Protection," *American Political Science Review,* 80.1, March 1986; Judith Goldstein, "The Impact of Ideas on Trade Policy," *International*

Organization, 43.1, Winter 1989, 31–71; Daniel Verdier, *Democracy and International Trade,* Princeton, N.J.: Princeton University Press, 1994.

79. Jagdish Bhagwati, *Protectionism,* Cambridge: MIT Press, 1988; Paul Krugman, *The Age of Diminished Expectations,* Cambridge: MIT Press, 1990.

80. Susan Strange, "Protectionism and World Politics," *International Organization,* 30, Spring 1985, 233–259.

ANNOTATED BIBLIOGRAPHY

C. Fred Bergsten et al. *No More Bashing: Building a New Japan-United States Economic Relationship.* Washington, D.C.: Institute for International Economics, 2001. Makes the case for rethinking Japan and its relationship to the United States.

Jagdish Bhagwati. *Protectionism.* Cambridge: MIT Press, 1988; Jagdish Bhagwati. *The World Trading System at Risk.* Princeton, N.J.: Princeton University Press, 1991. Both books offer a spirited and convincing case against the new protectionism.

Lonny Carlile and Mark Tilton (eds.). *Is Japan Really Changing Its Ways?* Washington, D.C.: Brookings Institution, 1998. A set of case studies examining the "embedded mercantilism" of the Japanese system.

I. M. Destler. *American Trade Politics.* 3rd ed. Washington, D.C.: Institute for International Economics, 1995. A detailed study of the political economy of trade during the 1980s and 1990s.

Dennis Encarnation. *Rivals beyond Trade: America versus Japan in Global Competition.* Ithaca, N.Y.: Cornell University Press, 1992. Traces the imbalance in U.S.-Japanese trade to asymmetries in foreign direct investment between these two countries.

David Friedman. *The Misunderstood Miracle.* Ithaca, N.Y.: Cornell University Press, 1988. Counters the MITI thesis and focuses on the impact of small- and medium-sized manufacturing in Japan.

Otis Graham, Jr. *Losing Time: The Industrial Policy Debate.* Cambridge: Harvard University Press, 1992. A detailed look at the political debate regarding an active governmental policy in supporting specific industries.

Jeffrey Hart. *Rival Capitalists.* Ithaca, N.Y.: Cornell University Press, 1992. Examines competitiveness in terms of differing forms of relationships between states and society.

Takashi Inoguchi and Daniel Okimoto (eds.). *The Political Economy of Japan,* Volume 2: *The Changing International Context.* Stanford, Calif.: Stanford University Press, 1988. A very insightful collection of essays.

Chalmers Johnson. *MITI and the Japanese Miracle.* Stanford, Calif.: Stanford University Press, 1982. An essential book on the evolution of Japan's business-government system.

Richard Katz. *Japan: The System That Soured.* Armonk, N.Y.: M. E. Sharpe, 1998. The best analysis of the dual nature of the Japanese economy.

Paul Krugman. *Rethinking International Trade*. Cambridge: MIT Press, 1990. A very important critique of free trade.

Helen Milner. *Resisting Protectionism*. Princeton, N.J.: Princeton University Press, 1988. An essential source for understanding the political economy of support for free trade.

Kenichi Miyashita and David Russell. *Keiretsu: Inside the Hidden Japanese Conglomerates*. New York: McGraw-Hill, 1996. A detailed and understandable description of Japanese *keiretsu*.

Theodore Moran. *American Economic Policy and National Security*. New York: CFR Press, 1993. Links economic competitiveness to military strength.

Joseph Morone. *Winning in High-Tech Markets*. Cambridge: Harvard Business School Press, 1993. Provides an analysis of competition in high technology from the firm perspective.

Michael Porter. *The Competitive Advantage of Nations*. New York: Free Press, 1990. An essential study of the competitiveness of firms as they operate in a national context.

Michael Porter et al. *Can Japan Compete?* Cambridge: Perseus, 2000. A very insightful critique of the government-based theory of Japanese growth.

Daniel Okimoto. *Between MITI and Market*. Stanford, Calif.: Stanford University Press, 1989. Brings the analysis of changes in MITI into the 1980s.

Adam Posen. *Restoring Japan's Economic Growth*. Washington, D.C.: Institute for International Economics, 1998. Argues that Japan's economic troubles are the result of macroeconomic mistakes.

David Rapkin and William Avery (eds.). *National Competitiveness in a Global Economy*. Boulder, Colo.: Lynne Rienner, 1995. An excellent collection of essays.

Wayne Sandholtz et al. (eds.). *The Highest Stakes*. Oxford, England: Oxford University Press, 1992. Offers an analysis of mercantilist tendencies in competitiveness thinking.

F. M. Scherer. *International High-Technology Competition*. Cambridge: Harvard University Press, 1992. An economist examines high-technology competition, using several case studies.

Leonard Schoppa. *Bargaining with Japan*. New York: Columbia University Press, 1997. A detailed examination of U.S.-Japanese negotiations in the 1980s and 1990s.

Carl Shapiro and Hal R. Varian. *Information Rules: A Strategic Guide to the Network Economy*. Boston: Harvard Business School Press, 1999. A very insightful analysis of the new world of information technology and business.

Karel van Wolferen. *The Enigma of Japanese Power*. New York: Vintage Books, 1990. Presents a very critical view of Japanese government and politics.

John Zysman and Laura Tyson (eds.). *American Industry in International Competition*. Ithaca, N.Y.: Cornell University Press, 1983. A dated but very helpful study of the political economy of firm competitiveness.

8

❖

Rich and Poor States
in the World Economy

The present level of international social and economic inequality is historically unprecedented. Before the past century, living standards had never diverged so widely across different countries and regions of the world. The moral and political issues raised by this inequitable distribution of resources take on added urgency when one considers the persistence of absolute poverty and hunger, rapid population growth, and the prospects of ecological disaster in many of today's poorer countries. Most disturbing, despite improvement in Southern living standards and the rapid economic growth of a handful of developing countries, the divide between rich and poor appears stubbornly resistant to amelioration. The total income of the richest 20 percent of the world's population was 30 times that of the poorest 20 percent in 1960. By 1998, the income of the top 20 percent had swelled to 82 times that of the poorest 20 percent.[1]

This development gap poses moral, political, and economic challenges for the relatively wealthy countries of the North.[2] Over the past three decades, Third World countries have continued to press the North to agree to reforms in the international economic order that might help spur Southern development. Issues of great concern to the North, such as Third World debt, illegal immigration, the destruction of the world's rain forests, and the illegal drug trade, can be traced indirectly to continuing Third World poverty. Failure to reach agreement between North and South on such problems could lead to serious consequences for countries on both sides of the divide. Inequality and economic deprivation can also contribute to the outbreak of violence and war, both within and among countries. Conflicts between North and South, as well as among Southern countries themselves, over the control of important resources, such as oil and strategic minerals, are likely to persist. Northerners also possess a direct economic stake in the success of Southern development efforts. Forty percent of U.S. exports, for instance, are destined for Southern countries, and two-thirds of the growth in U.S. exports since 1987 has been to developing countries.[3]

To cope more readily with the serious repercussions that the development gap holds for both rich and poor countries, we need to understand the political economy of North-South relations. This chapter and the five that follow will provide the background necessary to understand the nature of these relations by focusing on two related issues. The first of these concerns North-South bargaining over the distribution of gains from the economic ties between them. The development gap has rendered North-South economic relations more conflictual than the links among Northern countries. As a result, relations have rested less upon shared values than upon the exercise of political and economic power. We will examine the ways in which North-South bargaining has been influenced by asymmetries in power and the efforts of Third World states to offset the North's enormous power advantages.

The second major focus is the struggle of Third World governments to devise workable strategies of development in the international system. In particular, countries have varied in the degree to which they are willing to open their economies to trade and investment with the North. We argue that such choices are heavily influenced by the political and economic circumstances, both domestically and internationally, faced by particular Third World states.

The debate over appropriate strategies of development is, however, partly driven by disagreements over the origins and continuing sources of the development gap between North and South. Why did the North develop first? Can the South succeed by following the pattern established by the North? Or do the differing international conditions faced by Third World countries today dictate an altogether different path (or paths) to development? Do extensive economic ties with the North help or hinder Third World development efforts? These are some of the questions this chapter seeks to explore by examining alternative theoretical perspectives on the development gap.

To better set the stage for this discussion, however, it may be instructive to investigate the dimensions of the economic inequalities between North and South. We begin, therefore, by examining different methods for measuring development and by reviewing various statistical data relating to the development gap.

INDICATORS OF DEVELOPMENT

Economists have long sought a single, simple measure of economic development and human welfare. This sort of yardstick should, ideally, provide some sense of how far a society has progressed over time and how different nations compare with one another in economic performance. This is, however, an inherently difficult task. The concepts of development and human welfare are multidimensional and subject to varying interpretations. Overall averages calculated for societies as a whole tell us nothing about the status of particular groups or individuals and may hide gross inequities in the distribution of resources. Economic figures cannot capture the psychological, spiritual, cultural, or other nonmaterial aspects of human welfare. Even after a given measure has been selected, its meaningfulness can be called into doubt by the difficulty of collecting accurate and reliable data, particularly for Third World countries, where mechanisms for gathering economic information are less developed than in the North.

Because, however, governments, international agencies, and businesses require clear and comparable measures of development for planning and decision-making purposes, the issue cannot be easily sidestepped despite the difficulties involved. The most commonly cited statistical measure of economic development is per-capita income. This figure is calculated by adding up the value of all of the market transactions conducted within a given society over the course of a particular year and dividing by total population. Because inflation can appear to boost income without any real change in the standard of living, its effects are typically canceled out by recalculating income figures in terms of a given base year. To make comparisons over time in "real," inflation-adjusted income, measurements from years prior to the chosen base year are raised by the amount of intervening inflation, and figures for later years are lowered.

To allow for international comparisons, income figures for any given country are stated in terms of U.S. dollars. One way to accomplish this is to use exchange rates in the conversion. If, for instance, Mexico's yearly per-capita income is calculated at 30,000 pesos and the exchange rate is 6 pesos per dollar, then Mexico's annual per-capita income expressed in dollar terms would be $5,000 (these figures are hypothetical).

Using exchange rates to accomplish the conversion of income figures from local currencies into dollars does, however, introduce important distortions. Exchange rates may vary significantly, even over brief periods of time. These gyrations produce artificial and misleading shifts in comparative calculations of national income when exchange rates serve as the basis for conversion. When the value of the dollar falls vis-à-vis the Japanese yen, for instance, the same yen will be able to purchase more dollars than before. Although Japan's per-capita income level may not change at all—when calculated in yen—it will appear to rise when translated into dollars at the new exchange rate.

Also, local price levels vary significantly from country to country. Exchange rate-based income comparisons tell us, in effect, how well the average person from another country could live if all of his or her income were converted to dollars and spent in the United States on American goods and services. In reality, a haircut that costs $15 or $20 in the United States may cost only a fraction of that amount in most Third World countries due to lower labor costs. In other words, a given income level stated in dollars will go much further in a Third World country, where the overall price level is much lower, than it would in the United States. This distortion tends to understate the living standards of most Third World countries when comparisons with the North are accomplished via exchange rate conversions.

Economists have developed an alternative measure of per-capita income that attempts to correct for these problems. This new method of calculating income levels is called purchasing power parity (PPP). Income figures are adjusted to account for differences in local price levels. When PPP conversion is used to compare income, the gap between North and South, while still large, noticeably narrows. In particular cases, the different estimates produced by these two methods for calculating average national income can be striking. Using exchange rate conversion, for instance, the World Bank estimated China's per-capita GDP at $780 in 1999. But China's per-capita income jumps to $3,291, by the World Bank's estimate, when income conversion is accomplished by the PPP method. This astounding difference stems from vastly lower price levels in China as compared with the United States. When PPP figures are substituted for exchange rate figures, the World Bank's estimate of the Third World's share of total global output for 1999 jumps from 22 percent to 45 percent.[4]

Whichever conversion method is used, however, per-capita income has a number of disadvantages as a measure of development or welfare. It reflects only current income, not the amount of wealth accumulated over previous years. It provides us with no clue as to how equitably or inequitably income is distributed across the population. It does not reflect the value of goods and services that are not exchanged for money in the legal economy. Thus, for instance, household work, barter, illegal exchange, and subsistence production (for one's own use) are not measured by income figures.[5] Because all market transactions are treated the same, purchases of staple foods and housing are given the same weight as the money spent on cigarettes, junk food, or tanks, even though most people would agree that these various items make very different contributions to human welfare. The environmental costs of economic activity are ignored, no matter how real. The sale of timber obtained by clear-cutting a forest shows up as an addition to total income even if one result is to impose costs on nearby communities in the form of flooding during rainy seasons.[6]

The Human Development Index (HDI) was devised by researchers at the United Nations Development Program as a means for capturing some of the social dimensions of a nation's socioeconomic development that are neglected by income measures alone.[7] The HDI includes three components of human development: longevity (measured by life expectancy), knowledge (measured by a combination of adult literacy and mean years of schooling), and standard of living (measured by per-capita GDP, adjusted for the local cost of living by means of PPP conversion).

For each component, a nation's rating is determined along a scale ranging from 0 to 1. Zero represents the lowest possible measure for that component, and one represents the highest. So, for instance, a country with an adult literacy rate of 75 percent would score 0.75 on that component of the HDI. The

Table 8.1 Three Measures of Development: Selected Countries

	Human Development Index 1997	Real GDP per Capita (PPP$) 1997	GNP per Capita (US$) 1997
United States	0.927	29,010	29,080
Hong Kong	0.880	24,350	25,200
Korea, Republic of	0.852	13,590	10,550
Costa Rica	0.801	6,650	2,680
Mexico	0.786	8,370	3,700
Cuba	0.765	3,100	NA
Saudi Arabia	0.740	10,120	7,150
Philippines	0.740	3,520	1,200
Brazil	0.739	6,480	4,790
China	0.701	3,130	800
Indonesia	0.681	3,490	1,110
Vietnam	0.664	1,630	310
Nicaragua	0.616	1,997	410
Egypt	0.616	3,050	1,200
Botswana	0.609	7,690	3,310
Zimbabwe	0.560	2,350	720
India	0.545	1,670	370
Ghana	0.544	1,640	390
Kenya	0.519	1,190	340
Pakistan	0.508	1,560	500
Congo	0.479	880	110
Zambia	0.431	960	370
Tanzania	0.421	580	210
Guinea	0.398	1,880	550
Ethiopia	0.298	510	110
All developing countries	0.637	3,240	1,314
Least-developed countries	0.430	992	260
Industrial countries	0.919	23,741	27,174

*PPP$ = Purchasing Power Parity; N/A = not available

SOURCE: United Nations Development Program, *Human Development Report, 1999,* New York: Oxford University Press, 1999, Tables 1 and 11.

scores from all three components are then averaged to produce an overall measure of human development that can be compared across countries. Table 8.1 shows HDI scores for a range of countries, as well as aggregate scores for all developing countries, the least-developed countries, and industrialized countries. Notice that industrialized countries score more than twice as high as the overall average for the least-developed countries.

The HDI is a useful way to compare the overall quality of life across different countries. Life expectancy, for instance, reflects a country's overall nutrition

Table 8.2 Sources of Wealth by Region (percentage of total)

	Human Resources	Produced Assets	Natural Capital
World	64	16	20
High-income countries	67	16	17
Developing countries			
Sub-Saharan Africa	31	17	52
Eastern and Southern Africa	33	14	52
Western Africa	25	25	50
India and China	73	18	9
Other Asia	75	13	12
East Asia and Pacific	75	13	12
South Asia	76	16	9
Latin America and the Caribbean	50	15	35
Middle East and North Africa	39	29	32
Eastern Europe	41	16	43

SOURCE: The World Bank, *Monitoring Environmental Progress: A Report on Work in Progress,* Washington, D.C., 1995, Table 8.1, 63.

level, the quality of its health care, and the type of sanitary conditions under which people live. Adult literacy and mean years of schooling capture both the quality and the breadth of a nation's educational system. The HDI can reveal cases in which relatively high income levels fail to translate into a commensurate quality of life or, conversely, in which the population of a country with a relatively low per-capita income nevertheless enjoys relatively good health and education. Cuba, for instance, outscores Saudi Arabia on the HDI scale even though Saudi Arabia enjoys a per-capita income level more than three times that of Cuba.

Another way to measure development is to focus on wealth rather than income. Traditionally, wealth has been measured by estimating the market value of a nation's physical capital, including such things as factories, machinery, and buildings. This figure provides some sense of the size of the productive base upon which future economic returns depend. Yet a nation's future economic potential rests upon more than these so-called "produced assets." Both natural resources and the level of human skills possessed by a society's members are as important, and often more so, than the available stock of machines and factories.

For this reason, researchers at the World Bank have compiled a broader measure of national wealth that includes natural and human resources alongside manufactured capital.[8] For each nation, the World Bank attaches estimated monetary values to a set of natural resources, such as land, minerals, and water. Much the same is done for human or social resources, including education and skills. By this means, researchers can estimate the relative proportions of a nation's or region's wealth accounted for by human resources, produced assets, and natural capital (see Table 8.2).

This method for calculating wealth shows that on a global basis the value of the world's natural resources exceeds the total value of all manufactured wealth and that both of these together are far outweighed by the combined economic value of the world's human and social resources. This suggests that, from the standpoint of maximizing long-term economic health, nations are better served by focusing on ways to preserve and exploit scarce natural resources on a sustainable basis and on investing in human resources, such as education, than by placing sole priority on enhancing the nation's stock of factories, machines, and other hardware.

Notice also, however, that the relative weight of these different sources of wealth varies considerably from one set of countries to another. In India, China, and the countries of East and Southeast Asia, an overwhelming majority of wealth is accounted for by human resources, though these countries are relatively poorer in natural capital. Africa's wealth, by contrast, is heavily dependent upon natural capital, though its human resources contribute far less to the overall total. Latin America falls in between these extremes. These differences in the composition of wealth have important implications for each country's development strategy and help to determine where a nation's comparative advantage lies in world trade.

This way of measuring wealth also underlines the need for sustainable development strategies. Countries that rapidly deplete their mineral resources, cut down forests, or undermine the value of their land through shortsighted agricultural practices may increase their income in the short run or even translate revenues from these activities into physical capital. This will, however, only create the illusion of greater wealth. When adjusted for the depletion of environmental capital, for instance, the overall gross domestic savings rate in developing countries falls from 25 percent of total income to only 14 percent.[9] In the long term, such a pattern of development cannot be sustained and will erode the environmental basis for economic activity.

MEASURING THE DEVELOPMENT GAP

Northerners often find it tempting to adopt a fatalistic attitude toward the enormous development gap between North and South, based on the assumption that such disparities have always existed and therefore always will. Yet Latin America, Africa, and Asia each has served as the home of civilizations that once rivaled or surpassed European society in science and technology, culture, and economic productivity. In fact, the present concentration of global wealth and income is of quite recent origin.

It has been estimated, for instance, that per-capita GDP in what we now refer to as the North exceeded that of the South by only 50 percent in the mid-nineteenth century. Table 8.3, based upon data calculated by Paul Bairoch, shows just how recently development in the North began to outrace

Table 8.3 Relative Shares of World Manufacturing Output: 1750–1900 (in percentages)

	1750	1800	1830	1860	1880	1900
Europe	23.2	28.1	34.2	53.2	61.3	62.0
United States	0.1	0.8	2.4	7.2	14.7	23.6
Japan	3.8	3.5	2.8	2.6	2.4	2.4
Third World	73.0	67.7	60.5	36.6	20.9	11.0

SOURCE: Adapted from Paul Bairoch, "International Industrialization Levels from 1750 to 1980," *Journal of European Economic History*, 11, 1982, 296.

that in the South. In 1830 what is now the Third World accounted for over 60 percent of world manufacturing production as compared with 34 percent for Europe as a whole. Matters changed rapidly over the next 30 years, however, as the industrial revolution allowed Europe's share to rise to over 53 percent, while the Third World's share declined to just under 37 percent.

The North continued to expand its lead through the remainder of the nineteenth century and well into the twentieth century. In contemporary times, the social and economic contrasts between North and South have become truly stark. Consider, for instance, the following comparisons:

- Using PPP conversion figures, average per-capita income in those countries classified by the World Bank as high income exceeded average income in low- and middle-income countries by a ratio of more than 7:1 in 1998. The gap was even larger—at 20:1—if the comparison between Southern and Northern per-capita GDP is made in terms of exchange rate conversion.[10]

- Between 1990 and 1998, the average annual growth rate of private consumption per capita among high-income countries was 2.2 percent, compared with 1.9 percent for low- and middle-income countries.[11]

- Per-capita income has fallen in over 100 countries during the past 15 years.[12]

- In 1998 the typical Northerner could expect to live 78 years—13 years longer than the average Southerner.[13]

- The average Third World citizen must make do on a diet consisting of 20 percent fewer calories than the average Northerner consumes daily.[14] The United Nations World Food Program estimates that 830 million people (791 million of these located in the developing world) suffer from chronic malnutrition.[15]

- Of the 4.4 billion people who live in the developing world, 40 percent live in communities lacking basic sanitation, 33 percent lack access to safe drinking water, 25 percent lack adequate housing, and 20 percent are undernourished.[16]

- In 1993 Northern countries averaged 253 physicians for every 100,000 persons. The corresponding figure for the South was 76 physicians for every 100,000 people (and only 16 physicians per 100,000 in sub-Saharan Africa).[17]

- Whereas 6 infants out of every 1,000 born in the North die within their first year of life, the corresponding figure for the South is 64.[18]

- While 99 percent of Northern citizens meet minimal standards of literacy, only an estimated 71 percent of Southerners can read and write at a basic level.[19] In the North, secondary school enrollment amounts to 96 percent of total secondary school-age youths. The figure for the South is only 60 percent.[20]

- One-quarter of the world's population lives on less than $1 per day, while close to one-half lives on less than $2 per day.[21]

- Twenty-six percent of Americans use the World Wide Web, compared with two-tenths of 1 percent of Arabs and four-one-hundredths of 1 percent of South Asians. Eighty percent of all Web sites are posted in English.[22]

These aggregate figures hide the fact that the South's meager resources are not shared equally by the members of those societies. Glaring gaps between rich and poor exist within Third World societies. In fact, inequities in income, wealth, and landholding are typically much more pronounced in the South than in the North.[23] On average, for instance, 50 percent of all income in Southern societies goes to the richest 20 percent of the population.[24]

Nevertheless, if one looks at measures other than per-capita income, it is apparent that the gap between living standards in the North and those in the South has narrowed over recent decades. Table 8.4 shows that Southern performance across a range of social indicators has improved relative to the North since the 1960s and early 1970s. Indeed, over the past 30 years, the rate of malnutrition has fallen by one-third, infant mortality has been cut in half, fertility rates have declined by 40 percent, and life expectancy has risen by 10 years across the Third World as a whole.[25]

The structure of Southern economies and their relationship to the global economy differ markedly from those of Northern economies. Southern countries continue to rely more heavily upon commodity exports—including fuels, metals, and raw materials—than Northern nations. Agriculture plays a larger role in Third World economies, where it accounts for 12 percent of total GDP on average, than it does in the North, where agriculture comprises only 2 percent of total production.[26] The terms of trade deteriorated for the South throughout the 1980s. In other words, the average prices of Southern exports fell relative to the average prices of the goods the South imported. The same quantity of Southern exports that could buy $100 worth of Northern goods in 1980 could buy only $89 worth of the same products in 1988.[27]

Table 8.4 Narrowing the North-South Gap: Development Indicators

	REAL GDP PER CAPITA		LIFE EXPECTANCY		DAILY ADULT LITERACY		CALORIE SUPPLY		ACCESS TO SAFE DRINKING WATER		UNDER-FIVE MORTALITY	
	1960	1990	1960	1992	1970	1992	1965	1988–90	1975–80	1988–91	1960	1992
All LDCs As % of North	18	17	67	84	41	71	72	81	36	70	80	92

SOURCE: United Nations Development Program, Human Development Report, 1994, New York: Oxford University Press, 1994, 140–143.

Overall, Third World economies are less diversified and more vulnerable to international shocks than those of the North.

Geography and climate also distinguish North from South.[28] Ninety-three percent of the combined population of the world's 30 richest countries live in temperate and snow climate zones. Of the 42 highly indebted poor countries, on the other hand, 39 are located in tropical or desert climatic zones.[29] Overall, tropical countries had an average per-capita income only one-third that of temperate zone countries in 1995.[30] A tropical climate is less well suited for many kinds of agricultural production than a temperate climate and is given to extremes of heat and weather. Moreover, tropical countries are plagued by diseases not typically experienced in temperate climates. Ninety-five percent of all malaria cases, for instance, occur in the tropics, and between 1 million and 2.5 million people in tropical countries die each year from malaria. Tuberculosis is also more prevalent in the developing world, where it claims 2 million lives per year.[31] Because these societies are so poor, however, drug companies devote few resources to developing vaccines and other treatments for topical diseases. Of the 1,223 new drug compounds launched between 1975 and 1997, for instance, only 11 were designed to fight tropical diseases.[32]

CONTENDING PERSPECTIVES ON DEVELOPMENT

Scholars disagree over both the sources of the development gap and the likelihood that it can be narrowed in the future. There is also extensive debate over whether the South benefits from its extensive economic ties with the North. These disagreements revolve around much more than how to interpret the data. Fundamentally, they stem from differing assumptions about the nature of the development process itself. Here we identify and compare two contrasting theories about the problems of Third World development and North-South political economy.

These two theories, labeled *modernization* and *dependency,* are primarily scholarly in nature. As such, they provide a necessary conceptual introduction to some of the issues and debates that we will examine in a more substantive way in later chapters. Ultimately, this necessarily abstract discussion will provide us with the tools needed to sort through the complex and messy realities of North-South political economy.

Yet it is worth noting that these ideas have found their way from the sanctuaries of academia to the stormy citadels of the political world. In debates between representatives of the North and the South in the United Nations and elsewhere, arguments drawn from these two perspectives are often featured in the political rhetoric of the respective sides. Northern spokespersons often appeal, implicitly, to modernization theory, which emphasizes the benefits to the South of openness to trade and investment from the North. In the past, though less so today, Third World representatives have invoked dependency theory as a basis for demanding the reform of an exploitative world economic system. Therefore, aside from the merits of these two differing perspectives as explanations for the development gap, the modernization and dependency theories are worth examining for the insights they provide into the intellectual bases of political debates between North and South.

MODERNIZATION THEORY

Modernization theory views the obstacles to Third World development through the prism of the North's own development experience. The North grew rich, according to this theory not by exploiting the South but rather by discovering the secrets of sustained economic growth. The cultural values and social, political, and economic institutions that provided the keys to Northern development are embodied in the notion of modernity. The modernization of Europe involved the gradual shedding of traditional ways of organizing society. Although little of this process was planned, simultaneous trends in a number of different spheres of social life converged to create the basis for dynamic economic growth and industrialization.

What are the principal elements of modernity? The list of traits provided by different authors varies enormously.[33] But among the most commonly cited are secularization (or the declining centrality of religion in social and cultural life), urbanization, the rise of science and technology, increased social mobility, a system of social rewards based upon merit rather than upon inherited status, a tolerance for social innovation and intellectual diversity, the limitation of controls placed by political authorities on social and economic life (that is, the emergence of a "private" sphere), the ascendance of the rule of law, and the development of an extensive division of labor within society. All of these traits complement the development of modern market-based economies, in which economic decision making is decentralized among large numbers of producers, consumers, and laborers and is relatively free of direct control by political or religious authorities.

Traditional societies are dominated by religious authority, revolve around rural life, lack the capacity to generate scientific and technological discoveries, suffer from rigid social structures allowing little mobility, distribute social rewards based upon inherited status rather than upon merit, discourage innovation and new ideas, place few controls on the arbitrary exercise of political authority, and feature little social differentiation. The economies of traditional societies often rest upon either subsistence agriculture, in which extended families produce only for their own needs, or feudal or semifeudal landholding arrangements, in which relatively small numbers of large landowners live off the surplus produced by an indentured peasantry. Northern societies were once characterized by the traits associated with traditionalism, but they gradually made the transition to modernity over a period of centuries. According to modernization theorists, many Southern societies continue to be dominated by traditional values and institutions, though most have begun to embrace some elements of modernity.

The most critical element in the transition from a traditional society to a modern one, from the standpoint of economic development, is the emergence of a system of rewards for innovation. The society must not only come to expect and welcome change and to embrace the notion of progress but also willingly tolerate the inequalities that result from allowing individuals to reap handsome private returns for innovations that have high social value. For this to be possible, the state must devise means of organizing and protecting private property. By *property*, we refer not just to material possessions but also to the propriety that innovators must have over their own original ideas if others are not to profit from them instead. Although the state must protect property rights, it must at the same time allow economic decisions to be made in at least partial autonomy from political oversight and intervention. This is necessary because innovation is most likely to occur if decision making is decentralized through competitive market arrangements that encourage and reward new ideas while punishing inefficiency and stagnation. As this discussion suggests, the development of capitalist institutions lies at the heart of modernization, though the rise of capitalism in the North would not have been possible without the simultaneous transformations already mentioned in the noneconomic spheres of society.

Economists cite other factors besides the rate of innovation that may influence a country's potential for economic development. These factors include overall rates of savings and investment, the workforce's skill level, the relative abundance of natural resources, and the degree to which market prices are allowed to steer available resources to their most efficient uses.[34]

Modernization theorists suggest that before sustained and self-generating economic growth can become possible in the South, Third World societies must undergo the same transition from traditionalism to modernity previously undergone by the North. The path to development thus lies through emulation of the North. The principal obstacle to modernization arises from the persistence of traditional cultural values and institutions in the South that are incompatible with economic growth and industrialization.

Adherents to this school of thought disagree over just how likely it is that Third World societies will progress smoothly toward modernity. Perhaps the majority believe that the modernization of the Third World is an inevitable process. The agents of progress, in this view, are many. They include the modernizing political elites (often Northern educated) to be found in many Third World countries. Multinational corporations serve as transmitters of modern skills and values while also providing close-up examples of modern forms of economic organization. Exposure to international trade offers Southern societies incentives to embrace reform and change if they are to compete effectively. The penetration of Third World societies by European or U.S. culture through books, films, advertising, consumer products, and the media also helps Southerners to assimilate modern values and beliefs.

North-South economic interdependence is to be valued, according to modernization theorists, not simply for the mutual gains that routinely flow from market transactions but also for the beneficial impact that such ties have in helping to erode and undermine the traditional social values and structures that hold back development. Over time, both external and internal pressures will tend to shrink the traditional sector of the economy and society while the growth of the modern sector proceeds apace. Evidence of these trends at work, according to modernization theorists, can be found in growing urbanization, the development of a wage labor force, and broadened educational opportunities.

A minority of modernization theorists accept the distinction between traditionalism and modernity but question the assumption that Southern societies will necessarily modernize over time, leading eventually to a convergence between the social and economic structures of North and South. These authors instead see traditionalism as deeply embedded in the cultures and institutions of many Third World countries. Change may come slowly and not necessarily in the direction of a European-inspired ideal of modernity. Others who question the inevitability of modernization and convergence between North and South go further to suggest that economic development may well be possible in societies that embrace some elements of modernity but not others. There may be, in other words, multiple paths of development.

Modernization theory has been criticized on a number of grounds. It has been pointed out, for instance, that the concept of traditionalism is quite nebulous. In practice, the *traditional* label has been applied to virtually any social practices and institutions that are not modern or, in other words, not characteristic of present-day European and North American societies. To bundle all of the many varied Third World cultures that do not meet the criteria for modernity under the label *traditional* perhaps serves to obscure more than to illuminate.

Some critics also charge that modernization theory springs from an ethnocentric viewpoint. Certainly it is not difficult to deduce that most modernization theorists consider modernity good and traditionalism bad. This obviously reflects a Eurocentric bias. Whatever the merits of Northern societies, they are certainly not above reproach, and Southerners who embrace modernity in a general way may well hope to avoid some of the less appealing aspects of Northern societies even while seeking to match Northern living standards. Moreover, modernization theorists may be too dismissive of traditional societies, ignoring the possibility that they might contain redeeming traits worth preserving.

Some critics point out that modernization theory incorrectly assumes that the obstacles to Third World development lie solely in the persistence of the society's traditional sector. This ignores the possibility that the modern sector itself may be subject to contradictions and distortions that slow growth. Moreover, the movement from traditionalism to modernity is likely to be anything but smooth. Modernization in Europe proceeded in fits and starts, and the process often generated enormous dislocations such as war, revolution, unemployment, mass migration, and class conflict. There is little reason to expect modernization to be any less disruptive as it transforms Third World societies.

Modernization theorists are quite sanguine about the benefits of North-South economic exchange for Southern development. Whether it is true in general that links with the North spur modernization, most modernization theorists ignore the potential conflicts of interest between North and South. This is apparent in their tendency to downplay the North's potential economic power over the South. As we discuss later, the South's dependence upon the North offers the latter political leverage that can be used to capture a disproportionate share of the benefits flowing from North-South economic exchange.

Despite these criticisms, modernization theory offers important insights into the North's development experience. It would be surprising indeed, despite the changed context, if these insights did not hold useful lessons for those seeking to promote Southern development. Perhaps the most important of these is that capitalism, as a distinctive way of organizing economic relationships within a society, is a powerful mechanism for producing wealth. The development of capitalism, in turn, is dependent upon the evolution of supportive social, political, and cultural institutions in the noneconomic spheres of society. Whether these innovations can be successfully transplanted to a society from without or whether they must evolve indigenously is a crucial question in assessing the prospects for capitalist-led development in the Third World. This is, in fact, the central question raised by dependency theory, our second perspective on Third World development.

DEPENDENCY THEORY

Dependency theorists reject modernization theory's optimistic prediction that Third World states that imitate the cultural attitudes, institutions, and policies of the North can follow the same path toward development previously trod by present-day rich countries.[35] They point out that the international context facing developing societies today is vastly different from that which confronted the early industrializers. Capitalism developed largely indigenously in Europe, and the first wave of industrializers faced no competition from already developed rivals. Moreover, industrialization in Europe was helped along by the access that conquest provided Europeans to the raw materials and cheap labor of colonized lands.

Present-day developing countries face an entirely different set of international realities. Third World efforts to industrialize must cope with the formidable competition provided by the North's already well-established manufacturing capacities. Moreover, the infrastructure needed to support scientific and technological innovation is overwhelmingly located in the North. In general, capitalism was introduced to Southern societies from the outside on terms largely set by, and favorable to, Northern governments, merchants, and investors. Southern economies remain heavily dependent on external trade with the North, and Northern multinational corporations often dominate the most dynamic industries in many Third World countries.

Dependency theorists contend that these differences (and others) between early and late developers mean that the development experiences of the North hold little relevance for assessing the present-day prospects for Southern development. These distinctions are considered so important, in fact, that dependency theory locates the primary obstacles to Third World development in the international system rather than in the domestic political, cultural, and social characteristics of particular states. In other words, the international system, rather than the nation-state, is viewed as the appropriate unit of analysis.

Capitalism is the most important defining feature of the contemporary international system, according to dependency theorists. Capitalism is a distinct set of economic relations defined by the private ownership of property, wage labor, and market exchange. The capitalist world system, which some dependency theorists believe has existed since the sixteenth century,[36] involves two sets of exploitative relationships. Within firms, the owners of capital exploit workers by profiting from their labor. The second relationship of exploitation, and the more relevant one from our standpoint, exists between core and peripheral states in the world economy. Capitalism does not develop evenly. Instead, it tends to concentrate development in certain areas, called the core, that are characterized by advanced industrialization, rapid technological development, and high wage rates and living standards. Peripheral areas, which constitute the geographic bulk of the world economy, instead feature limited industrialization, little technological innovation, and relatively low wages and living standards.

The development of core countries is linked to the underdevelopment of the peripheral countries. The workings of the capitalist world system tend to perpetuate and reinforce economic inequalities among countries. As two prominent advocates of dependency put it: "Both underdevelopment and development are aspects of the same phenomenon, both are historically simultaneous, both are linked functionally and, therefore, interact and condition each other mutually."[37]

Third World countries were drawn into the capitalist world economy through colonialism as well as through the expansion of European trade and investment. European countries used their political domination to create and enforce a division of labor that reserved the most dynamic segments of the world economy for themselves. North–South trade was built around the movement of manufactured goods from North to South and the transfer of primary products, including minerals, raw materials, and agricultural goods, from South to North. Moreover, whereas Northern countries traded extensively with one another, Southern countries traded almost exclusively with the North. Colonialism left the economies of Southern countries geared more toward the needs of Northern markets than the domestic needs of their own societies. This set of economic relationships, dependency writers point out, outlived colonialism itself.

This position of Southern subordination to and dependence on the North is captured in Theotonio dos Santos's widely cited definition of dependency: "Dependency is a situation in which a certain number of countries have their economy conditioned by the development and expansion of another... placing the dependent country in a backward position exploited by the dominant country."[38]

Dependency theorists offer a number of mechanisms by which dependency hampers Southern development. Some cite changes in relative export prices as the primary means by which Northern societies extract surplus wealth from the South. The prices of the primary goods exported by the South, it is argued, tend to decline over time relative to the prices of the manufactured goods that Southern societies must import from the North. A country that finds itself in this situation—where, over time, a given quantity of the country's exports can purchase less and less of the imports it desires—is said to be suffering from declining terms of trade.

Northern multinational corporations are also viewed as instruments of exploitation. Foreign firms bring inappropriate technology, use their mobility and transnational links to evade taxes and regulations, drive out local competitors, manipulate Southern governments, refuse to hire and train top management drawn from the host country, and repatriate their profits rather than invest them locally.

Dependency theory asserts that these forms of Northern exploitation, along with others, such as foreign aid, commercial bank lending, and the influence of multilateral lending agencies, hinder Southern industrialization and development.

Dependency theorists differ over how severe and universal are the constraints that dependency places on Third World development. Some, especially among the early writers, argued that dependence allowed little latitude for development and was likely to continue to produce growing misery and poverty among most Southerners. The principal beneficiaries of dependence in the South would be a *"comprador"* class of elites who benefited from their privileged ties—whether political or economic—with the North and who acted as the local agents of imperialism.

Some dependency authors concede that dependency is not incompatible with economic growth and development, even including a degree of industrialization. Moreover, some countries are likely to progress further than others. These authors nevertheless maintain that dependence constrains development in most Southern countries, rendering economic growth and industrialization slower and less substantial than might otherwise be the case. They also generally argue that the overall relative position of the periphery in comparison with the core is unlikely to improve even where absolute gains are made.

A third set of authors argue that, although dependency is sometimes compatible with vigorous economic growth, it nevertheless produces a myriad of undesirable "distortions" that are peculiar to dependent Southern societies and economies. Among these distortions are growing income inequality, wasteful consumption, cultural degradation, and political repression. The main concern of these authors is not with whether "development" is occurring, but rather with the type of development produced under conditions of dependence.

Dependency theorists differ widely over the appropriate remedy for Third World dependency upon the North. Some favor inwardly directed development strategies that emphasize production for the domestic market. This would imply a curtailment of economic ties with the North through high protectionist barriers designed to nurture domestic industry and the strict regulation of foreign investment.

Others advocate some form of collective bargaining strategy whereby Southern states pool their political and economic resources to press for reforms in the international economic order, much as trade unions attempt to ameliorate capitalist exploitation of workers. This can take the form of resource cartels, such as OPEC, that are designed to reverse the declining terms of trade or broad coalitions that demand Northern assent to various specific reforms, such as the lowering of Northern protectionist barriers to Southern manufactured goods, commodity stabilization plans, or mandatory codes of conduct for multinational corporations. Those who advocate this strategy often stress the importance of improving economic ties, including the development of regional common markets, among Southern countries as a means of lessening dependence upon the North.

Finally, some dependency theorists argue that Third World states can escape dependence upon the capitalist world system only through socialist revolution and reconstruction. Such a strategy would involve the elimination of private capital and the development of nonexploitative links with other like-minded countries.

In short, although modernization theory asserts that Southern economic ties with the North are desirable because they transfer needed technology and skills, foster efficiency through competition, and break down cultural and institutional barriers to development, dependency theory views Northern economic and political penetration of the South as exploitative, producing a transfer of resources from the poor to the rich.

To evaluate dependency theory, we must distinguish between two lines of argument, each of which can be found, together or separately, in the writings of different authors. The first strain of dependency theory focuses primarily on economics. The concern here is with the way Third World states have been incorporated into the world capitalist system and the effects this process has had on their prospects for development. The second strain focuses on politics. In particular, this strain of dependency theory explores the asymmetries in power and interdependence that influence bargaining between North and South over the rules of the international economic system. Although both the economic and political dimensions of dependency theory derive from the same body of thought, each deserves separate treatment in any effort to assess the strengths and weaknesses of the dependency approach to Third World development and North-South relations.[39]

The economic dimension of dependency theory revolves around the suggestion that dependent capitalism, introduced to the South via Northern colonialism, trade, and investment, differs from the homegrown variety. The dependence of Third World economies on trade and investment with the North and their subordinate position in the international division of labor constrain the prospects for Southern development and lead to imbalances and distortions.

Critics of dependency theory have pointed to several difficulties with these claims.[40] One of these is that many of the features that are associated with dependency, such as penetration by multinational corporations and heavy reliance on external trade and technology, are also characteristic of many developed countries. Canada, for instance, is more dependent upon foreign direct investment than is India. Moreover, as any reader of Charles Dickens can surmise, the extreme social and economic inequalities that are painful features of most developing countries today were not unknown to the European societies of 150 years ago. This suggests that some of the inequities and distortions that have been attributed to external dependence may instead be characteristic of the early stages of capitalist development more generally.

Dependency writers might respond that the nature of North-North trade differs substantially from North-South trade. Northern countries trade principally in manufactured goods with one another. Southern trade with the North, by contrast, rests to a much larger degree upon the exchange of raw materials for manufactured goods. If, as dependency theorists assert, the latter form of trade is subject to deteriorating terms of trade for the kinds of goods that Third World countries typically export, then this division of labor works to the disadvantage of the South.

Yet, while recent years have indeed witnessed a deterioration in the South's terms of trade with the North, studies that have examined longer time periods have reached different conclusions. The prices of primary goods, such as raw materials and agricultural goods, do tend to fluctuate more widely than do the prices of manufactured goods—a pattern that leads to cycles of feast or famine for countries that depend upon only a few primary products for the bulk of their exports. The empirical evidence, however, shows no long-term tendency for the prices of primary goods to fall relative to manufactured goods over the course of the twentieth century. Even if trends in the terms of trade did favor manufactured goods, however, the implications of this would be complicated by the fact that some core countries, such as the United States, Canada, and Australia, depend upon primary goods for a substantial portion of their exports, while some developing countries, especially in East Asia, have become substantial exporters of manufactured goods.

As we discuss in a later chapter, multinational corporations often hold superior bargaining positions vis-à-vis Third World host states. This allows them to extract considerable benefits from their Third World operations and to escape some forms of regulation. Yet this does not establish that foreign direct investment stymies Third World development. The economic benefits that multinational corporations bring to Third World societies vary depending upon the nature of the investment. Manufacturing investments likely offer the host state more than do extractive investments, such as mining or agricultural production. Yet the package of assets that foreign firms bring to the country, including capital, technology, managerial expertise, and global marketing networks, often cannot be matched by local firms, whether private or state owned. In any case, the ability of Third World countries to maximize the benefits of foreign direct investment while minimizing the negatives varies across countries and across time.

Perhaps dependency theory's greatest shortcoming is that it has trouble explaining the enormous diversity of Third World development experiences. Whereas many Third World countries remain locked in poverty and show few signs of narrowing the gap with the North, a growing handful of countries have displayed impressive economic dynamism. Located primarily in East Asia, these so-called newly industrializing countries (NICs) have grown at rates far exceeding those in the North. As we discuss more thoroughly in the next chapter, they have also developed diversified economies that rest increasingly upon the production and trade of manufactured goods. Some have even become the originators of new technology.

Moreover, these countries have succeeded not by asserting greater autonomy from the North but rather by integrating themselves ever more thoroughly into the international economic system. Although the strategies pursued by these countries do not necessarily suggest a blueprint for success by other Southern nations, it does seem clear that the nature of the international economic system does not preclude the possibility of development for all Third World countries. Indeed, because the external constraints faced by the NICs did not differ radically from those facing many other Southern states, these cases of success should shift our attention toward those internal or domestic characteristics that can account for such different outcomes. This requires close attention to factors that are not typically included in dependency analysis.

The other strain of dependency theory emphasizes the disparities in political power between North and South. The most obvious power advantage possessed by the North lies in its preponderance of military resources over those of the South. Because economic conflicts are rarely resolved through the use of coercion, however, North-South bargaining is more directly influenced by other forms of power.

Northern leverage depends principally upon asymmetries in the relations of economic interdependence between North and South. Simply put, asymmetrical interdependence exists when two countries depend on trade, investment, and other economic ties with one another, but one country is significantly more dependent on the relationship than is the other. If the relationship were for some reason suddenly cut off, the more dependent trade partner would be hurt far more than the less dependent one. The less dependent country can therefore play upon the weakness and vulnerability of the more dependent country as a source of power or leverage.

A hypothetical case may help to clarify this point. Let us imagine that two countries, A and B, engage in trade with one another. For country A, its trade with country B constitutes only a small share of its overall trade with all countries and a much smaller proportion of its total national income. Were trade between A and B to be curtailed, country A would be only marginally hurt and could probably substitute for the losses by expanding its trade with alternative partners. Country B, however, is much smaller and less developed than country A. Trade with A constitutes a large portion of country B's overall trade and a significant increment of its national income. The loss of trade with country A would be devastating to country B's economy. Moreover, as a less developed nation dependent upon a narrow range of exports, country B might find it difficult to locate alternative buyers for its goods. This, in extreme form, is a relationship of asymmetrical interdependence. Country B's vulnerability to a rupture in trade provides country A with a source of power over B. Should political or commercial conflicts arise between the two countries, country A can reliably compel concessions from country B by threatening to withhold trade. Dependency theorists point out that this hypothetical case conforms rather closely to the actual realities of economic ties between many Northern states and many Southern states. As a result, the North's interests dominate in bargaining between the two.[41]

Dependency theorists are on much firmer ground with this line of argument than with their critique of dependent capitalism. Southern dependence upon the North may not pose an insuperable obstacle to development, but it does clearly give rise to disparities in power and influence both in relations between particular states and in collective negotiations over the rules and institutions of the international economic order.

Before we embrace these conclusions, however, several caveats are in order. It should be noted that the recognition that power flows from asymmetrical interdependence is not unique to dependency theory. Indeed, the concept of asymmetrical interdependence can, with appropriate modifications, be applied to the analysis of power in many different spheres of social, political, and economic life. Moreover, asymmetries exist not just between North and South but also among Northern countries themselves, though the resulting disparities in power are unlikely to be as wide in the latter instances as in the former. Finally, power relationships among states are not static. OPEC, for instance, managed to turn the tables on the North during the 1970s when it took advantage of the industrial world's enormous dependence on a particularly crucial resource.

CONCLUSIONS

What seems clear from our overview of modernization and dependency theories is that neither provides an entirely adequate overall understanding of the problems facing Southern countries as they attempt to close the development gap with the North. Modernization theory ignores some of the less appealing aspects of economic development under capitalism. It is also vague on some key theoretical points, such as the concept of traditionalism. Moreover, modernization theory overlooks the importance of power disparities between the North and the South. Dependency theory has weaknesses, as well, especially in its tendency to exaggerate the constraints that the international system places on development. The concept of dependence is vague, and the links between it and underdevelopment are tenuous. Dependency theory also provides us with few means for understanding why some Third World countries are rapidly developing while others are falling further behind. These shortcomings in the two principal alternative perspectives on development are perhaps a measure of the limits to our knowledge about the complex process of economic development.

Nevertheless, both modernization theory and dependency theory offer useful insights. On one hand, modernization theory provides a convincing account of the factors that contributed to the development of the North, and it points to a number of present-day obstacles to development in the cultures and institutions of Southern societies. It also makes a strong case for the proposition that the spread of capitalism and the incorporation of Third World states into the international economic system provide an overall positive contribution to Southern economic development. Dependency theory, on the other hand, reminds us that great power disparities flow from Southern dependence upon the North.

In general, we suggest that modernization theory is closer to the mark in contending that the gains to the South from North–South economic ties outweigh the losses. Indeed, as one might expect from market exchanges, both North and South tend to benefit. Yet this does not imply that both sides benefit equally. The gains from mutual trade and investment may accrue to both North and South, yet not in equal proportions. As dependency writers point out, market relations are not free from the exercise of power. Asymmetrical interdependence provides the North with leverage over the South. The use of this leverage can, as later chapters reveal, allow the North to bend the rules of the game in its favor to ensure that the benefits of North–South economic relations flow disproportionately its way. These insights, drawn from both modernization and dependency theories, will structure much of the discussion that follows. The South has been attracted toward greater involvement with the world economy by the promise of economic gain and accelerated modernization through exchange with the North. Yet it has also been repelled due to the dangers posed by overreliance upon the North and the risk that this dependence holds for exploitation.

Although modernization and dependency remain the principal general perspectives on development and North–South political economy, recent years have brought a shift in the terms of debate. New questions are being raised. Increasingly, scholars are turning to comparative studies that ask why countries facing similar international circumstances pursue differing development strategies. These policy choices, in turn, are seen as critical to economic outcomes.

Neither dependency theory nor modernization theory is well adapted to answering these sorts of questions. Dependency theory's emphasis on external constraints rules out domestically generated variation across countries. Modernization theory does look at domestic factors but emphasizes broad social and cultural traits that change slowly and are only loosely connected to specific policy choices. The newer literature, by contrast, pays close attention to the roles that political coalitions, as well as bureaucratic, institutional, and political structures, play in determining which development path a particular state is likely to choose. These sorts of factors are used to help explain, for instance, why the large countries of Latin America, including Brazil and Mexico, have generally pursued inward-looking development strategies stressing autonomy, whereas a number of successful East Asian countries, such as South Korea and Taiwan, have opted for outward-looking strategies based upon export expansion. The following chapter explores the issues raised by this recent literature at length.[42]

NOTES

1. Thomas Homer-Dixon, *The Ingenuity Gap,* New York: Knopf, 2000, 33.

2. Scholars, journalists, and politicians have invented many labels to distinguish the richer and poorer countries of the world from one another. Some use the terms North and South because most of the wealthier countries of the world are located in the northern latitudes, whereas the poorer countries tend to be south of the equator. The term Third World originated in an effort to distinguish the world's poor countries from the industrialized capitalist countries, called the First World, and from the industrialized communist countries, called the Second World. Southern countries are sometimes referred to as developing, less developed, or underdeveloped to contrast them from the advanced industrialized or developed countries. In general, these labels attempt to distinguish between relatively high-income countries that have undergone extensive industrialization and lower-income countries that remain at the earlier stages of industrialization. The latter countries often also share the experience of colonization. None of these labels is terribly precise. Some countries are difficult to classify. This is not surprising because development is a continuum, not an either-or proposition. Moreover, the use of these terms to place large numbers of states into broad categories often misleadingly implies a unity and a commonality among them that do not exist in reality. The label of "Third World" is particularly anachronistic given the end of the Cold War. Nevertheless, in deference to common usage, we shall employ these terms interchangeably throughout the text.

3. James Gustave Speth, "The Plight of the Poor," *Foreign Affairs,* May–June, 1999, 17.

4. World Bank, *World Development Report, 2000/2001,* New York: Oxford

University Press, 2000, Table 1, 274–275.

5. As a result, income figures for some Third World countries may be misleadingly low because some parts of the South still rely more on barter or subsistence production than do Northern countries.

6. For an interesting discussion of the deficiencies of GDP measures and alternative ways to measure economic welfare, see Clifford Cobb, Ted Halstead, and Jonathan Rowe, "If the GDP Is Up, Why Is America Down?" *Atlantic Monthly,* October 1995.

7. For a description of how the HDI is compiled, see United Nations Development Program, *Human Development Index, 1994,* New York: Oxford University Press, 1994, 90–93.

8. Peter Passell, "The Wealth of Nations: A 'Greener' Approach Turns List Upside Down," *New York Times,* September 19, 1995. For a more extended discussion on the topic of "green" accounting, see James Robertson and Andre Carothers, "The New Economics: Accounting for a Healthy Planet," *Greenpeace,* January–February 1989.

9. Vinod Thomas, "Why Quality Matters," *The Economist,* October 7, 2000, 92.

10. *World Development Report, 1999/2000,* Table 1, 231. Note that these figures differ from those that appear in Table 8.1 due to differences in which countries are counted in various categories.

11. *World Development Report, 2000/2001,* Table 2, 277.

12. Homer-Dixon, *The Ingenuity Gap,* 33.

13. *World Development Report, 2000/2001,* Table 2, 277.

14. *Human Development Report, 1999,* Table 20, 214.

15. Christopher S. Wren, "U.N. Report Maps Hunger 'Hot Spots,'" *New York Times,* January 9, 2001.

16. Speth, "Plight of the Poor," 14.

17. *Human Development Report, 1999,* Table 9, 175.

18. *Human Development Report, 1999,* Table 8, 171.

19. *Human Development Report, 1999,* Table 1, 137.

20. *Human Development Report, 1999,* Table 10, 179.

21. Dan Ben-David, Hakan Nordstrom, and L. Alan Winters, "Trade, Income Disparity and Poverty," Special Studies 5, World Trade Organization, 1999, 1.

22. Judith Miller, "Globalization Widens Rich–Poor Gap, UN Report Says," *New York Times,* July 14, 1999.

23. See Montek S. Ahluwalia, "Income Inequality: Some Dimensions of the Problem," in Mitchell Seligman (ed.), *The Gap between Rich and Poor: Contending Perspectives on the Political Economy of Development,* Boulder, Colo.: Westview Press, 1984, 14–21.

24. "Down the Rathole," *The Economist,* December 10, 1994, 69.

25. Gary Gardner and Brian Halweill, "Nourishing the Underfed and Overfed," in Worldwatch Institute (ed.), *State of the World 2000,* New York: Norton, 2000, 61: Lawrence H. Summers and Vinod Thomas, "Recent Lessons of Development," in Jeffrey Freiden and David Lake (eds.), *International Political Economy: Perspectives on Global Power and Wealth,* 3rd ed., New York: St. Martin's Press, 1995, 423.

26. *World Development Report, 2000/2001,* Table 12, 297.

27. *World Development Report, 1990,* Table 14.

28. For a comprehensive and insightful examination of how geography has influenced social and economic development over the span of human existence, see Jared Diamond, *Guns, Germs and Steel: The Fates of Human Societies,* New York: Norton, 1997.

29. Jeffrey Sachs, "Helping the World's Poorest," *The Economist,* August 14, 1999, 18.

30. Ricardo Hausmann, "Prisoner's of Geography," *Foreign Policy,* January–February, 2001, 46.

31. Sachs, "Helping the World's Poorest," 19.

32. "Balms for the Poor," *The Economist*, August 14, 1999, 63.

33. A partial list of works in the modernization tradition would include the following: Alex Inkeles and David H. Smith, *Becoming Modern: Individual Change in Six Development Countries*, Cambridge: Harvard University Press, 1974; David McClelland, *The Achieving Society*, Princeton, N.J.: Van Nostrand, 1961; Henri Avjac, "Cultures and Growth," in Christopher Saunders (ed.), *The Political Economy of New and Old Industrial Countries*, London: Butterworth's, 1981; Kalman Silvert, "The Politics of Social and Economic Change in Latin America," in Howard Wiarda (ed.), *Politics and Social Change in Latin America: The Distinct Tradition*, Amherst: University of Massachusetts Press, 1974; Myron Weiner (ed.), *Modernization: The Dynamics of Growth*, New York: Basic Books, 1966; Cyril Black, *The Dynamics of Modernization*, New York: Harper and Row, 1966; Gabriel Almond and James S. Coleman, *The Politics of Developing Areas*, Princeton, N.J.: Princeton University Press, 1960; and Daniel Lerner, *The Passing of Traditional Society*, New York: Free Press of Glencoe, 1958. For a critique of the modernization school, see Alejandro Portes, "On the Sociology of National Development: Theories and Issues," *American Journal of Sociology*, July 1976.

34. For a brief but accessible discussion of neoclassical growth theory and some of its recent variants, see "How Does Your Economy Grow?" *The Economist*, September 30, 1995, 96. For scholarly works exemplifying so-called new or endogenous growth theory, see Paul Romer, "Increasing Returns and Long-Run Growth," *Journal of Political Economy*, October 1986; Romer, "Endogenous Technological Change," *Journal of Political Economy*, October 1990; Romer, "The Origins of Endogenous Growth," *Journal of Economic Perspectives*, Winter 1994.

35. Among the major works in the dependency school are Theotonio dos Santos, "The Structure of Dependence," in K. T. Fann and Donald Hodges (eds.), *Readings in U.S. Imperialism*, Boston: Porter Sargent, 1971; Fernando Henrique Cardoso and Enzo Falleto, *Dependency and Development in Latin America*, Berkeley and Los Angeles: University of California Press, 1979; Fernando Henrique Cardoso, "The Consumption of Dependency Theory in the United States," *Latin American Research Review*, 12:3, 1977; Susanne Bodenheimer, "Dependency and Imperialism," *Politics and Society*, May 1970; Samir Amin, *Accumulation on a World Scale*, New York: Monthly Review Press, 1974; Andre Gunder Frank, *Capitalism and Underdevelopment in Latin America*, New York: Monthly Review Press, 1967; Frank, *Latin America: Underdevelopment or Revolution?* New York: Monthly Review Press, 1969; C. Furtado, *Devlopment and Underdevelpment.* Berkeley and Los Angeles: University of California Press, 1964; A. Emmanuel, *Unequal Exchange*, London: New Left Books, 1972; Paul Baran, *The Political Economy of Growth*, New York: Monthly Review Press, 1957; and Immanuel Wallerstein, *The Modern World-System: Capitalist Agriculture and the Origins of the European World-Economy in the Sixteenth Century*, New York: Academic Press, 1976.

36. For an interpretation concerning the origins of the capitalist world system, see Wallerstein, *The Modern World-System.*

37. Osvaldo Sunkel and Pedro Paz, *El Subdesarrollo Latinoamericano y la Teoria del Desarrollo*, Mexico, 1970, 6, quoted in J. Samuel Valenzuela and Arturo Valenzuela, "Modernization and Dependence: Alternative Perspectives in the Study of Latin American Underdevelopment," in Heraldo Muñoz (ed.), *From Dependency to Development: Strategies to Overcome Underdevelopment and Inequality*, Boulder Colo.: Westview Press, 1981, 25.

38. Quoted in Valenzuela and Valenzuela, "Modernization and Dependency," 25–26. Also see Teotonio dos Santos, "The Structure of Dependence," in K. T. Fann and Donald Hodges (eds.), *Readings in U.S. Imperialism.*

39. Our discussion of these two strains in dependency theory draws upon a similar distinction made in James Caparaso and Behrouz Zare, "An Interpretation and Evaluation of Dependency Theory," in Heraldo Muñoz (ed.), *From Dependency to Development*, 44–45.

40. For critical reviews of dependency theory, some more sympathetic than others, see David Ray, "The Dependency Model of Latin American Underdevelopment: Three Basic Fallacies," *Journal of Interamerican Studies and World Affairs*, February 1973; Sanjaya Lall, "Is Dependence a Useful Concept in Analyzing Underdevelopment?" *World Development*, November 1975; Richard Fagen, "Studying Latin American Politics: Some Implications of a *Dependencia* Approach," *Latin American Research Review*, Summer 1977; Raymond Duvall, "Dependence and *Dependencia* Theory: Notes toward Precision of Concept and Argument," *International Organization*,

Winter 1978; Tony Smith, "The Underdevelopment of the Development Literature: The Case of Dependency Theory," *World Politics*, January 1979; and Bill Warren, "Imperialism and Capitalist Industrialization," *New Left Review*, September–October 1973. For an effort to subject dependency propositions to empirical testing, see Vincent Mahler, *Dependency Approaches to International Political Economy: A Cross-National Study*, New York: Columbia University Press, 1980.

41. For a seminal discussion of how asymmetries in economic dependence can provide one party with potential power over another, see Albert Hirshman, *National Power and the Structure of Foreign Trade*, Berkeley and Los Angeles: University of California Press, 1969.

42. Two examples of research in this vein are Stephan Haggard, *Pathways from the Periphery: The Politics of Growth in the Newly Industrialized Countries*, Ithaca, N.Y.: Cornell University Press, 1990; and Sylvia Maxfield, *Governing Capital: International Finance and Mexican Politics*, Ithaca, N.Y.: Cornell University Press, 1990.

ANNOTATED BIBLIOGRAPHY

Cyril Black *The Dynamics of Modernization.* New York: Harper and Row, 1966. A widely cited statement of modernization theory.

Fernando Henrique Cardoso and Enzo Falleto. *Dependency and Development in Latin America* Berkeley and Los Angeles: University of California Press, 1979. An important study of Latin American political and economic development from a dependency perspective. Cardoso and Falleto offer a less deterministic and more historical and contextual approach to the study of dependency than do many of the earlier authors in this tradition.

Jared Diamond. *Guns, Germs and Steel: The Fates of Human Societies.* New York: Norton, 1997. A sweeping examination of how geography has influenced social and economic development across the course of human history.

Adam Hochschild. *King Leopold's Ghost.* New York: Houghton Mifflin, 1999. Disturbing portrait of the searing cruelties and immense costs of colonialism in turn-of-the-nineteenth-century Belgian Congo.

David Landes. *The Wealth and Poverty of Nations.* New York: Norton, 1998. Offers a historical perspective on the role that technological innovation has played in economic development across various societies.

Vincent Mahler. *Dependency Approaches to International Political Economy: A Cross-National Study.* New York: Columbia University Press, 1980. An attempt to subject dependency theory to empirical testing.

Kurt Martin (ed.). *Strategies of Economic Development: Readings in the Political Economy of Industrialization.* New York: St. Martin's Press, 1991. A collection of theoretical essays on development.

Robert Packenham. *The Dependency Movement.* Cambridge: Harvard University Press, 1992. A critical overview and assessment of the dependency school.

Alejandro Portes. "On the Sociology of National Development: Theories and Issues." *American Journal of Sociology,* July 1976. A critique of modernization theory.

Tony Smith. "The Underdevelopment of the Development Literature: The Case of Dependency Theory." *World Politics,* January 1979. A critique of dependency theory from a liberal perspective.

United Nations Development Program. *Human Development Report, 2000.* New York: Oxford University Press, 2000. Issued annually, these reports focus on the social, cultural, and economic aspects of development. Especially useful is the Human Development Index, which provides a composite measure of the quality of life in various countries. Contains ample charts and data.

J. Samuel Valenzuela and Arturo Valenzuela. "Modernization and Dependency: Alternative Perspectives in the Study of Latin American Underdevelopment." In Heraldo Muñoz (ed.). *From Dependency to Development: Strategies to Overcome Underdevelopment and Inequality.* Boulder, Colo.: Westview Press, 1981. Perhaps the best and most concise comparison of the modernization and dependency perspectives.

Bill Warren. "Imperialism and Capitalist Industrialization." *New Left Review,* September–October 1973. A critique of dependency theory from a Marxist perspective.

Charles Wilbur (ed.). *The Political Economy of Development and Underdevelopment.* 5th Ed. New York: Random House, 1992. A collection of classic and contemporary essays on Southern development, most written from a left perspective.

World Bank. *World Development Report, 2000/2001.* New York: Oxford University Press, 2000. Issued annually, these reports contain a wealth of information on all aspects of Southern economies. Each report focuses upon a different theme related to Third World development. In addition to the tables, charts, and boxes scattered throughout the text, an appendix titled "World Development Indicators" is provided at the end of each volume. This section contains comprehensive social and economic data on each country, displayed in 30 or more tables.

9

❖

Strategies of Southern Trade and Development

Third World development strategies have varied across nations and over
time. Some countries have enjoyed enormous success, whereas others
have stumbled along the path to a better life for their citizens. Various
models of economic growth and industrialization have shifted in and out of
fashion. This chapter examines the diverse ways in which Southern states have
managed the process of development and their nations' ties to the international economy. We distinguish between national and collective strategies for
overcoming underdevelopment and closing the gap between North and
South. National strategies involve policies designed to spur growth in a particular country. Collective strategies revolve around the coordinated efforts of
multiple Third World countries to enhance their bargaining power vis-à-vis
the North, to shift the rules of the international economic order to the
South's advantage, and to enhance South-South economic ties.

NATIONAL STRATEGIES OF TRADE
AND INDUSTRIALIZATION

Development strategies in the Third World have followed a rough historical progression. Under colonialism, Third World economies were forcibly
oriented toward trade patterns dictated by the colonial powers. The colonized lands provided raw materials and agricultural commodities to the

imperial center, which in turn sold consumer and industrial goods to the colonies.

For the most part, this arrangement precluded the possibility of industrialization in the South. Indeed, the colonial powers intentionally discouraged the development of manufacturing industries that might compete with their own. The British, for instance, dismantled thriving textile and handicraft industries in India when they arrived. The legacies of colonialism made it difficult for Southern countries to break free of this pattern even after the colonists departed. The colonial powers built infrastructures designed to service the colonial trading system. Roads and railways, for instance, linked mines or plantations with ports, bypassing population centers in the interior of the country. Although natives were often incorporated into the colonial bureaucracy, they were given few opportunities to learn entrepreneurial skills. Vast agricultural regions were converted from the production of staple foods for domestic consumption to cash crops designed for export. Without a domestic manufacturing capability of their own, the former colonies remained dependent on the revenues earned from these exports in order to finance consumer good imports. Many countries, in Africa, for instance, remain entrenched in the colonial trading pattern, reliant upon the export of a narrow range of agricultural goods or raw materials.[1] Heavy dependence upon raw material exports is often problematic since the prices of such goods fluctuate widely and relative prices have tended to decline over time.[2]

Beginning in the 1930s, however, a number of countries, especially in Latin America, began to develop a substantial manufacturing sector based upon a strategy known as import substitution industrialization (ISI). This strategy was forced upon Latin American countries during the thirties and early forties, when the Great Depression first eroded traditional export markets and then World War II interrupted the flow of consumer goods from the North. Initially as a necessity and then, after World War II, as a matter of conscious choice, Latin American countries began to seek greater self-sufficiency and domestic industrialization.

The difficulty in pursuing such a course after the war had ended was that Southern firms were generally too small and inexperienced to withstand direct competition from Northern exporters. In an effort to nurture these infant industries and to substitute domestic production for previously imported goods, Third World governments raised protectionist barriers to stymie foreign competition. The first industries to be offered protection were producers of consumer goods because the technical barriers as well as the capital requirements to this sort of production were lower. Due to the lack of experienced entrepreneurs, these firms were often created and owned by the state. Besides tariff protection, the new firms were offered other forms of assistance, including subsidized financing and preferential access to foreign exchange with which to purchase imported inputs. Where domestic industry lacked the knowledge or the capital to engage in certain types of production, Northern multinational corporations were encouraged to jump protectionist barriers and to serve local markets through domestic production rather than through exports.

Other policies were associated with ISI. Local currencies were kept over-valued. This cheapened the price of imported inputs such as oil, raw materials, and capital goods for ISI industries. Wage rates were allowed to rise, and social spending increased so as to encourage the growth of a domestic market for the consumer goods produced by ISI industries. Although the export of cash crops remained necessary in order to secure the foreign exchange needed for imported industrial inputs, the agricultural sector was generally squeezed. Investment was shifted from agriculture to industry, and surplus rural labor was channeled toward urban areas.

ISI produced impressive growth and industrialization during the 1950s in much of Latin America and elsewhere.[3] Yet by the 1960s, ISI began to run out of steam due to contradictions inherent to the strategy. After the potential for further growth in the consumer goods sector slackened, governments began to pursue the "deepening" of ISI by encouraging the development of manufacturing capabilities in basic and intermediate industries such as steel and capital goods. For the most part, these investments involved larger-scale commitments of capital and more-sophisticated technologies than had been the case in the consumer goods industries. This required foreign borrowing or massive government spending. Moreover, because the domestic market for such goods remained small in many countries, new factories could not operate at efficient economies of scale, leading to high prices and large government subsidies.

These were not the only problems encountered by countries pursuing ISI. The justification for protecting the initial ISI industries from foreign competition was that they needed a breathing spell until they attained sufficient size and experience to compete successfully on their own. In fact, many firms became dependent on protectionism and lobbied hard against lifting barriers. With little effective competition, moreover, these firms had few incentives to maximize efficiency or to innovate. They were also free to charge monopoly prices.

Financial difficulties also characterized the late stages of ISI. Government subsidies to industry and high social spending led to large budget deficits. Foreign borrowing, the repatriation of multinational corporations' profits, and the discouragement of exports due to overvalued currencies also led to external deficits and a growing debt, despite the substitution of domestically produced goods for imports. Growing wage levels, large budget deficits, and the high prices associated with inefficient and monopolistic ISI industries created severe inflationary pressures.

Among development experts, ISI is now largely in disrepute. Although ISI may once have played a necessary role in jump-starting industrialization in Latin America and elsewhere, many observers have concluded that the rigidities and inefficiencies that ISI policies produce have more recently served to hinder growth and development. The past two decades have brought great interest in an alternative path to development often referred to as export-led industrialization (ELI). This strategy entails an emphasis on the growth of manufacturing production aimed at the international market, in contrast to ISI, which focused on producing for the domestic market. ELI is rooted in theories of international trade which emphasize that countries are best off specializing in those goods for which they possess a comparative advantage while opening their economies to imports that can be produced more cheaply elsewhere. Whereas ISI's goal was to develop a well-rounded and relatively self-sufficient industrial economy, the goal of ELI is to exploit a country's particular advantages by finding a narrower, but profitable, niche in the world economy.

The most successful examples of export-led industrialization can be found in East Asia, a region where the total number of poor people fell from 400 million to 180 million between 1970 and 1990 despite a two-thirds increase in population.[4] Leading the surge among East Asian developing countries have been the "Four Tigers"—South Korea, Taiwan, Singapore, and Hong Kong.[5] These countries have sustained astonishingly high rates of economic growth over the past several decades and stand poised to join the ranks of the world's most highly developed nations.

A statistical portrait of these four nations underscores their economic dynamism.[6]

- Over the past four decades, all four countries have averaged annual GDP growth rates of 6 to 8 percent.
- All four have combined low unemployment rates with low inflation.
- In just 40 years, South Korea's population was transformed from 80 percent rural to 80 percent urban in composition.
- South Korea's shipbuilding industry is the world's largest. The country is a major producer of semiconductor chips, steel, and automobiles.
- Taiwan is the world's largest producer of notebook computers and controls one-half of the world market for local area networks (LANs). Taiwan also produces 95 percent of the world's scanners and 60 percent or more of the world's motherboards and monitors.[7]
- Fifty-nine per cent of Singapore's manufacturing exports fall into the high-technology sector.
- The proportion of scientists and engineers in the populations of South Korea and Singapore is triple the average for middle-income developing countries.
- Singapore has more Internet hosts per capita than either Germany or Great Britain and has launched an ambitious campaign to integrate the Web into the everyday lives of all of its citizens.[8]
- Singapore's infant mortality rate is significantly lower than that of the United States.
- Life expectancy in Taiwan jumped from 59 years in 1952 to 74 in 1988 while rising from 58 years in 1965 to 73 in South Korea.
- All four countries have strong primary and secondary education systems with close to universal age-group enrollment. Forty-five percent of young Taiwanese go on to gain some higher education and Taiwan graduates 50,000 new engineers per year.[9]

In much of Latin America, in contrast, economic development has been accompanied by extreme and growing inequalities in income and wealth. In Brazil, for instance, the top 10 percent of the population receive 47.6 percent of the national income, whereas the earnings of the bottom 20 percent amount to only 2.5 percent.[10] In Latin America as a whole, the ratio of the income of the top 20 percent of income earners to the bottom 20 percent is 19:1 (25:1 in Brazil).[11] This unfortunate pattern has been avoided among the East Asian newly industrializing countries (NICs). In Taiwan, for example, growth has generally brought more, not less, equity. The combined income of the top 10 percent of Taiwanese households amounted to 15 times the bottom 20 percent in the early 1950s. By 1980 this ratio had fallen to 4.2:1 (below that of many Northern countries, including the United States, Sweden, and Japan). Although inequality worsened slightly during the eighties, Taiwan remains highly egalitarian by comparative standards. Income distribution is even more equitable in South Korea, where the income of the top 10 percent is only 3.7 times that of the bottom 20 percent.

The Four Tigers have each based their strategies of development on rapid export growth and international specialization. Despite their small size, Hong Kong, South Korea, and Singapore are, respectively, the world's eleventh, twelfth and fourteenth largest merchandise exporting countries. After years of large trade surpluses, Taiwan had accumulated $90 billion in official foreign exchange reserves by 1995—among the largest in the world. From 1950 to 1991 Taiwan averaged annual export growth of 21 percent, while the comparable figure for South Korea exceeded 27 percent. These two countries plus Hong Kong and Singapore accounted for over 60 percent of all Southern exports of manufactured goods in 1990.[12]

Singapore and Hong Kong, both small city-states and centers of Asian finance and commerce, boast per-capita incomes exceeding those of Spain and Ireland. A consulting group known as the Business Environment Risk Intelligence Corporation has rated Singapore's workforce the best in the world, an important factor in explaining the large waves of foreign direct investment (FDI) that Singapore has succeeded in attracting.[13]

A group of export-oriented states in Southeast Asia has followed the path blazed by the Four Tigers (and before them, by Japan). From 1980 through 1999, Malaysia's exports increased at an average rate of 11 percent per year, and the corresponding figure for Thailand was 12 percent. During the same period, both countries enjoyed average annual income growth rates of roughly 6 percent.[14] Between 1985 and 1996, the share of high-tech goods in Malaysia's exports doubled to a total of 60 percent.[15] Between the early 1980s to the early 1990s, Indonesia experienced an eighteenfold increase in electrical output and a doubling of paved road miles, while economic growth averaged 7 percent per year from the mid-1960s to the mid-1990s. The proportion of Indonesia's population living in abject poverty fell from 60 percent in 1970 to 11 percent in 1996.[16]

Success has brought new challenges for the East Asian NICs. Wage levels rose rapidly in each of the Four Tigers in the late eighties and the nineties.

This has brought increasing competition from the lower-wage countries of China and Southeast Asia. As a result, Taiwanese and South Korean firms have moved much of their low-wage production to surrounding countries such as China, Indonesia, Malaysia, and Thailand. Between 1990 and 1998, 80,000 Taiwanese firms moved production facilities offshore.[17]

Hong Kong manufacturing firms have transferred much of their production to southern China. The share of manufacturing jobs in the overall Hong Kong workforce fell from one-half in 1979 to 15 percent in 1997. Similarly, the share of Hong Kong's GDP accounted for by manufacturing industries dropped from almost 25 percent to less than 9 percent over the same period. In place of manufacturing, Hong Kong has come to rely more heavily upon finance, trade, and tourism.[18]

The Four Tigers have also responded to a changing competitive climate by encouraging the growth of high-technology manufacturing and information-based service industries. Seeking to become a high-tech innovator rather than an imitator, Taiwan began pouring both public and private funds into research and development in the 1980s and 1990s. Taiwan's many small manufacturing firms, which are highly efficient but lack the capacity to engage in large-scale research or investment projects, have forged new links with bigger Japanese and American firms. The Hsinchu Science-Based Industrial Park, formed in 1980, offers an example of Taiwan's commitment to technological development. The government has channeled over $500 million into the development of Hsinchu, which is home to 13,000 researchers, 150 high-tech firms, and four national laboratories. Researchers at Hsinchu helped launch Taiwan's national semiconductor industry in the early eighties. It also serves to attract Taiwanese scientists, technicians, researchers, and entrepreneurs back from overseas jobs.[19] The payoff from this attention to high technology has been impressive. Taiwan is now one of the world's leading producers of computer equipment.[20] In recognition of Taiwan's success, Malaysia, Singapore, and Hong Kong have also built multibillion-dollar high-technology industrial parks.[21]

South Korea and Taiwan have begun to reduce their states' role in directing economic growth and to shift away from mercantilist trade policies. Between 1986 and 1990, average tariff levels fell from 28 percent to 10 percent in Taiwan and from 24 percent to 13 percent in South Korea. The South Korean government is engaged in efforts to loosen restrictions on foreign investment, raise social welfare spending at home, and increase the availability of credit to small businesses in an effort to curb industrial concentration.[22]

The East Asian NICs have some important commonalities that help to explain their success.[23] South Korea and Taiwan each received large sums of aid from the United States during the 1950s, a factor that helped jump-start the drive toward industrialization. U.S. aid financed 80 percent of South Korean imports in the fifties.[24] Each nation carried out extensive land reform in the early post-World War II period. These steps broke the political and economic power of conservative landholding elites while establishing the necessary conditions for relatively egalitarian growth patterns. Organized labor has been politically weak in both countries. Each was ruled over much of the postwar era by strong, centralized authoritarian states that governed largely independently of control by particular social groups.

South Korea and Taiwan passed through relatively brief phases of import substitution industrialization before switching to export-led strategies in the early 1960s. Each developed powerful economic ministries staffed by skilled technocrats, who have used tax incentives, subsidies, credit, and regulatory policies to promote favored industries. State industrial policies have sought to push development along a path of increasing technological sophistication. Both South Korea and Taiwan have carefully screened foreign direct investment.

Singapore and Hong Kong began their paths to prosperity as regional financial and marketing centers before broadening their economies to encourage manufacturing growth and exports. Both have nondemocratic political systems, skilled bureaucracies, and weak labor unions.[25]

Each of the Four Tigers has achieved stunningly high rates of domestic savings and investment. The overall savings rate in East Asia (excluding Japan) reached 36 percent in the early 1990s, double the average rate in Latin America. Singapore raised its savings rate from 1 percent in 1965 to 40 percent in the early nineties.[26] All have placed great stress on education. In South Korea, college enrollment rose from 142,000 in 1965 to 1.4 million by the late 1980s.[27] Yet whereas other Third World countries, such as those in Latin America, place a large share of their educational resources into higher education, the main emphasis in East Asia is on high-quality primary education and on the widespread proliferation of knowledge and skills. This focus on basic education promotes higher worker efficiency and allows for greater equity.[28]

Some interesting differences distinguish the East Asian NICs from one another. South Korea, the most statist of the four, has relied heavily upon large industrial conglomerates, both state-owned and private, whose growth has been fueled by cheap credit and heavy borrowing. Sales of the top four South Korean industrial groups, called *chaebols,* equaled one-third of all sales of Korean firms in 1993. The top 30 *chaebols* combined to account for 75 percent of the country's GDP.[29] South Korea has also accumulated a substantial foreign debt, a factor that rendered it vulnerable to the deleterious effects of the 1997 Asian financial crisis.

Taiwan's economy, by contrast, rests upon a collection of many small equity-based companies. Unlike South Korea, Taiwan has avoided extensive foreign borrowing. Hong Kong is alone among the four East Asian NICs in relying almost solely upon market mechanisms rather than aggressive state intervention to steer economic growth and development. Unlike South Korea and Taiwan, Singapore has depended heavily upon foreign direct investment to stimulate growth, even to the point of favoring foreign firms over local firms.

The World Bank and other development agencies have pointed to the East Asian NICs' success as examples to be copied by other Third World nations. Indeed, dozens of countries in Latin America, Asia, and Africa have abandoned the ISI strategies of previous decades in favor of more-liberal, open, and export-oriented economies. The recent experience of the Southeast Asian countries suggests that some of the nations seeking to emulate the Four Tigers will succeed. Yet it is far from certain that the East Asian model of industrialization can be generalized to large numbers of Third World countries.

For one thing, the so-called neoliberal version of ELI now being urged upon Third World countries by the World Bank and many development experts differs in subtle but important ways from the more mercantilistic strategy pursued by the East Asian NICs in the early stages of their economic takeoff. In South Korea and Taiwan, industrialization involved a heavy dose of state economic management and intervention. A recent World Bank study of East Asian development summed up the government's role in the South Korean economy: "From the early 1960s, the government carefully planned and orchestrated the country's development. [It] used the financial sector to steer credits to preferred sectors and promoted individual forms to achieve national objectives. [It] socialized risk, created large conglomerates (chaebols), created state enterprises when necessary, and molded a public-private partnership that rivaled Japan's."[30]

Both East Asia and Latin America experienced extensive state intervention. They differed, however, in whether industrial production was directed toward the domestic market or external markets. Contemporary advocates of ELI have typically embraced the export orientation of the East Asian countries while ignoring or rejecting the heavy state economic role that was characteristic of such nations until recent years. Whether the neoliberal version of ELI now being pursued by many Third World countries can match the accomplishments produced through the more mercantilist strategies adopted by the early export-oriented industrializing countries is an interesting but as yet unanswered question.

Also important, the successes of South Korea and Taiwan seem to be associated with a number of characteristics peculiar to the historical development of these societies. These characteristics include the rule of strong authoritarian governments, the development of skilled bureaucracies, the weakness of the landowning class, and low levels of labor mobilization. Each also enjoyed favored relations with the United States, bringing considerable economic aid as well as military protection during the early stages of their industrialization drives.

The issue of historical timing also deserves attention. The East Asian NICs adopted ELI at a time when most other Third World countries were pursuing inward-looking strategies. Northern markets were growing at a brisk pace, and trade barriers were falling rapidly. Conditions were ripe for the success of a strategy built around the targeting of Northern markets with goods manufactured by low-wage workers. In today's climate, by contrast, many Third World nations are competing to service the same Northern markets, and growth in Northern demand is sluggish.

Those who seek to emulate countries such as South Korea and Taiwan must also reckon with the less appealing consequences of rapid industrialization in East Asia. In South Korea, for instance, growth has brought staggering levels of industrial pollution. In one highly publicized incident, a large chemical leak on

March 14, 1991, contaminated a major reservoir that provided drinking water to nearby communities. Hundreds, perhaps thousands, of people became violently ill after drinking the polluted tap water. This episode led to an emotional debate among South Koreans over the environmental costs of development.[31]

The rush to development has also led to shortcuts that have compromised the quality of the region's infrastructure. During 1994 and 1995 South Korea witnessed a series of deadly disasters, including the collapse of a highway bridge (leading to 32 deaths), the explosion of a gas pipeline (100 deaths), the sinking of a ferry (29 deaths), and the disintegration of a major department store (400 deaths and 900 injuries).[32] South Korea also has the world's highest rate of industrial accidents and occupation-related illnesses.[33] In some respects, development has been directed by skewed priorities. Despite the success of South Korean manufacturing firms, for instance, the number of housing units nationwide in 1988 fell 40 percent short of the number of households. South Korea's capital, Seoul, was home to 2 million squatters out of a population of nearly 10 million.[34]

Most recently, the relevance of the "Asian model" as a blueprint for development has been called into question by the Asian financial crisis that began in 1997. These events are discussed in detail in Chapter 12 of this volume. For now, it is important to note that the financial crisis that spread across the region in 1997 revealed vulnerabilities in the development strategies of many of the region's states. It also set in motion policy changes that have significantly altered the development paths pursued by many countries.

The Asian financial crisis began in Thailand but quickly spread across the region. During 1997 and 1998, $115 billion in capital fled the Asia–Pacific region.[35] Stock markets plummeted, currencies lost value, banks accumulated bad loans on their balance sheets, and large industrial corporations were forced into bankruptcy. In addition, millions of people lost jobs, government tax revenues faltered, and exports suffered.

The International Monetary Fund (IMF) and the World Bank intervened after the crisis hit by lending money to countries in the region. IMF loans were conditioned upon austerity measures designed to restore financial stability. The IMF also, however, insisted that states liberalize and deregulate their economies and also privatize state firms. IMF conditions thus challenged the guiding role of the state that had previously been a distinctive feature of economic management in some Asian countries such as South Korea.

The crisis prompted the South Korean government, for instance, to take steps toward loosening the grip of the *chaebols* on the national economy. In 1998, government officials met with representatives of the largest Korean industrial conglomerates to insist upon the following package of reforms:[36]

- Improve transparency in business operations
- Publish more accurate accounting statistics
- Appoint external boards of directors and reduce overlap between the membership of board of different companies
- Make board chairs legally accountable

- Listen to minority shareholders
- Eliminate cross-guarantees between companies
- Cut corporate debt
- Aim for profits rather than sales growth
- Concentrate on core businesses and divest parts of the group in peripheral industries

Although change has been slow, South Korea's efforts to reform the *chaebols* has brought some results. Between 1997 and 2000, the *chaebols* have reduced their average debt from five times equity to less than twice equity.[37] One of the largest *chaebols,* Daewoo, is being broken up, with many subsidiaries sold off to pay massive debts.[38]

The banking sector has also been a target of reform in much of the region. While banks received government bailouts to retire mountains of bad debt, they have also been pressured to eliminate the close, long-term, and sometimes corrupt relationships that many held with particular firms or investors— a phenomenon sometimes referred to as "crony capitalism." Instead, banking reform is focused on transparency, accountability, and the importance of basing loan decisions on clear commercial standards.

The move to reduce state intervention and to break up tight linkages among banks and corporations represents a departure from traditional practice for many countries. Some view the move toward neoliberalism and the primacy of free markets as a consequence of globalization. Economist Doug Henwood has remarked: "It may be that as economies mature, throw off their own financial surpluses and get more involved in the global circuit of capital, it becomes impossible to sustain tight structures, whether Korean chaebol, Japanese keiretsu or German bank-industry links."[39]

TRANSITIONS TO EXPORT-LED
INDUSTRIALIZATION: THREE
COUNTRY STUDIES

Many Third World countries may find it difficult or impossible to duplicate the supportive domestic and international conditions that launched the East Asian nations along their path to prosperity or, if successful, to avoid the serious social and environmental drawbacks of rapid industrialization. The challenge that such countries face is to find ways of adapting an export-oriented strategy to their own unique circumstances.[40]

Three of the largest Third World countries to recently attempt the transition from inward- to outward-oriented development are China, India, and Brazil. This section examines the successes and failures that these three countries have experienced in their attempts to apply the lessons of the East Asian model to the special problems that each faces.

China

Beginning in 1979, a group of reformers in the Chinese Communist leadership, led by Deng Xiaoping, undertook a dramatic turnabout in China's strategy of economic development. Until this point, China's largely self-contained economy had been steered by traditional communist state planning and ownership. During the 1980s, however, Chinese leaders introduced a series of market reforms designed to speed up the process of economic modernization and open China to the world economy. Although the state-owned sector of the economy remained in place, a thriving private sector sprang up alongside it. At first, this economic experiment was limited to several special economic zones located along China's southern coast, but similar policies were later extended to other parts of the country. Chinese leaders gradually freed prices from state control, decentralized economic decision making, and encouraged foreign trade and investment. Reflecting the ideological tensions created by China's pragmatic turn, state officials contend that China is building a "socialist market economy." Somewhat more bluntly, Chinese leader Deng Xiaoping has succinctly declared that "development at a slow pace is not socialism."[41]

China's economy has responded with enormous vitality to the economic reforms introduced since 1979. Indeed, China's economic growth rate was the world's highest during the 1980s and 1990s. Per-capita income in China rose at a rate of 7.5 percent per year from 1975 through 1998.[42] Much of this growth has been fueled by rapid export expansion. Chinese exports rose at an average annual rate of over 19 percent during the eighties and 13 percent during the nineties.[43]

China's growth has also been aided by a massive influx of foreign direct investment. China attracted almost $44 billion in FDI in 1998 alone. This figure ranked third in the world, behind only the United States and Great Britain, and accounted for one-quarter of all foreign direct investment flowing to the developing world in that year.[44] A large proportion of FDI flows to mainland China have originated in Hong Kong, Taiwan, and other parts of East Asia. China was home to an estimated 450,000 expatriate business managers in 1995.[45]

Economic reform has ushered in an age of revolutionary social and economic change for the Chinese people. The lives of many Chinese citizens have been fundamentally transformed in a span of less than two decades. Whereas in 1970 one-third of all Chinese lived at or below the basic subsistence level, by 1990 this figure had fallen to 10 percent. Child mortality, which stood at 120 out of every 1,000 children under age five in 1960, declined to 47 by 1998. Average life expectancy rose by more than six years between the early 1970s and the late 1990s. As a result of government inoculation programs, in fact, a baby born in Shanghai is likely to live longer than a baby born in New York City. Overall, the Chinese consumed 2.5 times more meat, eggs, and milk in 1994 than they did in 1982. Per-capita housing space more than doubled in the eighties. In 1978 China possessed roughly 8 bicycles, 8 radios, and 0.3 televisions for every 100 people. By 1990 these figures had risen, respectively, to

34, 22, and 16.[46] From 1978 to 1990, the number of washing machines in China rose from virtually zero to over 97 million.[47]

Yet despite recent gains, China remains a relatively poor society, especially in the rural areas, where two-thirds of the population live. Among the 174 nations listed, China ranks ninety-ninth on the United Nations Development Program's Human Development Index.[48] China has only 70 main telephone lines for every 1,000 people-up from 6 lines per 1,000 in 1990 but far below the 661 figure for the United States. One-third of China's people lack access to safe drinking water and three-quarters lack adequate sanitation services.[49] Although China's "one child" policy has succeeded in slowing population growth, one result has been a skewed demographic age profile. As the birth rate drops, China faces a rapid aging of its population, with the share of China's elderly expected to rise from 10 percent of the population today to 22 percent in 2030. China's leaky social security system is poorly equipped to handle this demographic transition.[50]

Moreover, China's rapid economic growth has produced enormous social disruption and many unappealing side effects. One hundred million rural laborers are unemployed, and many are migrating to the cities in search of work. In 1993 20 Chinese provinces experienced peasant protests, 830 of which involved over five hundred people and 21 of which involved more than five thousand participants. Even urban areas have experienced increasing labor unrest, with 1993 witnessing over 12,000 significant labor disputes at Chinese factories. The conditions facing workers is often grim. While China produces one-quarter of the world's coal output, it accounts for 80 percent of the world's coal industry fatalities.[51]

Many unwelcome social changes are also evident. Crime has increased tenfold since 1979. Divorce rates have doubled. Most troubling to many Chinese is the pervasiveness of corruption in public life. In 1993 Chinese leader Deng Xiaoping warned that China had become "dominated by corruption, embezzlement and bribery." Chinese Premier Li Peng has stated that the fight against corruption among government officials has become a "life or death" struggle for China and its political leadership.[52]

China's once vaunted rural health system, charged with serving 800 million people, has virtually collapsed due to dwindling support from the central government. Although private clinics have opened in many areas, their services are too expensive for the majority of China's rural poor. Overall, rural health care costs rose between 400 percent and 500 percent from 1990 to 1997. As a result of deteriorating health care in rural regions, child immunization rates are down, infant mortality is once again on the rise following decades of decline, and the incidence of tuberculosis has quadrupled over the past 15 years.[53]

Inequality has added to the strains wracking China's social system. The gap between the top income earners and those at the bottom has more than doubled since the late 1970s. Urban residents now earn more than 2.5 times the average income of rural dwellers. And the economic gap between the relatively prosperous southern coastal regions and China's interior provinces has also widened.[54]

These serious problems pale, however, in comparison to the threats posed by environmental degradation and potential agricultural shortages. Due to a heavy reliance on coal in power production, sulfur dioxide levels far exceed international standards in virtually every major Chinese city. Air pollution has become the leading cause of disease in China. As many as 300,000 Chinese die premature deaths each year due to pollution-related lung diseases. Indeed, the air in Beijing is so dirty that local entrepreneurs have mounted a thriving business in "oxygen bars"—places where wheezy patrons stop off on their way home from work to purchase a whiff of fresh air delivered via oxygen canisters.[55]

Other environmental problems have reached disastrous proportions, as well. As a result of agricultural expansion and urban development, for instance, China's forest cover has shrunk to 13 percent of its total land area (compared with 31 percent for the world as a whole). Over 80 percent of China's sewage and wastewater enters rivers or lakes untreated. Sixty million Chinese cannot get sufficient clean water for their daily needs. One-third of China's cropland has been damaged by acid rain. Economists estimate that, overall, the financial costs of China's environmental deterioration and resource scarcities equals 8 to 12 percent of that country's GDP.[56]

Food offers another serious challenge for China. China's grain output rose from 150 million tons in 1960 to 456 million tons in 1993, with most of the increase occurring during the 1980s as a response to agricultural reforms.[57] Worker productivity in the agricultural sector almost doubled between 1980 and 1997.[58] Yet despite recent gains, China faces a serious agricultural crisis. China's ratio of arable land per farm worker is among the lowest in the world. Yet China has lost one-third of its farmland to industrialization, soil erosion, salinization, and other causes over the past 40 years. Agricultural land is expected to shrink another 10 percent over the next 15 years.

Providing food for China's growing population will pose the most important challenge of the next several decades. Increased food demand will stem from two sources. China's population, already 1.2 billion people, is expected to rise by 25 percent, or 300 million people, over the next 20 years. As incomes rise, moreover, the Chinese people will continue to increase and to upgrade their diets. Even without considering increased population, this factor alone will generate tremendous demand. If, for instance, the Chinese people increased their grain consumption to match the levels of South Koreans, China would need 600 million tons of grain each year. Assuming present Chinese grain production levels, China would have to import an amount of grain equal to all international shipments worldwide in 1994 in order to satisfy this level of consumption. If Chinese fish consumption rose to Japanese levels, China would consume all of the fish harvested worldwide.[59]

How China will manage this rising demand for food remains uncertain. With the major improvements registered during the 1980s, Chinese grain yields have already neared the limits of what appears possible, given present methods and technology.[60] As mentioned, presently cultivated land is expected to shrink in the coming years, and very little unexploited arable land remains available. The availability of water is also a problem. Due to extensive irrigation and other uses, the water table underlying the North China Plain, which produces 40 percent of China's grain harvest, is dropping at a rate of five feet per year.[61] Agriculture's share of total investment in the Chinese economy has, moreover, been declining in recent years.[62] Most likely, China will become a major food importer in future years, using industrial exports to pay for grain shipments from abroad.

One of the biggest puzzles facing China in the coming years concerns what to do about the hugely inefficient state-owned sector of the economy. Although the private economy has experienced explosive growth, state-owned enterprises (SOEs), concentrated in heavy industry, have not shared the same dynamism. The proportion of economic output accounted for by SOEs has fallen from 78 percent in 1978 to 43 percent in 1994. Despite tentative reforms, SOEs continue to act as a drag on the rest of the economy. Ten percent of such firms are virtually inactive, and one-third of the workforce in the state-owned sector is deemed "unproductive." Forty percent of SOEs showed a loss in 1994, and most carry heavy debt loads, cumulatively equal to one-third of China's GDP. One-half of the central government's budget is taken up by subsidies to SOEs, and 40 percent of all tax revenue goes to pay the interest and principle on existing government debt.[63]

Chinese authorities have allowed a growing number of SOEs to go bankrupt and have sought, with limited success, to attract foreign partners to help invigorate others. Officials have been reluctant to cut off subsidies, close down unprofitable firms, or engage in wholesale privatization for fear that such steps would lead to massive unemployment and social unrest. One-quarter of the Chinese population is dependent upon people employed by SOEs. It is estimated that 30 to 40 percent of all SOE employees would lose their jobs if such firms were run by commercial standards.[64]

The shrinkage of inefficient state-owned firms has created hardship for many workers. The year 2000 alone witnessed a net increase of 5 million laid-off workers from closed or downsized SOEs. Unemployment insurance in China comes to only $25 per month, and one study found that slightly less than one-half of dismissed SOE employees were successful in finding alternative employment.[65]

China's latest challenge is its entry into the World Trade Organization (WTO), which became official at the November 2001 WTO meeting. The WTO requires member countries to open their economies to world markets and restricts certain kinds of government intervention into both domestic and international markets. Bringing China into compliance with WTO rules will require major changes in China's commercial law, regulatory systems, and tax policy. Certain industries that have been relatively sheltered heretofore will face an abrupt rise in competition from foreign producers and investors. The necessary social dislocations and adjustments arising from China's entry into the WTO will be jarring, and the changing fortunes of different groups will divide Chinese society into winners and losers from liberalization. In the long run, however, greater openness ought to winnow out inefficient producers and strengthen those that successfully adapt to the growing competitive challenge. China's leaders are betting that the short-term political conflict unleashed by this new phase in market liberalization will not derail progress toward the long-term goal of creating a more competitive Chinese economy.

In light of these serious challenges, it is perhaps not surprising that one recent survey of urban Chinese discovered that only 36 percent are satisfied with current conditions. Much of the current dissatisfaction focuses on the unresponsiveness of China's political system to popular concerns. A 2000 survey of midlevel government officials found that 40 percent thought that reform was proceeding too slowly (compared with 12 percent in 1998) and 44 percent of the same group identified political reform as the most urgent priority.[66]

China has approached the transition from socialism to capitalism much differently than have many of the former Soviet bloc countries. China—rejecting the "shock therapy," or rapid and thorough transformation, adopted by Poland and several other eastern European countries—has followed a gradualist path that has nevertheless brought spectacular results.[67] Yet alongside the undeniable economic gains, China's dramatic experiment has produced many negative side effects, including growing crime, inequality, corruption, and environmental devastation. These outgrowths of economic progress were certainly not foreign to the experiences of today's developed countries as they passed through a similar stage of development. But whereas the process of development was spread over many decades, or even centuries, in the West, the speed of China's economic transformation is unprecedented. Can the world's most populous nation, ruled by an aging and politically inflexible elite, manage the stresses and contradictions loosened by rapid modernization without inviting a social and political explosion of some sort? The answer to this question will have important implications stretching far beyond China itself.

India

More than 50 years after gaining independence, India remains a country plagued by grinding poverty. In 1998 India ranked 128th of the 174 nations on the UN Human Development Index. India is home to one-quarter of the world's desperately poor, and 44 percent of the population lives in absolute poverty. Nineteen percent of Indians lack access to safe drinking water, 25 percent enjoy no access to health services, and 71 percent are without access to sanitation services. Fifty-three percent of India's children under age five are underweight for their age, and more than 10 percent of children born die before the age of five. For every 1,000 people, India possesses only 22 main telephone lines, 69 televisions, and 3 personal computers.[68]

For decades India was among the most devoted practitioners of an inward—looking strategy of development. The state controlled and directed strategic sectors of the economy; foreign investment was strictly limited and highly regulated; import substitution policies were designed to protect and nurture domestic industrialization; and India's currency, the rupee, was purposely overvalued.

After traveling to East Asia and expressing admiration for South Korea's model of development, however, newly appointed finance minister Mohammed Singh announced a dramatic shift in economic strategy in the summer of 1991. India would abandon ISI policies in favor of liberalization and a focus on exports. This turnabout was prompted by India's worsening financial straits, including persistent balance of payments deficits, dwindling foreign reserves, and a burdensome foreign debt that had risen from $20.5 billion in 1980 to $72 billion by 1991. India's predicament was exacerbated by a precipitous decline in previously significant levels of Soviet foreign aid as well as by the shrinkage of Soviet demand for Indian goods.

Following Singh's initiative, the Indian government pledged to devalue the rupee, eliminate the state budget deficit, cut subsidies to public firms while closing those that were particularly unprofitable, remove restrictions that discourage foreign investment, and reduce many barriers to imported goods. The World Bank and the IMF quickly rewarded India's shift from ISI toward a more liberal economic strategy by granting extensive new credits designed to relieve the immediate financial strains plaguing the country. Domestic reactions were more mixed, with many groups and individuals expressing worry and dismay that the new policies would produce increased unemployment and hardship among those reliant upon state support.[69]

India's reforms have brought a number of positive results. Between 1995 and 1997, economic growth averaged 7 percent, with rising industrial output leading the way. The rate of growth in exports doubled in the 1990s as compared with the 1980s, reaching an annual average of 11.3 percent. India's trade deficit declined during the nineties and official international reserves rose from $5.6 billion to $32.6 billion. The central government's budget deficit fell from 10 percent of GDP to less than 5 percent. Foreign capital began flowing into Indian stock markets, while annual foreign direct investment increased from $91 million in 1988 to $3 billion in 1997. In terms of social progress, India's adult literacy rate rose from 52 percent to 64 percent between 1991 and 1999.[70]

India has even found a niche in the global high-tech economy, focusing primarily on software programming services. India's computer software industry grew by 50 percent per year during the 1990s. By the end of the decade, revenues had risen to $8 billion per year. Overall, technology exports have now reached over $6 billion per year.[71]

Nevertheless, economic liberalization runs against India's historic tradition and has drawn fierce domestic opposition. The principal winners have been among India's relatively small middle class. Many others, especially those dependent upon state protection or vulnerable to growing international competition, feel threatened by India's turn toward greater reliance on market mechanisms. The public sector still accounts for one-half of India's industrial stock. The government has been slow to carry out widespread privatization or to allow unprofitable firms to go bankrupt. Indeed, large Indian companies, whether private or public, cannot lay off workers or close plants without government permission. Subsidies to rural farmers for water and power remain a substantial drain on government revenues. So too does interest on the public debt, which consumes 45 percent of the central government budget each year. Finally, India's international debt burden has continued to grow, reaching $98 billion in 1998.[72]

Foreign investors still face widespread hostility and distrust. In 1995 the regional government of Maharashtra, India's main industrial state, rejected the largest foreign investment project ever proposed for India—a $2.8 billion power plant to be built by Enron Corporation. Political instability has cast further doubt upon India's long-term commitment to liberalization. Support for the once hegemonic Congress Party has diminished, and recent years have witnessed a succession of weak coalition governments.[73]

Indeed, India possesses a set of traits that seems likely to make the successful transition to an outward-looking strategy of development especially difficult: a weak central government, extreme poverty, entrenched vested interests, cultural fragmentation, and a traditional distrust of the outside world. When one adds to these India's enormous size and still-burgeoning population, which recently surpassed 1 billion people, the prospects for a rapid improvement in the standard of living of most Indians appear slim.

Brazil

Brazil's ISI strategy, spectacularly successful in generating economic growth during the 1960s and 1970s, was derailed in the 1980s.[74] ISI succeeded in producing a diverse industrial structure in Brazil. Growth in GNP averaged 9 percent per year from 1965 to 1980. Yet massive foreign borrowing fueled much of this expansion. This accumulation of debt harmed Brazil's creditworthiness and led to a sharp contraction of foreign bank lending to the country in the eighties. Brazilian industry also became increasingly inefficient as it remained sheltered from international competition and was nursed along with government subsidies. Before March 1990, imports were simply prohibited in 1,000 categories of goods, while quotas restricted many other sorts of imports. Tariffs averaged 78 percent in 1984, and the central bank strictly controlled access to foreign exchange. Imports represented only 5 percent of Brazilian GNP in 1989, compared with 28 percent for South Korea and 33 percent for Taiwan. The 1980s witnessed the failure of Brazil's ISI strategy. Per-capita income stagnated, the number of Brazil's hungry rose from 25 million to 35 million, and inflation averaged 260 percent per year.[75]

Brazil's turn toward economic liberalization began in 1990. Since then, import bans have been lifted on hundreds of items, and average tariffs have fallen to 14 percent. Between 1989 and 1997, imports rose from $20 billion to $60 billion yearly. Exports also grew quickly, and $81 billion in foreign direct investment entered Brazil from 1996 to 1999.[76]

After years of negotiations, Brazil reached an agreement to reschedule its huge foreign debt to Northern commercial banks in 1993.[77] This paved the way for a vast wave of new foreign investment into the country. In 1994 it was estimated that an average of 300 American business representatives per day visited Sao Paulo, Brazil's largest industrial city.[78] Portfolio investment, in the form of stock and bond purchases, also rose dramatically. Sectors of the economy that were previously forbidden to outsiders, such as oil, mining, telecommunications, banking, and insurance, were opened to foreign investors.[79]

Yet the international fallout from the Asian financial crisis of 1997–1998 eventually created renewed instability in Brazil's international financial position. As portfolio investment fled Brazil in 1998, the government was forced to devalue Brazil's currency, cut spending, and accept a $41.5 billion bailout package from the IMF. Economic growth and exports both suffered. Brazil's external debt grew to $232 billion in 1998, the world's largest. Brazil's current account deficit for 2000 ballooned to $24.6 billion.[80]

Some sectors of Brazilian industry responded with alacrity to the increasingly competitive environment brought about by trade and investment liberalization. Brazil's automobile industry, for instance, experienced a 46 percent improvement in productivity between 1990 and 1993. Auto manufacturers introduced 10 new car models in 1993, compared with the usual two. Multibillion-dollar investment projects led to a doubling of Brazilian automobile production over the 1990s, reaching a level of 1.67 million vehicles in 2000. Similar changes have occurred elsewhere. Average prices for electronic goods fell by 40 percent between 1989 and 1993. The processed food sector introduced 600 new products in 1992, compared with 300 in 1991.[81]

Brazil's most intractable economic problem throughout the 1980s and early 1990s was an inflation rate of mind-boggling proportions. Successive anti-inflation plans failed to cure this malady until 1994, when new president Fernando Henrique Cardoso instituted a new initiative that included the issuance of a new currency and a sharp reduction in government spending. From a rate of 40 percent per month (the equivalent of 2,500 percent per year) in the first half of 1994, Brazilian inflation subsided to 1.5 percent in September. By 1999, Brazil's annual rate of inflation had fallen to only 5 percent.[82]

Cardoso's economic reforms extended to other areas as well. His government promoted the privatization of state enterprises, the reorganization of the social welfare system, the reduction of paperwork for imports, the transfer of health and education programs to the states, and the encouragement of foreign investment. Not all of these reforms have brought the promised results. In 1995, for example, Brazil privatized and deregulated the energy sector in hopes of creating a more efficient system for distributing power to consumers. In practice, however, these reforms led to higher prices, falling investment, and a decrease in quality of service. The most likely explanation is that privatization allowed the creation of commercial monopolies unconstrained by effective public regulation.[83]

Cardoso's own personal odyssey reflected the dramatically changed economic and ideological climate in Brazil and elsewhere in Latin America during the 1990s. Cardoso first gained fame as a left-wing sociologist who coauthored one of the seminal works in the dependency school[84] and who was a vocal critic of Brazil's right-wing military dictatorships of the 1960s and

1970s. Cardoso was drawn into mainstream politics beginning in the late seventies as Brazil gradually moved toward democracy. After serving as finance minister during the early nineties and presiding over Brazil's ultimately successful debt negotiations, Cardoso became the darling of international financiers. By 1994 this once radical sociologist could be quoted as saying: "Whoever tries to make decisions against the market is going to fail."[85]

The depth of neoliberal sentiment within the Brazilian political class, and within those of other Latin American countries as well, is evident in the reflections of Augusto Carvalho, a Brazilian congressman affiliated with the former Brazilian Communist Party, now known as the Popular Socialist Party: "I have changed, the left has changed, the Congress has changed. We're not against foreign capital that can create jobs and bring technology to the country."[86]

The biggest challenge facing Brazil today, however, is to find some way to reconcile this newfound commitment to free markets with the imperative of improving the life chances of those who lack the skills or resources to compete in this new economic environment. Brazil remains a country where the richest 20 percent of the population earns 26 times more than the poorest 20 percent. Regional disparities are striking. Compared with relatively prosperous southern Brazilians, residents of Brazil's largely rural northeastern region live 17 fewer years, suffer an adult literacy rate one-third lower, and receive average incomes of 40 percent less. One-half of the nation's farmland is concentrated in the hands of only 1 per cent of landowners. One-half of Brazil's 70 million workers have less than four years of schooling, and 15 percent have less than one year.[87]

In 1994 U.S. Undersecretary of Commerce for International Trade Jeffrey Garten predicted that "Brazil could be the big success story" of the coming years.[88] If this success is to be shared by all Brazilians, however, its economic managers must find a way to spread the benefits of renewed economic growth in a more inclusive manner than has been done in the past. Otherwise, an observation made by one of Brazil's military presidents during the boom years of the 1970s will once again hold true for the current period of economic transformation: "Brazil is doing fine. It's the people who are doing poorly."[89]

THE LEAST DEVELOPED COUNTRIES

Some analysts argue that the wave of market-oriented reforms currently sweeping the Third World will place Southern countries on the path to sustained economic growth. The East Asian NICs are often cited as beacons of the kind of future that could await other nations that follow their example. Yet these conclusions are not universally shared. Some argue that the successes of the NICs will be difficult to duplicate and that fundamental trends point toward the increasing marginalization of much of the Third World in the decades ahead.

Since World War II, the comparative advantage of most Third World countries has rested upon one of three sets of resources: strategic location, critical raw materials, and cheap labor. All three may well become less central to the functioning of the world economy in the years ahead.[90] A variety of Third World countries benefited from their perceived military and political importance to one or both superpowers during the Cold War. The United States and the Soviet Union carried their rivalry to the Third World by spreading vast sums of economic and military aid among scores of strategically vital allies. In some cases, these countries were compensated for their willingness to host U.S. or Soviet military bases. In others, the superpowers sought to bolster the allegiance or political stability of countries that sat astride strategic shipping lanes or provided militarily critical resources. Some countries received favor because they were located along the front lines of the U.S.-Soviet rivalry or because they had symbolic value as exemplars of capitalism or socialism.

With the end of the Cold War, the strategic and political significance of previously favored clients has evaporated. Foreign aid to many such countries has already declined and has been reallocated according to economic rather than political criteria. Spending for overseas bases has also fallen.[91]

Countries that depend upon the bulk export of a few varieties of raw materials will also suffer. In the past, the principal markets for such resources lay in the North. Yet as Northern economies become less dependent upon manufacturing and more heavily oriented toward services and the production and exchange of information, the demand for imported raw materials will fail to keep pace with overall economic growth. This trend is, in fact, already well established. Today, for instance, Japan uses 60 percent fewer raw materials to produce each unit of economic output than it did in 1973. Another important constraint on the export of Third World resources is the increasing tendency for Northern countries to devise synthetic substitutes for previously imported raw materials. Examples include artificial sweeteners and synthetic rubber.

Some types of industries will continue to shift production to the Third World in search of lower labor costs. But the most dynamic high-technology sectors are likely to remain in the North. For such industries, labor constitutes an increasingly small proportion of total costs. Far more important is access to capital, new knowledge, and a highly skilled work force. Factory managers must have direct and regular contact with Northern-based designers and engineers in order to carry out constant modifications in the production process as well as in the end product. Economic processes are also increasingly tied to communications networks and technological infrastructures that are lacking in the South.

None of this means that Third World development is at a dead end. It does suggest, however, that Third World countries must blaze different paths to development than in the past. It is tempting, under contemporary circumstances, to seek new orthodoxies or universal prescriptions to replace the old. Some experts point to the export-led strategy pursued by the East Asian NICs as a model for the remainder of the Third World. Such advice must be subjected to careful scrutiny. The development community has in the past often been given to faddishness. Witness the 1950s, when the now-discredited strategy of ISI was widely hailed as the cure to Third World underdevelopment.

Debates over the quickest path to industrialization, for instance, are of little relevance to much of the South. The great majority of people of the world's least developed countries continue to make their living off the land. In such societies, a premature emphasis on modern industry benefits the few at the expense of the many. Scarce resources have often been directed toward showcase industrial projects that end up as white elephants, failing due to poor infrastructural support, inadequate skills, and managerial inexperience or to an inability to afford the spare parts and imported energy needed to sustain the project.

The problems of the poorest countries are so serious that quick solutions are unlikely, and advice must be offered with a large dose of humility. Despite decades of development aid and plans real wages in Sub-Saharan Africa's 49 countries remain at the same level today as in 1970. Fifty percent of Africans live in poverty, and 40 percent suffer from hunger and malnutrition.[92]

Nevertheless, it seems clear that the first task for such societies must be to develop a modernized, diversified, and sustainable agricultural sector. There are several keys to successful agrarian development: avoid overconcentration of land ownership, allow markets to set realistic prices that provide incentives to producers, make credit and technical information available to small farmers, and encourage environmentally sound and sustainable agricultural methods. As efficiency gains raise rural incomes, it is possible to develop small-scale local industries aimed at providing the tools and implements needed by farmers, as well as a growing supply of consumer goods.

These tasks are, of course, easier said than done. Many Third World countries face harsh climates, unfavorable geography, burgeoning populations, political instability, widespread illiteracy, gross economic and social inequalities, and foreign interference. Though progress is possible, no tidy solutions to these problems are available. What seems clear about the future is that the diversification of the Third World will continue, with some countries experiencing healthy growth and development while others, perhaps the majority, struggle to keep up.

COLLECTIVE STRATEGIES
OF DEVELOPMENT

Some Third World countries have sought development not through industrialization and diversification of their economies but instead through attempts to turn the tables of traditional colonial trade patterns against the North. During the 1970s there existed great interest in the potential of resource cartels to enhance Southern wealth. The aim of this strategy was to exploit the North's dependence upon various Southern raw material or agricultural exports. Although no single Third World country controlled a sufficient market share to manipulate world prices for the commodities it exported, the major Southern producers acting collectively might successfully coordinate production and pricing decisions so as to maximize their joint revenues.

Although, for reasons we will discuss later, most such efforts failed, this strategy produced one spectacular success story: the Organization of Petroleum Exporting Countries (OPEC). The history of how the oil-exporting states gained control over their petroleum resources from Northern oil companies and accumulated enormous riches during the 1970s and early 1980s is a fascinating one. Yet this Third World success story is not unblemished. OPEC has been plagued by serious internal divisions, some resulting in war and violence, while since the early eighties the oil-exporting nations have witnessed a humbling fall in oil prices and revenues, punctuated by occasional and short-lived price spikes.

Prior to the 1970s, relations between the oil-exporting countries and the major Northern oil companies worked decidedly to the advantage of the latter. Seven large oil firms (sometimes called the Seven Sisters) came to dominate the world oil market. These included five U.S. firms (Esso, Mobil, Standard of California, Gulf, and Texaco), one British (British Petroleum), and one Anglo-Dutch (Shell). A French company, CFP, later became a major player as well. These large firms pioneered the global search for new oil reserves, striking major finds in most of the present-day OPEC countries between World War I and the early 1950s.[93]

The oil-producing countries initially found themselves almost entirely dependent upon the seven major firms for the development of their oil resources. None had the skills, technology, or marketing networks necessary to exploit its oil riches without outside help. Relations between oil-producing states and firms revolved around the concession system. Contracts negotiated between these parties gave particular firms or groups of firms the exclusive right to explore for oil in an agreed-upon territorial area within the country. Whatever oil was found belonged to the firm, which controlled all exploration, production, refining, and marketing decisions and activities. In return for these rights, Northern oil companies agreed to turn over a share of their revenues to the producing state in the form of taxes or royalties. This system gave the seven major firms control over production and pricing, although producing states sometimes attempted to influence such decisions.

Challenges to these arrangements were met with resistance not only from the oil firms themselves but also from Northern governments, which saw the major oil companies as agents of the national interest and key guarantors of Northern access to a critical resource. In the early 1950s, for instance, the seven major oil firms organized a boycott of Iranian oil after the nation's prime minister, Mohammed Mossadegh, ordered the nationalization of assets belonging to the Anglo-Iranian oil company. When the boycott failed to lead to a reversal of the nationalization decision, the United States helped to organize a coup d'état that toppled Mossadegh and returned Mohammed Reza Pahlavi to his previous position as shah.

As time went on, the major oil-producing states increasingly chafed under the traditional arrangements. Each found it difficult, however, to bring about fundamental change acting on its own. The oil companies adopted a united stand in negotiating with host countries and played oil producers off against one another.

In 1960, at the initiative of Venezuela, five major oil-producing countries (the other four were Iran, Iraq, Saudi Arabia, and Kuwait) attempted to improve their collective bargaining position by forming the Organization of Petroleum Exporting Countries.[94] The immediate precipitating factor was the decision by the major oil firms to lower prices in the face of a global glut of petroleum. Their revenues threatened, the oil-producing countries denounced the price cut and set out to gain greater control over the production and pricing of oil.

OPEC achieved relatively little of major significance during its first decade of existence. Beneath the surface, however, several trends were setting the stage for a revolution in the world of oil. Northern oil consumption rose at a rapid rate during the 1960s. At the same time, the growth of U.S. oil production began to slow and, by the early seventies, had reached a plateau. The juxtaposition of these two trends led to a tightening of world oil supplies, especially after the United States began importing increasing amounts of foreign oil to compensate for the stagnation of domestic production.

Other important factors contributed to OPEC's fortunes. A growing number of independent oil companies began to challenge the seven major firms for access to foreign oil reserves. These newcomers were often willing to strike bargains more favorable to the oil-producing countries, undermining the unity of the major oil firms. The oil-producing countries themselves came to acquire increasing competence in matters relating to oil, thus enhancing their confidence that they could manage their own industries with less reliance upon Northern firms. Also, OPEC gained a number of new members over the course of the 1960s, including Libya, Indonesia, Algeria, Qatar, Nigeria, and Abu Dhabi. By 1970 OPEC members accounted for 90 percent of world oil exports.[95] Finally, the emergence of radical nationalist regimes, such as in Libya, upset old arrangements between traditional rulers and the firms while increasing the aggressiveness of oil-producing states in their efforts to revise the old order.

With these elements in place, the major oil companies' dominant position quickly eroded, and events conspired to magnify OPEC's power over world oil markets. In 1970 Libya compelled Occidental Petroleum, an independent oil company, to raise the price of its Libyan-produced crude oil. OPEC moved quickly to exploit Libya's triumph. At an unprecedented meeting in Caracas during February 1971, 23 oil firms acceded to OPEC demands for an across-the-board price increase. The next two years brought further OPEC-dictated price rises along with the beginning of a widespread movement on the part of oil-producing states to nationalize all or part of oil company assets within their nations. Indeed, whereas in 1970 the Seven Sisters controlled 60 percent of world oil production outside the Soviet-controlled bloc, this figure had fallen to 14 percent by 1995, largely due to the effects of nationalist measures by the producing countries.[96]

In the midst of the October 1973 Arab-Israeli war, the Arab members of OPEC cut production by 5 percent and announced an embargo on deliveries of oil to Western supporters of Israel. In an already tight oil market, these actions led to a quadrupling of oil prices to almost $12 a barrel the following December. These high prices were sustained over the next five years, although inflation eroded the real value of OPEC oil revenues. The OPEC revolution triggered an economic recession in the North while generating a massive transfer of wealth from oil-importing countries to the oil-exporting countries. The United States largely failed in its efforts to organize a countercartel of oil-importing countries, although modest levels of cooperation among the principal Northern countries were institutionalized through the creation of the International Energy Agency.

OPEC again engineered a massive hike in oil prices in 1979 after the onset of the Iraq-Iran war removed 5 percent of world oil supplies from the market. The price of oil tripled to roughly $35 per barrel. Again, the drain of more-expensive oil, combined this time with tight monetary policies in the United States designed to reduce inflation, tipped much of the world economy into a major downturn.

Many Third World countries drew inspiration from OPEC's success during the 1970s despite the fact that Southern oil import bills rose along with those of the North. Countries who relied heavily upon natural resource exports viewed OPEC as a model for their own development efforts. Producers of bauxite, copper, tin, coffee, bananas, and other Third World commodities formed associations similar to OPEC in hopes of managing supply and driving up both prices and revenues. These ventures enjoyed little success. Beginning in the late seventies and early eighties, slowing demand in the North led instead to declining prices for many Southern raw-material and agricultural exports. OPEC's exceptional success stemmed from the critical role of oil in Northern economies, the concentration of vast oil reserves in a relatively small group of Southern oil-producing countries, and most important, the fact that market forces worked in OPEC's favor during the seventies.

OPEC's achievements also invigorated Third World efforts to negotiate a new international economic order (NIEO) with the North.[97] Beginning in the 1960s, Southern countries worked collectively through the United Nations and informal coordinating mechanisms such as the Group of 77 to hammer out a set of common demands for the reform of North-South relations.[98] The NIEO called for a variety of changes in the rules of the existing global economy: coordinated efforts to raise and stabilize commodity prices, the lowering of Northern barriers to Southern manufactured exports, increased Northern aid and financial assistance to the South, greater Third World voting power in institutions such as the International Monetary Fund and the World Bank, a global code of conduct for multinational corporations, debt relief, and greater Southern access to Northern technology. The Third World coalition counted upon OPEC's demonstrated power, along with its own unity, to provide the South with sufficient leverage to extract Northern concessions.

Indeed, fears that a stalemate in North-South bargaining might prompt desperate Southern responses harmful to the world economy prompted some prominent Northern commentators to embrace a strategy of compromise. Others in the North argued that wealthy countries shared an interest in reforms that might spur Southern growth and stimulate greater North-South trade.[99] For its part, OPEC endorsed Third World demands, pushed for the North to expand negotiations with the South, and increased its own aid to Southern countries harmed by rising oil prices.

Although the South's leverage proved sufficient to force the North into a series of global bargaining rounds over the NIEO proposals during the 1970s and early 1980s, it remained inadequate to bring about real change. Northern countries, particularly the United States, rejected the bulk of Third World demands. Northern leaders perceived the redistributive aspects of the NIEO as contrary to their own nations' interests. Moreover, Northern spokespersons argued that many NIEO provisions would hamper global economic growth by interfering with market mechanisms.[100] Ultimately, negotiations failed also because the South, as well as some in the North, had overestimated the Third World's true power. Southern nations often warned that the North's failure to accept reform would lead to radical Third World responses, such as the proliferation of resource cartels, debt repudiation, nationalization of multinational corporate assets, and political upheaval. In fact, few of these consequences followed from the failure of the NIEO negotiations. The underlying reality was that the South remained more dependent upon the North than vice versa. A serious break in economic relations between the two would hurt the South far more than the North. Southern power thus proved a chimera.

The 1980s were a difficult decade for OPEC. The high oil prices of the late seventies and early eighties stimulated successful conservation measures in the North, fuel switching to alternative sources of energy, and increased production from non-OPEC sources. Due to investments in energy efficiency, the amount of oil that OECD (Organization for Economic Cooperation and Development) countries needed to produce an extra dollar of GNP fell by 45 percent between 1973 and 1988. This contributed to a 20 percent drop in OECD oil consumption between 1979 and 1988. At the same time, the production of oil from non-OPEC sources, such as Mexico, the North Sea, and Alaska, grew by 20 percent from 1979 to 1986. Northern countries also began to diversify their sources of supply and to build up strategic stockpiles of oil in an attempt to rob OPEC of its power to control the oil market. Thus OPEC countries lost market share and became marginal producers—serving only that portion of world demand left unsatisfied after non-OPEC sources of supply had been exhausted.[101] OPEC's share of the world oil market (excluding the Soviet Union) fell from 63 percent in 1972 to 38 percent in 1985.[102]

OPEC responded to these challenges by attempting to limit production in an effort to bolster prices. Each member country was allotted a production quota to ensure that overall OPEC production did not breach agreed-upon ceilings. In practice, OPEC remained too divided to sustain this sort of cooperation. As prices softened, many countries attempted to avoid falling revenues by producing more oil than called for by their allotments. At first, Saudi Arabia compensated for this overproduction by reducing the rate of its own oil extraction and sales while attempting to persuade other OPEC producers to honor their quota agreements. The Saudis served, in other words, as a swing producer. By 1986, however, Saudi Arabia's market share and revenues had fallen precipitously, and jawboning had failed to curb widespread cheating within OPEC. At that point, the Saudis chose to discipline other OPEC members and to recapture lost market share by dramatically increasing their own oil production. This flood of oil onto world markets sent prices spiraling downward, falling by early 1988 to between $12 and $13 per barrel. In real terms (discounting for inflation), the price of oil now stood below the levels prior to the price hikes of the early 1970s.

The economic effects on OPEC were disastrous: between 1979 and 1988, per-capita income fell by 27 percent among OPEC countries taken together, while imports shrank by half.[103] Saudi oil revenues, which peaked at $19,000 per person in 1980, fell precipitously to $3,000 per person by 1994.[104] The Saudi government depends upon oil for 75 percent of state revenues. The combination of declining oil revenues, high military expenditures, and growing social welfare costs—a consequence of rapid population growth—have resulted in large budget deficits, reaching 11 percent of national income in 1998. By the year 2000, Saudi government debt had climbed to $133 billion, a figure greater than one year's total economic output.[105]

By some indicators, OPEC would appear well positioned to reassert dominance over world oil markets in the decade ahead. During the late 1980s and 1990s, oil prices fell too low to sustain expensive oil exploration projects or to spur additional investments in energy conservation. In the United States, virtually all gains in energy efficiency took place prior to 1986. By some measures, progress toward greater energy efficiency has been reversed. In 2000, for example, the average fuel economy of the U.S. auto fleet hit a 20-year low, due chiefly to the growing popularity of gas-guzzling sports utility vehicles.[106]

Production by some non-OPEC sources has fallen. U.S. oil production fell by 25 percent between 1986 and 1993, while imports rose from 28 percent of U.S. oil consumption in 1985 to 45 percent in 1994. Although U.S. oil producers spent $14 billion per year on exploration in the early 1980s, that figure declined to $5.3 billion in 1992. Declining investment and growing domestic demand have sharply cut Mexican oil exports. British and Norwegian production will decline in future years as the North Sea fields are exhausted. Falling investment levels, backward technology, and political instability have recently brought about a precipitous decline in oil production in the former Soviet Union. Russian production, which totaled 11.5 million barrels per day in 1988, fell to almost one-half that level by the mid-1990s, though it has since rebounded somewhat. Due to declining production and rising demand, some OPEC oil exporters, such as Qatar, Gabon, Nigeria, and Ecuador, will soon produce only enough oil for their own consumption. Thus the balance of power within OPEC seems likely to shift even more decisively in favor of the Persian Gulf states that possess enormous oil reserves. In 1990 five Persian

Gulf states accounted for two-thirds of the world's proven oil reserves. The share of current production accounted for by the Persian Gulf producers is expected to rise from 24 percent in 2000 to 32 percent in 2010. OPEC as a whole accounts for 75 percent of total world oil reserves and 40 percent of total output.[107]

Yet although OPEC's share of world oil production and sales seems destined to rise, this factor alone is unlikely to return OPEC to its glory days of the 1970s and early 1980s. Not only are prices expected to remain soft over the next decade, but also OPEC's ability to control overproduction by its own member states is in doubt.

Most observers predict that world demand for oil will grow only sluggishly in the coming years. From 1990 to 1998, global oil and natural gas consumption grew at an annual rate of only 2 percent per year.[108] Economic growth is projected to proceed at a modest pace in the mature economies of the major oil-importing countries. What growth does occur is unlikely to be associated with rising levels of energy consumption. As in recent decades, the share of energy-intensive, heavy-manufacturing industries in the overall economies of Northern countries will continue to dwindle, while the shift toward industries requiring relatively low inputs of energy, such as services and high technology, will continue apace. In transportation, highly efficient hybrid gas-electric cars have already hit the roads, while the coming integration of fuel cells into automobile technology promises even greater efficiencies.

Perhaps most important, ecological concerns about global warming are likely to spur efforts to reduce dependence upon fossil fuels. Carbon dioxide, a major product of burning hydrocarbons such as oil or coal, has been found to play a major role in exacerbating the greenhouse effect. Northern nations have pledged to stabilize or reduce carbon dioxide emissions over the next decade. Both conservation and fuel switching will be relied upon to achieve these goals. There remains great potential for conservation through the production of more-energy-efficient cars (including the growing use of electric-powered automobiles), appliances, homes, and factories.[109] Environmental concerns have combined with security concerns arising from excess dependence upon oil imports and recently rising prices to revive interest in renewable and nonfossil energy sources, including nuclear, solar, wind, hydroelectric, biomass, and geothermal, as well as natural gas, which is a relatively clean-burning hydrocarbon.[110] From 1990 to 1998, the annual rate of growth in production of wind power was 22 percent, while power from solar photovoltaics grew 16 percent per year. Moreover, the cost of producing a kilowatt of electricity from wind power declined from $2,600 in 1981 to $800 in 1998. Similarly, the cost of solar photovoltaic cells has declined by more than 50 percent since the mid-1980s.[111]

Moderate demand for additional oil in the North will, however, be partially offset by the increased energy needs of certain rapidly growing Southern countries. Oil demand in Asia is expected to rise rapidly as economies in that region recover from the Asian financial crisis. India and China, in particular, are expected to become major oil importers in the coming decade.[112] Nevertheless, global use of oil is expected to peak in 2005 and move downward thereafter.[113]

On the supply side, one-time fears that the world might be running out of oil have been proven unfounded, at least for the foreseeable future. Indeed, the world's proven oil reserves are 10 times as large today as in 1950. New technology has expanded the potential for exploiting known but previously inaccessible oil resources. The average exploratory well yields four times as much oil today as in 1980, while the exploration success rate rose from 23 percent in the 1970s to 29 percent in the 1990s. The average cost of finding oil has dropped by more than half since the 1970s.[114] It is estimated that the tar sands in the Alberta province of Canada contain oil deposits larger than the entire Middle Eastern oil reserves. Recent technological advances now suggest that it may be possible to extract oil from this dense, rocklike source at economically competitive prices.[115] Paul Portney, president of Resources of the Future, has predicted: "We will stop using oil long before we run out of it."[116]

The major constraint to expanding oil production lies in the huge investments required, combined with the weak incentives provided by low prices. Nevertheless, Western oil companies have begun to expand their activities in the many countries—such as Venezuela, Argentina, Colombia, Brazil, China, Vietnam, and Russia—that have recently lowered barriers to foreign direct investment in their oil industries or even begun to privatize formerly state-owned companies.[117]

One source of increasing oil production in the future will be the Caspian Sea countries of Central Asia. The former Soviet republics of Azerbaijan, Kazakhstan, Turkmenistan, Tajikistan, and Uzbekistan are thought to possess major oil and natural gas reserves. Western oil companies have initiated major new investments in this region. The principal problem facing governments and firms that stand to profit from these resources is the difficulty of getting the oil and gas to world markets. Large, lengthy, and expensive pipeline networks will be required. The question of which routes to use in transporting oil and gas from the Caspian oil wells has become a major source of political controversy. In such a politically volatile region, the wrong decision could carry considerable risks. There are fears of disruption as a result of war or political choice. The decision also carries economic consequences, as pipeline revenues could bring riches for the countries through which the networks run.

The Caspian countries themselves generally favor the most direct route, which would run through Iran to the Persian Gulf, where the oil could be offloaded to tankers. The United States, however, opposes this route due to its poor relations with Iran. Russia supports a pipeline running across the eastern Caspian to the Russian port of Novorossick, on the Black Sea. This route would, however, bring greatly increased tanker traffic, with accompanying environmental hazards, through the Bosporus Strait. Turkey objects to Russian plans for precisely this reason. The route preferred by the U.S. government would run from Baku in Azerbaijan through Georgia to the Turkish port of Ceylon. Sorting out these conflicting preferences is likely to take years.[118]

Thus, although OPEC's share of the world oil market may indeed rise, overall energy demand is likely to grow only slowly, while oil use may actually fall as it fills a declining proportion of total energy needs. The supply of oil, meanwhile, is plentiful, assuming that the needed investment is forthcoming. Oil prices are unlikely to rise dramatically in this climate. In contrast with the 1980s, however, when declining oil prices removed incentives for additional investments in conservation or alternative energy development, Northern governments will be inclined to mandate continued progress in these areas through the use of tax and regulatory policies.

Serious internal division among member states also threatens OPEC's economic power. As they often have in the past, these deep fractures may well hamper future efforts to coordinate production and pricing policies—both prerequisites to maximizing the cartel's overall revenues. The most obvious divisions are political. There exist deep ideological and political differences between the conservative monarchical regimes of the Persian Gulf region, the radical Arab nationalist governments of Libya and Iraq, and the fundamentalist Islamic republic of Iran, a non-Arab country.

The recent past has witnessed two instances of armed conflict among OPEC members, both involving Iraq. In each case, Iraqi aggression was partly motivated by considerations related to oil. The Iraqi invasion of Iran in 1980 was stimulated by Iraq's desire to gain exclusive control over a strategic waterway that lies astride the Iraqi-Iranian border. Lacking an adequate port along its short Persian Gulf coastline, Iraq sought a secure means by which it could off-load greater quantities of oil into tankers bound for Northern markets through the gulf. Iraq's violent attempt to solve this problem touched off an inconclusive eight-year war that claimed 1 million lives.

Oil also played a key role in Iraq's ill-fated decision to invade Kuwait in the summer of 1990. In the wake of its deadly war with Iran, Iraq faced huge reconstruction costs as well as an enormous foreign debt. Because the country exported little aside from oil, Iraq's hopes for economic revival rested almost exclusively on its ability to obtain higher oil revenues. Kuwaiti behavior presented a serious obstacle to this goal. In the first half of 1990, Kuwait consistently produced more oil than allowed by its OPEC quota. The failure of Kuwait and several other OPEC members to observe agreed-upon limitations on their oil production frustrated Iraqi efforts to engineer a hike in the world price of oil. Kuwait also angered Iraq by refusing to compromise over a dispute in which Iraq charged that Kuwait pumped more than its fair share of oil from a major field straddling the border between Iraq and Kuwait. Finally, Kuwait refused to forgive the $10 billion debt that Iraq accumulated from loans used to finance its war with Iran.[119]

The conflict between Iraq and Kuwait over production and pricing policies reflects broader and more enduring divisions among OPEC producers. OPEC has long been split between price "hawks" and price "doves." The former countries consistently push for higher oil prices, whereas the latter lobby for price moderation. With some exceptions, the doves, which include OPEC's most important member, Saudi Arabia, have generally won out in recent years.

The countries that favor higher prices share one or more of the following characteristics:

1. Dwindling oil reserves that are likely to be exhausted in the near- to medium-term future at historical levels of production
2. Large and growing populations
3. Relatively modest levels of investment in the wealthy oil-consuming countries of the North

These nations seek to maximize short-term revenues from a rapidly depleting resource while satisfying the demands for industrialization and a higher standard of living from large numbers of still relatively poor citizens.

OPEC members with abundant reserves, small populations, and extensive investments in the North have very different interests. For these countries, high prices would stimulate oil exploration, conservation, and fuel switching in the oil-consuming countries and thereby reduce the demand for oil in future decades. With small populations, these countries have a less urgent need to maximize present income. Moreover, as an increasing share of these nations' revenues comes from returns on foreign investment, they must worry that high oil prices might damage Northern economies and interrupt the flow of repatriated profits from abroad.

This division within OPEC overlaps with another: the split between integrated and nonintegrated producers. Several OPEC countries, including Venezuela, Saudi Arabia, Kuwait, and to a lesser extent, Nigeria, have aggressively integrated their oil production with the ownership of downstream operations, such as refining and retail sales, located in oil-consuming countries. Integrated producers not only desire the revenues from these downstream investments but also seek to lock up outlets for the sale of their own crude oil, thus reducing future uncertainties over foreign demand.

Nonintegrated OPEC producers, such as Iran, Iraq, and Libya, that lack these downstream connections face the risk of becoming marginal producers in the future. In other words, these countries would service only that portion of demand left over after the integrated producers have disposed of their output through refineries and marketing networks abroad. Integrated producers can use their control of downstream operations to assure steady, predictable levels of production and sales, whereas nonintegrated producers are likely to find themselves unable to locate buyers for all of their output if supply should exceed demand.[120] The largest integrated producing country, Saudi Arabia, has a long-term interest in maintaining market share and promoting price moderation and stability.

Despite its internal divisions and dismal long-term outlook, however, OPEC remains capable of acting to counter disastrous oil price declines, as evidenced by recent events. In 1998, oil prices dropped more than 40 percent to a range of $8 to $11 per barrel. In the face of a severe decline in revenues, OPEC countries agreed to lower overall OPEC oil production by 4 million barrels per day over the course of 1999. This renewed cooperation was facilitated by the coming to power of new political leadership in both Saudi Arabia and Iran, easing previously strained relations between the two countries. Moreover, newly elected Venezuelan president Hugo Chavez also fell behind a policy of pushing up oil prices. As a result of these efforts, oil supply fell below demand by up to 2.5 million barrels per day in early 2000. Oil prices rose rapidly, reaching over $30 per barrel in early 2000.[121]

Nevertheless, OPEC's leading members remain responsive to calls for price moderation so as to maintain good relations with major importing countries and avoid a global recession, which would depress energy demand. In February of 2000, the United States appealed to OPEC countries to increase oil output. The organization agreed to ramp up production by 1.7 million barrels per day. OPEC countries set a new target price range of $21 to $25 per barrel. Although heating, electricity, and gasoline prices remained high in the United States through the remainder of 2000 and early 2001, this was due less to the international oil market than to strained refinery and power plant capacity in the United States. Oil prices actually declined to $17 per barrel by November 2001.[122]

GLOBAL AND REGIONAL TRADE AGREEMENTS

Another form of collective effort to promote Southern development involves multilateral bargaining over the removal of barriers to mutual trade and investment. Southern countries pursue this path through both global and regional forums. In the global forum, groups of Third World countries often coordinate their demands in negotiations with the North over trade liberalization. In regional forums, Southern countries form smaller groupings that are intended to promote economic integration among member economies.[123] The following discussion addresses both settings.

The World Trade Organization

When the Uruguay Round global trade accord was signed in April 1994, many observers predicted significant gains for Southern economies. The Uruguay Round agreement required that Northern countries reduce barriers to Southern exports in the areas of agriculture, textiles, and clothing. One study estimated that such provisions would allow Third World exports to Japan and the European Union to rise by 15 percent on average.[124] Another study conducted jointly by the World Bank and the OECD Development Center predicted that the Third World as a whole would experience yearly gains of $213 billion by 2002 as a result of changes brought about by the Uruguay Round. These gains were not, however, spread equally across the Third World. The study also concluded that Africa and the Caribbean, for instance, were considered likely to lose from the accord.[125]

In practice, however, many Southern countries have been disappointed with the results of the Uruguay Round agreement. Northern governments have been slow to fulfill their commitments to lower barriers to Southern imports. The United States has used antidumping regulations to target steel imports from countries such as Brazil, Russia, and South Korea, as well as other products. Rich-country agricultural subsidies to farmers have continued to encourage overproduction of basic foodstuffs and undercut the export earnings of Third World food exporting countries. The stricter enforcement of intellectual property rights provided for in the Uruguay Round agreement has raised the prices of technology and medicines in many Southern countries.

Based upon such concerns, Third World governments demanded that the next round of global trade talks focus on issues of greatest interest to the South. The first attempt to launch a new round of negotiations failed when the 1999 Seattle meeting of the World Trade Organization (WTO) broke up without agreement. Multiple lines of conflict doomed the Seattle meeting. Tens of thousands of anti-globalization protesters took to the streets of Seattle to lambaste the WTO for its purported insensitivity to the environment and workers' rights. Many Third World governments objected, however, when President Clinton bowed to such pressures by suggesting that the next global trade agreement include labor and environmental standards. Southern representatives argued that such standards would be used as a hidden form of protectionism by the North and would rob Southern exporters of key sources of competitive advantage, such as cheap labor. Rich countries themselves were divided at Seattle over American proposals to reduce trade-distorting regulations and subsidies in areas such as agriculture, financial services, and insurance.[126]

The failure of the Seattle meeting threatened the credibility of the relatively new World Trade Organization, created by the Uruguay Round accord to strengthen the global trade system. A great deal of significance was therefore attached to the success of the WTO meeting scheduled for November, 2001 in Doha, Qatar. The purpose of this meeting was to draft guidelines for launching a new round of global trade negotiations that would stretch over coming years. The ultimately successful conclusion of the Doha meeting rested upon the willingness of various groups of countries to make the necessary trade-offs among their competing interests.

Third World countries played a much more assertive role in crafting the negotiating agenda laid out at Doha than they had in the Uruguay Round negotiations. Southern countries had several major goals:[127]

- *Pharmaceuticals:* Southern countries have long complained that Northern drug companies price drugs that are crucial for combating AIDS, tuberculosis, and other deadly diseases at levels far beyond the ability of Third World consumers to pay. Generic versions of the same drugs can be produced by drug companies in countries such as India, Brazil, and South Africa at only a fraction of the price set by the major pharmaceutical firms. Intellectual property rights regulations included in the Uruguay Round accord prevented Southern countries from purchasing cheaper generic versions of important drugs without violating the rights of patent holders. The final agreement at Doha bowed to Third World demands by accepting the principal that patent rights may be waived in cases where a major public health crisis can be demonstrated.

- *Antidumping Regulations:* The United States has long used antidumping laws to protect particular domestic producers from lower-cost imports. These regulations have been invoked to discourage imports of steel, semiconductors, and other goods in recent years. Southern exporters argue that antidumping laws allow the United States to ignore its international commitments through the WTO to open American markets. As part of the Doha guidelines, the United States agreed to open negotiations with the objective of narrowing the scope and application of antidumping laws.

- *Agricultural Trade:* Southern agricultural exporting countries called for reductions in tariffs and subsidies that discourage food exports to Europe, Japan, and other countries that use such mechanisms to protect their agricultural sectors. The Doha agreement set the reduction of barriers to trade in agricultural goods as a major goal of coming negotiations.

- *Textiles:* Southern countries wanted an agreement to speed up the process of phasing out Northern quotas on textile imports. Although the United States resisted such a step, American negotiators did agree to revisit this issue in 2002.

The WTO meeting at Doha established an agenda for a new round of trade negotiations. Actual revisions to the rules of the world trading system will only emerge after years of further negotiation. Although the new round of trade talks promises a variety of changes that could benefit Third World countries, success in realizing these aims will depend upon the hard bargaining yet to come.

Regional Free Trade Agreements

Between 1990 and 2000, the number of regional trade groupings worldwide grew from 50 to 200, with 70 more such agreements under negotiation.[128] The trend toward regional economic integration among Southern countries has moved most quickly in Latin America. Free trade agreements among Latin American countries are not new. The Andean Pact—comprising Bolivia, Colombia, Ecuador, Peru, and Venezuela—and Caricom, which encompasses eight Caribbean nations, both date to the 1970s. Recent agreements, however, are more comprehensive and far-reaching. Mercosur, an accord that lowers trade and investment barriers among Brazil, Argentina, Uruguay, and Paraguay, went into effect on January 1, 1995. The value of trade among the Mercosur countries rose from $4 billion in 1990 to $22 billion in 1998.[129] Mexico, Venezuela, and Colombia, the so-called Group of Three, have recently agreed to phase out trade barriers among their economies over the coming decade.

The movement toward economic integration in Latin America shows no signs of slowing. The Andean Pact countries are seeking a trade agreement with the Mercosur group. Ecuador is soon expected to join the Group of Three. Colombia plans to sign a free trade agreement with Caricom. Chile may soon become a member of Mercosur. And bilateral free trade arrangements have been concluded between Mexico and Bolivia, Chile and Peru, and Chile and Ecuador.

Led by Brazil, 19 Latin American countries agreed in 1994 to seek to merge these various commercial arrangements into a single trade pact covering virtually all of the Latin American continent. The Latin American Integration Association and the United Nations Economic Commission on Latin America have been charged with the task of comparing and reconciling the complex provisions of the existing accords so as to pave the way for full Latin American integration. At the Miami Summit of the Americas in December 1994, the United States agreed to join these efforts with the aim of eventually creating a free trade regime spanning the entire hemisphere, North and South.[130] Nevertheless, progress toward this goal has been glacial. After seven years of drift, the 34 nations represented at the 2001 Summit of the Americas renewed their pledge to create a hemispheric free trade zone by 2005. Many observers remained skeptical about such commitments given that previous declarations failed to produce concrete movement toward such a goal.[131]

Even before many of these plans are put into effect, Latin America's recent conversion to the gospel of free trade will have reshaped the continent's economies. Between 1991 and 1993 average tariff levels in Latin America dropped from 26 percent to 12 percent. For 10 South American countries and Mexico, intraregional exports increased from 11 percent of total exports in 1989 to 19.2 percent in 1993. Between 1987 and 1992 Latin American exports grew an average of 10 percent per year in real terms. Economies that were selectively sheltered from international competition and trade are being transformed and restructured as they are increasingly integrated into the global economy.[132] Nevertheless, regional free trade pacts have their critics, some of whom argue that such agreements serve as poor substitutes for global free trade. WTO director Michael Moore, for instance, argues that regionalism "leads not towards an open world economy, but an unbalanced system of hubs and spokes, with rich countries at the center, holding all the cards, and developing countries on the periphery."[133]

Moreover, some regional accords have brought disappointing results. While Mercosur brought down trade barriers between Brazil and Argentina, it did not reconcile the two country's incompatible currency systems. Brazil devalued its currency in 1998 as a consequence of the global financial crisis, whereas Argentina maintained its currency board system, which pegged the peso to the value of the U.S. dollar. Following Brazil's devaluation, Brazilian goods became cheaper and thus more competitive when sold in Argentine markets. The price of Argentina's goods sold in Brazil, by contrast, rose by 40 percent. These circumstances hurt Argentine producers and created friction between the two neighboring trading partners.[134]

The most controversial regional trade agreement involving Latin America has been the North American Free Trade Agreement (NAFTA), which provides for the gradual removal of most barriers to the movement of trade and investment among the United States, Canada, and Mexico. NAFTA, which took effect on January 1, 1994, after contentious ratification debates in all three countries, represented an extension of the earlier U.S.-Canada trade agreement completed in 1988. Besides addressing trade and investment, NAFTA and associated side agreements address issues such as intellectual property rights, the treatment of labor, and environmental standards.

Mexican president Carlos Salinas served as the driving force behind NAFTA. Salinas believed that Mexico's traditionally inward-looking and nationalistic development strategy had led to the economic crisis of the 1980s, featuring a crushing debt load and a sharp economic contraction. He therefore embraced and accelerated the neoliberal, or market- and export-oriented, policies of his predecessor, President Miguel de la Madrid. Salinas hoped that NAFTA would establish Mexico as a magnet for foreign investment, thus spurring economic recovery. A rebounding economy, in turn, would allow Mexico's longtime ruling party, the Institutional Revolutionary Party (PRI), to regain the prestige and authority that it had lost over the previous decade. In particular, Salinas sought to fend off the challenge posed by an invigorated Mexican left, which mounted a strong electoral showing in the 1988 presidential election. NAFTA would galvanize popular support around the image of a new, more "modern" Mexico. It would also serve to "lock in" the neoliberal policy shift championed by Salinas and make it difficult for successors to undo his legacy.

During the first year of NAFTA's implementation, U.S.-Mexican trade boomed, and foreign investors flocked to Mexico. The biggest beneficiaries were those associated with Mexico's export-manufacturing industries, located mostly along the border in the North. Mexicans from the poorer, rural southern part of the country, however, suffered from an influx of cheaper American grain and other agricultural goods. The anger of Mexico's peasants caused by this threat to their livelihood was symbolized by the opening of a guerrilla campaign launched by the Zapatista National Liberation Front, based in the southern state of Chiapas. The Zapatistas carried out their first armed attacks on Mexican authorities on the day that NAFTA took effect, underlining the central role that the agreement played in spurring rebellion.

The long-term effects of NAFTA on Mexico are still emerging. Roughly one year after NAFTA was implemented, Mexico suffered a severe financial crisis, involving a steep drop in the value of the peso and massive capital flight (see Chapter 12). The austerity measures taken to restore financial stability plunged Mexico into a deep economic recession from which it has been slow to recover. In 1999, average real wages in Mexico remained 25 percent below 1994 levels.[135] Although NAFTA did not cause Mexico's peso crisis, it may have played a contributing role by encouraging unrealistically large flows of capital into the country, thus allowing authorities to mask Mexico's large trade imbalance and the overvaluation of its currency.

Most economists expect that NAFTA will bring positive benefits to most Mexicans in the long run. Still, it is clear that NAFTA represents neither a magic cure for Mexico's underlying economic troubles nor a guarantee against economic instability.

Economic integration has occurred more slowly in East Asia.[136] The greatest progress has been made by subregional groupings. The most important of these is the Association of Southeast Asian Nations (ASEAN), which includes Thailand, Indonesia, the Philippines, Malaysia, Brunei, and Singapore. In 1992 ASEAN members agreed to gradually reduce or remove trade barriers among their economies. Other bilateral or subregional trade liberalization arrangements have been concluded among various East Asian nations.

It appears unlikely, however, that an exclusively Asian economic bloc encompassing the entire region will emerge.[137] In 1993 Malaysia advanced a proposal for such an organization, to be called the East Asian Economic Grouping. Notably, this bloc would have excluded the United States, Australia, and New Zealand. The United States expressed sharp disapproval, and most Asian nations, including Japan, showed little enthusiasm for the idea. The proposed members settled instead for the much looser East Asian Economic Caucus, which would serve as a consultative group to coordinate bargaining demands in global trade negotiations.

The cool response to Malaysia's proposal reflected several factors. Many East Asian nations depend heavily upon exports to markets outside the region, especially the United States. A free trade arrangement that excludes these target markets holds limited appeal. Also, a purely East Asian trade bloc would likely be dominated by Japan, raising historically based fears among those Asian nations who once suffered under Japanese colonial rule.

The largest and perhaps most promising regional trade organization to encompass East Asia is the Asian-Pacific Economic Cooperation (APEC) forum, created at Australia's initiative in 1988. In addition to Asian nations such as Japan, China, South Korea, Hong Kong, Taiwan, Australia, and New Zealand, APEC includes Pacific Rim countries from the Western Hemisphere, including the United States, Canada, Mexico, and Chile. Largely ineffectual during its initial years, APEC gathered momentum when a series of initiatives was passed at its 1993 and 1994 summit meetings. At the 1994 event, APEC members agreed to move toward full free trade by the year 2020. APEC nations also agreed to explore other integration measures, such as a regional investment code and the harmonization of product and environmental standards.

At APEC's 1995 meeting, member nations agreed to pursue the lowering of trade barriers through voluntary measures, forgoing the legal commitments involved in a more formal agreement. This unique method for pursuing multilateral liberalization promises to lead to speedier progress than would be possible through the slow and tortuous negotiation of a formal treaty. Yet this nonbinding approach will allow states to continue protection of politically sensitive sectors and may result in uneven progress across countries. Liberalization is likely to be less universal than a more formal approach. Ultimately,

APEC's future success will be determined by its ability to bridge the vast cultural, political, and economic differences among its members. It remains uncertain whether such a large, diverse, and geographically far-flung grouping can function as a unified or coherent economic bloc.[138]

The movements toward economic integration in Latin America and Asia have given rise to very different conceptions about the rationale and goals underlying these developments. For some, the goals of Southern regional cooperation are to encourage South-South trade, lessen dependence upon the North, gain greater Southern leverage in global economic negotiations, improve the South's bargaining position vis-à-vis Northern corporations, and promote Southern political unity. Others advocate a form of integration that ties groups of Southern countries to regionally dominant Northern countries, so as to facilitate Northern investment flows and ensure greater and continuing access to Northern markets.

The first model, represented by the Andean Pact in Latin America and by Malaysia's proposal for an East Asian Economic Grouping, seeks to weaken the ties of Southern dependence upon the North and to encourage greater Southern autonomy. The second model, represented by NAFTA in Latin America and by APEC in Asia, reinforces such dependence, though on terms that its advocates promise will be more favorable to the South. Although both models share some features, they lead to potentially different patterns of trade, investment, and political cooperation. Which vision prevails will help to determine the nature of North-South ties in the twenty-first century.

CONCLUSIONS

As is evident from this overview, Third World states have pursued a variety of development paths. It should also be clear that no single model or strategy of development is appropriate for all countries or all times. Progress toward economic prosperity is dependent upon the right fit or mix among three sets of factors:

1. The internal economic, political, and cultural attributes of a given country
2. The opportunities and constraints provided by the international political economy
3. The policy choices made by governing elites

Analysts are often led astray by focusing on the latter of these three, the choice of development strategy, in isolation from the first two. Yet policies that lack domestic political support or that are poorly tailored to a country's specific mix of economic resources are unlikely to succeed. Similarly, the continuing evolution of the international economic system means that policies that are feasible and desirable during one period may become less so as time goes on.

Table 9.1 Strategies of Development

	ORIENTATION	
	Inward	Outward
Type of Production		
Raw materials	Precolonial/ subsistence	Colonial trade resource cartels
Manufacturing	ISI	ELI

The evidence reviewed in this chapter reinforces the notion that policy success is dependent upon supportive domestic and international conditions. Among major Latin American countries, the shift to import substitution industrialization (ISI) was prompted by the disruptions in international trade produced by the Great Depression and World War II. These policies were sustained after the war by the rise of nationalist political movements at home. The initial stage of ISI proved successful until its growth potential was exhausted due to the limited domestic market for consumer goods. The deepening phase of ISI was accompanied by the emergence of authoritarian governments and growing international indebtedness. The internal contradictions of ISI, combined with unfavorable international economic conditions during the late 1970s and early 1980s, set the stage for a lost decade of economic stagnation in Latin America. The harsh realities of the eighties prompted the abandonment of ISI in many countries by the end of the decade and initiated a trend toward more-liberal economic strategies with still-uncertain consequences.

The East Asian NICs passed through brief ISI stages before shifting to export-led industrialization (ELI) strategies in the early 1960s. Domestic and international conditions proved favorable to the success of such strategies. Rising wage levels in the North made it possible for the first wave of export-led industrializers to target Northern markets for labor-intensive goods. The growing openness of the world economy combined with rapid economic expansion in the North also offered a congenial environment for ELI. Domestically, the East Asian countries featured strong, autonomous states free of serious challenges from either organized labor or landed elites. Technocratic bureaucracies were given the power to orchestrate state intervention so as to upgrade the levels of technology and skills in the economy and to target capital toward promising export industries. International and domestic factors thus supported a strategy of ELI. Whether other countries now attempting to emulate the success of the East Asian NICs will enjoy similar supportive internal and external conditions remains to be seen. This question is thrown into bolder relief by the 1997 Asian financial crisis and its consequences. The crisis revealed weaknesses in the "Asian model" of economic development and has compelled states in the region to adjust their strategies accordingly.

For decades, the oil-producing countries proved unable to fully exploit the economic potential of their vast petroleum reserves. Domestically, these countries lacked the skills, capital, and political will necessary to curb their dependence on the major international oil companies. Internationally, the lack of coordination among producing countries, the glut of oil on world markets, and the political influence of Northern consuming countries all weighed against the efforts of producing countries to boost oil revenues. These circumstances began to change in the 1960s, leading to OPEC's spectacular successes of the 1970s. Shifting market conditions, combined with disunity among oil producers during the 1980s, partially eroded the gains made during the seventies.

This suggests that it can be misleading to think of Third World development in terms of "models" that can be evaluated in the abstract and adopted or abandoned at will by given states. Instead, development strategies evolve historically, and their success or failure must be considered in light of the particular circumstances facing particular countries. It is not policy alone but rather the fit between an overall strategy of development and the domestic, as well as international, factors confronting public and private decision makers that determines the path of economic development.

NOTES

1. For a brief discussion, of colonialism, see Paul Harrison, *Inside the Third World,* 2nd ed., New York: Penguin Books, 32–46.

2. In 1998, for example, two major commodities indices showed that the overall average price levels of agricultural and resource commodities stood at a two-decade low (Jonathan Fuerbringer, "Commodities' Price Slide Victimizes Economies of Several Nations," *New York Times,* December 11, 1998).

3. For a discussion of Latin America's experience with ISI, see Robert Alexander, "Import Substitution in Latin America in Retrospect," in James L. Dietz and Dilmus D. James (eds.), *Progress toward Development in Latin America: From Prebisch to Technological Autonomy,* Boulder, Colo.: Lynne Rienner, 1991; and other essays in the same volume.

4. "A Survey of Asia," *The Economist,* October 30–November 5, 1993, 3.

5. For general treatments of the East Asian NICs, see Richard P. Appelbaum and Jeffrey Henderson (eds.), *States and Development in the Asia Pacific Rim,* Newbury Park, Calif.: Sage Publications, 1992; Ezra Vogel, *The Four Little Dragons: The Spread of Industrialization in East Asia,* Cambridge: Harvard University Press, 1991; Bela Balassa, *Economic Policies in the Pacific Area Developing Countries,* New York: New York University Press, 1991; Roy Hofheinz, Jr., and Kent E. Calder, *The Eastasia Edge,* New York: Basic Books, 1982; and Jon Woronoff, *Asia's "Miracle" Economies,* 2nd ed., Armonk, N.Y.: M. E. Sharpe, 1992.

6. Most of the following data on the "Four Tigers" is taken from World Bank, *World Development Report, 2000/2001,* New York: Oxford University Press, 2001.

7. "Survey Taiwan: Silicon Valley (East)," *The Economist,* November 10, 1998.

8. Michaelle Levander, "Nurturing the Cybercitizen," *Wall Street Journal,* October 25, 1999.

9. "Survey Taiwan."

10. "Demographics," *Latin CEO,* April, 2001, 76.

11. Nancy Birdsall, "Life is Unfair; Inequality in the World," *Foreign Policy,* Summer, 1998; United Nations Development Program, *Human Development Report,* New York: Oxford University Press, 1999, 39.

12. Stephan Haggard, *Developing Nations and the Politics of Global Integration,* Washington, D.C.: Brookings Institution, 1995, 47, 48.

13. See "Business in Singapore: A Snappy Little Dragon," *The Economist,* June 9, 1990.

14. World Bank, *World Development Report, 2000/2001,* New York: Oxford University Press, 2001, 294.

15. World Bank, *World Development Report, 1999/2000,* New York: Oxford University Press, 2000, 59.

16. Philip Shenon, "As Indonesia Crushes Its Critics, It Helps Millions Escape Poverty," *New York Times,* August 27, 1993; David Sanger, "World Bank Beats Breast for Failure in Indonesia," *New York Times,* February 11, 1999.

17. "Survey Taiwan."

18. "The Ever-Spreading Tentacles of Hong Kong," *The Economist,* June 18, 1998.

19. "Yin and Yang in Asia's Science Cities," *The Economist,* May 21, 1994.

20. "Taiwan's Big Prize," *The Economist,* April 15, 1995.

21. Mark Landler, "Malaysia Pushes Flagging Plan for Its Own Silicon Valley," *New York Times,* July, 13, 1999.

22. "Taming the Little Dragons" and "Korea's Anti-Mercantilists," *The Economist,* June 11, 1988.

23. For discussions of the East Asian development model and the political conditions that underlay it, see Stephan Haggard, *Pathways from the Periphery: The Politics of Growth in the Newly Industrializing Countries,* Ithaca, N.Y.: Cornell University Press, 1990; a special issue of *International Studies Notes,* Winter 1990, on the East Asian development model; various essays in Frederic C. Deyo (ed.), *The Political Economy of the New Asian Industrialism,* Ithaca, N.Y.: Cornell University Press, 1987; Bela Balassa, *The Newly Industrializing Countries in the World Economy,* New York: Pergamon Press, 1981; Leroy Jones and Il Sakong, *Government, Business, and Entrepreneurship in Economic Development: The Korean Case,* Cambridge: Harvard University Press, 1980; David Yoffie, *Power and Protectionism: Strategies of the Newly Industrializing Countries,* New York: Columbia University Press, 1983; Alice Amsden, *Asia's Next Giant: South Korea and Late Industrialization,* New York: Oxford University Press, 1989; Robert Wade, *Governing the Market: Economic Theory and the Role of Government in East Asian Industrialization,* Princeton, N.J.: Princeton University Press, 1990; and David C. Kang, "South Korean and Taiwanese Development and the New Institutional Economics," *International Organization,* Summer 1995.

24. Waldo Bello and Stephanie Rosenfeld, *Dragons in Distress: Asia's Miracle Economies in Crisis,* San Francisco: Institute for Food and Development Policy, 1992, 4.

25. Hong Kong was long a British colony. Sovereignty transferred from Britain to China in 1997, although China has allowed Hong Kong to retain a high degree of political and economic autonomy.

26. Michael Prowse, "Miracles beyond the Free Market," in Christian Soe (ed.), *Annual Editions: Comparative Politics, 95/96,* 13th ed., Guilford, Conn.: Dushkin, 1995, 223.

27. Paul Kuznets, *Korean Economic Development. An Interpretative Model,* Westport, Conn.: Praeger, 1994, 120.

28. "Survey of Asia," 6.

29. "South Korean Cars: Three's a Crowd," *The Economist,* June 11, 1994, 63.

30. Prowse, "Miracles beyond the Free Market," 223.

31. David Sanger, "Chemical Leak in Korea Brings Forth a New Era," *New York Times,* May 1991.

32. Sheryl WuDunn, "Koreans Ponder: Are Pillars of Postwar Miracle Shaky?" *New York Times,* July 18, 1995.

33. Bello and Rosenfeld, *Dragons in Distress,* 25.

34. Bello and Rosenfeld, *Dragons in Distress,* 39.

35. Jonathan Lemco and Scott B. MacDonald, "Is the Asian Financial Crisis Over?" in Helen Purkitt (ed.), *Annual Editions: World Politics 00/01,* 21st ed., Guilford, Conn.: Dushkin/McGraw Hill, 2000, 186.

36. "The Chaebol Spurn Change," *The Economist,* July 22, 2000, 59.

37. "The Chaebol Spurn Change," 59.

38. "South Korea: The Death of Daewoo," *The Economist,* August 21, 1999, 56.

39. Doug Henwood, "Asia Melts," *Left Business Observer,* no. 81, January, 1998.

40. For an argument that the success of the East Asian NICs cannot be duplicated by other Third World countries, see Robin Broad and John Cavanaugh, "No More NICs," *Foreign Policy,* Fall 1988.

41. Patrick Tyler, "Chinese End Austerity Drive in Favor of Yet More Growth," *New York Times,* November 23, 1993.

42. United Nations Development Program, *Human Development Report, 2000,* New York: Oxford University Press, 2000, Table 8, 185.

43. World Bank, *World Development Report, 2000/2001,* Table 11, 294.

44. World Bank, *World Development Report, 2000,* Table 21, 314.

45. "Multinationals: A Survey," *The Economist,* June 24, 1995, 13.

46. Data in this paragraph are drawn from Nicholas Kristoff, "Riddle of China: Repression as Standard of Living Soars," *New York Times,* September 7, 1993; "A Survey of Asia," 12; UN Development Program, *Human Development Report, 2000,* Table 9, 187; Robert Benjamin, "Big Changes in Diet Challenge the Chinese," *Des Moines Register,* February 27, 1994; Peter Nolan, "Introduction: The Chinese Puzzle," in Qimiao Fan and Peter Nolan (eds.), *China's Economic Reform: The Costs and Benefits of Incrementalism,* New York: St. Martin's Press, 1994, 11, 13.

47. "Survey: The Global Economy," *The Economist,* October 1, 1994, 28.

48. UN Development Program, *Human Development Report, 2000,* Table 1, 158.

49. UN Development Program, *Human Development Report, 2000,* Tables 12 and 4, 198–199 and 170.

50. "Credit Where It Is Due," *The Economist,* September 9, 2000, 94.

51. See "Survey China," *The Economist,* March 18, 1995, 19; and Jack Goldstone, "The Coming Chinese Crisis," *Foreign Policy,* Summer 1995, 48; Erik Eckholm, "Dangerous Coal Mines Take Human Toll in China," *New York Times,* June 19, 2000.

52. See Orville Schell, "China—The End of an Era," *The Nation,* July 17/24, 1995; and Seth Faison, "In China, Rapid Social Changes Bring a Surge in the Divorce Rate," *New York Times,* August 22, 1995.

53. Elisabeth Rosenthal, "Without 'Barefoot Doctors,' China's Rural Families Suffer," *New York Times,* March 14, 2001.

54. Minxin Pei, "In Other Words: Cracked China," *Foreign Policy,* September–October, 2001, 79.

55. BBC World Service broadcast, October 6, 1995.

56. Robert Benjamin, "Rapidly Developing China Faces Environmental Catastrophe, " *San Francisco Chronicle,* August 4, 1994. Elizabeth Economy, "Painting China Green: The Next Sino-American Tussle," *Foreign Affairs,* March–April, 1999, 15–16.

57. "Survey China," 20.

58. World Bank, *World Development Report, 2001,* Table 8, 288.

59. See Jack Goldstone, "Coming Chinese Crisis," *Foreign Policy,* Summer 1995, 36; "Survey China," 20–21.

60. Goldstone, "Coming Chinese Crisis," 36.

61. Lester Brown, "Challenges of the New Century," in Worldwatch Institute, *State of the World 2000,* New York: Norton, 2000, 7.

62. "Survey China," 19.

63. See "China Stirs Its Sleeping Giants," *The Economist,* August 17, 1994; Patrick Tyler, "China's Industries Battle Bankruptcy by Diversification," *New York Times,* May 5, 1994; Patrick Tyler, "Overhaul of China's State Industry at a Standstill," *New York Times,* December 16, 1994; "Survey China;" "China's Economy: Steady as She Slows," *The Economist,* September 11, 1999, 48.

64. "Shrinking the Chinese State," *New York Times,* June 10, 1995; "Out of Work, On the Move," The Economist, October 14, 1995.

65. Pei, "Cracked China," 79.

66. Pei, "Cracked China," 79.

67. For comparisons between the Chinese model and the "shock therapy" programs adopted in some eastern European countries, see Nolan, "Introduction: The Chinese Puzzle."

68. UN Development Program, *Human Development Report, 2000,* Table 7, 180, Table 4, 170, Table 9, 188, Table 12, 200.

69. See Bernard Weintraub, "Economic Crisis Forcing Once Self-Reliant India to Seek Aid," *New York Times,* June 29, 1991; Weintraub, "India Is Now in a New Ballgame," *New York Times,* July 8, 1991; "Indian Economy: Pepsi Generation," *The Economist,* June 9, 1990; and "India's Plan Is Backed," *New York Times,* September 23, 1991.

70. "The State of Reform in India," *The Economist,* August 6, 1994, 29; "How to Keep Investors Out," *The Economist,* June 11, 1994; "The Lure of India," *The Economist,* February 26, 1994; and Edward Gargan, "Shackled by Past, Racked by Unrest, India Lurks Toward Uncertain Future," *New York Times,* February 18, 1994; Marshall M. Bouton, "India's Problem is Not Politics," *Foreign Affairs,* May–June, 1998, 88–90; UN, Development Program, *Human Development Report, 1999,* 87; Swaminathan Aiyar, "Indians Do Better Than India," *The World in 2000 (The Economist),* 1999, 43.

71. Mark Landler, "India Optimistically Prepares for Slump in the US," *New York Times,* March 13, 2001.

72. Gargan, "Shackled by Past, Racked by Unrest"; "How to Keep Investors Out"; "The State of Reform in India"; and "India's Economic Nationalists," *The Economist,* August 12, 1995; World Bank, *World Development Report, 2001,* Table 21, 314.

73. "India's Economic Nationalists"; John F. Burns, "India Project in the Balance," *New York Times,* September 6, 1995.

74. For an overview of the history and development of the Brazilian economy, see Werner Baer, *The Brazilian Economy: Growth and Development,* 3rd ed., New York: Praeger, 1989; and Werner Baer and Joseph S. Tulchin (eds.), *Brazil and the Challenge of Economic Reform,* Washington, D.C. and Baltimore: Woodrow Wilson Center Press and Johns Hopkins University Press, 1993.

75. "Brazil's Economy: The Right Stuff," *The Economist,* June 9, 1990; James Brooke, "Brazil Opens Its Borders to Goods from Abroad," *New York Times,* August 16, 1993; James

Brooke, "A Hard Look at Brazil's Surfeits: Food, Hunger and Inequality," *New York Times,* June 6, 1993.

76. Brooke, "Brazil Opens Its Borders to Goods from Abroad"; James Brooke, "Brazil Cuts Its Tariffs on Many Goods," *New York Times,* September 12, 1994; James Brooke, "For Brazil, New Praise and Potential," *New York Times,* October 10, 1994; Simon Romero, "Carrying the Flag for Free Trade," *New York Times,* December 2, 1999; Simon Romero, "Brazil Has Become a Poster Child for Free Trade," *New York Times,* December 2, 1999.

77 "Brazil Signs Foreign Debt Agreements," *New York Times,* November 30, 1993.

78. James Brooke, "U.S. Business Flocking to Brazilian Ventures," *New York Times,* May 9, 1994.

79. Brooke, "For Brazil, New Praise and Potential"; Brooke, "Mexican Crisis Depressing Brazil and Argentina Stocks," *New York Times,* February 20, 1995.

80. Duncan Green, "The Failings of the International Financial Architecture," *NACLA Report on the Americas,* July–August, 1999, 32; Simon Romero, "Carrying the Flag for Free Trade," *New York Times,* December 2, 1999; "Investing in Brazil: Trouble in Paradise," *The Economist,* June 3, 2000, 63; "Latin American Index," *Latin CEO,* April 2001, 12; World Bank, *World Development Report, 2001,* Table 15, 302.

81. Brooke, "Brazil Opens Its Borders to Goods from Abroad"; "Brazil's Car Industry: Party Time," *The Economist,* September, 17, 1994; James Brooke, "Car Makers Shift to High Gear in Brazil," *New York Times,* March 28, 1995; "Latin American Index," *Latin CEO,* April, 2001, 12.

82. James Brooke, "Brazil's Mythic Inflation under Full Scale Attack," *New York Times,* March 3, 1994; Brooke, "For Brazil, New Praise and Potential;" World Bank, *World Development Report, 2001,* Table 1, 274.

83. Andreas Adriano, "Power Drought," *Latin CEO,* April, 2001, 58–59.

84. Fernando Henrique Cardoso and Enzo Falleto, *Dependency and Development in Latin America,* Berkeley and Los Angeles: University of California Press, 1979.

85. Brooke, "For Brazil, New Praise and Potential."

86. Brooke, "Brazil's Mythic Inflation under Full Scale Attack." For an interpretation of how neoliberal ideas came to dominate in most Third World countries, see Thomas J. Biersteker, "The 'Triumph' of Liberal Economic Ideas in the Developing World," in Barbara Stallings (ed.), *Global Change, Regional Response: The New International Context of Development,* Cambridge, England: Cambridge University Press, 1995.

87. Jacqueline Mazza, "Argentina, Brazil, Chile: Democracy and Market Economics," *Great Decisions,* Washington, D.C., Foreign Policy Association, 1994, 68; Paul Lewis, "U.N. Lists 4 Lands at Risk over Income Gaps," *New York Times,* June 2, 1994; "Survey Brazil," *The Economist,* April 29, 1995, 1; "Survey Brazil: A Better Life," *The Economist,* March 27, 1999.

88. Brooke, "For Brazil, New Praise and Potential."

89. Brooke, "A Hard Look at Brazil's Surfeits."

90. This discussion rests upon Alvin Toffler, "Toffler's Next Shock," *World Monitor,* November 1990, 34–38, 41–42, 44.

91. On the consequences of the Cold War's ending for the Third World, see Fred Halliday, "The Third World and the End of the Cold War," in Barbara Stallings (ed.), *Global Change, Regional Response,* 1995.

92. Salim Muwakkil, "Jesse Jr.'s Africa Challenge," *In These Times,* June 13, 1999, 20; Joseph Kahn, "World Bank Cites Itself in Study of Africa's Bleak Performance," *New York Times,* June 1, 2000.

93. For readable accounts concerning the relationship between the major oil firms and producing countries, consult Anthony Sampson, *The Seven Sisters: The Great Oil Companies and the World They Created,* rev. ed., London: Coronet, 1988; Daniel Yergin, *The Prize,* New York: Simon and Schuster, 1991; and John Blair, *The Control of Oil,* New York: Pantheon, 1976.

94. On the origins and evolution of OPEC, see Ian Skeets, *OPEC: Twenty-Five Years of Prices and Politics,* Cambridge, England: Cambridge University Press, 1988.

95. Robert Mortimer, *The Third World Coalition in International Politics,* 2nd ed., Boulder, Colo.: Westview Press, 1984, 44.

96. "Oil: A Very Crude Form of Politics," *The Economist,* May 6, 1995, 64.

97. On the negotiations surrounding the NIEO, see Mortimer, *Third World Coalition;* Jeffrey Hart, *The New International Economic Order,* New York: St. Martin's Press, 1983; Stephen Krasner, *Structural Conflict: The Third World against Global Liberalism,* Berkeley and Los Angeles: University of California Press, 1985; Jagdish Bhagwati and John Gerard Ruggie (eds.), *Power, Passions and Purpose,* Cambridge: MIT Press, 1984.

98. Despite its title, the Group of 77 eventually grew to include over 120 Third World countries.

99. For statements of this viewpoint, see Independent Commission on International Development Issues, *North-South. A Programme for Survival,* Cambridge: MIT Press, 1980; and Brandt Commission, *Common Crisis, North-South: Cooperation for World Recovery,* Cambridge: MIT Press, 1983.

100. For a critical assessment of the NIEO, see Robert Tucker, *The Inequality of Nations,* New York: Basic Books, 1977.

101. All data in this paragraph are from "The Cartel That Fell out of the Driver's Seat," *The Economist,* February 4, 1989.

102. Joseph Stanislaw and Daniel Yergin, "Oil: Reopening the Door," *Foreign Affairs,* September–October 1993, 83.

103. "The Cartel That Fell."

104. Agis Salpukas, "Long-Term Oil Strain Seen," *New York Times,* October 31, 1994.

105. F. Gregory Gause, III, "Saudi Arabia over a Barrel," *Foreign Affairs,* May–June, 2000, 83.

106. Nedra Pickler, "U.S. Gas Mileage Hits 20-Year Low as Guzzlers Soar," *Des Moines Register,* December 20, 2000.

107. The information in this paragraph has been taken from Mathew Wald, "Gulf Victory: An Energy Defeat?" *New York Times,* June 18, 1991; Saleh Billo, "Six OPEC Nations Have 70.5% of World's Proven Oil Reserves," *Oil and Gas Journal,* February 5, 1990; "The Cartel That Fell"; Salpukas, "Oil Strain"; Agis Salpukas, "Oil Companies Shifting Exploration Overseas," *New York Times,* November 8, 1993; Stanislaw and Yergin, "Oil: Reopening the Door"; Sabrina Tavernise, "A New Western Focus on Russia, 'Where the Oil Is,'" *New York Times,* December 5, 2001; and Larry Rohter, "OPEC's Unity Is Undercut by the Saudis," *New York Times,* September 29, 2000.

108. Brown, "Challenges of the New Century," 17.

109. To offer but one example, sales of energy-efficient compact fluorescent lamps jumped fourfold between 1989 and 1995. These bulbs are four times more efficient than incandescent bulbs and last ten times longer. The increased use of fluorescent rather than incandescent bulbs over the six years cited saved a quantity of energy equal to the output of 28 large coal plants. See Lester Brown, Nicholas Lenssen, and Hal Kane, *Vital Signs,*

1995: The Trends That Are Shaping Our Future, New York: Norton (Worldwatch Institute), 1995, 58-59.

110. A conservative estimate is that known natural gas reserves represent 145 years of supply at present levels of production, though actual reserves are probably much higher given that exploration has not been carried out in many parts of the globe. Some observers expect that natural gas will gradually replace oil in many uses and that gas production will exceed oil production by the year 2010. See Brown, "Challenges of the New Century," 17-18: and Brown, Lenssen, and Kane, *Vital Signs,* 48-49.

111. See Brown, Lenssen, and Kane, *Vital Signs,* 54-55, 57-58. On a more negative note, U.S. Department of Energy spending on energy research and development fell fivefold between 1978 and 1997 in real terms (Mary H. Cooper, "Oil Production in the 21st Century," in *Global Issues,* Washington, D.C.: CQ Press, 2001, 120).

112. Stanislaw and Yergin, "Oil: Reopening the Door," 90; Amy Myers Jaffe and Robert A. Manning, "The Shocks of a World of Cheap Oil," *Foreign Affairs,* January–February, 2000, 27.

113. Brown, "Challenges of the New Century," 18.

114. Jonathan Rauch, "The New Old Economy: Oil, Computers and the Reinvention of the Earth," *Atlantic Monthly,* January 2001, 47-48.

115. T. R. Stauffer, "Canada Is Ready to Exploit Huge Oil Reserves Locked in Sands," in Robert Jackson (ed.), *Annual Editions: Global Issues, 95/96,* 11th ed., Guilford, Conn.: Dushkin, 1995, 132.

116. Kenneth N. Gilpin, "Long Term Appears Turbulent for Oil," *New York Times,* December 20, 1999.

117. In general, the recent concentration of major Western oil companies— for instance, the mergers of Exxon with Mobil and BP with Amoco— are expected to enhance the bargaining leverage that firms possess in relation to producing countries (Youssef Ibrahim, "For OPEC's Richest, Natural Allies of Size," *New York Times,* December 3, 1998).

118. Note that China is moving ahead with a separate pipeline project that will bring oil from Tengiz across Kazakhstan to China's northwest (Cooper, "Oil Production," 129).

119. For more on the political divisions within the Arab world, as well as the factors that led to Iraq's invasion of Kuwait, see Yahya Sadowski, "Revolution, Reform or Regression? Arab Political Options in the 1990 Gulf Crisis," *Brookings Review,* Winter 1990/91; Geraldine Brooks and Tony Horwitz, "Brotherly Hate: Gulf Crisis Underscores Historical Divisions in the Arab 'Family,'" *Wall Street Journal,* August 13, 1990; and "The Middle East: New Frictions, New Alignments," in *Great Decisions,* New York: Foreign Policy Association, 1991. On the implications of the Gulf War for future energy security, see Robert Lieber, "Oil and Power after the Gulf War," in David N. Balaam and Michael Veseth (eds.), *Readings in International Political Economy,* Upper Saddle River, N.J.: Prentice-Hall, 1996.

120. Bob Williams, "OPEC Ventures Downstream: Industry Threat or Stability Aid?" *Oil and Gas Journal,* May 16, 1988.

121. Ibrahim, "Natural Allies of Size"; Martha M. Hamilton and William Drozklak, "OPEC's in the Driver's Seat," *Washington Post National Weekly Edition,* April 3, 2000; Jaffe and Manning, "World of Cheap Oil"; Larry Rohter, "OPEC's Unity Is Undercut by the Saudis," *New York Times,* September 29, 2000. Note that even at $30 per barrel, 2000 oil prices were, in real terms, only a little more than one-half of peak 1980 levels (Cooper, "Oil Production," 115.)

122. Hamilton and Drozklak, "OPEC's in the Driver's Seat"; David Barboza,

"OPEC's Pain Is US Gain," *New York Times,* November 16, 2001.

123. Although the following discussion focuses on Latin America and Asia, some movement toward regional economic cooperation is also evident in Africa. See Robert Browne, "How Africa Can Prosper," in Balaam and Veseth (eds.), *Readings in International Political Economy.*

124. "China Wants to Join the Club," *The Economist,* May 14, 1994, 35.

125. "For Richer, for Poorer," *The Economist,* December 18, 1993, 66.

126. For an analysis of the failure of the Seattle talks, see Ravi Kanth, "Why Seattle Talks Failed," *Business Times,* December 16, 1999.

127. For reports on the Doha negotiations, see Louis Uchitelle, "U.S. Industries Largely Favor Decision on Global Trade," *New York Times,* November 15, 2001; Joseph Kahn, "Nations Back Freer Trade, Hoping to Aid Global Growth," *New York Times,* November 14, 2001; and Richard W. Stevenson, "Measuring Success: At Least the Talks Didn't Collapse," *New York Times,* November 15, 2001.

128. Elizabeth Olson, "Regional Trade Pacts Thrive as the Big Players Fail to Act," *New York Times,* December 28, 2000.

129. Note, however, that trade among Mercosur member states dropped by 30 percent in 1999 due to exchange rate instability and regional recession ("Mercosur: Becalmed," *The Economist,* December 11, 1999, 34)

130. Information contained in the previous three paragraphs has been drawn from James Brooke, "The New South Americans: Friends and Partners," *New York Times,* April 8, 1994; Brooke, "Latins Envision a Single Trade Zone," *New York Times,* June 17, 1994; Brooke, "On Eve of Miami Summit Talks, US Comes Under Fire," *New York Times,* December 9, 1994; and Haggard, *Developing Nations,* 75–99.

131. David E. Sanger, "Biggest Obstacle to Selling Trade Pact: Sovereignty," *New York Times,* April 23, 2001.

132. "Reforming Latin America," *The Economist,* November 26, 1994; Shahid Javed Burki and Sebastian Edwards, "Consolidating Economic Reforms in Latin America and the Caribbean," *Finance and Development,* March 1995.

133. Olson, "Regional Trade Pacts."

134. "Mercosur's Trial by Adversity," *The Economist,* May 27, 2000, 37.

135. "Mexico's Trade Unions Stick to the Same Old Tune," *The Economist,* October 23, 1999, 35.

136. The following discussion of Asian regional economic cooperation relies upon Haggard, *Developing Nations,* 62-74; and Richard Higgott and Richard Stubbs, "Competing Conceptions of Economic Regionalism: APEC versus EAEC in the Asia Pacific," *Review of International Political Economy,* Summer 1995.

137. For a similar conclusion, see Karl J. Fields, "Circling the Wagons: Economic Integration and Its Consequences for Asia," Issues and Studies, December 1992, 28.

138. Andrew Pollack, "In a Move to Open Its Markets, China Pledges to Cut Tariffs on 4,000 Items Next Year," *New York Times,* November 20, 1995.

ANNOTATED BIBLIOGRAPHY

Robert Alexander. "Import Substitution in Latin America in Retrospect." In James L. Dietz and Dilmus D. James (eds.). *Progress toward Development in Latin America: From Prebisch to Techno-logical Autonomy.* Boulder, Colo.: Lynne Rienner, 1991. Provides a historical overview and evaluation of Latin America's experience with import substitution industrialization.

Bela Balassa. *Economic Policies in the Pacific Area Developing Countries*. New York: New York University Press, 1991. Balassa, a well-known liberal economist, attributes the success of the East Asian newly industrializing countries less to government industrial policy than to sound macroeconomic policies and high savings rates. He thus differs from those writers who characterize the economic strategies of these countries as mercantilist.

Waldo Bello and Stephanie Rosenfeld. *Dragons in Distress: Asia's Miracle Economies in Crisis*. San Francisco: Institute for Food and Development Policy, 1992. The authors explore the less favorable aspects of rapid growth in the East Asian newly industrializing countries. These include environmental destruction, political authoritarianism, and the repression of labor. They criticize the view that East Asia should serve as a model for other parts of the South.

Robin Broad and John Cavanaugh. "No More NICs." *Foreign Policy,* Fall 1988. The authors argue that the success of the export-oriented industrializers of East Asia will not be easily duplicated by other Third World countries. They outline an alternative path of development.

Thomas M. Callaghy and John Ravenhill (eds.). *Hemmed In: Responses to Africa's Economic Decline*. New York: Columbia University Press, 1993. A collection of essays, including both country and sectoral studies, focusing on how African governments and firms have attempted to cope with the prolonged economic downturn of the past two decades.

Frederic C. Deyo (ed.). *The Political Economy of the New Asian Industrialism*. Ithaca, N.Y.: Cornell University Press, 1987. An excellent collection of essays on the political factors underlying the economic strategies of the East Asian newly industrializing countries.

Peter Evans. *Embedded Autonomy: States and Industrial Transformation*. Princeton, N.J.: Princeton University Press, 1995. Examines the role that states play in promoting economic change. Argues that states work best when they achieve a balance between autonomy and "embeddedness" in their relationship to society.

Stephan Haggard. *Pathways from the Periphery: The Politics of Growth in the Newly Industrializing Countries*. Ithaca, N.Y.: Cornell University Press, 1990. An informative and provocative comparison of the development strategies pursued by the newly industrializing countries of East Asia and Latin America. Haggard emphasizes the role of external crises, state-society relations, and development ideas in determining the policy choices made by state officials, as well as their consequences.

Stephan Haggard. *Developing Nations and the Politics of Global Integration*. Washington, D.C.: Brookings Institution, 1995. Examines the political dynamics underlying the formation of regional trade and investment pacts among Southern nations.

Robert Mortimer. *The Third World Coalition in International Politics*. Boulder, Colo.: Westview Press, 1984. A comprehensive and detailed history of the rise and fall of the Third World's quest for a new international economic order.

Martha Brill Olcott. "The Caspian's False Promise." *Foreign Policy,* Summer 1998, 94–113. Details the political and geographic obstacles to the Caspian region's development and export of oil resources.

Barbara Stallings (ed.). *Global Change, Regional Response: The New International Context of Development*. Cambridge, England: Cambridge University Press, 1995. A collection of essays that examines how countries in different Third World regions have adapted their development strategies in response to recent global changes, including the end of the Cold War, increased competition among developed countries, new patterns in trade and production, the globalization of international finance, and new ideological currents.

Robert Wade. *Governing the Market: Economic Theory and the Role of Government in East Asian Industrialization.* Princeton, N.J.: Princeton University Press, 1990. Wade credits government intervention as a significant cause of rapid economic development in the East Asian newly industrializing countries. A very sophisticated and lucid treatment of the topic.

Marc Williams. *Third World Cooperation: The Group of 77 in UNCTAD.* New York: St. Martin's Press, 1991. A historical account of the efforts of Third World countries to bring about a new international economic order.

Meredith Woo-Comings (ed.). *The Developmental State.* Ithaca, N.Y.: Cornell University Press, 1999. A collection of essays that stress the importance of strong state institutions to economic development. This theme is pursued through the examination of country case studies and theoretical overviews.

Daniel Yergin. *The Prize.* New York: Simon and Schuster, 1991. This is a classic study of the politics and economics of oil. Written by a noted historian and energy analyst, this especially well written and accessible treatment makes for fascinating reading. Contains an extensive discussion of OPEC.

10

❖

Foreign Aid and Third World Development

Conceived through a marriage between idealism and self-interest, the birth of foreign aid was heralded by the world almost half a century ago.[1] Great things were expected of aid, not least of which was the conquest of world poverty. At present, however, foreign aid has settled into a beleaguered middle age, marked by unfulfilled dreams and scaled-down expectations. Sapped of their youthful spirit, many aid agencies find themselves engaged in a lonely battle to defend their very existence against legions of critics.

The high hopes that once surrounded foreign aid stemmed from its early accomplishments. Seeking to jump-start a slumping world economy and contain the spread of communism and Soviet influence, the United States poured 2.5 percent of its GNP into the reconstruction of Western Europe between 1947 and 1951.[2] Dubbed the Marshall Plan, U.S. assistance proved critical in hastening Western European recovery from the devastation of World War II.

Motivated by humanitarian impulses as well as pragmatic economic and security interests, the United States sought to replicate this success by expanding foreign aid to the developing world during the 1950s. The Point Four program, established in 1951 to provide technical assistance, was followed by the creation of the Development Loan Fund (a precursor of the present-day Agency for International Development), extending concessional financing for development projects and programs in Third World countries.

Meanwhile, the International Bank for Reconstruction and Development (IBRD), or World Bank, also began to shift its emphasis from European reconstruction to Third World development. A World Bank affiliate called the International Development Agency (IDA), which provided long-term, interest-free loans to finance development in the world's poorest countries, was created in 1960. The specialized agencies of the United Nations, such as the Food and Agricultural Organization and the World Health Organization, also grew in number and size during the 1950s and 1960s.[3]

Alongside the expansion of these multilateral agencies came the establishment of aid organizations in the developed nations of Western Europe and elsewhere. During the next 20 years, the bilateral assistance programs of these donors grew much faster than that of the United States. Whereas the United States accounted for 60 percent of the bilateral assistance provided by all member countries of the Development Assistance Council (DAC) at the time of the organization's founding in 1961, the U.S. contribution dropped to 13 percent of the total by 1999.[4] The 1970s also brought tremendous growth in the foreign assistance provided by a number of newly wealthy OPEC countries. During the 1980s, Japan rapidly expanded its foreign assistance, surpassing the United States to become the world's largest aid donor by the end of the decade.[5] By the early 1990s, official development assistance to the South had peaked at over $60 billion per year, although aid flows declined through the remainder of the decade.[6] An immense network of organizations and bureaucracies had evolved to administer this large flow of funds. Many of the world's poorest nations had become inextricably dependent upon outside aid.

Yet faith in aid has diminished even while the flow of assistance has increased. Early hopes that the success of the Marshall Plan could be duplicated in the Third World were soon dashed by the realization that Southern countries lacked not only capital and financing but also myriad other necessary prerequisites to development, including economic infrastructure, skilled and educated populations, competent bureaucracies, stable governments, and experienced entrepreneurs. A greater appreciation of the enormous challenges of Third World development dictated a more modest and reserved set of expectations toward foreign aid.

This was not the only source of disappointment. Critics increasingly questioned the purposes, philosophy, and methods of those who dispensed and received development assistance. Some charge that aid is a tool for serving the political and economic interests of donor countries. Moreover, aid may prop up repressive Third World governments, worsen inequality, and destroy the environment.[7] Others attack aid as a needless and costly subsidy that sustains bloated Third World bureaucracies and discourages recipient governments from carrying out needed policy reforms or supporting private sector growth.[8] Both the left and right condemn the inefficiency and corruption that too often plague foreign aid.

In recent years, criticisms of aid have become entwined with a broader grassroots movement against globalization. The World Bank, along with the IMF, has become a major target of protest. In 2000, for example, 12,000 demonstrators protested outside the joint World Bank/IMF meeting in Prague.[9] Seeking to avoid the spotlight brought on by such confrontations, the World Bank cancelled a major antipoverty conference that had been scheduled to meet in Barcelona, Spain in June 2001 after anti-globalization groups announced plans to protest at the event.[10]

The American public holds decidedly mixed views toward foreign aid. A survey conducted in January 1995 revealed that a large majority of respondents believed that the U.S. government spends too much on foreign aid and favored cuts in aid spending. The same survey also found, however, that Americans vastly overestimate the proportion of federal spending devoted to foreign assistance. Although in fact development aid constitutes less than four-tenths of 1 percent of government spending in the United States, the median estimate offered by survey respondents placed aid expenditures at 15 percent of the budget. Over 86 percent of respondents believed that the United States spent more than other countries on aid. Yet the United States actually ranks last among 24 major donor countries in aid as a percentage of GDP. When informed as to the actual share of government spending accounted for by aid, only 18 percent of respondents still thought existing aid levels were too high.

The survey also discovered that humanitarian rationales for aid attract the strongest support. Americans are less inclined to favor aid programs that are designed to reward friendly countries or to win economic benefits for U.S. business. Military aid is also quite unpopular. But majorities ranging from 74 percent to 91 percent want to maintain or increase aid devoted to ends such as child survival, humanitarian relief, repairing the environment, family planning, and long-term economic development. There exists strong support for targeting aid toward the poorest countries. Americans are skeptical, however, that aid actually reaches those who need it or achieves humanitarian aims. Roughly 80 percent of respondents believed that too much aid went to undemocratic regimes, that aid is plagued by waste and corruption, and that foreign assistance programs often foster dependence on the part of recipients.[11]

Systematic data on Third World attitudes toward foreign aid are scarce, but anecdotal evidence of frustration abounds. Popular movements have arisen to protest the social dislocations and environmental destruction that have accompanied huge aid-funded projects in Brazil, India, and Indonesia. Widespread resentment over the suspected misuse and theft of aid funds played a role in the political upheavals that forced Ferdinand Marcos from power in the Philippines. The unpopular policy reforms demanded of major debtor countries in recent years by bilateral and multilateral donors as a condition for further funding have prompted rioting in various countries. In a small but perhaps symbolic incident that occurred in 1985, Haitian peasants waved machetes in an attempt to fend off U.S. helicopters attempting to deliver food aid. These farmers acted out of fear that cheap foreign food would depress prices and undermine their livelihood.[12]

These critical responses to the growth of foreign aid are not surprising. Indeed, the emotionally charged debate over aid may flow inevitably from the fundamental nature of foreign assistance. Aid's very existence can be traced to the

persistent gap between rich and poor in the world economy. From a Third
World standpoint, aid is often viewed as a poor substitute for structural reforms
in the international economic order, which might more directly reduce this inequality between the haves and have-nots of the world. Moreover, stark contrasts
inevitably arise between the humanitarian declarations used to justify aid and the
political as well as economic motives that govern the allocation of assistance. This
clash between rhetoric and reality leaves aid givers vulnerable to charges of
hypocrisy. Finally, although aid may, on the whole, make a modest contribution
to Third World development and poverty reduction, it also fosters dependence.
The relationship between donor and recipient, never an equal one, is almost certain to provoke resentment and provide opportunities for manipulation.[13]

This chapter examines various controversies surrounding the relationship
between aid and development. After a brief discussion of the different types
and strategies of aid giving, we explore the effectiveness of foreign assistance
in spurring economic growth, reducing poverty, and enhancing environmental sustainability in the Third World.

THE RATIONALE FOR AID

The rationale for aid rests upon its presumed superiority in some respects over
private financial flows as an instrument for furthering Third World development. The World Bank, which lends $30 billion yearly in official develop-
ment assistance (ODA), cites the advantages foreign assistance offers in
promoting both efficiency and equity.[14]

Official aid, according to the World Bank, finances certain types of projects
that promise large social and economic returns but, nevertheless, seldom attract
the interest of private capital. These include investments in health, education,
agricultural research, and basic infrastructure. Many such projects pay off only
over 30 to 40 years, a time frame longer than most private investors are willing
to accommodate. Moreover, some types of technical assistance and policy advice
provided by official aid institutions are simply unavailable through private
sources. Aid's principal role in development is to complement, rather than substitute for, the private sector. The desired result is a more well-rounded and efficient pattern of economic growth. Aid is also justified on equity grounds.
Because most aid is provided on concessional terms, poorer countries gain access to resources that they would otherwise find unaffordable. Similarly, without
the subsidies made possible by concessional assistance, the poor within recipient
countries would be unable to pay the full costs for the services they receive.

STRATEGIES OF FOREIGN ASSISTANCE

The basic strategies and philosophies of development underlying foreign aid
have shifted markedly over time. We can distinguish among five major approaches. A "top-down" model, pursued most vigorously during the 1950s

and 1960s, sought to stimulate Third World development through the provision of infrastructure and technical advice. The 1970s brought a more egalitarian "bottom-up" strategy, designed to combine "growth with equity" through investment in the poor. During the 1980s, attention shifted to the strengthening of market mechanisms. New conditions placed on aid encouraged governments to remove barriers to trade and foreign investment, encourage private sector growth, and adopt more orthodox economic policies. The 1990s witnessed an emphasis on sustainable development and preservation of the environment. Finally, aid agencies have begun to incorporate democracy-promotion programs alongside their traditional missions.[15]

Early approaches to foreign aid were consistent with the theories of modernization then in vogue. Development was equated with industrialization and the expansion of the largely urban-based "modern" sectors of Third World economies at the expense of the "traditional" rural sectors. Most lending went to state-owned infrastructural projects, including such items as dams, roads, electrical grids, communications networks, and port facilities. The inadequacy of infrastructural development was considered a critical bottleneck to Third World growth and industrialization. Once this constraint had been overcome, economic growth would proceed according to the comparative advantage of various Third World countries.

This strategy relied heavily upon the creation of conditions likely to attract foreign investment. Multinational corporations would be enticed by cheap labor, abundant raw materials, and a growing Third World consumer market. Technical advice played a key role in providing state bureaucrats and local entrepreneurs with the skills and knowledge needed to manage a modern economy.

Agriculture took a back seat to industry, and the rural population was viewed primarily as an enormous reserve of potential wage labor, to be tapped gradually over time according to the expanding demands of the modern sector. Nevertheless, traditional agricultural exports were counted upon to generate foreign exchange that, in turn, could be put toward the importation of needed capital goods. Thus subsistence farmers producing basic food staples for their own consumption were encouraged to switch to specialized commodities that could be marketed abroad.

Although this strategy succeeded in stimulating industrialization in many countries, it became apparent by the late 1960s that the benefits of modernization were not trickling down to the poor majority as its proponents had hoped and had promised. In some countries, such as Brazil, income inequality worsened considerably, and the bottom 40 percent to 60 percent ended up both relatively and absolutely worse off than before.

These considerations led to a rethinking of traditional wisdom during the 1970s. Under the leadership of Robert McNamara (1968–1981), the World Bank, working particularly through its "soft" loan affiliate, the International Development Agency, began to focus more directly on eliminating the sources of Third World poverty.[16] This orientation was often referred to as "growth with equity." Around the same time, the U.S. Congress passed legislation designed to refocus the work of the Agency for International

Development (USAID) toward the needs of the poor majority. The Foreign Assistance Act of 1973 directed that USAID place greatest emphasis on "countries and activities which effectively involve the poor in development."[17] Many European countries followed suit.[18]

Concerns about equity were not the only ones driving this new attention to the plight of the poor. It was expected that poor people, if given the proper training and resources, could become productive contributors to development rather than drags upon it. This belief undergirded the two principal components of the new growth-with-equity strategy. The first was an emphasis on satisfying the basic needs of poor rural and urban dwellers. Proponents of this approach argued that the poor cannot become economically productive as long as they are afflicted by illness, malnutrition, illiteracy, inadequate shelter, and lack of access to clean water. Without these basic needs, the poor become locked in a continuing cycle of poverty, unable to earn a livelihood or to improve their economic circumstances.[19]

The strategy's second component followed from the first. After the poor were secure in their basic needs, they required new opportunities to begin providing for themselves and contributing to the remainder of society. The role of aid was to fund expanded education programs, agricultural extension schemes, rural cooperatives, small business development, and other projects designed to enhance the economic productivity of the poor.

Aid officials who embraced this growth-with-equity strategy rejected calls for more far-reaching efforts to redistribute wealth and income. The emphasis remained on growth. New-style investments were expected to produce economic returns as high or higher than more traditional projects.[20] Greater equity would emerge as a by-product of this strategy, however, as the retargeting of investment priorities allowed the poor to lay claim to larger increments of future growth.

This bottom-up approach to development drew criticism from a number of different directions. Some argued that, despite rhetoric about investing in human resources, the new lending programs did little more than subsidize consumption by the poor. Such "welfare" programs created only dependence, without providing the poor with the means to provide for themselves.

Others suggested that the aid community's new emphasis on aiding the poor amounted to less than met the eye. Poverty-oriented lending by the World Bank increased from 5 percent to 30 percent of total disbursements during the 1970s. Yet this left 70 percent of the bank's funds devoted to traditional projects. Moreover, some critics charged that much of the money allocated for the poor actually benefited those who were already relatively well-off in Third World societies, either because elites found ways of siphoning off aid for their own uses or because aid agencies used too sweeping a definition of who counted as poor.

In any case, enthusiasm for the new focus on poverty waned with the replacement of McNamara as head of the World Bank and the election of Ronald Reagan as president in the United States. Both the World Bank and USAID shifted priorities during the 1980s.[21] Previous approaches to foreign aid, it was argued, placed too little emphasis on the encouragement of free markets and private enterprise. The centerpiece of the new strategy designed to correct this oversight became known as "policy dialogue."

The World Bank began to expand program and structural-adjustment lending. These loans were not tied to specific projects, as in the past, but instead provided budgetary or balance of payments support. To qualify for such loans, however, governments were required to agree to policy reforms designed to reduce the state's role in the economy. These policy adjustments included the privatization of state-owned enterprises, decreased social welfare subsidies, trimmer government budget deficits, lower trade barriers, and the elimination of regulations that discouraged foreign investment. These demands were justified on the grounds that heavy state intervention stifled economic growth and that aid provided leverage to correct such impediments to development.[22] Indeed, as traditional aid has declined in relative importance as a source of new capital for Third World countries, aid agencies have begun to emphasize their role as consultants and sources of information and advice to Southern governments. Lynn Spire, World Bank research director, explains that in the future "the bank will become more of a knowledge-based institution, advising countries on developing their private sector."[23]

Alongside this emphasis on policy dialogue came a renewed effort to strengthen the roles of foreign investment and the private sector in Third World economies. The World Bank expanded funding for the International Finance Corporation, which, unlike other branches of the bank, made equity investments in partnership with private firms. Likewise, during the Reagan administration, a new entity known as the Bureau for Private Enterprise was created within USAID with much the same mission.[24] World Bank director James Wolfesohn has argued that the bank's key role is to "create the conditions for private capital to flow into all these countries."[25]

The 1990s brought two new programmatic objectives for foreign assistance: sustainable development and democracy promotion. The so-called Earth Summit, held in Rio de Janeiro, Brazil, in June of 1992, challenged both Northern and Southern governments to give greater attention to environmental sustainability when devising development plans. Although only modest amounts of new money have been devoted to environmental programs, aid agencies have reallocated some existing funds toward environmental projects and have begun to screen traditional projects more carefully for their environmental impact.[26]

The 1980s and early 1990s witnessed a wave of democratization in the Third World and the former Soviet bloc. The percentage of the world's governments classified as democratic rose from 30 percent in 1974 to 60 percent in 1998.[27] Northern countries, led by the United States, have directed a small but growing proportion of aid to programs designed to nurture and strengthen these fledgling democracies. USAID, for instance, has embraced democracy promotion as one of its four principal goals. This so-called political aid is devoted to promoting a democratic culture within the civil societies of targeted countries and often flows to nongovernmental organizations, such as labor unions, political parties, civic organizations, and educational institutions. Although democracy promotion is not directly tied to economic development, it has a number of indirect effects on the economic assistance programs that constitute our principal concern. Most obviously, democracy promotion projects compete for limited funds with traditional economic assistance programs. Moreover, many Northern countries have begun to condition economic assistance on the recipient country's respect for democracy and human rights.

Aside from the merits of any one approach, these frequent shifts in the assumptions and strategies favored by the aid community deserve further comment. The movement from one approach to another is less the result of steadily accumulating knowledge and insight into the process of development than a function of shifting political winds in the North. The top-down approach of the 1950s and 1960s must be understood in the context of the Cold War. The United States and its allies hoped that the emphasis on infrastructure would provide quick, tangible evidence of Western largesse, strengthen friendly governments, and by stimulating rapid growth, inoculate Third World societies against the appeals of socialism. The poverty-oriented focus of the 1970s reflected the liberal political climate of that era. In particular, the Vietnam War brought home for many the dangers of supporting narrowly based Third World elites without attention to the needs of the poor majority. The emphasis on markets and private enterprise during the 1980s stemmed from the conservative philosophy of newly elected Northern leaders such as Ronald Reagan and Margaret Thatcher. The focus on sustainable development during the 1990s was spurred by the growth of the global environmental movement, whereas democracy promotion reflected interest in nurturing the newly founded and still fragile democracies of eastern Europe and the Third World.

What difference does it make which approach to development is embraced by the aid community? Most obvious, the assumptions underlying foreign assistance affect project selection and design as well as the allocation of funds. Yet far more significant is the broader influence these ideas exert over the policies of the recipient countries themselves. The World Bank is one of the key sources of data and analysis on development issues. Its reports, publications, and activities are widely followed and play a pivotal role in debates among experts and government officials. As we have seen, the bank, along with other institutions, such as USAID and the IMF, actively seeks to shape the economic policies of Third World states. Changes in approach and philosophy at the largest aid agencies thus ripple through the entire Third World, altering, in both approach and emphasis, the development choices made by Southern governments.

This was particularly true during the 1980s and 1990s, when the World Bank and other agencies sought to expand and strengthen the scope of policy dialogue with recipient nations. Thus World Bank president Barber Conable's remark, in February 1990, about changing strategies of development in the Third World could be read as a measure of the bank's success in gaining acceptance for ideas it aggressively sponsored in recent years: "If I were to characterize the past decade, the most remarkable thing was the generation of a global consensus that market forces and economic efficiency were the best way to achieve the kind of growth which is the best antidote to poverty."[28]

THE EFFECTIVENESS OF AID

Does aid work? Has it contributed to efficient and equitable Third World development? Measuring the effectiveness of aid is a challenging task. It is difficult, for instance, to know what might have happened in the absence of aid. Moreover, success can be defined in different ways, depending upon whether one chooses to emphasize overall economic growth, poverty reduction, equity, or environmental impact. In addition, many factors besides aid affect a country's economic performance. Singling out aid's contribution is therefore tricky at best.[29]

Clearly, however, success stories are available, whether we are speaking of projects that have brought real benefits to targeted recipients or nations that have used aid as a tool for stimulating overall development. Among other things, foreign assistance programs have helped Southern countries to eliminate smallpox, immunize children against disease, spread family planning, reduce illiteracy, and increase grain yields. One study covering a 10-year period examined the economic rate of return for 504 World Bank projects where results could be estimated. On average, these investments brought a return of 18 percent, quite healthy by any standard.[30] The World Bank also points to South Korea and Indonesia as countries where aid played a major role during the formative stages of development to both spur growth and reduce poverty.

Many countries, however, such as Tanzania, the Sudan, Zaire, Mozambique, Niger, Togo, Zambia, and Haiti, have been and remain heavily dependent on external aid but show disappointing economic results. The difference between success or failure, the World Bank argues, has to do with a country's willingness to pursue sound, market-oriented policies. Aid works within a conducive policy setting but cannot compensate for the deleterious effects of poor economic decision making.[31]

Yet aid's critics suggest that foreign aid itself possesses inherent shortcomings stemming from the structure of the aid process as well as the priorities and motives of the donors. We take up seven of these criticisms in the sections that follow.

Poverty and the Misallocation of Aid

Perhaps the most widely accepted rationale for foreign aid lies in its potential for reducing Third World poverty. Indeed, as we have seen, public support for aid rests principally upon its purported humanitarian purposes; yet aid's success in ameliorating poverty is far from proven. After three decades of aid flows, the World Bank estimates that 1.2 billion people continue to survive on an income averaging $1 per day or less. Roughly 2.8 billion receive $2 per day or less in average income. Although the proportion of the world's population living in absolute poverty (defined as income less than $1 per day) fell from 28 percent in 1987 to 24 percent in 1998, this modest decline in relative poverty remains disappointing given overall levels of global economic growth.[32] Indeed, in a report reviewing the history of foreign aid, the Development Assistance Council (DAC) concluded that "the most troubling shortcoming of development aid has been its limited measurable contribution to the reduction—as distinguished from the relief—of extreme poverty, especially in the rural areas of both middle-income and poor countries."[33]

Part of the explanation for aid's disappointing record in attacking poverty is that political and economic considerations have influenced the allocation of foreign assistance. Substantial amounts of aid do not go to the countries that are most in need. To be sure, aid accounts for a significant portion of the income and investment in some of the world's poorest countries. Forty-seven countries count upon aid for 5 percent or more of their national income.[34] Yet in 1988, 41 percent of aid was distributed to middle- and high-income countries.[35] Aid receipts per capita bear little relation to average income. Indeed, Israel, a small and relatively wealthy country, is the world's largest recipient of foreign assistance. Overall, the richest 40 percent of all people living in the Third World receive twice as much aid per person as the poorest 40 percent.[36]

This misplacement of priorities is evident in the allocation of foreign assistance devoted to education. A disproportionate share of educational aid goes to higher education rather than primary schooling. In sub-Saharan Africa during the 1980s, for instance, official development assistance (ODA) to primary school education amounted to $1 per student, whereas aid to higher education equaled $575 for every student. Much the same pattern exists with respect to heath care, where rural clinics receive less aid than urban hospitals that cater to the middle class.[37]

The diversion of aid from poorer to relatively better-off Third World countries stems principally from the political and economic interests of donor countries. Historically, the influence of nondevelopmental considerations on aid allocation decisions has been most pronounced in the case of the United States. In 1986, according to the World Bank, development assistance to low-income countries accounted for only 8 percent of the overall U.S. aid budget.[38] One study found that among 17 donor countries, the United States ranked last in the degree to which it allocated aid according to the poverty-related needs of recipient countries.[39] Another study found that U.S. aid to relatively high-income countries amounted to $250 per person, whereas American assistance to very poor countries came to only $1 per person.[40] In 1994, only 26 percent of bilateral U.S. economic aid went to Asia, Africa, and Latin American combined. The remainder was allocated to the Middle East, Western Europe, and the former Soviet bloc.[41]

Over one-quarter of U.S. aid is channeled through the Economic Support Fund (ESF), which is administered by USAID. ESF aid is explicitly intended to reward friendly countries and promote political stability in areas considered important to U.S. interests. The great majority of U.S. ESF funding is directed toward Israel and Egypt as a reward for their willingness to enter into the Camp David Accords. Other countries, such as the Philippines, have received ESF funds as compensation for their willingness to allow U.S. military bases on their soil. Although some ESF aid goes to fund development projects, most provides general balance of payments support or finances commodity imports.

Developing-country governments also bear responsibility for the lack of progress in combating poverty within their societies. Corruption often diverts aid money from its intended beneficiaries (see the following discussion). Moreover, elites often show little interest in the plight of the poor. One study conducted by the United Nations Development Program found that only 29 percent of 140 countries surveyed had established dedicated antipoverty programs.[42]

The Ironies of Food Aid

The provision of food to alleviate hunger in the developing world has been a long-standing tool of foreign assistance. Food aid shipments rose from 7 million tons in 1997 to 14 million tons in 1999.[43] Yet food aid is among the most controversial forms of foreign assistance.[44] Sending food to hungry Southerners is popularly viewed in the North as a particularly humanitarian act. In fact, however, food aid sometimes does more harm than good.

The most straightforward form of food aid is emergency assistance designed to compensate for shortfalls during times of drought and famine. Under these circumstances, outside food can save hundreds of thousands or even millions of lives. The need for such assistance has grown rather than lessened over time, particularly in the case of many African countries that have experienced repeated food shortages over the last two decades. At the beginning of the 1990s, only one-third of all food aid shipments provided by the World Food Program were focused on emergency assistance. The remaining two-thirds were designed to serve longer-term development objectives. By the end of the decade, however, 80 percent of World Food Program food shipments were devoted to emergency needs.[45] In mid-2000 international experts estimated that over 20 million people in the four countries located in the Horn of Africa were in danger of starvation.[46]

Yet while emergency food aid has played a necessary role in alleviating much hunger and misery, such programs have been plagued by problems. Famine is rarely the result of natural factors alone. It is often exacerbated by government policies that discourage food production, the failure to set aside adequate food reserves during good years, slowness on the part of the governments and outside donors in reacting to signs of impending shortages, and the dislocations caused by war or political instability. These essentially political sources of hunger not only serve to heighten the probability of famine but also hinder efforts to assist the hungry after outside help becomes necessary. Conflicts between the local government and international relief agencies are common. Government authorities are often slow to acknowledge the prospect of famine for fear of shouldering the political blame for the country's desperate condition. Moreover, the distribution of food and medical supplies is fraught with political implications in severely divided societies. This often gives rise to intense bargaining between local governments and outside donors over the control of distribution activities.

These complexities are illustrated in the case of the 1990 Sudanese famine. Sudanese authorities repeatedly denied the prospect of food shortages despite increasingly urgent warnings of impending famine by outside observers and international relief agencies. The Sudanese government refused to request special assistance, effectively limiting donor access to the hungry. Moreover, aid personnel already working in the southern part of the country—where government troops were engaged in the suppression of an ethnic revolt—were forced to leave after authorities accused them of assisting the rebels.[47] This disturbing case is not unique. Almost identical events disrupted famine relief efforts in Ethiopia during 1984 and 1985.[48]

With some variations, a similar pattern repeated itself in Somalia in 1992–1993, where the collapse of any functioning government and the outbreak of intense clan warfare both exacerbated a worsening famine and interfered with the efforts of international aid agencies to feed a starving population. In this case, outside military intervention, in the form of United Nations and then U.S. troops, was required to restore some semblance of order and provide protection for relief efforts.

In 2000, famine again stalked Ethiopia, threatening the lives of an estimated 8 million people. Ethiopia's ability to marshal its own resources to combat hunger was compromised by an ongoing war with neighboring Eritrea, which consumed $1 million per day. Indeed, Ethiopian authorities refused to allow international relief agencies to funnel food aid into the country through the Eritrean port of Assab, thereby greatly slowing the distribution of crucial external assistance.[49]

Emergency aid often arrives too late or fails to reach those in greatest need. The European Community pledged food assistance in 1984 when much of sub-Saharan Africa faced famine conditions. Yet actual food deliveries did not begin until 400 days later. The slow response of the international community as well as that of local governments prompted many African farmers to abandon their land and migrate to enormous famine camps. Many who survived failed to return to their farms in time to sow new crops after the rains returned.[50]

After aid began arriving in 1985, the huge quantities of food overwhelmed port, storage, and transportation facilities. Only 75 percent of the food delivered to Ethiopia was distributed; the figure for the Sudan was 64 percent. Moreover, food aid failed to end when the famine finally lifted. Aid continued to pour into Kenya after returning rains allowed a record harvest in 1985. The overabundance of food flooded markets, depressed prices, and lowered rural incomes.[51]

A more ironic case of misdirected food aid occurred in the wake of the 1976 earthquake in Guatemala. Large quantities of food were delivered despite the fact that agricultural production remained unaffected by the quake and no food shortages existed.[52]

Despite the problems that surround emergency food programs, virtually all observers agree that such relief efforts are both necessary and useful. Other forms of food aid are more controversial. One form of food assistance, called "project aid," targets food toward specific purposes and populations. So-called "food for work" schemes, for example, provide food to the needy in areas where chronic hunger is widespread. In return, recipients are expected to work on projects with lasting development value, such as road and port construction, the repair of dykes and irrigation canals, the terracing of hillsides, and the replanting of denuded forest land.

A different form of project aid provides supplemental food for populations considered at risk, such as infants, schoolchildren, pregnant and breastfeeding mothers, and the elderly. Although useful in many instances, project aid may simply substitute for, rather than supplement, government social service assistance. Moreover, some projects go awry. One study of a child nutrition program found that the children's health actually improved after the project ended. While aid was available, mothers fed their children only the free grain and butterfat available through the program. Afterward, they reverted to a more balanced diet, including locally available fruits and vegetables.[53]

A great deal of food is distributed through so-called program aid. Food is simply provided free or sold at subsidized prices to governments to do with what they please. Governments generally resell the food within their own country, using the resulting revenue for other purposes. The motives behind this form of food assistance have less to do with altruism than with the political and economic interests of donor countries. Sir William Ryrie, former head of the British Overseas Development Administration, has observed that the bulk of food aid "is frankly more a means of disposing of European agricultural surpluses than of helping the poor."[54] The same, of course, is true of the U.S. Food for Peace program.[55]

Food aid is often distributed to friendly countries as a political reward. Owen Cylke, former acting director of the U.S. Food for Peace program, has commented that "it's used as a slush fund of the State Department to meet political requirements around the world."[56] In 1983, six of the top ten recipients of U.S. food aid were net food exporters. Egypt, a U.S. ally, received 20 percent of all cereal aid to the Third World in 1985–1986 and 50 percent of all such aid to Africa. This was despite the fact that Egypt's average caloric intake was 28 percent higher than necessary for a healthy diet. Because Egypt subsidizes food sales, bread is cheaper than chicken feed and is often fed to livestock. Patterns such as these prompted one World Bank study to conclude that "the distribution, quantity and nature of food aid sometimes bears little relation to dietary deficiency."[57]

The influx of cheap, subsidized Northern food into poor Third World countries can encourage dependence and vulnerability. Insecure governments prefer to keep food prices low so as to appease politically active urban populations. However, this practice denies rural farmers adequate revenue,

thus discouraging agricultural investment and production as well as perpetu-
ating rural poverty. The result is that cities swell with rural immigrants,
whereas the country becomes vulnerable should food aid levels fall due to
poor harvests and dwindling surpluses in the North.[58] Food aid is therefore
often resisted by rural residents, who make up the majority of the population
in many Third World countries. In 1990, Indonesian officials appealed to the
U.S. ambassador to stop the shipments of 700,000 tons of U.S. grain after
local farmers protested that they would be forced out of business due to the
influx of aid.[59]

Growth versus the Environment

Over the past decade, aid agencies have experienced enormous pressure from
groups in both the North and the South to give greater attention to the environmental, social, and cultural impacts of the projects they sponsor. The
World Bank, in particular, has come under attack for a series of controversial
projects that critics charge have brought devastating consequences to the environment and local inhabitants. Although the bank has taken steps to revise its
lending practices, many environmental groups remain skeptical about its commitment to reform.[60]

The environmental and social costs associated with the World Bank's emphasis on economic growth are plainly evident in the case of the Super Ther-
mal Power Plant and coal mine in India's Singrauli region. Funded by an $850
million World Bank loan, the project led to the forcible resettlement, with little compensation, of 23,000 local inhabitants. Ash from the coal-fired plant
has polluted neighboring cropland and a nearby reservoir, leading to the
growing incidence of tuberculosis and malaria among local residents. The
World Bank and Indian authorities were, moreover, slow to provide assistance
to resettled villagers.[61]

A migration project in Indonesia, financed by a $1 billion World Bank
loan, has led to the resettlement of 3 million poor people from Java and Bali
to outlying islands. Authorities hoped to relieve overcrowding and provide
peasants with small plots of new farmland. Millions of acres of tropical rain
forest have been cleared to make room for new settlers. The land of traditional
local inhabitants has also been seized, leading to violent confrontations with
the Indonesian army. Yet only one-half of the new farms have succeeded, due
largely to poor soils that are unsuitable for agriculture. Many settlers have mi-
grated back to the cities in search of work.[62]

A World Bank-funded colonization scheme in Brazil known as
"Polonoroeste" has brought similar results. Hundreds of thousands of poor
peasants have poured into the Rondonia and Mato Grosso provinces of the
Amazon region along a highway constructed with World Bank financing.
Huge tracts of virgin rain forest have been cleared and indigenous Indian populations displaced. Yet due to the leaching of minerals from the soil caused by
heavy rains, most farms prove productive for only a few years. Many resettled
peasants have responded by burning and clearing additional forest acreage. In

1987 it was estimated that the Amazon basin as a whole was afflicted by 6,000 forest fires, the great majority man-made.[63]

In May 1987, World Bank president Barber Conable conceded the bank's poor environmental record and promised a better performance in the future: "If the World Bank has been part of the problem in the past, it can and will be a strong force in finding solutions in the future."[64] The bank subsequently created a new environmental division staffed by 60 specialists. Some pending projects, including dams in India, Brazil, and Nepal, have been rejected on environmental or social grounds. New projects that exclusively address environmental problems have been approved, and environmental concerns have played a larger role in the planning of traditional projects. By 1990 the World Bank claimed that nearly one-half of all bank projects had environmental concerns built into them.[65] World Bank lending for free-standing environment projects increased to $2.4 billion in 1994, up thirtyfold from 1989 levels.[66] By 1997, the World Bank's loan portfolio included 153 environmental projects totaling $11.4 billion in loans.[67]

In 1991 the bank established the Global Environmental Fund (GEF), a new lending facility devoted to addressing environmental problems. In 1994 donor nations agreed to replenish the GEF with substantial new resources. Nevertheless, the World Bank has now been forced to share administrative responsibility over the GEF with the United Nations Development Program and the UN Environmental Program due to distrust of the bank on the part of Third World governments and private environmental groups.[68]

Despite the World Bank's new "green" image, critics argue that the bank's conversion has been less than complete. Peggy Hillward, director of forestry research for Probe International, charges that the World Bank is sponsoring "the same old projects with a few trees planted around the edges."[69] A congressionally mandated report issued in June 1990 by USAID cited 27 Bank projects that posed environmental or social dangers.[70] As of January 1990, an estimated 1.5 million people had been forcibly displaced by ongoing bank projects, and proposed plans threatened to displace a similar number.[71]

Despite growing concerns about the link between carbon dioxide emissions and global warming, the World Bank has shown little interest in energy alternatives to fossil fuels. Between 1992 and 1997, less than 3 percent of the bank's energy loans went toward renewable energy sources, whereas 78 percent were devoted to fossil fuel projects.[72]

Another concern is that a growing proportion of the bank's activities—namely, bank lending for structural adjustment purposes—is exempt from the new social and environmental assessments adopted in recent years. In the wake of the 1997 Asian financial crisis, structural adjustment lending rose to 63 percent of the bank's total loan portfolio in 1999.[73]

One underlying problem is that the serious environmental and social costs associated with some forms of development are not easily accommodated within the traditional models of economic growth embraced by most aid agencies. For this reason, the World Bank and other development organizations have begun to experiment with new models that include measures of ecological and resource depletion alongside long-accepted yardsticks of development (see Chapter 8).[74] These innovative measurements can reveal the hidden trade-offs underlying development. This new thinking about sustainable growth must be incorporated into project selection and design, however, before it will produce any widespread practical effect.

The Overreliance on Outside Experts

Development agencies have been criticized for relying too heavily on foreign experts in the design and implementation of aid projects while failing to take advantage of local talent or to consult with the poor about the plans that affect their lives. These tendencies often lead to poorly designed projects and feed resentment among recipients. Even worthwhile projects may wither over time if local people are not given the training, incentives, or responsibility necessary to sustain them. One study of aid-funded irrigation projects, for instance, found a 68 percent success rate in cases where beneficiary participation in the projects was high, whereas only 12 percent of those projects in which beneficiary participation was low were rated successful.[75]

The proclivity of aid agencies to manage aid projects through the use of imported expertise is pervasive. It has been estimated that at least 150,000 foreign-aid workers and consultants are employed in the Third World at any given time. The expense of keeping expatriate personnel in the field is considerable—$100,000 or more per year for each employee—usually much greater than that associated with the use of local labor.[76] The extensive overhead costs of administering aid projects often limits the amount of funding that actually reaches intended beneficiaries. Economist Abul Barkat of Dhaka University has estimated that only 25 percent of the foreign aid spent in Bangladesh since 1972 reached intended target groups. The remaining funds were spent on foreign consultants, bureaucrats, commission agents, contractors, and politicians.[77]

Not all of these foreign experts originate from the North. Many multilateral agencies, such as the United Nations Development Program, hire substantial numbers of Third World personnel. Yet these employees are often assigned to foreign postings. Only 10 percent of UN professionals, for instance, work in their home country[78] Paul Streeten, a consultant to the World Bank, notes that "a mediocre Indian, who might be useful within his competence in India, is recruited by the UN to work in Sierra Leone at ten times the salary he would earn at home, on a job for which he is ill-qualified, while a Sierra Leonean advises India.[79]

Foreign-aid workers are often clustered in separate project units, outside the recipient country's normal bureaucratic structure. This inhibits the accumulation of skills and learning experiences on the part of local officials and leaves aid projects without a strong constituency inside the regular bureaucracy. As a result, projects are often abandoned once outside aid is terminated.[80]

The work of this vast legion of aid emissaries is seldom effectively coordinated by various donor agencies. Some countries suffer from "aid overload."

The proliferation of aid projects from a multitude of donors simply over-whelms the capacity of the local bureaucracy to cope. In a single year, for in-stance, Burkina Faso was once visited by 350 separate aid missions. Project duplication is common and little standardization in equipment or design takes place. Donors provided Kenya, for instance, with 18 different varieties of water pumps for the country's rural water-supply system.[81]

Nor are the intended beneficiaries of aid typically given significant roles in designing or implementing aid projects. A study completed in 1988 by the World Bank's Operations Evaluations Department candidly concluded that "the principles guiding beneficiary participation in Bank-financed projects have been quite abstract and of limited operational impact. Beneficiaries were not assigned a role in the decision-making process, nor was their technical knowledge sought prior to designing project components."[82]

The consequences of failing to consult local knowledge can be devastating to project success. Three examples may help to illustrate this point. AID ex-perts relied upon a local irrigation canal to provide water to a fish farm proj-ect in Mali. Yet it was later discovered that the canal carried water for only five months out of the year. To prevent the fish pond from going dry during the remainder of the year, an expensive diesel-powered pump was installed to bring water from a source over two kilometers away. Moreover, fish food had to be imported because no suitable local source could be found. The in-creased costs of capital and inputs soon rendered the fish farm absurdly uneco-nomical. In a second such experiment, this time in the southern African nation of Malawi, a fish farm was located next to a bird sanctuary, providing the nearby population of fish-eating fowl with a tasty diet.[83] A third project, cited by USAID as a model, involved the planting of rows of trees as wind-breaks in the Majjia Valley of Niger. The purpose was to limit soil erosion by blocking destructive wind currents. In fact, however, the trees depleted the al-ready low water table and attracted birds and insects that pillaged nearby field crops. Moreover, the project brought on tensions between aid administrators and local herders over land rights.[84] The mistakes associated with these proj-ects, and others like them, might have been avoided had local expertise been tapped in the first place.

The Costs of Tied Aid

The common Northern practice of "tying" bilateral aid to the purchase of ex-ports from the donor country substantially reduces the real value of such assis-tance to Third World countries. The purpose of tied aid is to allow manufacturers in the donor's own country to capture a larger share of the sales stimulated by foreign aid. Tied aid also promotes future orders for donor coun-try exporters. Once an aid recipient installs machinery or equipment purchased from a particular supplier, it is likely to go back to that same firm for parts, supplies, and replacements. Thus tied aid generates a stream of business. In 1990, tied aid financed an estimated one third of the $25 billion to $30 billion in annual capital goods exports worldwide.[85] Overall, one-quarter of all ODA is tied to the purchase of donor country exports, a proportion that has declined over the past decade.[86]

When aid is tied in this way, however, recipient countries are forbidden to shop around for the least expensive or most appropriate equipment. On average, tying aid reduces its value by roughly 20 percent.[87] Moreover, Northern firms that benefit from tied aid serve as vested interests, lobbying for aid projects requiring heavy Northern inputs, whether or not these projects are the most appropriate from the recipient's point of view.

The Preference for Bigness

Some of the most persistent criticisms of aid have to do with the size and type of projects that donors typically sponsor.[88] Aid agencies tend to prefer large-scale, capital-intensive investments that require a sizable import component over smaller, labor-intensive projects relying principally upon locally produced inputs. Thus, in competition for the same funds, a single expensive infrastructure project, such as a dam, road, or port facility, will often win out over multiple smaller and less costly projects, such as rural health clinics or agricultural extension programs. Authors of the Wapenhans Report, an independent assessment of World Bank lending, concluded that loan officers gave priority to loan quantity over the quality of projects and were rewarded for the amount of money lent rather than the long-term success of projects.[89] These biases in project lending tend to skew development toward the modern urban sector of the economy to the detriment of the poorer rural areas and often contribute to an overdependence on imports.

The sources of this behavior stem from various bureaucratic needs of the aid agencies themselves. Most foreign assistance programs, for instance, finance only the foreign currency component of the projects they sponsor. This encourages recipient nations to maximize the proportion of total project costs that depend upon imported goods and favors reliance upon foreign suppliers over local firms. Future orders of parts and replacement equipment are likely to go to these same foreign companies, as well. Another consequence is that projects relying heavily on "hardware," such as imported capital equipment, are favored over those involving heavy labor costs that must be paid in local currency.

The preference for "bigness" is also related to bureaucratic factors. Aid agencies are under enormous pressure to "move money." Success is defined less in terms of the quality of projects or their contributions to development or poverty alleviation than in the total amount of funds dispersed. Within the agency, a good administrator is viewed as one who can lend the most money at the least cost in terms of bureaucratic overhead. Large projects are most efficient in this regard. The paperwork and worker hours required to initiate and review the progress of a small project are scarcely less than those needed to administer a large project. An overworked bureaucrat who seeks to impress his or her superiors with his or her productivity will thus find the oversight responsibilities associated with a single large loan far more manageable and rewarding than those that accompany many small loans. These incentives to think big become even more intense when the quantity of funds available to lend suddenly rises faster than the agency's workforce.

This syndrome is reinforced in the case of bilateral agencies that must spend their aid allocations within a given time period or lose access to the funds altogether. Moreover, if funding for a particular year is not fully dispersed, legislative overseers may conclude that future aid appropriations can be safely cut. These external funding constraints typically lead to an end-of-fiscal-year frenzy to spend all remaining funds. Under these circumstances, even marginal projects may be considered more favorably than before, particularly if they promise to move money quickly.

Recipient Country Corruption

Corruption, entrenched inequality, and the insensitivity of elites to the plight of the poor in many Third World countries seriously hamper even sincere efforts by outside agencies to reach those in need. According to Volkmar Kohler, then West German secretary for development, "We have to work with elites who have no interest in seeing the poorer classes in their societies advance."[90] Unrepresentative political regimes are many times plagued by officially sanctioned corruption. One World Bank staffer has admitted that Third World governments often demand financial kickbacks from firms involved in aid projects: "We know that it happens all the time. Its how business is done in those countries."[91]

In early 1999, a report prepared by an independent oversight arm of the World Bank concluded that bank officials had consistently overlooked massive corruption and mismanagement of aid funds on the part of the Indonesian government under President Suharto. The bank distributed $25 billion to Indonesia over the three decades of Suharto's rule. The report suggested that "issues of poor governance, social stress and a weak financial sector were not addressed." The bank feared that cutting off loans to Indonesia in response to the government's failure to follow bank advice would harm relations with Suharto, scare off foreign investors, and undermine the bank's public portrayal of fast-growing Indonesia as one of its great success stories. Julian Schweitzer, the bank's director for strategy and operations in East Asia, commented that "this is the great conundrum. That we didn't get it right in Indonesia is obvious, but understanding how to get it right is difficult. Issues of governance of a nation have not in the past been part of our agenda."[92]

A recent and disturbing example of how corruption can distort aid involves a group of international construction companies that won contracts with USAID to build water projects in Egypt. Over a period of years, these companies bilked USAID of tens of millions of dollars. Bribes were employed to fix the bidding process. The winning firms then realized profits of up to 60 percent through fraudulent billing.[93]

In recognition of the costs of corruption and poor management, democracy and good governance are increasingly viewed by many economists as a prerequisite to equitable development.[94] One United Nations study rated countries according to their achievements in "human development." It noted that 20 of the 25 nations scoring lowest on the human development scale were African dictatorships.[95] Donor countries have begun to take such considerations into greater account when allocating aid budgets. In 2000, the IMF placed more than distinct 60 conditions on a new loan to Kenya—the most detailed level of conditionality ever imposed—out of concern over rampant corruption in that country. Among other things, the IMF demanded that the Kenyan parliament pass a new anticorruption law and a code of conduct for public officials.[96] Canada and Britain, along with other donor countries, have conditioned their foreign aid on the recipient country's respect for human rights.[97]

Learning from Failure

The controversies dogging the major aid agencies have grown more frequent and intense in recent years. In 1992 an internal World Bank staff report found that over 37 percent of the bank projects completed in 1991 could be judged failures using the bank's own criteria. This represented a 150 percent increase in the bank's failure rate over the previous decade.[98] Another internal World Bank report, prepared in 1992 by the bank's Operations Evaluation Department, reviewed project completion reports through 1991 for 99 structural adjustment loans in 42 countries. The report found that two-thirds of the countries suffered declines in both public and private sector investment during the loan periods.[99] A similar internal International Monetary Fund review of structural adjustment programs in 19 low-income countries found that current account deficits and foreign debt loads actually worsened during the periods in which the IMF programs were in effect.[100] A report submitted by former World Bank employee David Knox has criticized the African Development Bank, arguing that it is bloated by bureaucracy, subject to political manipulation, and poorly organized to evaluate and monitor the projects that the bank funds.[101] A study conducted by Peter Boone, an economist at the London School of Economics, examined aid flows to 96 countries between 1971 and 1990. He concluded that the vast majority of aid financed consumption and that aid had little impact on overall economic growth rates.[102]

Japan has become a vocal critic of the neoliberal, free market policies espoused by the World Bank and the International Monetary Fund. Japanese officials argue that Third World countries need strong states to steer investment patterns, screen imports and foreign investment, and encourage the acquisition and development of technology. The activist state role favored by Japan is based upon that country's own experience, as well as those of other East Asian newly industrializing countries (NICs), including South Korea and Taiwan. Japanese officials are therefore skeptical about the advice offered Third World countries by the World Bank and other aid agencies, which tends to discourage state intervention in the process of economic development. This issue came to a head in 1993, when the World Bank published a study titled *The East Asian Miracle*. Although Japanese officials had originally requested the study, they were unhappy with its conclusions, which attributed East Asia's success to financial discipline rather than government industrial policy. Japan, a major contributor to both the World Bank and the IMF, has become increasingly bold in pressing for a reorientation of the development policies and models embraced by these institutions.[103]

These critical assessments, along with the problems reviewed earlier in this chapter, raise the important question of whether aid can be reformed. Can aid agencies learn from past mistakes and failures? One longtime development expert offers a pessimistic perspective, citing what he calls the "Three Rules of Development": "One, we never learn from our mistakes. Two, there is no bottom line. And three, no one ever gets fired."[104]

Yet a closer look reveals some significant evidence of institutional flexibility. As we have already seen, outside criticism of the World Bank's environmental record has led to significant progress toward a more ecologically sensitive method of operation.[105] This is not the only evidence of greater responsiveness in the aid community. Long criticized for its secrecy, the World Bank has become somewhat more open about its operations, allowing greater public access to internal documents. It has also created a new appeals panel that will consider complaints about bank projects from citizens of recipient countries.[106]

Another recent reform is USAID's move to channel a larger proportion of U.S. bilateral assistance through nongovernmental organizations (NGOs) rather than Third World governments. Called the New Partnerships Initiative, the program's objectives are to empower small businesses and entrepreneurs, strengthen local NGOs, and foster greater grassroots democracy. By working through NGOs, USAID hopes to reach the poor more directly and bypass the corruption and red tape often involved in working through governments.[107] The same trend is evident at the World Bank, where one-half of all projects now involve NGOs and 70 NGO specialists work in bank field offices.[108]

Improvements can be cited in other areas as well. By 1994, the World Bank had succeeded in bringing its failure rate down to 18 percent—still high, but a considerable improvement over a few years earlier.[109] Tied aid has declined as a proportion of the total. Over time, a larger proportion of assistance has been given in the form of grants rather than loans that must be repaid. An increasing share of aid has been funneled through multilateral institutions, which are less subject to direct political manipulation than bilateral programs and in which Southern countries have somewhat greater representation. Some donors have reduced or cut off aid to particularly repressive or inegalitarian regimes.[110] World Bank lending for health and education programs has tripled since 1990.[111] The proportion of World Bank dollars spent on traditional infrastructure projects has declined from $1 out of every $5 in 1995 to $1 out of every $50 in 2000.[112]

The World Bank has itself cited a number of lessons that it intends to incorporate in future lending programs. Developing countries must establish local "ownership" over aid projects. Recipients must be involved in all phases of project planning and implementation. Structural adjustment lending should focus on broad outcomes rather than imposing detailed conditions. A larger proportion of aid funding should be devoted to projects that directly improve the lives of the poor, such as education and the prevention and alleviation of disease.[113]

In cooperation with the IMF, the World Bank has also begun to require countries receiving structural adjustment funding to prepare Poverty Reduction Strategy Papers. This move followed growing criticism that bank- and IMF-sponsored structural adjustment programs led to particularly negative consequences for the poor in recipient countries.[114]

Efforts to reform foreign aid have in some cases been spurred by new ideas about the nature and sources of economic development. In the past, most foreign aid programs and projects focused on strengthening either states or markets. Recent theory and research, however, has pointed to the importance of "social capital" to successful development. The World Bank defines social capital as "the institutions, relationships, and norms that shape the quality and quantity of a society's social interactions."[115] A product of civil society rather than either the state or the market, social capital is the economic value of cooperative social activity. Examples include civic organizations, neighborhood associations, grassroots social movements, and other networks based on mutual trust and cooperation.

A number of studies suggest that societies that enjoy dense networks of social capital experience more robust economic development than those that suffer from a lack of social capital.[116] The economic advantages of dense associationalism are several: (1) High levels of trust and reciprocity reduce transaction costs; (2) strong social networks facilitate the dissemination of information and innovations; (3) social networks spread risk by serving as sources of support for individuals and groups during times of economic turmoil; (4) social capital allows groups to solve collective problems that would otherwise undermine economically beneficial undertakings.[117]

The World Bank has begun to build conceptions of social capital into the design of some of its lending projects. The bank is currently conducting a survey of social capital in 20 developing countries as a means for creating a database that will allow researchers to test various hypotheses related to the economic impact of variations in social capital. The World Bank's "Social Capital Initiative" has supported research into the linkages between social capital and development in particular sectors. The bank has also supported "Participatory Poverty Assessments" in over 50 countries as a means of both assessing and building levels of social capital in target societies.[118]

The aid community's interest in the positive potential of social capital as well as growing concern for poverty reduction are both evident in the movement by several major donor agencies, including the World Bank and USAID, to provide credit to the poor. Traditionally, aid agencies funded large-scale projects undertaken, in most cases, by governments. Critics argued that this form of assistance rarely benefited the poor directly. Indeed, most poor people lacked access to credit of any type, except through black-market lenders who charged usurious rates of interest. Commercial banks typically view the poor as bad credit risks. The fallacy of this assessment has been demonstrated by the Grameen Bank of Bangladesh. Founded 25 years ago by a visionary economist named Muhamad Yunus, Grameen lends small amounts of money, often equivalent to only a few hundred dollars, to small-scale cooperatives, most composed of poor women. These funds are used to establish small businesses, usually handicraft or livestock enterprises. Two million families in Bangladesh have received such loans. Loan volume approached $500 million in 1995, with a repayment rate of 97 percent. Following Grameen's lead, other "microcredit" institutions have been established elsewhere in the Third World over the past decade. The most effective microcredit programs combine loans with political organizing, training, business leadership education, lobbying, and project assistance.[119]

Encouraged by this success, the World Bank, USAID, and other official agencies have established programs that provide funding to hundreds of microcredit institutions in dozens of countries around the world. A Microcredit Summit held in Washington, D.C., in 1997 attracted 2,900 individuals representing 1,500 institutions in 137 countries. Conferees set the goal of reaching 100 million of the world's poor through microcredit by the year 2005. Although such an ambitious goal is unlikely to be met, over 1,000 microcredit organizations did serve almost 14 million clients during the 1997–2000 period, 75 percent of whom were women.[120]

These examples suggest that reform is possible. Like most bureaucracies, however, aid agencies prefer incremental change to wholesale shifts in policy and practice.[121] Most of the reforms discussed above have resulted when Northern governments and aid agencies have experienced outside political pressures and the glare of publicity from failed projects or programs. Only when the media, nongovernmental organizations, Third World governments, academic observers, or national legislatures take steps to expose serious problems has serious movement toward reform been forthcoming.

THE FUTURE OF FOREIGN AID

The prospect of significant future increases in Northern aid to the South seems slight. Since rising during the early 1980s, U.S. foreign aid has declined. Seeking to allocate its dwindling funds more effectively, USAID chief Brian Atwood announced plans in 1994 to restructure his agency over the coming few years. This reorganization led to the closing of missions in roughly one-half of the over 100 nations in which AID previously operated, cut 1,200 employees, and reduced USAID's list of priority goals from 33 to 4 (promoting democracy, protecting the environment, fostering sustainable development, and controlling population growth).[122] Despite these reforms, the Republican majority in the U.S. Congress continued to seek deep cuts in USAID funding and to lessen the agency's independence.[123] By 1997, U.S. aid had fallen to a level of only eight-one-hundreds of 1 percent of U.S. GDP.

The United States is not alone in reducing aid. Overall ODA flows fell from a peak of $61.9 billion in 1991 to $51 billion in 1998.[124] Measured in real per-capita dollars, ODA to 49 least-developed countries (LDCs) fell by 45 percent during the 1990s. In 1997, OECD members devoted less than one-quarter of 1 percent of their combined GDPs to aid, the lowest level ever.

Moreover, a rising proportion of aid is being diverted from long-term development projects to short-term disaster relief. Overall, the share of aid devoted to emergency relief rose by 500 percent during the 1990s.[125] In 1997, USAID responded to 27 declared disasters with assistance to over 40 million victims. These figures rose to 87 declared disasters and 140 million victims in 1998. USAID estimates that 418 million people were adversely affected by humanitarian crises in 2000.[126]

The lessening of Cold War tensions between East and West and the fall of communist regimes in Eastern Europe have had profound effects on aid flows to the South. During the Cold War, the United States and the Soviet Union each used aid as an inducement in their competition for Third World allies. With the waning of this rivalry, the United States no longer treats aid as a tool for countering the influence of a rival superpower, and Third World countries no longer enjoy the option of gaining increased assistance by appealing to Cold War fears.

Moreover, Third World countries have expressed alarm about the diversion of aid funds to Eastern Europe.[127] Although in 1988 the Soviet bloc countries donated a total of $5 billion in ODA to the developing world, these flows dried up almost entirely after the fall of communism. Shifting from donors to recipients, former Soviet bloc countries collectively received $6.7 billion in aid from the West in 1993.[128]

Although recipient countries may welcome Japan's growing commitment to foreign aid, they have less reason to cheer the conditions attached to such funds. Three-quarters of Japan's assistance is directed to countries in Asia and Oceania, where Japanese trade and investment levels are also high. Comparatively little finds its way to Africa or Latin America. Moreover, Japanese aid to the world's least-developed countries carries hard terms and contains a greater proportion of loans (versus grants) than is true for other aid donors. As we have seen, Japan ties a high proportion of its aid to the purchase of Japanese goods. Finally, a relatively large share of Japanese funds go toward infrastructural projects that bring few immediate benefits to the poor.[129]

CONCLUSIONS

This chapter has struck a largely pessimistic note regarding the effectiveness of aid in promoting development and alleviating poverty in the Third World. Such a conclusion does not imply that all aid is harmful or useless. Indeed, as we have also emphasized, aid comes in many shapes and forms. Not surprising, aid can claim many successes alongside its failures. Most projects probably have mixed effects, with costs and benefits spread unevenly across the affected population. Overall, aid may well provide measurable, and sometimes significant, economic benefits in many Third World countries. Indeed, it would be puzzling if the billions of dollars in aid that flow to the Third World each year did not have some positive impact.

Yet aid has surely failed to perform up to the hopes of its early proponents or, perhaps, even to the standards of its more modest defenders within the aid community today. We have surveyed a variety of specific criticisms that have been directed at aid. Three broader points take us to the roots of aid's shortcomings.

The contribution foreign aid can make to Southern development is limited in part by the modest size of aid flows. In 1992, foreign assistance from all sources amounted to 1.3 percent of overall Third World GNP, or roughly $11 for each Southerner.[130] To bring the limited contributions of aid into even clearer perspective, it has been estimated that the total value of Northern aid is exceeded by the costs to the Third World of Northern protectionism against Southern exports.[131] In 1996, ODA represented only one-quarter of all external finance flowing to developing countries, with private flows making up the remainder.[132] Although aid totals in the tens of billions of dollars may appear impressive, they seem less so when placed in the context of overall Third World needs. Moreover, as noted earlier, present aid levels seem likely to fall still further.

Another fundamental source of aid's limited success has to do with the poor state of our knowledge about the process of economic development. What seems clear is that there are many potential routes to development rather than a single model that can be successfully applied under all circumstances. This rather messy reality, however, makes it only more difficult to fashion aid strategies appropriate to each country. Changing academic and political fashions have combined with the inherent complexity of the development problem to produce a series of wrenching shifts in the strategies and philosophies embraced by the aid community. This inconsistency itself has detracted from aid's effectiveness.

Yet the most important constraints on aid are political. Why does aid often fail to reach the poor or to benefit them more directly? The fundamental answer is rather simple: the crucial decisions regarding aid are made by governments, over the heads of the poor themselves. Although aid is certainly not free of humanitarian motives and purposes, these often take a back seat to other concerns, including the pursuit of political power.

Donor governments use aid to reward friends and woo neutrals, to exercise leverage over the internal and external policies of recipients, to strengthen threatened allies, to pry open foreign markets, and to enhance the donor country's image at home and abroad. From the recipient government's standpoint, aid provides resources that help bolster the political power and legitimacy of the existing leadership. Political elites in these nations often use aid to reward supporters while denying resources to opponents, and sometimes indulge in direct corruption. Aid also encourages certain patterns of development that benefit different elements of society unevenly, perhaps, for instance, strengthening the modern, urban sector at the expense of the traditional, rural sector.

Seeing aid in terms of its effects on the political power of both donor and recipient governments helps us to understand why Third World political elites sometimes express ambivalent attitudes toward external assistance. Although aid may strengthen political leaders in relation to their domestic rivals, it also places them and their countries in a position of dependence upon aid donors. And dependence, of course, means increased vulnerability and the greater potential for external manipulation. This same aspect of the relationship makes the continuation of aid attractive to donor country leaders, even when foreign aid is unpopular among taxpayers and when evidence of its success in promoting development is ambiguous.

Given the political stakes associated with aid, the poor's lack of participation in the aid process is hardly accidental. Indeed, were aid to be reformed to focus more directly and effectively on the poor and to provide them with substantial input and control, aid would undoubtedly lose much of the appeal it presently holds for political elites in both donor and recipient nations. Ironically, taking the "politics" out of foreign aid might simply undercut the motivation for governments to go on spending and receiving foreign aid, leading to a massive contraction of such programs. This likelihood merely underscores the close association between politics and economics in North-South relations.

NOTES

1. Foreign aid takes many different forms, some beyond the scope of this chapter. We give little attention, for instance, to foreign military aid or assistance provided by private voluntary organizations. Our focus is on official development assistance (ODA).

2. World Bank, *World Development Report, 1985,* New York: Oxford University Press, 1985, 94.

3. On the United Nations agencies, see Douglas Williams, *The Specialized Agencies and the United Nations: The System in Crisis,* London: C. Hurst, 1987.

4. The DAC is an affiliate of the Organization for Economic Cooperation

and Development (OECD), which includes most major donor countries World Bank, *World Development Report, 1985,* 94; and James Gustave Speth, "The Plight of the Poor," *Foreign Affairs,* May–June, 1999, 17.

5. Anthony Rowley, "Flush with Funds," *Far Eastern Economic Review,* December 29, 1988, 52; and "Foreign Aid: Stingy Sam," *The Economist,* March 25, 1989, 26.

6. "Trends in Development Assistance," AID Fact Sheet, 1995.

7. For two examples among many, see Theresa Hayter and Catherine Watson, *Aid: Rhetoric and Reality,* London: Pluto Press, 1985; and Frances Moore Lappe, Joseph Collins, and

David Kenley, *Aid as Obstacle: Twenty Questions about Our Foreign Aid and the Hungry,* San Francisco: Institute for Food and Development Policy, 1981.

8. See, for instance, P. T. Bauer, *Reality and Rhetoric: Studies in the Economics of Development,* Cambridge: Harvard University Press, 1984, especially Chapters 3 and 4, 38–72; and Nick Eberstadt, "The Perversion of Foreign Aid," *Commentary,* June 1985.

9. Hans Greimel, "World Bank Calls Summit a Success," *Des Moines Register,* September 29, 2000.

10. "Spain: World Bank Cancels Meeting," Rueters, May 22, 2001.

11. All public opinion data are from Steven Krull, *Americans and Foreign Aid: A Study of American Public Attitudes,* College Park, Md.: Program on International Policy Attitudes, 1995. Also see Christine Contee, *What Americans Think: Views on Development and U.S.-Third World Relations,* New York and Washington, D.C.: InterAction and Overseas Development Council, 1987.

12. Lloyd Timberlake, "The Politics of Food Aid," in Edward Goldsmith and Nicholas Hildyard (eds.), *Earth Report: Monitoring the Battle for Our Environment,* Mitchell Brazley, 1988, 24.

13. For a general discussion of the tensions between aid givers and recipients, see the chapter entitled "Donors, Recipients and the Aid Giving Process" in Jeffrey Pressman, *Federal Programs and City Politics,* Berkeley and Los Angeles: University of California Press, 1975.

14. See World Bank, *World Development Report, 1985,* 99–100; Joseph Kahn, "World Bank Chief to Unveil an Ambitious Education Program," *New York Times,* April 27, 2000.

15. For useful overviews of the history of foreign aid and the shifting strategies of assistance, see Robert Packenham, *Liberal America and the Third World: Political Development Ideas in*

Foreign Aid and Social Science, Princeton, N.J.: Princeton University Press, 1973; World Bank, *World Development Report, 1985,* 94–99; Robert Wood, *From Marshall Plan to Debt Crisis: Foreign Aid and Development Choices in the World Economy,* Berkeley and Los Angeles: University of California Press, 1986; Stephen Hellinger, Douglas Hellinger, and Fred M. O'Regan, *Aid for Just Development: Report on the Future of Foreign Assistance,* Boulder, Colo.: Lynne Rienner, 1988, 13–32; and Brice Nissen, "Building the World Bank," in Steven Wasserman (ed.), *The Trojan Horse: A Radical Look at Foreign Aid,* Berkeley, Calif.: Ramparts Press, 1974.

16. For an examination of the World Bank's policies toward the poor during the McNamara years, see Robert L. Ayres, *Banking on the Poor: The World Bank and World Poverty,* Cambridge: MIT Press, 1983.

17. Hellinger, Hellinger, and O'Regan, *Aid for Just Development,* 22. Also on the impact of the "New Directions" legislation, see Robert L. Curry, "The Basic Needs Strategy, the Congressional Mandate, and U.S. Foreign Aid Policy," *Journal of Economic Issues,* December 1989.

18. See Steven Arnold, *Implementing Development Assistance: European Approaches to Basic Needs,* Boulder, Colo.: Westview Press, 1982.

19. For a discussion of basic needs, see Paul Streeten and Chahid Javed Burki, "Basic Needs: Some Issues," *World Development,* 6.3, 1978.

20. A study by the Overseas Development Council, based upon World Bank data through the early 1980s, suggests that poverty-oriented World Bank projects performed better than nonpoverty projects along a variety of economic criteria, including overall return on investment. Moreover, repayment rates were as high for poverty projects as for nonpoverty projects. Education directed at the poor offered the highest gains. See Sheldon Annis, "The Shifting

Grounds of Poverty Lending at the World Bank," in Richard Feinberg (ed.), *Between Two Worlds: The World Bank's Next Decade,* New Brunswick, N.J.: Transaction Books, 1986.

21. For discussions of these changing priorities at the World Bank and AID during the 1980s, see Clive Crook, "The World Bank," *The Economist,* September 27, 1986; John Sewell and Christine Contee, "U.S. Foreign Aid in the 1980s: Reordering Priorities," in John Sewell, Richard Feinberg, and V. Kallab (eds.), U.S. *Foreign Policy and the Third World,* New Brunswick, N.J.: Transaction Books, 1985; Christopher Madison, "Exporting Reaganomics—The President Wants to Do Things Differently at AID," *National Journal,* May 5, 1982; Christine Contee, "U.S. Foreign Aid in the 1980s," *Policy Focus* (published by the Overseas Development Council), no. 4, 1985; Joel Johnson, "Foreign Aid: The Reagan Legacy," *Policy Focus* (published by the Overseas Development Council), no. 2, 1988.

22. For a report on one such effort to link aid with policy reform, see John Felton, "Egypt: Aid Payments Used to Spur More Economic Reforms," *Congressional Quarterly,* August 26, 1989.

23. Paul Lewis, "A New World Bank: Consultant to Third World Investors," *New York Times,* April 27, 1995.

24. See Madison, "Exporting Reaganomics."

25. Lewis' "A New World Bank."

26. The topic of sustainable development is addressed at greater length in Chapter 13.

27. World Bank, *World Development Report, 1999/2000,* New York: Oxford University Press, 2000, 43.

28. Robin Broad, John Cavanaugh, and Walden Bello, "Development: The Market Is Not Enough," *Foreign Policy,* Winter 1990–91, 144. Broad,

Cavanaugh, and Bello offer a critique of the overwhelming emphasis on markets in the approach described by Conable.

29. For a detailed survey that attempts to assess aid's effectiveness, see Robert Cassen and Associates, *Does Aid Work?* Oxford, England: Clarendon Press, 1986.

30. World Bank, *World Development Report, 1985,* 103.

31. For the World Bank's views on aid's effectiveness, see its *World Development Report,* 1985, 101–105; and *World Development Report, 1990,* Oxford, England: Oxford University Press, 1990, 128–133. Also see Barbara Crossette, "UN Says Bad Government Is Often the Cause of Poverty," *New York Times,* April 5, 2000.

32. Dan Ben-David, Hakan Nordstrom, and L. Alan Winters, "Trade, Income Disparity and Poverty," Special Studies 5, World Trade Organization, 1999, 1.

33. World Bank, *World Development Report, 1990,* 127.

34. "Foreign Aid: The Kindness of Strangers," *The Economist,* May 7, 1994, 20.

35. World Bank, *World Development Report, 1990,* 127.

36. "Foreign Aid: The Kindness of Strangers," 19.

37. "Foreign Aid: The Kindness of Strangers," 20.

38. World Bank, *World Development Report, 1990,* 127–128.

39. Mark McGillivray, "The Allocation of Aid among Developing Countries: A Multi-Donor Analysis Using a Per Capita Aid Index," *World Development,* 17.4, 1989, 565.

40. "Foreign Aid: The Kindness of Strangers," 20.

41. "What Is USAID?" AID Fact Sheet, 1995.

42. Barbara Crossette, "U.N. Food Agency Says Famine Threatens 8 Million in Ethiopia," *New York Times,* February 24, 2000.

43. World Food Program, "Figure 4: WFP and Global Food Aid Shipments, 1997–2000" (http // www.wfp.org/statistics/2000/figure4.htm), accessed May 30, 2001.

44. For a brief survey and evaluation of various forms of food aid, see World Bank, *World Development Report, 1990,* 135. Also see Edward Clay and Olav Stoke (eds.), *Food Aid Reconsidered: Assessing the Impact on Third World Countries,* London: Frank Cass, 1991; and Vernon Ruttan (ed.), *Why Food Aid?* Baltimore: Johns Hopkins Press, 1993.

45. World Food Program, "World Food Programme: The Food Aid Organization of the United Nations," May 10, 2001 (http://www.wf p.org/info/intro/donors/index.html), accessed May 30, 2001.

46. George Gedda, "Africa Crisis Seen as Prelude to Famine," *Des Moines Register,* August, 2, 2000; Christopher S. Wren, "U. N. Report Maps Hunger 'Hot Spots,'" *New York Times,* January 9, 2001.

47. "African Famine: Yet Again," *The Economist,* January 5, 1991, 33; and Alyson Pytte, "Congress Is Using Aid as a Lever to Protest Rights Abuses" and "Somalia and the Sudan: Two Countries Plagued by Poverty, Famine and War,"*Congressional Quarterly,* May 13, 1989, 1132–1135. In March of 1991, Sudanese officials finally decided to make a formal appeal for emergency food aid and allow relief workers freer access to the country.

48. See the epilogue to William Shawcross, *The Quality of Mercy: Cambodia, Holocaust and Modern Conscience,* New York: Simon and Schuster, 1985.

49. Ian Fisher, "Ethiopian Hunger: Another Disaster Ahead?" *New York Times,* April 17, 2000.

50. Timberlake, "Politics of Food Aid," 24.

51. Timberlake, "Politics of Food Aid," 23–24.

52. Timberlake, "Politics of Food Aid," 24. For extended treatments of emergency and disaster assistance programs, see Randolph Kent, *Anatomy of Disaster Relief: The International Network in Action,* London: Pinter Publishers, 1987; and Lynn H. Stephens and Stephen J. Green (eds.), *Disaster Assistance: Appraisal, Reform and New Approaches,* New York: New York University Press, 1979. For a readable and interesting case study of international famine relief operations in Cambodia during the early 1980s, see Shawcross, *The Quality of Mercy.*

53. World Food Program, "World Food Programme; Timberlake, "Politics of Food Aid," 24–26.

54. Timberlake, "Politics of Food Aid," 27.

55. Martha Ann Overland, "Lawmakers Seek to Remove Politics from Foreign Aid," *Des Moines Register,* July 22, 1990.

56. Overland, "Lawmakers Seek to Remove Politics from Foreign Aid."

57. Timberlake, "Politics of Food Aid," 27–28. Also see Overland, "Lawmakers Seek to Remove Politics from Foreign Aid."

58. Timberlake, "Politics of Food Aid," 29.

59. Overland, "Lawmakers Seek to Remove Politics from Foreign Aid." For a defense of food aid, see H. W. Singer, "Food Aid: Development Tool or Obstacle to Development?" *Development Policy Review,* 5, 1987.

60. For a discussion of bargaining between environmental advocacy groups and the World Bank, see Pat Aufderheide and Bruce Rich, "Environmental Reform and the Multilateral Banks," *World Policy Journal,* Spring 1988. Also see Bruce Rich *Mortgaging the Earth: The World Bank, Environmental Impoverishment, and the Crisis of Development,* Boston: Beacon Press, 1994, which offers a critical evaluation of the World Bank's environmental record.

61. See Art Levine, "Bankrolling Debacles?" *US News & World Report,* September 25, 1989, 43–44; and Graham Hancock, *Lords of Poverty: The Power, Prestige and Corruption of the International Aid Business,* New York: Atlantic Monthly Press, 1989, 130–131.

62. See Levine, "Bankrolling Debacles?" 46–47; and Hancock, *Lords of Poverty,* 133–138.

63. Hancock, *Lords of Poverty,* 131–133.

64. Aufderheide and Rich, "Environmental Reform," 301.

65. On the bank's reforms, see Philip Shabecoff, "World Bank Stressing Environmental Issues," *New York Times,* September 24, 1990; Jeremy Warford and Zeinab Partow, "Evolution of the World Bank's Environmental Policy," *Finance and Development,* December 1989, 5–9; and Bruce Rich, "The Emperor's New Clothes: The World Bank and Environmental Reform," *World Policy Journal,* Spring 1990.

66. Hilary F. French, "Partnership for the Planet: An Environmental Agenda for the United Nations," Worldwatch Paper no. 126, July 1995, 36–37.

67. UN Non-Governmental Liaison Service, *The NGLS Handbook of UN Agencies, Programmes and Funds Working for Economic and Social Development,* 2nd ed., Geneva, Switzerland, 1997, 277.

68. "Greened," *The Economist,* December 4, 1993; Paul Lewis, "U.S. and Other Donor Nations Plan $2 Billion for Environment," *New York Times,* March 17, 1994.

69. Shabecoff, "World Bank Stressing Environmental Issues."

70. Levine, "Bankrolling Debacles?" 43.

71. Rich, "Emperor's New Clothes," 313.

72. Daphne Wysham and Jim Vallette, "Changing the Earth's Climate for Business: The World Bank and the Greenhouse Effect," *Multinational Monitor,* 18.10, October, 1997.

73. Carol Welch, "In Focus: Structural Adjustment Programs and Poverty Reduction Strategy," *Foreign Policy in Focus,* 5.14, April 2000.

74. For a brief discussion of these issues, see James Robertson and Andre Carothers, "The New Economics: Accounting for a Healthy Planet," *Greenpeace,* January–February 1989. On how these ideas have crept into World Bank thinking, see Warford and Partow, "World Bank's Environmental Policy."

75. World Bank, *Assessing Aid: What Works, What Doesn't and Why,* New York: Oxford University Press, 1998, 22.

76. Hancock, *Lords of Poverty,* 115.

77. Tabibul Islam, "Development— Bangladesh: Time to Look beyond Aid, Experts Say," Inter-Press Service, May 9, 2001.

78. Hancock, *Lords of Poverty,* 117.

79. Hancock, *Lords of Poverty,* 115.

80. World Bank, *World Development Report, 1990,* 132.

81. Cassen, *Does Aid Work?* 221, 223.

82. Hancock, *Lords of Poverty,* 125–126. For more on this problem, see Hellinger, Hellinger, and O'Regan, *Aid for Just Development.*

83. Both cases are discussed in Hancock, *Lords of Poverty,* 123–124.

84. Stryk Thomas, "Milk Shakes in the African Desert," *This World,* July 3, 1994, 9.

85. Clyde Farnsworth, "US Will Tie Aid to Exports in Bid to Curb the Practice," *New York Times,* May 14, 1990.

86. "Measuring Up for Aid," *The Economist,* January 8, 2000, 44.

87. C. J. Jepma, "The Impact of Untying Aid of the European Community Countries," *World Development,* 16.7, 1988, 804.

88. The discussion that follows in this section is drawn principally from Judith Tendler, Inside Foreign Aid, Baltimore: Johns Hopkins University Press, 1975.

89. World Bank, *Assessing Aid*, 118.

90. "Playing the Aid Game," World Press Review, February, 1989, 51.

91. Levine, "Bankrolling Debacles?" 44.

92. David Sanger, "World Bank Beats Breast for Failure in Indonesia," *New York Times*, February 11, 1999.

93. Kurt Eichenwald, "Global Conspiracy on Construction Bids Defrauded U.S.," *New York Times*, April, 13, 2001.

94. "Democracy and Growth," *The Economist*, August 27, 1994.

95. Paul Lewis, "Poorest Countries Seek Increases in Aid," *New York Times*, July 3, 1990.

96. "Dancing in Kenya to the Donor's Tune," *The Economist*, August 5, 2000, 43.

97. "Summit Leaders Link Human Rights to Foreign Aid," *Des Moines Register*, October 17, 1991.

98. "World Bank's Failure Rate," *New York Times*, April 14, 1993; Pratap Chatterjee, "World Bank Failures Soar to 37.5% of Completed Projects in 1991," in Kevin Danaher (ed.), *50 Years Is Enough: The Case against the World Bank and the International Monetary Fund*, Boston: South End Press, 1994.

99. "Cameron Duncan," Internal Report Card Looks Bad for Structural Adjustments," in Kevin Danaher (ed.), *50 Years Is Enough, 1994.*

100. "Foreign Aid: The Kindness of Strangers," 22.

101. "Development Banking: Double Trouble," *The Economist*, May 14, 1994.

102. "Down the Rathole," *The Economist*, December 10, 1994, 69.

103. John Judis, "World Bank," *In These Times*, December 13, 1993.

104. Robert L. Strauss, "My Road to Nowhere," *Stanford Magazine*, May–June, 2000, 78.

105. For an examination of how institutional learning took place in the World Bank as it grappled with criticisms of its environmental record, see Phillipe Le Prestre, *The World Bank and the Environmental Challenge*, Cranbury, N.J.: Associated University Presses, 1989.

106. Lewis, "A New World Bank."

107. Barbara Crossette, "Private Groups to Get More Foreign Aid," *New York Times*, March 13, 1995.

108. "The Non-Governmental Order," *The Economist*, December 11, 1999. Also see The NGLS Handbook of UN Agencies, Programmes and Funds Working for Economic and Social Development, UN Non-Governmental Liason Service, Geneva, Switzerland, 2nd ed., 1997. Note that some development experts believe that heavy reliance on NGOs skews development projects toward NGO priorities, even where these conflict with local needs. Some experts therefore stress stronger partnerships with local governments. Barbara Crossette, "UN Says Bad Government is Often the Cause of Poverty," *New York Times*, April 5, 2000.

109. Lewis, "A New World Bank."

110. For data relating to these points and a generally optimistic perspective on the willingness and ability of aid agencies to undertake reform, see David Lumsdaine, Moral Vision in International Politics: The Foreign Aid Regime, 1949–1989, Princeton: Princeton University Press, 1993.

111. Lewis, "A New World Bank."

112. Joseph Kahn, "International Lenders' New Image: A Human Face," *New York Times*, September 26, 2000.

113. "Development Finance: Old Battle, New Strategy," *The Economist*, January 8, 2000, 74. Also, see World Bank, *Assessing Aid.*

114. Welch, "In Focus: Structural Adjustment Programs."

115. World Bank, "Social Capital Initiative" (http://www.worldbank.org/poverty/scapital/scindex.htm), 2000.

116. See P. Whiteley, "Economic Growth and Social Capital," paper presented at the ECPR workshop on Social

Capital and Politico-Economic Performance, University of Bern, Switzerland, April 1997; and Stephen Knack and Philip Keefer, "Does Social Capital Have an Economic Payoff? A Cross-Country Investigation," *Quarterly Journal of Economics,* 112.4, November, 1997.

117. For key sources on social capital, see James Coleman, "Social Capital in the Creation of Human Capital," *American Journal of Sociology,* 94, supplement S95–S120, 1988; Peter Evans, "Government Action, Social Capital and Development: Reviewing the Evidence for Synergy," *World Development,* 24.6, August, 1996, 1119–1132; and Robert Putnam, "The Prosperous Community: Social Capital and Public Life," *The American Prospect,* no. 13, Spring 1993, 34–42.

118. World Bank, "Social Capital Initiative."

119. Patrick E. Tyler, "Banker Is Star at Parley on Women," *New York Times,* September 14, 1995; David Bornstein, "The Barefoot Bank with Cheek," *Atlantic Monthly,* December 1995. For more on the story of the Grameen Bank, see Muhammad Yunis, *Banker to the Poor: Micro-Lending and the Battle against World Poverty,* New York: Public Affairs, 1999.

120. Christopher Wren, "World Banks Seeking Funds for Small Loans to the Poor," *New York Times,* July 17, 1995; Lise Adams, Anna Awimbo, Nathanael Goldberg, Cristina Sanchez, "Empowering Women with Microcredit: 2000 Microcredit Summit Campaign Report" (http://www.microcreditsummit.org/campaigns/report00.html), 2000. For a skeptical look at the Grameen Bank model, see Gina Neff, "Microcredit, Microresults," *Left Business Observer,* no. 74, October, 1996.

121. A telling example is the controversy within the World Bank over preparation of the bank's 2000 *World Development Report.* The first draft of the report, prepared under the direction of bank official Ravi Kanbur, came under fire from within the agency for its alleged "antigrowth" bias and its emphasis on empowering the poor. A second draft was revised to correct these ostensible flaws. Kanbur subsequently resigned from the bank ("The Washington Dissensus," *The Economist,* June 24, 2000, 89).

122. "Foreign Aid: The Kindness of Strangers"; Steven Holmes, "State Department Seeks Funds of Other Agencies," *New York Times,* November 11, 1993; "U.S. Agency for Development Plans to Cut Aid to 35 Nations," *New York Times,* November 20, 1993; Andrew Cohen, "Clinton Doctrine: The Help That Hurts," *The Progressive,* January 1994; "Creating a New USAID" and "USAID Mission Closeouts," AID Fact Sheet, 1995.

123. Steven Greenhouse, "Foreign Aid and G.O.P.: Deep Cuts," *New York Times,* December 21, 1994; and Paul Lewis, "Rubin Says World Economy in 'a Pause,'" *New York Times,* October 4, 1995.

124. "Measuring Up for Aid," *The Economist,* January 8, 2000, 44.

125. "Foreign Aid: The Kindness of Strangers," 19; "Least Developed Countries Report," UNCTAD press release, October 12, 2000; World Food Program, "World Food Programme."

126. USAID press release, "Testimony by J. Brady Anderson, Administrator, USAID," House International Relations Committee, March 15, 2000 (http://www.usaid.gov/about/usaidhist.html), accessed May 30, 2001.

127. Paul Lewis, "Poorest Countries Seek Increases in Aid."

128. Roger Riddell, "Aid in the 21st Century," Discussion Paper Series, Office of Development Studies, United Nations Development Program, 14.

129. For data on Japanese aid, see Row-ley, "Flush with Funds," and Row-ley, "On Toyko's Terms," *Far Eastern Economic Review,* March 9, 1989, 78. More extended treatments include Shafiqul Islam (ed.), *Yen for Development: Japanese Foreign Aid and the Politics of Burden-Sharing,* New York: Council on Foreign Relations Press, 1991; Bruce M. Koppel and Robert M. Orr, Jr. (eds.), *Japan's Foreign Aid: Power and Policy in a New*

Era, Boulder, Colo.: Westview Press, 1993; Margee M. Ensign, *Doing Good or Doing Well? Japan's Foreign Aid Program,* New York: Columbia University Press, 1992.

130. United Nations Development Program, *Human Development Report,* 1994, New York: Oxford University Press, 1994, 167.

131. "Foreign Aid: Stingy Sam," 26.

132. 132. *World Bank, Assessing Aid,* 8.

ANNOTATED BIBLIOGRAPHY

Robert L. Ayres. *Banking on the Poor: The World Bank and World Poverty.* Cambridge: MIT Press, 1983. A detailed examination of the World Bank's poverty lending programs during the 1970s.

P. T. Bauer. *Reality and Rhetoric: Studies in the Economics of Development.* Cambridge: Harvard University Press, 1984. Chapters 3 and 4 present a conservative critique of foreign aid.

Edward Clay and Olav Stoke (eds.). *Food Aid Reconsidered: Assessing the Impact on Third World Countries.* London: Frank Cass, 1991. A collection of essays, mostly case studies, on the effects of food aid.

Robert Cassen and Associates. *Does Aid Work?* 2nd Ed. Oxford, England: Clarendon Press, 1994. A detailed, thorough, and balanced effort to measure the contributions of foreign aid to Third World development and poverty reduction.

Kevin Danaher (ed.). *50 Years Is Enough: The Case against the World Bank and the International Monetary Fund.* Boston: South End Press, 1994. A collection of short essays that, taken together, offer an impassioned critique and condemnation of the policies and effects of the world's two largest multilateral financial organizations.

Jonathan Fox and L. David Brown (eds.). *The Struggle for Accountability: The World Bank, NGOs and Grassroots*

Movements. Cambridge: MIT Press, 1998. A collection of essays examining the relationship between the World Bank and grassroots nongovernmental organizations.

Graham Hancock. *Lords of Poverty: The Power, Prestige and Corruption of the International Aid Business.* New York: Atlantic Monthly Press, 1989. A biting critique of foreign aid written by a journalist with extensive experience in the Third World. Criticizes the hypocrisy and ineffectiveness of the foreign aid bureaucracy.

Theresa Hayter and Catherine Watson. *Aid: Rhetoric and Reality.* London: Pluto Press, 1985. A radical critique of foreign aid.

Stephen Hellinger, Douglas Hellinger, and Fred M. O'Regan. *Aid for Just Development: Report on the Future of Foreign Assistance.* Boulder, Colo.: Lynne Rienner, 1988. Presents proposals for reforming foreign aid.

Carol Lancaster. *Transforming Foreign Aid: United States Assistance in the 21st Century.* Washington, D.C.: Institute for International Economics, 2000. Examines recent reforms in U.S. foreign aid and trends in thinking about the future direction of foreign assistance.

David Lumsdaine. *Moral Vision in International Politics: The Foreign Aid Regime, 1949–1989.* Princeton, N.J.: Princeton University Press, 1993. A unique book. Lumsdaine argues that foreign aid has been chiefly motivated by altruism rather than self-interest and that the humanitarian thrust of aid has become stronger over time. Aid is submitted as an illustration that morality does matter in international affairs.

Michael Maren. *The Road to Hell: The Ravaging Effects of Foreign Aid and International Charity*. New York: Free Press, 1997. An angry denunciation of the ineffectiveness of international relief aid by a former aid field-worker. Focuses on international efforts to relieve famine in Somalia in the early 1990s.

Paul Mosley, Jane Harrigan, and John Toye. *Aid and Power: Policy-Based Lending* (2 vols.). New York: Routledge, 1991. A sophisticated and comprehensive history, analysis, and evaluation of the World Bank's shift to policy-based lending during the 1980s. The first volume examines the rationale and goals of policy-based lending, using quantitative data; the second examines various country cases.

Judith Tendler. *Inside Foreign Aid*. Baltimore: Johns Hopkins University Press, 1975. Although dated, Tendler's book continues to offer important insights into how bureaucratic factors influence and hamper the performance of foreign aid agencies.

Sarah Tisch and Michael Wallace. *Dilemmas of Development Assistance: The What, Why and Who of Foreign Aid*. Boulder, Colo.: Westview Press, 1994. A basic primer on foreign aid.

Robert Wood. *From Marshall Plan to Debt Crisis: Foreign Aid and Development Choices in the World Economy*. Berkeley and Los Angeles: University of California Press, 1986. A theoretical and empirical examination of the post–World War II foreign aid system. Links foreign aid and the debt crisis with an approach drawing upon both dependency theory and regime analysis.

World Bank. *Assessing Aid: What Works, What Doesn't and Why*. World Bank Policy Research Report. Oxford, England: Oxford University Press, 1998. Lessons for effective development aid from the World Bank's perspective. Argues that foreign assistance can work only in cases where it is married with good policies, strong institutions, and innovative ideas.

Robert Zimmerman. *Dollars, Diplomacy, and Dependency: Dilemmas of U.S. Economic Aid*. Boulder, Colo.: Westview Press, 1993. A balanced assessment of U.S. foreign aid written by a former aid official.

11

❖

Multinational Corporations in the Third World

The growth of the multinational corporation (MNC) is one of the most revolutionary and controversial phenomena in the development of the world economy during this century. MNCs are business firms that own or control production in more than one country. In practice, the largest MNCs orchestrate an ensemble of investments scattered across dozens of countries. Tied together by a vast communications web, these firms match various corporate functions, such as research and development, production, and marketing, with locales around the globe that feature the right mix of necessary ingredients, whether these be the skills and wage rates of local labor, the tax and regulatory policies of governments, the availability of needed infrastructure, or the supply of natural resources.[1] The sheer size of many MNCs, combined with their economic efficiency and international mobility, not only provides such firms with a key place in the world economy but also endows them with considerable political power and influence.

In recent decades, MNCs have expanded in numbers, size, and economic clout. Between 1980 and 1997, global foreign direct investment (FDI) grew at an annual rate of 13 percent, compared with 7 percent per year for exports. In 1999, total FDI outflows from developed countries reached $595 billion. The number of firms worldwide that engage in FDI has more than tripled over the past three decades. By 1997, 54,000 parent MNCs controlled 449,000 foreign affiliates around the world representing an overall investment valued at $3.4

trillion. The world's 200 largest corporations now account for more than 25 percent of all global economic activity. U.S. MNCs earn twice as much in revenue from manufacturing operations abroad as from exports. Indeed, one-third of all world trade takes place on an intrafirm basis—among different units of the same global company. The yearly sales of the largest MNCs dwarf the annual GNPs of a vast majority of Third World countries, and the annual sales of the world's largest MNCs exceed the combined national incomes of 182 countries. Among the 200 largest MNCs, 62 are based in Japan, 53 in the United States, and 23 in Germany. Only 2 of the top 200 are headquartered in the developing world.[2]

The large-scale movement of modern foreign direct investment to the Third World dates from the turn of the last century. The earliest MNCs to invest in the developing countries focused on agricultural goods and the extraction of raw materials. The demands of rapidly growing Northern industries as well as the ris-ing affluence of European and North American consumers created a healthy market for Southern resources and cash crops. Very little Northern investment in the South flowed into manufacturing at this stage. In 1914, for instance, mining, oil, and agriculture accounted for 70 percent of all U.S. FDI located in develop-ing countries, whereas manufacturing amounted to only 3 percent.[3]

The composition of FDI in the Third World began to change during the interwar period. U.S. firms, in particular, established growing numbers of manufacturing subsidiaries in Latin America. By 1939 Latin America was the home of 200 foreign-owned manufacturing operations, two-thirds of the total for all developing countries.[4] Yet foreign investment in Third World manufac-turing did not really take off until after World War II. Today the subsidiaries of Northern-owned MNCs account for substantial shares of invested capital, employment, and output in the manufacturing sectors of most Third World countries. Their dominance is greatest in the most technologically advanced types of products and manufacturing processes.

Nevertheless, despite growth in the absolute levels of foreign investment in the South, FDI has expanded even more quickly in the North. On the eve of World War I, FDI located in the developing countries accounted for 60 per-cent of the total worldwide. By the early 1960s, the Third World share of FDI had fallen to one-third. This proportion fell further, to roughly one-quarter, in the mid-1980s.[5] By this latter period, over one-half of all U.S. FDI was lo-cated in only five developed countries (Britain, Canada, Germany, Switzer-land, and the Netherlands).[6]

The relative significance of FDI to Third World economies has varied considerably over time. MNC investment in the South grew from an annual average of $2.6 billion during 1967–1969 to $12.8 billion in 1979–1981. Largely due to rising levels of commercial bank lending, however, the share of FDI in overall private financial flows to the Third World declined from over 50 percent in 1970 to 20 percent in 1985. Indeed, levels of new foreign in-vestment fell absolutely during the early 1980s, dropping to an annual average of roughly $10 billion. A modest turnaround began in 1986 as the flow of FDI to developing countries increased to $12.5 billion. During the same year,

FDI again accounted for almost 50 percent of private financial flows. This was largely due, however, to a collapse in bank lending to the Third World.[7]

The 1990s witnessed a major resurgence in FDI flows to the Third World, reaching $163 billion in 1997. If portfolio investment, in the form of stocks and bonds (see Chapter 12 for a discussion of portfolio investment), and bank lending are included, total net private investment flows from North to South reached $299 billion in 1997. The South's share of overall FDI inflows also increased, to 37 percent in 1997. Yet these foreign investments are highly concentrated in a handful of relatively prosperous Southern countries. In 1998, for example, 10 countries accounted for 70 percent of all FDI flows to the developing world. The least-developed countries, by contrast, receive a combined share of only one-half of 1 percent of total global FDI.[8]

This revival of FDI flows to the Third World has been prompted by a variety of factors: falling interest rates in the North, the loosening of regulations on foreign investments in the South, rapid economic growth rates in some of the principal host countries, the emergence of debt–equity swaps as a tool for transforming Third World debt into equity investments, and new opportunities to purchase previously state-owned firms recently privatized by Third World governments.

MOTIVES FOR FOREIGN DIRECT INVESTMENT IN THE THIRD WORLD

Northern firms have a variety of motives for investing in Third World countries. Some seek access to Southern resources. Extractive industries, such as mining, oil, or timber, are attracted by the presence of raw materials or mineral deposits. Many Southern countries, by virtue of their climate or geography, are particularly well suited to the production of cash crops desired in the North, such as sugar, coffee, cocoa, or tropical fruits. Northern agribusiness firms invest in the production, processing, and packaging of such agricultural commodities in the South.

Manufacturing firms have greater freedom over where they locate their investments than do natural resource producers. The former often have a choice between servicing foreign markets through export or foreign investment. Decisions to invest in the Third World are influenced both by competitive pressures in particular industries and by the incentives created by government policies. One school of thought, known as product life-cycle theory, suggests that firms that gain a monopoly position as a result of successful innovation will move abroad in search of new markets or lower costs as a means of preserving higher-than-normal profits after imitation has begun to erode their initial advantage over rivals at home.[9]

Most manufacturing FDI in the Third World produces commodities aimed at the local market. This sort of investment is most common in the larger, more prosperous Southern countries that have sizable and therefore attractive consumer bases. MNCs may decide to produce in such countries rather than export in order to better adjust to local tastes or to take advantage of lower labor or capital costs.

Often, however, the decision to invest abroad is prompted by the necessity of jumping protectionist barriers to gain access to Third World markets. Southern governments may erect tariffs or other sorts of barriers precisely to discourage imports while encouraging local production of the protected goods. The aim of this strategy, often referred to as import substitution, is to spur industrialization. Many MNCs have discovered ways to benefit from such policies. A single large factory can service the entire local demand for a given product in many Third World countries. Thus the first foreign firm to gain entry can profit handsomely. Freed from competition due to the umbrella of protection and the limited size of the domestic market, the local subsidiary of the MNC can establish an effective monopoly, allowing it to charge higher prices and earn greater-than-normal profits. This very fact has engendered local resentment toward foreign firms.

For some firms, the primary incentive to invest in the Third World is to escape environmental regulations or higher taxes in their home country. Indeed, those Southern countries with a particularly urgent need for foreign investment have often explicitly molded their tax and regulatory policies to attract the interest of Northern multinationals.

Finally, foreign-owned assembly operations have been established in many Third World countries in order to take advantage of the low wage rates characteristic of Southern labor markets. Typically, products assembled in such factories are exported back to Northern markets, where they can be priced competitively vis-à-vis similar goods produced by other firms with more expensive Northern labor.

THE BENEFITS OF FOREIGN DIRECT INVESTMENT TO THIRD WORLD HOST COUNTRIES

Our primary concern in this chapter is with the impact of foreign direct investment on the Third World and the relationship between MNCs and host countries. Considerable debate surrounds these topics. Defenders of MNCs argue that FDI stimulates economic growth and development. MNCs augment scarce local resources and bring with them a package of assets that can seldom be matched by indigenous firms.[10] Elements of this package include:

Capital

Many Third World countries are characterized by low rates of domestic savings. As a result, their economies are dependent upon external capital flows to finance new investment. FDI offers one means by which scarce local capital can be supplemented. To be sure, MNCs demand a price for injecting fresh capital into the host country's economy. Specifically, foreign investors prefer to repatriate a large portion of the profits they earn abroad. Yet the terms of FDI often compare favorably with those accompanying other sources of external financing. Commercial loans from Northern banks, for instance, carry interest charges that must be paid regardless of whether the local investment they finance proves profitable. In contrast, although MNCs share in the benefits from FDI, they also bear much of the risk. If one of its Third World subsidiaries loses money, an MNC will find that there are no profits to repatriate. Indeed, the headquarters of the firm may well choose to inject new capital into the failing subsidiary in an attempt to turn the operation around and salvage its initial investment. FDI also offers certain advantages over foreign aid. Although foreign assistance may be provided on favorable financial terms, it often comes with political strings attached, whether implicit or explicit. This is seldom the case for FDI.

Technology

Although some Third World countries have managed to establish impressively modern manufacturing sectors, the vast majority of the new technology created worldwide still originates in the laboratories and universities of the North. Indeed, MNCs account for 80 percent of all civilian research and development expenditures worldwide.[11] MNCs provide one mechanism by which Northern technology is transferred to the Third World. MNCs tend to invest in the most technologically advanced sectors of Third World economies, supplying goods and services that are beyond the technological capacity of local firms to produce efficiently. MNCs also aid in technological diffusion through means such as licensing technology to other firms or passing along knowledge, skills, and techniques to local partners through joint ventures.

Management Expertise

The Third World subsidiaries of MNCs often organize production more efficiently than do local firms due to superior management skills and techniques. MNCs possess great experience in managing large-scale enterprises. Branch plant managers can draw upon the vast storehouse of information and expertise contained within the corporation as a whole. Knowledge of modern management methods is spread through the training of indigenous personnel, whose representation in the ranks of management typically grows at the expense of expatriates the longer the MNC subsidiary is in place.

Marketing Networks

Even where local firms can match MNCs in price and product quality, they may lack easy access to the extensive foreign marketing networks available to Northern firms. MNCs often possess long-standing relationships with, or even control over, Northern wholesale and retail outlets, enjoy greater information about market demand and consumer tastes, and command larger advertising resources.

THE COSTS OF FOREIGN DIRECT
INVESTMENT TO THIRD WORLD
HOST COUNTRIES

Critics argue that the economic and political costs of FDI often outweigh the benefits.[12] Many criticisms center around differences between foreign and domestic firms and the ways they do business.

MNCs are accused of earning excessive profits in Third World countries, made possible by their oligopoly position in local economies.[13] The largest proportion of these profits is repatriated to shareholders in the firm's country of origin rather than reinvested locally. According to some studies, MNCs also overcharge for technology transfers to their own subsidiaries and rely more heavily upon imported parts and machinery than do domestic firms. Each of these practices tends to reflect negatively in the host country's balance of payments position.

Critics contend that MNCs often borrow from the already scarce supply of local capital rather than bring new investment funds into the country. Because of their size and resources, foreign firms typically receive preferential terms from local banks when borrowing money, as compared with local firms. Another criticism is that MNCs discourage local entrepreneurship by often entering a country through the acquisition of an existing Third World firm or using superior resources to drive native competitors out of business.

Third World governments particularly object to a common MNC practice known as "transfer pricing." MNCs resort to this technique in an attempt to lower their overall tax burden or to evade restrictions on the repatriation of profits. Transfer pricing is essentially an accounting practice applied to intrafirm trade. Different branches or subsidiaries of the same firm, located in different countries, often exchange goods. A U.S.-based manufacturer, for instance, might produce parts in a factory located in Texas but ship these parts to a plant in Mexico for assembly. In turn, the assembled product is transported back to the United States for final sale. The price that the home firm charges the Mexican subsidiary for the parts or that the subsidiary charges the home firm for the assembled product is essentially arbitrary because these transactions take place within the same company and are not exposed to market forces. If, let us say, Mexico imposes a higher tax on corporate profits than does the United States, then the MNC can lower its overall tax bill by overpricing the parts shipped to Mexico while underpricing the assembled products that are "sold" back to the home firm in the United States. By manipulating the prices on intrafirm trade in this way, the Mexican subsidiary will show little profit on its books, thus avoiding the high Mexican tax rate, while the profit of the home firm will be artificially boosted—allowing it to be taxed at the low U.S. rate. This sort of practice is hard to detect because it is difficult to know what the products might have sold for in arm's-length transactions among independent firms. Because most Third World countries tax the profits of foreign corporations at relatively high rates, they are often targets of transfer pricing schemes and suffer a loss of potential tax revenue as a result.

Some forms of FDI represent attempts to export pollution from Northern countries, where environmental enforcement is stringent, or to exploit reserves of cheap labor. In Ilo, Peru, for instance, local villagers suffer from serious respiratory and other health problems stemming from the air and water pollution produced by a nearby copper smelter plant owned by three large American corporations. The plant emits up to 2,000 tons of sulfur dioxide into the air each day—10 to 15 times the legal levels for similar operations in the United States—as well as streams of toxic wastes that make their way into the local water supply.[14]

Mexico is host to 4,500 product assembly plants located along the border, a number that has doubled since 1994. Called *maquiladoras,* one-half of these plants are U.S.-owned, and the majority of their output is shipped to U.S. markets. In total, the *maquiladora* sector employs 1 million Mexicans and generates $10 billion per year in foreign exchange for the Mexican economy. Some of the U.S.-owned plants relocated to Mexico to take advantage of lax Mexican environmental laws and to break free of stricter regulations in the United States. A study by the American National Toxic Campaign found that of 23 such factories sampled, 17 were responsible for significant toxic waste discharges. Compared with nearby San Diego, California, Tijuana's waste water contains ten times more chromium, eight times more nickel, and three times more copper. Much of Southern California's furniture industry has moved across the border to escape severe air pollution controls on solvent emissions.

Mexico has recently taken steps to tighten its environmental laws and to crack down on polluters, but its enforcement mechanisms remain inadequate. Only 15 environmental inspectors are available for the entire state of Chihuahua, which includes the major city of Juarez. Mexico's single landfill site for the disposal of toxic wastes is capable of handling only a small fraction of the country's toxic waste production. Most of the rest is dumped illegally, despite laws mandating that toxic wastes be returned to the country from which the raw materials originated. The NAFTA side agreement between the United States and Mexico set up the Commission for Environmental Cooperation. The commission may investigate complaints by citizens that environmental laws in their own country are being ignored, but its recommendations are not binding on governments.

In addition to the environmental problems associated with *maquiladoras,* critics point out that the jobs created through these factories are extremely low paying and that work conditions as well as health and safety standards are far below those in the United States. The factory cities that have mushroomed along the border in recent years have proven unable to add new infrastructure fast enough to keep up with growing populations. Eighteen percent of Mexican border towns have no drinking water, 30 percent have no sewage treatment, and 43 percent have insufficient garbage disposal. Moreover, *maquiladoras* have developed few backward linkages to the rest of the Mexican economy. Of the $23 billion in physical inputs consumed by the *maquiladora* industries yearly, only 2 percent is supplied by Mexican sources.[15]

FDI also carries political risks. MNCs may appeal to their home government to exert pressure on a host state when disputes arise. The Hickenlooper Amendment, passed by the U.S. Congress in 1962, requires that aid be denied to countries that nationalize the assets of U.S. corporations without prompt and adequate compensation. The law has been applied, or its use threatened, on several occasions. More dramatically, the United States, through the use of CIA covert operations and economic pressure, took part in the overthrow of governments in Iran (1953), Guatemala (1954), and Chile (1973) after the assets of firms from the United States and other Northern countries were nationalized. Although other factors influenced these decisions, U.S. officials' desire to defend U.S. corporate interests abroad played an important role in all three instances.

A BARGAINING FRAMEWORK
FOR ANALYZING MNC-HOST
COUNTRY RELATIONS

Are MNCs a boon or a burden to Third World host countries? The answer is more complex than either of the two perspectives just outlined would suggest. Whether the benefits of FDI outweigh the costs depends substantially upon the balance of bargaining power between the firm and the host state. This bargaining relationship determines whether a state will have the capacity to control the activities of foreign investors and thus limit negative impacts. In this section, we first review the various types of regulation that Third World states have attempted to impose upon MNCs in the past. We then examine the sources of bargaining power available to each party.

Regulating MNC Behavior

During the 1970s, in particular, Third World states adopted a variety of regulations designed to control and channel the activities of MNCs. Many countries exclude foreign direct investment in certain crucial sectors of the economy such as public utilities, mining, steel, retailing, insurance, and banking. In some cases, foreign investors are required to form joint ventures providing majority control to local partners. A number of Latin American countries limit profit repatriation and technology payments by foreign-owned subsidiaries. Requirements that a stated percentage of production must be exported are common. Some countries require that indigenous labor be hired into middle- and upper-level management positions. Several countries have placed limits on MNC access to local capital markets in an effort to encourage greater contributions of external financing for new investments. Finally, attempts have been made to encourage MNC subsidiaries to carry out local research and development.[16]

These controls have been imposed most successfully by the larger, more prosperous Third World countries, which are in a relatively strong position to bargain over the terms of FDI. In addition to the risk that demanding regulations will simply scare away foreign investors, smaller, less-developed countries have a more difficult time enforcing investment rules.

Indeed, impressively strict regulations designed to enhance local control often have surprisingly little effect on MNC operations in practice.[17] Consider the common stipulation that MNCs must enter into joint ventures providing majority ownership to local partners. Compliance with this regulation is often achieved through fictitious means. A foreign firm will simply lend to the local partner the capital needed to acquire majority ownership. Or the original equity investment in the project is held artificially low so as to make it possible for the local partner to come up with the required money. The enterprise then funds its operations through debt rather than equity, often borrowing funds from the parent company of the foreign partner. These sorts of nominal shareholding arrangements create the illusion, without the reality, of a large local stake in the enterprise.

Even where local partners legitimately put up the majority of capital to fund a project, they seldom exercise real control. The MNC typically provides raw materials, equipment, spare parts, financing, technology, managerial skills, and marketing services. Because the keys to the success of the enterprise are in the hands of the foreign partner, so is effective control over how it is run. Foreign control may in fact be formalized in basic agreements concluded at the outset of the venture that reserve key functions to the MNC.

Many countries attempt to ensure that MNCs hire, train, and promote local workers into management positions or require that a certain proportion of the final product consist of locally produced parts. Yet the first restriction is often waived when foreign subsidiaries attest that people with the requisite skills and experience are not available locally. In some cases, local managers are hired but given little responsibility. Local-content rules can be circumvented by using creative accounting to inflate the value of the portion of the overall product accounted for by local inputs.

The Andean Pact represents one attempt to overcome the poor bargaining position of small countries. In December 1970 Bolivia, Colombia, Chile, Ecuador, and Peru (Venezuela was added in 1973; Chile abandoned the group in 1976) announced Decision 24—an agreement on "common treatment for foreign capital, trademarks, patents, licensing agreement, and royalties." This agreement imposed a common set of new regulations on MNCs operating in pact countries. These regulations included the exclusion of FDI from certain economic sectors, limits on profit repatriation and access to local lending, a phased-in reduction of foreign ownership in MNC affiliates to a maximum of 49 percent, and controls on technology transfer and royalty payments. The impact of these regulations has been mixed. Technology payments were rene-gotiated downward after implementation of the pact, and local participation in MNC operations increased. Due to incomplete data, however, the effect of Decision 24 on flows of new FDI is difficult to judge with precision. Invest-ments by U.S. MNCs in pact countries continued to increase during the late 1970s, but at a slower pace than in the rest of Latin America.[18]

The difficulty with national, or even regional, controls is that MNCs can reallocate their investment flows toward countries that offer less interference. Thus many Third World countries have long called for a strict, binding global code of conduct for MNCs.[19] Northern countries, however, have resisted these demands. Instead, in 1976 the Organization for Economic Cooperation and Development (OECD) sponsored a weaker, voluntary code that lacked Third World approval.[20] In the late 1980s, negotiations over international reg-ulation of MNC activities resumed under the auspices of the United Nations Center on Transnational Corporations (UNCTC). After several years of North-South stalemate, however, these negotiations were quietly set aside, and the UNCTC was itself disbanded.

A very different effort during the 1990s to forge global rules for interna-tional investment also ended in failure. Northern governments and corpora-tions pressed in the mid-1990s for a new accord to be labeled the Multilateral Agreement on Investment (MAI). The principal purpose of the MAI was to insure greater respect for corporate property rights in host countries and to gain broad acceptance of the principle that foreign corporations should be regulated according to the same rules that apply to locally owned firms. The MAI was vigorously opposed by a coalition of nongovernmental organizations (NGOs) which believed that the proposed agreement would weaken the abil-ity of governments to regulate corporate behavior in the name of broader public interests. As a result of NGO opposition, along with unresolved differ-ences between the United States and some European governments, the MAI negotiations were allowed to lapse without success in 1998.[21]

In the wake of the collapse of the MAI negotiations, the OECD updated its voluntary code of conduct for MNCs after extensive consultation with a group of 75 environmental and human rights NGOs. The revised code sets new labor and environmental standards, as called for by many critics of corpo-rate behavior. Although NGOs continued to press for a binding rather than voluntary code, a spokesperson for the NGO coalition called the new rules "a first step in the right direction of achieving true corporate accountability."[22]

THE DETERMINANTS OF RELATIVE
BARGAINING POWER

MNCs and Third World states are engaged in an interdependent relationship. Each party wants something from the other. The MNC's principal concern is to maximize profits. To accomplish this, it must gain access to the resources, markets, and/or cheap labor of the Third World country where an investment opportunity presents itself. The goals of the host state are diverse. Third World political leaders are attracted to the jobs, skills, output, technology, and global marketing power that MNCs offer.

Although the goals and interests of the two parties are potentially compatible, the MNC's desire to maximize profits may, as we have seen, lead it to engage in practices that reduce the benefits accruing to the host country. Third World countries are therefore often inclined to regulate and control MNC behavior so as to maximize host countries' share of benefits from the investment.

The host country's ability to successfully set the terms under which foreign investors do business in that country is constrained by its relative bargaining power. The country's principal bargaining advantage is its capacity to control access to the country and to exert legal control over foreign business operations after an investment has been made. The MNC, however, is far from helpless. Its power derives both from the package of assets it has to offer the host country and from its mobility. If the host state drives too hard a bargain, imposing regulations so onerous as to substantially erode the profit-making potential of foreign-owned subsidiaries, MNCs may take their business elsewhere or, less drastically, simply devise ways of evading regulations.

The balance of bargaining power between foreign firms and host countries may vary according to (1) the characteristics of the host country, (2) the characteristics of the investment, and (3) changes in the international economic environment.[23] We review each of these factors in the following sections.

Characteristics of the Host Country

Host countries possessing characteristics that render them attractive to foreign investors are likely to find themselves in a relatively strong bargaining position. The more lucrative the investment, the more likely it is to be made in spite of heavy host state regulation. Thus Third World countries with large domestic markets, skilled and disciplined work forces, bountiful natural resources, and well-developed infrastructures can afford to drive hard bargains with foreign firms that, presumably, will be eager to gain access to the country and its many economic opportunities.

The host country's position is also strengthened to the extent that it has available alternatives to foreign investment. If, for instance, the country already possesses a strong industrial structure, whether public or private, or is able to accumulate capital locally due to a high domestic savings rate, then its dependence on FDI is lessened. The price that the host state can demand of foreign investors for the right of entry is likely to go up.

Finally, states with large, sophisticated, and honest bureaucracies will be in a better position to bargain on an equal basis with highly skilled MNC negotiators. They will also possess a greater capacity to gather critical information, monitor MNC behavior, and enforce relevant laws and regulations.

Some Third World countries, such as Brazil, Mexico, and South Korea, possess many, though not all, of these characteristics. Yet most Southern countries lack, in varying degrees, a considerable number of the crucial characteristics that might place them in a favorable bargaining position with foreign firms.

Characteristics of the Investment

The bargaining relationship between governments and firms may vary across different investment projects within the same country. Some types of industry are more easily regulated than others. Bargaining leverage shifts to the host state when projects involve well-known and slowly changing technologies. In such cases, it is well within the capacity of state-or locally owned private firms to manage the production facility in question or to establish competing projects. Low-technology foreign investment is therefore often subject to heavy regulation, intense local competition, or even outright nationalization.

Investment projects resting upon more sophisticated or rapidly changing technology are less vulnerable to state demands. In these cases, the local skills and knowledge needed to manage the project or to create competitive local alternatives may not exist. Moreover, the success of such ventures depends upon continuous infusions of new technology from the home firm. This increases the host state's dependence upon a foreign firm and places the latter in a strong bargaining position.

Much the same logic applies with respect to the foreign marketing requirements associated with production for export. Products marketed through complex networks, especially when the latter are controlled by the multinationals themselves, may require the cooperation of foreign firms if they are to be exported successfully. When products can be more readily sold abroad by state-or locally owned private firms, it is easier for Third World governments to escape dependence on foreign capital and to assert control over local production.

Capital-intensive projects typically require large fixed investments in factories and machinery. After these are in place, the foreign firm is hostage to state control due to high sunk costs. Only continued production and sales will allow the firm to recoup its sizable initial outlay. Where fixed investment is low, however, a firm can more easily close up shop and relocate to a different country should state demands prove intolerable. Thus the size of the initial investment influences relative bargaining power.

Related to this point is the fact that potential foreign investors have greater bargaining power before a project is established than after. Knowing that the host state may be eager for additional investment, the firm will seek explicit pledges of favorable treatment prior to committing to a project. MNCs often attempt to play countries off against one another in an effort to strike the best and most reliable deal. After the project is in place, however, the firm's threat to relocate becomes less credible, and further concessions will be difficult to obtain. Indeed, Third World states often seek to alter the original bargain in their own favor.

In general, Third World bargaining power has been greatest with respect to mining and raw materials investments. These projects typically involve well-known and slowly changing technologies, simple marketing requirements, and high fixed investments. Owing to these factors, many foreign-owned extractive operations were nationalized by Third World governments during the 1970s.

MNCs usually have greater leverage in manufacturing industries, especially those involving sophisticated and changeable technologies, complex foreign marketing requirements, and low fixed investments. Indeed, it is in just such industrial sectors that the concentration of MNC ownership is highest in the Third World.

Changes in the International Economic Environment

The balance of bargaining power between states and firms can vary over time due to a changing international economic environment. During the 1970s, for instance, external conditions tended to strengthen Third World states relative to MNCs. Growing competition among MNCs made it easier for governments to play firms off against one another in an attempt to achieve a more favorable bargain. In particular, previously dominant U.S. firms now faced growing competition from European and Japanese MNCs. After falling from a high of over 60 percent during the 1960s, the U.S. share of the total world stock of foreign direct investment declined further, from 46 percent in 1980 to 25 percent in 1993. Although the United States accounted for 31 percent of new FDI flows from 1980 through 1984, this proportion fell to 17 percent from 1985 through 1989.[24] Moreover, European and Japanese firms often proved more tolerant of state regulation than did U.S. corporations.

Another international economic factor that favored Third World states during the seventies was the growing availability of commercial bank lending. This provided an alternative source of capital and lessened Third World dependence upon FDI. Able to do without MNCs more easily, governments of developing countries tightened regulations and funneled borrowed funds into state-owned corporations that sometimes served as direct competitors to existing foreign firms.

Finally, the seventies were a time of relative growth and prosperity for many Third World countries. Manufacturing exports expanded rapidly. Moreover, world prices for raw material commodities were high during the first half of the decade. The wave of Third World nationalizations of foreign investments in extractive industries was largely prompted by host state efforts to ensure that the benefits of these soaring prices would be captured locally rather than carried abroad in the repatriated profits of MNCs.[25]

These favorable conditions changed rapidly during the 1980s. A Northern recession led to declines in both Southern manufacturing exports and commodity prices. These, combined with higher oil prices and rising interest rates, led to a financial squeeze that culminated in the Third World debt crisis. As many countries teetered on the brink of insolvency, Northern banks drastically contracted their lending operations in the Third World.

Suddenly, many Third World countries came to view increased flows of FDI as one of the few available options that might allow them to sustain economic growth while simultaneously digging their way out from under a mountain of debt. Yet just when it was most needed, flows of FDI to the South entered a period of absolute decline. This was prompted in part by the dire economic circumstances in most Third World countries, but it was also a result of the strict regulations and controls that many MNCs confronted in developing nations.

Faced with an unfavorable international economic environment and chastened by declining investment flows, most Third World states as the eighties progressed were led by their weakened bargaining position to loosen controls on foreign investment. Mexico entirely revamped its foreign investment codes, removing many of the restrictions imposed during the seventies. Venezuela has done the same and has recently decided to invite back many of the same international oil companies whose assets it nationalized in 1976 to help with the exploitation of the Orinoco Belt.[26] Many developing nations, especially in Asia, now offer special incentives to MNCs willing to set up assembly operations in so-called export-processing zones. Governments seek to attract export-oriented production by offering tax, tariff, and regulatory concessions to foreign firms that agree to establish factories in these special areas.[27] Other common elements of deregulation include guarantees of unrestricted profit repatriation, tax breaks, special electrical rates, the removal of export and local-input requirements, and streamlined approval procedures.

These relaxed controls and new incentives have contributed to the renewed interest of multinational corporations in the Third World and have stimulated new investment flows. They also reflect, however, the weakened bargaining positions that most Third World states possess vis-à-vis foreign firms. The terms of the typical investment deal have swung decidedly in favor of the latter during the past two decades.

This bargaining framework approach to understanding the relationship between host states and foreign firms offers considerable advantages over treatments that exaggerate either the virtues or the villainy of MNCs in the Third World. Southern states can potentially influence the balance between the costs and benefits of FDI by setting the terms under which the subsidiaries of MNCs must operate. Whether a given government can do so effectively without discouraging desired flows of investment depends upon the relative bargaining strengths of the state and the firm. This, in turn, varies across countries and industries as well as across time.

A bargaining approach does, however, contain one major drawback. This sort of analysis is based upon the assumption that state managers in developing societies are motivated only by the desire to serve the national interests of their own country. The primary goal of the political leadership is to maximize the economic welfare of the society as a whole through the bargains it strikes with foreign investors. In some cases, however, this is an unrealistic assumption. Some observers argue that, although political elites in Third World countries may sometimes possess the capability to bargain effectively with foreign corporations, they often lack the political will to do so.

This is most obviously the case when MNCs use their considerable resources to win favors through bribery and corruption. In one example, five nations banded in 1974 to form the Union of Banana Exporting Countries. Each government agreed to place an export tax on banana exports. One of the affected corporations, United Brands, paid a $1.25 million bribe to the Honduran minister of economics. In return, the Honduran government partially reneged on its agreement with other banana-exporting countries by cutting its export tax from 50 cents to 25—a move that would have saved United Brands $6 million to $7 million yearly. In this case, United Brands's efforts backfired. Unlike most such episodes, news of the deal leaked to the public, and the Honduran government was overthrown[28]

Northern governments have recently undertaken efforts to root out the nexus between foreign investment and corruption. In 1997, the 34 members of the OECD agreed upon a clean practices convention designed to curtail corporate bribery and corruption in their dealings with host country officials. As of mid-2000, however, only 18 of the 34 signatory countries had ratified the pact[29]

Corruption is not the only threat to host state autonomy. Some Third World elites maintain power in part through close military, economic, and political relationships with the home governments of local MNC affiliates. Vigorous efforts to control MNC activities may threaten to sour these relationships. One study, for instance, has found that the U.S. government regularly brings political and diplomatic pressure on host governments to win special consideration for U.S. firms seeking to invest in Southern countries.[30]

Conversely, political motives may sometimes prompt Third World leaders to adopt an overly restrictive stance toward MNCs, purposely discouraging investments that could bring considerable benefits to the country. This might be the case, for instance, when the legitimacy of a government rests upon its nationalist appeal. Under these circumstances, MNCs may provide convenient scapegoats, perhaps diverting attention from government responsibility for other pressing national problems. Finally, some Third World governments may be divided on the question of foreign investment and thus unable to adopt any consistent bargaining position.

These considerations suggest the need for caution in applying a bargaining analysis to host state-MNC relations. Nevertheless, considerable evidence suggests that host states have in fact proven eager, in most instances, to strike better deals with MNCs when their bargaining position so allows. The extremes of co-optation or destructive defiance appear the exceptions rather than the rule.

RECENT TRENDS IN MNC-HOST
COUNTRY RELATIONS

Several important trends are reshaping the nature of foreign investment in the Third World. The geographic locus of investment flows has shifted from Latin America and the Middle East to Asia. Three long-term shifts in the sectoral orientation of MNC activities in the Third World are also continuing.

Manufacturing investments are increasingly favored over those in the extractive industries, while, within the manufacturing sector, export-oriented production is growing faster than production for the domestic markets of the Southern host countries. Recently, however, FDI growth has been swiftest in the service sector of Third World economies. Finally, the terms of MNC entry into Third World countries are changing dramatically, with foreign firms increasingly shedding the risks of outright ownership in favor of more-limited and -indirect forms of involvement in the Third World.

East Asia's share of global foreign direct investment rose from 3 percent in 1987 to 22 percent in 1997.[31] China alone attracted $270 billion in FDI from 1992 to 1999, almost half of all FDI flowing to the developing world during that period.[32] The redirection of foreign direct investment toward East and Southeast Asia is both a response to and a partial source of the rapid economic growth rates experienced over the past three decades by many countries of the region, including China, South Korea, Singapore, Taiwan, Hong Kong, Thailand, Malaysia, and Indonesia.

The initial surge of FDI to East and Southeast Asia was led by large Japanese firms beginning in the mid-1980s. Japanese investment in the surrounding region was prompted in part by the accumulation of vast financial resources as a result of Japan's export successes. Japanese firms also sought low-cost manufacturing sites abroad as a way of compensating for increasing Japanese wage levels and the rise of the yen. Between 1985 and 1989 the flow of Japanese capital, including FDI, to other Asian economies grew sixfold in dollar terms. Japanese firms focused on countries with well-educated and disciplined workforces, such as Thailand and Malaysia.[33]

Although Japanese FDI to Asian countries slowed in the mid-1990s, the slack was picked up by American and European firms. The Asian financial crisis that began in 1997 dramatically curtailed bank lending and portfolio investment flows to that region and stymied economic growth for a time. Yet FDI flows to Asian countries fell only slightly during this period, reflecting the longer time horizon of MNCs as compared with stock and bond holders.[34]

Although Asia attracted the largest share of FDI among developing regions in the 1990s, other Southern countries have benefited from growing FDI flows, as well. Latin America attracted 14 percent of global FDI in 1997.[35] Brazil captured $31 billion in FDI in 1999, while Mexico and Argentina remained popular with investors, as well.[36]

In 1997, only 1 percent of global FDI was directed toward Africa, even though profit rates for FDI were higher there than in any other region of the world between 1991 and 1997. One factor discouraging more investment in Africa and elsewhere is the prevalence of violent conflict in many of the world's poorest countries. The U.S. State Department lists 74 countries in which the risks to physical security are high, while 34 countries were experiencing civil war or rebel insurgencies in 2000. In Algeria, for instance, international oil companies devote 8 to 9% of their local budgets to security for facilities and personnel. Despite these obstacles to foreign investment, average annual FDI flows to the world's 44 poorest countries tripled, from $1 billion for the 1987–1992 period to nearly $3 billion in 1998.[37]

The shift in the sectors targeted by foreign investors, from extractive industries to manufacturing and from production for domestic consumption to exports, is illustrated by data on U.S. MNC affiliates located in the Third World. Between 1950 and 1984 the share of U.S. Third World FDI located in extractive industries fell from over one-half to less than 40 percent, whereas the proportion accounted for by manufacturing rose from 15 percent to 37 percent.[38] The share of exports in the total sales of U.S. MNC subsidiaries in the South grew from 8.4 percent in 1966 to 18.1 percent in 1977 and has continued to rise.[39] In addition to the manufacturing export sector, multinational corporations have increasingly been attracted to the Southern service industries, including banking, insurance, transportation, shipping, tourism, construction, retail sales, advertising, and telecommunications. Service industries are likely to capture an increasing share of North-South investment flows over the coming decade.

Perhaps the most important trend in Third World host country-MNC relations during recent years has been the development of new, more flexible forms of investment.[40] Traditionally, foreign investment entered the Third World in the form of a tightly integrated package owned and controlled by the MNC. Elements of this package included capital, technology, managerial expertise, and marketing. Foreign investors typically resisted pressures from the host country to break up this package by allowing greater local control over various elements. Third World governments often responded by attempting to steer the behavior of foreign firms through the imposition of external legal and regulatory controls.

Out of these conflicting perspectives emerged a set of arrangements that satisfied neither party. Third World governments argued that foreign control over all aspects of investment concentrated too much economic power in foreign hands, especially in critical sectors; limited the spin-off of skills, technology, and other benefits to the rest of the local economy; and led to abuses such as those surveyed earlier in this chapter. MNCs, for their part, became increasingly frustrated by government regulations that raised costs, cut profits, and hemmed in their autonomy. The result was a standoff: governments resorted to more-extreme measures of control, such as outright nationalization, while MNCs increasingly steered clear of new commitments in the Third World.

In recent years, however, each side has begun to abandon previously rigid positions and to seek out more-cooperative arrangements designed to reconcile conflicting interests. As we have seen, Third World governments have dismantled many of the regulatory controls that previously served to discourage new foreign investment. MNCs, meanwhile, have largely abandoned their insistence on formal ownership and control over all phases of investment, thus removing one of the concerns that prompted Third World governments to impose onerous controls in the first place.

Although the older forms of MNC investment in the Third World persist, a host of new ventures involves foreign firms as limited partners in projects often initiated and largely controlled by Third World businesses or governments. Typically, foreign firms provide only those elements of the overall project that local participants can't provide for themselves. The once monolithic packaging of capital, technology, management, and marketing has given way to a new division of labor in which local and foreign partners perform different functions, depending upon the particular strengths they bring to the project.

These partnerships take many forms. In joint ventures, local and foreign firms team up to provide capital and management while dividing up profits. Or Third World firms may subcontract to provide components of a larger product or to carry out assembly operations for a foreign firm. In some cases, foreign firms provide the missing ingredients for a project that is predominantly controlled by Third World partners. For instance, a foreign firm may, in return for a fee, license technology to a Third World firm to be used in the production or design of a particular product. Foreign firms may also provide managers for a project that is locally owned. So-called turnkey contracts call for foreign firms to construct factories that are then turned over to a Third World firm for operation. Product-in-hand contracts are like turnkey contracts, except that the foreign partner also trains local managers in how to operate the plant. Finally, some Third World businesses act as franchisees, putting up the capital or paying royalties and providing management while the franchiser provides technology and trademarks along with direction in how the operation is to be run.

Malaysia's effort to develop a domestic automobile industry provides one example of the new flexibility in MNC-host country relations. The government forged a partnership with the Japanese firm Mitsubishi to produce a small economy car called the Proton. In return for one-third ownership, Mitsubishi provided the necessary design, technology, and machinery. When difficulties plagued the plant after it opened under Malaysian management, Mitsubishi was called in to provide managerial expertise as well. The operation has become profitable and has begun to generate exports on top of healthy domestic sales.[41]

These new arrangements satisfy many Third World concerns about foreign involvement in their economies. Much greater control is vested in local parties. This limits the potential for MNC abuses while contributing to the local accumulation of skills, knowledge, and experience. Third World governments, which often take a direct role in such ventures, gain greater say over which projects are initiated and how they are run, thus lessening the need for indirect controls and regulations. At the same time, some of the benefits that foreign investment can provide are preserved, such as access to skills and technology unavailable locally. Another benefit is less obvious. Many of the Northern firms involved in such deals are small- to medium-sized businesses and have little prior experience in Third World markets. Their growing presence opens new channels for foreign investment in the Third World and presents established MNCs with greater competition. Overall, this improves the bargaining climate for Third World countries in their relations with foreign capital.

These new "designer deals" do, however, hold potential drawbacks for the Third World. By gaining greater control, Third World governments and private firms also shoulder higher risks. When the role of MNCs is lessened, MNCs give up responsibility for assessing the wisdom of investment decisions. If a project fails, the losses are felt much more directly in the Third World itself and much less in the bottom line of MNC spreadsheets.

This shift of responsibility, risk, and uncertainty to the Third World partners is precisely what makes the new forms of involvement attractive to many MNCs. Often they profit by providing services under contract without the necessity of putting their own capital at risk. The lower profile of these new investment forms also removes the political spotlight from foreign business involvement in the Third World, lessening the prospect of populist and nationalist agitation against their presence.

MNCS AND NGOS

Even as MNC relations with host governments have generally entered a more cooperative phase, challenges to MNC conduct have arisen from another direction-transnational NGOs. In recent years, labor, human rights, and environmental NGOs have become more vocal in their criticisms of MNC behavior, especially in developing countries. This phenomenon symbolizes a broader backlash against globalization that has mobilized elements of civil society in both North and South.

Critics have accused MNCs of colluding with repressive governments in countries where they do business, exploiting workers in Third World "sweatshops," and dumping toxic waste and other forms of pollution in host countries. NGOs have fought these corporate practices through a variety of tactics, including consumer boycotts, shareholder protests, publicity campaigns, direct action, legal challenges, and appeals to governments for new laws and regulations.

The anticorporate NGO movement seeks to redefine the meaning and scope of corporate responsibility. In this view, corporations have ethical obligations to workers, communities, and the environment that go beyond the traditional goal of maximizing profits. Aron Cramer, vice president of Business for Social Responsibility, argues that "more and more, the [public] is looking at what the private sector is doing on human rights."[42]

One corporate response to these criticisms has been to pledge better behavior in the future. Following NGO charges that it profited from child labor and abusive working conditions in its factories abroad, for instance, the sports shoe and equipment maker Reebok agreed to allow independent monitoring to insure that its products made in poor countries are free of child labor. Reebok also constructed a school in Pakistan as part of an effort to move children from factories to school. The company has created the Reebok Human Rights Award, adopted a human rights code of conduct, and funded a program to provide activists with hand-held cameras to allow them to document human rights abuses.[43]

Shell Oil Company came in for a blast of negative publicity after the Nigerian government executed poet and political activist Ken Saro-Wiwa in 1995 for his protests against the environmental and human costs of Shell oil operations in southern Nigeria. Royal Dutch Shell was accused of contributing to the Nigerian government's repression of its people and of ignoring the environmental devastation caused by leaking oil rigs and pipelines. Since then, Shell has adopted a corporate code of conduct on human rights and provided over $30 million toward local community development in areas where it does business in Nigeria.[44]

In response to the Nigerian case and others like it, a number of international oil and mining firms have agreed to a voluntary code of conduct dealing with human rights concerns. NGOs have pointed to numerous cases in recent years in which security forces belonging to host governments or those hired directly by corporations have committed human rights abuses against local peoples whose political activities were considered a threat to oil or mining investments. In response, the U.S. and British governments brought together a group of major corporations, including Freeport-McMoRan, British Petroleum, Shell, Chevron, Texaco, Conoco, and the Rio Tinto mining company, with a coalition of NGOs to hammer out an agreement that commits the firms to publicize and protest human rights abuses in host countries and to weed out security employees guilty of abusive behavior.[45]

In July of 2000, Kofi Annan, secretary general of the United Nations, presided over a meeting of 50 MNCs and 12 labor, human rights, and environmental groups in which corporate representatives agreed to a voluntary "global compact" addressing issues of corporate conduct. At this meeting, a number of large and well-known corporations, including Bayer, Dupont, Ericsson, Healtheon, Daimler-Chrysler, Shell, and Nike, pledged to support human rights, the elimination of child labor, the freedom of workers to organize into labor unions, and responsible environmental safeguards wherever they do business, even when host governments have inadequate laws or enforcement mechanisms to ensure such standards.

Amnesty International and the World Wildlife Fund were among the NGOs that endorsed this global compact. Other NGOs, including Greenpeace, refused to support the agreement on the grounds that it called upon corporations to pledge adherence to a set of vague and nonbinding principles but fell short of committing the firms to a detailed code of conduct. Dissenting NGOs also argued that the participating corporations saw the global compact as a means to clean up their tarnished images and forestall stronger and more binding restrictions at the national and international levels. Some NGOs were especially critical of UN involvement in sponsoring the meeting, which in their view served to "bluewash" corporate misconduct.[46]

In other cases, corporations have fought against restrictions on their business practices abroad. In recent years, dozens of state and local governments in the United States have passed "selective purchasing" laws, which bar these governments from purchasing products from or investing funds in firms that do business in foreign countries whose governments have particularly odious human rights records. Similar methods were used in the 1980s to discourage MNCs from doing business in South Africa in an effort to bring an end to apartheid in that country.

One such law was passed by the state of Massachusetts in 1996. The state government was ordered to attach a 10 percent penalty to bids for state contracts placed by companies that did business in Burma, whose government is widely considered guilty of serious human rights violations. Other states and local governments followed suit by passing similar legislation. Massachusetts's so-called "Burma law" was challenged in the courts in a lawsuit brought by the National Foreign Trade Council, which represents 550 major U.S. firms. Ultimately, a federal appeals court threw out Massachusetts's Burma law on the grounds that it usurped the constitutional right of the federal government to control U.S. foreign policy. This ruling has placed other selective purchasing laws elsewhere in the United States into legal uncertainty.[47]

The U.S. Congress itself has passed various pieces of economic sanctions legislation that restrict U.S. trade or investment with over 60 countries around the world. To combat these growing legal restrictions on the ability of U.S. corporations to do business in many parts of the world, 600 firms have formed a lobbying organization called "USA*Engage," which seeks the repeal of such legislative sanctions.[48]

In general, the clash between large MNCs and their NGO critics can be expected to continue and intensify in coming years, punctuated on occasion by efforts on both sides to find common ground.

CONCLUSIONS

Many MNCs make handsome profits on their Third World operations. Southern countries often benefit from the capital and know-how that accompany such investments. The potential for mutual gain has indeed perpetuated the ongoing relationship between Northern firms and Southern host governments. Yet although each party is, in varying degrees, dependent upon the other, the interests, purposes, and perspectives of MNCs and Third World states diverge in some essential respects. These differences have given rise to a history of conflict. The "rules of the game" governing foreign investment in various Third World countries have changed greatly over time, often in response to changes in relative bargaining power. Efforts to devise a lasting and mutually acceptable framework for MNC-Third World relations have generally produced disappointing results.

The fundamental source of MNC-Third World conflict stems from the varying attributes of the two parties. MNCs are economic entities that seek to maximize profits on a global scale. Although, in practice, FDI may contribute to the development of a host country's economy, this is, from the firm's perspective, an incidental result, not the investment's primary purpose. Changes in corporate practice that might maximize the benefits to a host country appeal to corporate executives only if the changes also happen to make sense in terms of overall profitability—a circumstance that is probably rare.

Third World states are political entities bounded by territorial borders. The principal concerns of Southern leaders are to promote economic development while also reducing their countries' vulnerability to foreign manipulation. From the Third World perspective, MNCs represent both opportunity and threat. FDI brings economic assets that are scarce in most Third World countries. Yet in the absence of effective regulation, these assets are subject to foreign control. Decisions made outside the country's borders ultimately determine both the economic and political effects of FDI.

MNCs would prefer a world without borders. Yet they must operate in a system of sovereign states. MNCs cannot escape the realities of fragmented political authority in the international system, but they can and do attempt to minimize the interference of national regulation on their global operations by translating their mobility, knowledge, and resources into bargaining power.

Short of outright nationalization, host states cannot alter the MNC's global or transnational character. They can, however, use their legal and territorial control to impose regulations designed to ensure that FDI takes place on terms that further national development goals. Their ability to do so without disrupting the stream of foreign investment depends upon the stringency of the regulatory regime that the state seeks to impose as well as upon its relative bargaining power.

The tensions between Northern MNCs and Southern host states may tighten or relax over time. The outcomes of bargaining between them may vary as well. But the fundamental character of their relationship is likely to persist. Conflicting interests and desires will continue to weigh against the mutual dependence of firms and states upon one another, ensuring a stormy marriage between the two.

The controversial nature of MNCs and their growing role in the world economy is also underscored by the emerging conflict between large international firms and their NGO critics. The differing perspectives that divide these two sets of actors derives from fundamentally divergent assessments of the costs and benefits of globalization. Yet even here—where the boardroom meets the barricade—there exists room for negotiation among representatives from the worlds of business and civil society.

NOTES

1. The internationalization of production has been greatly facilitated by the declining costs of transportation and communication. In 1990, sea freight costs were only one-half of 1930 levels, air transportation costs were only one-sixth of 1930 levels, and a transatlantic telephone call from New York to London cost only 1 percent as much as in 1930 (United Nations Development Program, *Human Development Report, 1999,* New York: Oxford University Press, 1999, 30).

2. Data in this paragraph are taken from Richard Barnet, "Lords of the Global Economy," *The Nation,* December 19, l994, 754; "The Discreet Charm of the Multicultural Multinational," *The Economist,* July 30, 1994; Reema Datta, "Business, the U.N. and the Millennium: Where Are We?," *The Interdependent,* 25.4, Winter 2000, 13; Padma Mallampally and Karl Savant, "Foreign Direct Investment in Developing Countries," *Finance and Development,* March 1999, 34–35; Sarah Anderson and John Cavanaugh, "Top 200: The Rise of Corporate Power," Corporate Watch, 2000; "The World's 200 Largest TNCs: Home Country, Revenues and Profits," *Le Monde Diplomatique,* April 1997, 16.

3. Rhys Jenkins, *Transnational Corporations and Uneven Development: The Internationalization of Capital and the Third World,* New York: Methuen, 1987, 5.

4. Jenkins, *Transnational Corporations and Uneven Development,* 5–6.

5. Jenkins, *Transnational Corporations and Uneven Development,* 5 and 13.

6. John R. O'Neal, "Foreign Investment in Less Developed Regions," *Political Science Quarterly,* 103.1, 1988, 137–138.

7. Gerald Pollio and Charles H. Riemenschneider, "The Coming Third World Investment Revival," *Harvard Business Review,* March–April 1988, 114; and Stephen Krasner, *Structural Conflict: The Third World against Global Liberalism,* Berkeley and Los Angeles: University of California Press, 1985.

8. World Bank, *World Development Report, 1999/2000,* New York: Oxford University Press, 2000, Table 21, 271; and Mallampally and Sauvant, "Foreign Direct Investment," 35; Datta, "Business, the U.N. and the Millennium," 13.

9. For elaboration, see Charles Kindleberger, "The Monopolistic Theory of Direct Foreign Investment," and Raymond Vernon, "The Product Cycle Model," both in George Mod-

elski (ed.), *Transnational Corporations and World Order: Readings in International Political Economy,* San Francisco: W. H. Freeman, 1979.

10. For a detailed empirical comparison between foreign and local firms in one country, see Larry N. Willmore, "The Comparative Performance of Foreign and Domestic Firms in Brazil," in Sanjaya Lall (ed.), *Transnational Corporations and Economic Development,* New York: Routledge, 1993.

11. "TNCs: Owners of Intellect and Life," *The Guardian* (Australia), 2000, reproduced on the Global Policy Forum Web page (http://www.globalpolicy.org/socecon/tncs/propright.htm), accessed May 20, 2000.

12. For critical treatments of MNC operations in the Third World, see Richard Barnet and Ronald Muller, *Global Reach: The Power of the Multinational Corporations,* New York: Simon and Schuster, 1974; Volker Bornschier and Christopher Chase-Dunn, *Transnational Corporations and Underdevelopment,* New York: Praeger, 1985; John Cavanaugh and Frederick Clairmonte, *The Transnational Economy: Transnational Corporations and Global Markets,* Washington, D.C.: Institute for Policy Studies, 1982; Stephen Hymer, "The Multinational Corporation and the Law of Uneven Development," in Jagdish Bhagwati (ed.), *Economics and World Order,* New York: Macmillan, 1972; Richard Newfarmer, "Multinational and Marketplace Magics in the 1980s," in Jeffrey Frieden and David Lake (eds.), *International Political Economy: Perspectives on Global Power and Wealth,* New York: St. Martin's Press, 1991; Osvaldo Sunkel, "Big Business and 'Dependencia,'" and Johan Galtung, "A Structural Theory of Imperialism," both in Modelski, *Transnational Corporations;* and Jeremy Brecher and Tim Costello, *Global Village or Global Pillage?* Boston: South End Press, 1995.

13. Business concentration is especially high in many extractive sectors. Data from the 1970s indicate that three MNCs shared 70 percent of the world

production, marketing, and distribution of bananas. Six firms controlled 70 percent of world aluminum production capacity. Fewer than ten corporations dominated the global production and processing of the following commodities: copper, iron ore, lead, nickel, tin, tobacco, and zinc (Garrett Fitzgerald, *Unequal Partners,* New York: United Nations, 1979, 11–12).

14. Calvin Sims, "In Peru, a Fight for Fresh Air," *New York Times,* December 12, 1995.

15. Data on Mexican *maquiladoras* are from William Burke, "The Toxic Price of Free Trade in Mexico," *In These Times,* May 22–29, 1991; Robert Reinhold, "Mexico Says It Won't Harbor U.S. Companies Fouling Air," *New York Times,* April 18, 1991; "Survey: Mexico," *The Economist,* October 28, 1995, 16; Lore Saldana, "Tijuana's Toxic Waters," *NACLA Report on the Americas,* November–December 1999; "A Greener, or Browner, Mexico?" *The Economist,* August 7, 1999; Robert Bryce, "Toxic Trade Imbalance," *Mother Jones,* January–February 2001.

16. For general discussions of Third World efforts to regulate FDI, see Jenkins, *Transnational Corporations and Uneven Development;* Krasner, *Structural Conflict;* Robert Cohen and Jeffrey Frieden, "The Impact of Multinational Corporations on Developing Nations," and Robert Kurdle, "The Several Faces of the Multinational Corporation: Political Reaction and Policy Response," both in Kendall Stiles and Tsuneo Akaha (eds.), *International Political Economy: Reader,* New York: Harper-Collins, 1991; Francisco Orrago Vicuna, "The Control of Multinational Corporations," in Modelski, *Transnational Corporations;* and Stephen Guisinger, "Host Country Policies to Attract and Control Foreign Investment," in Lall (ed.), *Transnational Corporations and Economic Development.*

17. The material in this and the next two paragraphs relies upon Franklin B. Weinstein, "Underdevelopment and Efforts to Control Multinational Corporations," in Modelski (ed.), *Transnational Corporations.*

18. Jenkins, *Transnational Corporations and Uneven Development,* 173–175; Cohen and Frieden,"The Impact of Multinational Corporations on Developing Nations," 169; R. N. Gwynne, "Multinational Corporations and the Triple Alliance in Latin America," in C. J. Dixon, D. Drakakis-Smith, and H. D. Watts, *Multinational Corporations and the Third World,* London: Croom Helm, 1986, 128.

19. See United Nations, "Resolution Establishing the Commission on Transnational Corporations and Charter of the Economic Rights and Duties of States," in Modelski (ed.), *Transnational Corporations.*

20. OECD, "Declaration on International Investment and Multinational Enterprises and Guidelines for Multinational Enterprises," in Modelski (ed.), *Transnational Corporations.*

21. "Uncivil Society," *Financial Times,* September 1, 1999, 14.

22. Guy de Jonquie'res, "OECD Agrees Global Company Code," *Financial Times,* June 28, 2000.

23. This section relies heavily on Theodore Moran, "Multinational Corporations and Dependency: A Dialogue for Dependentistas and Non-Dependentistas," *International Organization,* Winter 1978. Also see Franklin Weinstein, "Underdevelopment and Efforts to Control Multinational Corporations," in Modelski (ed.), *Transnational Corporations;* and John Stopford and Susan Strange, *Rival States, Rival Firms: Competition for World Market Shares,* New York: Cambridge University Press, 1991.

24. United Nations Center on Transnational Corporations, *World Investment Report, 1991: The Triad in Foreign Direct Investment,* New York: United Nations, 1991, 32; Peter Dicken, "Transnational Corporations and Nation-States," in Timothy C. Lim (ed.), *Stand! Contending Ideas and Opinions: Global Issues,* Bellevue, Wash.: Coursewise, 1999.

25. Pollio and Riemenschneider, "Coming Third World Investment Revival."

26. John McClean, "Venezuela Reverses Economic Course," *Chicago Tribune,* May 27, 1991.

27. Joseph Grunwald and Kenneth Flamm, *The Global Factory: Foreign Assembly in International Trade,* Washington, D.C.: Brookings Institution, 1985.

28. Not long afterward, the chairman of United Brands committed suicide by leaping from the forty-fourth floor of a New York skyscraper (Paul Harrison, *Inside the Third World,* Middlesex, England: Penguin Books, 1981, 349).

29. George Gedda, "Survey: U.S. Leans on Foreign Government for Trade," Associated Press, January 21, 2000 (available on the Global Policy Forum Web page, http://www.globalpolicy. org/socecon/tncs/usbrib.htm [accessed May 20, 2000]).

30. Gedda, "U.S. Leans on Foreign Government."

31. "The Gorgeous East," *The Economist,* July 16, 1994, 56; Mallampally and Sauvant, "Foreign Direct Investment in Developing Countries," 35.

32. "Infatuation's End," *The Economist,* September 25, 1999, 71.

33. See "Asia's Emerging Standard-Bearer," *The Economist,* July 21, 1990; and David Sanger, "Power of the Yen Winning Asia," *New York Times,* December 5, 1991.

34. Mallampally and Sauvant, "Foreign Direct Investment in Developing Countries," 35.

35. Mallampally and Sauvant, "Foreign Direct Investment in Developing Countries."

36. "Investing in Brazil: Trouble in Paradise," *The Economist,* June 3, 2000, 63.

37. "Business in Difficult Places," *The Economist,* May 20, 2000, 85–86.

38. Jenkins, *Corporations and Uneven Development,* 7.

39. United Nations Center on Transnational Corporations, *Transnational Corporations and International Trade: Selected Issues,* New York: United Nations, 1985, 6.

40. This discussion relies upon Lapper, "Dressed for Designer Deals"; Pollio and Riemenschneider, "The Coming Third World Investment Revival"; and C. P. Oman, "New Forms of Investment in Developing Countries," in Lall (ed.), *Transnational Corporations and Economic Development.*

41. "New Car for Malaysia, New Influence for Japan," *New York Times,* March 6, 1991.

42. Laurent Belsie, "At the Intersection of Business and Human Rights," *Christian Science Monitor* (available at the Global Policy Forum Web page, http://www.globalpolicy.org/ socecon/tncs/coresp.htm [accessed May 20, 2000]).

43. Belsie, "Intersection of Business and Human Rights."

44. Norimitsu Onishi, "In the Republic of Chevron," *New York Times Magazine,* July 4, 1999 (available at the Global Policy Forum Web page, http://www.globalpolicy.org/ socecon/nations/chevron.htm [accessed May 20, 200]).

45. "A Pact against Oil Company Abuses," *New York Times,* December 28, 2000. Blue is the symbolic color of the United Nations.

46. Blue is the symbolic color of the United Nations. Joseph Kahn, "Multinationals Sign U.N. Pact on Rights and Environment," *New York Times,* July 27, 2000.

47. Interpress Service, "Multinationals Win US Court Victory over Activists," June 24, 1999 (available at the Global Policy Forum Web page, http://www.global policy.org/socecon/tncs/court99.htm [accessed May 20, 2000]).

48. Russell Mokhiber and Robert Weissman, "When the People Speak, the Corporations Squeak," *Multinational Monitor,* May 10, 1999 (available at Global Policy Forum Web page, http://www.globalpolicy.org/socecon/ tncs/mnc-ngo.html [accessed May 30, 2000]).

ANNOTATED BIBLIOGRAPHY

Volker Bornschier and Christopher Chase-Dunn. *Transnational Corporations and Underdevelopment.* New York: Praeger, 1985. A conceptual analysis of international capital flows employing world systems theory-a school of thought that is closely related to the dependency perspective.

Jeremy Brecher and Tim Costello. *Global Village or Global Pillage?* Boston: South End Press, 1995. A radical critique of globalization and the spread of multinational corporations, written for a general audience.

Peter J. Buckley and Jeremy Clegg (eds.). *Multinational Enterprises in Less Developed Countries.* New York: St. Martin's Press, 1991. A collection of theoretical and empirical essays on the role that multinational corporations play in Third World countries.

Paul N. Doremus, William W. Keller, Louis W. Pauly, and Simon Reich. *The Myth of the Global Corporation.* Princeton, N.J.: Princeton University Press, 1998. Challenges the view that multinational corporations are "stateless" entities. Argues that MNCs remain heavily dependent upon home country economies and governments.

Rhys Jenkins. *Transnational Corporations and Uneven Development: The Internationalization of Capital and the Third World.* New York: Methuen, 1987. A comprehensive treatment of MNCs in the Third World written from a dependency perspective. Contains a wealth of data, history, and theoretical analysis.

David Korten. *When Corporations Rule the World.* West Hartford, Connecticut: Kumarian Press, 1996. A critical look at corporate globalization.

Sanjaya Lall (ed.). *Transnational Corporations and Economic Development.* New York: Routledge, 1993. An excellent collection of essays, new and old, on the economic dimensions of foreign direct investment in the Third World.

George Modelski (ed.). *Transnational Corporations and World Order: Readings in International Political Economy.* San Francisco: W. H. Freeman, 1979. Although dated, this reader contains a number of classic theoretical works on the politics and economics of foreign direct investment.

Theodore Moran. "Multinational Corporations and Dependency: A Dialogue for Dependentistas and Non-Dependentistas." *International Organization,* Winter 1978. A seminal source on the bargaining approach to analyzing MNC-host country relations.

John Stopford and Susan Strange. *Rival States, Rival Firms: Competition for World Market Shares.* New York: Cambridge University Press, 1991. Examines interfirm competition among multinational corporations and bargaining between firms and states.

Van Whiting. *The Political Economy of Foreign Investment in Mexico: Nationalism, Liberalism and Constraints on Choice.* Baltimore: Johns Hopkins University Press, 1991. A detailed case study focusing on Mexican efforts to regulate foreign direct investment.

12

❖

Third World Debt and North-South Finance

L ike a relentless and perpetually moving tornado, the winds of financial crisis careened around the developing world in the 1980s and 1990s, leaving economic destruction in their wake. Latin America, Africa, and Asia have each experienced episodes of financial turmoil at different times. Each new crisis serves as the occasion for tense negotiations between Northern creditors and Southern debtors and much hand-wringing over the need for reforms that might provide a long-term solution.

The debt problem underlines the degree to which increasingly close financial ties have entangled the economic interests of both North and South. It also underscores the power asymmetries between developed and developing countries. This chapter will explore the political economy of Third World debt and North-South financial ties. Our aim is to better understand the sources and consequences of the periodic financial crises that have so defined these relations over the past two decades, as well as the possible solutions. After surveying the costs of the debt problem and the actors involved, the remainder of our discussion is divided into two parts. We first examine the debt crisis that centered on Latin America in the 1980s and early 1990s. We then shift our attention to the Asian financial crisis of 1997–1998 and its subsequent spread to Russia, Brazil, and Argentina.

THE COSTS OF THIRD WORLD DEBT

Hovering menacingly over a shifting array of developing countries, a dark cloud of debt and financial instability dimmed prospects for Southern economic growth over the 1980s through today. The dimensions of Southern debt have reached almost unimaginable proportions. In 1970 Third World debt to Northern banks, governments, and multilateral lending institutions totaled $70 billion. By 1997, developing country debt had grown to over $2 trillion.

The burden of paying the stream of principal and interest due each year on this enormous debt has imposed severe costs on people throughout the Third World. Forced to squeeze domestic consumption in order to free the resources needed to satisfy the debt burden, governments have adopted measures that invariably produce economic hardship. As Jamaica's former prime minister Michael Manley observed in 1980, officials in debtor countries often face a cruel choice between "using your last foreign exchange to pay off Citibank and Chase Manhattan or buying food and medicines for your people."[1]

The debt crisis also engendered social and political instability in many countries. Between 1985 and 1992, 56 major "IMF riots," so called because they followed announcements of new government austerity policies demanded by the IMF in return for new loans, broke out in various developing countries around the world. In 1989, these incidents of unrest left 14 dead in Argentina, 200 dead in the Dominican Republic, and 300 dead in Venezuela, not to mention the many injured and the millions of dollars in losses from supermarket looting and vandalism. Wrenching economic reforms launched by Brazil during 1990, designed in part to prepare the country for renewed debt negotiations, led to severe economic recession and immense political and social turmoil. In June of that year an estimated 1.5 million workers participated in 330 separate strikes in protest of spreading unemployment and a declining standard of living. Striking workers at a Ford plant demolished cars and computers, and a peasant organization announced a "massive and radical offensive" of land occupations.[2] The story is similar in many parts of Africa. Urban insurrection in Sudan following the introduction of IMF reforms in 1985 toppled the government of Gaafar al-Nimeiry, while similar policies have led to rioting in Nigeria, Tunisia, and Morocco.[3]

More recently, financial crises in Asia and Latin America have triggered similar episodes of political instability and popular unrest. In 1998, over 500 lives were lost in Indonesian rioting after the IMF ordered the government to end a popular fuel subsidy. Continued public demonstrations eventually forced Indonesia's President Suharto to leave office after a 33-year reign.[4]

In May 2000, 40,000 people gathered in the streets of Buenos Aires when an IMF delegation visited the presidential palace to negotiate changes in Argentina's economic policies as a response to the country's financial crisis. As the Argentine crisis moved to a climax in late 2001, the eighth national strike in two years was held on December 13. Violent protests and street battles with police during the same period claimed 27 lives with 2,500 injuries and 4,000 arrests. After failing to arrive at a successful strategy for meeting international debt obligations while also restarting the stalled economy, Argentina's president resigned from office.[5]

ACTORS

The largest Third World debtors are generally located in Latin America and Asia. As a proportion of national income, however, African countries carry the largest debt burdens. Whereas most borrowing was carried by governments in the 1970s and 1980s, the private sector contracted a growing proportion of overall debt in the 1990s. Also, whereas the great bulk of debt in the earlier period consisted of bank loans, portfolio investment became an increasingly important source of debt in the nineties. (See Table 12.1.)

Most commercial lending to Third World countries is organized through bank syndicates. Many banks working together contribute, in varying proportions, to large "syndicated" loan packages to a given Third World country. The big banks that put up the largest amount of money negotiate with borrower countries on behalf of all the other banks. These deals often involve an enormous number of banks. Six hundred banks were party to negotiations over rescheduling agreements with Mexico in 1983, while similar negotiations with Brazil during the early 1990s involved 750 creditors.[6] Yet although many banks have some stake in the debt crisis, Third World lending has been overwhelmingly concentrated with a very few large banks. In the mid-1980s, nine large institutions together accounted for 63 percent of all Third World lending by U.S. banks.[7]

Northern governments are major creditors to the Third World through their foreign aid programs. Much Northern aid is given in the form of loans rather than outright grants, although usually at less than market interest rates. The major Northern creditor governments hammer out common strategies in their negotiations over debt issues with Third World countries through an informal consultative arrangement known as the "Paris Club."

Northern governments play other roles in the debt crisis, as well. They provide capital to the International Monetary Fund and World Bank and control the policies of those organizations through their preponderance of voting power. Government authorities in the North regulate the behavior of banks falling under their jurisdiction. Northern governments have provided temporary financing designed to help debtor countries avoid default. And finally, the United States, in particular, has intervened in the relationship between debtor countries and their creditors with comprehensive proposals for managing the debt problem.

Portfolio investors play a major role as creditors through their purchase of developing country stocks and bonds. Many of these funds are placed through mutual funds, which combine the capital of both small investors and large institutions, such as pension funds and insurance companies.

Table 12.1 Most Heavily Indebted Countries, 1998

Ranked by: Total External Debt (in millions of US$)		As % of GNP	
Brazil	232,004	Republic of Congo	280
Russia	183,601	Angola	279
Mexico	159,959	Nicaragua	262
China	154,599	Dem. Rep. of Congo	196
Indonesia	150,875	Zambia	181
Argentina	144,050	Indonesia	169
Rep. of Korea	139,097	Mauritania	148
Turkey	102,074	Syria	136
India	98,232	Ethiopia	135
Thailand	86,172	Sierre Leone	128

SOURCE: World Bank, *World Development Report, 2000/2001,* New York: Oxford University Press, 2000, Table 21, 314–315.

The International Monetary Fund is the multilateral lending agency most directly involved with Third World debt, though the role of the World Bank has grown in recent years. The IMF's principal purpose is to lend money to countries experiencing shortfalls in their current accounts. Fund loans must be repaid within one to three years. Each member country gains the right to borrow foreign exchange from the IMF by contributing a combination of the country's own currency and gold to the IMF's reserves. Each member's contribution is roughly proportional to the size of its economy.

Beyond certain credit limits (which vary according to the country's original contribution), however, IMF authorities may set conditions on additional borrowing. Before lending large amounts to a member country, in other words, the IMF extracts promises from the government that it will undertake various policy reforms that the IMF believes are necessary to correct existing current account deficits and to earn the foreign exchange needed to repay loans issued by the IMF. The terms of IMF policy reform packages are generally based upon the assumption that countries that run large deficits or borrow heavily abroad are living beyond their means by consuming more than they produce. Fund-supported "stabilization programs," as they are commonly known, are designed to reduce domestic consumption and consequently to lower the country's demand for imported goods and foreign loans.

The specific package of policy reforms sponsored by the IMF usually includes a number of the following measures: abolish or liberalize foreign exchange and import controls; reduce growth in the domestic money supply and raise interest rates; increase taxes and reduce government spending; abolish food, fuel, and transportation subsidies; cut government wages and seek wage restraint from labor unions; dismantle price controls; privatize publicly owned firms; reduce restrictions on foreign investment; and depreciate the currency.

The economic hardships these policies typically produce make them politically unpopular. The IMF's ability to compel governments to pursue these reforms stems less from the size of the loans that the IMF itself has to offer (which are typically only a portion of the country's overall needs) than from the fact that Northern banks will not extend new credits or reschedule old debts with a country that has not reached an agreement with the IMF. A debtor country's international credit standing rests upon its ability to obtain an IMF seal of approval. An accord with the IMF signals to private lenders that, in the IMF's view, a debtor country is pursuing the appropriate course necessary to correct past and present financial imbalances.

The World Bank has played an increasingly important role alongside the IMF in managing the Third World debt crisis. Although the World Bank once focused overwhelmingly on "project" lending, whereby loans were tied to specific investments, such as a hydroelectric dam or a new road, more recently the bank has shifted a large portion of its resources toward "structural adjustment" loans. This latter type of lending links balance of payments financing to reforms in broad sectors of the economy. The sorts of reforms supported by the bank are similar to those sponsored by the IMF; indeed, the two institutions often coordinate the advice they give client countries.

THE ORIGINS AND EVOLUTION
OF THE THIRD WORLD DEBT CRISIS

The fundamental origin of the debt crisis lies in the dependence of many Third World countries on external capital rather than on internal savings to finance economic growth. During the 1950s and 1960s, outside capital flowed to the Third World principally through Northern aid and foreign direct investment (FDI). Beginning in the late sixties, these sources declined in relative importance as commercial banks stepped up their lending to Third World countries. Whereas official development assistance from the North dropped from 58 percent of total Third World financial receipts in 1960 to 30 percent in 1978, the share accounted for by bank lending rose from 2 percent to 33 percent during the same period.[8]

This change in the composition of financial flows from North to South was perhaps as important as the dramatic increase in the total volume in contributing to the Third World financial crisis. From the recipient's standpoint, foreign aid and foreign direct investment offer advantages over bank borrowing. Foreign aid normally includes a concessionary element, sometimes taking the form of outright grants. Even when assistance must be paid back, aid funds come with little or no interest attached. As for FDI, the physical assets transferred to a host country through foreign investment are unlikely to be dismantled and removed. FDI often produces a transfer of skills and technology as well. Although a stream of profits from the investment may leave the country, this will occur only so long as the investment is productive and generating output, wages, and tax payments locally. If the investment goes sour, the outward flow of profits ceases, and the costs of coping with a bad business decision are shared between the multinational and the host nation.

The terms attached to commercial bank loans are more strenuous. Unlike foreign aid, all commercial bank lending must be repaid at market interest rates. In contrast to foreign direct investment, the principal and interest on these loans fall due on a regular basis regardless of whether the investment financed by the loan is generating revenue.[9] Indeed, the cost of the debt may rise for reasons beyond the debtor's control. Two-thirds of the Third World loans issued from 1973 to 1983 carried variable rather than fixed interest rates, meaning that Southern debt payments rise or fall with changes in Northern interest rates.[10] Commercial borrowing places much of the risk on the borrower.

The demanding and inflexible terms of commercial bank lending thus played a role in the origins of the Third World debt crisis of the 1980s. But why were the risks that accompanied the explosion of bank lending to the South so clearly underestimated by both the banks and the Third World borrowers?

Despite its rigorous conditions, there is no inherent reason why borrowing money from a bank should lead to economic ruin. Indeed, large corporations routinely borrow from banks to finance expansion plans. The key to assessing the riskiness of any given loan is to ask whether the productive activities financed by the loan are likely to generate revenues sufficient to allow the borrower to pay back the principal, with interest, over an agreed-upon time period. If so, then both lender and borrower will be well served by the transaction. If not, then the results are likely to be less happy.

The Misplaced Optimism of the 1970s

The debt crisis of the 1980s was built upon the misplaced optimism of the 1970s. Banks lent money to Third World countries based upon hopes that the ambitious development schemes espoused by government planners would fuel rapid Southern growth and export expansion. This faith, shared by bankers and borrowers alike, was eventually shattered when it became clear that too few of the funds borrowed from the North found their way into projects capable of paying for themselves.

There were several reasons why bankers took such imprudent risks. The first is a lack of historical memory. Latin American debt crises were common in the nineteenth and early twentieth centuries. Prior to the current crisis, the most recent such episode occurred in the 1930s, when many Latin American countries defaulted on their outstanding loans. Few bankers, unfortunately, took serious note of such cautionary precedents.[11]

Why, though, did Northern banks suddenly rediscover the Third World in the 1970s? Many found themselves awash in lendable funds early in the decade but experienced great difficulty attracting creditworthy borrowers in the North. With no place else to turn, the banks sent the surplus South. These surplus funds came from two sources. During the 1960s and early

1970s, the United States routinely ran balance of payments deficits. Many of these dollars remained overseas, finding their way into dollar-denominated accounts at banks abroad. Because the bulk of these dollars ended up in European banks or in the subsidiaries of American banks located overseas, they came to be referred to as Eurodollars.

This accumulation of overseas dollars expanded dramatically when OPEC nations, finding themselves with far more money than they could possibly spend after the quadrupling of oil prices in 1973, also began to make huge deposits of their largely dollar-denominated oil revenues in Western banks. These developments allowed the Eurodollar market to grow from $315 billion in 1973 to $2 trillion in 1982.[12] For the banks to profit from these new deposits, of course, they had to find customers willing to borrow the funds they contained. Yet partly as a consequence of the OPEC-engineered oil price rise, most Northern nations slipped into economic recession during 1975. Businesses cut back plans for expansion, and consumers put off big-ticket purchases. With money to lend and few prospects in the North, banks began to look South.

There they discovered many eager customers. The newly industrializing countries (NICs) of the Third World, particularly those in Latin America, found themselves amidst an explosion of manufacturing production and exports. To sustain this growth, Third World countries needed financing to pay for increasingly expensive oil imports as well as for the purchase of imported capital goods, such as the machinery used in newly built Southern factories. Rapid Third World growth was fueled not only by increased manufacturing exports but also by the strong prices that most Third World commodities fetched on world markets early in the decade. Commodity prices rose by 13 percent in 1972 and a further 53 percent in 1973.[13] Overall, the Third World's share of world exports increased from 18 percent to 28 percent during the seventies.[14]

Normally reserved bankers expressed an almost giddy sense of elation at the growth and promise of the profitable new markets of the South. Some portrayed commercial lending as a magical cure for underdevelopment. Foreign debt was seen as a badge of honor and success, not shame, for Third World countries. This bravado is reflected in the comments of G. A. Costanzo, then a vice president at Citibank, on Mexico's economic prospects: "Mexico... is in a particularly favorable position as it enters the 1980s.... Mexico's external debt may surpass that of Brazil during this decade, reflecting not an uncontrolled deficit but the recognition of unparalleled investment opportunities."[15] Southern borrowers shared this optimism. From their perspective, moreover, Northern loans looked like bargains. Due to high inflation levels, real interest rates were remarkably low, while the dollar's weakness made dollar-denominated loans seem cheap.

Alongside these economic motivations, Third World governments welcomed bank financing for political reasons as well. Nationalist sentiment ran strong in many countries. Seeking to harness these passions to their own benefit, many Third World politicians directed nationalist agitation toward multinational corporations—the most obvious and intrusive forms of Northern penetration in Southern societies. Moreover, Southern governments chafed against the superior bargaining power that many MNCs derived from their mobility. Particularly in Latin America, therefore, governments sought to create alternatives to the MNCs by buttressing state-owned firms. A strong publicly owned sector of the economy strengthened the hand of Southern governments in bargaining with MNCs while also providing political leaders with greater direct control over the economy and with a means of asserting their nationalist credentials. Because reducing dependence upon MNCs required access to alternative sources of capital, Third World governments looked to Northern banks that, in a relatively low-profile and unobtrusive manner, provided funds subject to the direct control of state bureaucrats and politicians.[16]

For a variety of reasons, therefore, both Northern lenders and Southern borrowers were well motivated to deepen their relationships with one another, and favorable conditions made international lending seem a good bet for all concerned. The eagerness of the banks to cash in on this huge and profitable new market was, moreover, relatively unrestrained by normally cautious Northern government bank regulators. Eurodollar funds were largely beyond the reach of government regulations designed to limit risky lending behavior. U.S. dollars deposited overseas escaped the jurisdiction of U.S. banking officials, while European bank regulations applied only to local European currencies, not to foreign currency-denominated accounts. This lack of normal oversight contributed to overlending.[17]

Northern banks found overseas lending quite profitable for a time. Earnings from the foreign operations of the seven biggest U.S. banks climbed from 22 percent of total profits in 1970 to 60 percent in 1982. Many bankers waved aside the concerns of those who questioned whether the large buildup of foreign debt by still-poor Third World societies was sustainable. Citibank chief Walter Wriston, whose bank epitomized the frenetic climate of international banking in the 1970s, predicted that "this fear that banks have reached a limit will turn out to be wrong tomorrow, as it always has in the past."[18]

The Bottom Falls Out:
The Fickleness of the World Economy

Yet the economic conditions that nurtured the growth of Third World borrowing during much of the 1970s shifted dramatically as the decade drew to a close. After several years of relative stability in oil markets, OPEC managed to engineer a trebling of world oil prices in 1979. The oil bill of oil-importing Third World countries leapt from $7 billion in 1973 to almost $100 billion in 1981.[19] This proved a bitter pill to swallow for the NICs of the Third World, whose appetite for additional oil was rising just as prices rocketed skyward.

Far more devastating in the long run, however, was the North's reaction to OPEC's price hike. In the United States, the Federal Reserve clamped down on the U.S. money supply in an effort to wring inflation from the economy.

This had several undesirable effects from the standpoint of Third World borrowers. Interest rates climbed to an average of 15.5 percent from 1979 to 1982. This meant higher payments on most commercial bank loans to the Third World. The U.S. economy, along with those of other Northern countries, entered the worst economic downturn since the Great Depression. Global growth averaged only 1.1 percent from 1979 to 1982, and world trade actually shrank. Slow growth hurt Southern exports to the North. Commodity prices fell by one-fourth between 1980 and 1982 as demand slackened.[20] Southern manufacturing exports were dampened not only by the economic slowdown itself but also by increased Northern protectionism as economic hardship in the North pushed governments to attempt to save jobs in industries threatened by Southern imports.[21] The dollar, strengthened by high interest rates in the United States, rose to record highs, forcing Third World governments to expend more in their local currency to obtain the dollars necessary to pay back the banks.

Peter Nunnenkamp has estimated that external factors over which Third World governments had little or no control accounted for $570 billion in new debt accumulation between 1974 and 1981.[22] By 1982 debt payments consumed 70 percent of the export revenues of the 21 largest non-oil-exporting debtors, up from 36 percent in 1973, and the overall current account balance for all non-oil-exporting Third World countries reached a deficit of $97 billion.[23]

Southern Mismanagement and Capital Flight

Unfavorable international developments were not the only forces working to transform Third World debt from a problem into a crisis. Internal factors such as poor policy choices and capital flight served to further aggravate matters.[24] Many Third World governments, particularly in Latin America, supported artificially high exchange rates during the late 1970s and early 1980s in an effort to control inflation without recession.[25] Overvalued currencies badly hurt exports, encouraged import growth, and led to large trade deficits that were covered by further borrowing from abroad.[26]

As conditions worsened, it became clear that these overvalued currency rates could not be sustained and that severe currency depreciation lurked just around the corner. Holders of liquid assets in these countries feared that the value of their cash holdings might take a nosedive. In response, the wealthy began converting their assets into dollars in massive amounts and sending the proceeds abroad. As further incentive for this so-called capital flight, interest rates in many Third World countries were held artificially low by legal ceilings even as rising inflation rendered the real rate of return on savings accounts negative. Just the opposite was true in the United States, of course, where monetary policies were at the same time producing skyrocketing real interest rates.

This combination of factors led to a hemorrhaging of foreign exchange toward the North. For the years 1976 to 1984, the World Bank estimated that

Mexico experienced $54 billion in capital flight (57 percent of Mexican external debt), that Argentina saw an outflow of $28 billion (60 percent of external debt), and that $35 billion fled Venezuela (a sum greater than Venezuela's entire external debt).[27] In 1985, IMF estimates put total Third World capital flight at $200 billion—a figure that by 1989 would rise to $340 billion for the 15 largest debtors alone.[28]

With high interest rates, a buoyant stock market, and a stable political system, the United States attracted roughly one half of all Latin American flight capital. Between 1977 and 1985, deposits by Mexican investors in U.S. banks increased 570 percent; for Argentineans, the increase in deposits was 450 percent; and Peruvian deposits rose 750 percent.[29]

Capital flight exacted a steep price from Third World debtors. During 1983 and 1984, Northern banks accepted more money in deposits from Southern sources than they dispersed to Third World countries in new loans. Capital flight took a toll on foreign exchange reserves, domestic investment, and tax revenues in Third World countries. Mexico lost an estimated $3.2 billion in taxes between 1977 and 1984 due to capital flight.[30]

Staggered by these blows, Third World governments attempted to maintain the momentum of growth by continuing to borrow. The banks, again flush with deposits from OPEC nations, proved willing to accommodate Third World demands for additional funds; however, they began to exact higher spreads, premiums tacked onto base interest-rate levels, as compensation for the greater riskiness of the new loans.[31] Ominously, most of the new lending during this period went not to finance promising development projects but instead to allow debtors to make payments on past debts. This expedient succeeded in staving off default for a time. Meanwhile, bankers and Third World governments hoped that the newly unfavorable world economic climate would change again for the better and allow the resumption of Third World growth.

The World Holds Its Breath: The Mexican Crisis

These hopes proved illusory. The bubble of optimism burst in August 1982, when Mexican officials announced that their country, then the world's second-largest debtor, lacked the funds to cover scheduled loan payments and stood on the verge of involuntary default. Ironically, given the role of the 1979 OPEC oil price hike in worsening the indebtedness of so many Third World countries, the first large debtor to approach default was a major oil exporter. In addition to the external circumstances mentioned earlier, such as higher interest rates and Northern recession, the Mexican predicament was exacerbated by unrealistic government economic policies.

The Mexican economy grew at the explosive rate of 8.1 percent per year between 1978 and 1981. This growth curve was clearly unsustainable in the face of an unfavorable international economic climate. Most significant, oil prices began to slide during the early 1980s, causing a $6 billion drop in Mexican oil revenues between 1980 and 1981.[32] Yet officials attempted to maintain a feverish pace of economic growth through massive government spending. By 1982 the government budget deficit, largely financed by foreign borrowing, reached a stupendous 16.3 percent of Mexican GNP. Seeking to quickly exploit large, newly discovered oil deposits, Mexico also borrowed heavily to finance the import of capital equipment for expansion of the oil industry. Lastly, Mexican officials maintained an overvalued exchange rate, thereby encouraging imports and discouraging exports.[33]

Mexico's day of reckoning arrived when Northern banks balked at providing enough additional financing to cover the large payments falling due on old debts plus the continuing demand for new funds needed to pay for the excess of imports over exports. The prospect of Mexican default set off alarm bells in Northern governmental and banking circles as the stark realization finally sank in that the stability of the entire Northern financial system stood in jeopardy. Mexico owed Bank of America and Citibank roughly $3 billion each.[34] Citibank's Mexican exposure equaled two-thirds of its net corporate assets.[35] A long-term interruption of Mexican debt payments could have spelled disaster for a number of the largest U.S. banks.

At this point, the U.S. government, abandoning its previously aloof stance toward Third World debt, stepped in to provide emergency short-term financing designed to keep Mexico solvent until a longer-term solution could be found. As part of the deal, the United States also made an immediate $1 billion advance payment for discounted Mexican oil and provided Mexico with $1 billion in credits toward the purchase of surplus U.S. grain. Mexico subsequently entered into negotiations with the IMF and its private bank creditors, during which debt payments were suspended for 120 days. Ultimately, the IMF provided almost $4 billion, and the banks $5 billion in new financing, while payments on almost $19 billion in old debt were stretched out over a longer period. In return, Mexico agreed to follow a stabilization plan designed by IMF officials that, among other things, required the government to close its budget deficit and devalue the peso.[36]

The most difficult phase of the negotiations revolved around the bankers' reluctance to lend new money to Mexico. Additional money was needed in order to finance necessary imports, complete ongoing investment projects, and roll over old debt. Without new funds, Mexican default seemed assured. Collectively, of course, the Northern banks all had an interest in avoiding this outcome. Yet individually, many bankers feared that Mexico would never pay its debts in full, and none wished to throw good money after bad. The Mexican deal almost came apart because many banks, especially the smaller ones, wished to benefit from a successful conclusion to the negotiations without, however, putting up new money of their own. If enough banks had maintained this attitude, of course, a successful deal would have proven impossible.

Drawing upon powers it had never previously exercised, the IMF provided the solution by compelling banks into involuntary lending. IMF officials, supported by the United States, threatened to withdraw their portion of the loan package, as well as their oversight of Mexican reforms, unless each bank contributed new funds proportionate to its previous stake in Mexico.[37] This persuaded the banks to follow the IMF's lead in the short run, but it failed to resolve the longer-term problem of the banks' newfound reluctance to provide even prudent amounts of new lending to Third World debtors.

The IMF Takes Charge

The IMF quickly assumed a role at the center of the debt crisis as more debtor countries experienced problems similar to Mexico's. During the 1970s, the IMF typically found itself drawn into negotiations each year with a few troubled debtors. In the wake of Mexico's troubles, dozens of countries on the verge of default, seeking to secure new loans and renegotiate the terms of old ones, approached the IMF and the banks. By 1983 the IMF had conditional lending programs in 47 countries.[38]

The IMF's cure for the problems of Third World debtors flowed from its diagnosis of the illness. Michel Camdessus, executive director of the IMF, attributed the debt crisis to "the criminal conduct" of "politicians who neglect to take care of urgent problems and prefer to wait for a miracle."[39] Having identified the cause of the debt crisis as economic mismanagement by debtor country governments, the IMF, supported by Northern governments and banks, placed the burden of adjusting to the crisis on the debtor countries themselves. Third World officials were expected to adopt correct economic policies, such as those previously discussed, and their citizens, having earlier lived beyond their means, would now have to swallow the medicine of austerity, no matter how unpleasant its taste.

In its deal with Mexico, for instance, the IMF demanded that subsidies on basic foodstuffs be reduced and that wages be restrained. As a result, authorities raised the prices of corn tortillas by 40 percent and bread by 100 percent. Wages were allowed to grow by only one third the inflation rate.[40]

The IMF prescription for Third World debtors generally led to substantial improvement in debtor country trade balances, but the price was frightening in lost economic growth and deteriorating social conditions. As a result, the IMF's remedy for Third World debt problems came under severe criticism. Many of these criticisms had to do with the economic soundness of the fund's policy prescriptions. One study found that low-income countries that followed IMF programs during the 1970s performed no better by a variety of economic measures than did countries not under the fund's guidance.[41] Another survey conducted by the IMF itself found that IMF-sponsored programs in sub-Saharan African countries met preestablished targets for growth, inflation, and trade in only a minority of cases.[42]

Some critics maintained that the IMF focused too exclusively on reducing Third World imports by dampening demand while neglecting supply—side measures that might stimulate debtor country exports. Domestic investment levels slumped during the 1980s in most Third World countries, declining, for instance, by 25 percent in Latin America between 1980 and 1988.[43] Among the 15 most heavily indebted countries, domestic investment plummeted from an average of 24 percent of GNP in 1971–1981 to 18 percent in 1982–1987.[44]

With insufficient investment in export industries, Third World countries found themselves limited in their ability to increase their export capacity or to enhance the efficiency and competitiveness of their products.

The effectiveness of another IMF tool—currency devaluation—proved a subject of controversy, as well.[45] One undesirable consequence of devaluing a nation's currency is higher domestic inflation as the prices of imported goods rise. Moreover, devaluation can produce effects contrary to its intended purposes. Some imported goods, such as oil, are so necessary that the increased prices caused by devaluation lead to only small declines in import volumes.[46] In such cases, the net effect of devaluation is to widen, rather than to narrow, the nation's trade deficit. Much the same is true with regard to export industries that rely heavily upon imported inputs, such as raw materials, parts, or capital goods. Part of the advantage that devaluation offers such industries by allowing them to sell their products more cheaply abroad is taken away by the higher costs that these same firms incur due to domestic inflation and more expensive imported inputs—both also consequences of devaluation.[47]

The widespread perception that IMF austerity policies often brought political instability also increased the reluctance of some governments to cooperate with the IMF. Perhaps the most feared element of the typical IMF package involves the removal of government subsidies for basic foodstuffs and other necessities, such as fuel oil and public transportation. Price rises in these sensitive areas have provoked unrest in many Third World countries.

Inching toward the Inevitable: The Brady Plan

Named after U.S. Treasury Secretary Nicholas Brady and presented in the spring of 1989, the Brady Plan included the first U.S. acknowledgment that debt reduction and forgiveness would have to comprise a part of any successful scheme for coping with the Third World debt crisis. The Brady Plan aimed at reducing Third World debt to private creditors. Brady originally set a goal of $70 billion in debt forgiveness for 15 heavily indebted countries to be achieved over several years. This would constitute roughly a 20 percent reduction in outstanding bank debt.

The heart of the Brady Plan consisted of a set of incentives designed to induce banks to forgive part of the debt owed them. Banks were offered the opportunity to exchange their old loans for new bonds carrying either a reduced principal or lower interest rates. The attraction of the new bonds, despite their discount, was that, unlike the old loans, they included guarantees of repayment secured by special funds set aside for the purpose. The new bonds thus carried a much lower risk of default than did the old debt. Only nations agreeing to adopt IMF-sponsored policy reforms were eligible for participation in Brady Plan deals. The special funds set aside as security for the new bonds were financed through new loans issued by the IMF, the World Bank, and Northern governments, especially Japan. Banks reluctant to provide interest or principal reduction were offered the option of lending new money. All private creditors were expected to accept one of these three forms of sacrifice (or a combination of them) in degrees proportional to their stake in the country's debt. Banks that initially refused experienced considerable pressure to participate from other banks and Northern governments.[48]

Mexico was the first country to reach an agreement with its bank creditors under the Brady Plan. The negotiations proved complex and arduous. Although the broad outlines were accepted in July 1989, the precise details of an agreement were not worked out until the following February. Roughly equal numbers of banks chose to reduce the principal on their loans by 35 percent or to accept a lower interest rate of 6.25 percent. A relatively small group of banks offered to extend new funds equal to 25 percent of their old loans. Mexico managed to lop $7 billion in principal off its total debt of $95 billion through the deal while also gaining reduced interest payments on a portion of the remainder and $1.5 billion in new lending. Mexico borrowed $5.7 billion, however, from the IMF, the World Bank, and Japan to finance the collateral fund set up to guarantee interest payments for a period of 18 months. Overall, Mexico reduced its yearly debt service burden by roughly 10 to 20 percent. By 1994, 18 large debtor countries had achieved similar Brady Plan deals with private creditors covering $191 billion in debt. Total debt reduction amounted to $61 billion.[49]

In late June 1990 President Bush announced an extension of the Brady Plan to cover official as well as private credit. In his "Enterprise for Americas" initiative, Bush offered to begin negotiations with Latin American countries that could lead to reductions totaling $7 billion in the debt they owed the U.S. government. The United States also promised to expand its support for collateral funds designed to guarantee payment on private bank debt and to increase U.S. assistance (contingent upon matching funds from Europe and Japan) for policy reforms designed to privatize publicly owned firms or to remove restrictions on foreign direct investment or currency exchange. Bush coupled these announcements with a call for negotiations on the creation of a hemispheric free-trade pact.[50] Latin American reaction was positive. Uruguayan president Luis Lacalle declared: "When, after years of our complaining of neglect, the most important man in the world offers his hand, then, I think we should grab it—and the arm and the elbow and the shoulder, too." Carlos Andres Perez, president of Venezuela, called Bush's plan "the most advanced proposal the United States has ever proposed for Latin America. It's revolutionary, historical."[51]

The Brady Plan, combined with renewed economic growth in Latin America, has helped to ease the debt burden of the largest debtor countries. For a group of 17 highly indebted middle-income countries, their ratio of net international debt to exports fell from 384 percent in 1986 to 225 percent in 1993. For these same countries, net external debt relative to GNP declined from 67 percent in 1986 to 42 percent in 1993. Nevertheless, debt repayments continue to absorb a substantial portion of export earnings and to render these countries vulnerable to negative external shocks.

The Brady Plan deals accelerated a trend in which bank debt was replaced by debt owed to official creditors, especially multilateral agencies. Of total external debt, the share owed to official multilateral lenders increased from 25 percent of long-term obligations in 1980 to 33 percent in 1997 for low-income countries and from 9 percent to 15 percent for middle-income countries over the same period.[52] As a result, the quality of the loan portfolios held by official multilateral creditors has declined. Indeed, arrears on the loans issued by the IMF reached a historic high of $4 billion in 1990, forcing the IMF to consider selling some of its gold holdings in order to replenish its liquid reserves.[53] More troubling from the perspective of Third World countries was that the bylaws of international lending agencies prevented them from forgiving outstanding loans. Thus a growing proportion of the remaining Third World debt was nonnegotiable.[54]

Also, the Brady Plan pushed the burdens of others' misjudgments onto Northern taxpayers. Not only were taxpayers asked to help fund increases in the lending resources of the IMF and the World Bank, but also, in the United States, they compensated for the revenues lost when U.S. banks deducted losses on foreign loans from their overall tax liabilities.[55]

The Heavily Indebted Poor Countries Initiative

Alongside the Brady Plan, which addresses the largest debtor countries, have come a variety of Northern initiatives designed to reduce the burdens of the poorest debtor nations, particularly those in sub-Saharan Africa. By the end of the 1990s, two-thirds of the least-developed countries in the world carried external debt burdens that were unsustainable by international standards. In the past decade, many of these countries have reduced import levels in order to make debt payments. Despite such measures, many have nevertheless fallen into arrears on their international debt.[56]

Responding to the plight of low-income debtor countries, the IMF and the World Bank in 1996 announced a joint program called the Highly Indebted Poor Countries (HIPC) initiative. This program was expanded in 1999, leading to the so-called Enhanced HIPC. The aim of this initiative is to provide debt relief to 41 eligible low-income debtor countries.

To qualify for HIPC aid, participating governments are required to follow an IMF-designed structural adjustment plan for three years, after which the IMF, World Bank and other official lenders write off a portion of the country's debt. The government must then continue to observe IMF-imposed economic policies for an additional three years. Those that fail to do so risk the reinstatement of the original debt obligations. A second condition for debt relief is that recipient country governments must prepare an acceptable Poverty Reduction Strategy Paper that outlines how resources freed from debt payments will be used to tackle poverty. HIPC proposes to reduce the external debt of poor country debtors to no more than 150 percent of annual export revenues. At this level, yearly debt payments would amount to roughly 15 percent of annual export income.[57]

Up through the year 2000, only a small handful of countries had qualified for HIPC debt reduction. Under pressure from an international coalition of nongovernmental organizations (NGOs), the IMF and World Bank greatly accelerated the pace of HIPC in 2001. By the end of that year, 24 countries had been approved for HIPC relief. For this group of countries, HIPC promised to cut their overall debt stock by 50 percent and to reduce debt loads from 60 percent of GDP to 30 percent. Yearly debt service payments would be reduced by one-third from actual levels in 1998–1999 (note that actual payments for the latter year fell short of obligated payments due to the buildup of arrears). As a result of the poverty reduction emphasis built into HIPC, it is estimated that two-thirds of overall debt relief will go to increased health and education spending within recipient countries. In addition to HIPC relief, some low-income countries will also benefit from the cancellation of bilateral official debt by some donor countries.[58]

THE POLITICS OF THIRD WORLD DEBT

In the late 1970s and early 1980s, many analysts predicted that Third World debt would provide these countries with enormous political leverage over the North—power that the Third World could use to wrest concessions from Northern nations on the reform of the international economic order. The reasoning behind this argument was captured by a well-worn saying: "If you owe the bank a thousand dollars, you have a problem. If you owe the bank a million dollars, the bank has a problem."

In fact, however, it was the North that gained leverage from the debt crisis. Early on, the nature, origins, and solutions to the debt crisis were defined largely by the North. The burden of adjustment fell upon the Third World in the form of IMF-administered austerity programs. Northern governments, the United States in particular, refused to alter related policies, such as those concerning interest rates or market access, to accommodate debtor country concerns. Nationalistic strategies of development in the South, meanwhile, gave way during the 1980s to policies long favored by the North, such as the lowering of barriers to Northern goods and investments.

By the early 1990s, the failure of earlier Northern-sponsored approaches had compelled Northern governments and bank officials to accept the prospect of limited debt reduction. Yet what remains striking about the history of the debt crisis during the eighties is the inability of the Third World to wrest greater concessions from the North and the reluctance of Southern officials to contemplate radical strategies for responding to the debt crisis. Before we turn to contemporary developments in North-South finance, it may be useful to reflect in greater depth upon the political dynamics of North-South bargaining over Third World debt issues during the eighties.

Why Not Repudiation?

The costs of attempting to repay their foreign debt have been high for many Third World countries, while the benefits have been few. Why, then, have more countries not simply repudiated their debts, refusing to pay on the grounds that their citizens have sacrificed enough? Although no major debtor country has flatly repudiated its foreign debt, several, including Peru, Brazil, and Argentina, have suspended or limited their debt payments for periods of time. These measures have been typically intended both to gain breathing space during periods when foreign reserves have run low and to be a bargaining tactic designed to force Northern banks to offer concessions in return for resumed debt payments.

Although debt moratoria can provide short-term relief and may bring concessions from creditors, they also involve costs for the debtor country itself. In particular, wayward debtors sacrifice their international creditworthiness. Countries fear that a defiant stance on debt repayment could result in a loss of access to short-term trade credit. Short-term credits, consisting mostly of loans issued for periods of days or weeks between the time of sale and the actual delivery of traded goods, are heavily relied upon to lubricate the wheels of international commerce. Without them, a nation must face the difficult prospect of conducting its trade with the outside world on a cash-only basis. The denial of trade credits is perhaps the ultimate sanction that banks have available for disciplining defiant debtors. Brazil accumulated $6 billion in arrears during its payments moratorium. However, according to John Reed, chair of Citibank in 1990, Brazil also lost access to some $3 billion in normal short-term lending.[59]

Actual debt repudiation might lead to even sterner sanctions, such as legal moves by bank creditors to seize a debtor country's assets abroad in fulfillment of its debt. The risk for any single country that decides to pursue a radical strategy is that it may rupture the entire web of relationships it holds with the international economic community. These calculations make clear the dependence of many, if not most, Third World states on the world economy. This reality is captured in Finance Minister Silva Herzog's recollection of deliberations among Mexican policy makers as they attempted to formulate a strategy for coping with the country's financial crisis in 1982: "We asked ourselves the question what happens if we say, 'No dice. We just won't pay'? There were some partisans of that. But it didn't make any sense. We're part of the world. We import 30 percent of our food. We just can't say, 'Go to Hell.'"[60]

Bargaining Power and the Debt: Southern Disunity and Northern Unity

If Third World debtors find it difficult to go it alone in defying Northern creditors, then why don't they pool their leverage through cooperation? The possibility of a debtors' cartel was a much discussed topic among bankers, academic observers, and government officials beginning in the early 1980s, when the idea was first seriously broached. Third World debtors indeed made sporadic attempts at cooperation in negotiating with the North during the eighties. Latin American countries were the most vigorous in their efforts to forge greater unity. Representatives from the region's major nations gathered frequently throughout the eighties to discuss their common debt problems.

These meetings typically produced declarations calling upon creditor governments and banks to share some of the burden of easing the debt crisis. Meeting in Ecuador in 1984, Latin American representatives appealed to creditors to "harmonize the requirements of debt servicing with the development needs of each country."[61] In November 1987 eight Latin American presidents meeting in Acapulco, Mexico, called for "mechanisms that will allow our countries to benefit from discounts in the value of the respective debts in the market and from the consequent reduction in the servicing of such debts" and for the establishment of "interest rate limits, in accordance with procedures decided upon between the parties."[62] This was followed in 1989 by a meeting of the 26 nations of the Latin American Economic System (SELA) to continue consultations on a common debt bargaining strategy.[63] Beyond Latin America, United Nations Commission on Trade and Development (UNCTAD), the Third World trade organization, issued a call in September 1988 for commercial banks to forgive 30 percent of the debt owed by the 15 most heavily indebted countries.[64]

The results of these consultations among debtor countries, however, seldom progressed beyond verbal expressions of unity. Latin American debtors rejected the notion of forming a true debtors' cartel. Even lesser forms of cooperation, such as coordinating the timing of debt renegotiations or agreeing on common terms, demands, and objectives in bargaining with the North, generally eluded debtor countries.

This disunity among debtors stood in contrast to the generally high degree of coordination among banks, Northern governments, and international organizations. Why, then, did debtor country cooperation prove so feeble? Part of the reason is that, despite their common interests, debtor countries were, and remain, in competition with one another for Northern funds. This rivalry can lead countries to seek the favor of creditors by adopting a more cooperative stance than their neighbors.[65] Governments may be slow to associate themselves with the radical positions sometimes taken by other debtors, for fear that their own creditworthiness will be marred.

This was the case in 1984 when President Raul Alfonsin of Argentina called for debtor country unity in confronting the IMF and the banks. Instead of rallying around Argentina in its time of need, other Latin American countries sided with Northern creditors and persuaded Argentina to back down from its confrontational stance. Neighboring debtor nations even went so far as to provide Argentina with the short-term financing needed to pay its overdue debt bill.[66] Commenting on this episode, one Mexican Foreign Ministry official pointed out: "We have a lot of incentives to convince the other nations to be cautious. We have suffered a lot to get where we are, and we don't want to see them upset it."[67]

A related obstacle to greater unity has to do with the differing timing of the countries' respective financial crises. When Argentina moved toward a more radical strategy in 1984, as we have seen, it was discouraged by Mexico and Brazil; both of these countries had reached agreements with their creditors and therefore felt less urgency about their debt problems. Peru unilaterally declared that it would devote no more than 10 percent of its export earnings toward debt payments in 1985. Still fearful of damaging their access to international credit, Mexico, Brazil, and Argentina refused Peru their support. Brazil and Argentina had new stabilization programs in place in 1986, when Mexico came close to suspending payments, and again, they refused to contemplate a more unified and confrontational course. Much the same was true in 1987, when Brazil declared a moratorium on payments to its private creditors. Mexico by that time had initiated a new stabilization plan in cooperation with its creditors, and Argentina was in no mood to rock the boat.[68]

Differences in size also impede cooperation. Small debtor countries have often been more supportive of a radical course than have larger debtor countries. Large countries receive more favorable treatment by Northern creditors than do small countries, precisely because the big debtors pose a greater threat to the world financial system. Large debtors also have better prospects of gaining renewed access to international credit markets in the future than do their smaller brethren and thus have more reason to protect their creditworthiness. For reasons of image and pride, moreover, large and relatively well developed countries like Brazil and Mexico do not wish to be lumped together with small poverty-stricken countries like Bolivia or Peru.[69] Finally, large debtor countries resent the prospect that small countries would be free riders on the efforts of the large countries in any cooperative endeavor. Small countries would benefit alongside large debtors from any favorable outcomes gained in bargaining with the North while contributing very little to the success of such a venture.[70]

Indeed, movement toward a debtors' cartel raises the problem of cheating. The North would inevitably seek to split any debtors' cartel by offering some countries special incentives to defect. This sort of obstacle has often stymied cooperation. Mexican officials, for instance, have at times believed that they could gain a better deal by relying upon their country's special relationship with the United States rather than by joining other debtor countries in a stance of defiance.[71]

Domestic factors also inhibit movement toward a radical strategy. The economic interests of the middle and upper classes in many Southern countries serve to sap governing elites of the will needed to confront the North over the debt issue. The well-to-do in many debtor countries invested substantial portions of their assets abroad during the 1980s. With large amounts of money in Northern banks, these individuals have little interest in endorsing methods that might wreak havoc on Northern financial institutions.[72]

Related to this is the presence of many technocrats in the economic ministries of most Third World countries. Often trained in the North, these internationalist-oriented bureaucrats share much of the ideology and outlook of organizations such as the IMF. They may lobby for compliance with IMF- or World Bank-sponsored reforms because they are convinced that such policies are conducive to long-term economic growth, regardless of the short-term costs. The outcome of internal battles between these policy makers and their more nationalist-oriented colleagues varies across countries and across time.

IMF and World Bank officials sometimes attempt to strengthen their allies in such conflicts so as to smooth acceptance of the policies they advocate. They do so indirectly by training Third World financial and development officials at special schools run by the IMF and the bank.[73] More directly, one study has documented efforts by World Bank officials to bypass and isolate nationalist bureaucrats, while cooperating with international technocrats, in the development and implementation of a structural adjustment program in the Philippines during the early 1980s.[74]

Northern banks also face a number of obstacles to mutual cooperation in their negotiations with debtor countries. Perhaps the largest of these obstacles stems from the sheer number of banks whose assent must be gained in any given deal. This is true of even relatively small-scale loans. A 1983 rescheduling agreement concerning Ecuador's $1.2 billion in overdue loan payments required the participation of over 400 banks.[75]

Coordination among this many actors would be difficult under most circumstances. But cooperation is rendered even more problematic by conflicting interests. Banks involved in international lending differ widely in their size and their proportional exposure to Third World debt. Smaller and less heavily exposed banks are typically more reluctant than are larger and more deeply committed banks to lend new money to help troubled debtors keep current on payments stemming from previous loans. Bankers are also divided by national origin. During the early 1980s, conflicts arose over the fact that U.S. banks were more heavily involved in lending to Latin America than were European banks, whereas the latter had lent more to Poland and other Eastern European countries than had those in the United States. Banks of different nationality also face varying regulatory requirements from their home governments.[76]

The relationship between banks and Northern governments has at times presented problems, as well. Tensions have arisen over the distribution of burdens between the two in coping with the debt crisis. Moreover, whereas banks are primarily concerned with profits, governments are motivated by broader political concerns, such as the maintenance of political stability or the spread of democracy in debtor countries. The potential for conflict between these outlooks is captured in a statement attributed to a Citicorp vice chair: "Who knows which political system works? The only test we care about is: Can they pay their bills?"[77]

During most of the debt crisis, however, Northern banks have been remarkably successful in maintaining unity among themselves, despite these obstacles, and in securing the cooperation of other actors. The difficulties of sustaining cooperation among large numbers of banks have been eased by the rules and practices of syndicated lending as well as by the web of ties that binds banks together. Most syndicated loan agreements, for instance, require two-thirds approval before a debtor can be declared in default. Because voting is weighted according to each bank's share of the total loan, this rule effectively provides the big banks with veto power over such decisions.

Less formally, large banks have developed procedures for monitoring small bank behavior and for pressuring them to cooperate in rescheduling deals. An advisory committee of 14 major banks carried out the bulk of negotiations with Mexico, for instance, in 1982. After a deal was reached, each of these banks took responsibility for bringing 10 regional banks on board. Each regional bank, in turn, sought to secure the cooperation of 10 nearby smaller banks. This arrangement became standard operating procedure in subsequent rescheduling negotiations. The major banks, as well as the debtor countries themselves, nudged recalcitrant banks toward cooperation in new lending by threatening to exclude the latter from future syndication deals. Due to their need to protect long-term business relationships with larger banks, small banks often found such threats compelling.[78]

Gaps in private cooperation are often filled in by the actions of public authorities. If pressure from the large banks is insufficient to induce cooperation on the part of a small bank, for instance, the latter might become the subject of informal pressure from U.S. Treasury Department or Federal Reserve authorities. The regulatory power that government agencies hold over banks provides authorities with a powerful means of influencing bank behavior.

The large banks have found the IMF and the World Bank generally responsive to their concerns and quite useful in protecting overall bank interests. The reasons for this are simple. Both institutions have weighted voting schemes that give the North far more voting power than the South. The top officials of both institutions are invariably drawn from the North and often have roots in the banking world. The IMF and World Bank also raise funds by issuing securities in Northern financial markets. Finally, both institutions are influenced by prevailing economic doctrines, which are predominantly shaped by Northern intellectuals.

These factors generally incline the IMF toward policies favored by the banks. Indeed, bankers treat the IMF's relationship with a Third World country as an indicator of the latter's creditworthiness. A country unable to resolve its differences with the fund will likely be snubbed by the banks as well. Banks find it too costly and difficult to develop detailed economic and political data concerning each Third World country. They instead rely upon the expertise and judgment of the IMF. The IMF is also in a much better position to impose, administer, and monitor policy reform programs in troubled debtor countries than are the banks. As a public institution that lends only to member countries, the IMF has an authority that is more legitimate than that of a private bank. Moreover, with the IMF in the lead, debtor countries find it more difficult to divide the bank coalition by striking special deals with some creditors but not with others. Finally, the fund sometimes defends the collective interests of all banks by compelling reluctant individual banks to shoulder their part of the burden of new lending.[79]

In general, Northern actors have been far more unified in bargaining over Third World debt than have their Southern counterparts. The resources at their disposal have also been greater. Yet, although still favoring the North, the balance of bargaining power has shifted somewhat in favor of debtor countries since 1989. Debtor countries began to pursue bolder tactics in their search for concessions from the North in the late 1980s. Banks, by allowing their new lending to the South to dwindle, diluted one of the incentives that previously had induced a more cooperative stance on the part of debtor countries. Conflicts intensified, moreover, between the banks and Northern governments. The Brady Plan called upon banks to make sacrifices not altogether to their liking. It was motivated in part by fears that lack of progress in defusing the debt crisis might lead to political instability in Latin America. This risk was driven home when left-wing candidates came close to winning the presidencies of both Mexico and Brazil in the late eighties. Broader political considerations, along with continuing pressure from U.S. export interests harmed by Latin American austerity, came to partially outweigh U.S. government responsiveness to banker preferences. These considerations serve as a reminder that power relationships, such as those that govern North-South economic ties, are never static and can shift for a variety of reasons.

NORTH-SOUTH FINANCE IN THE 1990s:

THE GROWTH OF PORTFOLIO INVESTMENT

The early 1990s brought a dramatic revival in North-South financial flows after the prolonged slump of the 1980s. The movement of all kinds of Northern capital to the Third World tripled between 1990 and 1993.[80] The composition and destination of these new financial resources differed substantially, however, from the recent past.[81]

Portfolio investment came to replace bank lending as the dominant source of foreign financing for many Third World countries. Bank loans accounted for 77 percent of all foreign capital that flowed to the Third World in 1981. By 1993 portfolio investment had come to represent 74 percent of such flows, overshadowing both bank lending and foreign direct investment. Between 1990 and 1997, the value of portfolio flows to the Third World increased sixfold. Sixty percent of portfolio investments during this period went to only six countries. Whereas the bank loans of the 1970s and early 1980s went primarily to Southern governments or state-owned firms, 60 percent of the portfolio funds of the 1990s went to the private sector.[82]

Portfolio investment takes two principal forms. In the first, foreign pension funds, mutual funds, investment banks, and individuals purchase stocks or equities in Third World firms. Typically, such investments are too small to provide actual control over the firm in question. Foreign investors take on a passive ownership role, forgoing participation in management of the company. This sort of stake differs from direct investment, where a foreign firm sets up its own operations in a host country or purchases a controlling interest in a local firm and takes on direct management responsibilities. A second form of portfolio investment involves the purchase of corporate- or government-issued bonds. This is a type of loan, extended directly from an investor to the bond-issuing firm. Investors receive a stipulated interest rate on the bonds they possess, with the principal to be paid back by a specified date.

The portfolio investment flows of the 1990s were stimulated by (1) the attraction of higher interest rates in the South as compared with those in the North, (2) growing investor confidence in the economic reforms being carried out by many Southern states, (3) more-successful management of Third World debt under the guise of the Brady Plan, (4) a loosening of Third World restrictions on many forms of foreign investment, and (5) the lure of investing in a growing number of previously state-owned firms that were sold off to private ownership by many Third World governments during this period.[83]

Portfolio investment has provided some Third World countries with a ready and welcome new source of international financial resources. As noted earlier, however, most Third World countries have been bypassed by Northern investors. Moreover, the drawbacks of portfolio investment are substantial. Many Northern investors know little about the firms in which they put their money. Most of these funds are provided on a short-term basis and do not offer the sort of "patient" or long-term capital that Third World countries most need. Portfolio funds are relatively liquid; they can be easily withdrawn at the first sign of trouble in a country's economy, quickly transforming a manageable problem into a deteriorating crisis as large quantities of capital flee the country.[84]

These dangers are clearly illustrated in the recent Mexican peso crisis. As 1994 dawned, Mexico was widely touted as a model of neoliberal transformation and as an example for other Latin American countries to follow. Over the previous decade, Mexican presidents had committed their country to a strategy of thorough liberalization, abandoning the traditionally dominant role played by the state in the Mexican economy. The once vast state-owned sector of the economy had been largely privatized. Hewing closely to IMF and World Bank policy prescriptions, Mexico was the first country to enjoy the debt reduction made possible by the Brady Plan. Mexico dramatically lowered import barriers during the early 1990s and entered into the North American Free Trade Agreement (NAFTA) with the United States and Canada. Once viewed with suspicion, foreign investors were now welcomed. Indeed, over $90 billion in foreign investment entered Mexico from 1990 through 1993, two-thirds of it in the form of portfolio investment. Following the deep economic downturn of the 1980s, GDP growth resumed at an average rate of 3.1 percent per year between 1988 and 1994, while annual inflation fell from nearly 145 percent to only 6 percent.[85]

By the end of 1994, however, this dreamy picture of economic health had given way to a nightmarish financial panic. Following a year of political upheaval and economic mismanagement, Mexico's peso crisis of December 1994 sent the economy into a tailspin and cast doubt upon both the wisdom of relying so heavily upon fickle international financial flows and the neoliberal policies that Mexico so well exemplified.

A number of factors prompted the wave of foreign investment that entered Mexico during the early nineties. The Brady Plan of 1989 and more-prudent government fiscal policies helped to restore a measure of faith in Mexico's creditworthiness. Investors welcomed Mexico's new, market-oriented economic strategy, and many believed that the impending NAFTA accord would spur Mexican exports and growth. The sell-off of state-owned enterprises created new opportunities for foreign investors to gain equity stakes in a set of large and stable firms at bargain prices. Moreover, low U.S. interest rates combined with recession north of the border prompted investors to look elsewhere, including Mexico, for profits.

Many of the funds that flowed to Mexico from the United States in the early nineties represented repatriated flight capital. Wealthy Mexicans who had deposited massive sums abroad during the depths of the Mexican debt crisis of the eighties brought these same funds back to Mexico after economic conditions there improved in the early nineties.[86]

Although Mexico briefly benefited from the renewed flow of international investment following the drought of the eighties, the gains were more apparent than real. Little of the huge torrent of portfolio investment that Mexico attracted in the early nineties found its way into new physical investments, such as factories or machinery. Most was geared toward short-term financial speculation on Mexican stocks and other securities. Moreover, the increased availability of foreign funds was substantially offset by a large drop in Mexico's own domestic savings rate—from 22 percent of GDP in 1988 to 16 percent in 1994.[87]

In fact, the main effect of increased foreign investment was to finance Mexico's uncontrolled import consumption binge of the early 1990s. Although Mexican exports grew strongly in this period, the country's import bill rose even more rapidly, producing a current account deficit of nearly $30 billion, equivalent to a whopping 8 percent of Mexican GDP, in 1994. This enormous trade deficit sapped Mexico's official reserves, which fell from $25 billion at the beginning of 1994 to only $6 billion by the end of the year. By early 1995 the government had issued $29 billion in short-term, dollar-denominated bonds, called *tesebonos,* to cover Mexico's foreign exchange shortfall.[88]

Mexico's worsening financial situation was exacerbated by both international and domestic factors. Internationally, rising interest rates in the United States, along with an economic recovery, attracted relatively liquid portfolio investment funds from Mexico and other Latin American countries back to U.S. financial markets.[89]

Domestically, Mexico suffered a series of political crises that undermined investor confidence. January 1994 brought an armed rebellion by a peasant organization called the Zapatistas in the southern state of Chiapas. Protesting NAFTA, Mexico's neoliberal economic policies, and the lack of genuine democracy, the rebels battled police and Mexican army forces for two weeks before both sides agreed to a tense cease-fire and subsequent on-and-off-again negotiations over rebel demands. In March a presidential candidate, Luis Donaldo Colosio, representing Mexico's longtime ruling party, the PRI, was assassinated. This was followed in September by the assassination of another high-ranking PRI official, party secretary general Jose Francisco Ruiz Massier. Both assassinations triggered allegations that they were the product of infighting and rivalries within the PRI hierarchy. In December renewed violence flared up in Chiapas.[90]

During this period, Mexico's financial authorities put off measures that might have eased the country's precarious financial circumstances. Despite a growing current account deficit, the government defended an overvalued peso out of fear that a devaluation might prompt so much pain as to endanger the election of the PRI's new candidate, Ernesto Zedillo, in August's presidential election.[91]

After Zedillo was elected, his government finally moved to devalue the peso by 15 percent on December 20. Coming on the heels of such a turbulent year, this move panicked investors and immediately set into motion a major financial crisis. Over the next two days, $5 billion fled the country. Mexican authorities proved unable to halt the free fall of the peso, which plunged in value from 3.5 pesos to the dollar in early December to 7.5 pesos to the dollar by March 1995. The Mexican stock market lost one-half of its value over the three months following the December 20 devaluation. The crisis quickly spread to other countries, such as Argentina and Brazil, where stock markets fell precipitously.[92]

Mexican interest rates briefly peaked at over 80 percent before settling back to a still-astronomical level of between 40 and 50 percent. Such high interest rates choked off domestic investment by Mexican firms. Later in the year, confidence in Mexico's currency dropped so low that many Mexican businesses refused to accept pesos in payment, insisting upon dollars instead. In January and February of 1995, at least 750,000 Mexican workers lost their jobs, and more cuts followed in succeeding months. The real wages of Mexican workers fell by 30 percent over the course of 1995.[93]

As during the 1982 crisis, Mexican authorities looked to the United States for relief. With its reputation tied to the success of NAFTA, the Clinton administration quickly responded. By the end of January 1995, with Mexico only days away from defaulting on its international debts, the United States had assembled a $50 billion international line of credit to Mexico, with $20 billion promised by the United States and the remainder pledged by the IMF, the World Bank, and other industrialized nations. Mexico offered its future oil export income as collateral for the borrowed U.S. funds, which were to be paid back within three to five years. The Mexican government drew upon over $12 billion of U.S. credit during 1995, most of it used to retire short-term *tesebono* bonds as they fell due.[94]

In mid-March, President Zedillo announced an austerity plan, including higher taxes and cuts in public spending, designed to restore international confidence in Mexico's creditworthiness. Higher interest rates were encouraged in an effort to attract investors and strengthen the peso.[95]

Although Mexico's economy shrank during 1995, many financial indicators showed improvement. The current account deficit virtually disappeared as a falling peso stimulated exports and dampened imports. Mexico's foreign reserves rose through the year, and the stock market partially rebounded. Still, the peso again came under attack late in 1995. The Zedillo government responded by announcing a pact with Mexican business and labor designed to restrain price increases, bolster wages, increase domestic savings, and spur public investment. The government also moved to bail out Mexico's own banks, which held vast amounts of worthless debt on their books. By 1999, the total cost of this bank bailout program had risen to $93 billion, an amount equivalent to 19 percent of Mexico's annual GDP.[96]

The Mexican crisis has led to international efforts to avert future episodes of this kind. In June 1995 a group of industrialized nations announced the creation of a $50 billion fund that could be used to stabilize Third World currencies and financial markets in response to rapid speculative movements of international capital. Only countries committed to strict fiscal and monetary policies would be eligible for assistance. The IMF simultaneously announced more sweeping requirements for financial and economic data from borrower countries so as to allow creditors a more accurate picture of each nation's financial health.[97]

This most recent Mexican crisis offers a number of important lessons. Most obviously, the Mexican case illustrates the dangers of relying upon volatile, short-term financial flows to finance unsustainable current account deficits. More broadly, there is no substitute for a strong domestic savings rate. Foreign capital can supplement domestic resources, but it is too unreliable to provide the basis for long-term growth in the absence of sustained domestic capital formation.

THE GLOBAL FINANCIAL CRISIS
OF 1997–1998

The global financial crisis (GFC) in the late 1990s affected many nations, but most intensely Thailand, South Korea, Malaysia, Indonesia, Russia, and Brazil. The combination of a downdraft in exchange rates, stock markets, and real estate prices was the result of a massive loss of confidence in these nations by global investors. And the crisis in developing states spread to the financial markets of advanced nations in Europe and North America. This crisis provides a fascinating case study of the benefits and the costs of globalization and of the political efforts required to stabilize the global economy. As such, interpretation of the causes and consequences of the crisis is linked to quite different ideological and theoretical perspectives. Further, the crisis raises a number of significant questions about the functioning of the world economy and the position of developing states in the system. Given that the crisis began in the rapidly growing economies of East Asia, we must wonder whether this marks the end of this cycle of dramatic growth. These economies were deeply integrated into the world economy through trade and capital flows, and the dramatic damage from the crisis has prompted many to question such a strategy. Others have suggested that the rapid liberalization of financial flows was not accompanied by comparable growth in political capacities for managing this system. This assessment raises the possibility of some significant modification of the mechanisms of global financial governance, especially the International Monetary Fund. And many have questioned the adequacy of decision making by international investors, both in their initial investments and in the rapid withdrawal. But evaluating these questions requires a basic overview of the origins and development of the crisis.

The origins of the GFC can be traced to the acceleration of the globalization of finance and production in the mid-1980s, specifically the currency realignments beginning in 1985, the relocation of production throughout Asia, and the increased financial flows that followed. In many respects, the GFC was a crisis of globalization itself. In 1985, with the Plaza Agreement, the major industrialized countries agreed to promote an increase in the exchange rates of most important currencies against the U.S. dollar. The main result was to realign the yen-dollar rate, which between 1985 and 1995 moved from 240 yen to the dollar to 80 yen to the dollar. This drastic shift in exchange rates had far-reaching consequences. And the reversal of this trend in 1995 created the circumstances for the global financial crisis.

The rising Japanese yen deeply undermined the competitiveness of internationally traded goods produced in Japan. But it also made the yen very valuable for purchasing assets in foreign countries. This combination pushed many Japanese companies to try to regain their competitiveness by shifting parts of their production abroad, mostly to Southeast Asia, where labor costs were much lower. Over the decade before the crisis began, first Japanese and later Taiwanese and South Korean firms launched an accelerating process of foreign direct investment to establish manufacturing facilities in Thailand, Malaysia, and Indonesia. Along with the Japanese firms came a series of government-sponsored aid projects designed to facilitate the investment of Japanese firms. Japanese banks were also ready to provide lending for the same purposes.[98]

The acceleration of investment had many important consequences. Several states in Southeast Asia became important (or more important) production and export platforms. The Japanese and Asian firms were soon joined by multinationals from other nations, and the exports of Thailand, Malaysia, and Indonesia soared along with their GDP growth. This began to attract more investors in the 1990s, and the inflows of capital became a tidal wave. To facilitate the inflows of capital, the United States urged Asian states to relax the restrictions on capital imports. Liberalization of the capital accounts of these countries came mostly after 1990 and did help accelerate these investments. In addition, many Asian states liberalized their domestic banking systems, often by permitting the formation of new kinds of banks with less governmental regulation. This liberalizing policy was consistent with the trends of the decade and brought these nations even more deeply into the world economy. A final measure designed to attract foreign capital was the linking of the value of local currencies to the dollar, which removed a major source of uncertainty for investors. By the 1990s, a larger proportion of incoming funds came as short-term investments, in areas like stock markets and quick maturing loans. But the benefits of joining the world economy seemed to overwhelm any potential downside. Over the 12 years from 1985 to 1997, Thailand, Indonesia, and Malaysia joined the largest 20 nations in global trade mostly as a result of the growing role of multinational corporations in domestic production and exports.[99]

The size and composition of the capital flows into emerging markets needs some detailed description and clarification. Some broad categories help us understand the speed and size of these flows. From 1988 to 1996, net private capital flows into emerging markets jumped from one-quarter of 1 percent of the GDP of these nations to more than 3 percent of their GDP and by 1996 totaled over $300 billion. In 1990, of the roughly $50 billion in private capital inflows, nearly two-thirds was in foreign direct investment (FDI). These funds were quite concentrated in terms of recipient countries: one-third to China; one-third to the combination of Malaysia, Thailand, Indonesia, and Korea; and nearly one-third to the group of Brazil, Mexico, and Argentina. Loans and portfolio flows were less than one-quarter of the totals. (Remember that FDI involves purchasing assets to be used to conduct a business and usually these assets are difficult to liquidate quickly. By contrast, those who purchase stock or make short-term loans can remove their funds much more quickly.) Only six years later, FDI had fallen to only one-third of the $300 billion inflow, whereas the shorter-term investments had ballooned to nearly $200 billion.

In some ways, the Asian economies were victims of their own success. By the mid-1980s, many Asian states had earned the tag "tiger economies" as a result of their rapid economic growth since the 1960s. Hong Kong, Singapore, South Korea, and Taiwan all made dramatic improvements in economic conditions, and the spreading of rapid economic growth to other Asian states after 1985 led many global investors to include these new "tigers" in their investment plans. Western mutual funds and banks became increasingly enchanted with Asia after 1990 and bought equities and made loans to reap the profits from this region.[100] Portfolio managers are judged primarily on how well they do in comparison with other portfolio managers; and much the same is true for bankers. Thus, as more managers and bankers invested and lent funds successfully, this success pulled in more funds from other managers and bankers.

Much of this money was from Europe and the United States, following Japanese money originally invested to establish offshore production facilities (see Table 12.2). The notion of a "herd instinct" in global capital movements is a controversial one. Liberals and defenders of the efficiency of free markets reject this notion because it violates their concept of the rationality of free markets, which are thought to allocate resources to their most efficient use.[101] Others, less enamored of markets, find evidence for a herd instinct in the global financial crisis. Funds flowed into Asia and other emerging markets in quantities greater than could be justified by a dispassionate analysis of the economic returns and risks; and when the sentiment turned, funds flowed out in a panicked effort to salvage principal and profits. In the wake of the Asian financial crisis, even highly placed officials came to acknowledge the fickleness

Table 12.2 Distribution of Loans By Nation of Origin, 1998 (billions of $US)

Borrower	Total	LENDER				
		France	Germany	Japan	U.K.	U.S.
Indonesia	58.7	4.8	5.6	23.2	4.3	4.6
South Korea	103.4	10.1	10.8	23.7	6.1	10.0
Malaysia	28.8	2.9	5.7	10.5	2.0	2.4
Thailand	69.4	5.1	7.6	37.7	2.8	4.0

SOURCE: *New York Times,* February 16, 1999.

of private monetary flows. Stanley Fischer, deputy managing director of the IMF, has observed that "markets are not always right. Sometimes inflows are excessive, and sometimes they may be sustained too long. Markets tend to react late, but then they tend to react fast, sometimes excessively."[102]

The boom in East Asia increasingly came to rest on a set of unsustainable arrangements. Opening the domestic system to capital flows—liberalization—often meant the creation or expansion of local financial institutions with little lending experience and weak regulation by the government. The governmental decision for liberalization frequently came as a result of pressure from a combination of the U.S. government, the International Monetary Fund, and global investors. And this choice was certainly swayed by the need to take advantage of an enormous growth bonanza. But liberalization of the flow of capital was a monumental step with major consequences. As one scholar put it:

> locals could open foreign bank accounts; banks could extend credit in foreign currencies in the domestic markets; nonbank financial institutions and private corporations could borrow abroad; foreigners could own shares listed by national companies on domestic stock markets; foreign banks could enjoy wider freedom of entry into the domestic banking sector; and offshore banks could borrow abroad and lend domestically.[103]

As the doors opened and the economy grew, foreign investors and domestic financial institutions began putting funds into less safe investments. The search for profits led to investments with higher and higher levels of risk, primarily in real estate. Real estate, especially for banks, looks like a safe basis for lending: it provides collateral with significant value. But in mid-1990s Asia, this promise turned illusory when growth helped make real estate into a speculative commodity and lending turned into speculation on real estate price appreciation. More generally, borrowed funds from abroad were frequently used for the purchase of nonproductive assets—assets that did not generate revenue to repay the loans and whose repayment depended on continuing price increases in real estate. By the end of 1996, for example, the real estate market of Bangkok, Thailand, had accumulated a backlog of $20 billion in new but unsold commercial and residential properties.[104]

A developing country, especially a rapidly growing one, often experiences a current account deficit. Thus is because developing nations need to import technology, production equipment, and various inputs for manufacturing. Along with this is the need to finance these purchases with external funds. Thus, the large deficit in the current account is financed by a surplus in the capital account. For this to continue, investors from abroad must continue to believe their loans will be repaid and their investments will be profitable.

Any number of events could operate to frighten off global investors, especially those with short-term commitments. The inflow of funds—often unregulated by the government and too often based on speculative decision making by investors—was increasingly unsustainable. A very substantial portion of the loans to Asian borrowers had maturity dates of less than one year—meaning the loan had to be repaid within 12 months or less. In 1995, for instance, roughly one-half of Thailand's $83 billion foreign debt was short term.[105] Additionally, many of these short-term loans were used to finance real estate construction linked to the boom in demand for office space and housing. The current account deficit meant that any interruption in capital inflows would force a sharp cutback in a variety of imports and would surely lead to a collapse in real estate and stock prices.

In the two years before the crisis broke out in July 1997, danger signals began to emerge that pointed to potential problems. Two were the most important. Remember that the huge inflow of funds was initially based on the rising value of the yen after 1985 and the great cost advantages for producing in and exporting from Asian states. The first warning sign came when the trends in the yen-dollar exchange rate began to reverse course in April 1995, with the dollar now rising against the yen. The currencies of each of the major Asian crisis states was fixed to the dollar, so their currencies also began to rise against the yen, thereby undermining some of their competitive advantage in global export markets. Because inflation in countries such as Thailand was higher than in the United States, many saw the existing fixed exchange rate between the Thai baht and the dollar (25 baht = US$1) as unsustainable. Further evidence of trouble came when Thai exports failed to rise in 1996. Without rising exports, the Thai current account deficit rose—meaning that even more foreign capital was needed to finance the deficit.

Into this arena of uncertainty and potential trouble came the global foreign exchange traders—the 800-pound gorillas of international finance, at least when their trading decisions tilt strongly in one direction.[106] The combination in Thailand of a large current account deficit, slowing export growth, rising inflation, decreasing international competitiveness, and sinking stock and property markets led many foreign exchange traders to the same conclusion: the fixed exchange rate of the baht and U.S. dollar could not be sustained. These traders began to speculate on a currency devaluation in the spring of 1997, prompting a vigorous effort by the Thai government to protect the currency's fixed rate by buying baht and raising interest rates. News of bad property loans contributed to renewed speculative attacks. With its foreign exchange reserves exhausted, on July 2, 1997, the Thai government capitulated and let the baht float. The rapid drop in the baht's value of more than 20 percent forced the government to turn to the IMF for help in stabilizing the currency.

The International Monetary Fund is a key actor in international financial crises, mainly as the one global institution able to provide for stabilization and able to tie aid to significant policy changes by affected governments. The IMF is one of the most important proponents of liberal globalization and has consistently pressed for freer markets in money and goods as the main path to development.[107] The entrance of the IMF into Thailand's financial crisis signaled an effort not only to prevent the crisis from spreading and damaging the global economy but also to require Thailand, in return for IMF assistance, to make some important changes. During July and August, the IMF and the Thai government negotiated the terms of an agreement to provide Thailand with a $17 billion loan. Thailand had to accept closure of many of its banks, more bank regulation, a large reduction in the current account deficit, cuts in government spending and tax increases, and increased opportunities for foreigners to own Thai businesses. These terms—fiscal austerity, regulation, and greater international openness—reflect the standard liberal concept of economic policy, one that surely advances the interests of globally competitive finance and industry.

The IMF effort to stabilize Thailand and prevent a spreading crisis failed. Soon after the Thai decision to float the baht, attacks on other currencies and rapid drops in stock markets spread across much of Asia. The GFC became one of the most serious of the now common financial crises, in large part because of a variety of processes that tended to amplify market declines. The decision to float the baht had the effect of virtually forcing other Asian states to permit their currencies to float, as well. The competitive dynamic of keeping each nation in the area on a par with others meant that, as the exchange rate of one fell, this placed considerable pressure on the others. The cumulative effect was to produce additional panic and speculative selling. October through November 1997 was especially difficult for Malaysia, Indonesia, and South Korea, with significant problems also encountered by Taiwan, Hong Kong, and the Philippines. The rapid drops in currency, real estate, and equity prices often led to new revelations about weaknesses previously unknown or only suspected, which generated additional price declines. For example, after three months of declines and crisis conditions in Southeast Asia, negative information about South Korean banks and corporate problems began to emerge. And this led to a downdraft in Korean currency and equity values.

Between fall 1997 and winter 1998–1999, the crisis in Asia deepened and expanded to the global level. The Clinton administration in the United States was very reluctant to intervene, for two reasons. First, far more of the international funds exposed to loss in the crisis were from Europe and Japan than from the United States (see Table 12.2). Second, after intervening in the Mexican financial crisis in 1994–1995, the administration had received considerable criticism from congressional Republicans who objected to bailing out international lenders with taxpayers' money.

The U.S. reluctance to intervene forced a heavy reliance on the IMF for solutions to the Asian crisis. As the crisis deepened, however, calls for action began to overcome conservative Republican hostility. The first large direct role for the U.S. government came after the crisis had spread to Korea and an IMF agreement failed to stem the tidal wave of stock market and currency (won) selling. Global investors and international banks concluded that the IMF agreement was inadequate for dealing with the large Korean short-term debts and expected Korea to default on these debts. These international lenders were unwilling to renew Korea's considerable short-term loans, which were due almost immediately and which the Koreans could not repay. This set up a series of dramatic Christmas Eve and Christmas Day meetings among the Korean government, the U.S. Treasury, the U.S. Federal Reserve, the IMF, and international bankers in New York. An agreement was reached to speed up IMF funds, obtain a Korean government guarantee of bank debt, and renew existing short-term loans.

Solving the Korean short-term debt crisis fell far short of stabilizing global financial markets. Between January and May 1998, the focus shifted back to Southeast Asia, especially to Indonesia. Another round of collapsing currencies moved back and forth across the region. The fourth largest nation by population, Indonesia was probably the country most damaged by this stage of the financial crisis. The commentators who point to the importance of crony capitalism as an element in exacerbating the crisis are often referring to Indonesia. Indonesia's political economy was based on an authoritarian state with a veneer of democracy, supported by the military and deeply involved in organizing and directing the economy so as to promote a state-backed capitalist class.[108] An elaborate system of state patronage provided subsidies to a multitude of groups but, most important, created a dense network of patrons in the government and clients in business. A elaborate system of licenses, monopolies, protection from competition, and state projects linked government patrons to favored businesses, many of which were operated by the military. This cronyism, or patrimonialism, was accompanied by close connections between government technocrats and international organizations like the World Bank. This helped promote the opening of the Indonesian economy to foreign investment after 1985.

Saddled with a very large short-term foreign debt, a substantial current account deficit, and a huge proportion of nonperforming loans, Indonesia was quickly hit with large drops in its currency. The financial crisis struck Indonesia especially hard: at one point the rupiah lost almost 80 percent of its value, with similar declines in the Indonesian stock market. Forced to turn to the IMF for help, the Indonesian government was confronted by demands for radical changes in its domestic political economy as a condition of receiving IMF aid. The initial agreement with the IMF in October 1997 called for the standard terms: major cuts in government spending and in the current account deficit, along with opening the economy to foreign ownership and closing failed banks. These terms clashed with the existing system of political economy, and the government under President Suharto repeatedly seemed unwilling or unable to carry out its commitments under the IMF aid plan. In

Table 12.3 Changes in Stock Market Valuations (billions of $US)

Country	6/97 Valuation	12/98 Valuation	Percent Change
Russia	84	12	−86%
Indonesia	111	22	−80%
Philippines	74	34	−54%
Thailand	60	35	−42%
Argentina	56	44	−21%
Malaysia	282	74	−74%
South Korea	157	111	−29%
Brazil	311	154	−50%
Hong Kong	427	348	−19%
Germany	766	1,181	+54%
Japan	3,312	2,448	−26%
United States	8,920	11,721	+31%

SOURCE: *New York Times,* February 16, 1999.

January 1998, Suharto's wildly unrealistic budget proposal prompted efforts by leaders from around the world to persuade him to change his policy. A plummeting rupiah forced changes, and on January 15 Suharto signed a new agreement, as IMF head Michel Camdessus "stood behind him with arms locked, photographed in a scene charged with the Javanese contextual significance of the surrendering ruler."[109]

But Suharto was still not finished, and soon he announced his intention to run again for president.[110] A scheme to tie the rupiah to the dollar (and perhaps protect the Suharto family's considerable wealth) was rejected by the IMF and international financiers as unworkable. A third IMF agreement was signed in early April, shortly after Suharto was reelected. This agreement once again attempted to force acceptance of restrictive conditions. International investors and bankers openly stated that the Suharto regime was unable to follow through on the changes needed to restore their confidence. Acting to meet the demands from the IMF and others, the government in early May slashed a series of subsidies, including one for fuel and gasoline. This prompted an outburst of riots and demonstrations across the country, and on May 21 President Suharto resigned. The financial crisis had destroyed the political stability of a nation with a deeply entrenched leader, mainly by undermining Indonesia's system of political economy. Suharto's vice president, B. J. Habibie, a longtime associate, assumed the presidency. The worst of the financial turmoil was over, but Indonesia continued to be plagued by a severe economic downturn and by political instability for the next two years. Nonetheless, a reasonably fair election replaced Habibie with Abdurrahman Wahid, a respected and moderate Muslim leader. One possible outcome of the financial crisis is the creation of a more democratic Indonesia.

Suharto's political demise did not end the turmoil in global markets. In short order, Russia and Brazil succumbed to financial chaos. Russia entered the summer of 1998 under the cloud of ballooning central government budget deficits (due in part to inefficient tax collection) and dangerous levels of short-term foreign debt. In July 1998, the IMF approved a $22.6 billion loan package designed to allow Russia to meet looming debt payments and to reassure financial markets while Russian officials devised a long-term plan for correcting the country's financial imbalances. Less than a month later, however, Russia's simmering problems boiled over into a full-scale crisis. Investors began selling roubles and pulling money out of the country. The Russian stock market plummeted, and many domestic banks ceased loaning money to one another.[111]

Over the coming months, Russian officials adopted a number of measures in an attempt to cope with the crisis, including currency devaluation, a partial moratorium on debt repayment, currency controls, domestic price controls on basic goods, and tougher steps to collect taxes. Russia also approached the IMF and Western nations on numerous occasions with requests for additional financing. The IMF resisted such calls and in fact threatened to delay or cancel distribution of remaining funds from the earlier package approved the previous July unless Russia complied with IMF-supported policy changes. Chief among these were demands that Russia reduce government spending and increase tax collection in an effort to turn a large budget deficit into a surplus. As the Russian economy steadily weakened, negotiations dragged on until March 30, 1999, when the IMF finally reached agreement with Russian officials on a new funding package of $4.8 billion in new loans (which were not actually dispersed until the following August). With over 200 conditions attached, the IMF agreement opened the way for Russia to renegotiate its international debts with Western banks and governments.[112]

Shortly after financial instability hit Russia in August 1998, the contagion spread to Brazil. Brazil carried an international debt load of $228 billion. The country suffered from a budget deficit that equaled 8 percent of Brazilian GDP and faced $70 billion in scheduled payments on its short-term debt in September and October 1998. Despite domestic interest rates of 50 percent, wealthy Brazilians began to move $1 billion per day out of the country during this period. The Brazilian stock market experienced its largest drop ever. Under IMF pressure, the Brazilian government announced a tough austerity plan in an effort to defend the fixed value of its currency, the real. Despite the announcement of an IMF-backed bailout package of $41.5 billion in November, these efforts failed, and the government was forced to allow the nation's currency to float in January 1999. This resulted in an immediate 15-percent decline in the real's value versus the dollar.[113]

Brazil's devaluation had a slow-motion effect on neighboring Argentina. Products produced in Argentina lost competitiveness to those produced in Brazil, worsening Argentina's already negative trade balance. As a result, Argentina's economy fell into a recession. Unemployment rose to 15 percent, and the country's current account deficit reached 3.3 percent of GDP. With its reserves dwindling and an international debt of $140 billion, Argentina was forced to adopt an IMF-sponsored austerity plan in March 2000. These measures produced large public protests and a series of national strikes. The government continued to defend the overvalued peso over the following 21 months while the economy remained in the doldrums.[114]

Matters worsened in Argentina toward the end of 2001. Industrial production dropped 11 percent in November amid continued financial chaos. On December 3, the government announced severe restrictions on the ability of Argentine citizens to withdraw cash from their bank accounts. Coupled with this move was a plan aimed at convincing private creditors to accept a debt restructuring in which new securities carrying lower interest rates would be issued in place of existing debts. Adding to the sense of crisis was a December 5 decision by the IMF to withhold a $1.26 billion loan installment because of the Argentine government's failure to meet budget targets. Massive protests followed, forcing the country's president to resign his office. New president Adolpho Rodriguez Saa announced a suspension of payments on $50 billion in international debt. Yet only a week later he also resigned.[115]

During this period, Argentine officials seriously considered declaring the U.S. dollar Argentina's official currency. Dollars were already widely held and exchanged among Argentines, and other countries, including Panama and Ecuador, had earlier taken such steps. In the end, however, this option was rejected. Instead, Argentina's fifth president in less than a month finally severed the peso's link to the dollar and allowed the currency to float in early January 2002. The peso quickly fell almost 40 percent in value while Argentina remained effectively in default on its massive foreign debt.[116]

With the exception of Argentina, which remains in crisis as of this writing, the countries of Asia, Russia, and Brazil eventually recovered from the financial crisis of 1997 and 1998. Interest rate declines in the United States, combined with IMF support and policy adjustments in the affected countries helped to speed the return to economic growth. Yet the continued outbreak of periodic financial crisis in emerging-country financial markets has forced many observers to question the soundness of the current international financial architecture.

REFORM OF THE INTERNATIONAL FINANCIAL SYSTEM

The inability of IMF and World Bank intervention to halt the spread and deepening of the Asian financial crisis set off a multisided debate over the appropriate policies for preventing and coping with financial instability. Some observers attributed the Asian financial crisis to the herd behavior of currency traders and short-term portfolio investors. The swift flows of unregulated money across international borders overwhelmed the ability of governments to defend the value of their currencies, even when a country's economic fundamentals were sound. Those placing this interpretation on events often argued for bringing back the type of currency controls that were common prior to the financial liberalization of the past two decades. As support for this position, advocates of currency controls often cited China, whose currency is not freely traded on international markets. Unlike many Asian countries, China escaped the Asian crisis relatively unscathed.

In the midst of the Asian crisis, Malaysia reimposed capital controls by forbidding investors from removing investment funds from the country. Malaysian prime minister Mahathir Mohamad asserted: "The free market system has failed and failed disastrously. The only way we can manage the economy is to insulate us... from speculators."[117] While most economists consider Malaysia's across-the-board currency controls too strict, some endorse the more limited measures adopted by Chile in 1991 (though later abandoned in 1998). Although Chile permitted international capital to enter the country freely, funds that subsequently left within a year were penalized by imposition of a tax. No tax was placed on capital that stayed for more than one year. This policy discouraged the kind of short-term money flows that have proven destabilizing in some countries while imposing no restrictions on longer-term flows. Under this policy, Chile succeeded in attracting ample amounts of foreign direct investment while maintaining a stable currency.[118]

An international version of the Chilean experiment would be the Tobin tax, an idea proposed in 1978 by Yale University economist and Nobel laureate James Tobin. Concerned about the financially destabilizing effects of speculative currency flows, Tobin suggested that governments around the world agree to impose a small tax—perhaps as little as one-tenth of 1 per cent—on such transactions. This would have the effect of discouraging currency trades that were merely speculative in nature, or in other words, not linked directly to trade and investment.

The rapid capital flight that characterized the Asian financial crisis has prompted renewed interest in the Tobin tax. Another source of renewed attention to Tobin's proposal is the fact that currency trading has become almost wholly detached from the real economy. In 1975, 80 percent of currency exchanges were associated with trade and investment in actual products and services. By 1998, this figure had fallen to 2.5 percent.[119] The remaining transactions were purely financial and directed mostly at profiting from the constant shifts in currency values. The Tobin tax would raise the costs of currency speculation and perhaps thereby restore greater stability in international financial markets. Governments would gain time to work out financial imbalances before being overwhelmed by massive attacks on the value of their currencies. Another potential attraction of the Tobin tax is that it would raise substantial funds, measuring in the tens of billions of dollars, that could be directed toward fighting poverty or environmental problems in the less developed countries.

Although most of the more ambitious schemes for reworking international financial institutions were shelved once Asian economies began to stabilize, the IMF has pledged to make a number of less sweeping changes based upon the lessons of recent experience. Internal evaluations of the IMF's own performance during the Asian crisis criticized the agency for failing to anticipate the crisis, responding too slowly once it emerged, and demanding policy reforms that imposed excessive costs on debtor country economies. IMF officials have promised to develop "early warning systems" that would allow them to better anticipate emerging financial problems and to respond in a more timely fashion. Member countries would be expected to gather and report relevant financial data in a fuller and more timely fashion. Also, the IMF has expressed an intention to scale back on the number and scope of conditions attached to its loans and to pay more attention to the implications of its policies for the poor and the health of each nation's social safety net. Whether these promises will be kept in practice remains to be seen.[120]

Nevertheless, even some of the IMF and World Bank's internal critics insist that the reforms considered so far are insufficient. One persistent problem concerns the political relationship between these international agencies and recipient country governments. In 1999, an independent assessment unit of the World Bank completed a study of the bank's relationship with Indonesia over several decades. The *New York Times* summary of the report's conclusions stated: "In a blistering evaluation of its own operations in Indonesia, the World Bank concludes that its officials turned a blind eye to corruption, growing repression and a collapsing financial system in the final years of President Suharto's 33 year rule... the Bank knew of many problems but did not want to offend Mr. Suharto's government or threaten the image the bank had promoted of Indonesia as one of its great success stories."[121] The IMF has similar problems in establishing the right balance between offering independent policy advice and maintaining close working relationships with governments. Even after the Asian financial crisis hit, for instance, the IMF found it difficult to ensure that governments followed the conditions placed on IMF financial assistance. In the case of Indonesia, the government met only 20 percent of the conditions demanded by the fund.[122]

Another sign of internal dissent at the World Bank came when Joseph Stiglitz, the World Bank's chief economist, resigned in December 1999, after criticizing the bank's handling of the Asian financial crisis. Stiglitz took the bank to task for focusing too much on macroeconomic stabilization, pushing recipient countries to privatize state-owned industries too quickly and with too little regulation and requiring the rapid liberalization of capital flows. Instead, Stiglitz argued that the bank and the IMF should pay more attention to establishing the rule of law and strengthening regulatory institutions.[123]

An increasingly potent source of opposition to IMF and World Bank policies has come from a global network of advocacy NGOs. Such groups have mounted major public demonstrations at the annual meetings of the IMF and World Bank in recent years. One such network was the international Jubilee 2000 movement, which demanded that the debts of the poorest countries be completely forgiven by the year 2000. Though 2000 came and went without realization of this goal, the movement did spur debate and continues in various forms.[124] Another group called 50 Years is Enough calls for a radical restructuring of the IMF and World Bank.[125] A broad coalition of such groups has banned together under an umbrella organization called Mobilization for Global Justice.[126] This group has issued a statement detailing four demands— endorsed by hundreds of organizations around the world—of the IMF and World Bank:

1. Open all World Bank and IMF meetings to the media and the public.

2. End all World Bank and IMF policies that hinder people's access to food, clean water, shelter, health care, education, and the right to organize. (Such "structural adjustment" policies include user fees, privatization, and economic austerity programs.)

3. Stop all World Bank support for socially and environmentally destructive projects, such as oil, gas, and mining activities, and all support for projects, such as dams, that include forced relocation of people.

4. Cancel all impoverished country debt to the World Bank and IMF, using the institutions' own resources.[127]

From the other end of the ideological spectrum, conservatives in the United States criticize the IMF for violating the sovereignty of debtor countries and the World Bank for competing with the private sector. In 2000, a commission headed by economist Alan Meltzer issued a report sponsored by the U.S. Congress that argued for scaling back the size and powers of both the IMF and the World Bank. The Meltzer Report suggested that the IMF serve only as a lender of last resort for financially troubled countries. Only short-term loans should be issued and conditionality should be strictly limited. The burden of financial adjustment should be left to market forces. The Meltzer Report also recommended that World Bank lending should be limited to the poorest countries and should focus solely on international public goods, such as funding for research in tropical diseases. Other types of investment should be left to the private sector.[128]

The IMF and the World Bank are clearly under fire from many directions at once. Although these institutions have so far responded to critics by adopting incremental reforms, the next major global crisis could create irresistible pressures for more far-reaching change.

CONCLUSIONS

Each episode of Southern financial instability can be traced to particular causes. The policies of specific Third World countries influence their varying degrees of vulnerability to financial crises. Yet the persistence of financial imbalances between North and South over a period of two decades and the fact that dozens of countries in all regions of the Third World have suffered from growing indebtedness and financial turmoil suggests that systemic factors are at work.

Periods of financial crisis are often preceded by periods of optimism and economic growth. The countries of Latin America were considered sound investment risks in the 1970s. The "miracle" economies of East Asia were thought immune to financial meltdown as investors poured funds into these countries in the early 1990s. This boom-and-bust cycle suggests a basic difficulty in assessing sovereign-country financial risk.

The financial liberalization of the past two decades has exposed developing countries to large, rapid, and fickle flows of capital and currency speculation. Because of the weak domestic financial institutions of many developing countries and the lack of sophisticated oversight and regulatory systems, the openness brought about by liberalization has led to increased levels of vulnerability across the Third World.

The policies of the IMF, the World Bank, and Northern governments also contribute to financial uncertainty. IMF responses to Third World financial crises often produce harsh economic consequences and political instability. The IMF's "one size fits all" approach often fails to take into account differences from one case to another. The fund's rejection of currency controls or other unorthodox policy tools may prolong financial turmoil and facilitate its spread to other debtors.

Most striking, however, Northern interests have largely dominated bargaining between developing and developed countries over how debt crises are handled. Many Southern countries have submitted to a degree of Northern supervision (via the IMF and other agencies) of their domestic and international economic policies that would have been unthinkable two decades ago. While Northern banks and governments have sometimes agreed to limited debt forgiveness schemes, the costs of adjustment have fallen disproportionately on the South. The financial "bailouts" organized by the United States and the IMF often serve mainly to insure that Northern banks and investors recover at-risk capital.

The persistent problem of Southern debt and financial instability illustrates the politics of asymmetrical interdependence. The South's greater dependence upon its ties with the North means that developing countries have more at risk in the web of relationships that bind North and South together. A more sweeping and lasting solution to developing country financial instability may await the day when increasing Southern political clout allows developing countries to bargain more effectively for changes in the international financial order.

NOTES

1. Quoted in Michael Moffitt, *The World 's Money: International Banking from Bretton Woods to the Brink of Insolvency,* New York: Simon and Schuster, 1983, 127.

2. James Brooke, "Brazil's Costly Trip to a Free Market," *New York Times,* August 6, 1990; George de Lama, "Latin World Teeters on Edge of an Abyss," *Chicago Tribune,* June 4, 1989; Alan Riding, "Rumblings in Venezuela," *New York Times,* March 7, 1989.

3. Ernest Harsch, "After Adjustment," *Africa Report,* May–June 1989, 48.

4. John Miller, "IMF under Siege," *Dollars and Sense,* July–August, 1998.

5. "Argentina: No Fund of Love for the IMF," *The Economist,* June 3, 2000, 39; Kevin Gray, "Violence, Looting Engulf Crisis-Riddled Argentina," *Des Moines Register,* December 20, 2001; Paul Brinkley-Rogers, "Leader Chosen as Violence Lulls in Argentina," *Des Moines Register,* December 22, 2001.

6. Vinod K. Aggarwal, "International Debt Threat: Bargaining among Creditors and Debtors in the 1980s," Policy Papers in International Affairs, no. 29, Berkeley and Los Angeles: University of California Press, 1987, 16; "Reforming Latin America," *The Economist,* November 26, 1994, 40.

7. Harold Lever and Christopher Huhne, *Debt and Danger,* Boston: Atlantic Monthly Press, 1985, 17.

8. Esmail Hosseinzadeh, "The Crisis of Third World Debt: Is There a Way Out?" in Roger Oden (ed.), *Proceedings of the Fifteenth Annual Third World Conference,* Chicago: TWCF Publications, 1991, 27.

9. For a comparison of bank borrowing and foreign direct investment, see Hosseinzadeh, "Crisis of Third World Debt."

10. Sarah Bartlett, "A Vicious Circle Keeps Latin America in Debt," *New York Times,* January 15, 1989. It was estimated in 1988 that every point rise in the rate of interest charged on Third World debt cost Southern debtors $3.5 billion annually. See Steven Greenhouse, "Third World Tells IMF That Poverty Has Increased," *New York Times,* September 29, 1988.

11. On the historical precedents for the international debt crisis of the 1980s, see Barry Eichengreen and Peter Lindert (eds.), *The International Debt Crisis in Historical Perspective,* Cambridge: MIT Press, 1989; Albert Fishlow, "The Debt Crisis in Historical Perspective," in Miles Kahler (ed.), *The Politics of International Debt,* Ithaca, N.Y.: Cornell University Press, 1985; and John Makin, *The Global Debt Crisis: America's Growing Involvement,* New York: Basic Books, 1984, 36–53.

12. Debt Crisis Network, *From Debt to Development: Alternatives to the International Debt Crisis,* Washington, D.C.: Institute for Policy Studies, 1985, 25.

13. Lever and Huhne, *Debt and Danger,* 36.

14. Andre Gunder Frank, "Can the Debt Bomb Be Defused?" *World Policy Journal,* Spring 1985, 729.

15. William Greider, *Secrets of the Temple,* New York: Simon and Schuster, 1987, 434.

16. Jeffrey Frieden, "Third World Indebted Industrialization: International Finance and State Capitalism in Mexico, Brazil, Algeria and South Korea," *International Organization,* Summer 1981.

17. See Miles Kahler, "Politics and International Debt: Explaining the Crisis," in Kahler (ed.), *The Politics of International Debt;* and Mary Williamson, "Banking Regulation and Debt: A Policy of Flexible Response," *Policy Focus,* Overseas Development Council Policy Paper no. 1, 1988.

18. Greider, *Secrets of the Temple,* 433.

19. Moffitt, *World 's Money,* 100.

20. Lever and Huhne, *Debt and Danger,* 38.

21. By 1988 the cost to the Third World in lost export revenues due to Northern protectionism amounted to twice the value of Northern aid to the South (Greenhouse, "Third World Tells IMF That Poverty Has Increased").

22. Hosseinzadeh, "The Crisis of Third World Debt," 9.

23. Debt Crisis Network, *From Debt to Development,* 32. Moffitt, *World 's Money,* 101.

24. Corruption also played a role in the worsening of the debt problems of some countries. Funds ostensibly borrowed to finance development often found their way into the pockets of Third World government officials or businesspeople. Ferdinand Marcos is said to have stolen and funneled into overseas investments $10 billion during his long reign. This compares with a Philippine foreign debt of $26 billion at the time Marcos stepped down in 1986. Similarly, it has been charged that $3 billion to $4 billion of Zaire's $5 billion external debt was diverted by President Mobutu Sese Seko for his own uses. See Graham Hancock, *Lords of Poverty*, New York: Atlantic Monthly Press, 1989, 175–179. For a general discussion of mismanagement and corruption as sources of the debt crisis, see George B. N. Ayettey, "The Real Foreign Debt Problem," *Wall Street Journal*, April 8, 1986.

25. Remember that high exchange rates tend to reduce the price of imports, which then act to keep other domestic prices from rising.

26. Rudiger Dornbusch, "The Latin American Debt Problem: Anatomy and Solutions," in Stallings and Kautman (eds.), *Debt and Democracy in Latin America*, 8.

27. "Latin American Debt: Living on Borrowed Time?" *Great Decisions, '89*, New York: Foreign Policy Association, 1989, 28.

28. Hosseinzadeh, "The Crisis of Third World Debt," 9; and Mike McNamee and Jeffrey Ryser, "Can This Flight Be Grounded?" *Businessweek*, April 10, 1989.

29. Frank Riely, "Third World Capital Flight: Who Gains? Who Loses?" *Policy Focus*, Overseas Development Council Policy Paper no. 5, 1986.

30. Riely, "Third World Capital Flight."

31. By pushing interest payments still higher, these added premiums worsened matters by increasing the burden placed on the many debtor countries already experiencing difficulties in servicing their loans (Debt Crisis Network, *From Debt to Development*, 33; Moffitt, *The World's Money*, 110).

32. Robert Bennett, "Mexico Seeking Postponement of Part of Its Debt," *New York Times*, August 20, 1982.

33. Lever and Huhne, *Debt and Danger*, 40–41.

34. Alan Riding, "Mexican Outlook: Banks Are Wary," *New York Times*, August 17, 1982.

35. "Latin American Debt: Living on Borrowed Time?" 28.

36. For a chronology of the Mexican debt rescheduling negotiations, see Aggarwal, "International Debt Threat," 66–67.

37. Robert Bennett, "Bankers Pressured to Assist Mexico," *New York Times*, August 21, 1982

38. "Latin American Debt: Living on Borrowed Time?" 29.

39. James Brooke, "Zaire Dispute with IMF Centers on Capital Flows," *New York Times*, September 29, 1988.

40. "Latin American Debt: Living on Borrowed Time?" 29.

41. John Loxley, *The IMF and the Poorest Countries*, Ottawa: North-South Institute, 1984.

42. Cited in John Loxley, "IMF and World Bank Conditionality and Sub-Saharan Africa," in Peter Lawrence (ed.), *World Recession and the Food Crisis in Africa*, London: James Currey, 1986, 96.

43. Greenhouse, "Third World Tells IMF That Poverty Has Increased."

44. Eduardo Borensztein, "The Effect of External Debt on Investment," *Finance and Development*, September 1989, 17.

45. For a critique of devaluation's effectiveness, see "When Devaluation Breeds Contempt," *The Economist*, November 24, 1990, 71.

46. Technically, economists refer to the demand for such products as price inelastic: a change in price produces a relatively small shift in the volume of sales.

47. IMF policies have also had unintended effects on South-South trade. Although the great majority of Southern exports are targeted toward Northern markets, the 1970s witnessed considerable growth in trade among Southern countries. This encouraging trend reversed itself in the 1980s because so many Southern debtors were simultaneously pursuing IMF-imposed austerity policies and thus cutting back on imported goods from all sources.

48. For descriptions of the Brady Plan's provisions, see Clyde Farnsworth, "World Bank and IMF Approve Plan to Cut Debt of Poorer Lands," *New York Times,* April 5, 1989; and Shafigul Islam, "Going Beyond the Brady Plan," *Challenge,* July–August 1989, 39–45.

49. On the Mexican deal, see Sarah Bartlett, "Reservations Expressed about Mexican Debt Accord," *New York Times,* July 27, 1989; and Larry Rohter, "Pact Is Signed to Cut Mexico's Debt," *New York Times,* February 5, 1990. Also see William Cline, "Managing International Debt: How One Big Battle Was Won," *The Economist,* February 18, 1995, 18.

50. Andrew Rosenthal, "President Announces Plan for More Latin Debt Relief," *New York Times,* June 28, 1990.

51. Quotes cited in Robert Pastor, *Whirlpool: U.S. Foreign Policy toward Latin America and the Caribbean,* Princeton, N.J.: Princeton University Press, 1992, 97.

52. Soren Ambrose, "Multilateral Debt Burden," *Foreign Policy in Focus,* 5.4, March 2000.

53. Clyde Farnsworth, "IMF Is Urged to Sell Gold as Hedge against Bad Loans," *New York Times,* February 1, 1990.

54. Jorge Castaneda, "Mexico's Dismal Debt Deal," *New York Times,* February 25, 1990.

55. Albert Fishlow, "Coming to Terms with the Latin Debt," *New York Times,* January 4, 1988.

56. "Least Developed Countries Report," UNCTAD press release, October 12, 2000.

57. Ambrose, "Multilateral Debt Burden."

58. World Bank, "The HIPC Initiative: Background and Progress Through December 2001" (available at Http://www.worldbank.org/hipc/progress-to-date/May99v3/may99v3. htm [accessed January 12, 2002]). The remaining 16 countries among the 41 targeted for HIPC assistance have yet to qualify for relief. The World Bank maintains that up to a dozen of these countries suffer from serious internal conflicts or governance problems that render them ineligible for HIPC aid at present.

59. "Brazil's Plan for Its Debt," *New York Times,* August 20, 1990.

60. Greider, *Secrets of the Temple,* 484.

61. "Latin American Debt," 31.

62. Mike Tangeman, "Safety in Numbers: Latin America Looks at Unity to Solve Debt Crisis," *In These Times,* February 3–9, 1988.

63. Merril Collett, "Brady's Debt Plan Is Short on Principle," *In These Times,* April 12–18, 1989, 2.

64. Tom Wicker, "The Real Danger of Debt," *New York Times,* December 2, 1988.

65. Aggarwal, "International Debt Threat," 31.

66. Richard Feinberg, "Latin American Debt: Renegotiating the Burden," in Richard Feinberg and Ricardo French-Davis (eds.), *Development and External Debt in Latin America: Bases for a New Consensus,* Notre Dame, Ind.: Notre Dame University Press, 1988, 59.

67. Aggarwal, "International Debt Threat," 32.

68. Alan Riding, "Brazil's Reversal of Debt Strategy," *New York Times,* February 22, 1988.

69. Feinberg, "Latin American Debt: Renegotiating the Burden," 59.

70. Aggarwal, "International Debt Threat," 52–53.

71. Feinberg, "Latin American Debt: Renegotiating the Burden," 59.

72. Feinberg, "Latin American Debt: Renegotiating the Burden," 60.

73. These are the IMF Institute and the World Bank's Economic Development Institute (Robin Broad, *Unequal Alliance: The World Bank, the International Monetary Fund, and the Philippines,* Berkeley and Los Angeles: University of California Press, 1988, 26, 31).

74. Broad, *Unequal Alliance.*

75. Charles Lipson, "International Debt and International Institutions," in Kahler (ed.), *Politics of International Debt,* fn. 14, 223.

76. Aggarwal, "International Debt Threat," 15–21.

77. Aggarwal, "International Debt Threat," 38.

78. On private cooperation, see Aggarwal, "International Debt Threat," 21–29; and Charles Lipson, "Bankers' Dilemma: Private Cooperation in Rescheduling Sovereign Debts," *World Politics,* October 1985.

79. On the relationship between the fund and the banks, see Aggarwal, "International Debt Threat," 35–44.

80. "Coping with Capital," *The Economist,* October 29, 1994, 86.

81. For an excellent overview of recent trends in North-South financial relations, see Stephany Griffith-Jones and Barbara Stallings, "New Global Financial Trends: Implications for Development," in Barbara Stallings (ed.), *Global Change, Regional Response: The New International Context of Development,* Cambridge, England: Cambridge University Press, 1995.

82. Kenneth Gilpin, "New Third World Fear: Investors Could Walk Away," *New York Times,* April 24, 1994; Ankie Hoogvelt, "Dependency Theory in the Age of Globalization: The Legacy," paper presented at the 2001 meeting of International Studies Association, Chicago, Illinois, February, 2001.

83. Masood Ahmed and Sudarshan Gooptu, "Portfolio Investment Flows to Developing Countries," *Finance and Development,* March 1993.

84. Gilpin, "New Third World Fear"; Stijn Claessens and Sudarshan Gooptu, "Can Developing Countries Keep Foreign Capital Flowing In?" *Finance and Development,* September 1994, 64.

85. "Survey: Mexico," *The Economist,* October 28, 1995, 4–5; Peter Passell, "Economic Scene," *New York Times,* January 12, 1995.

86. The Boom in Portfolio Investment," *Latin American Weekly Report,* April 15, 1993.

87. "Survey: Mexico."

88. "Survey: Mexico," 5–6; "Survey: Latin American Finance," *The Economist,* December 9, 1995, 19.

89. "Survey: Mexico," 6.

90. "Survey: Mexico," 6.

91. "Survey: Latin American Finance," 19.

92. "Survey: Mexico," 5–6; James Brookes, "Mexican Crisis Depressing Brazil and Argentina Stocks," *New York Times,* February 20, 1995.

93. Anthony DePalma, "In Land of the Peso, the Dollar Is Common Coin," *New York Times,* November 21, 1995; Anthony DePalma, "Mexicans Reach New Pact on the Economy," *New York Times,* October 30, 1995; Anthony DePalma, "Mexico Eager to Celebrate End to Crisis Despite Hardships," *New York Times,* April 27, 1995.

94. "Putting Mexico Together Again," *The Economist,* February 4, 1995; "Survey: Mexico"; Julia Preston, "Markets Skeptical, the Peso Falls Again," *New York Times,* November 9, 1995.

95. "Survey: Mexico."

96. "Mexican Banks: Fasten Seatbelts," *The Economist,* November 6, 1999, 77; DePalma, "Mexico Eager to Celebrate End to Crisis Despite Hardships"; "Survey: Mexico"; Julia Preston, "Intervening, Mexico Halts Slide in Peso," *New York Times,* November 10, 1995; Keith Bradsher, "Mexico: Absent from the White House Crisis List," *New York Times,* November 10, 1995; Preston, "Markets Skeptical, the Peso Falls Again"; DePalma, "Mexicans Reach New Pact on the Economy."

97. Paul Lewis, "IMF to Require More Data from International Borrowers," *New York Times,* October 6, 1995.

98. Walter Hatch and Kozo Yamamura, *Asia in Japan's Embrace: Building a Regional Production Alliance,* Cambridge, England: Cambridge University Press, 1996; David Aarse, *Buying Power: The Political Economy of Japan's Foreign Aid,* Boulder, Colo.: Lynne Rienner, 1995.

99. Waldo Bello, "The End of a 'Miracle': Speculation, Foreign Capital Dependence and the Collapse of the Southeast Asian Economies," *Multinational Monitor,* 19.1–2, January–February, 1998.

100. For a discussion of this process, see Nicholas Kristof and Edward Wyatt, "Who Sank, or Swam, in Choppy Currents of a World Cash Ocean?" *New York Times,* February 15, 1999.

101. For this liberal view of global financial markets, see "Capital Goes Global," *The Economist,* October 25, 1997; and "Is Contagion a Myth?" *The Economist,* October 31, 1998.

102. Bello, "The End of a 'Miracle.'"

103. Robert Wade, "The Asian Crisis and the Global Economy: Causes,

Consequences, and Cure," *Current History,* November 1998, 362.

104. Bello, "The End of a 'Miracle.'"

105. Bello, "The End of a 'Miracle.'"

106. For detail on the events of the Asian financial crisis, consult the "Chronology" developed by Professor Nouriel Roubini at: http://www.stern.nyu.edu/~nroubini/asia/AsiaHomepage.html (accessed June 6, 2002).

107. The IMF is joined in advocating liberal globalization by the World Trade Organization and the World Bank, by the leaders of international financial businesses (banks and investment firms), and by the leadership of the U.S. Treasury. For a discussion of the development of these ideas, see Robin Broad and John Cavanagh, "The Death of the Washington Consensus?" *World Policy Journal,* 16.3, 1999, 79–88.

108. Background on Indonesia can be found in Adam Schwartz, *A Nation In Waiting: Indonesia's Search for Stability,* 2nd ed., Boulder, Colo.: Westview Press, 2000; William Liddle, "The Relative Autonomy of the Third World Politician: Soeharto and Indonesian Political Economy in Comparative Perspective," *International Studies Quarterly,* 35.4 December 1991, 403–427; Alasdair Bowie and Danny Unger, *The Politics of Open Economies,* Cambridge, England: Cambridge University Press, 1997.

109. Judith Bird, "Indonesia in 1998," *Asian Survey,* 39.1, January–February 1999, 28.

110. Suharto had been in power in Indonesia since 1966.

111. "Investors Question Whether Russia Has Strength to Bear Financial Crisis," *Financial Times* (London), July 30, 1998; "Russian Markets Destabilize Again," *Tampa Tribune,* August 13, 1998.

112. "G7 Says Russia Must First Help Itself," *Financial Times* (London), August 19, 1998; "Russia Wants

More Money from West but Gets Only a Warning to Reform," *St. Louis Post-Dispatch,* August 29, 1998; Anna Dolgov, "In Bid for Loans, Russia Gives IMF an Economic Plan," *Boston Globe,* October 29, 1998; John Thornhill, "IMF Promises $4.8 Billion in New Loans to Bolster Russia," March 30, 1999; Joseph Kahn, "A Study Says IMF's Hand Often Heavy," *New York Times,* October 21, 2000.

113. Phil Davison, "Brazil Reels from 'The Vodka Effect,'" *The Independent* (London), September 19, 1998; Paul Blustein, "In Brazil, Fighting a Tide of Turmoil," *Washington Post,* September 20, 1998; Michael Astor, "Brazil Offers New Austerity Plan," *Ottawa Citizen,* October 29, 1998; "IMF Rescue of Brazil: Could More be Needed?" *Journal of Commerce,* November 16, 1998.

114. "Argentina: No Fund of Love for the IMF," 29; Robert Samuelson, "Is Argentina a Time Bomb?" *Newsweek,* April 23, 2001; Gray, "Violence, Looting Engulf Crisis-Riddled Argentina"; Clifford Krauss, "Argentina Limits Withdrawals as Banks Near Collapse," *New York Times,* December 3, 2001.

115. Harry Dunphy, "IMF to Re-evaluate Big-Money Bailouts," *Des Moines Register,* December 28, 2001; Brinkley-Rogers, "Leader Chosen as Violence Lulls in Argentina"; Bill Cormier, "Argentina Loses Another Leader," *Des Moines Register,* December 31, 2001; "Argentines Wonder How Low Money's Value Can Go," *Des Moines Register,* January 13, 2002.

116. Krauss, "Argentina Limits Withdrawals as Banks Near Collapse."

117. Mary H. Cooper, "Did Malaysia Shoot Itself in the Foot When It Adopted Currency Controls?" in *Global Issues,* Washington, D.C.: CQ Press, 2001, 82.

118. Cooper, "Did Malaysia Shoot Itself," 83.

119. Duncan Green, "The Failings of the International Financial Architecture," *NACLA Report on the Americas,* July–August, 1999, 31.

120. "IMF Must Correct Its Mistakes," *Business Times* (Malaysia), September 17, 1998; Jack Boorman, "IMF Draws Lessons from Asian Crisis," *Straits Times* (Singapore), January 21, 1999; Joseph Kahn, "World Financial Officials Pledge to Work to Block New Crises before They Happen," *New York Times,* April 20, 2001; Joseph Kahn, "A Study Says IMF's Hand Often Heavy," *New York Times,* October 21, 2000; Joseph Kahn, "I.M.F. Is Expected to Ease Demands on Debtor Nations," *New York Times,* June 30, 2000; "Development Finance: Old Battle, New Strategy," *The Economist,* January 8, 2000.

121. David Sanger, "World Bank Beats Breast for Failure in Indonesia," *New York Times,* February 11, 1999.

122. Kahn, "A Study Says IMF's Hand Often Heavy."

123. "Sick Patients, Warring Doctors," *The Economist,* September 18, 1999, 81; Louis Uchitelle, "World Bank Economist Felt He Had to Silence His Criticism or Quit," *New York Times,* December 2, 1999.

124. For the Jubilee USA Network, visit the following Web site at http://wwwjubileeusa.org/.

125. For 50 Years is Enough, visit their Web site at http://www.50years.org/.

126. For Mobilization for Global Justice, visit their Web site at: http://www.globalizethis.org/s30/.

127. For this list of demands, visit the following Web page: http://www jubileeusa.org/jubilee.cgi?path=/learn _more&page=rebuttal.html. For the World Bank's response to these demands, go to http://www.worldbank.org/html/ extdr/pb/pbfourdemands.htm.

128. "Slimming the Bretton Woods Duo," *The Economist,* March 18, 2000, 80.

ANNOTATED BIBLIOGRAPHY

Vinod Aggarwal. "International Debt Threat: Bargaining among Creditors and Debtors in the 1980's." Policy Papers in International Affairs, no. 79. Berkeley and Los Angeles: University of California Press, 1987. A brief but valuable conceptual treatment of North-South bargaining over solutions to the debt crisis.

Barry Eichengreen and Peter Lindert (eds.). *The International Debt Crisis in Historical Perspective.* Cambridge: MIT Press, 1989. A collection of essays that explores whether previous historical episodes of international debt crises hold lessons for coping with recent Third World indebtedness.

Morris Goldstein. *The Asian Financial Crisis: Causes, Cures, and Systemic Implications.* Washington, D.C.: Institute for International Economics, 1998. Focuses on the origins of the Asian financial crisis.

Stephan Haggard. *The Political Economy of the Asian Financial Crisis.* Washington, D.C.: Institute for International Economics, 2000. Examines the politics of the Asian financial crises through a series of comparative country case studies.

Miles Kahler (ed.). *The Politics of International Debt.* Ithaca, N.Y.: Cornell University Press, 1985. Although dated, this collection features a number of excellent political analyses of the evolution of the Third World debt crisis. Particularly useful as a source for relevant theories and concepts.

Miles Kahler (ed.). *Capital Flows and Financial Crises.* Ithaca, N.Y.: Cornell University Press, 1998. A collection of essays on the management of global and regional financial crisis.

Ethan Kapstein. "Managing the Global Economy's Managers." *Current History,* November 1998.

Howard Lehman. *Indebted Development: Strategic Bargaining and Economic Adjustment in the Third World.* New York: St. Martin's Press, 1993. Examines bargaining relationships among Southern states, Northern banks, and Northern governments over management of the debt crisis.

T. J. Pempel (ed.). *The Politics of the Asian Economic Crisis.* Ithaca, N.Y.: Cornell University Press, 1999. A collection of essays that examines why the Asian financial crises impacted some countries more than others.

David Woodward. *Debt, Adjustment and Poverty in Developing Countries* (2 Vols.). London: Pinter, 1992. A detailed study of the effects of the debt crisis on Third World economies.

13

❖

Hunger, Population, and Sustainable Development

The entire edifice of global economic activity rests upon a fragile natural ecosystem. The demands that humans place upon their natural environment have risen to unprecedented and destructive proportions in recent decades. Global population is expected to nearly double during this century, while rising incomes will lead to increased consumption. These trends raise questions about whether nature can accommodate ever-increasing resource demands for food, water, energy, minerals, and timber. Already, scientists warn that our massive appetite for fossil fuels may have altered the earth's atmosphere and set in motion an irreversible pattern of global warming, with dire consequences for future generations.

Biologists use the notion of carrying capacity to measure the limits of nature's ability to sustain increasing numbers of a given species. When nature's carrying capacity is breached, resource scarcity serves to correct excess population levels in a most brutal manner. Humans differ from other species, of course, in that they possess the ability to manipulate their natural environment and thus to extend its carrying capacity in various ways. Still, this biological metaphor aptly serves to raise the question of limits. How many people can the earth support? Where do the limits to rising consumption lie? What are the consequences should we overshoot the earth's carrying capacity?

These questions pertain in different ways to North and South. Northern societies today contribute to global environmental strains in far greater degree than do those in the South. Northern countries are home to less than one-quarter of the world's population, yet they account for five-sixths of global resource consumption. Rich countries also contribute 80 percent of global greenhouse gas emissions.[1] One estimate suggests that the average American will, during his or her lifetime, account for 13 times the environmental damage of the average Brazilian, 35 times that of an Indian, and 280 times that of a Haitian.[2]

Yet Southern resource consumption is expected to grow at a rapid pace over coming decades, due both to quickly rising populations and to increasing income levels. Moreover, whereas Northern societies possess the technology and wealth needed to cope with, reverse, or compensate for environmental threats in some degree, Southern societies are less capable of countering the effects of increasing air and water pollution.

These considerations have led many development specialists to recast notions of Southern development from visions of limitless increases in consumption to more environmentally sensitive notions of sustainability. Increasing consideration is being given to methods for limiting population growth and reconciling rising living standards with environmental protection. This re-thinking of the development process is complex and multifaceted. This chapter examines selected issues related to the challenge of sustainable development. The first two sections explore the relationships among population, hunger, and poverty. The third section discusses international efforts to support the movement toward sustainability, focusing on the 1992 Rio Earth Summit and subsequent developments. The final section examines the success and failures of environmental diplomacy aimed at countering two threats to the earth's atmosphere: ozone depletion and global warming.

POPULATION

As Table 13.1 shows, human population growth has accelerated at an alarming pace over the past two centuries. It took over a million years for the world's population to pass the 1 billion mark. Yet the passage from 5 billion to 6 billion in population was accomplished in little more than a decade. Much of this increase is concentrated in societies already too impoverished to provide the schooling, jobs, and social services that are necessary to offer a decent standard of living for rapidly growing numbers of claimants. Runaway population growth holds back economic development, contributes to social and political frictions, strains scarce resources, and triggers sometimes-destabilizing cross-border immigration flows. In myriad ways, rising population pressures are likely to play the dominant role in the political, social, and economic lives of many societies across the globe in the twenty-first century.

A variety of data shed light on the dimensions of the present population explosion. The rate of annual population growth peaked in 1963 at 2.2 percent and has since fallen, descending to 1.54 percent in 1994. In the past 30 years, the average number of children born per woman has fallen globally from 6 to 3.[3] Nevertheless, the absolute number of people added to the

Table 13.1 World Population Milestones

World Population Reached:

Level	Year
1 billion	1804
2 billion	1927 (123 years later)
3 billion	1960 (33 years later)
4 billion	1974 (14 years later)
5 billion	1987 (13 years later)
6 billion	1999 (12 years later)
Projections:	
7 billion	2009 (10 years later)
8 billion	2021 (12 years later)
9 billion	2035 (14 years later)
10 billion	2054 (19 years later)
11 billion	2093 (38 years later)

SOURCE: Population Information Network Gopher of the United Nations Population Division, Department for Economic and Social Information and Policy Analysis (table titled "World Population Milestones").

world's population continued to climb through the 1970s and 1980s, reaching a peak of almost 90 million per year in the early 1990s. This figure has since declined to about 78 billion additional people per year. In 1999 the world's population passed the 6 billion mark.[4] United Nations projections suggest that population levels will grow to around 10 billion people by the year 2050, although the actual figure could be higher or lower, depending upon the speed of progress in lowering birth rates.

Because birth rates in much of the developed world are already at or even below replacement levels, 98 percent of additional population growth in the years ahead will occur in the Third World.[5] Overall, Third World populations are expected to double in the next 30 years. Although the South's share of total world population stood at 68 percent in 1950, this proportion is expected to rise to 84 percent by 2025. Over the next two decades, Third World countries will face the challenge of finding jobs for 730 million new workers.[6]

Why are Southern populations expanding at such a rapid rate? Population experts believe that the Third World is passing through the same sort of demographic transition that led to growing population levels in Europe and North America from the late eighteenth through the early twentieth centuries. According to this theory, rapid population growth is essentially a by-product of the early stages of economic development. Prior to industrialization and economic development, population levels are generally stable. High birth rates are matched by high death rates. After development produces rising incomes and increased wealth, however, death rates begin to fall dramatically. Better nutrition and sanitation, combined with less physical toil and improved access to increasingly sophisticated medical care, lead to reduced infant mortality rates and rising life expectancy. Because birth rates are initially unaffected, a declining rate of death produces an imbalance that results in a population explosion.

As incomes continue to rise, birth rates begin to decline as well (for reasons explained later) and may eventually catch up with still-falling death rates. After birth rates and death rates are equalized at low levels, population stability again appears, only now on a much higher plateau. The sequence posited by the demographic transition theory is thus: (1) high death rate/high birth rate, (2) falling death rate/high birth rate, (3) falling death rate/falling birth rate, and (4) low death rate/low birth rate.[7]

Due to a phenomenon known as "population momentum," however, population growth will persist for a lengthy period even after couples begin to limit family size to the long-run replacement level of roughly two children each. Following a rapid burst of population growth, younger generations will account for a disproportionately large share of the overall population as compared with older generations. As these younger people move through their childbearing years, they will produce children at a faster rate than the comparatively small number of elderly people reach the end of their lives. Thus for birth rates to fall far enough to match death rates at low levels, two things must happen: family size must decline, and the age distribution must even out as the first generations produced by the population boom move past their childbearing years.[8]

As population growth slows and moves toward stability, one consequence is that the average age rises. North America, Europe, and Japan have already experienced this phenomenon, as fewer children are born and larger numbers of people live longer lives. Globally, the estimated median age was 25 in 1995. As population growth slows, the median age worldwide is expected to approach 40 by 2050. The proportion of the global population composed of persons aged 65 years or older is expected to rise from 6.5 percent today to almost 20 percent in 2050. Aging populations pose different sorts of problems. The need for education and other services for children declines, while the medical costs of caring for a growing elderly population rises.[9]

The demographic transition theory fits Europe's experience well. It also appears to explain trends in the Third World, although the South's population explosion has been far more intense than Europe's earlier boom. Due to the spread of antibiotics and other medical advances originating in the North, Southern death rates fell at a far steeper rate during the initial stages of development. Birth rates also fell more slowly in the South, thus extending the transitional period of high growth. Nevertheless, fertility rates have fallen across most Third World regions since the 1960s. Even areas such as Africa, where birth rates remain stubbornly high, have begun to witness declining fertility levels in recent years.[10] Overall, fertility rates have fallen beneath the replacement level of 2.1 children per woman in 61 of the world's 191 countries.[11]

The spread of modern contraceptives is helping to bring down birth rates in many places. In 1960 an estimated 10 percent of married women in Third

World countries used some method of fertility control. By 1994 this figure had risen to 51 percent, as compared with 75 percent for Northern women.[12] Although contraceptives help to avoid unplanned births, the majority of children born in Southern countries are conceived by choice. World Bank economist Lant Pritchett notes that "desired levels of fertility account for 90 percent of differences across countries in total fertility rates."[13] In some cases, the desire for large families is influenced by culture or religion. By and large, however, the incentives that most powerfully affect preferences about family size are economic. It is here, in the household economy of the family, that we can discover clues as to how best to go about restraining population growth.

Research has shown that the three most important factors affecting family size choices are income, education, and rural or urban status. Counterintuitively, poorer, less-educated rural families are likely to prefer larger numbers of children than are high-income, better-educated urban families. The reasons for this finding have to do with the economic costs and benefits of having additional children for families in differing circumstances.[14]

Poor rural couples have two strong incentives to prefer a large family. In Third World countries, agriculture is typically very labor intensive. On small farms, children provide a cheap source of added labor from a relatively early age. Their contributions can help to expand production and thereby augment family income. The costs of an additional child are relatively small for such households—chiefly, the expense's associated with food and clothing. At low income levels, moreover, it may be impossible for parents to save money for their old age, and few such families have access to the type of social security benefits that are available to elderly people in the North. For parents, then, a large number of offspring increases the chances that enough children will survive to adulthood and prosper sufficiently to take care of their parents after the latter are unable to provide for themselves.

As incomes rise, however, the incentives for rural families to prefer more children begin to diminish. A wealthier farmer may now have the means to hire skilled adult labor to help with the farm or to acquire labor-saving machinery. This lessens the family's degree of dependence upon the children's contribution. Better-off rural families are also more capable of setting aside savings for the parents' later years.

As households move from the countryside to the city, the incentives shaping choices about family size change still further. In urban areas, compulsory education laws are better enforced, and educational opportunities are more readily available. Thus children are more likely to be in school for longer periods rather than contributing to the family income through work. In any case, paid employment for children is scarce in urban areas, particularly where child labor laws are strict. The costs associated with each additional child, however, tend to rise in urban settings. Housing is more expensive. Moreover, urban parents are more likely to work at a distance from the home, increasing the costs of supervising a large number of children.

Education, particularly women's, also plays a role in reducing family size. Better-educated parents are more likely to use modern contraceptives. Education

Table 13.2 Third World Population and Growth Rates, by Region

	Total Population, 1999 (in millions)	Average Annual Growth, 1990–1999 (%)
East Asia and Pacific	1,836.9	1.3
Latin America and Caribbean	509.2	1.7
Middle East and North Africa	290.9	2.2
South Asia	1,329.3	1.9
Sub-Saharan Africa	642.3	2.6

SOURCE: World Bank, *World Development Report, 2000/2001,* New York: Oxford University Press, 2000, Table 3, 278–279.

is also associated with delayed marriage, reducing the opportunities for adding more children during a woman's childbearing years. As women gain more education and skills, they become more likely to engage in work outside the home, making a large family less attractive. Better-educated women also possess greater power within the marriage and are more likely to challenge traditional gender roles and expectations.

Indeed, the social status and education of women have been found to constitute the most powerful predictor of fertility rates. In societies where women have made progress against legal and social discrimination and where educational and economic opportunities are open to them, fertility rates are dramatically lower than in societies that offer women little social or economic power. India is a case in point. In southern regions of India, women enjoy much greater socioeconomic security than do women in northern parts of the country. Studies have found that women in southern India bear an average of only two children during their lifetimes, whereas northern Indian women give birth to an average of five children.

A recent World Bank study highlights the importance of women's education in curbing population growth. In parts of the Third World where women are excluded from secondary education, the average fertility rate is seven. Wherever at least 40 percent of women go on to the secondary level, the average number of children born drops to three. Similarly, illiterate women in Brazil bear an average of 6.5 children during their lifetimes, whereas Brazilian women who have completed secondary education have an average of 2.5 children.[15] The task of improving women's lives will be a huge one. Seventy percent of the world's poor are women. Twice as many women as men are illiterate. Many societies and cultures devalue women and continue to deny them access to education, the right to own property, or the freedom to engage in political life.[16]

The foregoing analysis suggests that population pressures are greatest among the rural poor. Bottom-up development strategies that seek to improve the income and status of the poor majority will also be the most effective at bringing down birth rates. Inequitable, top-down strategies that concentrate benefits at the top of the income scale will, however, fail to alter the incentives that give rise to exploding populations.[17]

At the 1994 UN-sponsored International Conference on Population and Development, held in Cairo, 180 nations endorsed a 20-year Program of Action on population control. Plans called for a rise in global spending on population control to $17 billion by the year 2000, with $5.5 billion of that figure provided by Northern aid agencies and the remainder by Third World governments. In addition to traditional population control measures, such as family planning outreach and the distribution of contraceptives, the conference focused on efforts to improve the socioeconomic and educational status of poor Third World women. Aside from their intrinsic value, such measures promise to bring down birth rates more quickly.[18]

THE AIDS PANDEMIC

The preferred method for slowing population growth, of course, is to lower birth rates relative to death rates. Rising death rates will have the same effect on population figures, albeit at a frightening human cost. Yet it is the latter prospect that some countries face as a result of the spread of HIV and AIDS. AIDS has now become the fourth biggest cause of death in the world. An estimated 34 million people presently suffer from this terrible disease and each day brings 15,000 additional cases of infection. Especially harmful from a social and economic perspective is the fact that one-half of those infected are between the ages of 15 and 24. AIDS has already claimed nearly 19 million lives. Some studies predict that over the next decade AIDS will claim more combined lives than all of the wars of the twentieth century.[19]

Ninety-five percent of AIDS sufferers are locating in the developing world. Hardest hit is sub-Saharan Africa, which alone accounts for 70 percent of all AIDS cases worldwide and where 2 million people died of the disease in 1999. In sixteen African countries, more than 10 percent of the population aged 15–49 carry the HIV infection that leads to AIDS. Seven of these countries have an HIV infection rate of more than 20 percent of the young adult population. The country most devastated by the AIDS crisis is Botswana, where one-third of all adults have HIV. By 2010, experts predict that the average life expectancy of a newborn baby in Botswana will have fallen to 29 years. In several of the hardest hit African countries, the probability that a 15-year-old boy will die of AIDS is over one-half.[20]

AIDS has produced almost 11 million orphans in Africa, a figure that is expected to rise to 40 million by 2010. In Zambia, an estimated 72 percent of all families care for one or more orphans. Paul De Lay, chief of the HIV/AIDS division at the U.S. Agency for International Development (USAID), has commented that "development in these countries has been set back forty years." The World Bank estimates that countries where HIV infection rates exceed 20 percent of adults can expect a resulting 1 percent annual decline in per-capita income.[21]

There is hope. In Africa, 80 percent of HIV infections are spread through heterosexual contact. The chances of infection can be greatly reduced through proper condom use. Senegal began an active anti-AIDS campaign in 1986 that increased condom use from 800,000 in 1988 to over 9 million in 1997. In contrast with its neighbors, Senegal has succeeded in holding its HIV infection rate to 2 percent. Uganda began a similar AIDS prevention effort in the early 1990s. As a result, Uganda's infection rate has dropped from 18 percent to 14 percent.

Forty percent of all babies born to mothers infected with HIV will also catch the virus during childbirth. This figure can be cut to 20 percent by treating the mother with antiviral medications just before childbirth. The use of infant formula can reduce chances of babies catching HIV from the mother as a result of breastfeeding. The use of infant formula itself, however, carries its own health risks if mixed with dirty water.[22]

The lives of individuals infected with HIV can be extended through drug treatment. Until recently, however, this has seldom been an option in the developing world. The anti-AIDS drug "cocktail" costs roughly $1,000 per month in the United States, a figure far beyond the financial means of the vast majority of Africans infected with HIV. A combination of pressures from AIDS activists, African governments, and media coverage has recently compelled large Northern drug companies to drastically cut their prices on AIDS drugs sold in Africa and other developing countries to cost or below. Also, generic versions of some AIDS drugs are already being sold in some African countries at cut-rate prices in violation of international patents. Regarding the patent rights of Northern drug companies, the director of the Ivory Coast's AIDS program has said: "Believe me, I don't care.... Our concern is what we can do for our people." In addition to dramatic price cuts in anti-AIDS drugs, the United States and Europe have announced new loan programs designed to finance the export of such drugs to Africa and other developing countries. Yet even considering these various efforts to reduce the costs of treating HIV-positive patients in Africa and elsewhere, the majority of those infected will still be unable to afford treatment.[23]

More promising are education and prevention programs. The UN estimates that spending on such programs in Africa would have to rise tenfold, to $3 billion per year, before the spread of AIDS could be slowed. The World Bank has recently committed itself to provide major funding toward the expansion of such programs.[24]

FOOD AND HUNGER

The Green Revolution, launched in the 1960s, harnessed modern science to the challenge of feeding a hungry world. Through crossbreeding techniques, scientists developed new varieties of wheat, rice, and other food crops that offered higher yields, better resistance to pests and disease, increased tolerance to environmental stresses, and quicker crop rotation. As a result, world grain production increased 2.6 times between 1950 and 1984; global rice production jumped from 257 million tons in 1965 to 468 million tons in 1985.[25]

Bountiful harvests helped to reduce the incidence of hunger in many parts of the world. India, a country repeatedly plagued by famine over the centuries, became self-sufficient in food. Across the Third World as a whole, the daily caloric intake per capita rose 21 percent between 1965 and 1990. The absolute number of malnourished people in the South fell by 20 percent between 1975 and 1994, despite massive population increases. The global food supply in 1995 equaled an ample 2,740 calories daily for each person on the planet. Although the world's population is roughly 6 billion, it is estimated that present levels of agricultural output could feed 7 billion people, assuming vegetarian diets and ideal distribution. One consequence of this bounty of staple foods is the fact that the prices of wheat and corn have each declined roughly 60 percent in constant dollars over the past 40 years.[26]

Yet despite these heartening statistics, the world food system has failed to provide for everyone, and its future effectiveness is even more uncertain. Roughly 830 million people remain undernourished, lacking sufficient calories or nutritional content in their diet to sustain health. One-third of all Third World children are underweight for their age. Most disturbingly, 15 million people, most of them children, die of hunger-related causes each year. Productivity losses due to malnourishment cost developing countries 1 to 2 percent of their overall GDP each year in lost wages.[27]

The tragedy behind these figures is caused not by an inadequate quantity of food in the world but rather by its inequitable distribution. Like other commodities, food is mainly allocated through the market. Using what income they have at their disposal, consumers bid for the food that is available. Those able to pay the market price receive the food they need, and sometimes more. Those lacking either the means to grow their own food or the money needed to purchase it in sufficient quantities simply go hungry. In short, the principal cause of hunger is poverty. Although nutritional programs run by governments or international agencies provide some relief, these efforts reach only a fraction of the chronically malnourished.

Yet although poverty and inequality account for much of the hunger in today's world, the future could bring genuine scarcity if food production fails to keep pace with population growth. Recent trends are troubling. After rising at a relatively steady pace of 3 percent per year throughout much of the post-World War II period, grain harvests have expanded at the anemic rate of only 1 percent per year since 1984. With the world's population growing at a much faster clip, this means that global per-capita grain production has been falling for over a decade. By the mid-1990s, global grain carryover stocks, as measured by days of consumption, stood at their lowest level in several decades, with the exception of a brief dip in the early 1970s. This trend is especially worrisome because grain is a staple of diets around the world and accounts for the majority of the food consumed by humans.[28]

Many observers once believed that the world's oceans could serve as a growing source of food. Until recently, data on global fish harvests showed steady growth through the 1990s. Scientists have recently discovered, however, that these estimates were distorted as a result of massive overreporting of fishing yields by China. Corrected data show that, in fact, global fish harvests have fallen by 360,000 tons per year as compared with 1988. Many scientists now believe that the world's fisheries are being overexploited and that only a drastic cut in fishing levels can assure sustainable harvests in the future.[29]

Using median population projections, food production must double by the year 2050 in order to maintain present levels of per-capita consumption. If the goal is to improve diets enough to eliminate malnutrition, then food production will need to triple in volume.[30]

Predictions as to whether this challenge can be met vary enormously. The director-general of the International Food Policy Research Institute, Per Pinstrup-Anderson, has declared: "Our estimates show that the world is perfectly capable of feeding 12 billion people 100 years from now."[31] To the contrary, population experts Paul Ehrlich and Anne Ehrlich argue in their book *The Population Explosion* that "human numbers are on a collision course with massive famines.... If humanity fails to act, nature will end the population explosion for us—in very unpleasant ways—well before 10 billion is reached."[32]

That knowledgeable and respected observers could reach such opposed conclusions provides some clue as to the complexity of the issues involved in charting the future relationships among food, hunger, and population. Many factors—political, economic, biological, and demographic—must be taken into account. The following discussion highlights some of the principal issues that are central to an analysis of world hunger in the coming decades.

One certainty is that much more food will be required in the future than is presently produced. Even if population control efforts are relatively successful, the number of consumers will continue to grow and, as living standards rise, those consumers will seek enhanced diets. Where will this additional food come from?

One way to increase food production is to expand the total land under cultivation. Growth in agricultural land was rapid between 1850 and 1950. The expansion of new farmland slowed considerably after World War II, however, and has actually reversed in the developed world and some Southern countries over the past decade. Between 1972 and 1989, the total land area harvested increased only 3.6 percent, and the amount of arable land per capita has been declining for decades. Since the early 1960s, 80 percent of increased food production has come as a result of higher yields, with the expansion of land under cultivation playing only a minor role in raising output.[33]

Nor is there much prospect that the growing food demands of coming decades can be met by opening new fields to production. Little arable land remains unexploited in Asia. There exists greater potential for expanding agriculture in Africa and Latin America, but the best land is already under production. Much of the arable land that remains is only marginally suited to support agriculture and is incapable of sustaining high yields. Indeed, the environmental costs of clearing new farmland are considerable because new land is typically obtained by burning or clear-cutting forests. Seventy to eighty percent of deforestation worldwide is a result of agricultural expansion.[34]

Against this, however, must be set the farmland lost to urbanization and the harmful effects of modern agricultural practices. Nearly 1 percent of all irrigated land is lost each year due to salinization or waterlogging, both attributable to poor drainage. If this rate of loss continues, nearly 50 percent of all presently irrigated land will be lost by 2050. Land is also lost to chemical pollution, a result of the overuse of fertilizers and pesticides. The greatest threat, however, comes from soil erosion. Topsoil is currently being lost at a rate many times faster than it is being replaced. If current trends persist, the world will be robbed of 30 percent of its global soil inventory by 2050. Overall, one study predicts that the area devoted to cereals production will grow by a total of only 5.5 percent between 1993 and 2020.[35]

If the net gain in agricultural land is likely to be small in coming decades, then the main burden for increasing food supplies must be placed on techniques designed to raise the productivity of existing land. This was the aim of the Green Revolution of the 1960s. Since then, scientific research into ways to enhance Third World food production has been conducted under the auspices of an informal international regime. International cooperation in this field began with the founding of the International Rice Research Institute (IRRI) in the Philippines in 1961. The IRRI developed new rice strains that dramatically raised yields throughout Asia. The Centro Internacional de Major-amiento de Maiz y Trige (CIMMYT), located in Mexico, soon duplicated this success by devising new wheat varieties that served to stimulate the Green Revolution in India, Pakistan, and elsewhere.

The Consultative Group on International Agricultural Research (CGIAR), founded in 1971, has meshed the efforts of a growing number of agricultural research organizations. CGIAR today encompasses 18 research centers and draws funding from 40 public and private sources, including Northern and Southern governments, development banks, private foundations, and international agencies. Although CGIAR's initial emphasis was on enhancing productivity through higher yields, it has since broadened its research into sustainable agriculture, including environmental concerns and resource management.[36]

In many ways, the work of implementing the Green Revolution is still unfinished. As of the mid-1980s, less than one-third of grain-producing farms in the Third World planted high-yielding Green Revolution varieties of grain. Bringing high-yield seeds into more common use throughout the Third World could lead to substantial gains in food output. Unfortunately, this goal is not easily met. Green Revolution grain varieties achieve their high yields by virtue of their responsiveness to liberal quantities of fertilizer and water. Irrigation is particularly important. Although only 16 percent of the world's grain-producing lands are irrigated, these fields produce 36 percent of all the grain harvested each year.[37]

But irrigation is expensive. The most bountiful and affordable sites for irrigated agriculture have already been exploited. Future expansion of irrigated land will require large investments. As previously mentioned, existing irrigated lands are threatened by salinization and waterlogging. In some cases, the dams and reservoirs upon which many irrigation systems depend are becoming clogged with silt. In other instances, underground water tables are being depleted much faster than they are being replenished. This is true of the aquifer that lies beneath India's bountiful Punjab wheat fields, which is falling by one meter per year. Although the area of agricultural land under irrigation grew by 2 percent per year between 1970 and 1982, that rate of growth fell to 1.3 percent per year from 1982 to 1994 and is expected to slow still further to 0.6 percent per year in coming decades. Overall, the per-capita quantity of irrigated farmland has declined by 6 percent since 1978. By 2020, the per-capita amount of irrigated land is expected to fall 17 to 28 percent below the 1978 peak.[38]

Fertilizers can boost yields substantially, especially if used in conjunction with modern seed varieties. Many owners of small farms in the Third World, however, lacking either self-generated capital or access to credit, simply cannot afford the expense of purchasing commercial fertilizers for their fields. In many places where fertilizer use is already heavy, farmers have begun to experience declining marginal returns. Additional quantities of fertilizer produce increasingly smaller enhancements to yield.[39]

Africa is one part of the Third World that has been almost entirely bypassed by the Green Revolution and other modern farming advances. As of the mid-1980s, only 1 percent of Africa's grain-producing fields were planted with high-yield Green Revolution varieties of seed. The fertilizer use rate in Africa is only 3 percent that of the United States. Due to the devastating effects upon livestock of diseases spread by the tsetse fly, only 16 percent of African farms rely upon animal power. Only 3 percent have access to modern farm machinery. Cereal yields in Africa are less than one-quarter those achieved in the United States, one-third of those in the Far East, and less than one-half those of Latin America. Moreover, the output of African farms has failed to keep up with the region's rapid population growth. Although African agricultural output rose by one-third during the 1980s, for example, overall population growth for the region grew even faster during this period. As a result, per-capita grain production has declined by 22 percent in Africa since 1967.[40]

When provided with adequate resources, African farmers are capable of substantially improved performance. Norman Borlaug, one of the founders of Asia's Green Revolution, helped to transplant Green Revolution techniques to 150,000 African farms between 1986 and 1992. These farms realized average increases in yield of 3.5 times previous levels.[41] A combination of factors, including general economic stagnation, rising debt burdens, repeated drought, and in many countries, civil violence, robs African agriculture of the investments needed to realize these sorts of results on a broad-scale basis. Should the necessary resources become available in the future, however, it is clear that Africa's farmland has the potential to produce far greater quantities of food than it does at present. This, then, offers some hope for the future.

Even where the Green Revolution has been pursued most vigorously, however, its effects have not been entirely positive. In many places, large farmers who could afford the investments required to reap the benefits from the new varieties of seed gained power and economic status relative to small farmers who lacked sufficient resources to undertake such investments. In the Punjab region of India, this led to an increasing concentration of land owner-ship, with nearly a quarter of all small farms disappearing between 1970 and 1980.[42]

The Green Revolution has also had negative environmental impacts that limit its sustainability, including increased soil erosion, the depletion of water tables, and chemical pollution. Moreover, because farmers in some regions have abandoned the plethora of traditional varieties of wheat or corn in favor of a small handful of new high-yielding varieties, a disturbing loss of genetic diversity is occurring. Native crops that may have useful characteristics, such as resistance to certain diseases, are threatened with extinction before scientists can even ascertain and exploit their beneficial qualities. The genetic unifor-mity of modern grain production also increases the risk that new diseases might wipe out entire crops or that pests will become increasingly resistant and invulnerable to modern pesticides. Traditional farming practices guarded against these risks by planting a variety of grains, each with different vulnera-bilities. This diversity reduces the chances that one disease will damage the entire crop.[43]

Despite these cautionary notes, scientific advances will undoubtedly play a role in boosting future food production. New rice varieties created by the In-ternational Rice Research Institute could raise total rice production by as much as one-quarter after they are planted on a widespread basis. Many such breakthroughs must be realized, however, if food production is to keep pace with growing populations. Yet funding for agricultural research and improve-ment has declined in recent years. The amount of official development assis-tance (ODA) targeted toward agriculture dropped by 57 percent between 1988 and 1996, while funding for CGIAR fell by 7 percent in real terms from 1992 to 1994. On average, developing-country governments devote only 7.4 percent of state budgets to agricultural development.[44]

Genetic modification offers one potential tool for tackling future food scarcity. Genetic marking, for instance, can greatly speed and simplify tradi-tional crossbreeding methods in the development of a given species of plant or animal. With knowledge of a particular plant genome, for instance, scientists can ascertain beforehand whether organisms have the specific gene that is de-sired for crossbreeding. This technology is relatively uncontroversial and may allow for swifter, though still incremental, gains in yield and pest resistance.[45]

Far more controversial are genetic engineering techniques that involve the transfer of genes from one species to another. The promise of such advances is alluring, although still largely unrealized to date. Most stunning has been the development of so-called "golden rice." Scientists have succeeded in produc-ing a yellow-hued strain of rice that is rich in vitamin A through transgenetic modification. This new rice could bring tremendous health benefits in the many parts of the developing world where vitamin A deficiency is a major problem. An estimated 124 million children worldwide suffer from a lack of sufficient dietary vitamin A. Two million children die of vitamin A deficiency each year, while another 500,000 go blind from the same lack.

Although its release has been delayed by patent disputes, cooperation involving the Rockefeller Institute and several agricultural research organizations and large biotechnology companies calls for the establishment of nonprofit holding companies that would distribute golden rice seeds free to poor farmers in the developing world. The vitamin-rich rice would be cross-bred with local varieties and the seeds saved for planting in future years.[46]

There exist other promising applications for these techniques. Some scientists, for instance, believe that genetic engineering could save an estimated 1 to 3 percent of the world's crops that are presently lost to pests and disease. Singapore, Taiwan, and a number of other developing countries are already heavily committed to research, development, and/or adoption of genetically engineered crops.[47]

Yet genetic engineering of modified foodstuffs has also encountered stiff opposition from some quarters. Environmentalists warn that the introduction of genetically modified organisms into natural ecosystems could produce unexpected and harmful effects, such as the development of fast spreading and pesticide-resistant "superweeds." Others express concerns about the consumption of genetically modified foods on human health. Scientific research into such risks has been scant thus far, and one authoritative review of existing studies concludes that it is not yet possible to draw firm conclusions about the safety of genetically modified foods.[48]

To date, little progress has been made toward developing widely accepted national or international standards and regulations with regard to genetically modified foods. Without such oversight, consumer confidence in the safety of such foodstuffs may stand in doubt. In 1999, negotiations on international rules regarding trade in genetically modified organisms based upon the Biosafety Protocol of the 1992 Convention on Biological Diversity ended in disagreement and failure. Later in the same year, efforts to establish a "Working Party on Biotechnology" under the auspices of the World Trade Organization also came to naught.

In general, the United States prefers open trade in genetically modified organisms and minimal regulation. Most European countries, in contrast, are highly skeptical about genetic engineering and the European Union has imposed what amounts to a near ban on the importation of genetically modified food and seeds. The EU's stance on this issue has slowed the spread of genetically engineered strains to developing countries, since the latter fear that the food grown from such seeds would be ineligible for export to European markets. Coming years promise to bring continued political strife over how to balance the promise and the risks of genetic engineering.[49]

Despite these points of controversy, however, the production of genetically modified foods is rapidly spreading. The global value of the transgenic seed market has grown from $156 million in 1996 to $3 billion in 2000. Overall, the acreage devoted to genetically modified food production grew 11 percent worldwide in 2001. Developing countries are beginning to embrace biotech crops. The acreage devoted to genetically modified crops increased 49 percent in Argentina and 66 percent in China during 2001 alone. Overall, the developing country's share of global biotech crop acreage increased from 18 percent in 1999 to 24 percent in 2000.[50]

There exist other measures that can help make more food available in the future. Better management should be able to save much of the 6 percent of all grain that is presently lost through poor storage and distribution practices. In the United States, 27 percent of all food is lost at the retail, consumer, and food service levels. In some places, land that presently produces only one crop per year could support two or more crops if properly managed.

The world's farms could feed far more people if a large proportion of the grain presently fed to livestock were instead consumed directly by humans. Livestock, such as cattle and sheep, now graze roughly one-half of the earth's total land area. One-quarter of the world's cropland is devoted to the production of grain and other feeds for livestock. These animals consume 38 percent of the grain produced worldwide.

Although the grain fed to livestock is converted to meat, which is eventually consumed by humans, the process is most inefficient. It takes seven kilograms of grain, for instance, to produce one kilogram of beef. Up to the point of slaughter, a 240 pound hog raised in the United States consumes 600 pounds of corn and 100 pounds of soybean meal. The meat thereby produced could supply one person with a diet of 2,200 calories per day for 49 days. The same corn and soybean, if consumed directly, could sustain one person at the same rate of caloric intake for 500 days. A decline in meat consumption would free up much grain for direct human consumption and help the world's agricultural system to accommodate the demands of a growing global population. Unfortunately, proportional meat consumption is more likely to rise than to fall in the coming years. Experience suggests that, as Southern incomes rise, people who had previously been able to afford only a vegetarian diet will begin to consume larger quantities of meat. Overall, the demand for meat in developing countries is expected to double between 1995 and 2020.[51]

Much will depend upon policy reform as well. If Southern agriculture is to modernize quickly enough to provide for rapidly growing populations, then the development priorities of many Third World governments must change. Three sets of policy biases common to many governments work against producers of basic staple food crops: an industrial bias, an urban bias, and a cash crop bias. Policy makers often equate development with industrialization. As a result, scarce capital is marshaled toward the manufacturing sector, whereas agriculture suffers from a scarcity of investment. Indeed, some governments deliberately manipulate food prices downward so as to please politically potent urban constituencies. The results of this urban bias are to depress rural incomes and to undermine both the ability and the incentive for farmers to modernize and expand production. Even within the agricultural sector, crucial inputs such as credit, infrastructure, and the best land are targeted principally at cash crops, such as coffee, tea, cocoa, or sugar, which can be exported to the North in return for scarce foreign exchange.

On balance, it seems possible, despite the obstacles, that the world can achieve sufficient increases in food production to avoid any dramatic lowering of present consumption levels and perhaps even to improve the diets of the millions of malnourished. Four factors appear critical to achieving this outcome: (1) continued progress must be made in reducing the rate of population growth; (2) ongoing scientific research must continue to devise increasingly reliable and higher-yielding staple crop varieties; (3) increased economic investment must be directed to agricultural modernization, particularly in the Third World; and (4) greater efforts must be made to bring about the more equitable distribution of food supplies. To say that these challenges can be met, however, is not to assume that they will be. Much will depend upon the priorities of political leaders in both North and South. What does seem apparent, however, is that the margin of error is slim when it comes to organizing the world's agricultural resources over the coming decades.

SUSTAINABLE DEVELOPMENT

Sustainable development can be defined as the ability of present generations of humans to provide for their own needs through economic activity without so harming the national environment as to endanger the ability of future generations to do the same. By this standard, there are growing indications that the current mode of global economic accumulation is, in the aggregate, clearly unsustainable. The warning signs are many. Consider, for instance, the following examples of human-produced environmental damage and resource scarcity:

- As carbon dioxide and other greenhouse gases accumulate in the earth's atmosphere, scientists predict that the earth's average temperature could rise by somewhere between 1.5 and 6 degrees Fahrenheit over the next century. Among other consequences, global warming could lead to a thawing of the polar icecaps and a rise in ocean levels of 20 inches.[52]

- In spite of international efforts to phase out chemical emissions that threaten the earth's ozone layer, 1998 and 1999 witnessed the largest, deepest, and longest-lasting ozone hole over Antarctica in recorded history. Recent years have also brought an alarming thinning of the ozone layer over parts of Europe and North America. Each 1 percent loss in stratospheric ozone results in an estimated 2 percent increase in skin cancers and a 1 percent rise in eye cataracts.[53]

- Twenty percent of the Amazon rain forest has already been lost. At current rates of deforestation, the Amazon will be entirely wiped out in 80 years.[54]

- By 2025, 18 nations will lack sufficient water resources to meet the basic needs of expected population levels.[55]

- The World Conservation Union estimates that 11,000 plant and animal species are at risk of extinction. Due to human effects on the environment, the current extinction rate is between 1,000 and 10,000 times higher than it would be under natural conditions.[56]

In light of these and other alarming data, the environment has moved to the top of national and international policy agendas. Yet the obstacles along the path to sustainable development are many and varied.

The most ambitious effort to date to chart a road map toward sustainable development has been the United Nations Conference on Environment and Development (UNCED), held June 3–14, 1992, in Rio de Janeiro, Brazil.[57] Popularly known as the "Earth Summit," this meeting brought together representatives from over 150 nations, including 118 heads of state, to focus on the connections between threats to the global environment and economic development. The UN General Assembly resolution authorizing UNCED established that its purpose was to "elaborate strategies and measures to halt and reverse the effects of environmental degradation in the context of increased national and international efforts to promote sustainable and environmentally sound development in all countries."[58]

Rio was also the site of a parallel meeting of 1,400 nongovernmental organizations (NGOs) called the Global Forum. Private environmental and citizens groups from around the world shared ideas, built ongoing networks, and lobbied government representatives on behalf of a more environmentally sustainable future.

The 1992 Earth Summit was modeled upon a similar conference held in 1972 in Stockholm, Sweden. That meeting, called the UN Conference on the Human Environment and attended by 114 nations, helped to stimulate development of the modern environmental movement. The earlier meeting also gave rise to the UN Environment Program and led to tighter environmental legislation in many Northern countries.

The Rio conference produced five major documents:

- The Rio Declaration established 27 basic principles of sustainable development.

- The Convention on Biological Diversity sought to address three major goals: (1) to commit governments to the preservation of endangered plant and animal species and habitats, (2) to encourage the sustainable use of biological resources, and (3) to establish the right of Southern nations to compensation from Northern commercial exploitation of products based upon Southern gene stocks.

- The Climate Convention addressed the problem of global warming brought on by the emission of so-called greenhouse gases, such as carbon dioxide. One hundred and fifty-three nations committed themselves to curbing the emission of such gases to 1990 levels by the year 2000.

- The Forest Principles document specified 17 nonbinding principles of sustainable forest management.

- Agenda 21, an 1,800–page document, provided a work plan, or agenda for action, covering all major areas of sustainable Southern development.

The most important new international institution to emerge from the Earth Summit was the Sustainable Development Commission. This organization was given responsibility for integrating the planning and activities of all UN bodies responsible for projects related to both environmental protection and economic development. The commission was also given the job of monitoring and reporting on progress toward fulfillment of the aims and programs spelled out in Agenda 21. National governments were invited to provide annual reports to the commission on the state of environmental and development goals within their countries. The Sustainable Development Commission will periodically hold high-level conferences on topics related to its mandate and will bargain with governments and international organizations on issues of mutual concern.

In many ways, the Earth Summit was a success. Never before had so many of the world's people and governments focused such concentrated attention on the major environmental challenges of modern life. With 8,000 journalists in attendance, media coverage was extensive. Broad agreement was reached on the critical importance of coupling environmental and economic issues and on many of the principles and strategies necessary to move in the direction of sustainability. The national reports prepared by most governments for submission at the summit enhanced the information base regarding environmental conditions in many parts of the globe. The creation of new institutions, such as the Sustainable Development Commission, will ensure continued international attention and regularized consultation regarding environmental problems. The Global Forum helped to strengthen cooperation among hundreds of nongovernmental environmental organizations from all parts of the world and illustrated the potential political clout of citizen-based groups.

Nevertheless, in other ways the Earth Summit fell short of its ambitious mandate. Disagreements plagued the deliberations surrounding many important issues. Due to differing interests and perspectives, final drafts of the forestry and climate change agreements were considerably watered down. Northern and Southern countries clashed over the assignment of responsibility for various environmental problems.

The most significant conflict emerged over how to finance the expensive programs elaborated in Agenda 21. UNCED's secretariat estimated that comprehensive implementation of the provisions of Agenda 21 in the South would cost $600 billion per year. The suggested share of this amount to be provided by Northern countries was $125 billion, with the remainder to be allocated by developing countries themselves. Yet there is little or no likelihood that either Northern or Southern countries will devote sums even approaching these recommended amounts to the pursuit of sustainable development. All of Northern foreign aid to the South amounted to roughly $60 billion in the early 1990s. Even if all of this aid were reprogrammed toward sustainable development projects (an unlikely prospect), it would still amount to less than half of the suggested total. In fact, the Rio conference produced Northern pledges of increased aid for environmental programs in the South amounting to only an estimated $6 billion to $7 billion. Between 1991 and 1998, the Global Environment Facility, created to combat global warming, ozone depletion, and other environmental threats, had allocated funds in the amount of less than $2 billion.[59] Nor are Southern states likely to come up with the hundreds of billions of dollars in annual funding necessary to implement Agenda 21 at a time when most are busy cutting public expenditures.

At best, Agenda 21 outlines a set of goals and strategies that can be realized only slowly through an incremental process. In the meantime, however, existing patterns of development will continue to inflict environmental damage to the land, sea, and air, sometimes in irreparable ways.

ATMOSPHERIC POLLUTION AND THE
TRAGEDY OF THE COMMONS

The world's atmosphere constitutes a classic "commons." Any resource that is freely available for common use by everyone and that is not easily partitioned by the allocation of exclusive ownership rights can be considered a commons. The earth's atmosphere meets these criteria. All nations, groups, and individuals have access to the atmosphere, whether to inhale its air or to emit pollutants. Atmospheric circulation patterns do not respect national borders and ensure that pollutants released in one country often travel to other parts of the globe.

The so-called "tragedy of the commons" refers to the fact that resources held in common are easily and often overexploited.[60] Individual users enjoy all of the benefits of exploiting common resources but are able to push the costs of doing so onto the community as a whole. The classic example is a village commons, where villagers can freely graze individually owned sheep. Each villager has an incentive to increase the size of his or her herd since more sheep means more wool and a greater income. When all follow this logic, however, the number of sheep feeding on the commons area quickly exceeds the carrying capacity of the land. The pasture gives out, sheep die for want of food, and the villagers all suffer.

This problem could be avoided in one of several ways. The commons could be divided into private property, with each villager taking a well-defined parcel. In this way, the costs of overgrazing would be born entirely by the individual herder and could not be passed along to the community. This would enhance the incentive for each herder to exercise restraint in managing herd size. Another solution would be to combine all sheep under community ownership, eliminating privately-held herds. Rather than each individual making separate decisions about the size of his or her herd, the community as a whole would balance costs and benefits in making a single decision that maximized the return to the village as a whole.

Neither of these solutions is available in managing the earth's atmosphere. As mentioned above, wind currents make it impossible to confine pollutants to the air space of the emitting country. So partition is not an option. Global ownership of the atmosphere under a single decision-making authority is conceivable but most unlikely given the division of the world into almost 200 sovereign nations.

A third solution is external regulation. Individuals continue to exploit the commons for their own gain, but under regulations imposed by some common authority. In the domestic sphere, this is the solution often adopted to protect local commons, such as streams and lakes. National or local governments impose limits on the activities of businesses and individuals.

At the global level, of course, there exists no world government that could impose binding regulations on states in relation to exploitation of the earth's atmosphere. Yet regulation remains an option if nations accept mutually agreed-upon rules and limitations on a voluntary basis. This is the approach that has been adopted in attempts to deal with the two most important threats to the world's atmosphere: ozone depletion and global warming. In both cases, global negotiations have aimed at agreement on a set of rules to which individual governments would voluntarily consent and comply.

The obstacles to the success of this approach to protecting the atmospheric commons are numerous. Agreement must be gained from all or most of those countries responsible for polluting the atmosphere. Yet states differ widely in power, economic interests, culture, political systems, and ability to adjust to new conditions. Nations have incentives to push the most difficult costs of adjustment onto others. The prospect that some countries will cheat or renege on agreements both makes such agreements more difficult to achieve and threatens their effectiveness once in force. These problems do not render environmental cooperation impossible, but they do raise questions about our ability to cope as a species with complex threats to the health of the global commons. The following sections examine and compare efforts to carve out voluntary global agreements dealing with the issues of ozone depletion and global warming.

Ozone Depletion

Over the past several decades, scientists have monitored the gradual thinning of the earth's ozone layer over certain portions of the planet.[61] Early findings focused on Antarctica. Subsequently, thinning has been detected in the Arctic region as well. Ozone "holes" over these areas have continued to expand and thinning has been detected in the populated areas of northern Europe, Canada, and the northern United States. The ozone hole over the Antarctica extends over an area larger than the size of the continental United States and reached its largest range to that point in the winter months of 1998 and 1999.[62]

The concerns raised by these measurements stem from the fact that the ozone layer in the upper atmosphere serves to protect plant and animal life on earth from the harm potentially done by the sun's intense ultraviolet rays. Scientists estimate that a 1 percent loss in stratospheric ozone leads to a 2 percent increase in the incidence of skin cancer among exposed humans and a 1 percent increase in eye cataracts.[63] Ozone loss endangers marine life through its harmful impact on sea plankton. Some types of terrestrial plant life are also threatened.

Ozone thinning was first linked to the release of chlorofluorocarbons (CFCs) into the atmosphere in the 1970s. Among other applications, CFCs are used as industrial solvents and as coolants for refrigeration. In the seventies, the United States was the first nation to take steps to limit CFC emissions by banning their use in aerosols. Over the subsequent years, scientists have identified other types of chemical emissions that deplete ozone, including halons, methyl bromide, and hydrochlorofluorocarbons (HCFCs).

The first steps toward multilateral regulation of CFCs began in the 1980s and culminated in the Montreal Protocol on Substances that Deplete the Ozone Layer, signed by representatives from industrial countries in 1987. The Montreal Protocol called for a 50 percent reduction in CFC production by the year 2000. As further scientific evidence revealed an accelerated loss of ozone in subsequent years, more far-reaching limitations were agreed to in the follow-up accords of 1992 and 1996. The latter agreement mandated a total phaseout of CFC production in Northern countries by 2000 and in the developing world by 2010. In 1995, international agreement was also reached to end production of methyl bromide by 2010. Another class of chemicals, called HCFCs, was originally considered an acceptable substitute for CFCs in many industrial uses. Subsequently, it was determined that HCFCs also contribute to ozone depletion, although they are less potent and less long-lasting compared with CFCs. HCFCs have also been found to worsen the global warming problem. HCFCs will now be phased out by 2030 under current agreements.

The initial moves to regulate CFC production were opposed by the chemical industry. Public pressure, along with the possibility of developing and marketing substitutes, eventually reduced the level of industry opposition. Southern countries were excluded from the Montreal Protocol at first. In 1996, however, developing countries agreed to phase out CFC production, albeit with a ten-year grace period.

Although the series of accords dealing with ozone depletion represent the most far-reaching and successful example of international environmental cooperation to date, it should be noted that the underlying problem itself has not been solved. CFC production continues in many Southern countries, and the deadlines for phasing out other classes of ozone-depleting chemicals still lie years into the future. Northern countries have yet to live up to their promises to provide financial assistance to Southern countries in making the transition to CFC substitutes. Moreover, CFCs remain active in the atmosphere for up to 100 years. In fact, the annual thinning of the ozone layer continues to worsen. Eventually, the ozone layer will recover as the previous buildup of ozone-destroying chemicals in the atmosphere subsides and new emissions continue to decline. But the threat and reality of ozone depletion will remain a serious concern for decades to come.

Global Warming

Global warming is perhaps the most serious environmental threat yet faced by mankind. The earth's surface temperature has warmed by almost half a degree since 1950, and nine of the ten hottest years on record since 1866 occurred in the period from 1990 to 2001. Scientists trace the recent warming trend to the human-induced buildup of so-called "greenhouse" gas emissions. Carbon dioxide accounts for roughly one-half of such emissions with methane, chlorofluorocarbons, and other greenhouse gases making up the remainder. Carbon dioxide is a by-product of the burning of fossil fuels and the combustion of plant life, such as forests. Methane is released during the cultivation of rice and the raising of livestock.[64]

As they build up in the atmosphere, these gases serve to trap solar radiation as it is transformed into heat by reflecting off the earth's surface. Greenhouse gases prevent this heat from escaping into space, much as a greenhouse captures the sun's rays to retain warmth within its walls even on a cold winter day. As the concentration of such gases in the earth's atmosphere has grown fourfold since 1950, the earth's average temperature has begun to climb. Scientists estimate that if current trends continue, the earth's surface will rise a further 1.5 to 6 degrees Fahrenheit over present levels by the year 2100.[65]

The consequences of uncontrolled warming could be severe. Scientists warn of rising sea levels as the polar ice caps recede, threatening to flood many islands and heavily populated coastal areas. Weather patterns could become more extreme, with more frequent episodes of hurricanes, severe hot spells, heavy rainfall in some areas, and drought in others. A warmer climate will allow tropical diseases such as malaria and dengue fever to spread to previously temperate zones. Ecosystems will be disrupted. Entire forests may die off as native tree species are suddenly exposed to climate conditions to which they are poorly adapted. While agriculture may flourish in some areas, many existing agricultural regions will suffer and the adjustment costs will be great. Overall, The United Nations Environmental Program has estimated that without decisive steps to reduce the rate of global warming, the consequences of a warmer earth could produce global costs of $300 billion annually by the year 2050.[66]

While these threats have prompted extensive international dialogue over what to do about global warming, the results so far have been disappointing. The Rio Earth Summit produced the UN Framework Convention on Climate Change, which came into force in March 1994 and has been ratified by 181 nations. The Framework Convention called for voluntary reductions in greenhouse gas emissions and committed the signatories to meet periodically to review progress and consider additional steps toward combating global warming. Such a meeting was held in Kyoto, Japan, in 1997. Eighty four nations signed the resulting Kyoto Protocol, which called for Northern countries to reduce their collective greenhouse gas emissions to 5.2 percent below 1990 levels by the year 2010. As of June 2001, however, only 22 states—none from the industrialized world—had ratified the Kyoto agreement.[67]

By the late 1990s, it became apparent that neither the loose voluntary commitments made in the 1992 Rio accord nor the more specific goals for emission reductions laid out in the Kyoto Protocol would be met. Only three countries—Great Britain, Germany, and Russia—had succeeded in meeting targets for reducing emissions. The United States was moving in the opposite direction. Between 1990 and 1998, U.S. carbon emissions actually grew by 10.3 percent.[68]

Developing countries refused to sign the Kyoto Protocol at all on the grounds that Northern countries were largely responsible for the buildup of greenhouse gases to date, accounting for 73 percent of global carbon dioxide emissions. Developing countries argued that those most responsible for creating the problem should bear the greater burden toward its solution. The United States, in particular, objected to the failure of developing countries to set targets for reducing their emissions, pointing out that rapidly growing energy production in the South meant that overall Southern greenhouse gas emissions would surpass the collective Northern total by 2010. The failure of Southern countries to sign the Kyoto Protocol has been cited by many congressional opponents for the U.S. failure to ratify the agreement.[69]

The Kyoto Protocol clearly falls short of providing a full and workable solution to the problem of global warming. Few nations are so far showing progress toward meeting the goals set out in the accord. Yet even if compliance with the Kyoto agreement were total, greenhouse gas concentrations in the atmosphere would continue to rise.[70]

In recognition of the Kyoto Protocol's limitations, signatory countries convened another meeting at the Hague in the fall of 2000 in an effort to hammer out more-detailed mechanisms for ensuring progress toward the goals set out in the earlier accord. These negotiations, however, collapsed in disagreement and failure in late November 2000. Although some governments and environmental groups held out for a compromise between polarized positions, in the end no common ground could be found. Dr. Michael Grub of Britain's Imperial College observed: "When something like this is killed, it is killed by an alliance of those who want too much with those who don't want anything." Business interests, led by large oil companies and represented at the meeting by over 300 lobbyists, argued that the emission reduction goals being considered were too stringent. Some environmental groups, in contrast, believed that the compromise proposals under discussion were too weak. According to Bill Hare of Greenpeace International: "We are better off with no deal than a bad deal."[71]

Subsequent to the failure of the meeting in The Hague, newly elected U.S. president George W. Bush declared, in March 2001, that his administration was no longer committed to the Kyoto Protocol despite the fact that the

United States had already signed (but not ratified) the accord under President Clinton. Bush stated that "I will not accept a plan that will harm our economy and hurt American workers."[72]

U.S. allies in Europe and other parts of the world harshly condemned Bush's repudiation of the Kyoto agreement and called for the United States to rejoin negotiations. Efforts to satisfy American objections to a pact on global warming continued through 2001. In April 2001, Dutch environmental minister Jan Pronk, chair of the United Nations climate change negotiations, proposed new compromises designed to bridge the gap between the United States and other countries prior to a major climate change conference scheduled for July 2001.

One element of contention concerned proposals for a global system for trading greenhouse emission reduction credits. Under such a system, countries that failed to meet their own goals for reducing greenhouse gas emissions could buy equivalent credits from other countries that had exceeded their own emissions reduction targets. In theory, credit trading system would encourage the reduction of emissions in places where it is least expensive to do so. One study suggests that the cost of cutting global emissions to 1990 levels by 2010 without an emissions trading system would be $57.5 billion. The same goal could be met at a cost of $9.3 billion if an emissions trading system were in place.[73]

In the Hague negotiations, European countries sought to limit the quantity of emissions credits that a country could purchase toward meeting its national target to one-half of the scheduled emission reductions. The purpose of this provision was to ensure that each country carried out some emissions reduction within its own borders. The United States argued that there should be no restriction on the number of credits that could be purchased toward the overall national emissions reduction goal.

Pronk's compromise proposal accepted the U.S. position on this point. Pronk also endorsed the U.S. demand—previously opposed by European nations—that countries be allowed to offset some of the carbon dioxide captured in forests and farmland toward national emissions limits and that reforestation be credited toward emission targets. Although Pronk's plan did not require that developing countries adopt emissions limits, as the United States would prefer, he did propose a multibillion-dollar global fund to finance emissions reduction projects in the developing world.[74]

Despite concessions to the U.S. position, the United States still refused to sign the Kyoto Protocol when, in November 2001, 164 nations agreed to a final version of the treaty. Even without U.S. support, the conclusion of negotiations on the Kyoto agreement represented a significant accomplishment. Nevertheless, the treaty will go into effect only when formally ratified by at least 55 nations, collectively accounting for 55 per cent of 1990 greenhouse gas emissions. If this goal is met, then industrial countries that are party to the agreement will be committed to reduce their overall greenhouse gas emissions to 5 percent below 1990 levels by the year 2012.[75]

COMPARISON OF THE OZONE AND
CLIMATE CHANGE NEGOTIATIONS

International negotiation has yet to provide full or lasting solutions for either of the major problems of atmospheric pollution reviewed above. Clearly, however, progress has been swifter and more significant in dealing with ozone depletion than in the case of global warming. Why the difference? What lessons can we learn from comparing these two cases?

Several points of comparison deserve attention. First, negotiations are more likely to succeed the smaller the number of key parties involved in seeking agreement. In the case of the Montreal Protocol, a relatively small number of industrial countries accounted for 85 percent of global production of CFCs and other ozone-depleting chemicals. Since developing countries contributed so little to the problem, they were granted a generous grace period before they would be expected to eliminate CFC production. In the case of global warming, much of past and present production was also accounted for by a small number of industrial countries. Yet future projections suggested that the developing world—especially China—would account for a rapidly growing share of greenhouse gas emissions in coming decades. Under these conditions, the United States was reluctant to carry the burden of reducing its own emissions without similar requirements for Southern countries. The South, however, was adamantly opposed to such a proposal. The broader scope of responsibility for greenhouse gas emissions led to disagreement over who should be included under the rules of an emerging global regime, thus greatly complicating negotiations.

Second, scientists offered a clearer and more urgent message in the ozone case. The scientific evidence linking ozone depletion to CFC emissions was overwhelming and the consequences of inaction were clearly spelled out. Moreover, the ozone hole could be easily monitored and graphically displayed to the public. As ozone thinning began to appear over populated areas in the middle latitudes, the dangers could no longer be ignored. It took longer for a scientific consensus to emerge over the reality of global warming, due in part to the difficulties of distinguishing human-induced temperature changes from natural fluctuations. Moreover, considerable uncertainty continues to exist over key questions, such as the pace and ultimate extent of warming, the eventual environmental consequences, and the best ways to either minimize or cope with these consequences.

Third, the economic and social costs and disruptions associated with proposed solutions were clearly far more manageable in the case of ozone depletion than in the global warming case. Coping with the problem of ozone depletion meant eliminating a relatively small class of chemical emissions for which substitutes could be developed at a reasonable cost. The chemical industry giants responsible for most CFC production could afford to eventually accept regulation because revenues from CFC sales accounted for only a small proportion of their total income. Moreover, the same companies could hope to profit from developing substitutes. In the case of global warming, a large share of the problem could be traced to carbon dioxide emissions, which are an inevitable product of burning fossil fuels. Given the world's overwhelming reliance upon oil, coal, and natural gas for current energy needs, the adjustment costs of lowering greenhouse gas emissions are potentially huge. This fact alone explains much of the reluctance to tackle the problem of global warming with more potent measures.

CONCLUSIONS

The model of economic development pioneered and pursued by Northern societies over the past two centuries has been premised upon visions of limitless growth. Nature has been viewed as an infinite provider. This vision has given rise to a set of affluent, highly industrialized economies located in North America, Western Europe, and Japan. The allure of these mass-consumption societies has spread across the world, with Southerners seeking to emulate the North's attractive living standards. As Southern countries themselves embarked upon the initial stages of economic development, falling death rates helped to spark a population explosion. It is this combination—of ever rising consumption for a rapidly growing number of people—whose viability is now in doubt.

In recent decades, the costs and limitations of the world's present economic and demographic course have become clearer and better understood. Many scientists and ecologists doubt that nature can sustain a doubling of the world's population over the coming century combined with a continuation in present rates of economic growth. Only recently, however, have serious efforts begun to work out the implications of these concerns for Southern development strategies. UNCED represented a breakthrough of sorts in promoting the idea that development must be judged not by growth alone but also by long-term environmental sustainability. Yet practical efforts to move toward sustainability have been modest thus far, and much evidence suggests that traditional thinking about development is hard to root out.

The stunning economic success of many East Asian countries, for instance, has led many to offer them as models for other Southern countries seeking to break free from poverty. Yet the example of these societies does little to suggest that the desire for rapid industrialization and rising mass consumption in the South can be reconciled with environmental sustainability. Indeed, the environmental costs of East Asian growth have been as impressive as the economic gains. A World Bank study recently concluded that the amount of sulfur dioxide, nitrogen dioxide, and total suspended particulates in the air increased by a factor of 10 in Thailand, 8 in the Philippines, and 5 in Indonesia between 1975 and 1988. Of the seven cities in the world with the worst air pollution, five are located in Asia. In Taiwan, asthma cases quadrupled during the 1980s due to severe air pollution, and 20 percent of the island's farmland is fouled with industrial waste. A 1985 survey showed that 59 percent of Taiwanese favored increased environmental protection over economic growth. Conditions in Asia are likely to worsen over the coming years because energy consumption in the region is doubling every 12 years and the number of motor vehicles in use is doubling every 7 years.[76]

Although a rethinking of both the means and the ends of Southern development may be desirable in its own right, any real progress in promoting environmental sustainability on a global scale must focus most intently on changes in the mass-consumption habits of Northern societies, which presently use far more resources and contribute to problems such as global warming in far greater degree than does the South. Ultimately, the notion of limits will increasingly come to exert an ever larger influence on all aspects of global economic relations.

NOTES

1. "Green Justice: The Facts," in Robert Jackson (ed.), *Annual Editions: Global Issues, 95/96,* 11th ed., Guilford, Conn.: Dushkin Publishing, 1995, 98–99.

2. Paul R. Ehrlich and Anne H. Ehrlich, *The Population Explosion,* New York: Simon and Schuster, 1990, 134.

3. Ezra Zwingle, "Woman and Population," *National Geographic,* October, 1998, 39.

4. Robin Wright, "Population of Earth Reaches 6 Billion," *Des Moines Register,* July 17, 1999.

5. Zwingle, "Woman and Population," 38.

6. Lester Brown, Nicholas Lenssen, and Hal Kane, *Vital Signs, 1995: The Trends That Are Shaping Our Future,* New York: Worldwatch Institute and Norton, 1995, 94–95; William Stevens, "Feeding a Booming Population without Destroying the Planet," *New York Times,* April 5, 1994; "New Era of Human Migration Has Begun, Experts Say," *San Francisco Chronicle,* August 9, 1994.

7. Charles Kegley, Jr., and Eugene R. Wittkopf, *World Politics. Trend and Transformation,* 5th ed., New York: St. Martin's Press, 1995, 305.

8. For a discussion of population momentum, see Kegley and Wittkopf, *World Politics,* 299–300.

9. On the future aging of the world's population, see Nicholas Eberstadt, "World Population Implosion?" in Timothy C. Lim (ed.), *Stand! Contending Ideas and Opinions: Global Issues,* Bellevue, Wash.: Coursewise, 1999.

10. Population Information Network Gopher of the United Nations Population Division, Department for Economic and Social Information and Policy Analysis, "New Fertility Declines in Sub-Saharan Africa and South-Central Asia."

11. Wright, "Population of Earth Reaches 6 Billion."

12. William Schmidt, "U.N. Population Report Urges Family-Size Choice for Women," *New York Times,* August 18, 1994; "Population: Battle of the Bulge," *The Economist,* September 3, 1994, 24.

13. "Population: Battle of the Bulge," 25.

14. The following discussion is based upon William W. Murdoch, *The Poverty of Nations: The Political Economy of Hunger and Population,* Baltimore: Johns Hopkins University Press, 1980, 15–58.

15. Barbara Crossette, "16% World Illiteracy to Grow, Study Says," *New York Times,* December 9, 1998.

16. William Stevens, "Green Revolution Is Not Enough, Study Finds," *New York Times,* September 6, 1994; "Population: The Battle of the Bulge," 25.

17. See Murdoch, *Poverty of Nations,* 59–83.

18. Schmidt, "U.N. Population Report Urges Family-Size Choice for Women."

19. Katherine Seelye, "Gore to Preside at Security Council Session on AIDS Crisis," *New York Times,* January 10, 2000; "Aid for AIDs," *The Economist,* April 29, 2000; Claire Nullis, "AIDS Massacres African Teenagers," *Des Moines Register,* June 28, 2000.

20. Harry Dunphy, "US to Offer Africa AIDS Funds," Associated Press, July 19, 2000 (available at http://home-news.excite.com/news/ap/000719/14/us-africa-aids); Nullis, "AIDS Massacres African Teenagers."

21. "A Turning Point for AIDs?" *The Economist,* July 15, 2000; "Orphans of the Virus," *The Economist,* August 14, 1999; Seelye, "Gore to Preside," "Aid for AIDs."

22. "A Turning Point for AIDs?"

23. Dunphy, "US to Offer Africa AIDS Funds;" Ellen Knickmeyer, "Africa Skirts HIV Drug Patents," *Des Moines Register,* March 20, 2001; Melody Peterson and Donald G. McNeil, Jr., "Maker Yielding Patent in Africa for AIDS Drug," *New York Times,* March 15, 2001.

24. Dunphy, "US to Offer Africa AIDS Funds"; Joseph Kahn, "World Bank Cites Itself in Study of Africa's Bleak Performance," *New York Times,* June 1, 2000.

25. Paul Kennedy, *Preparing for the Twenty-First Century,* New York: Random House, 1993, 65–66.

26. Henry Kendall and David Pimentel, "Constraints on the Expansion of the Global Food Supply," *Ambio,* May 1994, 199; John Bongaarts, "Can the

Growing Human Population Feed Itself?" *Scientific American,* March 1994; Brown, Lenssen, and Kane, *Vital Signs,* 146–147; Reid, "Feeding the Planet," 59.

27. Christopher S. Wren, "U.N. Report Maps Hunger 'Hot Spots,'" *New York Times,* January 9, 2001; Brown, Lenssen, and Kane, *Vital Signs,* 146–147; Anne Ehrlich and Paul Ehrlich, "Why Do People Starve?" *Amicus Journal,* Spring 1987, 44; Gary Gardner and Brian Halweill, "Nourishing the Underfed and Overfed," in Worldwatch Institute, *State of the World 2000,* New York: Norton, 2000, 73.

28. Debra MacKenzie, "Will Tomorrow's Children Starve?" *New Scientist,* September 3, 1994, 27; Brown, Lenssen, and Kane, *Vital Signs,* 26–27, 36–37, 42–43; "The Food Crisis That Isn't, and the One That Is," *The Economist,* November 25, 1995.

29. Erik Eckholm, "Study Says Bad Data by China Inflated Global Fishing Yields," *New York Times,* November 30, 2001.

30. Bongaarts, "Can the Growing Human Population Feed Itself?"

31. "Will the World Starve?" *The Economist,* June 10, 1995.

32. Quoted in Bongaarts, "Can the Growing Human Population Feed Itself?"

33. Bongaarts, "Can the Growing Human Population Feed Itself?"; Margaret R. Biswas, "Agriculture and Environment: A Review, 1972–1992," *Ambio,* May 1994, 192–193; Donald L. Plucknett, "International Agricultural Research for the Next Century," *BioScience,* July–August 1993, 433.

34. Bongaarts, "Can the Growing Human Population Feed Itself?"; Kendall and Pimentel, "Constraints on the Expansion of the Global Food Supply," 199.

35. Kendall and Pimentel, "Constraints on the Expansion of the Global Food Supply," 200; Per Pinstrup-Anderson, Rajul Pandya-Lorch, and Mark W.

Rosegrant, "The World Food Situation: Recent Developments, Emerging Issues and Long-Term Prospects," *Food Policy Report of the International Food Policy Research Institute,* Washington, D.C., 1997.

36. Plucknett, "International Agricultural Research for the Next Century."

37. Laura Tangley, "Beyond the Green Revolution," *BioScience,* March 1987; MacKenzie, "Will Tomorrow's Children Starve?"

38. MacKenzie, "Will Tomorrow's Children Starve?"; Bongaarts, "Can the Growing Human Population Feed Itself?"; Kendall and Pimentel, "Constraints on the Expansion of the Global Food Supply"; Sandra Postel, "Redesigning Irrigated Agriculture," in Worldwatch Institute, *State of the World 2000,* 40–41.

39. MacKenzie, "Will Tomorrow's Children Starve?"

40. Richard Critchfield, "Bring the Green Revolution to Africa," *New York Times,* September 14, 1992; Tangley, "Beyond the Green Revolution"; Kendall and Pimentel, "Constraints on the Expansion of the Global Food Supply"; Biswas, "Agriculture and Environment: A Review, 1972–1992"; Bongaarts, "Can the Growing Human Population Feed Itself?"; USAID Policy Paper, "Food Aid and Food Security," February 1995 (available at www.usaid.gov/pubs/ads/pps/foodse c/fs_measures.html [accessed May 30, 2001]).

41. Critchfield, "Bring the Green Revolution to Africa"; "Ethiopia: A Green Revolution?" *The Economist,* November 25, 1995.

42. Vandana Shiva, "The Green Revolution in the Punjab," *Ecologist,* March–April 1991.

43. Shiva, "The Green Revolution in the Punjab"; Kendall and Pimentel, "Constraints on the Expansion of the Global Food Supply"; Bongaarts, "Can the Growing Human Population Feed Itself?"

44. MacKenzie, "Will Tomorrow's Children Starve?"; Robert Paarlberg, "The Global Food Fight," *Foreign Affairs,* May–June 2000, 35.

45. Andrew Pollack, "Gene Research Finds New Use in Agriculture," *New York Times,* March 7, 2001.

46. Jon Christensen, "Golden Rice in a Grenade-Proof Greenhouse," *New York Times,* November 21, 2000.

47. George Anthan, "Many Countries Produce Biotech Food to Meet Shortages," *Des Moines Register,* December 15, 2000; Anne Simon Moffat, "Developing Nations Adapt Biotech for Own Needs," *Science,* July 1994.

48. Carol Kaesuk Yoon, "Modified-Crop Studies Are Called Inconclusive," *New York Times,* December 14, 2000.

49. Kristin Dawkins, "The International Food Fight: From Seattle to Montreal," *Multinational Monitor* January–February, 2000; Robert Paarlberg, "The Global Food Fight"; Kristin Dawkins, "Unsafe In Any Seed: US Obstructionism Defeats Adoption of an International Biotechnology Safety Agreement," *Multinational Monitor,* 20.3, March 1999; Barnaby Feder, "Rocky Outlook for Genetically Engineered Crops," *New York Times,* December 20, 1999.

50. Anne Fitzgerald, "Biotech Crops Spread Worldwide," *Des Moines Register,* December 30, 2001.

51. Kendall and Pimentel, "Constraints on the Expansion of the Global Food Supply"; Vaclav Smil, *Feeding the World: A Challenge for the Twenty-First Century,* Cambridge: MIT Press, 2000, 209; MacKenzie, "Will Tomorrow's Children Starve?"; Bongaarts, "Can the Growing Human Population Feed Itself?"; Reid, "Feeding the Planet," 74; C. Ford Runge and Benjamin Senauer, "A Removable Feast," *Foreign Affairs,* May–June, 2000, 40.

52. Daphne Wysham and Jim Vallette, "Changing the Earth's Climate for Business: The World Bank and the

Greenhouse Effect," *Multinational Monitor,* 18.10, October 1997.

53. Jessica Vallette Revere, "Ozone Depletion and Global Warming," *Foreign Policy in Focus,* 5.8, April 2000.

54. Michael Astor, "New Ideas Keep Amazon Alive," *Des Moines Register,* August 21, 1999.

55. "Water Fights," *The World in 2000 (The Economist),* 1999, 52.

56. Mara D. Bellaby, "Global Study Says 11,000 Plants, Animals Could Disappear Forever," *Des Moines Register,* September 29, 2000.

57. Much of the information given next on UNCED has been culled from Edward Parson, Peter Haas, and Marc Levy, "A Summary of the Major Documents Signed at the Earth Summit and the Global Forum," *Environment,* October 1992; Peter Haas, Marc Levy, and Edward Parson, "The Earth Summit: How Should We Judge UNCED's Success?" *Environment,* October 1992; and Jerald Schnoor, "The Rio Earth Summit: What Does It Mean?" *Environment, Science and Technology,* 27.1, 1993.

58. Haas, Levy, and Parson, "The Earth Summit: How Should We Judge UNCED's Success?" 8.

59. World Bank, *World Development Report, 1999/2000,* New York: Oxford University Press, 2000, 94.

60. The term itself was coined by Garrett Hardin in "The Tragedy of the Commons," *Science,* December 1968.

61. Unless otherwise indicated, information provided in the following section on ozone depletion is taken from Charles Kegley and Eugene Wittkopf, *World Politics: Trend and Transformation,* Boston: Bedford/St. Martin's, 2001, 386–388.

62. Jessica Vallette Revere, "Ozone Depletion and Global Warming," *Foreign Policy in Focus,* 5.8, April 2000.

63. Revere, "Ozone Depletion and Global Warming."

64. Kegley and Wittkopf, *World Politics,* 380; "This Year Was the 2nd Hottest, Confirming a Trend, U.N. Says," *New York Times,* December 19, 2001.

65. Kegley and Wittkopf, *World Politics,* 383; "Global Warming: Hotting up the Hague," *The Economist,* November 18, 2000, 81.

66. Kegley and Wittkopf, *World Politics,* 382; George Mwangi, "Report: Climate Change Would Mean Big Costs," *Des Moines Register,* February 3, 2001. For more on the science of climate change, see Curt Suplee, "Unlocking the Climate Puzzle," *National Geographic,* May 1998.

67. Daniel Sarewitz and Roger Pielke, Jr., "Breaking the Global-Warming Gridlock," *Atlantic Monthly,* July 2000, 58, 62; "Emission Impossible?" *Foreign Policy,* November–December 2000, 3l.

68. "Emission Impossible?" 31.

69. Kegley and Wittkopf, *World Politics,* 383; Sarewitz and Pielke, "Breaking the Global-Warming Gridlock," 62.

70. Sarewitz and Pielke, "Breaking the Global-Warming Gridlock," 62.

71. Andrew C. Revkin, "Odd Culprits in Collapse of Climate Talks," *New York Times,* November 28, 2000; "Corporate Campaign to Corrupt the Kyoto Protocol Continues after COP-6," *Corporate Europe Observer,* no. 8, 2000 (available at http://www.xs4all.nl/~ceo/observer 8/cop6.html [accessed June 1, 2001].

72. Cat Lazaroff, "UN Secretary General Denounces U.S. Global Warming Stance," *Environment News Service,* May 21, 2001 (available at http://ens.lycos.com/ens/may2001/2 001L-05-21-06/.html [accessed June 1, 2001]).

73. Estimate from a study carried out by the PEW Center on Global Climate Change, December 1999; conclusions cited in "Emission Impossible?" 31.

74. "New Climate Proposals Aim to Appease USA," *Environment News Service,* April 12, 2001 (available at http:www.ens.lycoes.com/ens/apr200 1/2001L-014-12-03.html [accessed June 1, 2001]).

75. "This Year Was the 2nd Hottest." While governments dither over how to cope with the prospect of global warming, some private companies are moving ahead with ambitious plans for reducing greenhouse gas emissions. In October 2000, seven large energy companies (DuPont, Shell, Alcan Aluminium, BP, Suncor Energy, Pechiney, Ontario Power Generation) announced plans to cut their emissions 15 percent below 1990 levels by the year 2010. The Environmental Defense Fund will audit emissions at company plants and offer technical advice (Andrew C. Revkin, "7 Companies Agree to Cut Gas Emissions," *New York Times,* October 18, 2000).

76. "Pollution in Asia: Pay Now, Save Later," *The Economist,* December 11, 1993, 361; Robin Broad, John Cavanagh, and Walden Bello, "Development: The Market Is Not Enough," in Jeffrey Frieden and David Lake (eds.), *International Political Economy. Perspectives on Global Power and Wealth,* 3rd ed., New York: St. Martin's, 1995, 436.

ANNOTATED BIBLIOGRAPHY

Lester R. Brown, Christopher Flavin, and Hilary French. *State of the World 2000.* New York: Norton, 2000. Statistic-laden and up-to-date collection of essays on various environmental trends and topics.

Lester R. Brown, Nicholas Lenssen, and Hal Kane. *Vital Signs, 1995: The Trends That Are Shaping Our Future.* New York: Worldwatch Institute and Norton, 1995. Revised yearly, this collection of reports on the state of the global environment is loaded with facts and figures. It is the best and most accessible source for those seeking a quick overview of current environmental issues.

Paul R. Ehrlich and Anne H. Ehrlich. *The Population Explosion.* New York: Simon and Schuster, 1990. A pessimistic and alarming perspective on runaway population growth and its consequences.

Al Gore. *Earth in the Balance: Ecology and the Human Spirit.* Boston: Houghton Mifflin, 1992. A broad survey of the threats facing the global ecosystem.

Thomas F. Homer-Dixon. *Environment, Scarcity, and Violence.* Princeton, N.J.: Princeton University Press, 1999. Examines the linkages between environmental scarcity, social cleavages, institutional stability, and communal violence.

William W. Murdoch. *The Poverty of Nations: The Political Economy of Hunger and Population.* Baltimore: Johns Hopkins University Press, 1980. An accessible look at the connections among population, hunger, and poverty. The author argues that structures of international and domestic inequality lie at the root of both rapid population growth and global hunger.

Bruce Rich. *Mortgaging the Earth: The World Bank, Environmental Impoverishment, and the Crisis of Development.* Boston: Beacon Press, 1994. More than a damaging critique of the World Bank's environmental impact, this book offers a philosophical meditation on the sources and implications of modern materialism. Rich challenges common assumptions about development, progress, and the relationship of human society to the ecosystem.

Vandana Shiva. *The Violence of the Green Revolution: Third World Agriculture, Ecology and Politics.* London: Zed Books, 1991. A radical critique of the Green Revolution.

Vaclav Smil. *Feeding the World: A Challenge for the Twenty-First Century.* Cambridge: MIT Press, 2000. A thorough and scientific look at the world's capacity to feed growing populations. Reaches cautiously optimistic conclusions.

14

❖

Charting the Future

Cooperation and Conflict
in the Global Economy

Our conclusion examines the prospects for successful management of the international economic system in an era of globalization. The presence of conflicting interests at both the domestic and international levels precludes the possibility of harmonious economic relations among states. Instead, international economic interdependence rests upon a complex mixture of cooperation and conflict. The balance between the two shifts over time, however, depending upon political and economic conditions within and among states.

The volatility of international economic relations is illustrated by the history of the past 65 years. This period can be broken into four distinct eras. The first spanned the decade of the 1930s, when competitive impulses overwhelmed cooperative efforts. Under the strains produced by the Great Depression, nations erected stiff protectionist barriers and formed economic blocs in vain efforts to preserve domestic production and employment. These actions led to a painful contraction of world trade and raised political tensions. Attempts to find cooperative solutions to the breakdown of the international economic order produced only limited results, due largely to the weakness of existing international institutions and the absence of any country with the power or willingness to exercise leadership. Ultimately, the international system collapsed into world war under the strains produced by spreading protectionism, economic depression, the spread of fascist and imperialist regimes, and interstate aggression.

The next era of international economic relations, stretching from 1947 to 1973, brought more serious and fruitful efforts at cooperation. A variety of new institutions and rules were created to help manage and encourage the growth of economic interdependence. Protectionist barriers fell dramatically, and levels of international trade and investment expanded rapidly, especially during the 1960s. All of this was made possible by a number of essentially political factors, including U.S. hegemony and leadership; the close security relationships forged among the United States, Western Europe, and Japan during the Cold War; and the lessons that political leaders learned from the harsh experiences of the 1930s. Nevertheless, economic cooperation did not extend to encompass the communist bloc, which remained largely isolated from the core capitalist countries, and much of the developing world pursued nationalist economic strategies during this period that limited their integration into the global economy.

The era stretching from 1973 through the early 1990s brought a wavering balance between the cooperative and competitive dimensions of the international political economy. Although economic interdependence continued to expand and deepen, it did so in an erratic manner. This era featured three major global recessions, three episodes of oil-supply disruptions, a major bout of inflation during the late 1970s, the growth of nontariff barriers and managed trade, periodic Third World debt crises, extreme imbalances in trade among the major economic powers, and the only-partially successful reintegration of the former command economies into the world economic system. International economic issues assumed heightened political salience in many countries, and the rules and institutions designed to manage international economic relations were subject to strains produced by changing economic realities as well as by disagreements among the major powers.

With unity and common purpose difficult to achieve, political leaders from various states nevertheless found ways to muddle through repeated crises and conflicts during the 1970s and 1980s, often devising temporary fixes or papering over differences. These expedients sufficed to avert a plunge into outright economic warfare. Indeed, the world economy continued to move toward deeper levels of economic interdependence. Yet gaps in the system's management and serious differences in perspective placed international cooperation under continuous strain.

Over the 1990s, the central tensions over international economic policy shifted from the international to the domestic sphere. With the important exception of the Asian financial crisis of 1997–1998, the global economy entered a period of relative stability from the early nineties onward. The United States economy, freed from Cold War burdens and fueled by a high-technology boom, experienced healthy and sustained growth. The European Union (EU) moved toward deeper levels of integration with the successful introduction of the Euro and a new European central bank. The EU accepted several new members, while the countries of the former Soviet bloc, including Russia, finally began to experience the benefits of market reforms.

Among the major powers, the competitive jockeying of the 1980s has given way to increased cooperation. The Uruguay Round of global trade negotiations reached a successful conclusion with the creation of the new World

Trade Organization (WTO) in 1996. Meeting in Doha, Qatar, the members of the WTO agreed in late 2001 to begin a new round of trade talks. Most importantly, elite opinion among political and business leaders in both the developed and the developing worlds has converged over the past decade around a neoliberal consensus over the need to encourage free markets and curtail state intervention in the economic realm.

Yet despite the revival in intergovernmental cooperation, popular dissatisfaction in many countries with the terms and consequences of globalization has produced a set of potent political movements whose aim is to slow or transform the process of growing economic integration. Labor, environmentalist, human rights, and cultural nationalist groups have attacked neoliberalism for its neglect of the poor and its disregard for the negative environmental effects of globalization. The principal institutions of global economic management, including the International Monetary Fund, the World Bank, and the World Trade Organization, have come under growing pressure to operate in a more open and democratic fashion. The division between popular and elite opinion over neoliberalism and globalization is both domestic and transnational in character. As the anti-globalization movement continues to grow, it has the potential to force a broadening of the agenda of international economic management to include new issues and concerns.

The remainder of this chapter examines the future prospects for successful management of the international economic order. Can political leaders successfully manage the complex process of globalization? Is it possible that traditional forms of economic nationalism and power politics might reemerge to threaten international cooperation? How will states, corporations, and the major international economic institutions respond to the growth of popular movements against globalization? Can cooperation triumph over competition and conflict?

HARBINGERS OF COOPERATION

The forces underlying international economic cooperation are significant and have generally outweighed the incentives for conflict over the past half-century. This section surveys the principal factors that incline states to seek economic openness and cooperative solutions in their relations with one another.

The Fruits of Interdependence

The most important reason for expecting the persistence of international economic cooperation in the future stems from the growing dependence of national economies on one another for essential goods, services, and raw materials. This global web of trade and investment has arisen partly from technological advances and economic processes. Improvements in transportation have greatly lowered the cost of moving goods, raw materials, and even people from one part of the globe to another. And the communications revolution has made it possible for large corporations to manage far-flung multinational empires. Firms interested in obtaining the cheapest labor and raw materials or in expanding into new markets have exploited these new opportunities for international growth.

These fundamental economic realities provide powerful incentives for policy makers to choose cooperative economic strategies. To be sure, interdependence threatens various values and interests, as we later suggest. As a result, states often seek to manage and regulate their relationship with the world economy. Nevertheless, policy makers are generally acutely aware that the costs of "going it alone" in today's world economy are prohibitively high. Indeed, an increasingly elaborate global division of labor has brought greater prosperity to the world economy as a whole. This trend has lent support to a key tenet of economic theory that holds that economic welfare is maximized when nations specialize in those goods that they can produce most efficiently while trading for products that they are poorly suited to produce.

There also exists a widespread understanding that the growth of trade and investment is impossible without a substantial commitment among states to openness, policy coordination, and cooperation in setting the rules and institutions needed to manage the system. The fear that spiraling political conflict could undermine the bases for international economic growth and prosperity inhibits policy makers from resorting to extreme nationalistic strategies and from pressing too hard for relative advantage. These shared perceptions do not preclude the possibility of serious differences among nations in the future, but they may set broad limits on the scope and intensity of conflict and competition.

International Institutions

In the post-World War II era, cooperation has become increasingly institutionalized under the auspices of a network of international organizations created for this purpose, including, among others, the International Monetary Fund, the World Bank, the Organization for Cooperation and Economic Development, the G-7, the European Union and, most recently, the World Trade Organization. States have invested considerable resources in strengthening the capacities of these institutions to monitor the global economy, attack specific problems, and implement relevant international agreements. Since these organizations serve important state interests, the incentives toward cooperation are strengthened by the desire of states to ensure the continued survival and health of the institutions themselves.

Over time, some of these organizations have acquired a degree of independence. The directors of the World Trade Organization and the International Monetary Fund, for instance, serve as lobbyists for the interests of their organizations, nudge states toward further cooperation, and sometimes act as brokers in difficult negotiations over areas of disagreement. In general, international institutions facilitate international cooperation and serve as prods to continued collaboration over time.

Internationalist Interest Groups

The impact of spreading interdependence on domestic interests and coalitions is less certain but may also favor stronger international cooperation. In most countries, economic policy making is influenced by more than simple calculations of the national good. Political leaders are dependent upon coalitions of particular interests. In the making of foreign economic policy, two sets of groups are usually most important: nationalists, who are harmed by the growth of economic interdependence, and internationalists, who directly engage in and benefit from foreign trade and investment.

Rising economic interdependence tends to heighten the political mobilization of both groups and intensifies the conflicts between them. With some important exceptions, however, high levels of trade can be expected to strengthen the power of internationalists, who favor cooperation and openness, at the expense of nationalists.

Nationalist coalitions typically emerge when large numbers of domestic industries begin to experience competition from more efficient foreign producers. The affected firms and workers seek government protection in the form of import restrictions or other sorts of regulations designed to counter the economic advantages possessed by foreign competitors. Such efforts are sometimes rewarded, especially under conditions that tend to strengthen the appeal of nationalism, such as prolonged periods of economic hardship or the persistence of negative trade balances.

Yet, although economic interdependence stimulates nationalist interests to mobilize in the defense of jobs and profits, it also, in the long run, weakens the political clout of nationalists by strengthening the relative economic weight of internationalist interests in the national economy. Even if uncompetitive firms or industries succeed in gaining a degree of state protection, this seldom reverses the shrinking importance of such sectors to the national economy as a whole over time. Internationalist coalitions, in contrast, tend to include many of a nation's largest, fastest-growing, and most competitive firms. As trade and investment grow, the absolute and relative number of firms with a stake in economic openness tends to grow over time, as well. Over the long term, economic success is a surer route to political influence than is failure.

The Neoliberal Convergence

The potential for future economic cooperation is also strengthened by a recent and rather unexpected trend: the growing convergence among nations around similar neoliberal economic strategies. The triumph of neoliberalism, which stresses international openness, free markets and a reduced state role in regulating economic outcomes, is evidenced by a number of recent developments. The Third World has retreated from demands for a new international economic order in which resources would be allocated according to political rather than market criteria. Nationalist import substitution strategies of development have also lost favor. Instead, country after country has, under the pressures of the debt crisis and poor economic performance, begun to privatize state industries, dismantle subsidies and price controls, lower overvalued currencies, and remove barriers to imports and foreign investment. The East Asian newly industrializing countries (NICs) have also begun to reduce the state's role in steering economic development. The same is true in Japan. As the Japanese economy matures and becomes more internationalized, the role of the Ministry of International Trade and Industry (MITI) and other bureaucracies has receded, while barriers to imports and foreign investment have eased. Most dramatic, of course, have been the movements of Eastern Europe and the republics of the former Soviet Union toward capitalism and reintegration with the world economy. Even socialist countries where communist parties remain strong or dominant, such as China and Vietnam, have begun to introduce market reforms and encourage greater trade, investment, and aid from the West.

Neo-liberalism's ascendancy among political and economic elites has paved the way for deeper forms of international cooperation. As discussed later, however, this consensus has come under attack from below by an increasingly vocal transnational populist coalition. Moreover, the Asian financial crisis and the disappointing results of market-oriented policies in some countries have opened cracks in the neoliberal consensus even among elites. The sustainability of the neoliberal model remains to be seen.

THE SOURCES OF CONFLICT

Despite the many factors favoring cooperation, there also exist powerful forces that could lead to heightened conflict and perhaps serve to undermine the basis for growing global interdependence. Some of these forces are quite traditional and stem from the tensions between national autonomy and economic interdependence as well as from the enduring sources of competitive rivalry among nations. Others are related to more recent trends and developments, such as shifts in relative power, the changing nature of bargaining over trade and other issues and the emergence of new social movements critical of globalization.

National Autonomy and Relative Gains

If it is rare for political leaders to isolate their country from the world economy, it is likewise rare for a government to permit trade and investment to take place entirely without regulation or restriction. Interdependence brings costs as well as benefits. In managing their nation's economic relationships with the rest of the world, policy makers attempt to balance the benefits and the costs of interdependence.

The most important political cost of interdependence is the erosion of national autonomy. Economic dependence can leave a country vulnerable to manipulation, as even the United States discovered during the 1970s, when it became dependent upon OPEC oil. In addition, interdependence can greatly complicate the task of economic policy making as decision makers must now take into account the reactions of foreign firms and governments when choosing among national economic policies and goals. Political leaders may also seek to limit trade and investment with nations that are military rivals for fear that such exchanges might allow the transfer of militarily relevant technologies.

Moreover, although trade between two countries may benefit both, there is no guarantee that both will prosper equally. Indeed, it is often possible for one nation to gain advantages over other states or to push burdens onto other states by restricting and regulating trade and investment in various ways. Because the competitive nature of world politics ensures that national leaders are concerned about relative power and position as well as about absolute economic gains, growing interdependence is bound to lead to increased struggle for national advantage alongside efforts at cooperation.

The Changing Nature of U.S. Hegemony

These enduring sources of competition and conflict are evident in the changing leadership role of the United States. At the height of its hegemonic power in the decades after World War II, the United States often placed the stable, long-term management of the international economic order above its narrow, short-term national interests. U.S. aid helped to rebuild the economies of Western Europe and Japan. The dollar served as a key currency. The United States opened its markets ahead of those of its competitors. And it carried a disproportionate burden in providing for the common defense among its allies. The Cold War provided a strong security rationale for American policies designed to strengthen the economic stability of its industrial allies despite the relative disadvantages of such policies for U.S. economic competitiveness.

By the 1970s and 1980s, however, the United States' relative dominance over Europe and Japan had diminished. Concerns about declining American economic competitiveness became a standard refrain in political debate. Moreover, the collapse of the Soviet empire at the end of that decade both freed the United States from some of its Cold War burdens and lessened previous concerns about the need to maintain allied harmony in the face of a common threat. The combination of these trends has transformed American economic and political leadership in important ways.

Over the past two decades, U.S. international economic policy has become more driven by narrow considerations of national interest and less focused on the pursuit of global economic stability for its own sake. The United States is less tolerant of foreign discrimination against American goods and more likely to seek ways to protect its own industries at home while promoting U.S. exports abroad. The United States drives harder bargains in negotiations over international trading rules and has sought to reduce its relative contributions to a host of international institutions. U.S. foreign aid has fallen dramatically in real terms. The United States is generally more attuned to the issue of relative gains in its relations with contending economic powers.

Although this changing orientation in U.S. leadership has led to greater conflict with other industrialized powers, serious ruptures have been avoided. This is partly because other countries remain acutely aware of their considerable dependence upon American markets and investments abroad. In short, continued U.S. power has ensured a degree of deference to its wishes even as American leadership has assumed a less generous, more self-interested form. Nevertheless, a number of conditions could bring about a downward spiral of international conflict: a global economic depression; the emergence of a new political and economic rival, such as China; a sudden loss of U.S. competitiveness or the strengthening of anti-globalization forces in a number of major countries. Were the United States to respond to such developments in an overly competitive fashion, cooperative management of the international economic order could easily falter.

Complexity and International Cooperation

The future of international economic cooperation is also clouded by the complexity of contemporary bargaining. The early stages of international cooperation in the decades after World War II, such as the Kennedy Round of trade negotiations, focused upon relatively simple goals, like the lowering of tariff barriers. Today, however, the goals are much more ambitious, the scope of the issues addressed is broader, and the intrusiveness of international commitments on the domestic sphere is much greater.

Trade negotiators must deal with more varieties of protectionism, many of them less visible and more subtle than tariffs. Bargaining has come to encompass areas once excluded from international trade rules, such as trade in agriculture and services, as well as nontraditional concerns, including protections for intellectual property and the rights and obligations of foreign investors. As the Structural Impediments agreements between the United States and Japan and the recent U.S.-Mexico free trade negotiations suggest, trade agreements are coming to affect policies that were once considered purely domestic in nature. Indeed, at issue are fundamental aspects of national economic structure.

All of this makes international cooperation more significant and substantial today than in the past. The issues are fundamental and the stakes higher. Yet it also suggests that cooperation at the cutting edge is becoming increasingly complex and politically salient, making agreements harder to reach or to implement and honor. The recent failure of negotiations over a proposed Multilateral Agreement on Investments illustrates the difficulties involved. In short, the easy part of building an open, liberal international economic order is past, and the hard part remains.

The Anti-Globalization Movement

Perhaps the most significant and novel sets of obstacles to cooperation arise from the multilayered backlash against globalization that has arisen in recent years. The critics of globalization include those domestic firms and laborers who are harmed by international economic competition, cultural nationalists who decry the erosion of traditional cultures that often accompanies mass commercialization, and environmentalists who question the ecological sustainability of the patterns of intensive consumption that have accompanied globalization. Groups campaigning against sweatshop labor or in favor of Third World debt relief champion those exploited or left behind by the process of globalization. These varied groups have coalesced into an increasingly potent transnational movement. Indeed, meetings of the World Bank, the International Monetary Fund, and the World Trade Organization are now routinely plagued by mass street demonstrations and the attendant negative publicity. While unlikely to stop or reverse globalization, these forces of resistance can and have deflected the process along less destructive avenues and forced governments and international organizations to take ameliorative action.

The critics of globalization view the neoliberal consensus discussed above not as simple agreement on how best to manage the global economy in the interests of all but as a manifestation of the growing power of international capital vis-à-vis both states and workers. As capital has become more mobile across national borders, states have had more difficulty regulating or controlling such flows in ways that promote traditional conceptions of the national interest. Moreover, states that pursue policies that fail to meet with the approval of large financial institutions or internationally mobile firms may suffer from capital flight, declining investment, job losses, and a falling currency. This is particularly true in the area of macroeconomic policy. If financial markets perceive that an expansionist monetary policy raises the risk of inflation, currency traders and investors are likely to diversify out of that nation's currency. Capital will flow to currencies and countries that follow a firmer anti-inflationary set of policies. Globalization has altered the balance of power between states and firms in favor of the latter and increased the incentives that governments experience to maintain "business confidence" in their policies.

In much the same way, international capital mobility decreases the power of labor. Compared with capital, labor is relatively immobile internationally, despite the increased immigration flows of recent decades. Nor in most cases, do nationally based labor movements have close transnational ties with labor organizations in other countries. The territorial constraints on labor and the weakness of international coordination among labor movements allow capital to play workers off against one another by threatening to relocate to a more hospitable country if concessions on wages, benefits, or work rules are not forthcoming. As a result, organized labor has lost clout and membership in many countries over recent years.

The increasing integration of global markets and the growing power of capital are thought by many to promote greater efficiency, productivity, and growth worldwide. The critics of globalization, however, point out that these trends have been accompanied almost everywhere by a worsening inequality in income and wealth and by a fraying of the social safety nets that many nations erected after World War II to aid the least-advantaged groups in their midst. Moreover, some fear that the weakening of national and international regulation of capital, especially in financial markets, may bring greater instability to the world economy as huge sums of capital are carried along by speculative booms and busts. The Asian financial crisis of 1997–1998 is often cited as an example of this sort of instability. Nonmarket values, such as the environment, may also fare poorly in a world where capital reigns supreme.

The anti-globalization movement has demanded that trade agreements include provisions designed to raise labor and environmental standards. They have also argued in favor of new restrictions on the mobility of international capital or taxation of speculative capital flows. Other demands include debt relief for poor countries, a greater emphasis on poverty reduction by aid agencies, and greater openness, transparency, and popular representation in international economic institutions. Corporations have also become targets as grassroots organizations have demanded that firms adopt corporate codes of conduct dealing with labor, environmental, and human rights practices. Many states, corporations, and international organizations have taken modest steps toward reform, but the central issues raised by the critics of globalization and neoliberalism remain the subjects of sharp contention.

CONCLUSIONS

The basic themes of this book have revolved around the struggle for power and wealth among nations. Two parallel yet interacting structures in the international system shape the pursuit of these goals. Fundamentally, nations seek power as a guarantee of survival in a competitive and anarchic state system characterized by territoriality, legal sovereignty, and self-help. Because there exists no higher authority capable of maintaining order in the international system, nations are left to their own devices in seeking ways of promoting their own security. Nations do so primarily through the accumulation of military might, yet a nation's military potential rests upon the size and technological sophistication of its economy. The combination of these military and economic resources determines a nation's power, or ability to influence others.

The competitive aspects of the international system largely derive from the fact that power is always relative. More power for one state means less for others. The relative nature of power thus ensures a degree of rivalry. This tendency manifests itself most clearly in arms races and war, but it also takes the form of economic conflict because political leaders must be concerned that relative economic gains by competing states could one day be translated into greater military might.

Alongside this competitive state system, however, exists the global marketplace, made possible by growing economic interdependence. In this realm, states, as well as firms and individuals, seek wealth for its own sake. States can bring about a higher standard of living for their citizens by encouraging the growth of trade and investment with other countries. Although the struggle for relative power engenders conflict, the pursuit of wealth through economic interdependence more often gives rise to cooperation because all can gain simultaneously.

Alongside the dynamics of cooperation and competition among states lies the struggle over interests and ideas carried out by a varied set of nonstate actors, including business firms, labor movements, and a growing number of nongovernmental organizations concerned with issues such as labor, the environment, and human rights. The interplay of societal interests intersects with and influences the policies of states and relevant international organizations. As the rise of new transnational social movements suggests, the globalization of economic life is accompanied by the globalization of social and political life. This rise of a new global civil society complicates our picture of the international political and economic order and presents challenges for both states and for academic analysts.

The study of international political economy requires an understanding of the complex relations that knit together the realms of politics, markets, and society. Although much will change in the international economic order in the years ahead, the struggle for power, wealth, and security across these connected areas of social life will continue.

Glossary

Absolute advantage A situation in international trade where one country is able to produce a good or set of goods at a lower cost than some other country or set of countries. See also *comparative advantage*.

Agency for International Development (AID) A bureaucratic arm of the U.S. State Department charged with dispensing and administering bilateral foreign aid funds.

Andean Pact An accord signed by five Latin American countries in 1970 in which each pledged to impose common regulations on foreign direct investment. This represented an attempt to increase host-country bargaining power vis-à-vis multinational corporations by limiting the ability of the latter to play small countries off against one another.

Asian financial crisis Currency and financial instability that afflicted many Asian countries in 1997 and 1998. The crisis began with Thailand and subsequently spread to other economies in the region.

Asian-Pacific Economic Cooperation (APEC) (Conference) A regional economic forum consisting of countries located in Asia and the Pacific Rim.

Asymmetrical interdependence A form of mutual dependence between two parties in which one partner is more dependent upon the relationship than the other. The less dependent party holds potential leverage over the more dependent party.

Autarchy An economic policy designed to promote an extreme version of economic self-sufficiency. This leads to closing off domestic markets from external trade as well as severely restricting exports. Such a policy frequently is designed to defend the nation against political and ideological imports that accompany trade along with organization of the economy for war.

Baker Plan Announced in 1985, this American initiative attempted to encourage renewed bank lending to Third World debtors in hopes that these countries could then grow their way out of the debt crisis. Although its immediate objectives were not realized, the Baker Plan represented the first partial step away from the previous reliance on Third World austerity as a solution to the debt problem.

461

Balance of payments   An accounting system designed to measure all transactions a nation has with the rest of the world over some period of time. See also *current account; capital account.*

Basic needs   A "bottom-up" approach to Third World development designed to enhance the living conditions and earning potential of the poorest segments of Southern societies. This developmental model was popular among aid agencies during the 1970s but lost favor in the 1980s.

Bilateral assistance   Foreign economic assistance administered directly by donor country governments.

Brady Plan   Announced in the spring of 1989, this American initiative was designed to alleviate the problem of Third World debt. The Brady Plan signaled, for the first time, official Northern recognition that debt reduction should play a role in the management of the debt crisis. The plan provided incentives for Northern banks to forgive a portion of the debt owed to them by certain Southern countries.

Bretton Woods   An agreement reached in 1944 at Bretton Woods, New Hampshire, that led to the creation of the postwar international economic order directed by the United States. Centered on the dollar, fixed exchange rates, and the International Monetary Fund, this system ended in 1971.

Capital account   An item in the balance of payments that measures the investment of resources abroad and in the home country by foreigners. See also *foreign direct investment; portfolio investment.*

Capital controls   Restrictions placed on the movement of capital across national boundaries. Governments impose controls in order to increase their ability to manage the domestic economy.

Capital liberalization   The process of removing and/or reducing capital controls.

Central bank   The government-owned and -run bank designed to manage the money supply of a nation. Examples include the Federal Reserve in the United States and the Bundesbank in Germany. In a financial crisis, the central bank provides

funds to the system when other lenders (usually private banks) have stopped making loans.

Collective goods   Benefits that meet two strict requirements: consumption by any one person or nation does not reduce the supply of the good, and no one can be excluded from consumption. An important issue in the theory of hegemony is the nature and extent to which hegemons provide collective goods to the international system.

Colonial trade system   A set of trading relationships typical of the colonial era. Colonized countries exchanged raw materials and agricultural commodities for manufactured goods produced by the imperial country. In the postcolonial period, most Third World countries have sought to alter this division of labor between North and South by developing their own industrial capacities.

Commission for Environmental Cooperation   Agency established through a NAFTA side agreement to facilitate environmental cooperation between the United States and Mexico.

Command economy   A system of political economy in most communist states in which decisions about what to produce and about prices for goods are made by central political authorities.

Common Agricultural Policy (CAP)   An important form of protectionism and income support for farmers in the European Community. Arranged in the 1950s and 1960s, CAP provides for funds to maintain high prices for farm products and for tariffs to protect these prices from external competition. See also *European Community.*

Comparative advantage   A strict definition refers to a situation in which one country may be unable to produce different types of goods more efficiently than another, but it nonetheless produces *some* goods better than others. This comparative advantage justifies a policy of free trade on economic grounds. A looser usage of the term refers to a country possessing an advantage in producing some goods and a disadvantage in others.

Competitiveness   The capacity of a nation to generate real growth in income for most persons in the country even when its economy is open to trade with the rest of the world.

Complex interdependence   A theoretical model of international relations that contrasts with traditional models of realism. Complex interdependence posits a world where economic issues are not less important than security issues, where linkages among nations reduce government control over foreign affairs, and where military power is essentially unimportant.

Convertibility   An arrangement in which a government permits the free exchange of its currency for that of other nations. See also *exchange rates*.

Cooperation   A situation in which two or more nations bargain over modifying their behavior and/or preferences in order to receive some reciprocal act from each other. The aim of these complementary concessions is coordination of their actions in order to gain some benefit they cannot have alone.

Corn Laws   Tariffs placed on food and grain products imported into Britain during the nineteenth century. Repeal of the Corn Laws in 1846 signaled a British turn toward free trade.

Creditor nation   This status is a reflection of a nation's net foreign position indicating that it holds more assets abroad than foreigners hold of its assets. See also *debtor nation*.

Current account   This is a summary item in the balance of payments that measures the net of exports and imports of merchandise and services, investment income and payments, and government transactions. See also *balance of payments*.

Dawes Plan   A proposal made in 1924 by Charles Dawes, calling for a reduction in reparations payments made by Germany to Britain and France and loans by U.S. banks to Germany.

Debt-for-equity swaps   A set of complex schemes for converting privately held bank debt into equity investments in the Third World, these deals became popular in the late 1980s, at a time when Northern banks sought to reduce their exposure to increasingly shaky Third World loans.

Debtor nation   This status is a reflection of a nation's net foreign position indicating that it holds less assets abroad than foreigners hold of its assets. See also *creditor nation*.

Debt service   The proportion of export earnings accounted for by the repayment of principal and interest on a nation's foreign debt.

Demographic transition   A theory which posits that rapid population growth begins when a country enters the initial stages of economic development but later slows as incomes reach moderate levels and the economy matures.

Dependency   A theory of development designed to explain the gap between living standards in the North and the South. Beginning with colonialism, Southern development has been constrained by the Third World's dependent or peripheral role in the international economy. North-South economic ties are marked by Northern exploitation of the South. Genuine, self-sustained economic development will require changes in the relationship of Southern countries to the international economic order.

Digital divide   Term referring to the division between those people with access to modern information technologies and those who lack such access.

Dirty float   A system of floating exchange rates in which governments occasionally intervene to prevent unwanted swings in the price of their currency. See also *exchange rates*.

Discount rate   The interest rate charged by a nation's central bank to its member banks when they borrow money. The discount rate is a major instrument used by the central bank in controlling interest rates for the economy as a whole and for influencing growth in the money supply. See also *central bank*.

Economic and monetary union (EMU)   The term for the elimination of all barriers to trade in the European Community by the end of 1992 and the development of a single currency later in the decade.

Elasticity A technique for precisely stating the relationship between a change in price and the resulting changes in demand or supply. When percentage changes in the quantity of demand or supply are greater than percentage changes in price, we speak of an elastic demand (or supply) of a product. When percent changes in demand are less than percent changes in price, this is a case of inelastic demand. For purists, this can be seen in the slope of the demand (or supply) curve.

Embedded liberalism A system of domestic and international political economy developed after World War II. Arrangements emphasizing free markets were tempered by broad acceptance of limits on the world economy's ability to influence developments in the domestic economy. Free trade was accepted only as a goal, and widespread limits on capital flows permitted nations to formulate independent domestic economic policies.

Emissions trading Proposal forwarded by the United States for reducing greenhouse gas emissions in a cost-effective manner. Countries that fail to reach greenhouse gas emission reduction targets could purchase pollution credits from other countries that exceed targets.

Euro A common European currency that came into widespread use in most European countries in 2001. The Euro replaced former national currencies.

Eurocurrency (Eurodollar) A development in the 1950s and 1960s in which dollars were deposited in European banks and came to be bought, sold, and borrowed. In the 1970s and 1980s, this expanded to include other currencies.

European Currency Unit (ECU) A weighted average of currencies in the Exchange Rate Mechanism of the European Community used as a benchmark to fix exchange rates among these nations.

European Monetary System (EMS) A monetary arrangement created after the breakdown of the Bretton Woods system and designed to maintain a fixed exchange rate system among some of the countries in the European Community. See also *European Currency Unit; exchange rate mechanism.*

European Union (EU) Officially begun in 1958, the European Economic Community established a set of stages for the elimination of tariffs and other barriers to trade. Originally composed of six nations, by 1986 the EEC expanded to twelve members and in 1991 agreed to add six additional members. In 1986, the nations of the EEC committed themselves to a single market by 1992 and to the political arrangements needed to achieve this result. The community became known as the European Union (EU) in 1993 as a result of the 1991 Maastricht Agreement, which also set the EU down the path toward monetary integration. See also *Common Agricultural Policy; European Currency Unit; economic and monetary union; European Monetary System; exchange rate mechanism.*

Exchange rate mechanism (ERM) The specific means by which a system of fixed exchange rates is maintained in the European Monetary System. Exchange rates are tied to the European Currency Unit (with small room for fluctuation). Governments act to peg interest rates to those in Germany and intervene in foreign exchange markets to maintain the fixed value of their currency. See also *European Currency Unit; European Monetary System.*

Exchange rate The price at which one currency can be exchanged for another. The system of exchange can be fixed, with governments acting to keep exchange rates within a certain agreed-on band, or floating (also known as flexible), in which demand and supply in a free market for currencies determine the price or rate of exchange. See also *dirty float.*

Export-led industrialization (ELI) Pursued most successfully by a group of East Asian newly industrializing countries, a strategy of export-led industrialization focuses on the production of manufactured goods for export to Northern markets.

Fiscal policy This refers to a government's policies on taxing and spending, in particular as these affect the level of economic activity.

Foreign direct investment (FDI) An investment in a nation by foreigners in which real assets are purchased. These include real estate or plant and equipment and involve some effort to manage. See also *portfolio investment.*

Foreign exchange reserves The amount of foreign exchange held by a government.

Free trade A particular international economic system in which barriers to trade have been eliminated. In practice, free trade exists only to a degree since some restrictions on trade across nations have always been present.

Free trade agreement A system of economic cooperation among nations in which tariffs, quotas, and other barriers to free trade are removed. Typically, this arrangement does not extend to establishing a common external tariff nor to the development of elaborate institutions for cooperation.

General Agreement on Tariffs and Trade (GATT) The system of treaties among more than 100 nations establishing rules for the conduct of international trade. Most rules relate to tariffs and quotas, though some arrangements have been made regarding other, nontariff barriers. The rules are the result of a series of negotiating sessions that began in the 1940s. See also *free trade; nontariff barrier.*

Genetically modified organisms (GMOs) Plants or animals that have been genetically altered to produce desired characteristics, such as pest or disease resistance.

Globalization The process of deepening and tightening of interdependence among actors in the world economy after 1973. Much higher levels of international financial transactions and increasing international production are key features.

Gold standard An international monetary system in which gold served as the medium for defining exchange rates. International payments were thereby made in terms of gold and sometimes actually in gold. This system existed from the 1870s to 1914 and briefly after World War I.

Grameen Bank The bank established in Bangladesh to provide credit to low-income entrepreneurs. The Grameen Bank set the model for the rapidly growing microcredit/microenterprise movement that has spread to many Southern countries.

Gross domestic product/gross national product (GDP/GNP) The total of all goods and services produced by a country over some period of time is its gross domestic product. Gross national product is derived by adding the income of nationals from foreign activity to GDP and subtracting income of foreigners from activity in the country measured.

Hegemony An international system in which one dominant state takes on the role of organizing and managing the world economic system. This means supplying capital, defining the rules for international trade, promoting political and military security, and having the state's money operate as a key currency.

Highly Indebted Poor Country (HIPC) Initiative A program offering partial forgiveness of official debt owed by low-income countries to Northern governments and multilateral lending agencies. Only countries agreeing to policy reforms are eligible for debt relief under this initiative.

Human Development Index (HDI) A statistical tool for measuring and comparing national development and human welfare. Developed by the United Nations Development Program, the Human Development Index is a composite of four individual measures of human welfare: life expectancy, adult literacy, mean years of schooling, and per capita income adjusted for the local cost of living. Scores on this composite index vary between 0 (the lowest measure of human development) and 1 (the highest measure of human development).

Import substitution industrialization (ISI) An inward-directed strategy of industrialization focused on the production of manufactured goods intended for sale in the domestic market. Typically, an ISI strategy provides trade protection or other forms of state assistance to import-substituting firms and industries.

Interdependence A situation in world affairs in which the linkages among nations makes their fate on certain issues mutually dependent. See also *asymmetrical interdependence.*

Interest rates Technically, this is the price of borrowing money. There are a vast array of interest rates, depending on who is borrowing and the length of time required to pay the money back. See also *discount rate; prime rate.*

International Monetary Fund (IMF) The international financial institution, funded and governed by member states, provides financing to countries experiencing balance-of-payments shortfalls. The IMF has played a key role in the Third World debt crisis by conditioning financial assistance upon debtor-country policy reforms.

Key currency Historically, this is the currency of the international hegemon that comes to be widely accepted as payment for international transactions. This acceptability depends on confidence in the stability of the currency's value and its reputation for acceptability in payment for goods or debts. In the nineteenth century the British pound and in the mid-twentieth century the U.S. dollar served as key currencies.

Keynesianism An economic policy common in capitalist societies after World War II and named in honor of the British economist John Maynard Keynes. The purpose was to reduce the severity of economic recessions through government spending, which often included deficits in fiscal accounts.

Kyoto Protocol The multilateral accord reached in 1997 in which signatory countries agreed to timetables for reducing the greenhouse gas emissions that contribute to global warming.

Liberalism A policy toward the world economy emphasizing the benefits of free markets and free trade. These views originated with Adam Smith and David Ricardo about 200 years ago and today infuse the policies of many governments, international businesses, and international economic organizations.

Liberalization A policy that leads to greater market freedom for firms through lower tariffs, reduced capital controls, or fewer restrictions and regulations.

Liquidity The level of cash held by a nation or firm. The term also refers to the ability to convert an asset to cash quickly.

Macroeconomic policy A governmental policy directed toward affecting the national economy as a whole. Examples include tax policy, spending policy, and monetary policy.

Maquiladora Special agreements between the United States and Mexico that created special export-processing zones inside Mexico. Here, parts from the United States and finished goods assembled in Mexico could cross the border without tariffs.

Market segmentation A situation in which the prices for similar goods are significantly different in different areas or markets.

Marshall Plan A proposal by U.S. Secretary of State George Marshall in 1947 calling for massive aid to Europe. The purpose was to secure a U.S. position of strength in Europe and reduce Soviet strength.

Mercantilism A policy designed to maximize exports while minimizing imports so as to generate the largest possible trade surplus. This was standard practice for nations prior to the mid-nineteenth century.

Mercosur The regional free trade agreement among the countries of Brazil, Argentina, Uruguay, and Paraguay that went into effect on January 1, 1995.

Ministry of International Trade and Industry (MITI) This is the unit of the Japanese government most responsible for planning and managing the Japanese economy. Although its powers have diminished since the 1950s, MITI (recently renamed the "Ministry of Economy, Trade and Industry") continues to play an important role in encouraging risk taking and product development by private enterprises in Japan.

Modernization A theory of development designed to explain the gap between living standards in the North and South. The North's economic prosperity is attributed to its successful transition from traditional to modern forms of social, political, and economic life. The economic backwardness of Southern countries is traced to the persistence of traditional social values and institutions. Southern development is thus dependent upon modernizing domestic reforms.

Monetary policy Decisions normally made by a nation's central bank concerning interest rates, the growth of the money supply, and exchange rates. See also *discount rate; open market operations.*

Multilateral Agreement on Investments (MAI) Proposed multilateral agreement setting rules for national treatment of foreign direct investment. Negotiations over the MAI ended in failure in 1998.

Multilateral assistance Foreign economic assistance that is channeled from donor countries through international organizations, such as the World Bank or United Nations Special Agencies.

Multinational corporation (MNC) A business firm that engages in the production of goods or services in more than one country.

New international economic order (NIEO) A package of proposed reforms in the international economic order sponsored by Third World countries during the 1970s. Largely rejected by the North, these proposals were intended to direct greater economic resources toward the South while also providing Third World countries with a greater role in managing the rules and institutions of the world economy.

Nontariff barriers Mechanisms other than tariffs used by nations to restrict trade, usually by inhibiting or blocking imports. These can include various kinds of regulations, quotas, or requirements attached to trading with a country that operate as an impediment to trade.

North American Free Trade Agreement (NAFTA) A regional free trade agreement among the countries of Canada, the United States, and Mexico.

Oligopoly A type of industry in which there are only a small number of producers and in which there are barriers preventing new firms from entering the industry. Usually, firms in an oligopolistic industry are able to affect prices and often engage in at least tacit collusion.

Open-market operations An action of a nation's central bank involving the sale or purchase of government securities in the market. The purpose is to drain funds from the economy—by selling securities, the central bank ends up with more money—or pumping funds into the economy—buying securities results in the central bank exchanging securities for money. This is a key instrument for managing the overall level of the money supply. See also *central bank; monetary policy.*

Organization of Petroleum Exporting Countries (OPEC) Formed in 1960, OPEC is a cooperative arrangement among many of the world's major oil-exporting countries. Its purpose is to facilitate common agreement among member states on matters relating to oil policy, such as production levels and pricing.

Portfolio investment An investment in a nation by foreigners in which debt or stock ownership is involved. The result is a claim on resources, but typically no participation in managing the company or assets is involved.

Post-communism A descriptive term used to refer to nations that have dropped some or all communist political and economic policies. In Europe and the former Soviet Union, this has meant an end to communist political control and an end to command economies. In Asia, it has meant significant economic liberalization directed by communist governments.

Prime rate The interest rate charged by banks to their best customers, usually large and well-run businesses.

Privatization A system for transferring control over government-owned enterprises to private hands. The focus of this effort is in postcommunist states of the former Soviet Union and Eastern Europe. Some successful transfers of government corporations to private hands took place in Great Britain during the 1980s.

Product cycle A set of stages in the development, production, and sales of a product that are associated with the comparative advantage of different countries.

The creation and development of a product usually takes place in advanced industrial countries with large scientific complexes, but once the method of production has matured, manufacture can take place where costs are lowest.

Productivity   Broadly, this is the quantity of output of a good or service measured by the amount of input. For example, the amount of a good one worker can produce in a period of time is a measure of productivity.

Protectionism   A policy of excluding the import of goods and/or services into a nation. Like free trade, this is always a matter of degree since total exclusion is exceedingly rare. See also *free trade*.

Purchasing power parity (PPP)   A statistical device designed to allow for more accurate comparisons of income and living standards across nations. The conversion of national income measures into dollars is adjusted for local purchasing power, or the cost of living.

Radicalism   Also closely linked to Marxism, this is a way of analyzing international political economy that emphasizes the way political and economic power are used to bias economic outcomes and garner special benefits for privileged and powerful groups and classes.

Regime   A relationship among nations in which there is a convergence of beliefs, expectations, norms, and procedures for making decisions relating to a particular problem or issue in international affairs. A regime is important to the extent that it affects the actions and choices of nations associated with the regime.

Rio Earth Summit   Formally the United Nations Conference on Environment and Development (UNCED), the Rio Earth Summit brought together representatives from 150 nations in June 1992 with the purpose of elaborating "strategies and measures to halt and reverse the effects of environmental degradation in the context of increased national and international efforts to promote sustainable and environmentally sound development in all countries."

Smoot–Hawley Tariff   A tariff proposal enacted in 1930 by U.S. protectionists during the Great Depression and signed by President Herbert Hoover. This led other capitalist states to adopt similar tariffs and contributed to a crushing decline in world trade and worsening depression in the United States and elsewhere.

Strategic alliance   An arrangement between two or more firms that creates some continuing cooperative relationship. This could involve production, marketing, and/or research and development, such that information, products, and/or production are shared and transferred.

Strategic trade   An international trade policy in which various forms of governmental aid are directed at a specific industry or industries to boost their competitive advantages in global markets. The industries selected for targeting typically have substantial positive consequences for the economy or have a cost or market structure that promotes a small number of producers.

Structural adjustment   In contrast with traditional project loans, which finance particular development investments or activities, the World Bank began shifting part of its lending to structural adjustment financing in the 1980s. Typically, this newer type of financing provides balance of payments support to countries that have committed themselves to bank-sponsored policy reforms.

Sustainable development   This term was first brought into common use by the World Commission on Environment and Development, also called the Brundtland Commission, in 1987. Brundtland defined sustainable development as that which "meets the needs of the present generation without compromising the needs of future generations."

Syndication   An arrangement whereby a collection of banks, usually organized by one or a few lead institutions, divide responsibility for financing a major loan package. Syndication was often used in lending to Third World countries during the 1970s. Syndication agreements typically stipulate that agreement among the participating banks is required before any renegotiation of debt arrangements can be implemented.

Tied aid   A condition attached to foreign economic assistance which requires that the aid extended to a recipient country be spent on goods and/or services produced by firms residing in the donor country.

Trade surplus/deficit　A situation in a nation's balance of payments in which exports exceed imports (surplus) or imports exceed exports (deficit).

Transfer pricing　An accounting practice by which multinational corporations adjust prices on intrafirm trade in order to shift profits from subsidiaries located in high-tax countries to those residing in low-tax countries or to escape restrictions of the repatriation of profits imposed by host-country governments.

World Bank　This term actually refers to a group of related international financial institutions, including the International Bank for Reconstruction and Development (IBRD), the International Development Agency (IDA), and the International Finance Corporation (IFC). Funded largely by capital infusions from Northern governments, these agencies provide financing for Third World development projects or programs.

World Trade Organization　A global trade organization created to oversee the implementation of agreements emerging out of the Uruguay Round of international trade negotiations.

Zaibatsu/keiretsu　Two related forms of industrial organization in Japan in which family-centered holding companies act to organize and integrate many different firms. Often, large banks operate to supply capital; in other cases, complex systems of manufacturers and suppliers are the main forms of organization. *Zaibatsu* refers to such enterprise systems prior to 1945; *keiretsu* refers to such systems after 1945.

Acronyms

APEC Asian-Pacific Economic Cooperation

ARPA Advanced Research Projects Agency

ASEAN Association of Southeast Asian Nations

BRITE Basic Research for Industrial Technology in Europe

CAP common agricultural policy

CFC chlorofluorocarbon

CGIAR Consultative Group on International Agricultural Research

CIMMYT Centro Internacional de Major-amiento de Maiz y Trige

DAC Development Assistance Council

DARPA Defense Advanced Research Projects Agency

EAEC East Asian Economic Caucus

EC European Community

ECB European Central Bank

ECU European Currency Unit

EEC European Economic Community

EFTA European Free Trade Area

ELI export-led industrialization

EMS European Monetary System

EMU economic and monetary union

ERM exchange rate mechanism

ESF Economic Support Fund

ESPRIT European Strategic Programme for Research and Development in Information Technology

EU European Union

EUREKA European Research Coordination Agency

FDI foreign direct investment

FTA free trade agreement

G-5 Group of Five

G-7 Group of Seven

GATS General Agreement on Trade in Services

GATT General Agreement on Tariffs and Trade

GDP gross domestic product

GEF Global Environmental Fund

GFC global financial crisis

GMO　genetically modified organism

GNP　gross national product

HCFC　hydrochlorofluorocarbon

HDI　Human Development Index

HIPC　Highly Indebted Poor Country

IBM　International Business Machines Corporation

IBRD　International Bank for Reconstruction and Development

ICBM　intercontinental ballistic missile

IDA　International Development Agency

IFC　International Finance Corporation

IMF　International Monetary Fund

IRRI　International Rice Research Institute

ISI　import substitution industrialization

JESSI　Joint European Semiconductor Silicon

LDC　least-developed country

LDP　Liberal Democratic Party

MAI　Multilateral Agreement on Investment

MFA　Multi-Fibre Arrangement

MITI　Ministry of International Trade and Industry

MNC　multinational corporation

MOF　Ministry of Finance

NAFTA　North American Free Trade Agreement

NATO　North Atlantic Treaty Organization

NGO　nongovernmental organization

NIC　newly industrializing country

NIEO　new international economic order

NTB　nontariff barrier

ODA　official development assistance

OECD　Organization of Economic Cooperation and Development

OEEC　Organization for European Economic Cooperation

OMA　orderly marketing agreement

OPEC　Organization of Petroleum Exporting Countries

PPP　purchasing power parity

PRI　Institutional Revolutionary Party

R&D　research and development

RACE　R&D in Advanced Communications-Technologies in Europe

RAM　random access memory

RTAA　Reciprocal Trade Agreements Act

SDR　special drawing right

SEA　Single European Act

SELA　Latin American Economic System

SOE　state-owned enterprise

TEU　Treaty on European Union

TRIP　trade-related intellectual property rights

UNCED　United Nations Conference on Environment and Development

UNCTAD　United Nations Conference on Trade and Development

UNCTC　United Nations Center on Transnational Corporations

UNDP　United Nations Development Program

USAID　United States Agency for International Development

VER　Voluntary Export Restraint

WTO　World Trade Organization

❖

Links to IPE Web Sites

Asia Crisis
http://www.stern.nyu.edu/~nroubini/
asia/AsiaHomepage.html
Comprehensive compilation of links and
resources on Asian financial crisis, created by Professor Nouriel Roubini of
the Stern School of Business, New
York University.

Asian Development Bank
http://www.asiandevbank.org/
The Asian Development Bank is a multilateral lending institution that finances
development projects in the Asia-Pacific region. Its Web site includes statistical data, speeches, project
summaries, business and consulting information, news releases, official documents, publications, and links.

Association of Southeast Asian Nations
(ASEAN)
http://www.asean.or.id/
ASEAN is an organization devoted to the
promotion of political, economic, and
security cooperation among a group
of nine Southeast Asian nations. The
ASEAN Web site provides background information, news, discussion

of major issues, a calendar of ASEAN
meetings and events, organizational
facts, a photo gallery, country profiles,
publications, and links to on-line
newspapers published in member
countries.

Bank Information Center
http://www.bicusa.org/index.htm
The Bank Information Center (BIC) is a
nongovernmental organization that
provides information and resources to
NGO networks working on issues related to the World Bank and other
multilateral development banks
(MDBs). BIC advocates greater transparency, accountability, and citizen
participation at the MDBs.

Berkeley Roundtable on the International
Economy (BRIE)
http://brie.berkeley.edu/~briewww/
BRIE is a research institute located at the
University of California, Berkeley.
Scholars associated with the institute
focus on issues related to technology
and national economic competitiveness. Associates include economists,
political scientists, legal scholars, and

business specialists. BRIE publishes books and working papers that address current issues, often with a focus on policy prescription. It also sponsors conferences and educational programs. BRIE's Web site includes information about the institute and access to some of its resources.

Canadian International Development Agency
http://w3.acdi-cida.gc.ca/virtual.nsf
Includes a comprehensive list of links to Web sites dealing with development issues organized by topics, countries, regions, and organizations.

Corporate Watch
http://www.corpwatch.org/
Corporate Watch is a media project designed to serve as a source of news and information about corporate abuses around the world. Corporate Watch is sponsored by a nongovernmental organization called Transnational Resource and Action Center (TRAC), based in San Francisco.

Europa: European Union (EU)
http://www.europa.eu.int/
This is the official Web site of the European Union. The EU is a regional organization devoted to political, social, and economic integration among European countries. The EU Web site is organized into four main sections: institutions, policies, news, and basic background information, including legal texts.

European Central Bank
http://www.ecb.int/
This is the official Web site for the ECB, which operates as the central bank for almost all of the nations of the European Union. The site contains considerable information about the Euro.

European Commission
http://europa.eu.int/comm/index_en.htm
This is the official site of the main governing body of the European Union. There are several useful documents and information about the workings of this institution.

European Network on Debt and Development (EURODAD)
http://www.oneworld.org/eurodad/
EURODAD is a network of European nongovernmental organizations (NGOs) from 15 countries working on issues related to debt, structural adjustment, and the accountability of the Bretton Woods institutions. EURODAD is partly funded by the European Union. The EURODAD Web site contains policy research papers and statistics related to international debt problems.

Focus on the Global South
http://www.focusweb.org/
Focus on the Global South in a nongovernmental organization based in Bangkok, Thailand, and affiliated with Chulalongkorn University. Focus generates research on international development issues (with an emphasis on the Asia-Pacific region) and seeks to facilitate cooperation among grassroots organizations. The Focus on the Global South Web site includes access to a series of on-line information bulletins dealing with international trade issues.

G-8 Information Center
http://www.g7.utoronto.ca/
This Web site at the University of Toronto provides contemporary and historical information related to the annual Group of Eight meetings. These conferences bring together heads of state and relevant officials from eight leading economic powers—Canada, France, Germany, Italy, Japan, Russia, the United Kingdom, and the United States—to discuss multilateral approaches to common economic issues and problems. The Group of Eight Information Center provides access to official documents, conference reports, news accounts, scholarly papers, and links related to these yearly summits.

Global Environmental Facility
http://www.gefweb.org/
This is a liberal organization whose goals are to promote sustainable development. It consists of governments

and private organizations and coordinates these efforts.

Global Reporting Initiative
http://www.globalreporting.org/
This is a broadly based effort to define criteria for evaluating the impact of global corporations on sustainable development. You can find a set of guidelines for engaging in such reports.

Global Trade Watch
http://www.tradewatch.org/
Global Trade Watch is a project of Ralph Nader's organization Public Citizen. Public Citizen has been critical of free trade and neoliberalism. Global Trade Watch's Web site includes resources for activists interested in changing U.S. trade policy.

Grameen Bank
http://www.citechco.net/grameen/bank/
The Grameen Bank, located in Bangladesh, was created by Professor Muhammad Yunus to provide credit to the poor. The Grameen Bank helped to spark a global microcredit movement and spawned many imitators in countries around the world. This site describes the history and philosophy of the Grameen Bank, along with relevant statistics and bibliographic resources.

Institute for Agriculture and Trade Policy
http://www.sustain.org/
This is an environmental organization with a broad array of interests focusing on agriculture.

Inter-American Development Bank
http://www.iadb.org/
The Inter-American Development Bank is a multilateral lending institution that finances development projects in Central and South America. Its Web site includes statistical data, project summaries, business opportunities, news, and publications.

International Forum on Globalization
http://www.ifg.org/
The International Forum on Globalization (IFG) is an alliance of 60 leading activists, scholars, economists, researchers, and writers formed to stimulate new thinking, joint activity,

and public education in response to economic globalization. Representing over 60 organizations in 25 countries, the IFG associates come together out of a shared concern that the world's corporate and political leadership is undertaking a restructuring of global politics and economics that may prove as historically significant as any event since the Industrial Revolution. The IFG is generally critical of liberal approaches to globalization.

International Monetary Fund (IMF)
http://www.imf.org/
The IMF is a multilateral lending institution responsible for assisting countries experiencing serious balance of payments deficits. The IMF has, since the early 1980s, played a major role in coping with developing country debt and financial crises. The IMF homepage provides historical background, recent news releases, official IMF speeches, publications, and reports and analyses of contemporary problems in international finance.

International Political Economy Network (ISA)
http://csf.colorado.edu/ipe/
This Web site is maintained by the International Political Economy (IPE) Section of the International Studies Association (ISA). ISA is an association of scholars interested in the study of international relations. The IPE section is specifically devoted to international issues that lie at the intersection of politics and economics. The IPE Web site provides visitors with access to an ongoing IPE discussion group. Thematic and geographic archives are available. Links are included to on-line IPE journals, dissertation listings, syllabi, graduate programs in IPE, and the homepages of ISA/IPE Section members.

Jubilee 2000
http://www.jubilee2000uk.org/main.html
Jubilee 2000 is an international campaign sponsored by a coalition of nongovernmental organizations devoted to the pursuit of debt relief for the world's poorest countries.

Labor Net
http://www.igc.org/igc/labornet/
Sponsored by the Institute for Global
   Communications, Labor Net provides
   a comprehensive and up-to-date guide
   to Web-based information on issues
   affecting workers around the world.
   An excellent site for gathering recent
   news often overlooked by the mainstream media.

Multinational Monitor
http://www.essential.org/monitor/
Multinational Monitor is a monthly magazine that tracks corporate activities in
   developing countries, with a focus on
   labor and environmental issues.

Office of the United States Trade
   Representative
http://www.ustr.gov/index.html
The Office of the U.S. Trade Representative is responsible for negotiating
   trade agreements with other countries.
   Its Web site includes relevant
   speeches, congressional testimony,
   press releases, reports, trade agreements texts, and access to official documents.

Organization for Economic Cooperation
   and Development (OECD)
http://www.oecd.org/
The OECD is an organization designed to
   promote economic cooperation among
   the 29 member countries. The OECD
   gathers statistical data and facilitates
   consultation among economic specialists drawn from member country governments. The official OECD Web
   site offers information about the organization's history, purposes, organization, and achievements. Visitors can
   also find statistical data, official reports, and news on upcoming events.

Organization of American States (OAS)
   Trade Unit
http://www.sice.oas.org/
The OAS Trade Unit Web site provides
   the full texts, as well as short summaries, of all major trade and investment agreements among countries in
   the Western Hemisphere. Also included are statistical data, a calendar of
   trade related events, and updates regarding ongoing trade negotiations.

Pacific Exchange Rate Service
http://pacific.commerce.ubc.ca/xr/
Operated at the University of British Columbia, this is a very useful site for information about foreign exchange.
   You can obtain historical data and up-
   to-date information about foreign exchange values, with very useful
   graphs. There is a useful discussion of
   the Euro at: *http://pacific.commerce.ubc.
   ca/xr/euro/menu.html*

South Centre
http://www.southcentre.org/
South Centre is an intergovernmental organization formed in 1995 through an
   agreement among 46 developing
   country governments. The South
   Centre carries out research and technical analysis focused on development
   and South-South cooperation.

The Development Group for Alternative
   Policies (GAP)
http://www.igc.apc.org/dgap/
This site is maintained by a nongovernmental organization that is critical of
   existing economic orthodoxy on development as promulgated by the
   World Bank, the IMF, and the World
   Trade Organization. Development
   GAP advocates alternative policies designed to promote greater equality,
   environmental sustainability, and the
   democratic functioning of national
   and international institutions. This
   Web site contains research reports and
   articles offering critical perspectives on
   development issues.

The Economist
http://www.economist.com/
This is certainly the best site for a liberal
   perspective on the global economy
   and perhaps the best overall source of
   information. Provides daily news and
   access to the magazine's Web site.

The Global Site
http://www.theglobalsite.ac.uk/
A searchable collection of original and
   reprinted articles, book reviews, and
   news on world politics, with an emphasis on issues in political economy.
   It is run by the University of Sussex,
   England.

The International Institute for Sustainable Development (IISD)
http://iisd1.iisd.ca/
IISD is a nongovernmental organization based in Canada that works to support the idea of sustainable development through policy research. The IISD Web site includes access to policy reports on a wide variety of economic, social, and environmental topics.

The North-South Institute
http://www.nsi-ins.ca/ensi/
The North-South Institute is a nonprofit research organization devoted to exploring and promoting political and economic ties between Canada and developing countries.

Transparency International
http://www.transparency.de/
Transparency International, a nongovernmental organization with chapters in 77 countries, is devoted to exposing and combating government corruption, particularly as it relates to the business world.

United Nations Conference on Trade and Development (UNCTAD)
http://www.unctad.org/
The UNCTAD promotes cooperation among developing countries on trade and development issues. Its Web site offers information about UNCTAD programs, news, and conference schedules.

United Nations Development Program (UNDP)
http://www.undp.org/
The UNDP seeks to promote social and economic development in Southern countries by providing relevant technical advice and assistance. The UNDP Web site includes background on the UNDP, news, statistical data, publications, and links to other Web sites.

United Nations Food and Agricultural Organization (UNFAO)
http://www.fao.org/
UNFAO provides development assistance, technical information, and policy advice to developing countries in the areas of food and agriculture. The UNFAO Web site includes statistical data, publications, news, and information about the organizations and its activities.

United Nations International Labor Organization (UNILO)
http://www.ilo.org/
The ILO is a specialized agency of the United Nations that provides technical assistance to member countries regarding labor issues. Its Web site offers information on ILO programs and conferences.

United States Agency for International Development (USAID)
http://www.info.usaid.gov/
USAID dispenses bilateral official development assistance on behalf of the U.S. government. USAID's Web site includes publications, policy statements, news, data, and links to dozens of development-related Web sites.

United States Federal Reserve System
http://www.federalreserve.gov/
This is the official site of the United States' central bank. There is considerable information about the structure and operation of this institution.

World Bank
http://worldbank.org/
The World Bank Group includes several distinct multilateral lending and development agencies, including the International Bank for Reconstruction and Development, the International Development Agency, and the International Finance Corporation. The World Bank's Web site provides basic information about these agencies and development data. Visitors can place orders for a wide array of World Bank publications.

World Business Council for Sustainable Development
http://www.wbcsd.ch/
The World Business Council is an organization sponsored by 130 international companies. The council offers a business perspective on issues relating to sustainable development. The council Web site includes policy research, news, and information.

World Trade Organization (WTO)
http://www.wto.org/
The WTO is a relatively new global multilateral institution created as a product of the Uruguay Round of world trade negotiations. The WTO is responsible for overseeing the trade rules agreed upon through the Uruguay Round, settling disputes, gathering informa-tion, and providing a forum for ongoing trade negotiations. The WTO Web site includes information and analyses on a wide variety of issues related to international trade and investment. It also provides access to news releases, publications, links, and legal texts.

Index

❖

A

absolute advantage, 19, 20, 21
absolute gains, 187 n. 4
Abu Dhabi, 287
acquis communautaire, 177
Advanced Micro Devices, 129
Advanced Research Projects Agency
    (ARPA), 4, 6, 218
Agency for International Development
    (USAID), 317–318, 333, 336
Agenda 21, 436–437
AIDS, population growth and, 425–426
Airbus, 5
Alfonsin, Raul, 390
Algeria, 287, 362
Amnesty International, 136, 366
Andean Pact, 182, 297–298, 355
Annan, Kofi, 366
anti-globalization movement, 457–459
APEC (Asian-Pacific Economic
    Cooperation), 183, 300
Argentina, 182, 297, 374–375, 382, 389,
    390–391
    global financial crisis and, 406–407
ARPA (Advanced Research Projects
    Agency), 4, 6, 218

ASEAN (Association of South East Asian
    Nations), 183, 300
Asian financial crisis, 273, 302, 459
Asian-Pacific Economic Cooperation
    (APEC), 183, 300
Association of South East Asian Nations
    (ASEAN), 183, 300
atmospheric pollution, 437–442
    global warming, 440–442
    ozone depletion, 438–440
Australia, 48, 108, 183
Austria, 167
autarky, 62–63
Azerbaijan, 292

B

Bairoch, Paul, 245
Baker, James, 158
balance of payments, 23–27
balance on current account, 23
Bank for International Settlements, 2
Bank of England, 27
Bank of Japan, 200
banks, Third World debt and, 375,
    392–393
Banque of France, 27